THE ALCHEMICAL BODY

THE ALCHEMICAL BODY

Siddha Traditions in Medieval India

DAVID GORDON WHITE

THE UNIVERSITY OF CHICAGO PRESS / CHICAGO AND LONDON

David Gordon White is associate professor of religious studies at the University of California, Santa Barbara. He is the author of *Myths of the Dog-Man* (1991), also published by the University of Chicago Press.

The University of Chicago Press, Chicago 60637
The University of Chicago Press, Ltd., London

Printed in the United States of America
05 04 03 02 01 00 99 98 97 96 1 2 3 4 5
ISBN: 0-226-89497-5 (cloth)

Library of Congress Cataloging-in-Publication Data

White, David Gordon.
The alchemical body : Siddha traditions in medieval India / David Gordon White.
p. cm.
Includes bibliographical references and index.
ISBN 0-226-89497-5 (cloth : alk. paper)
1. Siddhas. 2. Alchemy—Religious aspects—Tantrism. 3. Yoga, Haṭha. 4. Tantrism. 5. Nātha sect. I. Title.
BL1241.56.W47 1996
294.5′514—dc20 96-16977
CIP

∞ The paper used in this publication meets the minimum requirements of the American National Standard for Information Sciences—Permanence of Paper for Printed Library Materials, ANSI Z39.48-1984.

for Catherine

CONTENTS

Contents

PREFACE

In the new age India of the 1990s, it has become popular, even fashionable, to have the name of a *tāntrika*, a kind of all-purpose sexologist, medicine man, and shaman, in one's little black book of phone numbers. This same phenomenon has brought with it the appearance, preceding the title page of books on magic and tantra, of "disclaimers" to the effect that said book does not guarantee the results of the techniques it is treating and that its editors are not responsible for unhappy side-effects of said techniques when they are practiced in the privacy of one's home. The present work carries no such disclaimer because it in no way purports to be a "how-to" book for realizing immortality. Nor is this a study in the history of Indian medicine or science: a great number of Indian scholars and scientists as well as a growing number of western authors have written excellent works on the matters I will be treating from these perspectives, incorporating into their writings comprehensive overviews of Indian chemistry, human physiology, pharmacology, and therapeutics.

The present work is rather a history-of-religions study of the medieval Siddha traditions of Hindu alchemy and *haṭha yoga*, which formed two important fields of theory and practice within the vast current of Indian mysticism known as tantra. It is the religious and, more specifically, tantric features of these interpenetrating traditions that I will be treating in these pages, from both a historical and a phenomenological perspective. In the main, this will be a study of the *language* of mystic experience and expression, and it will be from the standpoint of language that I will chart out the theoretical, symbolic, and analogical parameters of the alchemical and hathayogic disciplines within their broader tantric and Hindu contexts. And, working from the semantic and symbolic fields of meaning that the alchemical material generates, this study will also look at a much wider array of Hindu and Indian phenomena through "alchemical eyes."

This will furthermore be a scholarly work, nearly entirely divorced from any ground of personal mystical experience. Apart from a short period of schooling in *haṭha yoga* undertaken in Benares in 1984–85, I have never experienced anything that one could qualify as a genuine master-disciple relationship. I have never levitated, read other people's minds, or even seen auras. This being the case, it may well be that I belong to the great mass of those who "must go on blundering inside our front-brain faith in Kute Korrespondences, hoping that for each psi-synthetic taken from Earth's soul there is a molecule, secular and more or less ordinary and named, over here—kicking endlessly among the plastic trivia, finding in each Deeper Significance and trying to string them all together like terms of a power series hoping to zero in on the tremendous and secret Function whose name, like the permuted names of God, cannot be spoken . . . to make sense out of, to find the meanest sharp sliver of truth in so much replication."[1]

Ultimate reality is beyond my reach, either to experience or express. I nonetheless hope that these pages may serve to bridge a certain gap between raw experience and synthetic description, and thereby contribute to an ongoing tradition of cultural exchange that is at least as old as the Silk Road.

In reading these pages, the reader may come to experience a sensation of vertigo, as the horizon of one mystic landscape opens onto yet another landscape, equally vast and troubling in its internal immensity. It may be that these landscapes,[2] with their dizzying multitudinous levels of self-interpretation, may inspire analysis by psychologists of both the armchair and professional varieties.[3] I believe, however, that the most useful western companion to the present study is the work of the French philosopher Gaston Bachelard entitled *The Poetics of Space*.[4] Bachelard's work is a phenomenological study of literary depictions of the experience of space, from cellar to attic, from Chinese boxes to the interiors of seashells. In these pages I will endeavor to follow just such a phenomenological approach, pointing out homologies where the sources would seem to indicate connections internal to the traditions themselves, without attempting to force the textual data into any preconceived model.[5]

I treat alchemical and tantric discourse as self-referential, as part and parcel of a self-enclosed network of specifically Indian symbols and signs, my assumption being that the words and images of these traditions are always referring, before all else, to other words and images.[6] Therefore, the best way to formulate a theory concerning the nature of the experiences for which these words and images are so many signposts is to generate a symbolic lexicon from the multitude of intersecting words and images the sources offer.[7] Rather than exposing the doctrines of any single school, movement, or exegetical tradition, this study seeks to lay bare the words, images, and logic that a wide swath of the Hindu, and particularly Śaiva (and tantric), population always already assume to be the case prior to giving voice to their doctrines.

This is, in the main, a study of a pervasive Indian worldview from a tantric and alchemical perspective. Now, if we follow Douglas Brooks when he maintains that Hindu tantrism has been treated as "an unwanted stepchild in the family of Hindu studies";[8] and if, as Betty Dobbs has written with regard to its rejection of alchemy as so much fuzzy mysticism, that "modern science, like adolescence, denies its parentage,"[9] then the subject of this study has a troubled family life. Perhaps it is the stepparents' and adolescents' judgment that one ought to question here.

This book is the fruit of twelve years of research begun at the University of Chicago, where I began to translate the *bānīs*, the mystic vernacular poems of Gorakhnāth, under the direction of Professor Kali Charan Bahl. The use of metaphor and imagery in these poems reminded me of similar language from an alchemical work entitled the *Rasārṇava* (The Flood of Mercury), which I had attempted to translate (with mitigated success) for a self-styled French mystic a few years earlier.

It was on the basis of these first tentative identifications that I embarked in earnest on the present research, going to India in 1984–85 under the auspices of a grant from the American Institute for Indian Studies. It had been my intention, in undertaking my research tour, to find a living yogin-alchemist and to sit at his feet until I had solved all the riddles the *Rasārṇava* and the *Gorakh Bānī* had posed for me. This endeavor was a total failure. There were no alchemists to be found in the places in which I sought them out (although I did meet a number of amateurs and charlatans), and the few Nāth Siddhas who struck me as genuine practitioners of the *haṭha yoga* taught by Gorakhnāth made it clear that they would be willing to divulge their secrets to me only after a long period of discipleship.

Being a westerner in a hurry, I spurned this path, in spite of its many attractions, for that of the textualist. First in India, under the guidance of a number of professors of Ayurvedic studies, and later in Europe and the United States, then in India and Nepal once again, under the auspices of a grant from the Council for the International Exchange of Scholars, I followed the leads the texts offered me. In spite of my rush at the outset, it is only now, after an additional ten years, that I feel myself capable of understanding these mystic disciplines sufficiently to be able to share certain of my insights on them. Let the reader be forewarned, then, that my interpretations of the language of the Hindu alchemical, hathayogic, and tantric traditions bear no stamp of approval from any Indian guru of any sect whatsoever. This is a textual study, one that is based, in any case, on a number of texts for which the all-important chain of transmission of oral tradition from teacher to disciple has long since been broken. In the absence of a teacher from the tradition itself, I have taken the difficult road of letting the texts speak for themselves and even communicate among themselves as the exemplars and followers of the medieval Siddha traditions under study here would have done. I hope they will speak to the reader of this work as well.

I feel somewhat justified in my textualist bias, however, since it is shared by the alchemical tradition itself. We read in three major alchemical works that "neither sequence (oral teachings) without written sources nor written sources without sequence [are acceptable]. Knowing the written sources to be conjoined with sequence, the person who then practices [alchemy] partakes of the *siddhi*s."[10] On still another score I also believe this to be an authentic work. The twelve years' preparation this book has required of me corresponds to the standard period of preparation of a yogin in the traditions under study here. Twelve years, the mystic homologue of a year of twelve months in which the seasons and the dance of sun and moon are brought full circle, seems to me to be an appropriate period for this scholarly exercise, which will have succeeded if its final transmutation of raw data into food for thought pleases the reader's palate.

Many are the people to whom I owe thanks for their help in the preparation of this book. A great number of these persons' names will be found in the text of this book itself or in the endnotes, under the rubric of "personal communication." This group includes several of the countless Nāth Siddhas who offered to share their *chillum*s and knowledge with me (usually in that order) as well as fellow academics from both India and the west. In India, these include Bhambhulnāth, the late abbot of the Hardwar monastery; Avedyanāth, abbot of the Gorakhpur monastery; and the great Nāth Siddha scholar Narharināth, abbot of the Caughera monastery in the Dang region of southern Nepal; Sivaprasad Dabbaral, Dr. Laxmi Chandra Sastri, Dr. Surya Kumar Yogi, Dr. N. Sethu Raghunathan, Dr. Rajendra Kumar

Agrawal of Gurukul Kangri University in Hardwar, Dr. Damodar Joshi of Benares Hindu University, Dr. Siddhinandan Mishra of Sampurnanand Sanskrit University (Benares), Dr. Hari Shankar Sharma of Gujarat Ayurved University (Jamnagar), Mahavir Prasad Gill of the Anup Sanskrit Library in Bikaner, Vijaya Shrestha of the Nepal National Archives in Kathmandu, and Thakur Nahar Singh Jasol, Director of the Mehrangar Museum Trust in Jodhpur.

Back in the west, a number of students in my undergraduate and graduate courses have played a catalytic role in the writing of this book, forcing me, through their stimulating discussions and questions, to shape and sharpen my thinking on a number of issues: Bryan Cuevas, Than Garson, Bill Gorvine, Paul Hackett, Chuck Jones, Spencer Leonard, Derek Maher, Amir Muhammadi, David Need, Mark Siebold, Kerry Skora, Phil Stanley, Dennis Swaim, and Steve Weinberger. I also wish to thank Bronwen Bledsoe, Véronique Bouillier, Douglas Brooks, Mark Dyczkowski, Morten and Jytta Madsen, Jan Meulenbeld, John Roberts, Bo Sax, Alain Wattelier, and Dominik Wujastyk for the scholarly and material support they afforded me at various stages of this book's development. I am especially indebted to Dr. Arion Roşu, the greatest living western historian of Indian medicine, for the fatherly guidance he has shown me over the past decade. To Alexis Sanderson, without whom the sixth chapter of this work would still be the shambles that it was when he first read it, I also owe special thanks. Finally, I owe a great debt of gratitude to the late Mircea Eliade—the greatest modern "midwife" of historians of religions—whose groundbreaking studies inspired me to explore the field of Indian alchemy,[11] and who helped me to publish my first article on the subject.[12]

Publication of this book was funded in part by the Office of the Vice Provost for Research at the University of Virginia.

NOTE ON TRANSLITERATION

Unless otherwise noted, all transliterations from the Sanskrit follow standard lexicographical usage, with the following exceptions: (1) toponyms still in use are transliterated without diacritics (thus Srisailam and not Śrīśailam), except in the case of sites identified with deities (thus Kedārnāth and not Kedarnath); (2) names of authors and editors from the colonial and postcolonial periods are transliterated without diacriticals; (3) the term *Nāth* is transliterated in its modern Hindi form as opposed to the Sanskritic *Nātha;* (4) proper names of historical Nāth Siddhas are transliterated with the *-nāth* suffix, as opposed to the Sanskritic-*nātha* (however, see note 8 to chapter 1).

ABBREVIATIONS

ĀK *Ānandakanda* of Mahābhairava.
ASL Anup Sanskrit Library, Lalgarh Palace, Bikaner, India.
BhP *Bhūtiprakaraṇa* of the Gorakṣa Saṁhitā.
GAU Gujarat Ayurved University, Jamnagar, India.
HT Sanjukta Gupta, Dirk Jan Hoens, and Teun Goudriaan, *Hindu Tantrism.* Handbuch der Orientalistik, 2.4.2 (Leiden: Brill, 1979).
HTSL Teun Goudriaan and Sanjukta Gupta, *Hindu Tantric and Śākta Literature* (Wiesbaden: Harrassowitz, 1981).
HYP *Haṭhayogapradīpikā* of Svātmarāma.
KCKT *Kākacaṇḍīśvara Kalpa Tantra.*
KCM *Kākacaṇḍeśvarīmata.*
KhV *Khecarī Vidyā* of Ādinātha.
KJñN *Kaulajñānanirṇaya* of Matsyendranāth.
KM *Kubjikāmata.*
KPT *Kakṣapuṭa Tantra* of Siddha Nāgārjuna.
MBhT *Mātṛkabheda Tantra.*
MSL Mahārāja Mān Singh Library, Mehrangarh Fort, Jodhpur, India.
NNA Nepal National Archives, Kathmandu, Nepal.
NSC Ramlal Srivastav, ed., *"Nāth Siddh Carit" Viśeṣāṅk (Yog Vāṇi*, special issue no. 1 for 1984). Gorakhpur: Gorakhnath Mandir, 1984.
Ocean *The Ocean of Story Being C. H. Tawney's Translation of Somadeva's Kathā Sarit Sāgara (or Ocean of Streams of Story)*, ed. N. M. Penzer, 10 vols. (London: Chas. J. Sawyer, Ltd., 1924–28).
RA *Rasārṇava.*
RAK *Rasārṇavakalpa.*
RC *Rasendracūḍāmaṇi.*
RHT *Rasahṛdaya Tantra* of Govinda.
RM *Rasendra Maṅgala* of Śrīman Nāgārjuna.
RPS *Rasaprakāśa Sudhākara* of Yaśodhara.
RRĀ *Rasaratnākara* of Nityanātha.

RRS *Rasaratnasamucchaya* of Vāgbhaṭṭa II.
RU *Rasopaniṣat.*
RV *Ṛg Veda.*
SDS *Sarvadarśana Saṃgraha* of Mādhava.
SSP *Siddha Siddhānta Paddhati* of Gorakṣanātha.
ṢSS *Ṣaṭsāhasra Saṁhitā.*
SV "Siddh Vandanāṃ."
SvT *Svacchanda Tantra.*
TĀ *Tantrāloka* of Abhinavagupta.
VRĀ *Varṇaratnākara*
YRM *Yogaratnamālā.*
YSĀ *Yogisampradāyāviṣkṛti*

ONE

Indian Paths to Immortality

The emperor Aurangzeb issued a *firman* to Ānand Nāth, the abbot of Jakhbar, an obscure monastery in the Punjab, in 1661 or 1662:

> The letter sent by Your Reverence has been received along with two *tolahs* of quicksilver. However, it is not so good as Your Reverence had given us to understand. It is desired that Your Reverence should carefully treat some more quicksilver and have that sent, without unnecessary delay. A piece of cloth for a cloak and a sum of twenty-five rupees which have been sent as an offering will reach (Your Reverence). Also, a few words have been written to the valiant Fateh Chand to the effect that he should always afford protection.[1]

The greatest Mogul persecutor of Hinduism in history offers his protection to a Hindu abbot named Nāth in exchange for twenty grams of treated mercury. What is the story behind this curious missive?

1. Sexual Fluids in Medieval India

Some time around the sixth century A.D., a wave of genius began to sweep over India, a wave that has yet to be stilled. This wave, which took the form of a body of religious thought and practice, has been interpreted in a number of different ways by Indians and westerners alike. What some have called madness and abomination, others have deemed a path to ecstasy or the sublime. Such have been the evaluations of this phenomenon, which has, over some fourteen hundred years, never ceased to enthuse and confound.

The Indians who innovated this body of theory and practice called it *tantra*, "the warp (of reality)." The word has a most ancient pedigree. Its root, *tan*, means "to stretch," as one would a thread on a loom (also called *tantra*) or, in Vedic parlance, a body (*tanu*) to be sacrificed on an altar within the ritual framework (*tantra*).[2] Those persons who followed the way of tantra were called *tāntrika*s, and their written and orally transmitted works the *Tantra*s.

Indian tantrism,[3] in its Hindu, Buddhist, and Jain varieties, did not emerge out of a void. It was on the one hand influenced by cultural interactions with China, Tibet, central Asia, Persia, and Europe, interactions which had the Silk Road and medieval maritime routes and ports as their venue. Much more important, however, were the indigenous Indian roots of tantrism, which was not so much a departure from earlier forms of Hinduism as their continuation, albeit in sometimes tangential and heterodox ways. This book explores the uniquely Indian foundation of tantrism. More specifically, this book is an inquiry into those Hindu sectarian groups that have come to be known as the *Siddha*s, which, appropriating traditions that were more ancient than those of tantrism itself, did not in fact fully flower until the twelfth and thirteenth centuries. As a loosely structured religious community identified with a particular body of practice, the Siddhas have had greater staying power than the tāntrikas and continue to form a visible part of the Indian religious landscape.

As a common noun, *siddha*[4] means "realized, perfected one," a term generally applied to a practitioner (*sādhaka*, *sādhu*) who has through his practice (*sādhana*) realized his dual goal of superhuman powers (*siddhi*s, "realizations," "perfections") and bodily immortality (*jīvanmukti*). As a proper noun, *Siddha* becomes a broad sectarian appellation, applying to devotees of Śiva in the Deccan (*Māheśvara Siddha*s),[5] alchemists in Tamil Nadu (*Sittar*s), a group of early Buddhist tāntrikas from Bengal (*Mahāsiddha*s, *Siddhācārya*s), the alchemists of medieval India (*Rasa Siddha*s)[6] and, most especially, a mainly north Indian group known as the *Nāth Siddha*s.[7]

These last two groups greatly overlapped one another, with many of the most important Nāth Siddhas—Gorakh, Matsyendra, Carpaṭi, Dattātreya, Nāgnāth, Ādināth,[8] and others—being the authors (if only by attribution) or transmitters of a wide array of revealed yogic and alchemical teachings. The medieval Nāth Siddhas and Rasa Siddhas further interacted with a third group. This was the *paścimāmnāya* (Western Transmission), a Śākta sect devoted to the worship of the goddess Kubjikā which, based mainly in Nepal, also incorporated tantric,[9] yogic, and alchemical elements into its doctrine and practice.

A major point of convergence between these three groups, within the broader tantric matrix, was their cult of the Siddhas who were for them not historical figures but rather demigods and intermediaries between the human and the divine. Cults of these semidivine Siddhas go back to at least the beginning of the common era; they and their peers the Vidyādharas (Wizards) are a standard fixture of Indian fantasy and adventure literature throughout the medieval period.[10] Central to these cults was their "popular" soteriology, which had little in common with the "authorized" soteriologies of Vedic and classical Hinduism. The worlds of the Siddhas and Vidyādharas were the closest homologue India has known to popular western notions of heaven as a place of sensual gratification and freedom from the human condition. Those capable of acceding to these atmospheric levels remained there, liberated from the fruits of their acts (*karma*) and forever exempted from the lower worlds of rebirth (*saṃsāra*) but not divested of their individuality as is the case with the impersonal workings of release into the Absolute (*mokṣa*). A precursor of the Puranic notion of the "seventh heaven" of *brahmaloka* or *satyaloka*, the world of the Siddhas was a place that endured even beyond the cyclic dissolution (*pralaya*) at the close of a cosmic eon (*kalpa*). This popular tradition, whose reflection is found in the lower hierarchies of the Hindu and Buddhist pantheons, in adventure and fantasy literature, and in humble shrines to these anonymous demigods, lay beyond the pale of brahmanic control and legitimation. So too would the medieval Siddha movements, which appropriated for themselves, with certain modifications, the preexisting Siddha soteriology.

The most important innovation of these medieval Siddha traditions (the Nāth and Rasa Siddhas in particular) was the concrete and coherent method they proposed for the attainment of the Siddha world and Siddha status. This is what had been lacking in the earlier Siddha cults: the belief system was there, but the notions of how to reach that blessed abode were vague at best. Certain traditions maintained that it could be reached through travel,[11] others through the miraculous intervention of the Siddhas one propiated,[12] others through more serendipitous means. The later medieval Siddha movements proposed the following working principle: mere humans could, through their tantric, yogic, and alchemical practice, climb the ladder of being and accede to the ranks of the semidivine Siddhas. In this new perspective one could, by perfecting oneself, transform perfected role models into colleagues. A trace of the notion of a primordial ontological difference between those born perfect and those who made themselves perfect (not unlike the difference between old money and new) remains in works which categorize the Siddhas into the three *ogha*s (streams)—the divine, the perfected, and the human—but the dividing line between them was a dotted one that could be crossed through a systematic body of esoteric practice.[13]

Apart from this common heritage, a second point of convergence between the Nāth Siddhas, Rasa Siddhas, and the Western Transmission lies in their common body of mystic doctrines and practices involving sexual fluids—male and female sexual fluids, to be sure, but ever so much more. Since the time of the Vedas, *rasa*—the fluid element found in the universe, sacrifice, and human beings—has been more or less identified by Indians with the fount of life. All fluids, including vital fluids in humans, plant resins, rain, the waters, and the sacrificial oblation, are so many manifestations of *rasa*.[14] So too, since at least the dawn of the common era,[15] Indians have known that the miracle of conception occurs through the union of male and female vital fluids, semen and uterine blood. With early tantrism, these procreative fluids came to be conceived as "power substances" for the worship of and ultimately the identification with gods and goddesses whose boundless energy was often portrayed as sexual in nature. Nearly always, the god in question was some form of Śiva, the god whose worship in the form of a *liṅga* (phallus) dates from at least the second century B.C.[16] The way to becoming a "second Śiva"—for this has nearly always been the goal of tantric practice in its various forms—was, in early tantrism, realized through the conduit of a horde of wild goddesses (which the tāntrikas identified with their human consorts), generally known as *yoginī*s. These "bliss-starved" goddesses, attracted by offerings of mingled sexual fluids, would converge into the consciousness of the practitioner, to transform him, through their limitless libido, into a god on earth.[17]

Following the brilliant tenth- through eleventh-century reconfiguration of Trika Kaulism by Abhinavagupta and others, most of the messy parts of tantric practice (at least outward practice) were cleaned up, aestheticized, and internalized in different ways.[18] For the later "high" tantric schools, the cult of the *yoginī*s and the ritual production, offering, and consumption of sexual fluids were continued, but only within the restricted context of the "secret practice" of an inner circle of initiates. Outwardly, however, ritual sexuality had undergone a paradigm shift. Sexual fluids themselves were no longer the way to godhead; rather, it was in the bliss of sexual orgasm that one realized god-consciousness for oneself.[19]

In certain cases, all such transactions involving sexual fluids became wholly internalized and incorporated into the so-called subtle body (*sūkṣma śarīra*). Here, all humans were viewed as essentially androgynous with sexual intercourse an affair between a female serpentine nexus of energy, generally called the *kuṇḍalinī*, and a male principle, identified with Śiva, both of which were located within the subtle body. An intricate metaphysics of the subtle body—its relationship to the brute matter of the gross body as well as to the universal divine life force within, the bipolar dynamics of its male and female constituents, etc.—was developed in every tantric school.[20]

It was especially within two tantric sects, the Western Transmission and the Yoginī Kaula (transmitted by Matsyendra), that a practical concomitant to this speculative—and in some cases gnoseological or soteriological—metaphysics came to be elaborated. This was *haṭha yoga*, the "method of violent exertion," whose system of the six *cakras* ("wheels [or circles] of transformation") became the centerpiece of the doctrine and practice of the Nāth Siddhas—who claim their origins in the person and teachings of Matsyendranāth.[21] For the Nāth Siddhas, the *siddhis* and *jīvanmukti* were the direct results of the internal combination and transformation of sexual fluids into *amṛta*, the divine nectar of immortality.

Matsyendranāth and the founders of the Western Transmission were not alone, however, in their persistent emphasis on the sexual fluids as (generally internalized) power substances, rather than simply as by-products of a transubstantiating experience of bliss. At about the same time as their hathayogic systems were being elaborated, the matter of sexual fluids was being broached from a novel and rather unexpected angle by a third group. These were the Rasa Siddhas, the alchemists of medieval India, whose doctrines are best summed up in a classic aphorism from the foundational *Rasārṇava: yathā lohe tathā dehe*, "as in metal, so in the body."[22]

In a universe that was the ongoing procreation of the phallic god Śiva and his consort the Goddess,[23] a pair whose procreative activity was mirrored in the fluid transactions and transformations of human sexuality, in a universe whose every facet reflected the fundamental complementarity of the male and female principles, the mineral world too had its sexual valences and fluids. In the case of the Goddess, her sexual emission, her seed, took the form of mica, while her uterine or menstrual blood was identified with sulfur. There are a number of reasons for these identifications, not the least of which are chemical: mica and sulfur are important reagents in the purification and activation of the mineral homologue to divine semen. This is mercury, and if there ever was an elective affinity to be found at the interface between chemistry and theology, this is it. For what a miraculous mineral mercury is! Mercury is a shining liquid, amazingly volatile, seemingly possessed of a life of its own: what better homology could one hope to find for the semen of a phallic god? But this is not all. Mercury's chemical behavior as well is nothing short of miraculous, and as such it stands, in the words of an early twentieth-century scholar alchemist as the "central idea upon which the whole structure of the Hindu Chemistry is erected: viz., the fact that mercury can be made to swallow, by special processes, a considerable quantity of gold or other metals, without any appreciable increase in the weight of the swallowing mercury."[24]

Mercury, which when "swooned" drives away disease, "killed" revives itself, and "bound" affords the power of flight,[25] is the presence in the mineral world of the sexual essence of the Absolute. As such, it is as all-absorbing as Śiva who, at the end of cyclic time, implodes the entire universe into his yogic body, thereby transforming existence into essence. This is precisely what occurs in alchemical reactions. A "seed" (*bīja*) of gold or silver is planted in mercury (whose powers of absorption have been massively enhanced through a series of treatments in sulfur, mica, and other mainly "female" elements), which then becomes possessed of a "mouth" capable of "swallowing," of absorbing into itself, according to the alchemical scriptures, millions, even billions and trillions, of times its mass in base metals. These are thereby transmuted into gold, and in a tradition in which "gold is immortality,"[26] that's saying a mouthful. All that remains is for the alchemist to swallow the mercury in question to himself become a second Śiva, an immortal superman (Siddha) whose every bodily secretion becomes transmutative and transubstantiating. In tandem with his work in the laboratory, the Hindu alchemist also engages in the practice of *haṭha yoga*, as well as a certain number of erotico-mystical tantric operations involving the sexual fluids that he and his female laboratory assistant generate in order to catalyze reactions between divine sexual fluids in their mineral forms. In the end, all is a continuity of sexual fluids.

2. Tāntrikas, Siddhas, and Yogis

The sole surviving heirs to this medieval legacy are the Nāth Siddhas, who continue to be revered, on a popular level at least, as India's masters of yoga and wizards of alchemy, the last living guides along the secret paths to supernatural power and bodily immortality. Theirs is a powerful legacy. On the one hand, they are perfected immortals who have chosen to remain in the world of men, moving through it even as they transcend its transience and attendant sorrows. On the other, for persons still trapped in this world, a good Siddha is hard to find.

Hindu tantrism disappeared as a major sectarian phenomenon a number of centuries ago, a victim of its own excesses.[27] These excesses were primarily of two orders. The first and best documented is nonetheless less important than the second. This excess was one of bad publicity. In seeking to truly live out their principles of nondifference—between god and creature, elite and preterite, squalor and grandeur, the exalted and the demented—many tāntrikas, openly indulging in cross-caste adultery, coprophagy, and all manner of other purity violations and antisocial behavior (or at least openly claiming to do so), were simply revolting to the general public. The second excess, which truly sounded the death knell of tantrism as an important religious movement, came as the result of a sea change in tantric theory and practice. Following Abhinavagupta, tantrism became transformed into an elite mystic path that was all too complicated, refined, and cerebralized for common people to grasp. The man on the street could not recognize himself in its discourse. It bore too little resemblance to his experience as a mortal being inhabiting a body doomed to age and die, entangled in the meantime within a network of family and social relations; wielding plowshares, hammers, and the like; living, loving, and dying on the trampled earth of a village his people had inhabited for hundreds of years. The thirty-six or thirty-seven metaphysical levels of being were incomprehensible to India's masses and held few answers to their human concerns and aspirations.

For the Nāth Siddhas, whose institutionalized sectarian orders (*sampradāyas*) mainly grew out of earlier and more heterodox Śaiva orders (the Pāśupatas and Kāpālikas in particular), the "brahmanization" of tantrism and its departure from the realm of the concrete into that of the sublime came as a boon of sorts. For whereas "high" tantrism was now mainly offering transcendence of the world, the Nāth Siddhas' path continued to offer concrete and relatively accessible *power* in the world. For the masses, as well as for kings whose concerns were often more this-worldly than those of brahman metaphysicians, the Nāths and many of their fellow Siddhas became the supernatural power brokers of medieval India. The Siddhas, yogins and alchemists that they are, have always been technicians of the *concrete:* specialists in the concrete transmutation of base metals into gold and the concrete transformation of mortal, aging man into a perfected, immortal superman, masters of the natural processes rather than mere victims of or bystanders to them. Theirs has always been a path to mastery and raw, unadulterated power—mastery over the forces of nature, including the inexorable processes of aging and death, and dominion over the temporal powers of even the greatest kings and armies.

In this context, the Nāth Siddhas have often been cast in the role of kingmakers, elevating untested boys to the thrones of kingdoms throughout medieval south Asia, at times bringing down mighty tyrants in the process.[28] But India has also always been a country of villages, and the Nāth Siddhas, whose backgrounds have generally been humble, have long been the special champions of village India. These are cowherd boys who, having performed minor miracles at an early age, were initiated into a Siddha order and grew up to be immortal, hail-stopping "god men." Many are the accounts I have heard, from traveling salesmen, university students, monastic novices, and village plowboys alike, of these perfected beings who have dotted and even defined the religious landscape of village India with their awesome, death-defying presence.

The Nāth Siddhas' persistent popular success, coupled with their generally humble social backgrounds, the relative accessibility of their path, and the this-worldly focus of their practices and goals, has long made them the object of scorn and censure on the part of India's social, cultural, and religious elites—the upper castes, urban intelligentsia, and cosmopolitan literati whose religious proclivities have tended more towards refined and cosmeticized orthodoxy or cerebralized tantrism. Indeed, the Nāth Siddhas have long been accused of being charlatans or mere conjurers—an accusation that India's street magicians have long used to their advantage, posing as yogins or tāntrikas in their performances.[29] It is in this context that we must introduce yet another important term to our lexicon. This is the term *Yogi* (*Jogi*, in vernacular parlance), which has to a certain extent supplanted the terms "tāntrika," "Kāpālika," and "heretic" in orthodox Hindu discourse. While *yogi[n]* is nothing more than an adjectival or possessive form of the term *yoga*, used to designate a practitioner of yoga, the term came to take on a sectarian and often pejorative connotation in medieval India, a connotation which has remained operative down to the present day. "Yogi" or "jogi" has, for at least eight hundred years, been an all-purpose term employed to designate those Śaiva religious specialists whom orthodox Hindus have considered suspect, heterodox, and even heretical in their doctrine and practice. On the one hand, the Yogis are defined (like the tāntrikas of an earlier time) by their nonconformity to and exclusion from orthodox categories: they are that troubling aggregate of sectarian groups and individuals whose language and behavior subvert the canons of

Vedic, devotional, and "high" tantric religion. On the other hand, they are defined by certain features of their sectarian affiliations and practices: heirs to the heterodox Pāśupatas and Kāpālikas of an earlier age, they are devotees of terrible forms of Śiva (usually Bhairava) who besmear themselves with ashes, leave their hair uncut, and continue to adhere to the practices of "primitive" tantrism. As such, their "yoga" is more closely identified, in the jaundiced eyes of their critics, with black magic, sorcery, sexual perversion, and the subversion of alimentary prohibitions than with the practice of yoga in the conventional sense of the term. In recent times, "Yogi" has been most specifically applied to the Nāth Siddhas, who are widely known as Kānphaṭa (Split-eared, for the very visible earrings they wear in holes bored through the thick of their ears, the hallmark of the order) Yogis or Jogis—a term that they themselves eschew.

This book, then, is about those tantric movements and sects which called themselves and continue to call themselves Siddhas, but which were—following the "brahmanization" of the tantrism with which they had interacted throughout their early development—branded as Yogis by the Hindu orthodoxy. That these Yogis were alchemists is borne out by no less a person than Marco Polo who, describing a group of *ciugi* (Jogis) whom he had encountered on the Malabar coast of India at the close of the thirteenth century, attributed their superhuman life spans of 150 to 200 years to their ingestion of an elixir composed of mercury and sulfur.[30] Some five hundred years later, Marco Polo's observations are seconded by the French traveler François Bernier, a Catholic man of letters, when he notes that the Yogis "know how to make gold and to prepare mercury so admirably that one or two grains taken every morning restore the body to perfect health."[31]

What links these two accounts in a most startling way is that their descriptions of Yogis both seem to define these figures as *alchemists.* Yogis were healthy, had good digestion, and lived for hundreds of years because they ingested mercury and sulfur as part of their daily regime. Here, let us also recall that the *firman* Aurangzeb sent to the Nāth Siddha abbot of the Jakhbar monastery was a request for treated mercury. These data, set against the backdrop of the vast wealth of yogic literature—as well as a sprinkling of alchemical works—produced by such illustrious Nāth Siddhas as Gorakhnāth and Matsyendranāth, can lead to only one conclusion. The Siddhas, the Yogis, of medieval India were both alchemists (Rasa Siddhas) and pioneers of *haṭha yoga* (Nāth Siddhas). Yoga and alchemy were complementary, interpenetrating disciplines for the medieval Siddhas.

The Rasa Siddhas and Nāth Siddhas, if they were not one and the same people, were at least closely linked in their practice. The balance of this book is devoted to proving this thesis.

3. The Quest for Immortality: The Vedic Legacy

The altogether human aspiration to be possessed of a body not subject to the trammels of death finds its earliest Indian expression in the ca. 1200 B.C. *Ṛg Veda*, in which a poet pleads "Deliver me from death, not from nondeath."[32] Here, the Vedic term *amṛta* is a polyvalent one, at once signifying nondeath (*a-mṛta*), immortality, the immortals (the gods), the world of the immortals (heaven)—and nectar or ambrosia (which is the Greek cognate of *amṛta*), the draft of immortality, by which the gods remain immortal. It is this final gloss that is the most pregnant with meaning for the later traditions I treat in these pages. In the Vedic context, the gods win and maintain their eternal life by offering *soma*, the miraculous herb of immortality, as a sacrificial oblation among themselves.

Here, the rich Vedic (and Indo-European) mythology of the theft of *soma*[33]—from either the atmospheric Gandharvas or the rival Asuras (antigods)—is given a particularly sacrificial gloss in the priestly tradition of the brahmanic literature. It is not enough to simply possess the *soma*—or any sacrificial oblation for that matter—to benefit from it. Rather, as the gods first discovered, it is by offering or surrendering the sacrifice to another (god) that its benefits accrue to the sacrificer. The brutish Asuras, unable to fathom this secret, each offered the oblation into his own mouth and so failed to win (the benefits of) the world of the sacrifice.[34]

In the Vedic present, humans who have now learned the secret of sacrifice come to reap its benefits by offering the sacrificial oblation (idealized as *soma* regardless of the oblatory material) to the gods. The oblation sustains the gods and maintains their immortality; moreover, the fruit of the sacrifice that accrues to the human sacrificer also takes the form of a certain order of immortality.[35] In addition to fulfilling to the more or less mundane aspirations of the brahmanic sacrificer—wealth in cows, faithful wives, sons, etc.—the principal fruit of the sacrifice was a mitigated immortality for a "full life span" (*viśvāyus*) of one hundred years. Therefore, in order to live a full life, one had to sacrifice constantly, "for a hundred years is tantamount to immortality."[36]

There were two ways in which sacrifice saved one from death. The first of these was the mechanism of sacrifice itself. According to brahmanic theory, the body one inhabited in life was in fact a loan from the gods or, more precisely, from Yama, the Lord of the Dead. As such, sacrifice was nothing other than a payment on a loan; failure to pay (i.e., offer sacrifice) resulted in repossession (i.e., death). In order that his debtors might keep up on their payments, Yama, Vedic Hinduism's cosmic "repo man," threw in a piece of land with the body he loaned: this was the parcel on which the sacrificer installed his household (*gārhapatya*) fire.[37] In this context, the English term "mortgage" (literally "dead pledge") for "the conveyance of real or personal property by a debtor to a creditor as security for a debt"[38] to be repaid within a fixed period of time takes on a new fullness of meaning. Under the terms of Yama's and the gods' contract, no human could occupy a body for more than one hundred years, since such would have been tantamount to (divine) immortality. Thus, once again, "a hundred years is tantamount to immortality."

The second way in which the sacrifice saved humans from death lay in the nature of the oblation itself. *Soma*, the divine nectar of immortality, was, in the time of the Vedas, considered (or fantasized) to be accessible to humans, whence such hymns as: "We have drunk the Soma; we have become immortal; we have gone to the light; we have found the gods. . . . Far-famed Soma, stretch out our lifespans so that we may live. . . . The drop that we have drunk has entered our hearts, an immortal inside mortals."[39]

Like fire (*agni*), *soma* is both a substance and the god identified with that fluid oblation.[40] Early on, however, Soma the god became identified with the moon (Indu, in Vedic parlance), which was considered to be a drop (*indu*) of nectar (*amṛta*), of *soma*, shining in the heavens.[41] But the moon, this drop of nectar, was nothing other than divine seed (*retas*),[42] which was identified by analogy with vital fluids both animal and vegetable (*rasa*),[43] as well as with the vivifying rains and waters (*āp*), which were so many medicines or remedies (*bheṣaja*) for all that ails mortal man.[44]

It is the fluid element (*rasa*), then, that the Vedic theoreticians conceived as the support of all life and indeed of nondeath for humans as well as gods. As I have already noted, however, the potential of the fluid oblation could not be activated or realized without the dynamic of sacrifice, which also brought two other elements into play: these were fire (*agni*), divinized as Agni, the god of fire; and wind (*vāyu*), the active element of exchange, which conveyed the essence of the sacrificial oblation from the world of humans to the divine realm. This trinity of elements (and gods) was complemented by another conceptual triad, which served and continues to serve as the ground for the network of homologies and analogies that are the framework of the entire sweep of Indian symbol systems. This is the triad constituted by the human being (microcosm), the mediating mechanism of the sacrifice (mesocosm), and the universe as a whole (macrocosm)—which is often conceived as the body of a universal man or god.[45] A passage from the *Śatapatha Brāhmaṇa* (9.5.1.11) plays on all of these interrelations: "When he [the sacrificer] has offered in the fire, he drinks [*soma*]; for that [fire altar] is his divine body, and this [the sacrificer's body] is his [the fire god Agni's] human one."

As I will show, this threefold structure, in combination with the triad of fluid-fire-wind, comes to inform both medical and yogic models of digestion, conception, metabolism, and bodily regeneration, as well as alchemical models of the chemical reactions between the fluid element mercury (called *rasa*) and the fiery element sulfur, transmutation in the laboratory, and the transubstantiation of the human body.

Already in Vedic traditions we find embryonic notions of this interplay between the human, divine, and sacrificial—and mineral—realms. In a hymn of praise to *odana*, the sacrificial porridge, the *Atharva Veda* (11.3.1–2,7–8) states that "of this porridge Bṛhaspati is the head, Bráhman the mouth, heaven and earth the ears, sun and moon the eyes, the seven seers the in- and out-breaths . . . dark metal its flesh, red metal its blood, tin its ash, gold its complexion."[46]

Later, the *Śatapatha Brāhmaṇa* (6.1.3.1–5) puts a mineral twist on one of its many accounts of the creation of the universe through the self-sacrifice of the cosmic god-man Prajāpati:

> Verily, Prajāpati alone was here in the beginning. He desired "May I exist, may I reproduce myself." He toiled, he heated himself with inner heat. From his exhausted and overheated body the waters flowed forth . . . from those heated waters foam arose; from the heated foam there arose clay; from the heated clay, sand; from the heated sand, grit; from the heated grit, rock; from the heated rock, metallic ore; and from the smelted ore, gold arose.

The Vedic ritual in which the exhausted and decomposed body of the creative self-sacrificer Prajāpati was restored to wholeness was called the *agnicayana*, the "piling of [the] Fire [altar]," of which an important moment was the installation of a golden image of a man (*hiraṇya-puruṣa*) beneath a corner of the altar emplacement. With this ritual, the *adhvaryu* priest intoned, "He is Prajāpati, he is Agni, he is made of gold for gold is light and fire is light; gold is immortality and fire is immortality. He is a man for Prajāpati is the Man."[47]

Let us note here that the thermal energy that transforms the body of Prajāpati into gold (and in other myths of this sort, the entire created universe in all its parts) is an inner fire or heat that is kindled through religious austerities. Within a few centuries of the composition of this Brāhmaṇa text, a revolution in Indian thought would issue into the notion that humans too could internalize the sacrifice and thereby entirely bypass the mechanism of external sacrifice. This inward turn, which would ground the entire gnostic and nondualist project of the Upaniṣads, also sowed the seeds for the innovation of a body of techniques for internal bodily transformation—i.e., for the practice of *haṭha yoga*. Here one's bodily fluids, and semen in particular, become identified with the oblation, the heat of inner austerities with fire, and breath with the dynamic element of wind.[48]

It is in the *Atharva Veda* in particular that we find the most important foundations for the later medical and alchemical traditions, which sought to extend (indefinitely) the life span of human beings. Indeed, it is in this text that one finds the greatest preponderance of healing hymns involving the use of charms and herbal remedies to restore the ailing patient to health. At the center of this practice stood the healer (*bhiṣaj*) who was also a possessed "shaker" (*vipra*) and an inspired master of incantation (*kavi*).[49] Part physician, part shaman, part sorcerer, the *atharvan* priest was viewed as both powerful and dangerous by Vedic society. For this very reason, perhaps, his heir, the itinerant Ayurvedic physician (*cāraṇa-vaidya*) was also regarded with suspicion by "good" brahmanic society.[50]

That the Hindu medical tradition (Āyurveda, the "science of longevity") is the self-conscious heir to the Atharvavedic synthesis is clearly evinced in the *Caraka Saṁhitā*, the textual cornerstone of this tradition: "The physician [*vaidya*] . . . should manifest his devotion to the Atharva Veda . . . because the Veda of the *atharvans* has discussed medicine [*cikitsā*] by way of prescribing donations, propitiatory rites, offerings, auspicious rites, oblations, observance of rules, expiations, fasting, and *mantras;* and because it indicates that medicine improves the quality of life."[51]

Within the Indian medical science of Āyurveda, the term employed for the prestigious body of techniques devoted to rejuvenation therapy is *rasāyana*, the "path of *rasa*," of which an important component consists in the application of herbal remedies, inherited in part from the *Atharva Veda*. This same term, *rasāyana*, is also used by the Rasa Siddhas to designate their alchemical "Work in two parts," with its dual emphasis on transmutation and bodily transubstantiation. In this alchemical context, *rasa* is a term for the fluid metal mercury, the mineral hierophany of the vital seed of the phallic god Śiva.

TWO

Categories of Indian Thought: The Universe by Numbers

1. Microcosm, Macrocosm, and Mesocosm

Of all the conceptual constructs I treat in this book, the most pervasive and persistent by far is that which treats of the multivalent relationships or homologies obtaining between the individual and the world, or the microcosm and the macrocosm. Spanning the history of ideas the world over, three broad strategies for describing this relationship have predominated. These are the monist (which maintains that creature, creation, and creator are essentially one), the dualist (all is two), and the atomist (all is many)—with a myriad of permutations, qualifications, and recombinations on these three basic organizing principles.

Although the sacrificial worldview of the Vedas was a dualistic one, it was one that nonetheless allowed for a breakthrough or transfer to occur —via the sacrifice—between man in the world and the gods in heaven, between the human world order and divine cosmic order (which together formed a whole called *ṛta*). As a transfer mechanism or template between the two orders of being, between the human (*adhyātman*) and the divine (*adhidevatā*), the sacrifice became possessed of an ontological status of its own. That which pertained to the sacrifice (*yajña*), to that pivot between the human and divine worlds without which neither could survive, was termed *adhiyajña*.[1] This tripartite configuration, undoubtedly the most pervasive structure to be found in the Indian world of ideas, has come to be applied to a myriad of domains, across a wide array of religions, philosophies, and scientific disciplines, including those of yoga and alchemy. I term the three members of this configuration—of human + mediating structure + divine—as *microcosm*, *mesocosm*, and *macrocosm*.[2]

Over time, the mechanism of sacrifice itself came to take precedence over both the humans who enacted it and the gods to whom it was offered, and so we find, in the tenth- through eighth-century B.C. body of revelation known as the *Brāhmaṇas* (Priestly Books), the notion that the sacrifice (or the ritual of sacrifice) is all that truly matters in the universe. Humans and gods become tributary to the sacrifice in this period, and the sole gods granted any importance are precisely gods of sacrifice. These are (1) Puruṣa/Prajāpati, the "Man" or "Lord of Creatures" whose primal (self-) sacrifice, which "created" the universe, stands as the model for every sacrifice that has followed; (2) Agni, "(Sacrificial) Fire," and (3) Soma, the "Fluid" god of the sacrificial oblation. In a sense, this brahmanic triad of sacrificial gods is itself a reworking of the triune Vedic universe, with two static elements (gods and humans, oblation and fire) being mediated by an active third element (the enacted sacrifice).

Throughout the history of Indian thought, no set of concrete elements has been as pervasive as this sacrificial triad—of fluid, fire, and air; of *rasa*, *agni*, and *vāyu*. Although the three members of this triad have, according to their specific fields of application, taken the form of moon-sun-wind, semen-blood-breath, or mercury-sulfur-air, they have always borne the same valences as they did in their original Vedic context. Much of this book will be devoted to describing the ways in which fluid, semen, moon, and mercury on the one hand, and fire, blood, sun, and sulfur on the other—always mediated by the active element of air, wind, and breath—have interacted with one another through the "sacrificial" structure of microcosm-mesocosm-macrocosm, across a dozen interpenetrating ritual and belief systems and some three thousand years of cultural history.

Two other features of the Vedic synthesis which have persisted through time need also to be mentioned here. The first of these is a fascination with number. If, as the Brahmanic sources assert, the sacrifice in all its parts is identical to the universe in all its parts, then it is necessary to enumerate all of those parts, and "cross-list" them with other parts. More than this, the number of parts in a given whole—for example, the 4 × 11 syllables of the *triṣṭubh* meter—has a significance which is independent of that aggregate of parts for which it is the numerical index. Thus, it was not uncommon for the priestly commentators on the ritual to wax poetic on the "eleven-ness" of the number eleven, and so on.[3] This Vedic fascination becomes a veritable obsession in tantrism, in which we witness nothing less than an explosion of numbers, categories, and numbers as categories. In the tantric case, the hallucinating proliferation of number-based homologies—between microcosm, mesocosm, and macrocosm—appears, in the final analysis, to serve to reassure the tantric practitioner of the efficacy of his ritual acts—something akin, perhaps, to the many numerical proofs for the existence of God that illuminated western savants have proferred over the centuries. Number and proportion become the very foundation of the good, the true, and the beautiful, in the petals of the lotus, just as they do in their western reflection, the Secret Rose.

Much of this chapter will be devoted precisely to this matter of numerical progression, from duality to ternarity and thence to pentads, the number sixteen, and the staggering figures given in Hindu reckonings of the duration of the cosmic eons (*kalpa*s). Out of all these dilations of number, however, there emerges a single bipolar[4] dynamic that has played itself out in the form of four interrelated temporal cycles that Hindus have employed, over the centuries, to situate the microcosmic individual within (or without) the macrocosmic flow of time. A series of charts will illustrate these interrelated cycles.

A second leitmotif concerns the dynamics of the sacrificial and later systems. The aggregate of microcosm-mesocosm-macrocosm would not be an interesting or useful one were an exchange not possible among the three levels. This is the exchange, nay the transformation, that is effected through sacrifice, that most exalted of human activities, in which men "do what the gods did in the beginning."[5] As I have already indicated, the sacrificial world order was dualistic: there was a sharp break between the human order and the divine, cosmic order, which only sacrifice could bridge. This it did as if magically: a pot broken in this world, that is, in the sacrificial context, becomes a whole pot in that world of the gods.[6] The metaphysics that flowed from this system therefore assumed the building blocks of reality to be discrete and impermeable. Its dynamic was one of differentiation and reintegration. This dualistic approach, which finds early expression in the Rgvedic "Hymn of the Man" (10.90), is restated time and again in later texts, sometimes taking on sexual valences (to describe a universe in which all is ultimately two), such as in a *Bṛhadāraṇyaka Upaniṣad* myth which depicts Prajāpati as splitting into male and female halves to incestuously reintegrate "himself" through all manner of human and animal forms.[7] This is the mythic foundation of Sāṃkhya, literally the "enumerating" philosophy, the earliest of the Indian philosophical systems.

Out of this dualist system, or perhaps in response to it, there emerged another current of thought, this a mystic and monistic one which, on the contrary, assumed a continuity of being, extending unbroken from the supreme absolute down to the lowest forms of inert matter. Because all being, every being, was emanated from a primal and ultimate source, it thereby participated in some way in the very Being of that Absolute. This gnoseological doctrine, first promulgated in the *Āraṇyaka*s (the ca. seventh-century B.C. "Forest Books") and the classic *Upaniṣad*s (the ca. sixth-century B.C. traditions of "Placing in Equivalence") maintained that all bodies, but especially all souls (*ātman*), participated in the nature of the absolute or universal soul (*bráhman*). If "*ātman* is *bráhman* in a pot [the body]," then one need merely break the pot to fully realize the primordial unity of the individual soul with the plenitude of Being that was the Absolute. To know it was to be it.[8] This early monism is known by the name of Vedānta, because it is broached in the Upaniṣads, that corpus which constitutes the "end (*anta*) of the Veda." As we will see later in this chapter, it was likely the concrete experience of yoga that gave rise to this mystical and monistic vision. All apparent oppositions—between god and man, between male and female, etc.—here become consumed as it were in the fires of yogic austerities (*tapas*) conceived as the internalization of the sacrifice. The notion of transfer (from one plane to another) becomes metamorphosed into one of transformation (one plane primordially and ultimately *is*—the same as—the other), with the human body itself becoming the seat of the sacrifice and the human soul the indwelling Absolute. These two dynamic systems, of dualist differentiation and reintegration and monist emanation and participation, inform, singly or in combination, all of the Indian traditions that pass in review in these pages. They are vital to an understanding of any and every Indian metaphysical system.

If we are to understand the dynamics of these systems, two further notions are absolutely essential here. The first concerns the nature of the "body" that transmigrates from the corpse of a deceased person to a world of intermediate afterlife, identified in Upanishadic Hinduism with the moon. This body, termed the "body of enjoyment" (*bhoga-śarīra*), is an elaboration on the subtle body (*sūkṣma śarīra*), i.e., the "living being" (*jīva*) that, according to nondualist thought, mediates between the eternal but wholly intangible soul and the gross body (*sthūla śarīra*) composed of the five elements: earth, water, air, fire, and ether. As I demonstrate, the subtle body—especially when it is "clothed" in the body of enjoyment—becomes *lunar* at certain points in its cyclic existence, filling out and diminishing, in the unending course of births and deaths, around the "core" of the immortal soul. Like the moon itself, this transmigrating body is also "fluid"; like the moon, the subtle body is composed of incremental digits or members (*kalā*s)[9] that come into being and pass away, to be renewed yet again.

The second basic notion concerns the five elements to which I referred a moment ago. In the individual, it is via these elements that a correlation exists between the subtle and gross body. To the five gross elements that are the building blocks of the gross body and the universe correspond the five subtle elements (as well as the five senses of grasping and of perception). More than this, the universal macrocosm and the human microcosm are essentially composed of a "layering" of the elements. Armed with the knowledge that the body is nothing more than a series of overlays of the five hierarchized elements, Indian mystic thought innovated a concrete technique for the return of being into essence, for the resorption of the human microcosm into its divine source. By first "imploding" the lower gross elements into the higher, the practitioner could thence implode, via the subtle ether, the gross into the subtle and by degrees telescope the subtle back into its essential source, the individual soul (*ātman*) which, as the Upanisadic gnosis never tired of reiterating, was identical to the universal Soul, the absolute *bráhman*. Later, Hindu Tantra would carry this reasoning to its logical conclusion, conceptually imploding body, individual soul, and divine Soul into One:

> Ultimately the conscious bits of the universe, like stones, are also God and hence consciousness, but a consciousness that has decided to conceal itself (*ātmasaṃkoca*) . . . The world of the Tantric, then, is ultimately all God, but it contains a vast range of things, from things as gross as stones to things as subtle as God . . . Looking from God downwards, we have the range from conscious to unconscious, the range from simple to complex, and the range from subtle to gross. These three ranges are co-ordinate; in fact they are different aspects of the same thing. Moreover, movement down the scale is precisely what happens when God creates the universe.[10]

2. Ternarity and Bipolarity in Veda and Āyurveda

Two practical disciplines that grew out of the Vedic matrix to interact with Hindu and Buddhist philosophical and mystic traditions well before the beginnings of the tantric age were Āyurveda and the body of physical and meditative techniques known as yoga. Both traditions have their origins in the Vedas, both emerge as systems of thought and practice in or around the sixth century B.C., and both continue to share common methods and goals down to the present day. When we go back to the very first use of term *yoga*, in the *Ṛg Veda* (7.86.8; 10.166.5), we find that it is part of a compound: *yoga-kṣema* means "harmonious adjustment."[11] As we will see, the principal aim of Ayurvedic practice is also adjustment: *sama-yoga* is the harmonious conjunction of microcosmic and macrocosmic "climates." Also growing out of the Vedic matrix is the metaphor of cooking for such transformative processes as sacrifice, cremation, digestion, aging, and the yogic austerities. As in Vedic sacrifice, so in yoga and Āyurveda: the body is to be "cooked to a turn" (*paripakvā*).[12]

The extent to which the yogic and Ayurvedic perspectives interacted with other nascent Indian traditions is incalculable. The organizing principles of the sixth-century B.C. teachings of the Buddha on suffering and its cessation were essentially medical;[13] conversely, one finds Buddhist terminology as well as an inductive method that is clearly Buddhistic[14] in the most venerable textual pillar of Āyurveda, the *Caraka Saṁhitā* (compiled between the third century B.C. and the fourth century A.D.).[15] This same source contains what is perhaps the earliest complete expression of Sāṃkhya philosophy that has come down to us.[16] Towards the end of this same period, such Upaniṣads as the *Praśna* (3.6), and *Maitrī* (6.22, 30; 7.11.2–5) were tentatively charting the yogic body and practicing yoga as a means to concretely experiencing the absolute in ways that were deeper than reason could know.[17] It is not our intention here to trace a chain of transmission of ideas from one tradition to another, but rather to present them as variations on a *sensus communis* that existed in India from a very early time, even before the recorded teachings of the Buddha, the proto-Sāṃkhya of Caraka, and the dualist Sāṃkhya and the monistic Vedanta of the early Upaniṣads. Here, we follow the French physician and historian of Indian medicine Jean Filliozat, when he states that "the Samkhyan concepts, like those of Āyurveda, are part and parcel of the intellectual baggage common to all Indian thinkers."[18]

According to Āyurveda, the human being is composed of a triad of psychic being (*sattva*), soul (*ātman*), and body (*śarīra*), which arises from yet is distinct from *puruṣa*, the transcendent self. Āyurveda is thus a dualistic system. Like all living creatures, the human being is possessed of natural characteristics (*prakṛti*), which are sixfold: the five gross elements (*mahābhūtas*) presided over by the *ātman:* "Earth is that which is solid in man, water is that which is moist, fire is that which heats up, air is breath, ether the empty spaces, *bráhman* is the inner soul (*ātman*)."[19] As such, the human self is an exact replica of the macrocosm: "Indeed, this world is the measure (*sammita*) of the man. However much diversity of corporeal forms and substances there is in the world, that much [diversity] there is in man; however much there is in man, that much there is in the world."[20]

When applied to the medical tradition proper, these concepts define the physician's craft: the treatment of imbalances between the bodily microcosm and the universal macrocosm, i.e., of diseases. Critical to the Ayurvedic understanding of the body and its metabolic functions is its conceptualization of the process of digestion. This is a seven-step process, in which the food one eats is serially "burned" or refined, over the seven "fires of digestion" (*dhātvagnis*) into the seven bodily constituents (*dhātus*).[21] In order, these are chyle (*rasa*),[22] blood (*rakta*), flesh (*māṃsa*), fat (*medas*), bone (*asthi*), marrow (*majja*), and finally, in men, semen or sperm (*śukra*, *retas*).[23] In women, the seventh *dhātu* is uterine or menstrual blood (*śoṇita*, *artava*), or, after childbirth, breast milk.[24]

Āyurveda further conceives of bodily metabolism in terms of an interaction between the *doṣa*s, the three "morbid states"[25] or humors, of phlegm (*śleṣma*), bile (*pitta*), and wind (*vāta*). While we may see in the humors a reapplication of the Vedic *rasa-agni-vāyu* triad, we should note that they also anticipate one of India's most important metaphysical constructs, that of the three "strands" (*guṇa*s) of manifest being, the discussion of which is first broached in the classic Upaniṣads. According to Sāṃkhya, the three strands—white *sattvā*, red *rajas*, and black *tamas*—remain in a state of equilibrium for so long as the universe persists in a nonmanifest state. It is an unexplained disturbance in their equilibrium that triggers a gradual fall into manifestation, which is cast as the self-reproduction of the original materiality (*prakṛti*).[26]

The Ayurvedic *doṣa*s are of the same order as the *guṇa*s in the sense that, for so long as a human being is not exposed to the outside world (when in the womb, for example), it enjoys a perfect balance of *doṣa*s.[27] When, however, it becomes exposed to the outside world, the *doṣa*s fall out of balance and the individual becomes subject to health disorders. It is in these cases that the Ayurvedic physician must intervene to restore the lost equilibrium between the bodily microcosm and the universal macrocosm, a macrocosm whose climatic changes are governed by the interactions of moon (*rasa*), sun (*agni*), and wind (*vāyu*).[28] As we will show, the physician's most powerful weapon against such humoral imbalances is the sequestering of his patient in an edifice identified with that womb within which his *doṣa*s had originally been in perfect balance.

The identification of the three *doṣa*s with the three components of sacrifice is also explicit in Āyurveda. The body's inner fire (*antarāgni*) is represented by the fiery liquid that is bile; phlegm is "lunar" (*saumya*) fluid, and the microcosmic wind bears the same name as it does in the macrocosm: *vāyu* (or *vāta*). Each of these three *doṣa*s is further subdivided into five types. In the case of the windy humor, the five breaths are known as: *prāṇa*, the in-breath that enters the body via the nostrils and sustains the body; *udāna*, the out-breath that is the vehicle of speech; *samāna*, the breath that moves food through the digestive organs and kindles the fires of digestion; *apāna*, the breath that voids the lower body of excretions; and *vyāna*, the breath that circulates throughout the body, vehiculating the inner fluids and producing bodily locomotion.[29]

Similarly, there are five "lunar" phlegms and five "fiery" biles, the first of which is the fire of digestion (*pacaka*). In the process of digestion, the product of each cooking process is of a more refined nature, but also of a lesser volume than that *dhātu* from which it is produced.[30] This is perceived as a long and even dangerous process. Over the period of twenty-eight days required for the "raw" food one consumes to be fully transformed into semen, the human microcosm is subject to a certain number of dangers. These dangers are of two orders. The first of these concerns only males directly. This is the sex drive, which inclines men to lose, in a single stroke, all that a full month of digestion has provided them: I return to this special problem at the end of this book. The second of these, of a more general order, is the nature of the universal macrocosm or ecocosm, the many climatic changes of which constitute so many threats to the human microcosm and so many challenges to the Ayurvedic physician.

The *vaidya* is armed with two powerful weapons for battling the humoral imbalances that so threaten the harmonious functioning of the digestive and metabolic processes. First, he may calm (*śamana*) the overaccumulation of a given *doṣa* internally, through dietary regimen and the use of pharmaceutical preparations, the scientific development of which owes much to the alchemical tradition in India. Should this fail, he may take recourse to external purifications (*śodhana*) through clinical therapy which in an unexpected way constitutes an adaptation of a number of yogic principles and techniques. We now turn to the conceptual foundations that undergird these two Ayurvedic techniques.

In a groundbreaking study written twenty years ago,[31] Francis Zimmermann set forth the Ayurvedic principles for adjusting the human microcosm to the universal macroclimate or ecocosm. Here, he outlined the ways in which the Ayurvedic physician, by employing dietary regimens, medicines, and clinical techniques appropriate to a specific locus in time and space (*ṛtu-sātmya*), is able to ensure the continuity of the good life. Ultimately, one may conceive of the physician's practice as one of confronting time—both the time that ages mortals and saps them of life (time as death) and the time that takes the form of seasonal or temporal changes which have more immediate effects on the human organism. In Vedic sacrifice, "articulating activity" (*ṛtu*) is the foundation of a universe that is well-ordered, regulated, or "articulated" (*ṛta*). Thus the Vedic god of sacrifice Prajāpati, who is also the year, is reordered, rearticulated, and reconstructed through the human activity of sacrifice.

With the last of the Brāhmaṇas, the *Gopatha Brāhmaṇa*, these notions become applied to the treatment of disease: "It is at the turning points between seasons that afflictions arise; therefore, sacrifices are performed at the turning points between seasons."[32] In Āyurveda, however, the situation becomes altered if not reversed: time is of two orders, both "objective" and "subjective," with the physician able to act on the latter alone, i.e., the internal evolution of the patient's disease, his imbalance of the three humors. External time takes the form of the changing of the seasons, which, when they are excessively unbalanced, constitute an excessive conjunction (*ati-yoga*) or insufficient conjunction (*a-yoga*) of time (*kāla*). Kāla, that all-conquering deity of the *Atharva Veda* (19.53.1–9), is capable of destroying life in this way; the physician pits himself against Time's excessive or insufficient conjunctions by adjusting the microcosm to the macrocosm: this is called *sama-yoga*.[33]

In Āyurveda, the excessive manifestations of time that the physician must most often combat are the three "extreme" seasons of the Indian year, seasons that correspond to the three *doṣa*s. To winter correspond accumulations and disturbances in the phlegm; the hot season is identified with excesses of wind; and the rainy season with excessive bile.[34] More important for our concerns than this tripartite division, however, is the bipolar structure underlying it. In models that were being developed simultaneously in Upanishadic and Ayurvedic circles, the round of the seasons and the cycles of life and death were ultimately reducible to a single dynamic: this was an ongoing tug-of-war, between sun and moon, in which the prize was moisture, in the especial form of vital fluids. So the year was divided into two semesters: the fiery (*āgneya*), in which a blazing sun, which rose higher in the sky with every passing day, drained (*ādāna*, "captation") the fluid life principle out of all living creatures, and the lunar (*saumya*), during which the moon, relatively higher in the sky than the lowering sun, poured (*vi-*

sarga, "release") more moisture into the world (through the rains of which it is the presumed source) than the sun was able to draw out.[35]

The first of these two semesters roughly corresponds to the period between the winter and summer solstices, during which the sun's angle of elevation increases and the point of sunrise moves northward along the horizon with each passing day; the second approximates the period between the summer and winter solstices, when the sun's angle of elevation decreases and its apparent movement along the horizon follows a southerly course. In India, these are known as the northern course (*uttarāyaṇa*) and southern course (*dakṣiṇāyana*), respectively: their "turning points" (*saṃkrānti*) fall on 14 January and (approximately) 14 July, respectively.[36] The northern course is, throughout much of the Indian subcontinent, a long period of increasing dessication, culminating in the blazing dry heat of the hot season; the southern course begins with the torrential rains of the summer monsoon and ends with the gentler winter monsoon. The latter is a life-giving season in which creatures thrive; the former—in which wind and heat are combined—can prove deadly to all. The latter is a time of life, even immortality; the former a time of death.[37]

It is precisely with the culmination of the northern course that the "ontological disease" of *rājayakṣma*, "royal consumption," is said to occur in humans. According to both medical[38] and literary[39] convention, the king who allows himself to become debauched in the clutches of too many passionate women also falls prey to "royal consumption": as a result, his kingdom, sapped of all its *rasa*, withers and dies. In Hindu mythology, the prototypical king to suffer from royal consumption is the moon itself, the same moon that is responsible for revivifying a dessicated world at the end of each hot season, the same moon whose substance, whose fluid *rasa*, has been identified, since at least the time of the *Taittirīya Saṁhitā* (2.3.5.2) with semen. In his mythic loss and recovery of his *rasa*, Candra, King Moon, is married to the twenty-seven (or twenty-eight) daughters of Dakṣa, who are the stars that make up the *nakṣatras*, the lunar mansions through which the moon passes in its waxing and waning phases. On each night, he dallies and makes love to his wives, but it is in the embrace of his favorite, Rohiṇī, that he passes the most time. It is here that Candra, at that point at which he is "closest to the sun," spends himself completely in the clutches of his starry wife, and the moon disappears. His *rasa*, his vigor, his semen completely dried up, the moon must perform a *soma* (which is both a name for and the stuff of the moon, the *rasa* par excellence) sacrifice in order to recover his lost *rasa*, and so the cycle begins anew.[40]

The importance of this myth, and of the conjunction of the disease of royal consumption and the height of the hot season, lies in the dire effects of sun and fire (*agni*) on moon and fluid (*rasa*). Here the parallel, between the fiery (*āgneya*) and lunar (*saumya*) semesters of the year on the one hand, and the waning and waxing fortnights of the lunar month on the other, is transparently evident. In both cases, that half of a temporal cycle characterized by dessication (of the ecosystem, of the moon's *rasa*) is associated with the heat of the sun and death. Royal consumption is most likely to occur at the end of the solar semester, just as the disappearance of King Moon occurs at the end of a dark fortnight during which he has dissipated himself by exposing himself to the draining heat of the sexual embrace of the starry woman Rohiṇī. King Moon's loss of *rasa* is manifested in the latter half of his monthly cycle, by the waning of the moon, by its diminution, by one digit (*kalā*) on each succeeding night. And, at the end of its dark fortnight, the moon, completely dissipated, disappears.[41]

The moon can and does, however, return to wholeness, over the fifteen days of the waxing fortnight; and versions of the myth of King Moon found in Ayurvedic sources demonstrate his rehabilitation (as well as that of humans smitten with the same ailment) through elixir therapy, *rasāyana*. Indeed, one of the earliest medical references we have to the internal use of mercury—also called *rasa*, the vital fluid of the god Śiva—prescribes it as a treatment for increasing the production of male semen (*śukravṛddhi*). The duration of the treatment is most significant: "like the moon (*śaśaṅka*), the bodily *dhātu*s are replenished over fifteen days."[42]

This connection, between the gradual replenishment, even rejuvenation, of a dissipated moon and that of dissipated human bodies takes us to the heart of the two crowning disciplines of the Indian medical tradition. These are *rasāyana*, elixir or rejuvenation therapy; and *vājīkaraṇa*, sexual rehabilitation therapy. Both of these branches of Āyurveda assume that youthful vigor is primarily a matter of good digestion which, when overly troubled by "excessive manifestations of time," must be restored through more radical treatments than special dietary regimens or purification techniques. As we have noted, the end product of digestion is, in males, semen—semen that is homologized with the *rasa* of the moon, *soma*, the nectar of immortality. As such, semen is called *saumya*, lunar, like the semester characterized by an outpouring of vitalizing moisture into the ecosystem. As such, microcosmic semen is subject to many of the same dangers as the macrocosmic moon. On the one hand, it takes either a lunar fortnight (as indicated above) or a lunar month (the same time it takes a woman's body to produce an ovum) for the food males ingest to become fully transformed into semen.[43] On the other, it requires a prodigious quantity of food to produce a single gram of semen.[44] These perceived dangers to the very survival of the male sexual fluid are compounded by an Ayurvedic identification of female uterine blood with the fiery (*āgneya*) sun that drains the ecocosm of all its vitalizing moisture in the first semester of the year:[45] the "lunar" semen a male is capable of producing is but a drop in the fiery maelstrom of his partner's sexual fluid.

In this context, the venerable Ayurvedic treatments for the replenishment of vital male fluids have come of late to enjoy a renaissance all across India. Ayurvedic *gupta rog* (the "secret" or "hidden affliction") clinics, which specialize in the treatment of "sexual disorders" whose prime symptom is the birth of daughters, have been mushrooming across India for the past several decades. The techniques these modern clinics employ, however, and the medicines they dispense are essentially the same as those employed over the past two millennia for such ailing kings (royal patrons of the medical and alchemical authors) as King Moon. In the classic Ayurvedic sources, *rasāyana*, the seventh branch of Āyurveda, is a holistic approach to increasing bodily longevity through the use of plant- and mineral-based elixirs in combination with clinical therapeutic techniques. Intimately associated with *rasāyana* is the eighth and final branch of Indian medical science. This is *vājīkaraṇa*, treatments for increasing male vigor and virility,[46] which the fathers of Āyurveda quite sensibly placed after *rasāyana*, reasoning that a long and healthy life was a necessary precondition to a long and happy sex life. This near identification of virility with longevity is a fundamental one in India, linking together the bodily processes of digestion, semen production and retention, conception, and reproduction.

Here, the most elaborate and prestigious body of *rasāyana* therapy once again refers back to the myth of King Moon. This is the treatment known as *kuṭīpraveśa*, "entering into the hut," in which the patient is sequestered within the triply enclosed (*trigarbhā*) innermost chamber of a hut called the "womb of the womb" (*garbha-garbham*). Any resemblance to the female reproductive system is altogether intentional here, with the rebirth of the patient being portrayed quite literally:

> The soma plant brought into the *kuṭi* . . . [is] cut with a gold implement, and [its] milk collected in golden cup. With one dose of soma milk in the *kuṭi*, a person passes through several severe states of cleansing in about ten days, and then begins to grow as quickly again.

> On successive days in the first week, he vomits, purges, and emits fluids . . . His hair, nails, teeth, and skin fall off and are soon regenerated. But before the regeneration begins, he is a ghastly sight . . .
>
> Very soon the skin of the man begins to grow normal . . . For some time, the person thus has to be nursed through all the growing stages of a new-born babe, oil smearing, bathing, feeding, and putting to sleep in [a] soft bed. Before the close of the first month, the person begins to develop a new set of teeth . . . After some more time . . . his old hair is removed and then he develops a luxuriant growth of jet black hair. Later still . . . exposure is practised as in the case of a child. [He is] carefully and gradually [taken] from the innermost room of the *kuṭi* into the second enclosure, then into the third, and finally into the open sun and air, all in the course of about thirty days. After nearly three months or more . . . he may be in a fit condition to go about in the world.[47]

This Ayurvedic technique bears striking parallels to sacrificial *dīkṣā*, in which the initiate is sequestered in and reborn out of a closed initiation hut. It also reminds us of the common perspective of early Āyurveda and Sāṃkhya, in which a fall into manifestation, triggered by a disturbance in the equilibrium of the *doṣa*s or *guṇa*s, is reversed through a return to the "womb" of nonmanifestation. Finally, it appears to work from the same principles and assumptions as do a number of yogic techniques for the generation of inner heat (*tapas*) and the production of a new transcendent self.[48]

It is here, at the level of the replenishment and maintenance of vital fluids, and most particularly the vital fluid that is semen, that the disciplines of Āyurveda and *haṭha yoga* intersect: the same semen that the physician identifies with male virility and vitality is the sine qua non of yogic practice: semen is the raw material and fuel of every psychochemical transformation the yogin, alchemist, or tantric practitioner undergoes, transformations through which a new, superhuman and immortal body is "conceived" out of the husk of the mortal, conditioned, biological body. In the royal consumption myth, we saw that King Moon lost his *rasa*, his semen, through sexual contact with fiery women close to the sun. In the hathayogic tradition, some of whose descriptions of the subtle body may be traced as far back as the sixth-century B.C. *Chāndogya Upaniṣad* (8.6.1–2, 6), we find a similar homology, one that becomes a commonplace in later yogic traditions. The yogin's lower abdomen (the solar plexus) is the place of the female, sanguineous sun, which provides the heat necessary to triggering the yogic process, but which can also, like Time (*Maitrī* 6.15), wholly consume the body, causing aging, disease, and death. The head, and more specifically the cranial vault, is the locus of the sun's counterpart, the cooling moon, a moon whose *rasa* is nothing other than semen that has been carried upwards by the yogic process and so been transmuted into nectar, *amṛta*, which is equivalent to *soma*, the draft of immortality.[49]

We should not conclude from these observations that an ideal world would be one in which there were no sun, fire, women, or uterine blood at all. Sacrifice, the medical year, and the rhythms of yoga are all *bipolar* systems in which two opposed principles interact, constructively and destructively, after the fashion of the up-and-down motion of a firing rod, piston, or camshaft, to produce a *cycle* characterized by alternations between fluid and fire, dry and rainy seasons, male and female offspring, and a death that leads to immortality. Indeed, the genius of each of these three systems—the sacrificial, Ayurvedic, and yogic—lies in the particular way with which each comes to terms with this bipolar fact of life. Whereas the Vedic sacrificer sought to regulate macrocosmic time as a means to ensuring cosmic and social order and the Ayurvedic physician strives to adjust microcosmic time to excesses in macrocosmic time in order to ensure bodily health, the yogin claims to be capable of imploding these two temporal orders into one another as a means to transcending both and freeing himself from time (and every other natural and cultural constraint) altogether.

In this, the hathayogic synthesis appears to subscribe to the same basic working principle as the erotico-mystic practices of Hindu tantrism, i.e., that one must, if he is to transcend the human condition, work *through*, rather than *against*, the overwhelming energy of the feminine. In Tantra, sexual intercourse, the abandonment of male semen (the sacrificial offering) into the fiery maw of the female sexual organ, is identified as a sacrifice, the benefits of which accrue to the sacrificer. During the act, the male practitioner will therefore recite, "Oṃ, thou the Goddess, resplendent by the oblation of *dharma* and non-*dharma*, into the fire of the self, using the mind as sacrificial ladle, along the path of the *suṣumṇā*, I who am engaging in harnessing the sense organs, constantly offer this oblation."[50]

Techniques for palliating or channeling the effects of this bipolar dynamic are by no means restricted to these elite traditions. In fact, the same sorts of principles and techniques also ground the cycles of the ceremonial year in modern-day popular Hinduism. This is particularly evident in the religious calendar of the hot season in north India, which is more or less framed by the vernal equinox and the summer solstice. In rural Madhya Pradesh, nearly all of the major religious festivals of this period are concerned with ritually "cooling down" goddesses who are considered to be malevolent, dangerous, bloodthirsty causes of disease. "Hot" diseases, with their attendant fevers arise, for example, from the anger of the smallpox goddess Śitalā (whose name means "cooling," a reference to her ideal nature, which manifests itself when she has been appeased through ritual), who is identified or associated with the "Seven Sisters," seven varieties of smallpox. The heat of these goddesses' fury is ritually distributed into wheat seedlings which, after eight days of sprouting, are carried in pots on women's heads before being immersed in water; it is also transformed into types of possession ("which comes on like a fever"), whose "seizures" are calmed by the imposition of cooling *nīm* (margosa) leaves. These "hot" goddesses are further appeased through songs of praise and the offering of blood sacrifices.[51]

All of these treatments—elite and popular, ritual, medical, yogic, erotic, and mythological—are ultimately grounded in a body of metaphysical assumptions that date back, in some cases, to the time of the classical Upaniṣads. Since at least the beginning of the common era, there have existed two more or less parallel models for depicting the bipolar interaction of fluid and fire in the microcosm and macrocosm. The first of these is the Ayurvedic model of the seasons in their interactions with the *doṣa*s. The second is a yogic model, which depicts yogic withdrawal from and return to mundane consciousness in terms of the interaction between the sun located in the lower abdomen and the moon located in the cranial vault of the subtle body. This model, which respects the Ayurvedic seasonal paradigms of solar captation and lunar release of vital fluids, can be effected only through the "regressive practice" (*ulaṭā sādhana*) that is the hallmark of hathayogic practice. I return to this model later in this chapter: suffice it to say here that it literally stands all other models "on their heads." There is also a third model which, dating from the earliest Upaniṣads, is chronologically prior to those of both the Ayurvedic and yogic syntheses. This model is based not on the dynamics of heat convection and fluid transfer, but rather on a photic opposition between darkness and light. This is, in fact, the earliest systematic statement of the doctrine of karma and rebirth—or, alternatively, liberation from rebirth—to be found in all of Indian literature. Here, in describing the fate of the soul after death, these

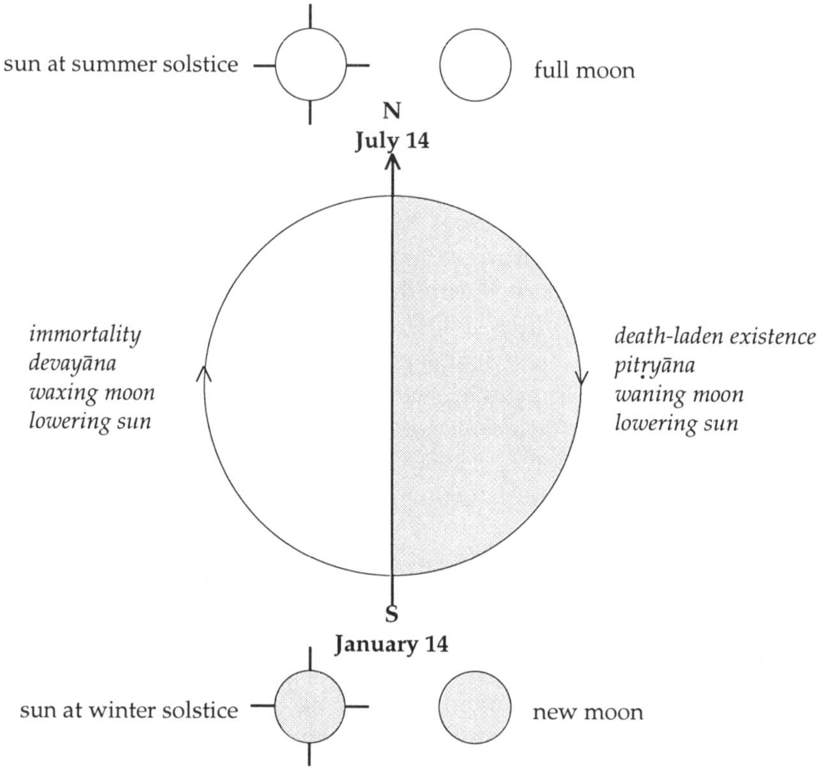

Figure 2.1. Upanisadic model of the year

sources state that those for whom liberation is promised go into the fire of the funeral pyre and thence into the day, the bright lunar fortnight, and the sun (along the path of the gods, the *devayāna*). Those, however, who must suffer rebirth go into the smoke of the funeral pyre and thence into the night, the dark lunar fortnight, and the moon (along the path of the ancestral fathers, the *pitṛyāna*), where, after they have been "eaten" by the gods, are "rained" down to earth again, and become part of the food cycle and thereby the cycle of rebirth.[52]

In this last case, the notion arises that some portion of the transmigrating human body is basically fluid and *lunar* in nature. In his commentary on this passage of the *Chāndogya Upaniṣad*, Śaṅkara, the great eight-century A.D. synthesizer of nondualist Advaita Vedānta philosophy, coherently delineates for the first time the relationship between the soul, the subtle body, the body of enjoyment, and the moon.

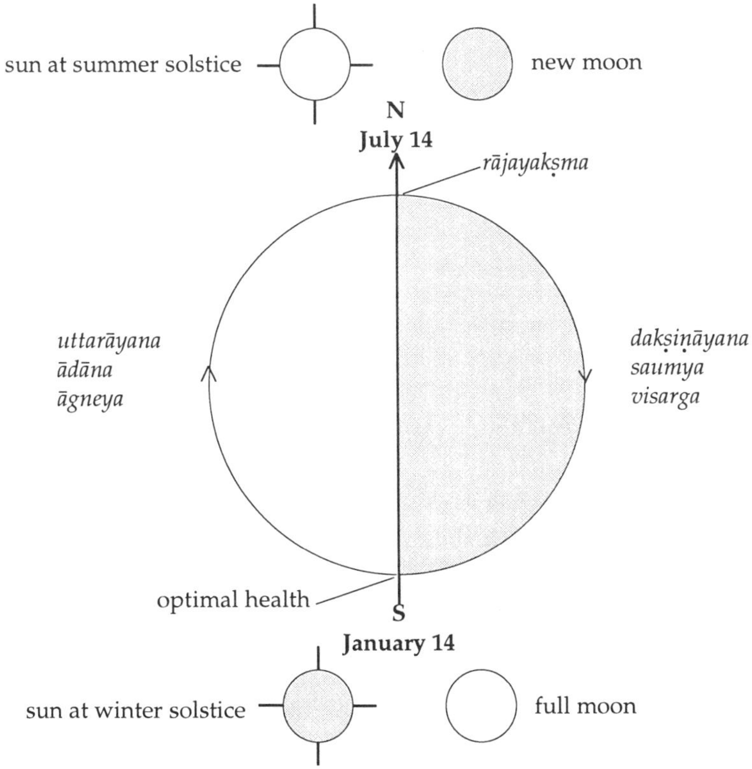

Figure 2.2. Ayurvedic model of the year

> On the lunar orb, [the dead, in compensation for their accumulated merits] obtain a body of aqueous nature for the enjoyment of pleasures. The liquid elements employed in the funerary rites combine with other elements, and reach the heavenly regions. There, they amalgamate with the structure of the moon and become the [new] bodies of those who have performed sacrifices, etc. [during their earthly existence]. When the final oblation [is] made into the funerary fire, and when the body [is] entirely consumed, the humors that arise from it fuse with the rising smoke and envelop the [subtle body of the] sacrificer. Upon reaching the moon, they form the primary matter of [his] new body, in the same way as straw and clay [serve to construct the ephemeral "statue" of a divinity].[53]

When this body of enjoyment has exhausted the merits that permitted it to enjoy its temporary lunar sojourn, it "melts" to once again become a vehicle for the subtle body. Returning to its prior state of an amorphous vapor, it fuses with the clouds, falls to earth with the rains, enters into the sap of plants and thence into the blood and seed of the animals and humans who eat those plants. Here, it enters, as it has done an infinite number of times before, into an embryo formed of the mixture of blood and seed produced in sexual intercourse to once again become a living creature.[54]

The "fluid" or "thermodynamic" and lunisolar Ayurvedic model of the year together with its mirror image, the "photic" but nonetheless lunisolar Upaniṣadic model are presented in chart form in figures 2.1 and 2.2. I present the yogic model later in this chapter.[55]

3. Physical and Metaphysical Factors of Five

Like the fingers on the hand, the number five in India has long been "good to think with." Even if its multiple pentads are expansions on the primal sacrificial triad—of fire (*agni*), oblation (*rasa*), and the wind (*vāyu*) that conveyed the smoke and aroma of the offering to the gods—the Hindu cosmos has been, for at least three thousand years, a fivefold one.[56] It is the Brāhmaṇas that, even as they continue the Vedic discourse of the triune universe, first elaborate the concept of the universe as fivefold. This they do most especially in their speculations concerning the piling of the great fire altar (*agnicayana*), which is composed of five layers of bricks. These five layers, the *Śatapatha Brāhmaṇa* tells us, are the five bodily constituents of the god Prajāpati, as well as the five seasons, the five directions, etc.[57] The brahmanic identification of this sacrificial god with the year and with food would in turn give rise, in the early *Taittirīya Upaniṣad* (2.1), to a hierarchical representation of the five elements in their relationship to the universal and microcosmic man: "From this ātman verily ether arose; from ether air; from air fire; from fire, water; from water, earth; from earth, herbs; from herbs, food; from food, semen; from semen, Man."

This notion of the physical universe as an aggregate of the five elements is one that informs, as we will see, not only the three great metaphysical systems of ancient and classical India (Sāṃkhya, Vedānta, and the Buddhist Dhamma), but also permeates commonsense discourse on the nature of life and death. The perennial expression *pañcatvam gamana*, "going to the fiveness [the five elements]," is particularly disclosive of this worldview. Indians have employed this term since at least the time of the epics as a euphemism for death, the dissolution of bodily integrity.[58]

This deconstruction of a perceived unity called "self" was a central concern of Buddhism, for which the reality of this world was nothing more or less than an ever-changing configuration of five "heaps" or "aggregates" (*khandhas*). Rather than there being bodies inhabited by individual souls thirsting for reintegration into a universal soul, as the Upaniṣads taught, the Buddha showed existence to be nothing other than a series of evanescent recombinations of appearances, sensations, conceptions, mental formations, and consciousness. The extinction (*nirvāṇa*) of suffering consisted in dissociating the five aggregates from any notion of "self," for this was what trapped one in existence.

Ultimately, however, the Buddha was working from the same basic problematic as were proto-Samkhyan and proto-Vedantic thought in the early Upaniṣads. Buddhism denied the reality of self in order to emphasize an ethical attitude towards an impermanent world characterized by suffering born of ignorance. Sāṃkhya affirmed the existence of a plurality of selves and the reality of the world for so long as spirit (*puruṣa*) remained confused with nature or original materiality (*prakṛti*). Vedānta asserted the identity of the individual soul (*ātman, jīvātman*) with the universal soul (*bráhman, paramātman*) while denying the reality of the phenomenal world.[59] Yet underlying these divergent philosophies, there remained a common ground that no subtlety of argumentation could efface. This was the concrete experience of the human body—and, as we shall see, most particularly the very concrete yogic experience of the body—in its relation to the external world.[60] Thus, despite the important points of divergence between the metaphysics of these three schools, the identity of microcosm and macrocosm—already evoked in Brahmanic speculations on the identification of the fire altar with the body of the cosmic man (Puruṣa-Prajāpati) and the universe—was constantly undermining the philosophical distinctions drawn between them. In the end, "wet" experience would win out over "dry" philosophical speculation.[61]

In the early Upaniṣads, the cosmogonic metaphysics that was generated to link the individual to the universe and its absolute source was nothing other than a reverse account of the stages by which the yogin withdraws from the external world to realize the absolute within.[62] For the monistic Vedantins, this was a process of resorption that was implied in the primal cosmic emanation: yoga was a remounting of those stages through which absolute poured itself out to form our manifold, manifest universe. This universe was a continuum, a single reverberation, out of the primal essence that was *bráhman*, down into subtle (*sūkṣma*) and gross (*sthūla*) forms of life and matter. All was interconnected, both structurally and materially; and because all being contained a trace of the absolute *bráhman* (in the form of the individual soul, the *ātman*) within, all was potentially, and thereby virtually, one with the universal essence. Yogic practice, meditation and insight (*jñāna*) were the means to realizing, in the gnoseological sense of the word, this inner potential.

Although monist, Vedānta constructed its model of an emanated universe upon a Samkhyan prototype, which was dualist. According to Sāṃkhya, the manifold universe in all its parts was essentially a mistake. That is, Spirit (Puruṣa), deluded (for reasons that are never clearly explained) into identifying itself with a rather scatterbrained Mother Nature (Prakṛti), moves her to undergo internal modifications that serially generate lower and lower strata of being. Rather than a process of emanation, this is one of differentiation: in spite of its temporary loss of discrimination, Puruṣa is wholly spirit and therefore not of the same stuff as Prakṛti or the lower differentiates with which he identifies himself. Puruṣa, spirit, and Prakṛti, the world, are proximate, though never in actual contact. Thus the various levels of metaphysical reality remain disconnected materially, with their structural sequentiality being the result of Puruṣa's "fall" into (identifying itself with these ever-descending mutations of) Prakṛti.[63]

In spite of the fundamental differences between them, the basic model employed by these two metaphysical systems is one and the same. The shape of reality is composed of five sets of five categories, headed by the "preternatural" pentad of *puruṣa*, *prakṛti*, *buddhi* (intellect), *ahaṃkāra* (ego), and *manas* (mind). Below this pentad are four parallel pentads, which interact with and interpenetrate one another. These are the five *buddhīndriya*s (sense-capacities: hearing, feeling, seeing, tasting, smelling); the five *karmendriya*s (action-capacities: speaking, grasping, walking, excreting, generating), the five *tanmātra*s (subtle elements: sound, touch, form, taste, smell) and the five *mahābhūta*s (gross elements: ether, air, fire, water, earth).[64] It is at the level of the twenty lower *tattva*s that another constant feature of the Indian worldview emerges. This is the pattern of corresponding hierarchies that proliferates throughout a wide variety of different yet parallel disciplines. In the case of the Samkhyan categories, there is a point-for-point correspondence between the members of each level of each of the four parallel groups. Thus, the *buddhīndriya* of hearing corresponds to the *karmendriya* of speaking, the *tanmātra* of sound, and the *mahābhūta* of ether, and so on, down to the correspondence between olfactory sensing, procreation, odor, and earth.[65] The Samkhyan system thus comprised twenty-five metaphysical categories, five hierarchical series of five. This system was taken as given by Vedantic thought in its description of emanated (as opposed to differentiated) reality and, as I now show, by tantric Buddhism and Hinduism in their maps of a theistic universe, in which the impersonal Puruṣa or *bráhman* was replaced by personalized Buddhas, or by forms of Śiva and the Goddess.

In the Hindu case, the metaphysical categories or cosmic principles (*tattvas*) of Sāṃkhya were deified, early on, in the form of the twenty-five faces of Mahāsadāśiva.[66] Because its was an "exploded" metaphysics that denied any primal essence, absolute or universal, Buddhism resisted the Samkhyan model for several centuries; but here too, yogic experience eventually prevailed. Already in Aśvaghosa's (A.D. 80) theory of "suchness" (*tathatā*), the unbridgeable gap that the Buddha taught between existence (*saṃsāra*) and its cessation (*nirvāṇa*) was beginning to yield to the irresistible force of yogic experience. A few centuries later, it would collapse completely with the Mahāyāna notion that the Dharmakāya—the "Buddha body" composed of the body of the Buddha's teachings—was an absolute or universal soul, a Buddhist equivalent of the Vedantin's *bráhman*, with which the practitioner entered into mystic union.[67] Once the inviolate gap between *saṃsāra* and *nirvāṇa* had been breached, the familiar corresponding hierarchies of the Indian cosmos came rushing in through the back door, as it were. Thus, while logicians like Śantideva and Diṅnāga were devising hair-splitting arguments by which to interpret the world as a void entity,[68] Buddhist tāntrikas were deifying and hypostasizing the Buddha into five emanated Buddhas or Tathāgatas: Amitabhā, Vairocana, Amoghasiddhi, Ratnasambhava, and Akṣobhya.[69] These five primal Buddhas were subsequently equated with the five elements,[70] the basic concept being that cosmic expansion, the multiplication of the absolute into fundamental forces, could be represented by lineages of gods just as easily as by metaphysical categories. Thus, each of the five primal Buddhas presided over five lineages of five *bodhisattvas* which, added to the transcendent Dharmakāya, generated a total of twenty-five divine beings, the same as the number of Samkhyan categories. Thus we read in the *Jñānasiddhi*: "Since they have the nature of the five Buddhas, the five constituents of the human personality are called *jīna*s (conquerers): and the five *dhātu*s (elements) correspond to the Buddha's *śakti*s . . . Therefore our body is a Buddha body."[71]

This complete turnabout, effected before the seventh century, gave rise to Buddhist tantra. Hindu tantrism as well came to generate clan or family lineages (*kula*s) of divinities that were so many deifications of the Samkhyan categories, adding, as had the Buddhists, transcendent categories (totaling as many as thirty-seven in the Trika Kaula synthesis) to underscore the superiority of its pantheon of supreme deities. In the Hindu case, the supreme god Śiva and his consort Śakti (or the Goddess by one of her many other names) are transparent appropriations, but now with a sexual reinterpretation, of the Samkhyan pair of Puruṣa and Prakṛti.

These tantric reworkings of the Samkhyan categories would have a myriad of practical applications in the fields of *haṭha yoga* and alchemy, both of which stressed the importance of the five elements. In the former system, the five lower *cakra*s were identified with the five elements, while in alchemy, mercury, the semen of Śiva, was viewed as incorporating the five elements in itself. I discuss these applications in detail in later chapters.

4. The Lunar Cipher of Sixteen in Veda, Yoga, and Tantra

In the royal consumption origin myth related above, the moon was revived and replenished in its bright fortnight through the offering of a *soma* sacrifice. Soma is the fluid essence of the moon, which, in the sacrificial context, must be bought. With what does King Moon buy back his vital fluids? With a red cow, whose name, *rohiṇī*, is the same as that of the starry woman who was the original cause of his woes.[72] The Brāhmaṇas offer another explanation for the moon's ability to wax anew, indeed, for its immortality. Of the moon's sixteen digits, the last is said to descend to earth to dwell in animals and plants: "Now this King Soma, the food of the gods, is none other than the moon. When he is not seen that night either in the east or west, then he visits this world; and here he enters into the waters and the plants. And since during that night he dwells (*vasati*) [here] at home (*amā*), that is called the new moon (*amāvāsyā*)." "Then, on the night of the new moon, entering by means of its sixteenth digit (*kalā*) into all that is possessed of breath, it [the moon] is reborn in the morning."[73]

What is this sixteenth, immortal digit of the moon? Clearly, it is to be identified with the immortal soul, which persists through an infinite series of rebirths and redeaths. Why the number sixteen? In all likelihood, the intimate association of this figure with the moon is the result of the Indian penchant for "rounding up" from a given set of aggregates to express the notion of perfect wholeness. In this case, the fifteen observable nights of a lunar fortnight are taken as fifteen separate units, to which is added an additional unit (the whole lunar fortnight as the sum of its parts). Here, the fifteen nights are also taken to be the spokes of a wheel, with its felly, the sixteenth, identified with the *ātman*. This transcendent sixteenth unit, the *amṛta-kalā*, "fills out," renders perfect, the fifteen units of the mundane lunar fortnight.[74] Let us dwell for a moment upon the Hindu concept of the *kalā*, the lunar digit, and most especially on the sixteenth, immortal digit (*amṛta-kalā*) of the moon as it applies to the yogic body.

In Ayurvedic parlance, the term *kalā* is used as a synonym for *dhātu*[75] or for the invisible supports (*dhāras*) of or divisions between each of the seven *dhātus*.[76] This usage probably originates from the original concept of sacrificial initiation (*dīkṣā*) in the Vedic tradition. Here, when the sacrificer's body is made anew, the embryo of his sacrificial body is symbolically generated by adding layer upon layer of bodily constituent: semen, blood, caul, placenta, etc.[77] Indeed, the original sacrificial body—that of Puruṣa-Prajāpati who is reconstructed time and again in brahmanic speculation—is said to be divided into sixteen *kalās*, which are each of his eight *dhātus*, taken twice.[78] An Upanisadic identification of Prajāpati's body with the moon would appear to reinforce this interpretation. Indeed, sixteen is also a key figure in Indian reckonings of a woman's menstrual cycle. In the words of the *Yājñavalkya Smṛti*, "sixteen nights are the season of a woman . . . from the appearance of menses, sixteen nights is for a woman the season, i.e. the time for the conception of the fetus." As with the moon, which fills out through an addition of layers (digits), so with the (re)constitution of sacrificial and embryonic bodies, as well as the ovum.[79] Elsewhere, in Śaiva Siddhānta ritual, the body parts of God, which the devotee superimposes upon his own body through the recitation of mantras, are called *kalās*.[80]

A similar perspective appears to underlie a popular ritual observance found throughout modern north India: the "sixteen Mondays vow," during which one fasts and offers coarse wheat-flour cakes to Śiva on sixteen successive Mondays. As in English, Monday means "moon-day" (*soma-vāra*) in the modern Indo-Aryan languages; this ritual observance may be interpreted as a practice by which to fill out the moon—through the intermediary of Śiva, the god whose semen is identified with *soma*—in successive phases, until it is sixteen *kalās* full.[81]

The original use of the term *kalā* is found in the *Ṛg Veda*, where it was used to signify "any single portion of a whole, especially a sixteenth part."[82] It was somewhat later that the term came to be applied to each of the sixteen digits of the moon, but by that time its meaning had already expanded to encompass a wide array of other sets of sixteen.[83] The standard number of priestly specialists (excluding the *yajamāna*) in a brahmanic *soma* sacrifice was sixteen;[84] already in the Brāhmaṇas, the number sixteen was identified as the numerical attribute of *bráhman*, the absolute.[85] When the identification of the universal macrocosm, ruled by *bráhman*, and the corporeal microcosm, ruled by *ātman*, was made, the sixteen attributes of *bráhman* translated into the aggregate of the five breaths, the five organs of action (*karmendrīyas*), the five organs of sensation (*jñānendrīyas*) and the mind,[86] or into the sixteen components of the living being of which only one-sixteenth is unmanifest (*avyakta*) and transmigrates.[87]

Nowhere, however, does the notion of wholeness and perfection translate more fully, on both microcosmic and macrocosmic levels, than in the dynamics of the waxing and waning of the moon, in the increase and diminution of lunar digits, the *kalās*. The moon fills out with each lunar month to become brimful of this nectar, which it pours into the world in the form of vivifying rain, the fluid source of every creature's vitality.[88] In this context the invisible sixteenth *kalā*, that digit that makes the moon fully whole, takes on its fullness of meaning as the *amṛta-kalā*, the "digit of immortality."

The increase and diminution of the moon, both in its lunar fortnights and in its relationship to the sun in the system of the solar and lunar semesters of the year, is intimately tied into yogic theory and practice relative to the subtle body. This is a bipolar body that is divided into two halves at the level of the navel. Of these, the lower half is associated with femininity, with male semen that is "prey" to blood and to the fire of the sun; and the upper with masculinity, with semen that has been refined into nectar identified with the moon. The lower half is further identified with mundane existence, with the dispersal of the individual's life into a myriad of worldly concerns paralleled by the dispersal, in his lower body, of his seed: this is *pravṛtti*, extroversion. The upper half, on the contrary, is identified with supermundane consciousness, with the reintegration of all that is normally dispersed in mundane existence: this is *nivṛtti*, introversion.

In this system, human life itself is seen as dependent upon the maintenance of the immortal digit of lunar nectar. Even at such times as an individual is not practicing yoga, he remains alive by virtue of the sixteenth digit of nectar that endures in the cranial vault, identified as the abode of *bráhman* or Śiva (both of whom are identified with the number sixteen) in the subtle body: this is the microcosmic homologue of the single immortal lunar digit that dwells in the world on new-moon nights.[89] The realization of supernatural powers and bodily immortality requires that that same moon in the cranial vault be replenished to its fullness and shine with all of its sixteen digits. It is, however, impossible for these sixteen digits to be regenerated without the "seed" that is the immortal digit, also known, in yogic parlance, as the *nivṛtti kalā*, the digit of yogic introversion.[90]

The subtle body is in fact composed of two sets of sixteen digits, the one solar and fiery and the other lunar and fluid. In the body of a nonpractitioner, it is the former set that holds sway: the sun or fire of time in the lower abdomen burns with all of its *twelve* digits[91] and thus consumes, ages the body. In addition to these twelve solar digits, there are also said to be *four* fiery digits in the body.[92] These are located in the medial channel of the subtle body, the *suṣumṇā nāḍī* or *brahmamārga* (the "path of *bráhman*"), which runs up the spinal column from the lower abdomen to the cranial vault. Yoga, and most especially *haṭha yoga*, involves forcefully controlling, even reversing the body's natural tendencies through the combined techniques of breath control, fixed postures, and meditation. What these techniques aim to reverse is the aging process, which yogic traditions identify with the predominance in the body of the solar and fiery digits. This yogic battery of techniques for reversing the course of nature and time is variously called *ulaṭā sādhana* (regressive practice), *kāya kalpa* (bodily reintegration), and *parāvṛtti* (retroversion). Yogic practice reduces the influence of the sixteen digits of the lower body while simultaneously increasing that of the sixteen lunar digits of the moon located in the cranial vault. This it does, in practical terms, by raising the yogin's semen from his lower abdomen along the length of the medial channel until it fills out the moon in his head. As it rises, this same semen is gradually transformed into *amṛta*, the stuff of the macrocosmic moon, the divine nectar of immortality which pours itself into the world in the form of vivifying rain.

The way in which this transformation occurs lies at the heart of hatha-yogic theory and practice. *Haṭha yoga* is the forceful channeling and control of the vital breaths (*prāṇa*s) and of the thermal energy (*tapas*, *yogāgni*) of the subtle body. Yogic transformation begins when the yogin concentrates all of his vital breaths at the base of his medial channel, in the region of the subtle sun that is burning with all of its twelve digits. This concentration of breaths opens the medial channel, the mouth of which had theretofore remained closed, at which point the process of yogic reversal truly begins. Through heroic efforts of mental concentration and physical exertion, the yogin now initiates a controlled raising of his seed, the heat of his solar fires, and his breath along the medial channel.[93] At each stage of this pro-

July 14
full sun
mundane consciousness

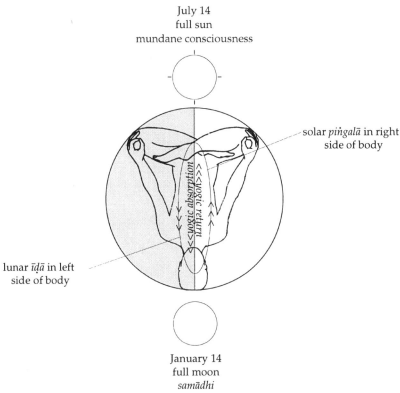

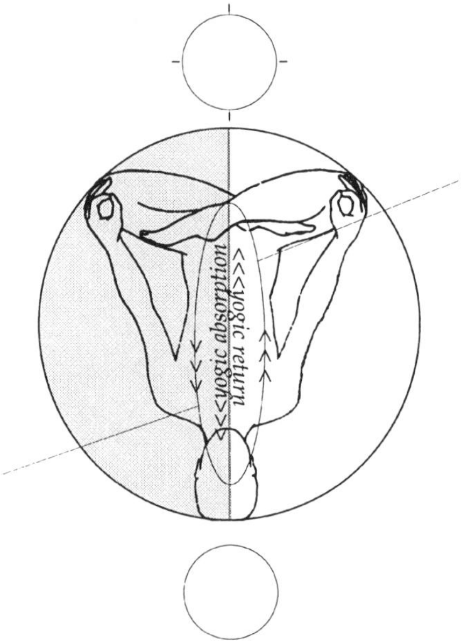

solar *piṅgalā* in right side of body

lunar *īḍā* in left side of body

January 14
full moon
samādhi

Figure 2.3. Yogic model of the year

cess, the fire of the sun in his abdomen decreases incrementally: what the yogin is in fact doing is burning up the fire of death (*kālāgni*) with the immortalizing fire of yoga (*kālāgnirudra*).[94]

In its simplest terms, this channeling of vital fluid, breath, and heat energy is a six-stage process. These six stages are described as the piercing (*bheda*) by these vital elements of six energy centers or circles of transformation called the *cakras*. The six *cakras*,[95] strung along the length of the spinal column in the subtle body, are, in order, the *mūlādhāra* (at the level of the anus), *svādhiṣṭhāna* (at the level of the genitals), *maṇipura* (navel), *anāhata* (heart), *viśuddhi* (throat), and *ājñā* (between the eyebrows).

The prodigious heat generated with the piercing of each *cakra*, coupled with the fact that upward movement is here equated with absorption, allows for a homologization of each circle of transformation with a cremation ground, the place of the final sacrifice, and a *pralaya*, a cosmic dissolu-

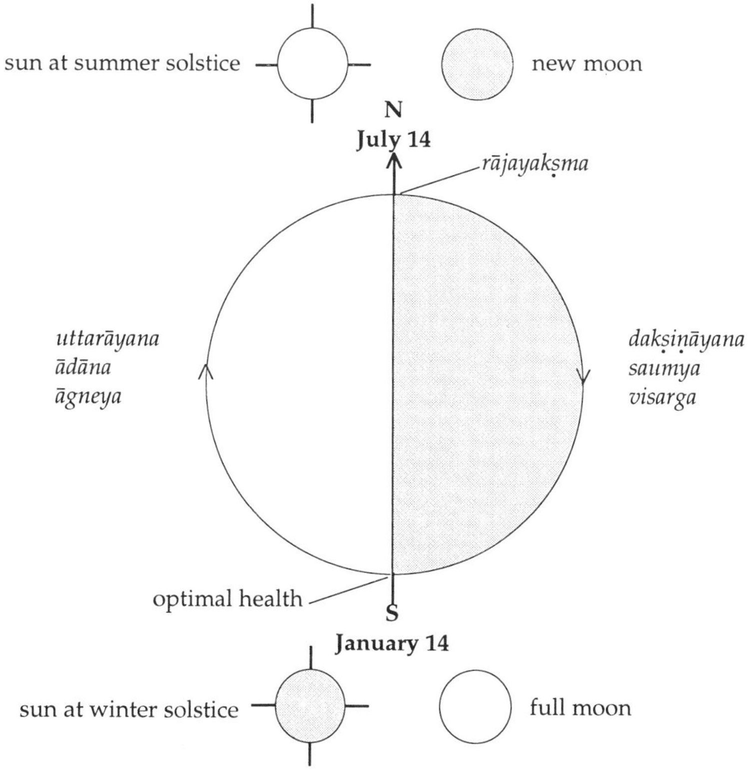

Figure 2.4. Ayurvedic model of the year

tion.[96] This heat, concentrated within the infinitesimal space of the medial channel, effects the gradual transformation of "raw" semen into "cooked" and even perfected nectar, *amṛta;* it is this nectar that gradually fills out the moon in the cranial vault such that, at the conclusion of this process, the lunar orb, now brimming with nectar, is possessed of its full complement of sixteen digits. The brimming downturned moon in the cranial vault is also identified as a thousand-petaled lotus: this is the so-called "seventh" *cakra,* the *sahasrāra.* This transformation of semen into nectar wholly transforms the body, rendering it immortal.

Because the yogin reverses all natural tendencies (inertia, being-towards-death, extroversion) through his practice, he quite literally reverses the flow of time; because his is a "regressive practice," it stands the conventional models of the temporal cycles on their heads. Here, we illustrate with a chart these reversals—between the interplay of the macrocosmic sun and moon in the *visarga* and *ādāna* semesters of the Ayurvedic year on the one hand and the cyclic interplay of lunar and solar *kalā*s in the subtle body of *haṭha yoga* on the other (figs. 2.3 and 2.4).

The application of the hathayogic model—of a full, male, immortalizing moon in the upper body and a blazing, female, deadly sun in the lower body—becomes greatly expanded in the Puranic reckoning of the great cosmic time cycles, the *kalpa*s or eons. Here, a divine, cosmic yogin triggers the creation or dissolution of the universe through his cycles of yogic withdrawal from (which corresponds to cosmic dissolution) and return to (which corresponds to cosmic emission) mundane consciousness.[97] Here as well, the phases into which eons are divided, i.e., of nonmanifestation and manifestation, are termed *niṣkala* and *sakala*, with *kalā*s and without *kalā*s, respectively.[98]

In fact, time (*kāla*) is always lurking in the background of any discussion of the *kalā*s, because to each *kalā* there corresponds a lunar day (*tithi*):[99] with each passing *kalā*, another day goes by. Normally, man is the victim of this relentless passing of the *kalā*s, the march of time, which, just as it diminishes the moon in its waning fortnight, wears down the human body and brings man a day closer to his death. Only the yogin, through his regressive practice, can effect a return to a primordial plenitude, thereby enabling himself to stave off and even reverse and gain back "lost time." So it is that as he enters deeper and deeper into his practice, the yogin turns back the hands of time, moving backwards through his earlier life and prior existences and thereby annulling the karma, the effects of the accumulated fruits of past acts, attached to them. Still deeper into his yogic trance, when he has remounted the emanated order of creation back to its very source—a source prior to sameness and difference, life and death, male and female, ego and other—he realizes a state of being that is unconditioned even by Time itself. The yogin then becomes a *kāla-vañcaka*, a "tricker" or "skewer" of Time,[100] and many are the myths of Siddhas who harrow hell and give Death a thrashing for his having presumed to hold sway over one of their fold. For the Indian yogin, following the example of the yogic god whose withdrawal from and return to mundane consciousness synchronize the arising and passing away of the cosmic ages, time need not merely move forward: there are also the options of fast forward and reverse. It is in this way that the yogin, even though he employs the same bipolar system for time reckoning as do all other Indians, relates to time in his own unique way. Rather than being a slave to time, he is its master. He becomes a "second Śiva," the master of a universe he knows to be of his own making.

Following their supreme fusion in *haṭha yoga*, the lunar digits and the number sixteen seem to pursue separate careers in later Hindu traditions. On the one hand, the number sixteen becomes expanded, through an inflationary tendency quite endemic to Hinduism, into eighteen. On the other, *kalā* becomes a tantric metaphysical category more or less divorced from its prior associations with the waxing and waning moon. It is especially in the context of the phonematic emanation of the tantric universe, in which the self-manifestation of the absolute is effected through the garland of the fifty-one ordered phonemes (*varṇa-mālā*) of the Sanskrit alphabet—which are at once acoustic matrices and mother goddesses (*mātṛkā*s)[101]—that the term *kalā* is most broadly employed in nondualist tantra. Here, through the "particularizing energy" of the *kalā*, the unmanifest acoustic nature of the absolute, called *nāda*, "resonance," becomes condensed into the differentiated phonemes of manifest speech.[102] It is here that tantrism coopts, in its own way, the notion of the *kalā*s as lunar digits: the fifteen vocalic phonemes of the Sanskrit language, together with a nasalization called the *bindu*, are identified with the first fifteen digits of the moon. The sixteenth *kalā*, the invisible and immortal digit that is present in all that flows from it, becomes the turning point between vowels and consonants in the order of the emanated phonemes: this is the *visarga*, the surd aspirate often found at the end of Sanskrit words. As such, the sixteenth phonemic *kalā*, the *visarga* is pictured as the point of intersection or union between utterance and meaning, between language and event, signifiant and signifié.[103] These sixteen phonemic *kalā*s, while identified with Śiva, are only enlivened through his interaction with his manifest aspect, the goddess Śakti.[104] As such, this group of sixteen may also be identified as sixteen divine mothers.[105]

In addition to its extended applications of the full complement of lunar digits in its theory and practice, tantrism also expands on the number of digits in the full moon, raising it to eighteen. This is a process that was already under way prior to the time of the tantras themselves. The numerical attribute of the absolute *bráhman* is raised, in the *Mahābhārata*, from sixteen to eighteen.[106] Likewise, in the writings of the Mahāyāna philosopher Asaṅga, as well as of certain Nāth Siddhas, the number of inner "voids" (*śūnya*s) alternates between sixteen and eighteen.[107] Finally, in Hindu tantra, the number of *kalā*s is raised from sixteen to eighteen, to accomodate for additional metaphysical categories.[108]

There is yet another important sphere of Hindu life in which the number sixteen plays an important role. These are the *saṃskāra*s, the Hindu

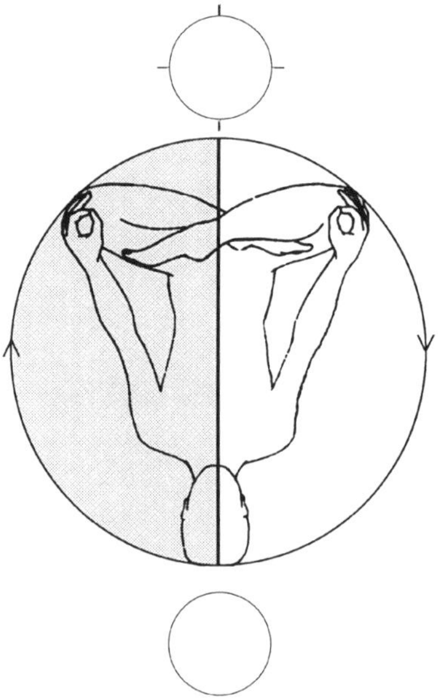

Figure 2.5. Yogic model of the cosmic year (Kalpa)

"sacraments" or "life-cycle rites," which, extending from conception to cremation, respect the numerical determinism of the number sixteen.[109] Over the millennia, this term has come to take on a wide range of applications, one of which is an alchemical one: the series of 16 + 2 processes which lead to the transformation of mercury, the "lunar" semen of Śiva, into a transmuting agent, are called the *saṃskāras*.[110] The alchemical *saṃskāras* moreover retain a number of the "lunar" elements intrinsic to the number sixteen. Thus, the alchemical *Bhūtiprakaraṇa*, in a clear reference to the myth of the origin of royal consumption, states that the mineral *rasas* arose from the union of Bhairava and Rohiṇī, the erstwhile spouse of King Moon. The same source goes on to state that it is only under a waxing or full moon that alchemical operations leading to bodily rejuvenation will succeed.[111] We will return to a detailed discussion of the alchemical *saṃskāras* in chapter nine.

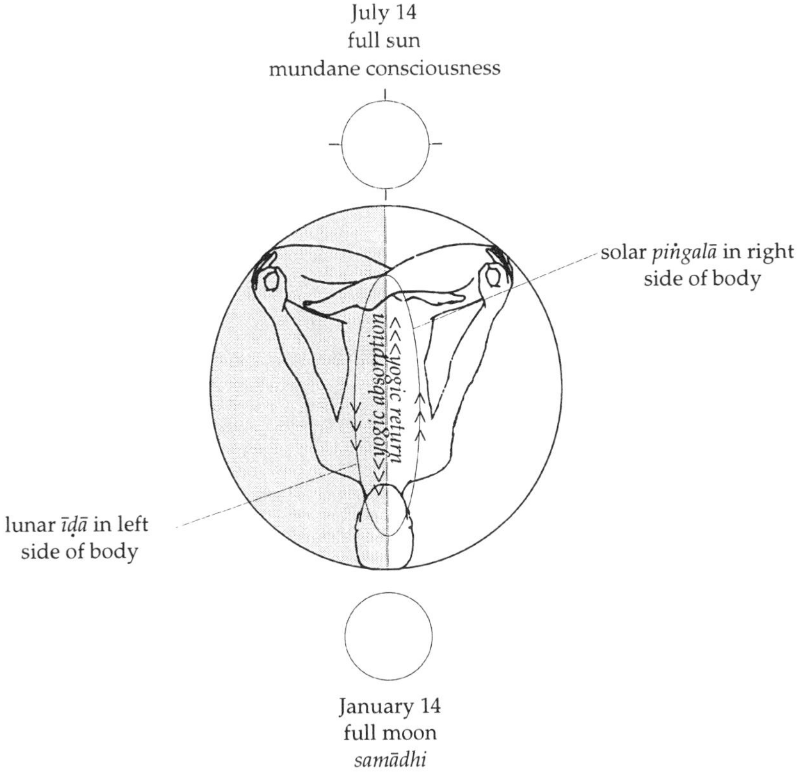

Figure 2.6. Yogic model of the year

5. Yogic and Cosmic Cycles

In *haṭha yoga,* the principal motor behind the transformations of mundane semen into divine nectar of immortality—and of mundane mind (*manas*) to a state beyond mind (*unmanā*)—is a pneumatic one. It is wind, the dynamic element in the ancient Vedic triad, which here, taking the form of controlled breathing, plays a crucial transformative role in the hathayogic system. When the breath is stable, mind and semen are stabilized; but more important, when through breath control (*prāṇāyāma*) the base of the medial channel is opened, that same breath causes the reversal of mundane polarities. Rather than descending, semen, energy, and mind are now forced upwards into the cranial vault, effecting total yogic integration (*samādhi*), a reversal of the flow of time, immortality and transcendence over the entire created universe.

The importance of yogic *prāṇāyāma* is underscored in Indian systems of time reckoning, especially as concerns two extreme units of measurement. It is here that we find not a mere dilation of number—as has been the case with two, three, five, and sixteen—but a veritable explosion thereof, with numerical progressions raising these figures to powers of fourteen or factors of trillions. Yet, as always, the same phenomena, of bipolarity and homology, lie at the root of such mathematical exultation.

We have already outlined the correspondences between the semesters of the solar year and the fortnights of the lunar month. Moving down the scale from these temporal units, we find that each of the days in a lunar month is divided into bright (day) and dark (night) halves and so on until one arrives at the basic "bipolar time unit" of human, or more particularly yogic, respiration. This is the *mātra* ("measure"),[112] or the elapsed time of a yogic inhalation (homologized with the day, the bright lunar fortnight, and the northern path) and exhalation (homologized with night, the dark lunar fortnight, and the southern path). Ninety-six *mātra*s constitute one *ghaṭa;* sixty *ghaṭa*s one day and night; thirty days one month (a day of the ancestors); twelve months one year (a day of the gods); 12 × 360 × 1000 years a *mahāyuga* (a day of the god Brahmā); and one thousand *mahāyuga*s a *kalpa* (a day of the cosmic yogin Viṣṇu). According to nearly every yogic and tantric tradition, Śiva is an even greater yogin than Viṣṇu. As such, a *kalpa* of Viṣṇu is but a single *mātra,* a divine inbreath and an outbreath for Śiva—the proof of this being the garlands of skulls, of Brahmās and Viṣṇus of innumerable past creations that he wears around his neck. In the words of the twelfth-century Vīraśaiva poet Basavaṇṇa,

> When the ghosts read the writing on the skulls
> Śiva wears around his neck,
> they know, "This one is Brahmā, this one is Viṣṇu,
> this one is Indra, this is Death,"
> as they play happily with them,
> Śiva smiles, he laughs, our god.[113]

In the monistic or pneumatic perspective of the yoga-based Indian gnoseologies, it is ultimately breath, breathing in and breathing out, that unites the microcosm to the macrocosm (indeed, *ātman* can be translated as "spirit" or "breath, re-spir-ation").[114] The lunar months, solar years, etc. are so many temporal mesocosms, so many levels at which the human becomes joined to the absolute, through the bipolar dynamic of breathing in and breathing out. It is for this reason in particular that breath control plays such a paramount role in the entire yogic enterprise.

With these remarks, I present two final charts which compare the basic bipolar model of yogic withdrawal and return on the one hand and the kalpic cycle of divine withdrawal (dissolution, *pralaya*) and return (emission, *sṛṣṭi*) on the other (figs. 2.5 and 2.6).

THREE

The Prehistory of Tantric Alchemy

1. Six Alchemical Accounts

a. The Zawgyis or Weikzas, the alchemist-monks of Burma whose esoteric alchemical tradition dates from the fifth century A.D., are indebted at least in part to India for their knowledge of the mercurials with which they are expert in "pickling" their bodies. A Burmese legend set in the time of the eleventh-century king Anawrahta also betrays an Indian connection:[1]

> [A monk, having saved two boys from drowning] discovered that they were . . . Indians by race. He took them to his monastery and, naming them Byat-wi and Byat-ta, he brought them up as his pupils. Years passed and the boys became fully grown young men. One day the monk found on the hill-side the body of an alchemist who had died during the final stages of his experiments, and he instructed his pupils to carry it to the monastery and roast it. After the body had been roasted, the monk said, "Look here, pupils, the roasted flesh of the alchemist is to be eaten only by the Great King of Thaton, so that he will become a mighty man of endeavour and protect our country from its enemies. So I must go to the city to invite the King to dinner" . . . In the darkness, the roasted body of the alchemist shone like gold, and it gave out such a sweet flavour that the two youths yearned to taste the strange flesh . . . "Let us just take a bite each," and they cut off a tiny part of the roasted body and ate it, but as the flesh tasted so good they greedily went on eating until the whole body was finished . . . The elder brother [said] ". . . let us enjoy ourselves." Then, feeling gay and strong, he lifted the monastery from its foundations and turned it upside down. "Is that all you can do?" mocked the younger brother, and he lifted a huge rock and placed it on the

> path . . . The monk saw the huge rock and the upside-down monastery and realized that the worst had happened. "Alas, Lord King," he exclaimed, ". . . I fear that my boys have eaten the roasted alchemist, and unless they are quickly apprehended they will rebel against you."

b. The seventh-century Indian author and playwright Bāṇabhaṭṭa provides the earliest literary account we have of an Indian tāntrika in the comic description he gives of a south Indian (Draviḍa) ascetic who superintended a temple of the goddess Caṇḍikā on the road to Ujjain:[2]

> He had a tumor growing on his forehead that was blackened by constantly falling at the feet of the mother Goddess . . . and was blind in one eye from a batch of invisibility salve [*siddhāñjana*] given him by a quack . . . He had brought a premature fever on himself with an improperly prepared mercurial elixir [*rasāyana*] used as a vermifuge . . . He had a collection of palm-leaf manuscripts containing material on conjuring, *tantra*, and *mantra*, which were written in letters of smoky-red lacquer. He had written the doctrine of Mahākāla as such had been taught to him by an old Mahā-pāśupata. He was afflicted with the condition of babbling about buried treasure and had become very windy on the subject of transmutational alchemy [*dhātuvada*] . . . He had increased his grasp on the *mantra-sādhana* for becoming invisible, and knew thousands of wonderful stories about Śrīparvata.

c. Alberuni, the Muslim savant who accompanied Mahmud of Ghazni in his conquest of western India between A.D. 998 and 1030, relates a number of Indian alchemical legends, including the following:[3]

> In the city of Dhâra,[4] the capital of Mâlava, which is in our days ruled by Bhojadeva [1000–55], there lies in the door of the Government house an oblong piece of pure silver, in which the outlines of the limbs of a man are visible. Its origin is accounted for by the following story:—Once in olden times a man went to a king of theirs, bringing him a *Rasāyana*, the use of which would make him immortal, victorious, invincible, and capable of doing everything he desired. He asked the king to come alone to the place of their meeting, and the king gave orders to keep in readiness all the man required.
>
> The man began to boil the oil for several days, until at last it acquired consistency. Then he spoke to the king: "Spring into it and I shall finish the process." But the king, terrified at what he saw, had

not the courage to dive into it. The man, on perceiving his cowardice, spoke to him: "If you have not sufficient courage, and will not do it for yourself, will you allow me myself to do it?" Whereupon the king answered, "Do as you like." Now he produced several packets of drugs, and instructed him that when such and such symptoms should appear, he should throw upon him this or that packet. Then the man stepped forward to the cauldron and threw himself into it, and at once he was dissolved and reduced into pulp. Now the king proceeded according to his instruction, but when he had nearly finished the process, and there remained only one packet that was not yet thrown into the mass, he began to be anxious, and to think what might happen to his realm, in case the man should return to life as an *immortal, victorious, invincible* person, as has above been mentioned. And so he thought it preferable not to throw the last packet into the mass. The consequence was that the caldron became cold, and the dissolved man became consolidated in the shape of the said piece of silver.

d. In the account he gives of his travels in India in the last years of the thirteenth century, Marco Polo offers the following description of a group of persons he encountered on the Malabar Coast of India:[5]

> Here these Braaman live more than any other people in the world. . . . Moreover they have among them regulars and orders of monks . . . who are called *ciugi* [Yogis, Jogis] who certainly live more than all the others in the world, for they commonly live from 150 to 200 years . . . And again I tell you that these *ciugi* who live so long . . . eat also what I shall explain . . . I tell you that they take quicksilver and sulphur and mix them together with water and make a drink out of them; and they drink it and say it increases their life . . . They do it twice on the week, and sometimes twice each month . . . and without mistake those who live so long use this drink of sulphur and quicksilver.

e. At the close of the seventeenth century, the French traveler François Bernier, a Catholic man of letters, gives a more nuanced account of the religious practices he observed in Mogul India. While he either ridicules or shows disgust or contempt for nearly all that he sees of Hindu religious life, one group, whom he calls, as had Marco Polo, Yogis, seems to command his respect:[6]

There are others quite different from these [other Hindu sectarian groups]; strange fellows these, almost constantly travelling hither and thither; these are people who scoff at everything, and whom nothing troubles. They are people with secrets who, it is said, even know how to make gold and to prepare mercury so admirably that one or two grains taken every morning restore the body to perfect health and so fortify the stomach that it digests very well, such that it is nearly impossible for them to eat their fill.

f. Two hundred years after Bernier, John Campbell Oman, a relatively open-minded[7] subject of the British Empire—for whom, however, western superiority and the propriety, even the necessity of the colonial and missionary enterprise were never open to question—gives a report of an Indian alchemist that is less flattering than those of his two western predecessors:[8]

A learned Sikh told me of an . . . unfruitful experience he had with a gold-making Nirmali *sadhu*. This man made friends with the Sikh, and insinuated himself into his confidence. He . . . revealed, under the seal of secret, that he was acquainted with the occult art of transmuting metals. The Sikh . . . was much excited at finding that his new friend was a potent alchemist . . . The transmuter of metals seemed to live very well, yet occasionally borrowed money, showing special favour to the Sikh in this matter . . . One day the *sadhu* showed the Sikh a common bronze . . . coin, and then in his presence put it into a small furnace along with various leaves and roots he had collected. After an hour or so he produced from his crucible a golden fac-simile of the [coin]. The Sikh, not to be taken in even by his dear friend, asked to be allowed to have it tested by a goldsmith. Permission was given and acted upon, with the result that the experts in the bazaar pronounced it gold of the purest quality. The Sikh was now agog to learn the important secret of gold-making, and many were the rupees he willingly lent the *sadhu*, in the hope that he would accept him as a pupil. But the saintly man of science suddenly and unexpectedly decamped. "Alas," said the Sikh after he had narrated these circumstances to me, "I lost more than sixty rupees through that imposter. I have since learned how he fooled me, but never a Nirmali *sadhu* has, since those days, had so much as a drop of water from my hand!"

2. Religious Alchemy in India: Three Typologies

The six accounts presented here epitomize the historical evolution and devolution of *religious alchemy* in India. The Burmese folktale and Bāṇabhaṭṭa's seventh-century caricature typify *magical alchemy*, which held the field from the second to the tenth century A.D. Al-Biruni's eleventh-century account is a legendary portrayal of an operation proper to *tantric alchemy*, which enjoyed its golden age from the tenth to the fourteenth century. Marco Polo's and François Bernier's descriptions of Yogis document the tradition of *Siddha alchemy*, which thrived from the thirteenth to the seventeenth century. The decline of Siddha alchemy, already hinted at in the Aurangzebian *firman* with which this book opened, is chronicled in Oman's nineteenth-century account.

We may begin to generate a working definition of religious alchemy by distinguishing it from what it is not. Throughout the three phases I have evoked, religious alchemy interacted with, and was at times even indistinguishable from, other theoretical and applied sciences in which mercurial and mineral-based preparations played a central role. The most important of these (though perhaps not the earliest)[9] was Āyurveda, whose two foundational works, the *Caraka Saṁhitā* (ca. A.D. 100)[10] and the *Suśruta Saṁhitā* (ca. fourth century A.D.),[11] contain references to external, therapeutic uses of mercury. Following these, the sixth- to seventh-century A.D. *Aṣṭāṅga Saṃgraha* of Vāgbhaṭṭa the Elder contains the earliest Indian reference to the internal use of mercury for therapeutic ends.[12]

In spite of the fact, however, that Ayurvedic uses of mercury predate those of the tantric and Siddha alchemical traditions that will concern us, and although Āyurveda later incorporated many of the technical discoveries made by tantric alchemy (especially following the decline of the latter in the fourteenth century), its use of mercurial and mineral-based preparations falls, for the most part, outside the purview of this study. The reason for this is that the goals of the Ayurvedic "mercurial science" (*rasa śāstra*)—i.e., mineral-based pharmacy—are essentially therapeutic (*rogavāda*),[13] whereas the hallmark of religious alchemy is its dual emphasis on transmutational (*lohavāda*) alchemy and elixir (*dehavāda*) alchemy, on the bodily transformation of the living practitioner into a perfected immortal, a Siddha, Vidyādhara, or a "second Śiva." The Ayurvedic tradition has no such pretensions. The Ayurvedic physician's goal is to heal the man and not to create a superman. Because, however, a vast wealth of religious alchemical doctrine has remained fossilized as it were within the canons of Āyurveda and *rasa śāstra*, we will have the occasion to refer to a wide array of medical and pharmacological sources throughout this study.

I have chosen the term *magical alchemy* to designate the earliest phase of religious alchemy for a simple reason: it is, for all intents and purposes, the stuff of fairy tales. Transmutation and bodily immortality are its stated goals, but the means to these ends are a matter of serendipity throughout this period. Its watchword is the term *rasa-rasāyana*—a mercurial elixir cum philosopher's stone and one of the eight magical *siddhi*s of Mahāyāna Buddhism,[14] as well as medieval Hinduism[15] and Jainism[16]—but this is a power or object to be won or wrested from gods, demigods, or demons rather than produced in the laboratory. While most of the alchemical lore of this period is found in Buddhist sources, the secular literature of the time (of which Bāṇa's *Kādambarī* is a prime example) also contains its share of accounts of Hindu alchemical heroes and buffoons. Indeed, the Gupta age was a period of great syncretism between Hinduism and Buddhism. Both the Burmese folktale and Bāṇa's account also square with a number of other features of the alchemy of this period, not the least salient of which is that it rarely seems to work. Also, as Bāṇa's account intimates, alchemy appears to be a mainly *south* Indian phenomenon in this period, as evidenced in frequent mentions of Srisailam-Śrīparvata in period sources. Since India's original fascination with alchemy most probably arose out of early contacts with a China (India was exporting Buddhism to China in this period) whose Taoist speculative alchemical tradition had been developing since the second century A.D., one might conclude that such traditions reached south India via a maritime route.[17]

While Bāṇa's seventh-century description of the hydrargyriasic Draviḍa ascetic also contains India's earliest literary reference to tantric manuscripts, it would not be until some three centuries later that *tantric alchemy*, as I define it, actually emerged. Here, Alberuni's eleventh-century legend proves to be nothing other than the narrativization of an actual alchemical operation, as described in the final verses of the *Rasārṇava* (*RA*).[18] Alberuni's legend is entirely faithful to the tantric spirit of the *RA* and other texts of this period. The goal of tantric alchemy is bodily immortality, invincibility, and transcendence of the human condition. The tantric alchemist, like most of his brother tāntrikas, seeks through his practice to render himself godlike, a second Śiva.

The means to this end also distinguishes tantric alchemy from magical alchemy as well as from the therapeutic uses of mercurials proper to the Ayurvedic tradition. In the procedure of which Alberuni's text is a mythologization, the alchemist is instructed to first "test out" his mercury on metals before throwing himself into his alchemical cauldron. Only mercury that has proven itself capable of transmuting ten million times its mass of base metals into gold will suffice here.[19] This dual focus is indeed the watchword of the tantric alchemical method, which the *RA* summarizes with the pithy formula: *yathā lohe tathā dehe*—"as in metal, so in the body . . . first test [mercury] on a metal, then use it on the body."[20] Moreover, the two elements placed in relation here, metals (*loha*) and bodies (*deha*), define the two branches of the tantric alchemical synthesis: these are *lohavāda*, "transmutational alchemy" and *dehavāda*, "elixir alchemy." As this verse makes clear, however, the transmutation of base metals into gold is not an end in itself, but rather the necessary means to the ultimate end of bodily immortality.

Not only are the goals of tantric alchemy consistent with those of the broader Hindu tantric tradition, but so are its means to attaining those goals. The alchemical Tantras abound in references to tantric formulae (*mantra*s) and diagrams (*maṇḍala*s), as well as in descriptions of divine hierarchies, yogic and meditative techniques, sexual and ritual practices, and the Śākta-Śaiva devotionalism that are the hallmarks of the tantric tradition as a whole. Many of the major alchemical works of the period call themselves Tantras and are cast as the revealed teachings of Śiva (often in his tantric Bhairava form) to some tantric form of the Goddess. For reasons that will be made clear shortly, tantric alchemy was, in the main, a Hindu rather than a Buddhist occult science. Alberuni's account is set in Dhāra, the capital of the great king Bhoja of the Paramāra dynasty, located in western Madhya Pradesh—and it was indeed in western India that the greatest flowering of tantric alchemy occurred.

What truly sets tantric alchemy apart from magical alchemy is the rigor of its method and the remarkable breadth of the botanical, mineralogical, chemical, geographical, religious, and technical knowledge it mobilizes in the pursuit of its ambitious ends. Seemingly out of nowhere, the alchemical science burst upon the Indian scene in the tenth century with a laboratory full of specialized equipment and mineral and botanical raw materials in its theoretical inventory which magical alchemy had in no way anticipated. While Chinese (Taoist alchemy) and Persian (the Shi'a Jabirian school) traditions no doubt interacted with tantric alchemy, the Indian material is so specifically Indian—as much in the subcontinental provenance of its *materiae primae* as in its nearly exclusively Hindu religious and metaphysical presuppositions—as to preclude any possibility of this being a matter of wholesale borrowing. The roots of the revolution that was tantric alchemy may be traced back to the powerful impact of tantrism on Indian mystic and metaphysical speculation on the one hand and to developments within the medical schools on the other. In this latter context, a gradual phasing out of the practice of surgery (*śalyatantra*)—a development some attribute to the pervasive influence of the Buddhist ideal of noninjury (*ahiṃsa*)—seems to have been counterbalanced by discoveries and innovations in the field of mercurial and mineral-based medicines.[21] Tantric alchemy would have inherited some portion of its science from these new developments, which begin to appear both in Ayurvedic works and such tantric alchemical classics as the *Rasahṛdaya Tantra* (*RHT*) and *RA* in the tenth to eleventh centuries.

Sometime in the fourteenth century, we witness the gradual disappearance of tantric alchemy and the appropriation of its techniques and goals of transmutation and transubstantiation by other Indian systems of thought and practice, both old and new. As already noted, many of the techniques of tantric alchemy were churned back into the Ayurvedic tradition from which they had, at least in part, originated. Here the legacy of tantric alchemy is *rasa śāstra*, Ayurvedic pharmacy, a sine qua non of Ayurvedic practice and a discipline that continues to be taught in Ayurvedic universities and colleges in India down to the present day.[22]

I have already qualified this reapplication of transmutational and elixir alchemy to therapeutic ends as *rogavāda*, the "medical alchemy" specific to north Indian Āyurveda. Another development of the same order is *rasacikitsā*, "mercurial medicine." Although this school retains certain of the religious elements of tantric alchemy (its devotional cult of mercury, for example), it nonetheless shifts the emphasis of the latter away from transmutation and bodily immortality towards therapeutic ends. The *rasacikitsā* school continued, for centuries, to thrive—and even to rival classical Āyurveda—in south India, the eastern states, and the Sind and was exported along with classical Āyurveda to Tibet, China, southeast Asia, and Sri Lanka.[23] Yet another spin-off of the decline of tantric alchemy was the emergence of transmutational alchemy as an independent pursuit. Here, aurifaction, the production of alchemical gold, became an end in itself, rather than a means to the tantric end of bodily transubstantiation and immortality. Kings interested in increasing the royal treasury are known to have taken a lively interest in this discipline.[24]

The fourth evolute of tantric alchemy was the tradition I will call *Siddha alchemy*, which is most readily identified by its emphasis on the combined use of mercurial preparations with techniques of *haṭha yoga* for the attainment of immortality and a mode of being on a par with that of the divine Siddhas and Vidyādharas. In this, it bears certain similarities with the physiological alchemy (*nei-tan*) of Taoist traditions.[25] The complementarity of these two modes of practice is intimated in the accounts of Marco Polo and François Bernier, inasmuch as both present figures they call "Yogis" (*yogins*, practitioners of yoga) who are long-lived and healthy because they eat mercury. An important Indian witness to this complementary emphasis is the fourteenth-century Mādhavācārya, who devotes chapter nine of his *Sarvadarśana Saṃgraha* to the "Raseśvara Darśana," the "revealed system of the Lord of Mercury."[26] What is significant in Mādhava's synthesis is that, while he mainly draws on the tantric alchemical classics (the *RA*, etc.) to expound the basic principles of the alchemical doctrine, the inferences he draws from them relate specifically to the characteristically dual emphasis of Siddha alchemy, and to its emphasis on stabilizing and immortalizing the body through yoga.[27]

The south Indian *ciugi* alchemists were, in the words of Marco Polo, an "order of monks," while those whom Bernier chronicles in the north were a itinerant order "almost constantly travelling hither and thither." Now, while there were many monastic orders and even many orders of itinerant monks circulating in medieval India, there was only one such order whose highly mobile members enjoyed a reputation as alchemists in this period, and these were the Nāth Siddhas, also known as Nāth Yogis. The Siddha alchemists were, by and large, Nāth Siddhas; and because the Nāth Siddhas were itinerant, they made Siddha alchemy a pan-Indian phenomenon.

A significant number of alchemical works from this period are attributed to Nāth Siddhas, although it must be said that none—with perhaps two important exceptions[28]—are as weighty or innovative as the tantric alchemical classics. Two reasons may be adduced to explain this phenomenon. The first of these is that the Nāth Siddhas were, for the most part, not members of the Indian literati. Sons of the people—if not the salt of the earth—they simply *practiced* their alchemy, and when they wrote about it, it was more often in compact, even elliptical, poetry cribbed down in the vernaculars of the day than in Sanskrit. Had the Nāth Siddhas written in Sanskrit, more of their alchemical works would perhaps be extant today. However, their forte was not writing Sanskrit, but rather living and speaking in the popular speech of their time. The second reason for the relative paucity of Siddha alchemical works is that the old tantric alchemical classics contained all that needed to be known to carry out the alchemical complement to the hathayogic practices proper to a two-pronged approach to bodily immortality. This is clearly the purport of the *RA* (1.18b) when it states: "Mercury and breath [control] are known as the Work in two parts." It was the complementary discipline of *haṭha yoga* that required further explanation, and in this field of expertise the Nāth Siddhas simply had no rivals. Nearly all of India's hathayogic classics are the works of Nāth Siddhas (with the most important of these being attributed to Gorakṣanātha, i.e., Gorakhnāth), and all date from the period of Siddha alchemy. Furthermore, as we will demonstrate, the language of the Nāth Siddhas' *haṭha yoga* is often nothing other than a projection of alchemical discourse upon the human body. The human body is an alchemical body.

3. Magical Alchemy

The term "Siddha" is an ambiguous one, given that a great number of Hindu and Buddhist schools, sects, and traditions have been so identified—either by themselves or (retrospectively) by others—since the Gupta period. The original referent of the term was a class of demigods: in Buddhist and Hindu traditions alike, the Siddhas shared the interface between earth and sky—mountaintops and the atmospheric region—with a horde (*gaṇa*) of semidivine beings. In the words of the fifth-century *Amarakośa*, "The Wizards (*Vidyādharas*), Nymphs, Dryads, Protectors, Celestial Musicians, Centaurs, Ghouls, Hidden Ones, Perfecti (*Siddhas*), and Beings: these constitute the class of the demigods."[29] Gradually, however, the notion arose that the world or level of the Siddhas and Vidyādharas was one to which humans too could accede, and so it was that throughout the Indian middle ages, a growing pool of such Siddhas came to be shared, together with an expanding body of legend on their subject, by Hindus, Buddhists, and Jains alike.[30]

Vyāsa, a fifth-century commentator on Patañjali's *Yoga Sūtras*, provides us, albeit in an apophatic way, with what may be called the "Siddha charter"; that is, a comprehensive account of the goals of the human who aspires to Siddha-hood. This he does in his commentary on *Yoga Sūtra* 3.51, which states: "When invited by the celestial beings, that invitation should not be accepted nor should it cause vanity because it involves the possibility of undesirable consequences." Vyāsa's commentary reads:

> The celestial beings residing in high regions noticing the purity of the intellect of those who have attained unalloyed truth . . . try to invite them by tempting them with enjoyments available in their regions in the following manner: "O Great Soul, come and sit here and enjoy yourself. It is lovely here. Here is a lovely lady. This elixir prevents death and decay. Here is a vehicle which can take you to the skies. The tree which fulfils all wishes is here . . . here are the perfected Siddhas and the great seers. Beautiful and obedient nymphs, supernormal eyes and ears, a body of adamantine strength, all are here."[31]

In his *Jātakamālā*, Aryaśūra refers to experts in demonology or "demonic medicine" for the exorcism of demons (*bhūtavidyā*, the fourth limb of Āyurveda), as Siddhavidyās, persons versed in the occult knowledge of the Siddhas.[32] At first blush, there appears to be no connection between these two fields of expertise. Yet, upon closer inspection, we in fact find a number of uncanny correspondences, of which many are specifically south Indian, between the two. To begin, the classic work on Ayurvedic demonology, the *Kumāra Tantra*, is attributed to the great arch-demon of the south and villain of the Sanskrit *Rāmāyaṇa*, Rāvaṇa.[33] In the ca. twelfth-century Tamil *Irāmāvatāram* of Kampaṅ, the daughters of Rāvaṇa are said to be the wives of the Sittars, the Tamil equivalent of the Siddhas.[34] In his commentary on *Yoga Sūtra* 4.1, Vyāsa glosses *auṣadhi*, "botanicals"—which Patañjali designates as one of the four means to obtaining *siddhi*s—with *rasāyana*, which he says may be found "in the dwellings of Asuras ['anti-gods,' 'demons']."[35]

Vyāsa's association of botanicals with Asuras is echoed in later commentaries, including that of the ninth-century Vācaspati Miśra, who also glosses *auṣadhi* as *rasāyana* into which, he says, a man may be initiated "by alluring Asura maidens."[36] A similar reading is found in the *Bhāgavata Purāṇa* (5.24.13), which employs the term *rasa-rasāyana* to refer to the medicinal herbs employed by the many denizens of the subterranean regions to ensure eternal youth and good health.[37] Even today, the Sittar physicians of south India qualify one class of treatment as *rākṣasa*.[38]

The great wealth of the subterannean Asuras[39] is also enjoyed, according to epic and Puranic traditions, by the Yakṣas (the Dryads of India, whose leader Kubera is the god of wealth in both Hindu and Buddhist traditions), and the Nāgas, Serpent deities, subterranean plutocrats as well, and India's version of the archetypal dragon who lies atop hoards of buried treasure.

The Asuras and the subterranean locus of their wealth seem to be connected to an obscure passage from the eleventh-century *RA*, which describes the types of persons best adapted for "Treasure Practice" (*nidhi-sādhana*), and "Hole in the Ground Practice" (*bila-sādhana*): the former are identified by the digging tools they carry, and the latter by their resemblance to male Asuras (who are ugly and terrible, in contradistinction to their female counterparts).[40] With regard to the Serpents as custodians of fabulous underground treasures, a living tradition among the self-proclaimed "Jogis" of the Sind province of Pakistan, who claim descent from the great magician and serpent master Gūgā Chauhan, is highly illustrative:[41]

> Jogi tradition has it that seven jogis are required to catch a single cobra because although the cobra strikes only two and a half times, it spits out a substantial amount of venom that can be lethal even from a distance. The seven jogis make seven dunghills, dig seven ditches behind them, fill these with water and climb inside with only their heads visible on the surface. Then they start playing their enchanting tunes on their *beens* to lure the cobra, silently reciting magical *mantar*s [Sanskrit: *mantra*s] at the same time . . .
>
> Explains Punoo Jogi, "When the *sheesh nang* ["king cobra": Sanskrit *śeṣa nāga*] is provoked, he strikes at the first dung heap and sets it aflame. While he strikes, the jogi submerges himself in water so that no harm comes to him. Then he lunges again, and yet again but with less force. Once he has disgorged all his poison, he can no longer fight. You should see his rage then. In one final blow, he strikes at the treasure he has been guarding for years and destroys it before finally succumbing to the seven jogis.[42] That is why the jogis have never found the treasure that the *sheesh nang* guards."

The Dryads and Serpents, perhaps the most archaic divinities of India, were gradually absorbed, quite literally, as "props" for the high gods of Hinduism and Buddhism when these became the great religions of the subcontinent. In classical Hinduism, it is a Serpent that serves to support the entire universe atop his bejeweled hood; at times when the universe is nonexistent (exactly half the time), he supports the sleeping god Viṣṇu, in whom the universe is contained in a nonmanifest state, serving as his couch.[43] Like Viṣṇu, the Buddha too is sheltered by the hood of a Serpent, and the earliest iconographic depiction of such is in fact Buddhist rather than Hindu. This is the third-century A.D. sculpted image of the Buddha, on a Serpent couch, from Nagarjunikonda (Andhra Pradesh) in south India. It is precisely in this region that the ca. third-century A.D. Buddhist *Gaṇḍavyūha* locates the seat of the bodhisattva Mañjuśrī, whom it says converted many indigenous Serpents to Buddhism.[44] This region is also one that produces a great number of figures with names containing *Nāga* (serpent): the most illustrious of these is Nāgārjuna, whom a number of later traditions identify as a Siddha alchemist hailing from Śrīparvata.

The ca. first-century A.D. south Indian play, the *Mṛcchakaṭikā* (The Little Clay Cart), the first literary source to make mention of what is apparently a human Siddha, is the work of an author from Andhra Pradesh, who very likely would have hailed from Śrīparvata (also mentioned in the text).[45] This Siddha reminds us once more of Bāṇabhaṭṭa's hapless south Indian Śaiva ascetic who had lost his sight in one eye due to an invisibility salve called *siddhāñjana* ("perfected, super ointment"), and who knew myriads of stories concerning Śrīparvata. Slightly prior to Bāṇabhaṭṭa, the south Indian author Subandhu provides an early mention of mercury (*pārada*), as well as of Śrīparvata, in his comic play, the *Vāsavadattā*.[46] Now, *śrīparvata* (or *śrīśailam*)—generally identified with a holy peak located in the central Deccan plateau (Kurnool district, Andhra Pradesh) of south India[47]—is a highly generic term for a mountain or hilltop in the Sanskrit and Hindi languages: both simply mean "splendid, auspicious, or excellent peak." Therefore, while the greatest wealth of Siddha lore, both Hindu and Buddhist, is attached to this toponym, we cannot be certain that it is always the Srisailam or Śrīparvata of the east central Deccan that is being evoked.

The earliest Hindu mention of Srisailam is found in the *Mahābhārata* which, precisely, identifies it as a place at which to attain *siddhi*s, the stuff that Siddhas are made of.[48] It is the Buddhist religious literature, however, that contains the greatest wealth of early references to Śrīparvata-Srisailam. Located in the heart of the Andhra country, a south Indian "Buddhist fief" in the first centuries of the common era, this site was a launching point for missionaries to Kashmir, China, Bengal, and Sri Lanka.[49] There are, however, no mentions of *siddhi*s (*ṛddhi*s in Pali) or Siddhas in Buddhist evocations of Śrīparvata,[50] unless one chooses to see in the name of the third-century A.D. heretical "Siddhāthaka" school of that region a forerunner of the term Siddha.[51] Buddhism was fast losing ground to Śaivism in the region by the seventh century, with temples to Śiva Siddheśvara ("Lord of the Siddhas") beginning to appear at Srisailam at that time.[52]

It is a figure from Tamil Nadu, some distance to the south of the Andhra country, who first talks about the Siddhas in an informed way. This is the seventh-century Tirumūlar who, while he is generally held to be the first of the eighteen Sittars (i.e., the Siddhas of Tamil tradition) and the founder of the Sittar school, speaks of the Siddhas—although it is unclear whether he means the semidivine or the human variety—as if they were already an established institution. In his *Tirumantiram*, Tirumūlar defines the Siddhas as those "who have experienced divine light and divine energy [*śakti*] from within and through yogic integration [*samādhi*]."[53] Sittar tradition maintains that Tirumūlar was the disciple of the alchemist Nandi(keśvara); while a certain alchemist by the same name is cited in a number of post-twelfth-century sources, these never attribute any alchemical texts to him, nor are there any extant works of his to prove he was ever anything more than a legendary human or a god of alchemists.[54]

The discipline of Siddha medicine, butressed by a Siddha alchemy that is in fact a synthesis of hathayogic and alchemical practice, is the present-day legacy of the Sittars in Tamil Nadu. While the extant alchemical works of the eighteen Sittars,[55] the storied founders of these traditions, turn out to be quite recent,[56] the body of legend attached to these figures carries us back, once again, to the lore of magical alchemy.

A limited number of documents indicate that a historical figure named Nandi may have lived in the same century as Tirumūlar. This Nandi, a Buddhist monk from central India, left India in the middle of the seventh century, traveling by sea to Sri Lanka and southeast Asia before arriving in China in A.D. 655. A year later, the emperor of China shipped him off to sea again to collect medicinal herbs. He returned to China in 663.[57] Prior even to Nandi, according to Sittar tradition, was the alchemist Bogar (or Pokar or Bhoga), whose links with China are also remarkable. The Sittar Bogar, who is said to have lived in the third to fifth centuries A.D., is today worshipped at that site in the Palani Hills of Tamil Nadu where he is said to have practiced and taught alchemy.[58] Traditions concerning Bogar cast him either as a Chinese philosopher who came to India for the study of medicine, traveling first to Patna and Bodhgaya before taking up residence in Madras; or as a south Indian Sittar, who traveled to China and taught alchemy to a ruler named Koṅg (his disciple Koṅganar,[59] according to Sittar tradition) before returning to south India.[60]

The greatest historical value of these accounts of Bogar and Nandi lies in their references to early maritime exchanges between India and China. The sea trade between India's southeast coast and Han China (via the entrepôt of Hanoi), already well under way by the beginning of the common era, especially thrived during the golden age of Sino-Indian exchange—of religious ideas as well as goods—of the third to eighth centuries A.D. This was, of course, the period that first saw the export of Buddhism from India to China and, slightly later, the introduction of certain elements of Taoism into Indian religion and culture. (Overland trade along the Silk Road—which brushed India's northwest frontier at Takṣaśila and Peshawar, and slightly above the Jhelum River in the Punjab—and its spurs, which ran down into the subcontinent's great trading hubs at the port of Bhṛgukaccha (Broach), Ujjain, and Patna (via Kathmandu), had already been flourishing since about 110 B.C.).[61]

We have already seen that Taoist alchemical speculation and experimentation had already reached an appreciable level of sophistication by the time of these exchanges.[62] Here let us also note the important fact that nearly all the mercury the Indian alchemists would later use came from China: given the fact that there exist no mercurial deposits on the subcontinent, China was India's nearest and obvious supplier.[63] It is therefore rather curious that the majority of historical notices from this period indicate that it was China that was looking to India for alchemical drugs and data. When the Han emperors first asked for instruction in the Buddhist faith, they also requested a "drug of immortality" they supposed India to possess.[64]

While the Chinese have no record of having been visited by an Indian alchemist named Nandi, they do mention an Indian scholar named Nārāyaṇasvāmin, who was captured and held in the Chinese court in about A.D. 649 because he knew of an elixir of life; later, in 664, an Indian physician named Lokāditya would be summoned there to serve as an alchemist-in-residence.[65] Slightly earlier, in about A.D. 646, the Chinese offered a Sanskrit translation of the *Tao te ching* to the king of Kāmarūpa (Assam), purportedly in exchange for information concerning transmutational and elixir alchemy.[66]

In charge of that translation was the great seventh-century Chinese pilgrim Hsuan-tsang who would, in his *Su yu chi* (Buddhist Records of the Western World), record accounts he had heard in the court of King Harṣa concerning the famed Indian alchemist Nāgārjuna.[67] Yet this was the same royal patron for whom Bāṇabhaṭṭa wrote his description of the hydrargyriasic south Indian ascetic, in his *Kādambarī*;[68] and the same seventh-century India in which the Chinese pilgrim I-Ching reported, in the account he gave of his travels there between A.D. 671 and 695, cases of grave misuse of mercuric ores as elixirs.[69] It was also an India in which a sixth-century

Indian king (of Udyāna, in the Swat region of present-day Pakistan) quizzed two Chinese Buddhist visitors to his court on the "Taoist matters" of medicine and science and the silver and golden palaces of the Immortals.[70]

The picture that emerges from this period is one of an ongoing exchange between India and China regarding matters alchemical, matters in which China, even if it appears always to have been ahead of India in innovations throughout this period, nonetheless looked to India for inspiration.[71] Such is perhaps understandable, given the incredible impact Indian Buddhism was having on China.

If, however, Indian religion and science were in vogue in China, so too were Chinese traditions in India. More than this, whatever India exported over the mountains to China seemed to come back, in altered form, to be reappropriated by the Indians a few centuries later. A prime example is the Indian yogic tradition, which China received, in a fairly unsophisticated state, along with Buddhism, in the third century A.D. But the Taoist China of the time was already experimenting with what it termed "embryonic respiration" and the "feeding of the vital principle"—practices that were more or less equivalent to Indian yogic techniques, but which, in the Chinese context, already bore a veneer of alchemical symbolism. A yogic technique of apparent Chinese origin, called *huan-ching* or "making the Yellow River flow backwards," identified with either the practice of urethral suction or that of internally raising semen along the spinal column, would first make its appearance in Indian Mahāyāna sources[72] and later reappear as an erotico-yogic technique of the Nāth Siddhas.[73] Indeed, Indian tantra first appeared at points of contact with Taoist China and, in the words of Joseph Needham, upon whose masterful *Science and Civilisation in Ancient China* I have been relying throughout this section, "the Taoist department of Buddhism was Tantrism." So it was that when Indian tantrism was first introduced into China in the eighth century by the Buddhist monks Śubhākarasiṁha, Vajrabodhi, and Amoghavajra, a certain number of its techniques were merely "returning" to their country of origin, from which they had been exported but a few centuries earlier.[74]

The principal Sino-Indian points of contact in this period of exchange were (1) the mountain passes located in the northwestern region of the subcontinent (Himalayan Pakistan and Afghanistan) and (2) Assam to the east—these being the two regions through which the Indian spurs of the Silk Road passed—as well as (3) the major seaports on the coastlines of Tamil Nadu and Gujarat, which linked India to China and the west via the maritime routes of the day. According to the evidence at our disposal, two illustrious travelers along these trade routes in this period would have been the "Chinese goddess" Tārā and the element mercury (*pārada*),[75] whose entrances into the subcontinent appear to have been curiously linked. Both are said to be sixth-century imports from "greater China" (*mahācīna*, a blanket Sanskrit term applied to both China and Tibet) into a nascent Indian Buddhist tantric tradition, and both are purported to have been brought to India by none other than Nāgārjuna.[76]

The question then arises: Did "Nāgārjuna" bring Tārā and mercury to India by land or by sea? Both mercury and Tārā are mentioned in the sixth-to seventh-century south Indian *Vāsavadattā*,[77] which would indicate a maritime link with eastern China; but both are also mentioned in the sixth-century *Aṣṭāṅga Saṃgraha*,[78] which was probably composed in Ujjain, in western Madhya Pradesh. The earliest recorded case of Tārā worship in India comes to us from seventh-century Nalanda, the great Buddhist complex located in modern-day Bihar (whose main links to China were overland, via Patna to the north);[79] a century later, we read of a temple built to the "Chinese goddess" in Kāñci, on the coast of Tamil Nadu.[80]

This coastal location reminds us of what may have been Tārā's original role: she was a goddess of navigation, of sea crossings—*tārā* is generated from the verb *tṛ*, to cross over the sea.[81] A fanciful eighteenth-century Tibetan source, the *dPag-bsam-ljon-bzan*, brings these elements together in a unique way. Saying that Nāgārjuna was born in Kāñci, it goes on to describe how he sailed across the sea on a craft made of two fig leaves, until he came to an intermediate continent, from which he brought a gold-making elixir back to his monastery at Nalanda.[82]

Now, Tibet's source of mercury has long been Yunnan, in southeastern China,[83] which shares a border with Annam (Vietnam), of which Hanoi was the major port for maritime commerce with India and southeast Asia. That the back country of Annam was rich in mercurial ores is demonstrated by a historical anecdote from China: the great mercurial alchemist Ko Hung (ca. A.D. 300) requested and received a transfer to that province, into an administrative position unworthy of his rank in the imperial bureaucracy, in order that he might have ready access to the cinnabar (red mercuric sulfide) he needed to conduct his experiments![84] We further know that mercury was carried in the cargo holds of the ships that plied these Sino-Indian trade routes in later centuries. On the one hand, we find a report of over a ton of the stuff being warehoused in the Malaysian port of Malacca;[85] and on the other, we know that the Indian port cities of Surat

(Gujarat), Murshidabad (Bengal), Calcutta, and Madras have long been centers for the fabrication of synthetic cinnabar and calomel (mercurous chloride), using native Indian minerals and imported mercury, since at least the sixteenth century A.D.[86] Also supporting a direct Sino–south Indian maritime link in matters alchemical is the fact that Sittar alchemy and medicine have always been more mineral based and "Taoist" than the more herb-based northern traditions.[87]

Against a maritime link, and in favor of an overland connection in the mercury and Tārā trade, we can marshal the following evidence. The Tibetans themselves have historically purchased their mercury from Chinese traders who transported it to Tibet; here, the obvious link would have been an overland one.[88] So too, the mercury that reached Varāhamihira (author of the *Bṛhat Saṁhitā*) and Vāgbhaṭṭa the Elder in northwest India quite certainly traveled overland, via the Silk Road or one of its spurs. What of Tārā? On the strength of two passages from the third- to eleventh-century A.D. *Sādhanamālā* (The Garland of Practice), Tārā is generally considered to have been brought to Nalanda, directly from Bhoṭa (Tibet) by Nāgārjuna. Yet, in fact, the passages in question concern two different forms of Tārā, named Vajra ("Diamond") Tārā and Ekajaṭā ("One Lock of Hair").[89] Now, Ekajaṭā is also known as Mahācīnatārā, as if to emphasize her Tibetan roots. In the Tibetan Buddhism of the Dragon Kaju sect, Ekajaṭā is in fact the consort of an "ancient" Nyingma divinity named Quicksilver (i.e., mercury), identified with Bhairava Yamāntaka ("Terrible Slayer of Death"). In the Padmaist literature of the same Nyingma school, she is the consort of the god Amṛtakuṇḍali, who is also known by the epithet "King of Elixirs."[90]

With this, we perhaps arrive at the source of the tradition that Nāgārjuna brought "mercury," together with Tārā, from Tibet in this period. Yet if Nāgārjuna did indeed bring Tārā and mercury to India from Tibet, it is curious that the sixth- to seventh-century *Aṣṭāṅga Saṃgraha*, which mentions both Tārā and mercury, should make no mention of Nāgārjuna. More than this, Tibetan tradition itself maintains that the worship of Tārā was introduced into that country from Nepal—in the seventh century, i.e., later than the earliest mentions of her in Indian sources![91] This would make the claim that Nāgārjuna introduced Tārā to India "from Tibet" an untenable one, unless it is the two specifically Tibetan forms (Vajratārā and Ekajaṭā) of the goddess that are intended. As we will shortly see, the alchemist Nāgārjuna manages to elude the historian at nearly every turn.

I have already noted that there are no mercurial ores native to the Indian subcontinent. The same, in fact, holds true for Tibet, which means that if Nāgārjuna brought mercury to India from Tibet at the end of the Gupta age, then it was very likely Chinese mercury that he brought from there; for it is from Yunnan in southeastern China that the Tibetan supply came.[92] This Chinese source likely lies at the origin of one of the many Sanskrit terms employed for cinnabar, the most commonly occurring mercurial ore in the world. This is the word *cīnapiṣṭa*, "Chinese powder." Many of the other terms for mercury or its ores also indicate regions to the northwest of India (and west of Tibet) as its region of provenance. *Pārada*, the most common alchemical term for mercury, refers to Pārada-deśa, the land of the Parthians or Pāradas of Transoxiania or the Baluchistan region; *darada*, red cinnabar, to Darada-deśa, the modern Dardistan, in northern Kashmir; *hiṅgula*, cinnabar, to Hiṅglāj (-Devi) in Baluchistan or to a country called Hiṅgula. The term *mleccha*, "(proper to) the (central Asian) barbarian (races)" would have been a more blanket term.[93] Cinnabar and other mercurial ores occur naturally throughout the trans-Himalayan regions of central Asia, as well as in Chitral (Pakistan), Garmshir (Afghanistan), and Yunnan, and it was from these regions that India's supply of mercury would likely have come.[94]

4. Desperately Seeking Nāgārjuna: The Buddhist Evidence

The origins of Indian alchemy are closely linked to the figure of Nāgārjuna, who, whenever one attempts to pin him down as a historical personage, proves to be quite as protean and mercurial as quicksilver itself. One has the feeling that if it were only possible to extract Nāgārjuna the alchemist out of the welter of the Nāgārjunas who dot the mythology and history of Indian religions and medicine, one would be well on the way to generating a coherent history of Indian alchemy.[95] Yet, there are so many Nāgārjunas to choose from. In addition to the Nāgārjunas I have already mentioned to this point (the Nāgārjuna who purportedly brought mercury and Tārā to India, and the Nāgārjuna who sailed to the intermediate continent on a fig-leaf boat to recover a "gold-making elixir") there are perhaps a dozen other figures with the same name—who may or may not have been the same person, and who, all told, would have authored over a hundred works on a wide array of subjects[96]—connected in some way with the Indian alchemical tradition. These include Nāgārjuna the Mādhyamika philosopher, Nāgārjuna the tantric Buddhist author and commentator, Nāgārjuna the Hindu tantric sorcerer, Nāgārjuna the Nāth Siddha, Nāgārjuna the north Indian medical author, Nāgārjuna the south Indian medical author,[97] Nāgārjuna the Buddhist alchemist, Nāgārjuna the Jain alchemist, Nāgārjuna the northern Hindu alchemist, Nāgārjuna the southern Hindu alchemist,[98] Nāgārjuna the eye doctor, Nāgārjuna the sexologist, Nāgārjuna the *parfumeur*—so many Nāgārjunas, so little time! Whereas Albert Grünwedel called him the "Faust of Buddhism,"[99] Max Walleser, the western scholar who probably toiled the longest at attempting to identify the historical Nāgārjuna, concluded that no Nāgārjuna ever existed![100] Tibetan historians have had it both ways, simply allowing that a single figure named Nāgārjuna alchemically prolonged his life for 529 to 1000 years, during which he found the time to dabble in or master all of the fields mentioned above.

Nāgārjuna bursts upon the stage of intellectual and religious history as the south Indian founder (ca. second century A.D.) of the Mādhyamika school of philosophy within the then-nascent current of Buddhism called Mahāyāna.[101] An extremely prolific writer, he was the author of the seminal Mahāyāna text, the *Prajñāparamitāśāstra*, a commentary on the revealed "Teachings of the Perfection of Wisdom" (*Prajñāparamitā Sūtras*). According to legend, these teachings had been preserved for millennia in the netherworld of the Nāgas, before being restored to the world by Nāgārjuna. Chinese sources relate that a great serpent (*mahānāga*) opened a seven-jeweled chest for Nāgārjuna, from which he recovered the Vaipulya (Mahāyāna) teachings;[102] according to later Tibetan legend, he was initiated by the Nāgas (whence his name) and received the Perfection of Wisdom texts directly from them.[103]

A number of sources, whose historical veracity is equally suspect, indicate that the Mādhyamika philosopher Nāgārjuna was the protégé and companion of a certain ruler of the Śātavāhana dynasty which ruled over the Andhra country between the first century B.C. and the second century A.D.[104] Bāṇabhaṭṭa speaks in his *Harṣacarita* of "a monk named Nāgārjuna" who had presented Śātavāhana with an elixir in the form of a jewel called "Pearl-Wreath Mandākinī," which had been given to him by the king of the Nāgas.[105] According to Hsuan-tsang, the Chinese pilgrim who was Bāṇa's contemporary at the court of Harṣa, the "Bodhisattva Nāgārjuna" was so skilled in the art of compounding medicines that he had produced a pill with which he had extended his own life as well as that of his royal companion for many hundreds of years. Later, as Hsuan-tsang relates, it happened that the king ran out of funds while building a monastery for Nāgārjuna at

Bhramaragiri, "Black Bee Hill." At this point, "the Bodhisattva Nāgārjuna (Lung-Mêng Phu-Sa) scattered some drops of a numinous and wonderful pharmakon over certain large stones, whereupon they all turned to gold," thus resolving Śātavāhana's problems and his own.[106] While there is good evidence that such a monastery was built in the Andhra country, we cannot be sure that it was built prior to the fifth century A.D., at which time it is mentioned by the Chinese pilgrim Fa-hsien (who identifies it with Śrīparvata).[107] Hsuan-tsang further describes a meeting he had, somewhere in the northeastern Punjab, with a brahmin disciple of bodhisattva Nāgārjuna who, although he was seven hundred years old, looked to be only thirty.[108]

Even in those Chinese, Tibetan, and Indian legends in which the philosopher Nāgārjuna is made out to be an alchemist of sorts—the possessor of an elixir of long life and some rudiments of transmutational alchemy—there is never any specific mention of the raw materials (such as mercury) or techniques he employs in his craft. This omission is of a piece with the magical alchemy of the period on the one hand and, on the other, with a handful of vague references to aurifaction contained in a number of Mahāyāna texts, of which at least two are attributed to the philosopher Nāgārjuna. These are the *Mahāprajñāparamitāśāstra*, which contains four references to transmutational alchemy; and the *Avataṃsaka Sūtra* (attributed to Nāgārjuna by Fa-hsien and translated into Chinese in A.D. 699).[109] In addition to these sources, references to magical alchemy are found in the fourth- through sixth-century *Mahāyāna Saṃgraha Bhāṣya* (a commentary on Asaṅga translated into Chinese in about A.D. 650 by Hsuan-tsang) and the *Abhidharma Mahāvibhāṣa* (translated and considerably lengthened over a fifth-century recension by Hsuan-tsang himself, in A.D. 659).[110]

Given the paucity of alchemical references in writings attributed to the second-century philosopher Nāgārjuna, one wonders why this figure should have been perceived, in the seventh-century sources I have been citing, to have been such a great alchemist. The most plausible explanation would be that Bāṇabhaṭṭa and Hsuan-tsang had heard of another Nāgārjuna, a near contemporary of themselves, and had conflated this later figure with the renowned Mādhyamika philosopher—a not-untenable proposition, given the tradition that he had produced an elixir of long life. A number of lineage lists identify a Nāgārjuna who would have lived in the first half of the seventh century as the disciple of Sarāha at the great Buddhist monastic university of Nalanda, where alchemy was reputedly part of the curriculum.[111]

It is just such an assumption that a number of Sanskrit, Chinese, and

Tibetan sources make, mainly in the form of retrospective prophecies concerning the Buddha. These prophecies, which begin to appear in the fourth- through fifth-century *Mahāmegha Sūtra*, are the reef against which every attempt to locate the historical Nāgārjuna has foundered. The pivot of these so-called prophecies—a figure whom tradition identifies as "Siddha Nāgārjuna"—would have been an important seventh- or eighth-century teacher in the fledgling tantric Buddhist tradition. It is this Nāgārjuna who is said to have been Sarāha's disciple at Nalanda and to have brought mercury and the goddess Tārā from Tibet to India.

Before we proceed any further, two points need to be made clear concerning "Siddha Nāgārjuna." The first of these is that he is nowhere referred to as "Siddha" in the period (ca. seventh through eighth centuries) in which he purportedly lived. He is either simply called Nāgārjuna or has the title *Arya* prefixed or the ending *-pā* (or *–pāda*) suffixed to his name.[112] The Siddha appellation is, as we will see, an ex post facto categorization on the part of later tantric genealogists who, in the eleventh century, began to refer to their founding gurus as the Siddhācāryas ("perfected teachers"), Mahāsiddhas, or simply the eighty-four Siddhas. However, just as persons living in Palestine prior to the birth of Jesus Christ did not refer to their age as "B.C.," so the Indian innovators of tantric Buddhism did not call themselves "Siddhas."

Second, the confusion of this seventh- to eighth-century figure (whom later convention identifies as "Siddha Nāgārjuna") with the second-century philosopher of the same name likely derives from the fact that each was associated with a figure named Aryadeva. Nāgārjuna the philosopher was the teacher of Aryadeva, while "Siddha" Nāgārjuna's disciple Karṇaripā was also known as Aryadeva.[113] Grafted to this composite Nāgārjuna are associations—which I have already noted in the writings of Hsuan-tsang and others—with a king named Śātavāhana and the site of Śrīparvata. The most baroque concatenations of these data are the work of the Tibetans, whose "prophecies" concerning Nāgārjuna maintain that he was born in Saurashtra (Gujarat) 400 years after the Buddha's *parinirvāṇa*[114] and lived for over 500 years, passing the first 200 years of his life at Nalanda, the second 200 "in south India,"[115] and the final 129 or 171 years at Śrīparvata, where he voluntarily gave up his life at the request of Śātavāhana's son. In nearly none of these prophecies—neither those of the Tibetans nor the Indian or Chinese sources upon which they drew—is Nāgārjuna ever referred to as a Siddha; on the other hand, the name of this figure alternates between Nāgārjuna, Nāgabodhi, Nāgāhvaya, and Nagarāja.[116]

His amazing longevity is a tenable proposition only if one is prepared to accept the notion, as the Tibetans did, that Nāgārjuna's alchemy served to dilate his life span.

It is only in the late Tibetan sources, moreover, that we find explicit references to Siddha Nāgārjuna as an alchemist. The fourteenth-century historian Bu-ston states that Nāgārjuna procured a gold-making elixir from the intermediate continent and so saved Nalanda from the ravages of famine. In the early seventeenth century, Tāranātha expatiates on this theme, stating that "with the help of the art of alchemy, he maintained for many years five hundred teachers of the Mahāyāna doctrine at Śrī Nalendra [*sic*]." Later, he adds that "from the time he became a *rasāyana siddha*, his face shone like a gemstone." In a similar vein, another late Tibetan source states that after Nāgārjuna had received his tantric initiation from his guru, the Siddhācārya Sarāha-pā, he "attained success . . . especially in *rasāyana*" such that his body became as hard as a diamond (*vajrakāya-siddhi*). This, however, runs against the teachings of his guru, given the fact that Sarāha-pā criticizes those who practice *rasa-rasāyana* in one of his vernacular songs.[117] Of the fifty-nine works attributed to Nāgārjuna and translated, in the twelfth through thirteenth centuries A.D. into Tibetan in the *Tanjur*, none contains any alchemical material.[118] One would therefore have to assume that if a seventh- through eight-century Nāgārjuna did practice alchemy at Nalanda, he left no written records of his work there.

Elsewhere, the Tibetan mythology of the eighty-four Siddhas casts a number of "debates" between Buddhist and Hindu figures as so many "*siddhi*-contests." So we read that Lalitavajra had a contest of magic power with the Hindus in the kingdom of Naravarmā in the west. "The teacher swallowed a quantity of poison and two wine-jars full of mercury. Still he remained unaffected. The king was full of reverence."[119] If, however, the Buddhists won this particular battle, in the end they lost the Indian war: a victim of the Muslim invasions that were overtaking the continent, as well as of its own growing resemblance to Hindu Tantra, Buddhist Tantra and Buddhism effectively disappeared from the Indian subcontinent by the twelfth century. In a sense, the early alchemical tradition epitomized a syncretistic trend that had been ongoing since the origins of Tantra, with *mantras*, clan lineages, and divinities converging with one another.[120] The alchemists' gods were precisely those divinities who had come to occupy the no-man's-land of the Hindu-Buddhist tantric divide: Tārā and Akṣobhya, of whom Hindu forms would emerge in about the tenth century; Avalokiteśvara, whom the Hindus would identify with Śiva Lokanātha; Vajrasattva-Ādibuddha, whom they would identify with Ādinātha; and Bhairava, Bhairavī, and Mahākāla, whom Buddhism borrowed from Hinduism. In concrete terms, Indian Buddhism was losing its specificity, and thereby its royal patronage, a situation which, in the face of the Muslim conquests, proved fatal.

Of course, export Buddhism of a tantric stamp continues to flourish in Tibet (into which it was introduced, from eastern India, perhaps from Nalanda itself, in the eighth century) down to the present day; and it is precisely in Tibet that we may glimpse what became of the Buddhist alchemical tradition. What is intriguing about the alchemy of Tibetan Buddhism is that it more closely resembles earlier Taoist practices and contemporary Hindu erotico-mystical techniques than it does the procedures and goals of transmutational and elixir alchemy. For all intents and purposes, external alchemy disappears from Buddhism at about the same time as Buddhism disappears from the Indian subcontinent. So it is that we find very few Tibetan references, apart from those cited a moment ago, to the practice of any sort of alchemy by the Siddhācāryas—i.e., by the teachers who founded the tantric Buddhist path, between the seventh and twelfth centuries A.D. Karṇari-pā obtains an elixir from urine; Carpaṭā-pā gains the power to transmute as well as an elixir of immortality from a boy's penis and anus, respectively; and Vyāḍi-pā produces an alchemical elixir with the aid of a prostitute; this last figure is also the author of two of only four Indian alchemical works to be translated into Tibetan and included in the *Tanjur*.[121]

The *Kālacakra Tantra*, with its early eleventh-century *Vimalaprabhā* commentary, offers us the most penetrating view we have of any specifically Buddhist alchemical system.[122] In contradistinction to the "external" Hindu tantric alchemy that was emerging in the same century, Buddhist alchemy was headed in an "internal" direction. This is precisely what we find in the *Kālacakra Tantra* tradition: the external manipulation of metals and mercurials, which it calls gold making (*gser 'gyur*), has been declared "mundane" and inferior to the "transmundane" inner alchemy (*rasāyana*) of "channels and winds," which can lead to direct enlightenment.[123] Those passages of the *Vimalaprabhā* which do, however, speak of external alchemy, are remarkable in their resemblance to portions of the eleventh-century Hindu tantric alchemical classic, the *RA*.[124] But from a closer perspective—or at least from the perspective adopted by both the Padmaists of the Nying-ma school[125] and the encyclopedist Bo dong—inner alchemy is tantamount to an "extraction of the essence" (*bcud len*) that is quite identical to the Taoist, Mahāyāna, and Hindu hathayogic techniques of urethral suction and the "hydraulic" raising of the semen along the spinal column. In Vajrayāna parlance, "alchemy" consists of the fixing of the *bodhicitta*—by combining the ambrosial essences (*bdud rtsi*) of Prajñā (the goddess "Wisdom") and Upaya (the male "Skill in Means")—and the cultivation of a "rainbow body" (*ja' lus*) or a "body of light" (*'od lus*).[126] In concrete terms, the goal of tantric Buddhist alchemy is to produce the nectar of immortality and wisdom through a combination of semen and uterine blood that is at once yogic and sexual. Hindu alchemy employs the same techniques, but complements these with the mineral-based elixirs of external alchemy. Whereas the erotico-mystical practices of tantra (which Hindu yogins would later term *vajrolī mudrā*) become identified as "alchemy" in Tibetan Buddhism,[127] erotico-mystical practice and external alchemy remain two complementary yet distinct disciplines in Hindu tantric alchemy.

It is apposite to note that the tenth-century twilight of magical alchemy is also the dawning of no fewer than three distinct forms of tantric practice from within and beyond the borders of India. On the one hand, we observe the emergence of tantric alchemy, which combines an "external" transmutational and elixir alchemy with the "internal," but nonetheless concrete (and explicitly hydraulic) practices of *haṭha yoga* and tantric sexual techniques. Its goal is the production of an immortal yet concrete *diamond body* that transcends the laws of nature. Second, there is the Tibetan Buddhist internalization of alchemy into a meditative and ritualized form of yoga, whose goal is the acquisition of a spiritualized *body of light.*[128] Third, there is the Hindu Trika Kaula, which sublimates the same concrete hathayogic and sexual techniques into a meditational and ritual system whose goal is the acquisition of a divinized *body of sound.*[129] All three of these emergent systems were in fact refinements upon an original tantric synthesis, which was based, to a great extent, on the worship of terrible, ravenous deities, with the fluids produced in sexual intercourse. All three were, like the matrix from which they arose, *soteriologies*, individual paths to salvation from the trammels of human existence,[130] and all three were unique and innovative inasmuch as they professed self-divinization—of three different types—as the means to such transcendence.

The India that Buddhism left behind was in many ways tantric, and a number of Buddhist elements find their way into Hindu tantrism in this period. These include a number of Buddhist deities, the four Buddhist *pīṭhas*,[131] various elements of Buddhist discourse and practice and, as we shall see, a significant number of Buddhist teachers, in whose number Nāgārjuna figures prominently. Elsewhere, we may attribute uncanny parallels between the Buddhist and Hindu tantrism of this pivotal period to the simple fact that the two traditions were, in spite of their professed mutual animousity, so close to one another.[132] Most striking in this regard is the resemblance between Tibetan alchemy's "extraction of the [innate, divine] essence [from the gross corporeal body]" and a Hindu tantric practice described by Bhavabhūti in his eighth-century play, *Mālatī-Mādhava*. Here, a female Kāpālika tāntrika named Kuṇḍakapālā attains the power of flight by extracting the quintessence (*pañcāmṛta*) of her five bodily elements. This same passage is also a Hindu watershed inasmuch as it constitutes the earliest mention in Indian literature, sacred or secular, of the six energy centers (*cakra*s) of the subtle body in the practice of *haṭha yoga*. It may be herein that the original sense of the term *rasāyana* lies: it is the "coming forth" (*āyana*) of the fluid essence (*rasa*).[133]

Now, the Hindu[134] tantric schools in whose works the six *cakra*s of hathayogic practice make their earliest appearance are the *paścimāmnāya* or Western Transmission and the Yoginī Kaula founded by Matsyendranāth, which predate the Trika Kaula reformer Abhinavagupta, who makes veiled allusions to both in his ca. A.D. 1000 *Tantrāloka*.[135] As we will show in some detail, these two Kaula sects were closely related, mainly through the person of Matsyendra, whom the Nāth Siddhas would later claim as their founding guru. Matsyendra's classic work, the *Kaulajñānanirṇaya* (*KJñN*) (Discussion of the Kaula Gnosis), revealed in Kāmarūpa (Assam) in the ninth or tenth century, is important inasmuch as it constitutes the earliest explicit account we have of Hindu India's earliest Siddha clans or sects, the Siddha and Yoginī Kaulas.[136] The revelations of the *KJñN* were "brought down" (*avatārita*) at a site called Candradvīpa ("Moon Island"), a toponym which further links Matsyendra's Siddha and Yoginī Kaulas to the Western Transmission, whose textual canon was "brought down"—by a figure variously called Śrīnātha, Śrīkaṇṭha, Ādinātha, or Siddhanātha—at a lunar location called Candragiri, Candradvīpa, Candrapurī, or Candrapīṭha.[137] In one such canonical text, the *Kubjikānityāhnikatilaka*, we find an account that appears to dramatize the changes that were occuring on the Indian tantric landscape in this period. Here, we are told that Śrīnātha—with the aid of three Siddhas named Sun, Moon, and Fire—founded the tantric *kula* tradition, "at the beginning of the Kali Yuga," at a site called Candrapurī ("Moon City"), located in Koṅkaṇa, in coastal western India. The original core of this new *kula*, the text continues, was composed of nine Nāths who, originally Buddhist monks, had converted when, through a miracle produced by Śrīnātha, the roof of their monastery had collapsed![138]

This "conversion," from Buddhism to Hinduism, carries much further in this context. First of all, a lineage found in the *Grub thob*, a ca. fourteenth-century Tibetan translation[139] of Abhayadatta's eleventh- to twelfth-century *Caturaśītisiddha Pravṛtti* (Acts of the Eighty-four Siddhas), identifies two figures, Vyāḍi and Kubjika, as disciples of "Siddha Nāgārjuna."[140] As already noted, Vyāḍi is an alchemist (he is the last of the eighty-four Siddhācāryas); as we will see, he is an alchemist who figures prominently in *Hindu* lists of the Rasa Siddhas (the traditional founders of the alchemical tradition), lists that appear in a number of the major alchemical tantras. Such also appears to be the case with Kubjika: the same name is applied to a *male* Siddhācārya in Buddhist tantrism and to a *female* deity (Kubjikā) in Hindu tantrism. Whether it was the Hindus or the Buddhists who had the first claim to these figures is a moot question; what is important here is that both, like the Nāgārjuna with whom they are associated in this particular lineage, are pivotal figures in the Buddhist-Hindu tantric syncretism. With the departure of Buddhism from the subcontinent, the alchemist Vyāḍi, the goddess Kubjikā, and the polymath Nāgārjuna become transformed, in medieval India, into exclusively *Hindu* figures—figures who are closely linked, moreover, to the history and mythology of tantric alchemy. They also become linked with figures—divine, symbolic, or (super)human—identified as "Nāths" or "Siddhas."

But, just as was the case with tantric Buddhism and its Mahāsiddhas or Siddhācāryas, the Hindu application of the terms Nāth, Siddha, and Nāth Siddha to semihistorical human figures is an ex post facto one. Once again, it is not until the eleventh or twelfth century that we find these terms being applied, retrospectively, to such historical and legendary figures as the Hindu Nāgārjuna, Vyāḍi, Gorakṣa, or Matsyendra. (While this last figure defined the Siddha Kaula, and was retrospectively identified as the guru of Gorakhnāth, founder of the Nāth Siddhas, he is nowhere referred to as "Matsyendra Siddha" or "Siddha Matsyendranāth" prior to the fourteenth century). I by no means wish to imply that such figures did not live during the period I have been chronicling. There can be no doubt that historical figures named Nāgārjuna, Matsyendra, Gorakṣa, etc., defined the religious landscape of a certain Gupta and post-Gupta India. It must, however, be allowed that these figures' lives, acts, and words became fused, in the popular imagination, with those of gods and demigods, in whose number the *divine* Siddhas and Vidyādharas must be counted.[141]

We can also argue that by the tenth century, human individuals or orders known as Siddhas already existed in everything but name in India. In the centuries that followed, these individuals and their real or alleged writings would come to be collated, anthologized, canonized, and institutionalized into (1) Siddha lists, (2) a massive body of Siddha literature, and (3) a loosely structured confederation of Siddha religious orders. All of these post-tenth-century enumerations, canonizations, and institutionalizations would look to the age of magical alchemy for their origins, and invariably find them, in a name, a text, or a real or imagined lineage. The self-proclaimed Siddhas of later history *invented* their past as a means of justifying their own lives, works, and institutions: the "charismatic" superheroes of the past—fast on their way to becoming "divinized" through an identification of them with the Siddhas and Vidyādharas of earlier cults—were also becoming "institutionalized" into the sectarian founders they never had been.[142]

As I demonstrate in the next chapter, historiographers of the medieval Siddha traditions have failed to come to terms with this fact, and have therefore always found themselves struggling to bridge unaccountable gaps of hundreds of years between the legendary "biographies" of many of these Siddhas and their literary productions or institutional roles. Their efforts have been in vain: just as new individuals named Nāgārjuna or Matsyendra appeared on the Indian religious landscape once every one to two hundred years, so too *entire founding lineages* were created or reappropriated by self-proclaimed Siddha traditions at several centuries' remove from the time in which their founders may have lived.[143]

Before turning to the Hindu side of the Siddha phenomenon, I must attempt to account for the alchemical reputation of the Buddhist "Siddha Nāgārjuna" for the period just discussed, the seventh to tenth centuries. As with the case of the philosopher Nāgārjuna, there is little hard evidence to go on, beyond the body of legend bequeathed to us by Hsuan-tsang and others. In this light, it appears significant that the seventh-century Chinese scholar-pilgrim claimed to have met an alchemical disciple of Nāgārjuna who looked to be only thirty, in spite of his seven hundred years. If he was indeed thirty, or slightly older, then we have grounds to believe that a reputed alchemist named Nāgārjuna did in fact live in the first half of the seventh century.

The *Yogaśataka*, datable to either the seventh or ninth century and the work of an "Ācārya Śrī Nāgārjuna," is mainly devoted to herbal, rather than mercurial, remedies, although some of its preparations are called "elixirs" (*rasāyanas*) or "nectars" (*amṛtas*).[144] This same Nāgārjuna may have been (1) the editor of the *Suśruta Saṁhitā* responsible for the appendix entitled "Uttara Sthānā" (although this section contains no innovative data on mercurial medicines);[145] (2) the figure singled out by the ninth-century Vṛnda as having carved instructions for the ophthamological use of black mercuric sulfide—a preparation he calls *nāgārjuna-varta*—into a pillar at Pāṭaliputra (Patna, the capital of modern-day Bihar);[146] (3) an alchemist whom the eleventh-century Alberuni mentions as having lived some one hundred years prior to himself;[147] and (4) the author of a work on metallurgy referred to as the *Lohaśāstra* of Nāgārjuna by Cakrapāṇidatta, in the ca. A.D. 1075 *Cikitsāsaṃgraha*, a commentary on the *Caraka Saṁhitā* and itself an Ayurvedic watershed in the use of mercurial medicines.[148] This composite ninth-century Nāgārjuna would therefore have had to have been a figure distinct from the seventh-century Nalanda alchemist-monk, if one ever existed.[149]

To conclude, then, we can very tentatively identify three Nāgārjunas from what has been called the period of "magical" alchemy. These are (1) the ca. second-century A.D. Mādhyamika philosopher whose only alchemical feats were mythical; (2) the early seventh-century disciple of Sarāha, and resident of Nalanda and Śrīparvata, whose alchemical reputation reached the ears of Hsuan-tsang (who was himself the translator of two Mahāyāna texts containing references to magical alchemy), but who left no alchemical works for posterity; and (3) the ninth-century author of the *Yogaśataka* and the appendix to the *Suśruta Saṁhitā*, about whom Alberuni heard reports in the early eleventh century. It is only some two to three centuries after Alberuni that we encounter an alchemical author named either Siddha or Śrīman Nāgārjuna in chapter colophons. These are three extant Hindu works, which shade in their content from tantric sorcery into alchemy—the *Kakṣapuṭa Tantra*, the *Yogaratnamālā* (also called the *Āścaryaratnamālā*) and the *Rasendra Maṅgala*.

Finally, I close this chapter on the age of magical alchemy with a note of caution to anyone who would attempt to interpret the general history of this period. This I do mainly as a corrective to south Indian historians of Siddha medicine who maintain that the Sittar alchemists had already perfected their craft long before the time of the sixth- to seventh-century Tirumūlar and Nandi.[150] First, there is no evidence to show that any alchemy—even as practiced by persons who may already have been calling themselves Siddhas—prior to the tenth century A.D. was anything but "magical." Second, while most of our data concerning magical alchemy is of southern provenance, this in no way implies that it was of Tamil origin. In fact, nearly all signs from this period point either to the Andhra country (Śrīparvata-Srisailam) or to western India as the cradle of the alchemical art in India. It is, moreover, in these two regions that the so-called Māheśvara Siddhas begin to appear in the tenth century and that magical alchemy became transmuted, as it were, into tantric and Siddha alchemy.

FOUR

Sources for the History of Tantric Alchemy in India

1. Medieval Lists of Rasa Siddhas and Nāth Siddhas

Among the most valuable historical documents we have at our disposal for charting the period in which (1) "outer alchemy" disappeared from Buddhism, (2) Buddhism disappeared from India, and (3) Hindu Siddha alchemy emerged out of a fusion of tantric alchemy with the discipline of *haṭha yoga* are retrospectively compiled lists of Siddhas (both Buddhist and Hindu) and Nāths (exclusively Hindu), that proliferated throughout the Indo-Tibetan world between the eleventh and fifteenth centuries. It is in these sources that the appellation *Siddha* comes to be used extensively, as a blanket term covering most of the figures—some historical, others legendary, others divine, and still others clearly undecided—whose lives and acts I review in these pages.

While we cannot be certain that such was the case, the ordering of the names in the Siddha lists at times appears to correspond to *guruparamparās*, i.e., to the clan lineages[1] of teachers and disciples through which the mystic Siddha doctrines were transmitted. Here, the Siddha lists would constitute simplifications of an earlier set of models. These were the ca. ninth-century A.D. idealized "post-scriptural systematizations"[2] of the major tantric sects and texts. These records often took the form of mystic diagrams (*maṇḍalas*), in which the clans (*kulas*) of the divinities and legendary preceptors of the major sectarian divisions of Hindu tantrism were set forth schematically. Such *maṇḍalas* or *yantras* were at once divine and human genealogies, ritual and meditational supports, and models of and for microcosmic, mesocosmic, and macrocosmic reality, in which color, number, direction, divine name, vital breath, activity of consciousness, sensory organ, etc., were so many simultaneous proofs for the coherence of the world system they charted: structure and function were congruent.[3]

In the absence of anything comparable to a systematic theology (for which god would one choose?) or a religious anthropology, Puranic Hinduism lent much attention to what one scholar has termed "systematic geography," the elaboration of a spatial grid of the great chain of being, from the highest gods to the most abject demons, via the realms of humans, demigods, sages, and all manner of other creatures.[4] In the tantric context, however, it is perhaps more proper to speak of "systematic genealogy" rather than systematic geography or cosmology, given the fact that the cardinal directions to which the major clans of the tantric *maṇḍala*s were assigned appear to bear no correlation whatsoever to the geographic locations of these sects or their founders. Rather, these were, in a quite literal sense, organizational "flow charts," in which the flow in question was of sexual fluids emanating first from the godhead and radiating outwards, through the biological transmission, via goddesses and yoginīs, of the clan nectar (*kuladravya*), into the various sectarian clans, orders, and sects. Through their systematic genealogies, the tāntrikas at once located themselves within the cosmic chain of being and within a network of socioreligious institutions.

The major tantric classificatory systems that will concern us here—inasmuch as certain names found in them correspond to names found in the Siddha lists detailed below—are those of the *pīṭha*s and *āmnāya*s. While the former term is nearly always employed to denote a "footstool" or pilgrimage site of the Goddess in Śākta devotionalism, there also emerged, around the time of the *Brahmayāmala Tantra* (ca. ninth century A.D.) a tradition of four "literary" *pīṭha*s. Here, the major texts (together with the practices and methods they espoused) of earlier tantrism were classified, purportedly on the basis of the principal subjects they treated—but in fact rather artificially—under the headings of *vidyā*, *mantra*, *mudrā*, and *maṇḍala pīṭha*s. Most of the important texts of this classificatory system fell under the rubrics of the *vidyāpīṭha*[5] and *mantrapīṭha*.

Somewhat later,[6] the classificatory system of the *āmnāya*s ("lines of transmission") was devised to classify Kaula sects and texts. While sectarian cleavages based on the name of the major cult goddesses figure most prominently here, the theoretical classifications are geographical. The four *āmnāya*s are the eastern (Trika, whose cult centers on the three Parā goddesses), northern (Krama, which worships Kālī), western (which worships the goddess Kubjikā, the "Contracted One," an alloform of the hathayogic *kuṇḍalinī*), and southern (Śrīvidyā, which worships the goddess Trīpurasundarī) transmissions.[7]

While it is likely that the historical value of the Siddha lists is as limited as that of the *maṇḍala*s of tantric *pīṭha* and *āmnāya* classifications,[8] a comparative overview will offer insights into what the medieval mystics of India—Buddhists, Hindus, Jains (and later, Muslims), yogins and alchemists alike, from Tibet to south India—considered to be their heritage. In the words of Giuseppe Tucci, the "Siddhas are the most eminent personalities of medieval India's esoterism and represent the ideal link between Śivaism and Vajrayāna, indeed the expression of the same religious and mystical endeavor, translated through analogous symbols."[9] These figures were always first and foremost Siddhas, and it would be erroneous to maintain that the inclusion of a figure's name in a Buddhist Siddha list made him a Buddhist, or that a name figuring in a Rasa Siddha list necessarily made that person an alchemist. The Siddhas, a pool of wizards and demigods, supermen and wonder-workers that all south Asians (and Tibetans) could draw on to slake the thirst of their religious imagination, were the most syncretistic landmarks on the religious landscape of medieval India.[10]

Our presentation of the medieval Siddha lists will, with a single exception, be a chronological one: we will insert the list from the fifteenth-century *Haṭhayogapradīpikā* (*HYP*) of Svātmarāma before two fourteenth-century lists (from the *Varṇaratnākara* and the *Ānandakanda* [*ĀK*]) because its content corresponds more closely to that of earlier eleventh- to thirteenth-century lists than do the latter. We will begin our survey with the Indo-Tibetan lists of the eighty-four Mahāsiddhas or Siddhācāryas. Two nearly identical lists are found in the *Grub thob*,[11] a mid-fourteenth-century Tibetan text based on a ca. eleventh- to twelfth-century Sanskrit work attributed to the Indian Abhayadatta; and the A.D. 1275 *Sa-skya-bka'-'bum*,[12] which purports to be a list of the gurus who taught at the Saskya monastery between A.D. 1091 and 1275. In these lists, the *-pā* endings to many names are shortenings of *-pāda:* these endings, rather than the term *Siddha*, are the authentic mark of the eastern Indian figures and lineages that founded tantric Buddhism. Following what has become a scholarly convention, we will assign numbers to these figures, in accordance with their ordinal placement in these various lists:

1. Luī-pā/Matsyendra
8. Mīna-pā
9. Gorakṣa-pā
10. Caurangi-pā

12. Tanti-pā
16. Nāgārjuna
17. Karāha-pā/Kānha-pā
18. Karṇari-pā/Aryadeva
30. Kambala-pā/Kamari-pā
46. Jālandhara-pā
64. Carpaṭā-pā
71. Kanthali-pā
72. Kapāla-pā
76. Nāgabodhi-pā
77. Dārika-pā
84. Bhali-pā/Vyāli-pā

In fact, the names of many of the figures in these lists are identical to those of the authors of the earliest mystic poetry of "Buddhist" tantrism, the so-called *Caryāpadas*[13] (composed in Old Bengali in eastern India before the twelfth century), as well as of a number of authors whose writings are found in the Sanskrit *Sādhanamālā*, which dates from the same period.[14] Exceptions to this rule are (9) Gorakṣa, (10) Cauraṅgi, (16) Nāgārjuna, (64) Carpaṭā, (71) Kanthali, (72) Kapāla, (76) Nāgabodhi, and (84) Vyāli, whose "signatures" are found in neither the *Caryāpadas* nor the *Sādhanamālā* (Nāgārjuna is the author of two *sādhanas* in this latter work). A later Tibetan recension of the *caryā* songs, incorporated into the *Tanjur*, includes works by Ghorakṣa (*sic*), Cauraṅgi, and Carpaṭā/Carpaṭi not found in the original anthology.[15]

Six of these names—Cauraṅgi, Nāgārjuna, Carpaṭi, Kapāla, Nāgabodhi, and Vyāli—figure in another enumeration of Siddhas. These are the lists of the twenty-seven *Rasa Siddhas*, as such are found in three alchemical works.[16] Two of these—a list found in the thirteenth- to fourteenth-century *Rasendra Maṅgala* [*RM*] of Śrīman Nāgārjuna[17] and a list in the fourteenth-century *Rasaratnasamucchaya* [*RRS*] (1.2–4) [a] of Vāgbhaṭṭa II[18]—are nearly identical; whereas a second list, found in both the thirteenth-century *Rasaratnākara* [*RRĀ*] (3.1.66–69) of Nityanātha Siddha[19] and the *RRS* (6.51–53) [b], differs slightly from the first. Furthermore, certain recensions of the *RRS* supply as many as forty additional names (following 1.5) to the original list of twenty-seven: we will call this supplementary list *RRS* [c].[20] Figures whose names have already appeared above, in the Tibetan lists, are given here in *italics*.

RM/RRS[a]	*RRĀ/RRS*[b]
1. Ādima/Āduma[21]	
2. Candrasena	2. Candrasena
3. Laṅkeśa	3. Laṅkeśa
4. Viśārada	22. Śārada
5. *Kapāla*/Kapālī	
6. Mata/Matta	
7. Māṇḍavya	10. Māṇḍavya
8. Bhāskara	
9. Śurasena/Śūrasenaka	12. Śūrasena
10. Ratnaghośa/Ratnakośa	6. Ratnaghośa
11. Śambhu	20. Śambhu[rloka]
12. Ekaratna/Sāttvika	19. Tāttvika
13. Vāhana	4. Naravāhana
14. Indra[da]	
15. Gomukha	
16. *Kambali*[22]	
17. *Vyāḍi*	1. Vyālācārya
18. *Nāgārjuna*	5. Nāgārjuna
19. Surāvida/Sūrānanda	7. Surānanda
20. *Nāgabodhi*	14. Nāgabuddhi
21. Yaśodhara/Yaśodhana	8. Yaśodhara
22. Khaṇḍa	15. Khaṇḍa
23. Kāpālika	16. Kāpālika
24. Brahma/Brahmā	
25. Govinda	25. Govinda
26. Lampaka	21. Lampaṭa
27. Hari	17. Hara

Nine names included in the *RRĀ/RRS* [b] list do not accord with those found in the *RM/RRS* [a] list. They are: (3) Subuddhi; (9) Indradyumna; (11) Carpaṭi; (13) Vāḍava/Agama;[23] (18) Kāmāri/Kāmalī; (23) Bāṇāsura; (24) Muniśreṣṭha; (26) Kapila; and (27) Bali. All of these names, however, figure among the forty additional Rasa Siddhas listed in *RRS* [c]. We now present the lists of these additional Rasa Siddhas as they occur in the continuation of *RRS* [a] (1.5–7) and *RRS* [c], names which, as Vāgbhaṭṭa II explains, are "names of authors of other alchemical texts." To these, we juxtapose data from another list, that of thirty *mahāsiddha*s "who had broken Time's rod" found in the *HYP* (1.5–9). This list is nearly identical to a list drawn up by Caturbhujamiśra, a 15th- to 16th-century commentator on the *RHT*, with the difference that the latter identifies the twenty-four names on his list as Rasa Siddhas.[24] As before, names occurring in Tibetan lists are *italicized;* those already noted in *RRS* [b] have their numbering from that list shown in parentheses.

RRS 1.5–10 [c]	*RRS* 1.5–7 [a]	*HYP* 1.5–9
28. Rasāṇkuśa	28. Rasāṅkuśa[25]	
29. Bhairava	29. Bhairava	4. Bhairava
30. Nandi	30. Nandi	
31. Svacchandabhairava	31. Svacchandabhairava	
32. Manthānabhairava	32. Manthānabhairava	10. Manthānabhairava
33. Kākacaṇḍīśvara	33. Kākacaṇḍīśvara	23. Kākacaṇḍīśvara
34. Mahādeva	40. Mahādeva	
35. Narendra	41. Narendra	28. Naradeva
36. Ratnākara		
37. Harīśvara	43. Harīśvara	
38. Koraṇḍaka		13. Koraṇṭaka
39. Siddhabuddha	39. Maithilā[hvaya]	11. Siddhirbuddha
40. Siddhapāda		15. Siddhipāda
41. *Kanthaḍī*		12. Kanthaḍi
42. Ṛṣyaśṛṅga	35. Ṛṣi Śṛṅga	
43. Vāsudeva	42. Vāsudeva	
43. Kriyātantrasamucchayī	36. Kriyātantrasamucchayī	
44. Rasendratilaka	37. Rasendratilaka Yogi	
45. Bhānukarmerita	38. Bhāluki	27. Bhāluka
46. Pūjyapāda		18. Pūjyapāda
47. *Kaṇerī*		17. Kaṇerī
48. Nityanātha		19. Nityanātha
49. Nirañjana		20. Nirañjana
50. *Carpaṭi* (11)		16. Carpaṭi
51. Bindunātha		22. Bindunātha
52. Prabhudeva		24.[Allama] Prabhu
53. Vallabha		
54. Vālākhilya-jñā [Bālākiryanjā]		
55. Ghoḍacoli		25. Ghoḍācolī
56. *Tiṇṭanī*		26. Tiṇṭini

RRS 1.5–10 [c]	*RRS* 1.5–7 [a]	*HYP* 1.5–9
57. Kālācārya		
58. Subuddhi (3)		
59. Ratnaghośa (6)		
60. Susenaka		
61. Indradyumna (9)		
62. Āgama (13)		
63. *Kāmāri* (18)		
64. Vāṇāsura (23)		
65. Muniśreṣṭha (24)		
66. Kapila (26)		
67. Vali (27)		

Apart from its parallels with the *RRS* lists, the *HYP* list also appears to borrow a number of its Siddhas from the Tibetan *Grub thob*. To these parallel lists we also juxtapose data from yet another source, the ca. A.D. 1300 *Varṇaratnākara* (*VRĀ*)[26] list of seventy-six Siddhas:

HYP 1.5–9	*Grub thob*	*VRĀ* 7
2. Matsyendra	1. Luī-pā/Matsyendra	41. Mīna
3. Śābarānanda	5. Śābara-pā	43. Śavara
5. Cauraṅgi	10. Cauraṅgi-pā	3. Cauraṅginātha
6. Mīnanātha	8. Mīna-pā	1. Mīnanātha
7. Gorakhnāth	9. Gorakṣa-pā	2. Gorakṣanātha
16. Carpaṭi	64. Carpaṭā-pā	31. Carpaṭi
	17. Kānha-pā	13. Kānha
21. Kapālī		11. Kapāli
26. Tiṇṭini	13. Taṇṭi-pā	5. Taṇṭi-pā
	16. Nāgārjuna	22. Nāgārjuna
	30. Kamari-pā	12. Kamārī
	46. Jālandhara-pā	19. Jālandhara
	77. Dārika	9. Dāri-pā

The *Varṇaratnākara* further accords with various Rasa Siddha lists in its mention of Carpaṭi, Kapāli, Nāgārjuna, Kamārī—listed above—as well as of (71) Govinda (no. 25 in three lists) and (73) Bhairava (no. 29 in two lists). The (1) Ādima of the *RM/RRS* [a] list is to be identified with the (1) Ādinātha of *HYP* 1.5: *ādi* denotes origins; Ādinātha is therefore the original and divine Rasa Siddha or Mahāsiddha: as such he is sometimes identified with Matsyendranāth. The relationship here between Gorakṣanātha and his guru Mīnanātha in the two Hindu works listed here is symmetrical to that obtaining between the figures Gorakṣa-pā (9) and Mīna-pā (8) in the Tibetan *Grub thob.* This squares, moreover, with the statement made by Gorakṣa in the second verse of his earliest work, the *Gorakṣaśataka*, that his guru was Mīnanātha. It is a later conflation (as in the 15th-century "Sidh Vandanāṃ," below) that identifies Matsyendra (the second Siddha, listed after Ādinātha, in the *HYP* list) or Luī-pā (the first Siddha of the *Grub thob* list) with Mīna. The identification is a simple one: all three of these names include the term *fish.* As I will demonstrate, the historical Gorakṣa or Gorakhnāth was a 12th- to 13th-century figure, whereas Matsyendra, his purported guru, could not have lived later than the 10th century; it is another figure, named Mīna, who was Gorakhnāth's guru.

The final two lists to be reproduced here also begin—both logically and chronologically—with Ādinātha, the Lord of Beginnings. The first of these is the 14th-century *Ānandakanda* [*ĀK*] (1.3.47–51),[27] certainly the longest extant alchemical text, and also the most convoluted in many ways. Behind its complexity, however, we may glimpse a number of Siddha lineages which it was attempting to decant into a single authoritative list. Of exceptional interest is the fact that it divides its list of twenty-five names into a set of "Nine Nāths" and "Sixteen Siddhas." In this, as well as in a number of other unique hathayogic elements found in this, but no other alchemical source, we find ourselves in the presence of a truly syncretic Siddha alchemical tradition. The data it contains will also lead us, in a moment, into a second corpus, the myriad lists of the Nine Nāths. The list we will juxtapose here with the *ĀK* is quite unusual, inasmuch as it purports to constitute a list of the "eighty-four Siddhas"[28] *and* "nine *yogeśvara*s (Lords of Yoga)"—but which in fact only lists fifty-six names. This vernacular work, entitled "Sidh Vandanāṃ" [SV][29] (Praise of the Siddhas) is relatively late, given that it mentions the 15th-century Kabir as its fiftieth Siddha. For purposes of comparison, we juxtapose elements from the *HYP* list with those of the *ĀK* and the SV. We will list the Nine Nāths and sixteen Siddhas of the *ĀK* list continuously, numbering from 1 to 25. *Italics* refer to names that also appear in Rasa Siddha lists from earlier sources:

ĀK 1.3.90–93	SV 1–27	*HYP* 1.5–9
1. *Ādi*-nātha	1. Ādināth	1. Ādinātha
2. Mīnanātha/Mūlanātha	2. Machindra	6. Mīnanātha
3. Gorakṣa	3. Gorakṣa	7. Gorakṣa

ĀK 1.3.90–93	SV 1–27	*HYP* 1.5–9
4. Koṅkaṇeśvara		
5. Jālāndhreśa	10. Jalandharī	
6. Kanthanīśa	28. Kanthaḍ-pāy	11. Kanthaḍī
7. Uḍḍīśa		
8. Ciñc[h]inīśvara		
9. Cauraṅgi	27. Cauraṅgi	5. Cauraṅgi
10. Cauraṅgi[30]		
11. *Carpaṭa*	4. Carpaṭa-rāy	16. Carpaṭi
12. Ghoḍacūli		26. Ghoḍācolī
13. Rāmadvaya		
14. Bhola/Bāla	14. Bālanāth	
15. *Govinda*-siddha		
16. *Vyāḍi*		
17. *Nāgārjuna*		
18. Koraṇḍa		16. Kodaṇḍa
19. Śūrpakarṇa/Śūrpadhuṇḍhī		
20. Muktayī/Duktayī		
21. Revaṇa/Reṇava		
22. Kukkurapāda		
23. Śūrpapāda		
24. Kaṇairika	23. Kāṇerī	17. Kaṇerī
25. Kiṅkinika/Tiṇṭini	26. Taṇṭanī	27. Tiṇṭini
	30. Kapālī	21. Kapālī
	32. Kāg Caṇḍ	23. Kākacaṇḍeśvarī
	33. Kāg Bhuśaṇḍ	
	34. *Sūrānand*	14. *Sūrānanda*
	35. Bhairū Nand	4. Bhairava
	36. Śāvarā Nand	3. Śāvarānanda

2. The *Ānandakanda* List and Medieval Western Indian Śaivism

A number of apparently incongruous names in the *ĀK* list may be shown to correspond to names of Nāth Siddhas found in southwestern Indian sources. The names Śūrpakarṇa ("Shovel Ears") (19) and Śūrpapāda ("Shovel Feet") (23) resemble that of Śūrpanāth who—according to a thirteenth-century inscription from the Nāth Siddha monastery of Kadri, located on the northern outskirts of Mangalore (Karnataka)—would have lived in the early part of that century.[31] According to Maharashtran traditions dating from at least the final quarter of the thirteenth century, Revaṇa (21) is listed as one of the Nine Nāths. Elsewhere, the Vīraśaivas, who have always been concentrated in southwestern India, revere Revaṇa (or Reṇuka) Siddha as one of their five great founders.[32] Uḍḍīśa (7) is the name of a work on tantric sorcery[33]; and Kukkura-pāda (22) is a Mahāsiddha (no. 34) from the *Grub thob* list.

Other names on this list are found to correspond to those of certain of the eighteen Sittars, the alchemist-physicians of Tamil Nadu.[34] The Sittar lists—of which there exist at least eighteen variants—are infuriatingly heterogeneous. No two are alike, and any one is likely to include names of Vedic sages (Agastya, Loma Ṛṣi), demons (Pulastya), and nymphs (Urvaśī), as well as classical Hindu gods (Rāma, Dakṣinamūrti, Subrahmanian), the divine or semidivine founders of Āyurveda (Dhanvantari), yoga (Patañjali), Advaita Vedānta (Śaṅkarācārya), and south Indian orthodox Śaivism (Iḍaikkādar, Pambatti, Auvai, Manika Vachagar, etc.),[35] and the odd European (Yacoppu, i.e., Jacob). In addition to these, however, we also encounter names found in the *Ānandakanda* list: Tirumūlar (whom the Nāth Siddhas call Mūlanātha [2a]), Macchendrar (= Matsyendranātha [2b]); Korakkar Nādhar (= Gorakhnāth [3]), and Koṅganar (Koṅkaṇeśvara [4]). One exemplary list of the eighteen Tamil Siddhas[36] enumerates the following (names from earlier lists are italicized): *Nandi* (1), *Mūlanātha* (2), Kālāṅganātha (3), Bhoga (4), *Koṅkaṇa* (5), Agastya (6), Pulastya (7), *Bhuśuṇḍa* (8), Romamuni (9), Dhanvantari (10), Saṭṭaimuni (11), *Matsya*muni (12), Kaṅva (13), Pidinākkīśa (14), *Gorakṣa* (15), Terayar (16), Yūhimuni (17), and Iḍaikkāḍar (18).

The last chapter discussed alchemical lore on the subject of two other recurring names from the Tamil lists, Bogar and Nandi; as was noted, Koṅganar was the disciple of one of these two alchemical gurus.[37] Also worth noting here are the Sittars named Kambali Siddhar (number 15 in the *RM/RRS* [a] list); Navanādhar (*navanātha*, the "Nine Naths"), and Sattaināthar (Satyanātha). This last figure, whom Tamil traditions credit with having authored twenty-one alchemical works, is identified by the Nāth Siddhas with the historical founder of one of its twelve (modern) subdivisions, as well as with a yogic incarnation of the god Brahmā.[38]

Ādināth, Mūlanāth, Koṅkaṇeśvara (4), and Ciñcinīśvara (8) belong to another sectarian tradition that interacted with the Nāth Siddhas and Rasa Siddhas throughout this period. This is the *paścimāmnāya*, the Western

Transmission. To begin, we find lists in this tradition's fourteenth-century *Kubjikānityāhnikatilaka* and twelfth-century *Manthānabhairava Tantra* that are structurally identical to that of the *ĀK:* that is, they are subdivided into a set of nine and a set of sixteen of teachers. Two consecutive chapters in the *ṢSS*, itself an expansion on the *Kubjikāmata* (*KM*), treat of the Kubjikā revelations that were brought down to earth by Ādināth (1) and Mūlanāth (2). That these sources are in some way related is further supported by the fact that the Koṅkaṇa in Koṅkaṇ-eśvara—the "Lord of Koṅkaṇa"—is precisely the (western) coastal region in which the Western Transmission claims to have been founded, through the agency of a group called the "Nine Nāths."[39] In a list of the Nine Nāths that probably originates from the Deccan, one of the group is named Koṅkaṇanāth.[40]

The name Ciñcinīśvara (8) evokes the title of another important Western Transmission work: this is the Nepali *Ciñcinimatasārasamucchaya*, which states in its first verse that the cult of Ciñcinī was founded by a figure named Siddhanātha. Ciñcinī ("tamarind") is moreover identified with Kubjikā, the goddess whose cult lies at the heart of the Western Transmission.[41] Siddhanātha is, according to a number of texts, an alternative name for Matsyendranāth, whose name is also cited in the *Kubjikānityāhnikatilaka* as one of the appellations of its fifth teacher.[42]

Inasmuch as he stands as the prototypical Siddha, I return to the pivotal figure of Matsyendra throughout this and the next chapter. In addition to having a role within the Western Transmission, Matsyendra is also considered to have founded a number of other tantric clans. More than this, he is at once revered as the superhuman intermediary who transmitted—or "brought down" (*avatārita*) from the divine to the human plane—the original tantric revelation *and* as the human reformer responsible for having transformed the old Kula tradition into "reformed" Kaulism.[43] As such, his principal teaching, the *KJñN*, is a watershed for all manner of tantric and Siddha traditions. In this work, Matsyendra describes himself as an adherent of the sectarian Siddha Kaula, the founder of the Yoginī Kaula, and revealer of the (hathayogic) doctrine of Matsyodara ("Fish Belly"). The *KJñN* is, in fact, one of the earliest Indian texts to make wide and general use of the term "Siddha"; moreover, it anticipates the *haṭha yoga* of later Nāth Siddhas (who also claim Matsyendra as their founder) and contains a wide array of original data on tantric theory and practice.

Abhinavagupta singles out "Macchanda Vibhu" (Matsyendra) for praise in the opening lines of his monumental A.D. 1000 *Tantrāloka*[44] and incorporates Matsyendra's Yoginī Kaula cult into the secret ritual of the Trika Kaula virtuosi.[45] Elsewhere, Abhinavagupta calls Macchanda the great Kaula master of his age, the *kali yuga;* and, following earlier scriptural tradition, places Macchanda, together with his consort Koṅkaṇā, in the northern quadrant of the *Siddha Cakra.*[46] In this way as well, Matsyendra may be identified with Koṅkaṇeśvara (4): he is the lord (*īśvara*) of his consort Koṅkaṇā.

Now, it happens that both the scriptures of the Western Transmission[47] and the early works of Matsyendranāth have, for centuries, been extant in Nepal alone. How is it that revelations transmitted at a "Moon Island" (Candradvīpa) or "Moon Hill" (Candragiri) either on the west (the Western Transmission's Koṅkaṇa) or east (the Yoginī Kaula's Kāmarūpa) coast of India should now find themselves in a landlocked Himalayan valley? An abundance of local legends explain Matsyendra's "transfer" from Kāmarūpa to Nepal.[48] As for the latter toponym, a geographical explanation is possible: Candragiri is the name of a hill located at the western end of the Kathmandu Valley which was, according to myth, originally flooded, prior to being drained by Mañjuśrī: this western Moon Mountain would originally have been a Moon Island.[49] Another probable explanation is of a historical order. There exist significant medieval links between southwestern and eastern India on the one hand, and Nepal on the other, by which the transplantation of these cults can be explained. From the early twelfth century onwards, the Kathmandu Valley was penetrated first by religious proponents of south Indian Śaivism and subsequently by kings from the Deccan region. Following the fourteenth-century Malla restoration, priests from Bengal and the Deccan officiated in temples in the city of Bhaktapur, at the shrine of Paśupatināth, and elsewhere in the Kathmandu Valley.[50] A number of Nepali religious institutions and traditions reflect this historical connection, down to the present day.[51] A third, esoteric, explanation for these toponyms will be discussed in chapter eight.

Nepal's relative isolation has also fostered the preservation of forms of Hindu tantrism that have long since disappeared from India itself. The Kathmandu Valley remains a "living museum" of both Hindu and Buddhist tantrism, in which *caryā* songs belonging to the same tradition as that of the seventh- through twelfth-century Siddhācāryas continue to be sung at religious performances, where the old Western Transmission cult of Kubjikā continues to be observed,[52] and where hordes of tantric Bhairavas and Kālīs continue to receive blood sacrifices on a massive scale.

3. Excursus: The Nine Nāths, the Twelve *Panths*, and the Historical Gorakhnāth

At this point, it becomes necessary, for historiographical reasons, that we trace the origins of the Nāth *sampradāya* or Nāth *panth*, the institutionalized religious order or sect of the Nāth Siddhas. The reason for this is simple. It is entirely impossible to make historical sense of the Nāth Siddhas if we fail to separate pre-thirteenth-century legend from post-thirteenth-century historical fact. Armed with this interpretive tool, we will be able to neatly bypass such burning nonissues as whether Gorakhnāth was originally a Buddhist living in eastern India and at the same time dovetail historical and geographical evidence for a western Indian origin of the Nāth Siddhas with data concerning the Rasa Siddhas, such as that found in the *ĀK* list.

The point I wish to make here is that the Nāth *sampradāya*, a great medieval changing house for western Indian sectarian Śaivism, could not have emerged prior to the late twelfth to early thirteenth century A.D. I will show that this was not a monolithic order, but rather a confederation of groups claiming a similar body of Śaiva and Siddha tradition, the basis for whose unity was and remains (1) the identification of the twelfth- through thirteenth-century historical Gorakhnāth with earlier historical, legendary, or divine figures named Gorakh or Gorakṣa; (2) the retrospective association of this or some earlier Gorakh—often in the role of guru or disciple—with founders of other Siddha or Śaiva sects and clans, many of which came to be absorbed into the Nāth *sampradāya*, (3) the transformation of the abstract concept of the Nine Nāths into a number of quasi-historical lineages; and (4) the continued appropriation, in later centuries, by groups outside the Nāth *sampradāya*, of the names Gorakh and other of the Nine Nāths as a means to integrating themselves into that order.

We begin our discussion by undertaking a conceptual archaeology of the Nine Nāths (*navanātha*). To date, no scholar has ever doubted that these were ever anything but a group of legendary, if not historical figures. But what we find when we look at the Nine Nāths historically is that they were, at least a century prior to their transformation into historical lineages, an abstract or symbolic category belonging to the Western Transmission. The earliest veiled reference that we find to this group is found in the *Kubjikāmata* which calls a (presumably divine) Nāth the "lord of the nine *cakras*" (*nātho navacakreśvaraḥ*), "founder of all the Siddha [lineages]" (*sarvasiddhānām . . . saṃvyavasthitaḥ*), and "governer of the six cities [*cak-*

ras?], lord of the Kaulas and leader of the Kula" (*ṣaḍpurādhipatirnāthaḥ kauliśaḥ kulanāyakaḥ*).[53] We have already mentioned a later text belonging to the same tradition: this is the *Kubjikānityāhnikatilaka*, which relates that the clan was founded, in Koṅkaṇa, by Śrīnātha, who was accompanied by "twice nine Nāths." He emanated into three Siddhas, who had nine sons whom they made their disciples; from these originated the sixteen disciples.[54] Two later works place an equally allegorical gloss on the Nine Nāths: the *Tantrarāja Tantra* correlates the Nine Nāths with the nine bodily orifices,[55] while the *Tantra Mahārṇava* identifies eight Nāth Siddhas with the eight cardinal directions. This latter list places Ādināth at the "center" of the Indian universe, in the land of Kurukṣetra; a location that would correspond to a widespread Kaula doctrine, which calls the central *pīṭha* of its mystic universe the Ādipīṭha.[56] According to the Western Transmission, the supreme goddess (Parā, Kubjikā) dwells in a *pīṭha* of the same name: radiating out from her are eight other such centers, at each of which is found a Nāth through whom she generates her empowering energy.[57] Here, the Nine Nāths appear to be nothing other than a nonuplication of Matsyendranāth: they are the superhuman intermediaries who brought the Western Transmission teachings down to earth.[58] In the *ṢSS* and the *Saṃvartārthaprakāśa*, two other works of the Western Transmission, this group of nine (abstract) Nāths is doubled into a set of eighteen Nāths or Siddhas. In this light, it is noteworthy that Tamil tradition holds that there were originally nine Sittars, before their number was doubled to eighteen.[59] Finally, the abstract or symbolic becomes merged with the historical in the vernacular *Gorakh Upaniṣad*, whose list of the Nine Nāths begins with seven stages in an emanatory schema, followed by a set of eight "historical" Nāth Siddhas, of which Matsyendra is the first and Gorakh the last.[60]

When, however, the aggregate of the Nine Nāths came to be identified, some time in the twelfth to thirteenth century, with the legendary or historical founders of the Nāth *sampradāya*, the "historical" name that headed most lists was that of Matsyendra. If, as many have done,[61] we conflate Matsyendra[-nāth] with Mīna[-nath] and Luī[-pā] (all three names can be loosely taken to mean "Lord of Fishes"), we find that it is he whose name figures the most frequently (together with Gorakṣa, Carpaṭi, and Nāgārjuna) in the Siddha lists we have compared to this point (six times). Next in frequency are Cauraṅgi, Vyāḍi, Ādināth, Taṇṭi / Tiṇṭini, Karṇarī / Kaṇerī, and Bhairava (five times), followed by Jālandhara, Kanthaḍī, and Govinda (four times). Of these, the following names appear in all three types of Siddha lists—i.e., of the Indo-Tibetan Siddhācāryas, Indian Mahāsiddha yogins, and Indian Rasa Siddhas: Matsyendra-Mīna, Gorakṣa, Nāgārjuna, Carpaṭi, Cauraṅgi, Taṇṭi / Tiṇṭini, Karṇarī / Kaṇerī, and Kanthaḍī. In fact, many of these names correspond to most frequently appearing names in the myriad lists of the nine "historical" Nāth Siddhas. The most commonly occurring names in such lists are (1) Matsyendra, (2) Gorakh, (3) Carpaṭi, (4) Jālandhara, (5) Kaṇerī, and (6) Cauraṅgi. Also figuring in many lists are (7) Nāgārjuna, (8) Bhartṛhari, and (9) Gopīcand (Govinda-candra, who is never identified with Govinda the alchemist).

There exist a seemingly infinite number of permutations on this set of nine, with historical and subsectarian variants abounding. Ādināth is often added to head the list, in the role of creator god or demiurge: this is a tradition that dates back at least to the *Kulārṇava Tantra* (6.63), which places him at the head of the divine stream (*divyaugha*) in its enumeration of the founding Kaula gurus.[62] Furthermore, there are regional variations in the name employed for any given Nāth Siddha: just as Matsyendra can become Mīna; so Nāgārjuna can become Nāgnāth or Arjun Nāga; Kaṇerī either Karṇarī, Kṛṣṇapāda, or Kānha; Gorakh Gorakṣa; Carpaṭi either Karpaṭi or Carpaṭa; Cauraṅgi Pūraṇ Bhagat; and Jālandhara Hāḍi-pā. By way of illustrating such variants, I offer four lists of the nine founding Nāths, all of which date from the thirteenth through sixteenth centuries. In Bengal, two sources dating from the seventeenth century but harking back to earlier traditions[63] provide the following data (in which the ninth Nāth is lacking): (1) Ādināth (identified with Śiva) is the founder of the order; his two disciples are (2) Mīnanāth (Matsyendranāth) and (3) Jālandhari-pā (Hāḍi Siddha); (4) Gorakhnāth is the disciple of Mīnanāth; (5) Queen Mayanāmatī the disciple of Gorakhnāth; (6) Kānha-pā and (7) Gopīcand the disciples of Jālandharī-pā; and Bāil Bhāḍāi (8) the disciple of Kānha-pā. According to a thirteenth- to fourteenth-century Maharashtran source,[64] the divine founder of the clan is (Viṣṇu-)Dattātreya, who is the guru of (1) Matsyendranāth and (2) Jvalendra (Jālandharanāth). Matsyendra is the guru of (3) Gorakhnāth, (4) Carpaṭi, and (5) Revaṇa; while Jvalendra is the guru of (6) Kariṇa-pā (Karṇarī-pā); (7) Bhartṛhari and (8) Gopīcand. Gorakhnāth is the guru of (9) Gahaṇināth. The third list is found in a ca. A.D. 1400 Telugu text from Andhra Pradesh, the *Navanātha-caritra* of Gauraṇa, which was written at the behest of the abbot of a Śaiva monastery at Srisailam.[65] The fourth list is adapted from a ca. sixteenth-century *paramparā* recorded in the Punjab,[66] which gives the following succession: Śakti and Śiva (1) initiated Ude (2), second of the Nine Nāths and founder of the Jogi *panth*. His descendants were two demons, Rudragaṇ and Jālandhar. Descended from Jālandhar, the demon convert and initiate, were Matsyendra (3) and Jālandharī-pā (4). Matsyendra was the guru of Gorakh (5), Arjan Nāga (6), and the father and guru of the two Jain *tīrthaṃkaras* Nīmnāth and Pārasnāth (7). Jālandharī-pā's disciples were Bārtrināth (Bhartṛhari) (8) and Kāṇipā (Kānha-pā) (9).[67]

Bengal	Maharashtra	Andhra	Punjab
1. Ādi	Matsyendra	Śivanāth	Śiva
2. Mīna	Jālandhara	Mīna	Ude (Udaya)
3. Jālandhari	Gorakh	Sāraṅgdhara[68]	Matsyendra
4. Gorakh	Carpaṭa	Gorakṣa	Jālandharī-pā
5. Mayanāmatī	Revaṇa	Meghnād	Gorakh
6. Kānha-pā	Kariṇa	Nāgārjuna	Arjan Nāga
7. Gopīcand	Bhartṛhari	Siddhabuddhū	Nīm-/Pāras-nāth
8. Bāil Bhāḍāi	Gopīcand	Virūpākṣa	Bārtrināth
9. ———	Gahaṇi	Kaṇika	Kāṇipā

Elsewhere, multiple lists of names of the founders of the twelve "official" subdivisions of the Nāth order (*bārah panth*)—generally disciples of either Matsyendra or Gorakh—often include Bhartṛhari, Gopīcand, Cauraṅgi, Nāgnāth, and Satyanāth (or Satnāth).[69] Once again, the lineages of masters and disciples (*guruparamparās*) of these subdivisions are useful in dating the origins of the Nāth Siddhas as a structured religious order (*saṃpradāya*), as opposed to an idealized list of names, a body of legend, or a corpus of literature. All of these data point to a twelfth- to thirteenth-century western Indian watershed, which witnessed a major realignment of a number of preexisting Śaiva religious orders, the creation of a number of new orders, and the appearance of a "canon" of literature on the technical and experiential aspects of *haṭha yoga*. This historical convergence lends credence to the notion that a historical figure, named Gorakhnāth, actually founded a new religious order—the Nāth *saṃpradāya*—in this period.

By way of demonstration, let us look at the suborder of the Nāth *saṃpradāya* known as the Vairāg panth, which was, according to tradition, founded by Bhartṛhari, a thirteenth-century disciple of Gorakhnāth.[70] The current head of this suborder is a householder Nāth named Nārāyaṇ Nāth, whose family compound, in a village named Padu Kala (Meerta City tehsil, Nagaur district, Rajasthan) is attached to a temple containing a dozen extremely worn burial tumuli (*samādhis*). These are, according to Nārāyaṇ Nāth, the tumuli of Bhartṛhari's immediate disciples, as well as of certain of the twenty-six other Nāth Siddhas—most of whom he could name from memory—who had intervened between Bhartṛhari and himself as titular leaders of that subsect. If these *samādhis* do indeed contain the bodily remains of seven centuries of Nāth Siddhas (and they certainly appear to be very ancient), they constitute stronger evidence for the actual institutional existence of this sect than do the lists, legends, and even writings of its purported founders that have come down to us.[71]

Another piece of archaeological evidence, also from the thirteenth century, is an A.D. 1279 inscription from Karnataka (Jagalur tāluka), which records the donation of a village by a general of the Yādava king Rāmacandra to a "yogi world-conquerer" (*yogi cakravarti*) named Prasāda Deva. In this inscription, we find what appears to be an enumeration of Prasāda Deva's lineage: "Ādigadedunātha Caturaraginātha Gorakhanātha Vistāradevī . . . nātha Kāhaḷinavi [Kanthaḍī?] Śurppāṇanātha Lonanātha Naranātha pantha." Although no one of the twelve modern subsects of the Nāth *sampradāya* appears to ever have been based in Karnataka, the ancient and prestigious monastery of Kadri, located on "Jogi Hill" on the northern outskirts of Mangalore, is a permanent fixture of Nāthdom, and it is the founding lineage of the abbots of this monastery that is recorded in this inscription.[72] Located in the monastery precincts at Kadri is a certain Mañjunātha temple, whose principal image, of Lokanātha, was dedicated in A.D. 968. In the inscription that records that dedication, it is stated that "the image of the god Lokeśvara [was placed] in the beautiful *vihāra* of Kadirikā." Now, *vihāra* is a term that can refer only to a *Buddhist* monastery; this, in conjunction with a number of other indices (Lokanātha-Lokeśvara's three-faced image conforms with northern descriptions of the Buddhist Avalokiteśvara, etc.), indicates that coastal Karnataka and Kadri were Buddhist until shortly before the end of the tenth century. All of this is most interesting, in the context of the ca. twelfth-century Western Transmission legend, related above, which stated that the "Nine Nāths" of Koṅkaṇa converted from Buddhism to Hinduism *after the collapse of their monastery*,[73] and in light of the fact that Nāth Siddha traditions at Kadri maintain that the Mañjunātha appeared, in the form of the three-faced image of Lokanātha, to the three Jogi gurus Gorakhnāth, Matsyendranāth, and Śārṅganāth. Shrines to these three founders enclose the *vihāra*-temple of Mañjunātha.[74] The Kadri monastery is also the venue for a number of Nāth legends, and is mentioned by the Italian traveler Pietro della Valle, who in 1624 visited "the famous hermitage of Cadiri" to see the "Batinate [*panthi nāth?*], called King of the Gioghi [Yogis]."[75] It was also on this coast that Marco Polo encountered his "Ciugi" alchemists, in or around the year 1295.

While we can be certain that a historical Matsyendranāth lived and wrote at least two centuries before the symbolic Nine Nāths begin to appear in twelfth-century Western Transmission sources, the notion of nine historical figures who, taken as an aggregate, constituted the Nine Nāths probably did not solidify until the foundation, by Gorakhnāth, of the Nāth *sampradāya* as an institutionalized religious order, in the twelfth to thirteenth century. Additional datable evidence from this period includes the Maharashtran Jñāneśvara's ca. A.D. 1290 reference to Gorakhnāth as his guru's guru's guru;[76] and a reference in Viśobakhecara's thirteenth-century *Ghaṭasthala* to the founders of his lineage as Ādināth, Mīnanāth, and Gorakhnāth. This proof is also supported, apophatically, by further evidence from Maharashtra. Less than a century prior to Jñāneśvara, Mukuṇḍarāja, the first poet to write in the Marathi medium, gives an account of his lineage in his *Vivekasindhu*. Ādinātha, who founded the lineage, had Harinātha (A.D. 1159–86) for his disciple. Harinātha's disciples were Surendranātha, Bhāratīnātha, Janārdana, Nāgnātha, Viśvambharnātha, and Raghunātha—with the last of these being Mukuṇḍarāja's guru.[77] Here, we are presented with a lineage founded by Ādinātha, and in which a large number of individuals whose names end in *-nātha* are figured, but from whose number Gorakhnāth is conspicuously absent. Another early Marathi-language work, the twelfth- to thirteenth-century *Līlā Caritra* of Cakradhara Svāmī, founder of the Mahānubhava *sampradāya*, also lists number of familiar Nāth Siddhas, with the significant omission of Gorakhnāth.[78] Gorakhnāth's appearance, in Jñāneśvara's A.D. 1290 *Jñāneśvarī*, as the disciple of a semidivine Matsyendra and as Jñāneśvara's guru's guru's guru, indicates the appearance of the historical reformer Gorakhnāth on the western Indian scene in the late twelfth to early thirteenth century.

Additional evidence of the same order may be elicited from an A.D. 1030 inscription from Karnataka (Nelamangala tāluka) which commemorates the founding of a Siddheśvara ("Lord of the Siddhas") temple there. While this inscription names the Candrapurī ("Moon City") of Western Transmission tradition, a founding guru named Ādinātha, and a number of other figures with names ending in *-nātha*, as well as the orthodox Śaiva textual corpus (*śaivāgama*), it makes no reference to Gorakh or any one of the "authorized" nine founders the Nāth Siddhas:[79]

> At the foot of a wonderful tree in Candrapurī, [which is] situated in the Western Ocean, Ādinātha is installed. By merely recalling his excellent lotus feet, the residual effects of acts commited in past lives are destroyed. His disciple . . . was Chāyādhinātha ["Shadow Ādinātha." His disciple was Stambhanātha] . . . His son, versed in the meaning of the Kālāgama, was the *yati* Dvīpanātha . . . His disciple was born Mauninātha *munipa*. The bearer of the latter's commands was Rūpaśiva [the priest given charge of the temple] . . . devoted to the *śaivāgama*.

As is common practice, the founder of the Siddheśvara temple traces the lineage of its priest back to the divine founder of his sectarian tradition. As such the greatest historical interest of this *guruparamparā* lies in the fact that it does *not* mention the traditional "historical" founders of the Nāth Siddhas (who figure in the later A.D. 1279 Kadri inscription, from the same region, mentioned above), even as it commemorates the founding of a "Siddha" temple. In this, it supports the proof elicited from the Maharashtran data a moment ago. There were, prior to the thirteenth century, a number of groups, mainly Śaiva, who called themselves Siddhas, as well as groups whose founding gurus had the suffix *-nātha* appended to their names. There were, however, no groups calling themselves Siddhas with names ending in *-nātha* who traced their lineage back to a founder named Gorakhnāth prior to this time. It is not until the thirteenth century that such specifically "Gorakhnāthi" lineages suddenly appear, in at least half a dozen places in western India.

It is, moreover, to the same period that the major Sanskrit-language hathayogic works of Gorakhnāth, as well as a "canonical" body of vernacular mystic poetry—attributed to Gorakhnāth and others and written in a mixture of Old Rajasthani (Diṅgal), Old Punjabi, Khaḍī Bolī, and Apabhraṁśa—are dated.[80] We also find external references to Gorakhnāth in (1) the *haṭha yoga* section of the *Śārṅgadhara Paddhati*, a work dating from the thirteenth to fourteenth century;[81] (2) the A.D. 1372 foundation of the important Nāth monastery at Dhinodara (Kacch district, Gujarat) by Dharamnāth;[82] and (3) two Kathmandu Valley inscriptions, dating from A.D. 1382 and 1391, left by "a follower of the sect of Gorakha," and by a Yogi named Acintanāth.[83] Prior to this surge of solid historical data, reinforced by the literary evidence of the thirteenth-century "canon" attributed to Gorakhnāth, we have little but legend to go on.

A significant volume of evidence, then—archaeological, literary, and inscriptional—points to the institutionalization of the Nāth *sampradāya*, via the recognition of Gorakhnāth and other figures as its historical founders, in the thirteenth century. What appears to have occurred was the "Gorakhization" of disparate monasteries (Kadri), lineages (the Vairāg panth), and even entire religious orders (the Pāśupatas and Kāpālikas), which became absorbed into this new institutional entity. In the case of the latter two old Śaiva orders, an A.D. 1287 inscription from Somnath (Junagadh district, Gujarat), the original homeland of the Pāśupata sect, is significant, inasmuch as we find in it the name of Gorakh appearing together, for the first time, with that of the "Lākulīśas" (i.e., of Pāśupatas).[84] In many ways, the Nāth Siddhas appear to be the direct heirs to the Pāśupatas and Kāpālikas.

Śaiva sectarianism in fact begins, some eleven hundred years before the advent of Gorakhnāth, with this former order, whose teachings were revealed by Śrīkaṇṭha or Nīlakaṇṭha Śiva himself to the sect's founder Lakulīśa—the "Lord with the Stave"—who hailed from Kāyāvarohana (the modern Karvan, Baruch district, Gujarat) in the first half of the second century. The Pāśupatas were the prototypes of the Śaiva ascetic, whose daily "bathing" in ashes, antisocial behavior, sectarian markings, goals of *siddhi*s and bodily immortality, and even an emphasis on "yoga"[85] have been passed down to present day Śaivites via such sects as the Kāpālikas. This latter group, which emerged in the beginning of the first millennium of the common era, constituted the more heterodox, left wing of Śaiva sectarianism. Situated at the orthodox end of the Śaiva spectrum in this period were the Kālamukhas, mainly based in Karnataka, and the Śaiva Siddhāntins, who were based in both south (Tamil Nadu in particular) and north (Madhya Pradesh, Kashmir) India.

While the Pāśupatas and Kāpālikas were clearly the forerunners of the Nāth Siddhas, and whereas the disappearance of the Kālamukhas more or less coincided with the appearance of the Vīraśaivas in the Deccan, it is the Śaiva Siddhāntins who have defined mainstream Śaiva ritual devotionalism for the past twelve hundred years or more. Śaiva Siddhānta was, by the ninth century, the Śaiva orthodoxy of both north and south India.[86] Following this ninth-century watershed, however, a north-south rift developed, with much of Kashmir Śaiva metaphysics being propelled in the direction of a nondualist idealist gnoseology by such great theoreticians as Abhinavagupta and the south remaining dualist and more concerned with external practice than inner realization. Because, however, the Nāth Siddhas have historically subscribed to none of the central tenets or canons of the Śaiva Siddhānta orthodoxy—devotion to Śiva, external worship, conventional behavior—this important tradition need not concern us further.[87]

A number of Nāth Siddha traditions maintain that there originally existed twelve Śaiva subgroups—the "Yogis" of the post-Gupta age; i.e. Pāśupatas, Kāpālikas, Kālamukhas, etc.—to which Gorakhnāth added another twelve of his own creation.[88] These figures are indirectly supported by a list from the relatively recent *Śabara Tantra* (quoted in the ca. seventeenth-century *Gorakṣa Siddhānta Saṃgraha*) of the "twelve Kāpālika teachers" and their twelve "disciples." The former list, which is headed by Ādinātha, contains names that hark back to the older Śaiva orders: Kāla, Karāla, Mahākāla, Kālabhairava-nātha, Vāṭuka, Bhūtanātha, Vīranātha, Śrīkaṇṭha, etc. In the latter list, of the twelve "disciples" of these teachers, we recognize the names of the traditional founders of a number of the twelve *panth*s of institutionalized Nāthdom: Nāgnāth (or Nāgārjuna), Satyanāth (or Satnāth), Gorakṣa, Carpaṭa, Vairāgya (Bhartṛhari), Kanthādhārī (Kanthaḍī), Jālandhara, etc.[89]

Nāth Siddha tradition further maintains that the twelve Śaivite orders and the twelve Gorakhnāthi orders battled one another, with all but six of each of the two groups being destroyed. These twelve surviving orders were confederated by Gorakhnāth to form the twelve original *panth*s of the Nāth *sampradāya*.[90] All of these twelve original subsects were based in Śaivism's ancient heartland, i.e., the northwestern part of the Indian subcontinent (Gujarat, Punjab, Sind, Rajasthan), with one group, the Rāwals or Nāgnāthis, having its base in Afghanistan.[91] This configuration or confederation has changed over the centuries: twentieth-century enumerations of the twelve *panth*s base two of these in Bengal, one in Orissa, one in Nepal, and one (the important Gorakhpur monastery) in Uttar Pradesh.[92]

The emergence of the Nāth Siddhas or Nāth *sampradāya* was probably of a less dramatic order than that described in this legend. Its coalescence, both prior and subsequent to the institutional organization founded by Gorakhnāth, was more likely a gradual process, catalyzed by the itinerant lifestyles of India's *sādhu*s and the oral communications network they have always maintained at the many pan-Indian pilgrimage sites they have frequented over the past seven centuries. The end result of this process was the loose confederation of lineages that is today known as the *bārah panth*, a hydra-headed group with no single leader,[93] which holds general assemblies of sorts on the occasions of major religious festivals (for example, at the *kumbha melā*s at Hardwar and Allahabad).[94] The term *panth*, "path," is a significant one here; one who belongs to a *panth* is a *panthi*, a "path-taker," and an itinerant lifestyle has long been the hallmark of the Nāth order.

For our purposes, it is most important to note that the twelfth- to thirteenth-century Gorakhnāth, while he was a reformer, innovator, and systematizer, did not innovate either the techniques of *haṭha yoga* or the Nāth *sampradāya* out of whole cloth. There was already something there: an embryonic hathayogic tradition, a body of legend in which there already figured a Siddha or Vidyādhara named Gorakṣa or Gorakh, and several religious orders and sects, some of whose adherents were already calling themselves "Nāth" or "Siddha" before Gorakhnāth appeared on the scene.[95]

While such may, at first blush, appear to be overly facile, we may quite safely characterize the emergence of the Nāth Siddhas as a marriage between Nāths (i.e., Śaiva groups—Pāśupatas, Kāpālikas, and Śāktas—for whom Śiva had long been called Nāth, "Lord") and Siddhas (Māheśvara and Rasa Siddhas and Sittars, as well as the Buddhist Siddhācāryas)[96] which took the institutionalized form of the Nāth *sampradāya*. Starting in this period, all manner of preexisting Śaivite and Siddha clans, lineages, or sects would have funneled themselves into the Nāth suborders or have been identified as Nāth Siddhas by outside sources. In addition to groups already mentioned, we also find the Vaiṣṇava Avadhūta *sampradāya* (founded by Dattātreya),[97] Dasnāmī Nāgas, Jains, Sufi Muslims, and a group of snake charmers claiming allegiance, in the fourteenth and later centuries, to one or another of the twelve subsects.[98] By claiming descent from Gorakh or Matsyendra, or some other founding Nāth Siddha, these various groups grafted themselves onto what they considered to be a past with a future.[99]

It appears that, from the outset, there have always been more candidates for the twelve "slots" than there have been *panth*s, which has made for a protean aggregate.[100] Indeed, even the correct name for members of the aggregate I have been blithely referring to as the Nāth Siddhas is a matter of disagreement. Other terms include: *Yogi* or *Jogi*, which is both too broad a term, covering as it does all manner of itinerant *sādhu*s, including certain of the historical forerunners of the present order,[101] and too pejorative, since *Jogi* has long been the name of a scheduled caste in India;[102] *Kānphaṭa* ("split-eared") *Yogi*, which applies to the sectarian marking of some, but not all, cenobitic members of this order, who wear great earrings (*kuṇḍala*s, *mudrā*s, *darśana*s) through the thick of their ears, which are bored open upon full initiation; *Gorakhnāthi*, which evokes the name of the founder or reformer of the institutional order (however, many suborders trace their lineage back to Matsyendra or Jālandhara, and not Gorakh, and those who claim descent from Jālandhara generally eschew the *kuṇḍala* earrings, even upon full initiation, and call themselves "Aughars," rather than "Kānphaṭas" or "Darśanīs");[103] and *Nāth Panthi* or *Nāth Sampradāyi*, which appear to be overly institutional in their emphasis.

If we are to judge from recent publications coming out of the important Gorakhpur monastery, *Nāth Siddha*, the term I employ, is the term most favored by the leadership of the order itself.[104] This is also a term that acknowledges the historical Śaiva and Siddha roots of the sect, roots evoked in the *Yogabīja* of Gorakhnāth, which evokes both the *siddha-mata* (Siddha doctrine), and the *nātha mārga* (Nāth path).[105] It also acknowledges the fact that most adherents to this sect suffix their names with *-nāth*.[106] Having said this, we must allow that the reality of the situation cannot be decanted into the neat typologies I have been attempting to generate here. So it is that we find, under the umbrella heading of Nāth Siddha, Nāth *sampradāya*—or any of the other alternatives enumerated—notions of both sect and subcaste (especially among the large communities of householder Nāths found scattered throughout north India) and a wide array of lineage claims, as well as variations in dress, vows, devotional worship, and forms of behavior that appear to be both regional and sectarian in origin.[107]

At this point, let us return to the *ĀK* list, which was the point of departure for this long excursus on the sectarian origins of the Siddhas. Our hypothesis—that the Nāth *sampradāya* emerged in the early thirteenth century as a great medieval changing house of Śaiva and Siddha sectarianism—is supported by this source. Here, our thirteenth-century *terminus ante quem* is clearly demonstrated by the fact that no alchemical source prior to the fourteenth-century *ĀK* lists the "Nine Nāths," including Gorakh (whose name it sanskritizes to Gorakṣa), in its Rasa Siddha lists. In the final analysis, the myriad Siddha lists of eleventh- to fifteenth-century India provide us with the pool of names, mystic disciplines, and sectarian orientations that would come to funnel themselves into the Nāth order, confederated in the late twelfth or early thirteenth century by the western Indian reformer Gorakhnāth. This order, which inherited the techniques of tantric alchemy from the Rasa Siddhas, would transform that discipline into what we have termed Siddha alchemy, the melding of external alchemy with internal hathayogic practice, as such was taught by the tenth-century Matsyendra and systematized by the twelfth- to thirteenth-century Gorakh. It is in this sense that all manner of medieval Indian traditions have been quite correct in their *retrospective* identifications of the Nāth Siddhas with the tantric alchemists, the semidivine revealers or transmitters of

Śaiva and Sākta traditions,[108] as well as with the seventh- to twelfth-century founders of tantric Buddhism, known as the Mahāsiddhas or Siddhācāryas.

4. Sorting Out the Siddhas

While the Nāth Siddhas have left us burial tumuli and a living (though perhaps not thriving) institutional order—in which disciples are initiated by gurus, often in a monastic setting, within the *bārah panth* structure—all that the Rasa Siddhas have bequeathed us are lists of names and a corpus of alchemical literature. Just as there are no gurus initiating disciples into alchemical orders or lineages today,[109] we can be quite certain—in spite of the Rasa Siddha lists and scattered references one finds to the Raseśvara doctrine (*darśana*, *mata*), or to alchemical initiations of disciples by gurus—that there never were institutionalized orders of alchemists in medieval India.

This is supported in the classic *RA*, which, like a number of other alchemical sources, discusses alchemical gurus, disciples, and initiation, but which simply states, on the subject of lineages, that the guru should be "devoted to the *kula-mārga*" and "the member of a true order (*satsampradāyin*)."[110] More significant is its contention (1.27) that "to those who say this [alchemical] order (*sampradāya*) is not a 'womb,' it is maintained that mercury is a 'womb.'"[111] In the context of tantric doctrines according to which initiation into an order, i.e., a clan, consists in partaking of the "clan-nectar" that streams from the womb of the Goddess, this statement is a defense of the fact that the medieval alchemists were "biologically" linked through initiation, even if theirs was not an institutionalized sect. Quicksilver entrepreneurs, they took their initiation directly from Śiva.

This squares with the rare autobiographical data the alchemical authors offer in their own writings, which indicate that these figures were attached to royal courts, rather than to any monastic or religious order. The mercury-eating regular and secular orders about which Marco Polo and François Bernier wrote belonged to "Yogi" (i.e., Siddha alchemical), and not Rasa (i.e., tantric alchemical) lineages.

At this point, we must clarify the position of yet another Siddha tradition, an aggregate that overlaps many of the other Siddha groups I have been discussing. This is a group called the Māheśvara Siddhas. As their name indicates, this group defines itself by its devotion to Śiva, the Great Lord (*maheśvara*); and in fact nearly every Śaiva sect, school, or institution—the Pāśupatas, Kāpālikas, Kālamukhas, Śaiva Siddhāntins, and Vīraśaivas (or Liṅgāyatas)—has called itself or been called Māheśvara.[112] Etymology and logic would then lead one to conclude that the term *māheśvara siddha* ought to apply to any mystic devotee of Śiva Maheśvara who has perfected (*siddha*) himself through his practice. The specific use of the term is more restricted, however, and relates directly to our subject. The Māheśvara Siddhas were, generally, alchemists who did not seek bodily immortality (*jīvanmukti*) as the final goal of their practice, but rather aspired to another sort of liberation (*parāmukti*). Rather than a perfected (*siddhadeha*) or adamantine (*vajradeha*) physical body, the Māheśvara Siddhas' goal was a divine body (*divyadeha*) of a more ethereal, even incorporeal nature. At times, one has the impression that the Māheśvara alchemists (the authors of the *Rasahṛdaya Tantra* [*RHT*] and *Rasopaniṣat* [*RU*] are examples) were seeking the same sort of liberation (*mokṣa*) that nearly all mainstream Hindus aspire to—i.e., the absorption of the individual soul (*ātman*) into the absolute (*bráhman*)—and that their alchemy was merely a means to prolonging the lives of bodies within which their hearts and intellects could discover their innate unity with the universal essence. Such is also the purport of the "Raseśvara Darśana" chapter of Mādhavācārya's fourteenth-century *Sarvadarśana Saṃgraha*, which opens with the statement: "Other Māheśvaras there are who, while they hold to the identity of self with Parameśvara, insist upon the principle that the liberation in this life taught in all the systems depends upon the stability of the body, and therefore celebrate the virtues of *rasa* . . . as a means for stability of the body." As minister to King Bukku I (A.D. 1356–77) of Vijayanagara (modern Hampi, Bellary district, Karnataka), Mādhavācārya identified what he termed the "revealed system of the Lord of Mercury" with the doctrines of the Māheśvara Siddhas, who were active there in his time.[113] This emphasis differs radically from that of both the Nāth Siddhas and the *RA*, whose powerful rhetoric regarding the this-worldly nature of bodily liberation will be discussed in chapter six.[114]

In practical terms, the alchemy of the Māheśvara Siddhas was more therapeutic than transmutational, for which reason it funneled directly into south Indian Siddha medicine. In certain sources, the distinction between this group and the Rasa or Nāth Siddhas is cast in more subtle terms, with the distinction between *viśuddha-māyā* and *mahā-māyā* categories being emphasized. A legend from a Vīraśaiva source illustrates the difference between the two sectarian and philosophical perspectives. Gorakhnāth and Allama Prabhu (also known as Prabhudeva, no. 52 in the *RRS* [c] list) have a *siddhi* contest. When Allama Prabhu takes a sword to Gorakh, its blade shatters on his adamantine body; when Gorakh does the same to Allama Prabhu, it passes through his body, which is wholly ethereal. Allama Prabhu then chides Gorakh, saying that such bodily density is merely the mark of a density of illusion.[115] Another Vīraśaiva source maintains that it was Allama Prabhu who initiated Gorakh and Nāgārjuna into the alchemical arts at Srisailam. Yet the same Allama Prabhu (and he was not alone in this) scorns Gorakh and the Nāth Siddhas for the "this-bodily" emphasis of their alchemy.[116] We may therefore conclude that while all or some of the Māheśvara Siddhas may have been alchemists, and while certain of the Vīraśaivas may have even been itinerant alchemists, they were not alchemists of the same stripe as the Nāth Siddhas, the Siddha alchemists of medieval India.

The Māheśvara Siddhas were concentrated in the Deccan and western coastal region of India.[117] As noted, a Siddheśvara temple was dedicated, in A.D. 1030, in coastal Karnataka. Several centuries earlier, a number of temples to Śiva Siddheśvara were constructed in the Srisailam region of Andhra Pradesh, in the Deccan.[118] Elsewhere, architectural or archaeological data provide us with very few clues to the history of tantric alchemy. The *Viṣṇudharmottara Purāṇa*, a ca. eighth-century Kashmiri text that is most attentive to the iconography and plastic reproduction of divine images, contains descriptions of mercurial preparations used to coat stone sculptures and thereby increase their resistance to the elements.[119] The alleged presence of mercury and other elements in a number of metal images from the Buddhist monastic university complex at Nalanda (Bihar) would indicate that alchemy was part of its curriculum prior to its destruction in the twelfth century.[120] A ca. twelfth-century sculpted image, dominating the southern facade of the *sikhara* of the Menāl (Mahānādakāla) temple in the Bhilwara district of southeastern Rajasthan is said to be a representation of Siva Raseśvara.[121] In Malaysia, the foundations of a twelfth- to thirteenth-century Śiva temple containing a mercurial *liṅga* and other alchemically prepared elements are evidence for the spread of medieval Hindu alchemy to greater India.[122]

This paucity of hard evidence and a plethora of mythic references have spawned a number of wild hypotheses concerning the origins and chronology of Indian alchemy. A persistent theory has it that the Muslim conquests drove the Buddhist alchemists in residence of such intellectual centers as Nalanda (Nalanda district, Bihar) south into the Deccan or up into the northern perimeter of the subcontinent, where they converted to Hinduism or took on Hindu disciples. According to this theory, the great works of Hindu tantric alchemy would have issued from this diaspora, in such far-flung places as Bhutan, Srisailam, Devagiri (the capital of the Yādavas, in present-day Maharashtra), and Junagadh (Gujarat). A parallel theory, dear to historians of medieval Hindu sectarianism, maintains that the Nāth Siddhas were originally a group of Buddhists who apostasized in the face of the Muslim invasions in order to continue their tantric practices. Both theories, attractive as they may appear as explanations for the medieval emergence of the Rasa Siddhas and Nāth Siddhas respectively, are seriously flawed.

Through the compounding of a scholarly error, first promulgated by Prafulla Candra Ray[123] in 1903, and later amplified by Sylvain Lévi, Jean Filliozat, and Mircea Eliade,[124] it has been standard practice, in the historiography of Indian alchemy, to identify a work, attributed to Nāgārjuna and entitled *Rasaratnākara* (*RRĀ*), as India's primal and primordial alchemical classic. However, in an article written in 1983, Dominik Wujastyk[125] proved that the so-called *RRĀ* of Nāgārjuna was a conflation of three separate texts: the *RRĀ* of Nityanātha, and the *RM* and *Kakṣapuṭa Tantra* (*KPT*), both authored by Nāgārjuna. The youngest of these three works, the *RM*, a derivative source which borrows extensively from other Hindu alchemical tantras, is a thirteenth- to fourteenth-century work. It is unique, however, in its dramatic presentation of a portion of its data (most of its fourth chapter, which it shamelessly cribs from the *RA*)[126] in the form of a dialogue, atop Srisailam, between the Mādhyamika philosopher Nāgārjuna, the Buddhist goddess Prajñāparamitā, King Śālivāhana,[127] a *yakṣiṇī* haunting a sacred fig tree, and a host of mainly Buddhist luminaries, including Ratnaghośa, Śūrasena, and Nāgabodhi. A smattering of Buddhist terminology completes the tableau, leaving the superficial impression that the Nāgārjuna who authored the *RM* was the same figure as the Nāgārjuna who had received the Perfection of Wisdom teachings a millennium earlier.

In spite of the fact that this text is in every other respect a straightforward Hindu alchemical Tantra, which terms mercury *harabīja* (the seed of Hara, i.e., Śiva), and invokes Śaiva gods, goddesses, and tantric practices, Ray finds in its fourth chapter proof positive that "the *Rasaratnākara* [*sic*] seems to us to be a typical production representing the Mahāyānist period of intellectual activity and we may not be wide of the mark if we put down 7th or 8th century A.D. as its latest date." From here, Ray passes from the specific to the universal: "From the 5th to the 11th century A.D. the colleges in connection with the monasteries of Pāṭaliputra, Nālandā, Vikramaśīla, Udaṇḍapura, etc., were the great seats of learning . . . and alchemy was included in the curricula of studies." Therefore, Ray concludes, most of the early alchemical tantras were Buddhist.[128] Later, in a very ambiguously worded passage, Ray notes that the (then) recently discovered *Kubjikāmata* "presupposes the existence of other schools and we have the distinct mention of the Mahāyāna"; then, vaguely citing Shastri's *Catalogue*, he quotes a passage from this work in which "Śiva himself speaks of *pārada* (mercury) as his generative principle and eulogises its efficacy when it has been killed six times."[129] The Sanskrit, which he gives in a footnote, is nowhere to be found in Shastri's description of the *Kubjikāmata*, nor have I been able to locate it in the manuscript which Ray claims was Shastri's source (NNA MSS no. 1–285 *ka*). Yet, Ray's confabulations have been duly reiterated by scholars, including me, throughout the twentieth century.[130]

In addition to the western scholars cited above—who accepted the Buddhist cachet of Nāgārjuna's "*Rasaratnākara*" as authentic, and who thereby subscribed to the theory that the foundations of Hindu tantric alchemy were Buddhist—P. V. Sharma, India's most respected historian of Āyurveda, is clearly following Ray when he states that

> when, due to the 12th century advance of [Muhammad] Bakhtyar Khilji, the universities of Nalanda and Vikramaśīla were deserted, their scholars and scientists fled, some to Nepal, Bhutan, and Tibet, and others to south India—most especially to Devagiri, where they took refuge in the courts of the Yādava kings . . . In south India, *rasa śāstra* continued to develop under the custodianship of the Siddhas [Sittars]. The Siddhas are said to have been eighteen in number . . . They have been dated to the 10th century and after.[131]

In spite of the fact that the Muslim scholar Alberuni himself maintained that the invasions of his own patron, Mahmud of Ghazni, was the cause for the flight from western India of "the Hindu sciences,"[132] a number of data militate against this hypothesis. The first of these is the absence of any extant medieval Buddhist alchemical works outside of the *Kālacakra* and Tibetan Nying-ma traditions.[133] Once one allows that the *RM* and *RHT* were not Buddhist works, and when one takes into account the fact that the Tibetan *Tanjur*—which seemingly incorporated *every* extant Buddhist text into its voluminous mass—contains only four alchemical works, of which none bears a clearly Buddhistic stamp, one begins to wonder who the armies of university-trained Buddhist alchemists were who flocked to the Himalayan kingdoms, the Deccan, and Tamil Nadu. Elsewhere, Sharma musters ample evidence to prove that the Yādavas of Devagiri were indeed great patrons of the alchemical arts.[134] Yet, as he himself demonstrates, on the basis of solid historical evidence, the Yādavas' twelfth- and thirteenth-century alchemist protégés were a highly mobile group. Bhāskara circulated between Kashmir, south India, and Devagiri; his son Soḍhala between Devagiri and Gujarat (where Muslim penetration had begun in the closing years of the tenth century); and so on.[135]

One does not have the impression that the Hindu scholars of this period were huddling in Hindu refuges from Islam; why would the Buddhists have done so? Moreover, there is good evidence that Hindu physicians and alchemists were welcomed into the courts of Muslim princes whose thirst for immortality, increased virility, and the philosopher's stone would have been stronger than their religious fervor.[136] Finally, we know that Muslim physicians, alchemists, and mystics were avid for the wisdom of their Indian counterparts, as evidenced by the translation, in the sixteenth century, of a treatise on *haṭha yoga*, attributed to Gorakṣa, entitled the *Amṛtakuṇḍa* (The Pool of Nectar).[137] Some time prior to the seventeenth century, it may have been a Bengali Muslim, Sheikh Fayzullā, who glorified the exploits of Gorakh, Matsyendra, and other Nāth Siddhas, in his *Gorakṣa* (or *Gorakha*) *Vijay*.[138] Elsewhere, the venerable and powerful Nāth monastery at Gorakṣanāth Ṭilla (Jhelum district, Punjab, Pakistan) has been a center of Hindu-Muslim syncretism since a very early date.[139] Finally, as we indicated on the opening page of this book, at least one highly placed Muslim—the fanatically anti-Hindu Mogul emperor Aurangzeb—was still petitioning the Nāth Siddhas for their alchemical expertise well into the seventeenth century.

Theories concerning relations between the Nāth Siddhas and Buddhists in the period of the Muslim conquest bear a certain resemblance to those I have reviewed on the subject of India's alchemists, with a number of scholars maintaining that certain of the founders of the Nāth *sampradāya* were originally Buddhists hailing from eastern India.[140] Such theories generally take the Siddha lists as their starting point. Seven of the figures whose names most frequently occur in enumerations of the nine "historical" Nāths—Matsyendra (Luī-pā; Mīna), Gorakṣa, Cauraṅgi, Nāgārjuna, Kaṇerī (Kānha–pā; Kāṇipā; Karṇarī), Jālandhara (Hāḍi-pā), and Carpaṭi (Carpaṭā)—figure in the Buddhist Siddhācārya lists. In addition, a number of scholars evoke the "Buddhist" terminology (*śūnya*, *sahaja*, etc.) employed in the poetry and technical works of the Nāth Siddhas to indicate that the "origins" of the Nāth Siddhas were something other than Śaiva.[141]

Armed with this data, writers since at least the time of Tāranātha, the Tibetan author of the A.D. 1608 *History of Buddhism in India*,[142] have advanced all manner of argument to demonstrate the following thesis: that due to the similarity between names of Siddhācāryas and many of the nine founding Nāth Siddhas beginning with Luī-pā (who was one of the founders of the Siddhācārya lineage) and Matsyendra[nāth]),[143] and because Luī-pā and other early Siddhācārya figures (including Kānha-pā and Jālandarī-pā) authored a number of the pre-twelfth-century *Caryāpada*s, which were written in Old Bengali, some or all of the Nāth Siddhas, whose legendary founding guru was named Matsyendra, were originally Buddhists based in eastern India, who abandoned the faith as a means to escaping Muslim persecution in the first half of the thirteenth century. Tāranātha does not mince his words: "At that time, most of the Yogi followers of Gaurkṣa [Gorakṣa] were fools; driven by the greed for money and the honour offered by the *tīrthaka* [Hindu] kings, they became the followers of Īśvara. They used to say 'we are not opposed even to the Turuṣkas [Turks, i.e., the Muslims].'"[144]

To be sure, certain of the Siddhācārya *guruparamparā*s, as preserved in both the *Caryāpada*s and Tibetan sources, parallel data on the original Nāth Siddhas found in pre-seventeenth-century Bengali sources.[145] So, for example, in *caryā* song no. 11, Kānha-pā calls himself a "Kāpālika" disciple of Jālandharī-pā, and mentions the unstruck sound (*anāhata*) and the wearing of earrings (*kuṇḍala*) that are hallmarks of Nāth Siddha theory and practice.[146] It is also significant that the Nāth Siddha lineage (*pantha*) founded by Jālandhara is the sole lineage in which initiates' names are suffixed with *-pā* or *-pāda*, rather than *-nāth;* and that the *-pā* suffix is employed only by Nāths or Siddhas in the eastern part of the subcontinent: Uttar Pradesh, Bihar, Bengal, Nepal, and Tibet.[147] While there is no explicit legend on this subject in the *Grub thob* (which, it must be recalled, is a mid-fourteenth-century translation of an eleventh- to twelfth-century Sanskrit source), a legend concerning the Siddhācārya Cauraṅgi (Siddhācārya no. 10)—who is dismembered after being falsely accused by an evil stepmother—does bring a cowherd (*go-rakṣa*) into play, who is instrumental in restoring Cauraṅgi's limbs. The sole figure to be identified as a yogin in this account is, however, Mīna-pā (no. 8), and not Gorakṣa (no. 9). Later, in Tāranātha's seventeenth-century work, it is Gorakṣa rather than Cauraṅgi who is the dismembered and restored yogin.[148] Finally, the existence in eastern India of large "Jogi" and "Kāpālika" subcastes is marshaled as evidence for a mass apostasy, from Buddhism to Hinduism (and thence to Islam!), that would have been led by "Gorakhnāth."[149]

However, just as Tāranātha gets Gorakṣa's legend wrong, so too he and scholars who follow him are wrong when they attempt to make Nāth Siddhas out of those seventh- to twelfth-century A.D. Buddhist Siddhācāryas who were based in eastern India. First, while there were indeed Vajrayāna figures named Gorakṣa, Luī-pā, Kānha-pā, Jālandhara-pā, and so on, their writings, as preserved in the *Tanjur*, are either clearly Buddhist or heavily indebted to Hindu sources.[150] Second, it makes no sense that Gorakṣa—if he lived, as the *Grub thob* says he did, in the time of the ninth-century king Gopāla[151]—would have had to have led his mass conversion of Buddhist Siddhas to Hinduism some four hundred years prior to the Muslim conquest (1256–60) of Bengal! In fact, there are no extant Bengali works by anyone named Gorakṣa or Gorakh and no tradition whatsoever of there ever having been a Bengali Siddha author named Gorakṣa. A very short work on the physiology of the subtle body, attributed to Ghorakṣa (or Ghorakha, but not Gorakṣa, i.e., Siddhācārya no. 9), is included in volume 21 of the *Tanjur*.[152] This work, included in the "Tantra" section of the *Tanjur*, may date from as late as the fourteenth century, as might a number of *caryā* songs attributed to the same author, found in the same source. The *Amṛtakuṇḍa*, attributed to a certain Gorakṣa from Kāmarūpa (Assam), cannot be dated prior to the late sixteenth century, [153] and Bengali literary versions of the *Gorakṣa Vijay* postdate fifteenth-century Nepali and Maithili versions of the same by at least two centuries. If these data constitute proofs for the existence of a pre-thirteenth-century "historical" Gorakṣa in eastern India, it nonetheless remains the case that the contents of these two works in no way resemble the hathayogic summa of Gorakhnāth (even if this figure's name is sanskritized to "Gorakṣanātha" in these works). The existence of a ninth- to eleventh-century eastern Indian Gorakṣa is unproven; a more likely scenario would have the works of the twelfth- to thirteenth-century western Indian Gorakhnāth being transmitted back to Bengal and attributed to a Bengali Gorakṣa in the thirteenth through fourteenth centuries.

Prior to this thirteenth-century watershed, the sole Gorakṣa in Bengal or eastern India would have been a Siddha demigod worshipped by cowherds for the protection of their livestock, with no connection to the historical author and reformer Gorakh. Indeed, he is portrayed as a cowherd in his *Grub thob* legend.[154] This figure may well have been "Buddhicized" into a Vajrayāna deity in the northeastern Indian subcontinent: three juxtaposed images in a monastery in Sikkim are identified as the divine Buddha Amitabhā, the human founder Gautama Buddha, and Gorakṣanātha![155] Another striking piece of evidence comes from Gorakhpur, where

> Gorakhnāth . . . discovered at the site of the present [Gorakhnāth] temple a shrine sacred to the god Gurakh or Gorakh, who appears to have been a deity of great fame in the Nepal country; and having devoted himself to the service of this deity, practiced the greatest austerities. He . . . took the name of Gorakhnāth or servant of Gorakh. Shortly after his death . . . members of the [ruling Satāsi] family establish[ed] themselves near the shrine, from which the town they founded took the name of Gorakhpur.[156]

I have already noted that images of Gorakṣa were being worshipped from an early date at both Kadri and Somnath. Elsewhere, the sixteenth-century alchemical *Rasakaumudī* (3.50) prescribes the worship of the Nine Nāths. The worship of a semidivine Gorakh or Gorakṣa, as well as of many other Nāth Siddhas, remains widespread in India and Nepal down to the present day.

To conclude: since no extant tantric or Siddha alchemical works, either Hindu or Buddhist, emerged out of Bengal prior to the thirteenth century, we need not concern ourselves any further with the imagined east Indian Buddhist origins of Gorakhnāth or the Nāth Siddhas.[157] Elsewhere, the Nāth Siddhas were, more than any other medieval Hindu sect, most amenable to syncretism with Islam. Many are the Nāth Siddhas who are known as "Guru" or "Nāth" by their Hindu devotees and "Pīr" by Muslims. The Bāuls of Bengal are a prime example of such a phenomenon: they are often Muslims who revere Gorakh and other Nāth Siddhas, and whose sung poetry curiously resembles that of the Buddhist Mahāsiddhas.[158] The prominent place occupied by Jogīs in Indian Sūfī hagiography is a further indication of this syncretism, a subject that is only now beginning to receive the scholarly attention it deserves.[159]

The volume of legend surrounding Gorakh, Matsyendra, Kānha, Gopīcand, Bhartṛhari, Carpaṭi, Cauraṅgi, and the other major Nāth Siddhas is so massive as to constitute an entire field of study in itself. The names of these traditional founders, common enough to begin with, have over the centuries been constantly reappropriated in such a way as to generate a plethora of figures with the same names and often the same gurus and disciples, but living in different centuries, under different kings, and in different regions of India. Our discussions of the historical and legendary data pertaining to the major Nāth Siddhas will therefore be limited to those cases which serve to trace the history and doctrines of tantric and Siddha alchemy.[160]

5. Western India: The Heartland of Tantric and Siddha Alchemy

As soon as we turn away from Buddhism and eastern India and towards Śaivism and the west of the subcontinent, the alchemical trail suddenly becomes hotter. I have already noted that all of the original twelve *panth*s of the Nāth order were based in western, and especially northwestern, India.[161] As I will show, nearly all the historical data we have at our disposal indicate that the medieval alchemists, too, were centered in western India, although further to the south than the Nāth Siddhas' original haunts. However, as already noted, the Nāth Siddhas were also an important presence at Kadri in Karnataka; and we know too that their well-traveled network of sacred pilgrimage sites also drew them north into the Himalayas and as far south as Srisailam. In broad terms, the geographical area of convergence between the medieval Nāth Siddhas and Rasa Siddhas covers a region roughly corresponding to the modern Indian states of Rajasthan, Gujarat, Maharashtra, and Karnataka.

a. Srisailam

Our survey begins, however, with Srisailam, perhaps the same site as the Śrīparvata of Buddhist fame around which an early body of alchemical lore concerning Nāgārjuna coalesced. As already mentioned, from the seventh century onwards, a number of temples were dedicated, on or around this peak, to Śiva Siddheśvara. Already mentioned in the sixth-century *Vāsavadattā* (together with the goddess Tārā and the element mercury) as a site at which liberation could be realized, Srisailam was portrayed, in descriptions from two thirteenth- to fourteenth-century Hindu alchemical sources, as an alchemical wonderland.[162] It was also a center for the Pāśupatas, Kāpālikas, and Kālamukhas, three sects that rode the wave of Śaivism that swept Buddhism out of western and southern India, from the seventh century onwards. Indeed, it was these sects that controlled Srisailam down to the twelfth century, at which time they were supplanted or absorbed there by the Vīraśaivas who, under the leadership of Basava, were emerging as an important south India sect, in much the same fashion as were the Nāth Siddhas further to the north.[163] The *jyotirliṅga* named Mallikārjuna, the heart of the Śaiva cultus at Srisailam, was reconsecrated there by the Vīraśaivas.[164]

Following Bāṇabhaṭṭa's seventh-century description of the hydrargyriasic south Indian Śaiva ascetic who, in his mercury-provoked delirium, recounted "thousands of wonderful stories about Śrīparvata," we also encounter references to Kāpālikas from Srisailam in Bhavabhūti's eighth-century *Mālatī Mādhava* and Kṣemīśvara's tenth-century *Caṇḍakauśika*. The former of these is also important inasmuch as it contains the earliest extant Indian literary reference to the yogic physiology of the six *cakra*s and the ten *nāḍī*s; in the latter drama, the Kāpālika hero is cast as a divinized alchemist.[165] Following the twelfth-century advent of Vīraśaivism, alchemical references to Srisailam multiply. The *Vīramāheśvarāgama* maintains that Gorakhnāth was schooled in alchemy, by a Māheśvara Siddha, on the shore of the Tungabhadra River. He, in turn, taught what he had learned to Raseśvara Siddhas in the "Antarvedī" region of Maharashtra.[166] According to the sixteenth-century Telugu *Prabhuliṅgalīla* of Piḍapatti Somanātha Kavi, Gorakhnāth and Nāgārjuna were both initiated into the alchemical art by the Vīraśaiva teacher Allama Prabhu at Srisailam itself.[167] The Tamil Sittars echo the same tradition, tamilizing Gorakh's name to "Korakkar"; and adding that Nāgārjuna established a transmuting (*sparśavedhī*) *liṅga* of Śiva there.[168] According to a work by the Sittar Koṅganar, Korakkar had an animated mercurial pill called "bogi" [*bhogi?*] which, when he held it in his mouth, afforded him the power of flight.[169] He was the author of a work entitled *Korakkar Malai Vagatam* (Korakkar's Mountain Medicines), the lore of which he collected during his life in the Deccan region.[170]

Perhaps influenced by earlier Buddhist traditions, Nityanātha Siddha—who was very likely a Nāth Siddha—states in his *RRĀ* that Nāgārjuna set up an alchemical laboratory on Srisailam.[171] The A.D. 1400 *Navanāthacaritra* of Gauraṇa indicates that Gorakh attained yogic bliss (*yogānanda*) in a cave near a subterranean stream of the Ganges River, somewhere below the sacred peak.[172] The same source has Nāgārjunanāth teaching his son, Siddha Nāgārjuna, the "gold-making" *siddhi* at Srisailam. When the young alchemist sets about to transmute the entire mountain into gold (in an obvious retelling of accounts of the alchemist Nāgārjuna of Buddhist legend) his experiments are halted by Viṣṇu.[173] Here, the alchemical trail from Srisailam ends. What is most troubling is the fact that there exists no hard evidence—geological, chemical, archaeological, or epigraphical—to indicate that mercurial alchemy was ever practiced at Srisailam![174] Inasmuch, however, as it was a hub of Śaiva activity, prior to and following the advent of the Vīraśaivas (whose links with the Māheśvara Siddhas were strong), Srisailam was in fact linked to those regions, to the west and north, in which both alchemical raw materials and expertise were abundant.[175]

b. Maharashtra.

The highly generic *Śrīśailam*, "excellent peak," has been identified, throughout history and across several regional traditions, with a number of mountains of the Indian subcontinent. In addition to the two or even three candidates for this toponym within Andhra Pradesh itself, there have also been peaks called Srisailam in western Uttar Pradesh (at Devalgadh, a hill eighteen kilometers northeast of Srinagar, in Pauri Garhwal district), Kerala,[176] and Maharashtra. The Garhwal toponym is closely connected to Satyanāth who, according to the *Śaṅkaravijaya* of Ānandagiri, conversed with Śaṅkarācārya atop this peak in the Himalayan foothills. The Nāth Siddhas identify this Satyanāth with the Sittar author of twenty-one alchemical works.[177] Elsewhere, the *KJñN* clearly identifies Srisailam with the *pīṭha* of the Goddess at Kāmākhyā; the *KM* locates a *śrīśaila-vana* above the *brahmarandhra* and the four *pīṭhas*; and Siddha Nāgārjuna, in his *KPT*, refers to Śrīparvata as a *kula-parvata* or "clan peak." These three identifications ought, however, like the "Nine Nāths" of the Western Transmission, to be consigned to the realm of the subtle physiology of the bodily microcosm, rather than to the geography of the Indian subcontinent.[178]

Nāth Siddha traditions locate a Maharashtran Srisailam in the vicinity of the upper Godavari River,[179] a region that was, for at least three centuries, an important center of activity for Nāth and Rasa Siddhas alike. It was near the headwaters of the Godavari that Devagiri (modern Daultabad, Aurangabad district, Maharashtra), the capital city of the Yādava kings, was situated.[180] In the centuries prior to the fall of their kingdom to the sultans of Delhi in 1318, the Yādavas appear to have directly patronized all of the groups I have been discussing in this chapter. Bhillama (1175–91), the founder of the dynasty, was the royal patron of Bhāskara, the guru of the Nāgārjuna who authored the *Yogaratnamālā*.[181] Bhillama's successor, Jaiṭugi, was instrumental in introducing Śaivism into the Kathmandu Valley; Jaiṭugi's successor Siṅghaṇa was himself an Ayurvedic physician and a great patron of *vaidya*s and alchemists.[182] Thirty years after his demise, it was during the reign of the Yādava king Rāmacandra (1271–1311) that the Nāth Siddha Jñāneśvara wrote his *Jñāneśvarī* and *Yogisampradāyāviṣkṛti* (*YSĀ*), and that a grant of land was made by that king to the same Nāth order in the Jagalur tāluka of Karnataka in 1279.[183] According to Nāth Siddha tradition, Jñāneśvara's guru Nivṛttināth fully realized his yogic practice at Tryambaka Kṣetra ("Plain of the Three-Eyed [Śiva]"), the source of the Godavari.[184] Gahaṇināth, the disciple of Gorakhnāth and guru of Nivṛttināth in Jñāneśvara's lineage, is mentioned together with "Gorakṣanāth" by Nityanātha in his thirteenth-century alchemical *Rasaratnākara*, an indication that this was a Maharashtran work. The *Tantra Mahārṇava*, possibly a Western Transmission text, maintains that Nāgārjuna hailed from "a forest near the Godavari"; still another states that Gorakh was born on (yet another) Candragiri, on the banks of the Godavari.[185] The Avadhūta subsect of the Nāth Siddhas, said to have been founded by a twelfth- to thirteenth-century figure named Dattātreya, was also originally based in this region; the Dharamnāthi subsect is presently based there.[186]

Another pan-Indian toponym found this region is Kadalī-vana ("Plantain Forest"), which rivals Moon Mountain and Moon Island as the most frequently recurring venue of Nāth Siddha legend. A Plantain Forest, located in the vicinity of Tryambaka Kṣetra[187] corresponds to a toponym found in the *RA:* this is Kadalī-nagara ("Plantain City"), which this text too locates on the Godavari. In fact, in all of the rare cases in which the *RA* gives specific geographical data—most of it on the subject of "magical waters"[188] (hot springs, corrosive mineral waters, poisonous waters, etc.)—the locations it details are clustered around the headwaters of this river; when the discussion is more general, it is locations in southwestern India that predominate. So, for example, this work's Plantain City description states that "in the south . . . is a pure and auspicious river, as renowned as the Ganges, called the Godavari. On its southern shore is a city called Plantain City; to its south is the world-famous mountain called Kṛṣṇagiri ('Black Hill'); nearby is a town called Ambika, where *sañjīvinī jalam* ('resuscitating water') is found."[189]

Yet another *RA* (12.260–62) reference to this region designates a location in the Sahyādri (Vindhya) range to the north of the Godavari as the site of a hot spring (*uṣṇodaka*); a Nāth Siddha source, the *Kadalīmañjunātha Māhātmya*, locates the Plantain Forest on the southern flank of the same range.[190]

This data, together with what appears to be a reference, in the *RRS*, to the author of the *RA* having indirectly passed down the formula for a mineral preparation to Siṅghaṇa—the Yādava king of Devagiri from A.D. 1210 to 1247—make it likely that this, India's most important work on tantric alchemy, was compiled along or near the upper Godavari, albeit prior to the A.D. 1175 founding of the Yādava dynasty.[191]

c. Gujarat

One of the physicians who graced the Yādava court was Bhāskara, who came to Devagiri from Kashmir in the latter half of the twelfth century. Two of Bhāskara's disciples, however, were based in Gujarat. The first of these was his son Soḍhala, who was the author of the an Ayurvedic lexicon entitled *Soḍhalanighaṇṭu*, and the second was Nāgārjuna, who eulogizes this Bhāskara as his teacher in the opening verse of his *Yogaratnamālā*. This same Nāgārjuna may have been the author of the *Kakṣapuṭa Tantra:* both are works on tantric healing and sorcery, and a number of verses, formulae, and colophons in both works are identical.[192] We can be more or less certain of the date of the *Yogaratnamālā* because its important "Laghu Vivṛtti" commentary, written by Śvetāmbara Bhikṣu Guṇākara, is dated to A.D. 1239. While Guṇākara was, as his title indicates, a Jain, he was also very likely a tāntrika (a Jain tantric tradition did indeed exist alongside the Hindu variety) with a knowledge of alchemy. He was also from Gujarat, as evinced in the use he makes of a number of vernacular terms.[193]

Now, Gujarat has long been a stronghold of Jainism in India, and it is here as well that Jain alchemical lore is the most frequently encountered. So, for example, two Śvetāmbara Jain sources, the A.D. 1304 *Prabandha Cintāmaṇi* of Merutuṅga and the A.D. 1349 *Prabandhakośa*, give accounts of a Nāgārjuna who is a *Jain* alchemist, accounts which appear to borrow freely from Buddhist and Hindu lore on his subject. According to the latter work

> Nāgārjuna is born the son of the snake king Vāsuki and the human princess Bhopalā, from Mt. Dhāṅka, [a peak identified with the sacred Jain site of Mt. Śatruñjaya, also in Gujarat], an alchemical wonderland.[194] He grows up to become the preceptor of a Śātavāhana king, but leaves him to go to Paliṭṭanakapura, the city of the Jain wizard Pādalipta.[195] After a series of incidents, Pādalipta accepts him as his student, and instructs him in the preparation of an elixir of immortality (*rasasiddhi*), with the aid of a magical image of the Jain *tīrthaṃkara* Pārśvanātha, and a chaste woman to stir [grind] the po-

> tion. He manages to secure both, and prepares the elixir on the shore of the Sedi River, with the aid of his royal patron's queen Candralekhā. Her two sons kill him before he can benefit from the elixir (but not before he buries some of the elixir on Mt. Śatruñjaya); the site on the Sedi where he made it becomes the Jain pilgrimage site called Stambhana Tīrtha, the "holy site of immobilization," for this is where Nāgārjuna solidified his [mercurial] elixir.[196]

A number of elements found in this legend link it to other sites on the Kathiawar peninsula of Gujarat, as well as to a site in Assam. Mount Śatruñjaya/Dhāṅka was a peak renowned for wells and springs said to contain the elixir of immortality. A mid-fifteenth-century work, the *Śatruñjayakalpa*, relates a story in which a young man learns from a Jain monk of a well of *rasa* at the site, which is only visible to persons who perform religious austerities in front of an image of the Jīna Śantinātha and make a nocturnal offering to a snake goddess named Vairothya. Satisfied by the young man's acts, Vairothya opens the well for him, and he gains the elixir. This account closely resembles a myth from the ca. fourteenth-century *Siṁhāsanadvatriṃśika* (Thirty-two Tales of the Throne), in which King Vikramāditya, by offering his own head to the tantric goddess Kāmākṣī, affords access to a Siddha who has been attempting, without success, to enter into a sealed cave, next to Kāmākhyā *pīṭha*, in which a vessel containing the elixir is hidden.[197]

The second connection concerns the toponym Dhāṅka. According to another Jain source, the A.D. 1277 *Prabhāvakacarita*, Nāgārjuna was born not on a peak named Dhāṅka-Śatruñjaya-Paliṭṭanakapura, but rather in the town of Dhāṅka. On the urging of Dominik Wujastyk, who had been there two years previously, I visited this site in the winter of 1993. A series of caves behind the Śiva Duṅgareśvara temple to the west of this village contain old bas-reliefs and a sculpted image which the local residents say is a representation of Nāgārjuna. It was in these caves that Nāgārjuna would have practiced his alchemy.[198]

A third connection lies in the many mountains that become conflated in the Jain sources. In addition to the three mentioned a moment ago, a fourth, Valabhī-śaila—either another name for the same peak (identified with the modern Palitana, in Bhavnagar district) or another peak in the area—is also reputed to have been a center for Jain alchemy.[199] Valabhipur is the name of a town (twenty-five miles north of Palitana) which, moreover, becomes the focal point for what has to be the most oft-repeated legend in Gujarat. This is the legend of the sudden destruction of a city by fire, through the agency of an angry holy man (often a Nāth Siddha) or in some connection with alchemy. In Kathiawar, the name of the destroyed town is Valabhī; in Kacch, it is called Pattan.

The historical source of the Valabhī version of the story was the sack of the city by Amru ibn Jamāl of the Sind in A.D. 788.[200] Apparently, physical traces of this destruction remained visible for several centuries after the event and gave rise to a body of legend. An early account is that related by Alberuni in the first half of the eleventh century, according to which a merchant who had become fabulously wealthy through the possession of an alchemical touchstone had managed to buy up an entire town, which a king named Vallabha was also eager to own. The merchant entered into an alliance with a "Lord of Almanṣūra," who made a night attack on King Vallabha and destroyed his town.[201] Alberuni concludes: "People say that still in our time there are such traces left in that country as are found in places which were destroyed by an unexpected night attack."[202] At the town of Dhank some one hundred miles to the west of Valabhipur, blackening on certain of the outer facades of Nāgārjuna's caves is identified by the local people as traces of the sack of Valabhī.[203]

Some one hundred miles to the northwest of Dhank, on the southern coast of Kacch, is a town named Mandavi. According to Nāth Siddha legend, a city named Pattan was once located two miles to the north of Mandavi. Unfortunately for Pattan, the Nāth Siddha Dharamnāth, who was on his way east from Peshawar in the fourteenth century, chose to stop near this town and sent two of his fellow Yogis to beg alms there. With a single exception, the hard-hearted people of Pattan gave nothing; and for this, Dharamnāth upset his alms bowl and cursed the people saying, "be fallen [*pāttan*] all the Pattan cities." So it was that all the cities in Kacch bearing this name were swallowed up, together with their inhabitants.[204] (The source of all of these legends may in fact be a *Liṅga Purāṇa* myth of a demon named Jālandhara, in which it is stated that with the fire from his third eye, Śiva destroyed two cities of the Sind, which fell into the ocean.)[205] In his *Kakṣapuṭa Tantra*,[206] Nāgārjuna refers to what appears to be the fall of a city named Pattan; this would further support the theory that he was a Gujarati author.[207]

In about the year 1030, Alberuni indicates that a Nāgārjuna practiced his alchemy some one hundred years before him—i.e., in the early tenth century—at a site north of Somnāth that he calls "Fort Daihak"; this would appear to correspond to the toponym Dhank, which was mentioned a moment ago in the context of Nāgārjuna legends. Now, if a tenth-century Gujarat-based Nāgārjuna indeed wrote a treatise on alchemy, that work has been lost: none of his extant Hindu alchemical works predate the thirteenth century. It is, however, worth noting that the sole text attributed to Nāgārjuna in the Jain canon is a *rasa tantra*.[208] Elsewhere, the Jain equivalent of the Buddhist *Caryāpada*s, the *Pāduha-doha* written by Muni Rāmasiṁha in the Apabhraṃśa vernacular in about the year A.D. 1000, contains an alchemical poem.[209] An untitled anonymous Jain work on Āyurveda, written in Gujarati script, is perhaps the earliest Indian medical work written in a medieval vernacular. It dates from the twelfth century.[210] These vernacular works aside, a number of major Hindu alchemical works, written in the Sanskrit medium and straddling the line between tantric alchemy and therapeutic alchemy, are Gujarati productions. The most important of these are the twelfth- to thirteenth-century *Rasendracūḍāmaṇi* of Somadeva, a resident of (the lost Gujarati city of) Bhairavapura; and the thirteenth-century *Rasaprakāśa Sudhākara* of Yaśodhara Bhaṭṭa, who hailed from Junagadh.[211]

Surat, on the Saurashtra coast of Gujarat, has long been a center for the manufacture of synthetic cinnabar, through the sublimation of imported mercury with native sulfur. Gujarat moreover continues to be a leader in alchemy and Ayurvedic *rasa śāstra*, down to the present century. The Goṇḍal Rasāyanśāla (Gondal, Rajkot district) was, throughout the first half of this century, a center for the edition of the major alchemical texts by the resident *vaidya*, Yādavjī Trikamjī Ācārya. It was at the Gujarat Ayurved University in Jamnagar that the first critical edition and translation of the *Caraka Saṁhitā* was compiled; and at the same site that alchemical gold was most recently synthesized, in 1968. Many of India's greatest present-day specialists in *rasa śāstra* have received their training there from Professor Hari Shankar Sharma.[212]

Some twenty minutes by scooter rickshaw to the south of Junagadh is the magnificent peak of Girnar which, according to the A.D. 1333 *Vividhatīrthakalpa* of Jīnaprabhāsuri and the *Skanda Purāṇa*, is also a site abounding in mercurial pools (*rasa-kūpika*) and alchemical miracles.[213] Girnar is also a peak abounding in Jain temples, as well as caves and crags sacred to the Nāth Siddhas, and, to all appearances, the two groups have been enjoying a symbiotic relationship there for centuries. Girnar is dotted with shrines to a number of important Nāth Siddhas (Gorakh, Dattātreya, Bhartṛhari, Gopīcand), and has been an important pilgrimage site for the order since at least the thirteenth century; the site is already mentioned by

Hsuan-tsang, in connection with "supernatural *ṛṣis*," by which Pāśupatas of the sort described by his contemporary Bāṇabhaṭṭa are likely intended.[214] The beautiful Jain temples located on its southern flank date from the thirteenth century, but Jains may well have been there from an earlier date as well. Gujarat is also a region with a relatively high concentration of Nāth Siddhas, who have monasteries and temples throughout the state.[215]

d. Rajasthan

Another western Indian site at which one finds a similar sort of symbiosis between Nāth Siddhas and Jains is the equally ancient sacred site of Arbuda Devī (Mount Abu, Sirohi district, Rajasthan), located some 250 miles to the northeast of Girnar as the Siddha flies. Like Girnar, Abu has an alchemical reputation: in the early stages of my fieldwork, I was assured by Yogi Narharināth, abbot of the Caughera monastery (in the Dang Valley of the inner Terai region of Nepal) and the most illustrious Nāth Siddha scholar of our time, that I would find living, practicing alchemists at that site.[216] In fact there is a curious symmetry between Girnar and Abu, beginning with the fact that both are located on east-west ridges comprising a series of three peaks. At the base of both pilgrimage routes, one encounters Nāth establishments called "[Gorakh] Ṭileti."[217] From these, the pilgrim's west-to-east progress first passes through the Jain temple complexes, followed by shrines devoted to the Hindu goddess Ambā (on the first peak) and other mainstream Hindu deities; on the second peak is a Nāth shrine (Gorakh at Girnar; Gopīcand at Abu);[218] and both pilgrimage routes terminate or culminate, at their easternmost points, at sites identified with Dattātreya. This last peak is called Guru Śikhara, the "Guru's Pinnacle," at Abu, while it is simply called Dattātreya at Girnar. So too, the central peak at Girnar is referred to not as *Gorakh kī Dhūnī* (Gorakhnāth's Fireplace), which is technically more exact, but simply as Gorakhnāth.

The reason for these Girnar toponyms goes back, I believe, to the archaic Buddhist and Hindu cults of *divine* Siddhas and Vidyādharas, who were denizens not only of the atmospheric regions, but also, in the Hindu popular imagination, of mountaintops. The Girnar peaks of Gorakhnāth and Dattātreya are so called not because they feature shrines to these Nāth Siddhas, but because they *are* these Siddhas.[219] In fact, one might quite aptly summarize the legacy of the Nāth Siddhas by calling theirs a conquest of high places. From identifications with the Siddhas and Vidyādharas identified with such heights, to Pāśupata spells to gain power over the same Vidyādharas, to the yogic cultivation of the power of flight (*khecara*), to the claim they have laid to the high places of the Indian subcontinent, to the widespread practice of using cannabis as a means to "getting high,"[220] the Nāth Siddhas have always been upward bound.

The Jain temples at Abu and Girnar alike feature massive images of Nemīnātha (in black stone) and Pārśvanātha, who are considered to have been the twenty-second and twenty-third *tīrthaṃkaras* of that faith. It will be recalled that it was a miraculous image of the former that was employed by Nāgārjuna to produce an alchemical elixir in the Jain legend recounted in the *Prabandhakośa*. Pārśvanāth's name can in fact be simply read as "Lord of the Touchstone" (*pārśva*, *pāras*), making the alchemical connection an obvious one. There is another dimension, however to this figure and his successor, which moreover aids us in understanding the apparent Jain–Nāth Siddha symbiosis encountered at Abu and Girnar. This is the body of Nāth legend that transforms Pārśva and Nemī into Nāth Siddha sons of Matsyendra. In a variant on the classic myth of Matsyendra's brush with death in the form of sexual dissipation in the Kingdom of Women in Assam, Matsyendra becomes a king in Siṁhala (generally identified with Sri Lanka), and fathers two sons, Pārśvanāth (or Pārasnāth) and Nemīnāth (or Nīmnāth). In a classic ruse, Gorakh seeks to "disenchant" Matsyendra by killing the two boys, skinning them, and hanging their hides out to dry. When Matsyendra grieves for his sons, Gorakh decries his attachment to the gross bodily husk and revives the two boys. Matsyendra returns to the yogic path and initiates his sons as Nāth Siddhas. They become the founders of the Nīmnāthi and Pārasnāthi *panths*, the two Jain suborders of the Nāth *sampradāya*.[221] In such a syncretistic milieu, we should not be surprised to find Hindu and Jain alchemists exchanging expertise with one another or Hindu and Jain sectarians sharing sacred mountains.

There also exist historical connections between the two sites, connections which account in part for the significant numbers of Marwari and Mewari Hindus who travel to Girnar and of Gujarati Hindus who come to Abu (of course, Jains from both regions circulate between the two sites as well). Southeastern Rajasthan and Gujarat are linked, both culturally and linguistically, in a number of ways that point to a common historical legacy. This legacy dates back to the time of the Maitraka kings of Valabhī. According to legend,[222] when Valabhī was sacked and Silāditya VI, its last ruler, slain, his queen, Puṣpavatī, was returning to the capital from a pilgrimage to Ambā Bhavanī, in her native land of Candravatī, a short distance to the south of Abu.[223] Great with child, she hid herself in a cave in the mountains of Malia to give birth to a son. She then committed suttee. Her son, raised by a foster mother, was named Guha, "Cave-Born." The child, who grew up among the aboriginal Bhils of nearby Idar (Sabarakantha district, Gujarat)—in the Rajasthan-Gujarat border region—was later elected to be their king. So it was that he became the founder of the Guhilot (from Guha) clan, the family of the future Rānās of Mewar.[224] Ninth in line from Guha was Bāppā ("father") Rāwal, who, according to the fifteenth-century *Ekaliṅga Māhātmya*, founded the kingdom of Mewar in A.D. 728 and the Ekliṅgjī temple (fourteen miles north of his capital of Udaipur). In fact, there is no extant epigraphical mention of Bāppā Rāwal prior to the A.D. 971 Ekliṅgjī inscription of Naravāhana.[225]

The *Ekaliṅga Māhātmya* and a number of other legends further associate Bāppā Rāwal with sectarian forerunners of the Nāth Siddhas. According to these sources, the young Bāppā, forced to live in forest exile after the slaying of his father Nāgāditya by the Bhils,[226] encounters an itinerant Śaivite ascetic named Hārīta Rāśi, who accepts him as his disciple. Hārīta Rāśi agrees to initiate Bāppā into his Śaiva order and thereby imbue him with immortality and supernatural powers. But when Bāppā comes to the appointed initiation site, the ascetic has already begun an ascent to the atmospheric realms. Before rising out of sight, however, he spits down upon his disciple, commanding Bāppā to receive his expectorate in his mouth. "Bāppā showed his disgust and aversion by blinking, and the projected blessing fell on his foot, by which squeamishness he obtained only invulnerability by weapons instead of immortality."[227] With these, he grows up to defeat his father's slayers and become the founder of the Mewar kingdom. As I show in chapter ten, this common theme of Śaivite and Nāth Siddha legend has important philosophical and practical implications.

Legend has it that another itinerant ascetic whom Bāppā met in his wanderings in the wilds of Udaipur, and who gave him a two-edged sword with which to defeat his enemies, was none other than Gorakhnāth. Of course, this is chronologically impossible. However, inscriptional and numismatic evidence supports the Ekliṅgjī temple's claims to antiquity and Bāppā's connection with the Śaivas of his time. A gold coin from the time of his reign is inscribed with the words *Śrī Voppa* on the obverse, together with a trident, a Śiva *liṅga*, and a bull; below is the image of a man, prostrate, having large pierced ears, the holes exaggerated.[228] As such, this seal would appear to be a representation of Bāppā's initiation, featuring the ear boring that has so long been identified with the Nāth Siddhas. Given the chronology, however, it is far more likely that Bāppā's ear-boring initiation was performed by a Pāśupata. This is further supported by the name of his initiator: *Rāśi* was a common name ending among the Pāśupatas.[229] It is certain, however, that the custodianship of the temple passed through the hands of the Nāth Siddhas before being given over to the Rāmānandīs in the sixteenth century.[230]

Following his initiation, Bāppā assumed the title of "Rāwal" (from the Sanskrit, *rāja-kula*, "royal lineage") whence the name by which he is known to history: Bāppā Rāwal. According to Hazari Prasad Dvivedi, Rāwal was, already in the eighth century, a clan name proper to the Pāśupatas which, in the thirteenth century, became the third of the old Śaivite clans absorbed into the Nāth *sampradāya*. The Rāwals have, in the course of the intervening centuries, become transformed into a Muslim suborder, based for the most part in Pakistan and Afghanistan.[231] These were "great wanderers" (they give the Persian *rawinda*, "wanderer," as the etymological root of their name), who were to be found peddling quack medicines and other wares of a dubious nature in nineteenth-century Europe and who continue to sell their services as hail stoppers in Kumaon, where they are called Oliyas, "hail men." Rāwals are also based in Andhra Pradesh, Himachal Pradesh (Jwālamukhī), and Hariyana (Asthal Bohar).

As a suborder, the Rāwals are closely associated with the Dharamnāthis, Satnāthis, Pāgalpanthis, and Pārasnāthis.[232] They are also known as Nāgnāthis, by virtue of which fact they are said to bear some connection to the Nāth Siddha known as Arjun Nāga or Nāgārjuna, whose suborder is based at Jwālamukhī in the Kangra district of Himachal Pradesh. If only by virtue of his name, this figure is identified as an alchemist. Elsewhere, Gorakh refers to an unnamed Rāwal Yogi as an alchemist in one of his *bānī*s.[233] Nāgnāth, the legendary founder of the Rāwal suborder, is said to have been a disciple of Gorakh; since, however, this clan was originally Pāśupata, it predates Gorakhnāth by several centuries. Another early Nāth Siddha hailing from the present-day region of Himachal Pradesh is Carpaṭi, who is said to be the disciple of Matsyendranāth. A historical Carpaṭi is named in a tenth-century *vaṃśāvali* from Camba, and his *samādhi* is located at Chambādevī (Chamba district), to the north of Jwālamukhī.[234] Jwālamukhī was already a pilgrimage site in the time of the *Mahābhārata*;[235] at present, the Nāth Siddhas control a subsidiary shrine—a miraculous pool of cold boiling water—at the site.[236]

Today, it is the Nāgnāthi-Rāwals who accompany pilgrims to the far-flung western *pīṭha* known as Hiṅglāj Devī (Las Bela district, Baluchisthan,

Pakistan).[237] A gas vent and "fireplace of Gorakhnāth" are maintained there down to the present day.[238] In spite of the inaccessibility of her original worship site, Hiṅglāj Devī remains an important goddess for Hindus in western India, and temples consecrated to her are found throughout this region.

Tradition links Pāśupata forerunners of the Nāth Siddhas with the founding of yet another dynasty in western Rajasthan. These were the Rāwal kings of Jaisalmer.[239] According to the bardic chroniclers who were the informants of Colonel James Tod, the founding of this dynasty occurred in the following fashion:

> Deorāj [b. A.D. 836], the future founder of the Rāwal dynasty, is a prince without a kingdom. One day, he is visited by a Jogi named Rita who bestows upon him the title of *Sid[dha]*. Rita, who possesses the art of transmuting metals, one day goes away, but leaves his tattered cloak [*jarjari-kantha*] behind. Inside the folds of this cloak is Rita's elixir vessel [*rasa kumbha*], from which a drop falls upon Deorāj's dagger, turning it to gold. Deorāj decamps with the elixir vessel, and uses it to raise an army and the walls of a fortified city. Rita is well aware of the theft, and later comes to visit Deorāj in order to legitimate the latter's possession of his stolen property. This he does on the condition, however, that Deorāj become his disciple and, as a token of his submission and fidelity, adopt the external signs of his order. He gives him the ochre robes of his order, places the earrings (*mudrā*) in his ears, the little horn [*siṅgnād*] around his neck, and loincloth [*laṅgoti*] about his loins; in this garb, and with gourd in hand, Deorāj then perambulates around the dwellings of his kin, exclaiming *alakh! alakh!* Then, having exacted that these sectarian rites of initiation should be continued to the latest posterity, Rita disappears. Thereafter, the title of Rao was abandoned for that of Rāwal.[240]

If this account is historically accurate, then the ninth-century western Rajasthani forerunners of the Nāth Siddhas were already Nāth Siddhas in everything but name. The *jarjari-kantha*, *mudrā*s, *siṅgnād*, and use of the expression *alakh* ("attributeless," an apophatic description of the absolute) are all hallmarks of the sect. If it contains elements from a later time than it purports to describe, it nevertheless portrays the Nāth Siddhas as wonder-working king-making alchemists.[241] Given the chronology, Deorāj's itinerant Yogi Rita would, like Bāppā Rāwal's H*ārīta*, have been a Pāśupata rather than a Nāth Siddha.

FIVE

Tantric and Siddha Alchemical Literature

In an important theoretical work written in 1981, Marcel Detienne argues that "raw myth," if such a thing ever existed, would have taken the form of lists or catalogues of names, lists from which generally oral native *exegesis* would have subsequently generated genealogies or lineages, and which written *interpretation* would later have transformed, from the vantage point created by the act of writing, into mythology. The myth, fragile and evanescent, is metamorphosed into something else as soon as it is recounted. Therefore, for all intents and purposes, the myth does not exist: it is rather mythology, the exegesis and interpretation of myth that scholars study, whether they be located "inside" or "outside" the tradition in question.[1] With the lists of Rasa and Nāth Siddhas that grounded our discussion in the preceding chapter, we seemed to find ourselves in the gray area between the ground zero of myth (catalogues of names) and the first impulse of native exegesis, i.e., the organization of list into lineage. We also witnessed the written interpretation, and thus the transformation of these original "myths" into mythology, in the legends of the eighty-four Mahāsiddhas; the creative appropriation, in chapter four of the *RM*, of certain of the names figuring in the Rasa Siddha lists; and the proliferation of mythology generated by the multiple lists of the Nine Nāths. By reading between the lines of these mythologies, I attempted to glean a certain number of elements to aid in reconstructing a history of the medieval Siddha traditions. In the present chapter, I attempt to effect a similar hermeneutics of retrieval, this time through a survey of the alchemical literature.

1. General Survey of Alchemical Literature in the Sanskrit Medium

Of what value are the Rasa Siddha lists for anyone who would attempt to reconstruct the history of Hindu alchemy? Nearly half of the names on the early lists (*RM; RRS* [a]; *RRĀ*) appear to be so many *voyageurs sans baggages*, with either no alchemical texts, attributions, or citations connected to their names in later sources, or, at best, unverifiable references in this or that solitary source.[2] Many appear to simply be the names of gods. As we have already noted, Ādima (1) is none other than a variant on Ādideva or Ādinātha, the Lord of Beginnings. Śambhu (11), Brahmā (24) and Hari (27) are the three gods of the so-called Hindu trinity. Ratnaghośa (10) is a Buddhist figure, while Kambali (16) and Nāgabodhi (20) are names carried over from the Buddhist Mahāsiddha lists. These would appear to be names of figures classified as divine or semidivine Siddhas.[3]

Another group of names are so many black holes in an alchemical void. Who were Viśārada ("Skilled"), Matta ("Intoxicated"), Ekaratna ("One Jewel"), Indrada ("Gift of Indra"), Surānanda ("Joy of the Gods"), and Khaṇḍa ("Portion")? Were they teachers of known alchemists and as such mute links in lost alchemical lineages? If they were authors of alchemical works, were their works lost to or simply disregarded by all later alchemical authors? Or have their works and the works of later authors who may have cited them all been lost? Indeed, certain south Indian historians of alchemy maintain that all of the major alchemical works were originally committed to writing in the medieval Grantha script of Tamil Nadu and that certain of these were never transliterated into the north Indian Devanagari script. As evidence, they note the fact that many south Indian alchemical works cite alchemical sources of which north Indian traditions ignore the existence.[4] Another possibility is that these were individuals whose teachings were oral, rather than written; or that these were people who were living exemplars of the alchemical arts. Such persons may be living, even today, in bodies immortalized through the use of mercurial preparations. Or, like the Zawgyi alchemists of Burma, they may have lived fast, died young, and left good-looking corpses (for mercury does indeed tend to "pickle" one's epidermis, in life and after a premature death), prior to realizing a certain modicum of immortality in the Rasa Siddha lists.

The most likely explanation is that these unaccountable names, like so many of the "begats" of the Old Testament, were fillers in "systematic genealogies" that manuscript copyists dutifully passed on to posterity for the simple reason that copyists copy. Or again, they were names that filled the lotus petals of so many lost alchemical worship *maṇḍala*s. Elsewhere, my remarks concerning the interplay between divine and human Siddhas and Vidyādharas appear to be apposite: a number of the Rasa Siddhas were gods whose divine works have yet to be revealed to humanity. Whatever the case, I will follow the lead of the tantric and Siddha alchemical authors themselves and generally disregard those Rasa Siddhas whose names they but rarely mention, save in the lists reviewed in the last chapter.

A number of names from the early lists appear to correspond to authors of various works. Candrasena (2) is said to be the author of a lost work entitled *Rasacandrodaya.*[5] Laṅkeśa (3) is generally identified with Rāvaṇa—Laṅka's Lord (*laṅka-īśa*)—who authored the *Kumāra Tantra*, an early and important text on the treatment of childhood diseases, and whose daughters are said, in the tenth- to eleventh-century Tamil *Irāmāvatāram* of Kampaṉ, to be the wives of the eighteen Tamil Sittars.[6] Māṇḍavya (7) is the name of an Ayurvedic teacher cited by Vāgbhaṭṭa the Elder in the *Aṣṭāṅga Saṃgraha* and the author of a lost alchemical work entitled *Rasavāridhi.* He is also cast, in a passage from the fourth chapter of the *RM*,[7] as a conversation partner to Nāgārjuna and [co-]author of a work entitled *Vasiṣṭamāṇḍavya.* (As we have already indicated, however, the historicity of many of the figures introduced as alchemists in the *RM*—including Ratnaghośa [10] and Nāgabodhi [20][8]—is doubtful). Somadeva, the twelfth- to thirteenth-century Gujarati author of the *Rasendracūḍāmaṇi* [*RC*],[9] mentions Bhāskara (8) and Śambhu (11), but gives no details on who they were or what they wrote.[10] Since Somadeva was himself from Gujarat, however, the Bhāskara he invokes may well have been the guru of the twelfth- to thirteenth-century Nāgārjuna who authored the *Yogaratnamālā.* Śūrasena (9) is purportedly the author of the lost *Rasendrasuraprabhāva*, Naravāhana (13) that of the lost *Rasānandakautuka*, and Lampaṭa that of the equally lost *Lampaṭa Tantra.*[11]

It is with the names that appear in the latter portions of the older lists, as well as a number of names from the later lists (*RRS* [b] and [c]), that we appear to move from the realm of legend into that of textual history: many correspond to known authors of often extant alchemical texts. As was mentioned in the last chapter, Vyāḍi (17) is an alchemist whose legend was known to the eleventh-century Alberuni and two of whose alchemical works were translated into Tibetan in the *Tanjur.* In addition, the *Garuḍa Purāṇa* praises Vyāḍi as an authority on gemstones.[12] Nāgārjuna's (18) alchemical pedigree is solid: we will return to him shortly. Govinda (25) is the name of the author of the ca. tenth- to eleventh-century *RHT*, very likely the earliest extant Hindu alchemical tantra. Carpaṭi—the figure whose name appears the most often, after Nāgārjuna, in lists of both Nāth and Rasa Siddhas, is the author of two short post-fourteenth-century vernacular alchemical works, entitled *Carpaṭ Rasāyan* and *Carpaṭ Nāth jī ke ślok*—as well as of two lost Sanskrit works, entitled *Svargavaidyakāpālika* and *Carpaṭi-siddhānta*. Conclusive textual evidence (a local *vaṃśāvalī*; and the *Grub thob*, which names him as Vyāḍi's guru)[13] indicates that a Carpaṭi lived in the kingdom of Camba (Himachal Pradesh) in the tenth century; if this figure was the author of the two Sanskrit alchemical works mentioned above, he would have been one of the earliest of the Hindu alchemists.[14] Carpaṭi is also the subject of alchemical legend in both Tibetan Buddhist and south Indian traditions and is cast as an alchemist in a Sikh work, the *Prāṇ Saṅkalī*.[15]

By far the biggest name-dropper among the alchemical authors was Somadeva, whose *RC* was mentioned a moment ago. In addition to naming Bhāskara, Śambhu, Govinda, and Nāgārjuna, he also mentions Nandi (no. 30 in the *RRS* [a] and [c] lists) and Bhāluki (no. 38 in the *RRS* [a] list), as well as Manthānabhairava, Svacchandabhairava, Bhairavācārya, Śrīkaṇṭha, and others. Śrīkaṇṭha, whose name appears in none of the lists passed in review here, is simply another name for Śiva: the Pāśupata teachings were revealed to Lakulīśa by Śrikaṇṭha (or Nīlakaṇṭha). He is cast as codiscussant (with the goddess Umā) in an alchemical work that has recently been edited under the title of *Gorakṣa Saṃhitā:* it is likely to this work that Somadeva is referring.[16] Although Manthānabhairava (no. 32 in *RRS* [a] and [c]) does not appear in the Rasa Siddha list of the *RM*, this work mentions him elsewhere and, after the fashion of nearly every other post-eleventh-century alchemical work, describes an elixir called *manthānabhairava rasa*. According to P. V. Sharma, Manthānabhairava would have been the author of the *Ānandakanda* (*ĀK*) and personal physician to the king of Siṁhala (Sri Lanka?). I have found no evidence to support this claim. On the one hand, the *ĀK* as a text is at least a century younger than any of the references to Manthānabhairava found in other tantric alchemical works; on the other, the *ĀK*'s chapter colophons state that it was revealed by Mahābhairava.[17] The eleventh- to twelfth-century *Manthānabhairava Tantra* is, however, one of the most important works of the Western Transmission, and one that is moreover linked to the *Gorakṣa Saṃhitā*.[18] As we will see shortly, a *RM* reference to a text entitled *Manthānabhairava* may be a clue to the presence of an eponymous figure in the Rasa Siddha lists.

Apart from the *ĀK*, three other important tantric alchemical works are also cast as divine revelations transmitted by human authors who chose to remain anonymous. One of these presents us with no problems, however. This is the *Kākacaṇḍeśvarīmata* (*KCM*), a text revealed by Śiva to Kākacaṇḍeśvarī—the "Fierce Crow[-faced] Goddess"—and clearly the text attributed to the alchemical author Kākacaṇḍīśvara (no. 33 in *RRS* [a] and [c]).[19] The two other such works are more problematic. The *Rasopaniṣat* (*RU*) is, according to Siddhinandan Misra, the work of a certain Kāpālika master, which evokes the name "Kāpālika," the twenty-fourth Rasa Siddha in the *RM/RRS* [a] lists. In its first chapter, the *Rasopaniṣat* itself states that it is nothing other than an abridgement, in eighteen chapters, of an earlier work, in twenty-nine chapters, entitled the *Mahodadhi*.[20] Now, there is a tradition according to which a certain Kapālī (no. 5 in the *RM/RRS*[a] list) authored an alchemical work entitled *Rasarāja-mahodadhi*. If this is the case, then the *Rasopaniṣat* author who epitomized the *Mahodadhi* in his work could have been a "Kāpālika"—i.e., a follower of Kapālī rather than a member of the "skull-bearer" Śaiva sect—or both. A lost work, simply entitled *Mahodadhi*, is attributed to a certain Śivanāth Yogi; if this is the work to which the *Rasopaniṣat* refers, then Misra's theory is untenable (unless Śivanāth Yogi was a Kāpālika).[21]

The last work in this group is the most tantalizing of all, given that the anonymous *Rasārṇava* is truly the summum of tantric alchemy. According to P. V. Sharma, the history of this text is intimately connected to a Yādava king named Siṅghaṇa (1210–47), who was one in a series of great royal patrons of the medical and alchemical arts.[22] Sharma maintains that a certain "Bhairavānanda Yogi"—whom the *RRS* (16.126) names as having indicated (*vinirdiṣṭā*) a preparation called the "Lokanātha packet" (*poṭali*) to a King Siṅghaṇa—was the author of the *RA*. Three manuscript copies of the *RA*, held by the Anup Sanskrit Library in Bikaner, carry the following colophon: "thus concludes Īśvara's alchemical dialogue . . . the great treatise [entitled] *Rasārṇava* . . . [as] uttered by Yogānanda."[23] By metathesizing the two components of this latter name, one arrives at Ānanda-yoga. The work is, moreover, cast as a dialogue between Bhairava and Bhairavī: by juxtaposing the name of the divine revealer of this work to that of the figure who recounted it, one could conceivably generate the name Bhairava-ānanda-yog[i]. If, however, we accept Sharma's argument that the Bhairavānanda Yogi who indicated an Ayurvedic preparation to Siṅghaṇa was also the author of the *RA*, this pushes the date of this work forward to the early thirteenth century, which is chronologically impossible.[24] The *RRS* passage cited by Sharma, which concerns a preparation called the Vaiśvānara packet, states that "this preparation was declared by king Siṅghaṇa . . . Its application is known [to be the same as that of] Siṅghaṇa's packet called Lokanātha, which was handed down (*vinirdiṣṭā*) by Bhairavānanda Yogi." The operative term here is "handed down": the *vi-* prefix here indicates that the Bhairavānanda Yogi who handed down this alchemical preparation was not a contemporary of Siṅghaṇa.[25] It is moreover curious that the preparation the *RRS* attributes to Bhairavānanda Yogi is nowhere to be found in the *RA*. As I will demonstrate, the *RA* is an eleventh-century text. It therefore follows that its author is not to be identified with the figure to whom Siṅghaṇa attributes the invention of this preparation. The author of the *RA* would more likely have lived under the imperial predecessors of the Yādavas, i.e., the Cālukyas of Kālyāṇī, whose tenth- through twelfth-century kingdom covered most of the same western territory of India as did that of the Yādavas.[26]

It is much easier to simply identify the *RA* with its divine revealer, which is what I believe Somadeva does when he refers to "Bhairavācārya" and what Vāgbhaṭṭa II (*RRS* [a] and [c]) does when he lists Bhairava as its twenty-ninth Rasa Siddha. The evidence of the *RRS* lists is all the more compelling for the fact that the Rasa Siddha whose name immediately precedes that of Bhairava is Rasāṅkuśa: throughout the *RA*, Bhairava describes the worship of his own and the Goddess's alchemical forms. Whereas he is called Rasabhairava, the "Mercurial Bhairava," she is always referred to as Rasāṅkuśī, the "Elephant Goad of Mercury." It follows that the two should appear together in the Rasa Siddha lists.[27]

The *RRS* ([a] and [c]) also lists a third Bhairava—named Svacchandabhairava—as a Rasa Siddha (no. 31). This figure is cited as an alchemical author in the thirteenth-century *RPS* of Yaśodhara Bhaṭṭa and the sixteenth-century *Rasakalpa*.[28] In its chapter colophons, the so-called alchemical *Gorakṣa Saṁhitā* calls itself (among other things) the *Svacchanda-śaktyavatāra* ([The Revelation] Brought Down by Svacchanda Śakti). A number of references are made in this text to the cult of Svacchanda (Bhairava), and the opening chapter intimates that this is an abridgment of a greater alchemical work in twenty-five thousand verses originally revealed by Svacchanda.[29] As already noted, however, this work is a dialogue between Śrīkaṇṭha and the goddess Umā. Moreover, in the final verses of a number of manuscripts of this work, the "Nāth [named] Gorakṣa" is mentioned.[30] Like Manthānabhairava, and Bhairava *tout court*, Svacchandabhairava is first and foremost the name of an important tantric divinity;

and a number of important tantric texts, including the massive *Svacchanda Tantra* (*SvT*), quite naturally bear his name.[31] It is therefore uncertain whether this Rasa Siddha was a human alchemist or an alchemists' god. Indeed, the alchemical god Rasabhairava, whose iconography is described in the *RA* (2.63–64), is an ectype of Svacchanda Bhairava.[32]

With this, we return to "signed" alchemical works. Rasendratilaka Yogi (no. 37 in *RRS* [c]) is the name of the author of the *Rasasāratilaka*. Vāsudeva (no. 42 in *RRS* [c]) is the purported author of the lost *Rasasarveśvara*.[33] The name Kriyātantrasamucchayī (no. 43 in *RRS* [c]), literally the "Compiler of the Kriyā Tantra," is likely a reference to the ninth- to tenth-century *Kriyākālaguṇottara Tantra*, an early work on tantric sorcery and healing. This work is, however, revealed by the ubiquitous Śrīkaṇṭha.[34] Śrīnātha, who doubles with Śrīkaṇṭha as the divine revealer of the Western Transmission texts, is also the purported author of an alchemical work entitled the *Rasaratna*. This work has also been attributed to Manthānabhairava.[35] Ghoḍā Colī (no. 55 in *RRS* [c]) is the author of a short Sanskrit alchemical work entitled *Ghoḍā Colī*, or *Ghoḍācolī Vākya*.[36] He is also identified with Colīnāth, the founder of the Āī *panth*, one of the original twelve Nāth suborders.[37] We have already noted the south Indian traditions concerning Allama Prabhu (also known as Prabhudeva, no. 52 in *RRS* [c]), a founder of the Vīraśaiva sect and considered, in Tamil traditions, to be an incarnation of the alchemist Nandi.[38]

Ratnākara and Nityanātha (nos. 36 and 48 in *RRS* [c]) may be one and the same figure: Nityanātha is the author of the thirteenth-century *Rasaratnākara*, the same text from which Vāgbhaṭṭa II would have copied his second ([b] = *RRS* 6.51–53) list of Rasa Siddhas verbatim. The fifth division of the *RRĀ*, entitled "Siddha Khaṇḍa" or "Mantra Khaṇḍa," is the manifest source of the *KPT* of Siddha Nāgārjuna, a work on tantric sorcery.[39] Like the "Mantra Khaṇḍa," the *Śabaracintāmaṇi*, which treats mainly of tantric sorcery, is also a work of Nityanātha Siddha, "son of Pārvatī"; in it, the author states that the teachings of his work were originally expounded by Matsyendra.[40] In addition to being listed as a Rasa Siddha in the *RRS*, Nityanātha is also listed, in the *HYP* (no. 19), as one of the yogic Siddhas who had "broken Time's rod." Was Nityanātha, as his name and his writings would seem to indicate, a Nāth Siddha? Chances are that he was. Certain manuscript colophons to the *Siddha Siddhānta Paddhati*, generally attributed to Gorakh, call it a work of Nityanātha Siddha.[41] If this is the case, then Nityanātha, whose *RRĀ* is dated to the thirteenth century, was a Nāth Siddha polymath who, not unlike his near contemporary Gorakh, would have been well versed in the alchemical, yogic, and tantric disciplines. It may be, on the other hand, that Nityanātha Siddha and Nityanātha, son of Pārvatī, were two distinct persons, in which case the double listing—as Nityanātha *and* "Ratnākara" in the *RRS* [c]—would be an accurate one.

The authors of approximately half of the major extant tantric alchemical works are found to correspond to names figuring in the Rasa Siddha lists. These texts are the *Rasahṛdaya Tantra* of Govinda, the *Kākacaṇḍeśvarīmata* and *Kākacaṇḍīśvara Kalpa Tantra* attributed to Kākacaṇḍīśvara, the *Rasendra Maṅgala* of Nāgārjuna, the *Bhūtiprakaraṇa* (or *Svacchandaśaktyavatāra* or *Gorakṣa Saṁhitā*) attributed to Gorakṣa, and the *Rasaratnākara* of Nityānātha.

Major extant alchemical texts by authors whose names do not figure in the Rasa Siddha lists all date from the thirteenth century or later and decrease in the originality of their content with the passing centuries. Moreover, following a paradigm shift that occurred in the thirteenth to fourteenth century, the content of most of these later works tends to shade from an emphasis on tantric elixir alchemy towards either therapeutic or purely transmutational ends. These works include the ca. 13th-century *Rasendracūḍāmaṇi* of Somadeva, *Rasaprakāśa Sudhākara* of Yaśodhara Bhaṭṭa,[42] and *Rasapaddhati* of Bindu;[43] the 13th- to 14th-century *Rasaratnasamucchaya* of Vāgbhaṭṭa II and *Rasādhyāya* of Kaṅkāla Yogī;[44] the 14th-century *Rasarājalakṣmi* and *Rasasindhu* of Viṣṇudeva or Viṭṭhala;[45] 14th- to 15th-century *Rasasāra* of Govindācārya;[46] the 15th-century *Rasaratnadīpika* of Rāmarāja;[47] the 15th-century *Rasacintāmaṇi* of Anantadeva Sūri;[48] the 15th-century *Rasendracintāmaṇi* of Ḍhuṇḍhukanātha;[49] the 15th-century *Rasasaṅketakālikā* of Camuṇḍakāyastha;[50] the 15th- to 16th-century *Śivakalpadruma* of Śivanātha;[51] the 15th- to 16th-century *Rasarājaśiromaṇi* of Paraśurāma;[52] the 16th-century *Rasakalpa*, *Pāradakalpa*, *Gandhakakalpa*, and *Dhātukalpa* (all of which spuriously claim to be portions of the *Rudrayāmala Tantra*, and authored by Nāgārjuna)[53] and *Rasapradīpa* of Prāṇanātha;[54] and the 17th-century *Rasendrakalpadruma* of Rāmakṛṣṇabhaṭṭa.[55] The reader will have noted that a significant number of these texts are the work of authors whose names end in *Yogi* or *Nāth*. There is, however, little or no internal evidence to indicate that any of these—with the possible exceptions of the *RRĀ* of Nityanātha and the *Rasendracintāmaṇi* of Ḍhuṇḍhukanātha—were in fact the work of Nāth Siddhas.

In addition to these works on Hindu alchemy, a number of other sources lend an important place to alchemy, even though their main subject matter is of another order. So, for example, we find a sizable corpus of works on tantric sorcery—works that may be classified under the general heading of Kriyā Tantras—which include chapters on or references to alchemical preparations and procedures.[56] The earliest of these is the *Kriyākālaguṇottara Tantra*, a work dating from the ninth to tenth century. This text, which takes the form of a dialogue between Śrīkaṇṭha (identified with Śiva) and Kārttikeya, is a work on tantric healing through the use of mantras, amulets, rituals and sorcery.[57] Another later work, the *Yogaratnāvali* of a Śaiva master named Śrīkaṇṭha Śiva, is a so-called "poison tantra" dating from perhaps the fifteenth century. Its sixth chapter contains alchemical data.[58] From the same period is another work on tantric sorcery, the *Kautukacintāmaṇi* of Pratāpadeva, which contains a significant amount of data on generally "magical" alchemy—potions for invisibility, magical flight, attraction, projection, etc.[59]

Two texts dating from the twelfth to thirteenth century—the *KPT* and the shorter *Yogaratnamālā* (or *Āścaryaratnamālā*)—are both the work of a Siddha (or Śrīman) Nāgārjuna. Their content, moreover, is so similar that they are likely the work of one and the same author: the former work, however, is little other than a reworking of a portion of the *RRĀ* of Nityanāth Siddha.[60] Both the *RRĀ* and the *KPT* postdate the *Dattātreya Tantra* and the *KCM;* all three cite their sources in their opening verses; apart from a nearly identical list of four works (in which both give "Kālacaṇḍeśvara" for *Kākacaṇḍeśvara*), the *RRĀ* and *KPT* both add another twenty-four sources not mentioned in the *Dattātreya Tantra.*[61] A final text belongs to a category all its own. This is the ca. thirteenth-century *Mātṛkabheda Tantra* (*MBhT*), a Śākta-Śaiva work on the tantric worship of Śiva and the Goddess, whose first, fifth, and eighth chapters contain original alchemical data mainly pertaining to the fabrication of mercurial *liṅga*s.[62] This is also the sole alchemical work under discussion here to betray an east Indian origin.

Also containing data on tantric alchemy are a number of medieval compendia and encyclopedias, all of which are of western Indian origin. These include the ca. A.D. 1040 *Rājamārtaṇḍa* of Raja Bhoja of Mālava; the A.D. 1131 *Mānasollāsa* of the Cālukya king Someśvara III "Bhulokamalla";[63] the fourteenth-century *Śārṅgadhara Paddhati;*[64] and the fourteenth-century *Sarvadarśana Saṃgraha* of Mādhavācārya. Those portions of the *Mānasollāsa* that are devoted to yoga closely resemble passages of the *Yogaśīkhopaniṣad*, which is one of nine works from the south Indian corpus of 108 Upaniṣads that borrow visibly from works by Gorakh and other Nāth Siddhas.[65] Also contained in this work are discussions of elixir (*rasāyana*) therapy (including the technique of *kuṭīpraveśa*, "entering into the hut"), and the cultivation of a divine body, possessed of the *siddhi*s of flight, etc.[66]

2. Matsyendra and Gorakh: The Nāth Siddha Literature

The two greatest modern contributions to the historiography of the vernacular literature of the Nāth Siddhas have been a critical edition of the mystic poems of Gorakhnāth, compiled by Pitambaradatta Barthwal in 1942[67] and that of a corpus of poetry attributed to a number of other Nāth Siddhas, compiled by Hazariprasad Dvivedi in 1957. Both editors, who consulted a number of manuscript sources in the preparation of their works, found that "standard anthologies" of the poetry of Gorakhnāth on the one hand and a number of later Nāth Siddhas on the other have existed since at least the fourteenth century and that these standard anthologies have not been greatly altered over time. There is, moreover, general agreement that the language of these poems appears to be a blend of Diṅgal (Old Rajasthani), western Punjabi, Khaḍī Bholī, and Apabhraṃśa.[68] Following Gorakhnāth, whose literary output (at least by attribution), in both the medieval vernaculars and Sanskrit media, dwarfs that of any other Nāth Siddha or, for that matter, nearly any other medieval poet, we find the following frequently recurring "signatures" on the medieval mystic poetry of the order. These authors, in order of the volume of their anthologized literary production, are (1) Gorakh, (2) Jatī Hanavant, (3) Carpaṭi, (4) Gopīcand, (5) Bhartṛhari, (6) Mahādev, (7) Dattā[treya], (8) Ghoḍā Colī, and (9) Jālandhara/Hāḍi-pā.

Two of the names listed here—Jatī Hanavant (2) and Mahādev (6), who figure in none of the lists of the nine Nāth Siddhas—will not concern us here. A single verse from a poem by Bhartṛhari (5) is alchemical.[69] There are no alchemical works attributed to either Cauraṅgi, Kaṇerī, or Gopīcand (4), nor do alchemical references appear in any of their mystic poems. All do, however, have much to say about *haṭha yoga*, and alchemical motifs recur in all of their legends. The sparse extant alchemical works of Carpaṭi (3) and Ghoḍā Colī (8) have already been surveyed; a poem contained in Dvivedi's anthology, the "Śrī Carpaṭ jī kī sabadī," is a short treatise on the subtle body. Carpaṭi also figures in a number of alchemical legends.[70] The two short poems by Nāga Arjan found in Dvivedi's anthology contain no references to alchemy,[71] and it is doubtful that this is the same figure as any of the candidates for the historical alchemist named Nāgārjuna. While none of his poems in the Nāth Siddha anthologies treat of alchemy, the figure of Dattātreya (7) does in fact bear a tenuous connection to the alchemical tradition: the *Dattātreya Tantra*, a ca. twelfth-century work attributed to him, contains a chapter on "magical" alchemy. A lost alchemical work perhaps attributed to him is the *Rasaratnāvali* of Guru Datta Siddha.[72] Belonging to Dattātreya's Maharashtran lineage is Revaṇa [Siddha], to whom two lost alchemical works have been attributed: the *Rasadarpaṇa* and *Rasarājaśiromaṇi*.[73]

Major Nāth Siddhas who are conspicuous by their relative absence from these vernacular anthologies are Ādinātha (no poems), Matsyendra (one poem), and Cauraṅgi (four poems). The "Prāṇ Sāṅkalī," Cauraṅgi's contribution to the standard anthologies is, however, exceptional in its length, content, and antiquity. The literary productions of Matsyendra and Nāgārjuna are nearly wholly restricted to the Sanskrit medium.

There are a number of Sanskrit works attributed to Ādinātha. As with Dattātreya and Śrīkaṇṭha, however, it is difficult to determine whether we are to take these as the works of a historical author, or rather the received revelations of Śiva, the "Lord of Beginnings." Some of these works belong to the Western Transmission;[74] however, the principal work attributed to Ādinātha, as far as our interests are concerned, is the ca. fourteenth-century *Khecarī Vidyā*, the "Aviator's Science." This Sanskrit work, which places itself squarely in the hathayogic tradition of the Nāth Siddhas, is unique in that its final chapter is devoted to a description of the alchemical complement to yogic practice. As such, it is an exemplary work of Siddha alchemy.[75]

None of the eight works[76] attributed to Matsyendranāth—either in Sanskrit or vernacular languages—contains any alchemical data. This notwithstanding, his teachings are recognized by a vast number of later tantric authors as fundamental to their own syntheses, as I demonstrate in this and later chapters. A mention of the Siddha[-amṛta] Kaula in Matsyendra's masterwork, the *KJñN* (16.47a, 48b; 21.4–7), is significant inasmuch as Śiva-Bhairava is praised as the leader of the Siddha Kaula in an opening verse of the *RA* (1.4b); the same alchemical work (18.228a) closes with—and perhaps takes its title from—a verse it appears to borrow from the *KJñN* (15.7a). It also mentions worship of the Siddha Cakra (*RA* 14.24), a tantric "systematic genealogy" in which Matsyendra figures prominently.[77] In this, we may see that, in addition to his pivotal role within the broader tantric tradition, Matsyendra also constituted a bridge between mainstream works of the Hindu tantric tradition and the alchemical tantras.

Matsyendra's *KJñN* is itself a synthesis of the Siddha and Yoginī Kaula traditions, inasmuch as it portrays the latter as emerging out of the former.[78] The *Mṛgendrāgama*, a ninth- to tenth-century Śaivasiddhānta work, casts the two as separate but equal groups: "The sages know of eight [other] currents, connected respectively to Śiva, the Mantreśvaras, the Gaṇas, Gods, Ṛṣis, Guhyas, the Yoginī Kaula and the Siddha Kaula . . . The Yoginīs received a wisdom that immediately causes yoga to shine forth. It was called *yoginīkaula* because it never went beyond the limits of their circle. The same is the case for the other [i.e., the Siddha Kaula current]." This relationship between Matsyendranāth the Siddha and the *yoginīs* of Kāmarūpa (Assam) becomes the subject of a rich body of Nāth Siddha legend in later centuries.[79]

Matsyendra also constitutes an early and vital link between two perennial heartlands of tantric practice: eastern India (Assam, Bengal, Orissa) and Nepal. While his *KJñN* was revealed in Kāmarūpa, both the oldest manuscript of the work and the oldest mythology of Matsyendra hail from Nepal.[80] Nepal has also long been the homeland of the Western Transmission and its cult of Kubjikā, and it is in the Kathmandu Valley that nearly all the important manuscripts of the Western Tradition scriptures are found. A great number of other data, some of which I have already noted, further link Matsyendra (and later Gorakh) with this latter Kaula tradition. Both the revelations of Matsyendra's Yoginī Kaula and the Western Transmission were "brought down" at the "lunar" site of Candra-dvīpa (or Candra-giri)[81]—even if, in Matsyendra's case, Candradvīpa is to be identified with coastal Assam and the Western Transmission's Candradvīpa or Candragiri with coastal Karnataka. The *YSĀ* locates Gorakh's birthplace at Candragiri, "on the shore of the Godavari River" in western India.[82]

The *KJñN* of Matsyendra and the Western Transmission's *KM* contain the earliest extant references we have to the six *cakras* of hathayogic practice. Whereas the earliest mention of the six *cakras* of Hindu[83] *haṭha yoga* appears in an eighth-century A.D. literary source, the *Mālatī Mādhava* of Bhavabhūti,[84] a number of scholars maintain that it was in such Western Transmission works as the *Kubjikāmata* (*KM*) that these practices were first discussed systematically.[85] Here, I offer evidence to the contrary. In fact, Matsyendra's *KJñN* gives a more extensive account of the subject than does the *KM*. In *KJñN* 17.2b–4a, Matsyendra lists the six *cakras* by their locations i.e.: (1) *gūḍha* (anus), (2) *guhya* (genitals), (3) *nābhi* (navel), (4) *hṛd* (heart), (5) *ghaṇṭikāgrantha* (throat), and (6) *bhrūmadhye* (between the eyebrows), to which he adds the crowning *brahmarandhra*;[86] he notes the techniques of *prāṇāyāma* and *kapālabheda* (20.2b–3a), *khecarī mudrā* (6.18–19), "binding" and "piercing" (4.11); and one may discern in *matsyodara* ("fish-belly"), the name he gives for his sect in the fourth and present age, the Kali Yuga, an occult reference to the hathoyogic technique of diaphragmatic retention (*kumbhaka*).[87] There is, moreover, no conclusive evidence to prove that Matsyendra's Yoginī Kaula and *KJñN* are later than the Western Transmission's Kubjikā cult and *KM*. On the one hand, the earliest manuscript of the *KJñN* is older than the oldest Kubjikā manuscripts;[88] Abhinavagupta mentions Macchandanātha[89] and the *KM*;[90] and both Abhinavagupta[91] and the *KM*[92] mention Matsyendra's Yoginī Kaula. On the other hand, Matsyendra makes no direct mention of either the goddess Kubjikā, the Western Transmission, or Abhinavagupta's Trika Kaula.

Matsyendranāth's pivotal role in the history of tantric sectarianism became further expanded when the myth of his "recovery" of the original tantric teachings of Śiva related in the *KJñN* (16.27–36) became appropriated as the origin myth of the Eastern Transmission (*pūrvāmnāya*), that tradition within which the Trika Kaula scriptures were classified. It is moreover through an appropriation of this myth that Abhinavagupta was able to reincorporate—into the "secret worship" of the same Trika Kaula whose reforms had removed such practices from the public sphere—the orgiastic, power substance–based observances that had been inherited from the Kāpālika practices associated with the scriptures of the old Vidyā Pīṭha. This he did by adapting into his synthesis the diagrammatic rendering of that Eastern Transmission "systematic genealogy" known as the Siddha Cakra, the "Circle of the Siddhas." This diagram was used as a support for the tantric worship of the Kaula lineage deities (Kuleśvara, Kuleśvarī, and the eight Mother Goddesses together with their Bhairava consorts), as well as of the *yuganātha*s, the "Nāths of the Cosmic Ages," i.e., the Kaula masters who taught in the four *yuga*s. Of these four mythic Nāths, each of whom bore an animal name, the fourth and last, associated with our own Fourth Age was Macchanda (i.e., Matsyendra).[93] While Macchanda was identified with the northern direction in the Siddha Cakra, his female consort was named Koṅkaṇā, whose name again evokes the region in which Śrīnātha and the "Nine Nāths" founded the Western Transmission. The Siddhas as a group are placed in the southern quadrant of this diagram, and the *siddhaugha* ("Siddha stream") in the western quadrant.[94] We may therefore see in this diagram evidence both for the tantric reappropriation of the preexisting cult of the *divine* Siddhas and for the incorporation of certain human or divinized Siddhas, led by Matsyendra, into that elite circle.

The Trika Kaula considered Macchandanātha to have been the founder of the *kula*, the line of transmission of the Kaula tantras. This is explained in a myth according to which Macchanda fathered twelve sons, sending six of them out (from Srisailam) into the Indian subcontinent to found six Kaula orders in the Fourth Age: these are the six *ovalli*s ("currents of doctrine") of the Trika Kaula.[95] Elsewhere, it is likely that Matsyendra's teachings also influenced the development of the Buddhist Kāpālika-Yoginī cult within the highest yoga tantra (*anuttarayoga*) current of Vajrayāna Buddhism.[96]

To what are we to attribute Matsyendra's pivotal role? The answer to this question may be elicited from a passing reference made by Abhinavagupta to the distinction between the earlier Kula practices of primitive tantrism, and the later Kaula traditions, for which Matsyendra's reforms would have constituted a watershed. In the words of Alexis Sanderson,

> The distinction between Kula and Kaula traditions . . . is best taken to refer to the clan-structured tradition of the cremation-grounds seen in the *Brahmayāmala-Picumata*, *Jayadratha Yāmala*, *Tantrasadbhāva*, *Siddhayogeśvarīmata Tantra*, etc. (with its Kāpālika *kaulikā vidhayaḥ*) on the one hand and on the other its reformation and domestication through the banning of mortuary and all sect-identifying signs (*vyaktaliṅgatā*), generally associated with Macchanda/Matsyendra.[97]

In other words, Siddha Matsyendra, founder of the Yoginī Kaula, shifted the emphasis of early tantrism away from the "terrible" practices and clan-based (Kula) system featured in the scriptures of the Vidyā Pīṭha, and towards the erotico-mystical practices that became the bedrock of later Kaulism. In the ninth and tenth centuries, we witness the emergence and three-stage evolution of Trika Kaulism, which reached its peak of refinement, in the eleventh century, in the exegetical summa of Abhinavagupta and his disciple Kṣemarāja. While publicly carrying Matsyendra's reforms to a still higher level of abstraction (in order to render Trika ritual acceptable to the broader Kashmiri Śaiva community), the Trika reformers preserved, as a cult of their virtuosi,[98] the erotic ritual of Matsyendra's Yoginī Kaula, described in the *KJñN*. Whereas early (pre–A.D. 800) Trika and the *KJñN* both emphasized the cult of *yoginī*s (who were to be invoked with offerings and the communal consumption of blood, flesh, wine, and sexual fluids),[99] Abhinavagupta's later synthesis toned down the grimmer side of the public cult while promulgating a "sublimated" form of its erotico-mystical practices for public consumption.[100] (The notion of the *kula* nevertheless remains operative in the Kaula context. The Kaulas are those persons who belong to a *kula*, i.e., to a clan lineage, a particular tantric line of transmission through a series of masters and disciples, and who make use of the power substance of the Goddess's sexual emission, also called *kula*).[101] Abhinavagupta's reinterpretation of the *kula* practices turned especially on the matter of sexual orgasm and the use of its by-products:

> While its principal purpose in the Vidyāpīṭha was to produce the power-substances needed to gratify the deities, here the ritual of copulation is aestheticised . . . the emphasis has now moved to orgasm itself. It is no longer principally a means of production. It is a privileged means of access to a blissful expansion of consciousness in which the deities of the Kula permeate and obliterate the ego of the worshipper.[102]

Even as he plays to the Kashmir Śaiva gallery, Abhinavagupta does in fact retain the concrete use of sexual fluids in the secret ritual of those initiated into the Trika Kaula.[103] In certain cases, he prescribes, for the attainment of *siddhi*s, the consumption of sexual fluids after intercourse. Here, the partners are to pass these fluids from mouth to mouth prior to placing them into a collecting vessel as an offering to the gods of the tantric "sacrifice."[104] In the Siddha Cakra worship of the *yuganātha*s, the officiant offers to Bhairava (with whom he has identified himself), as well as to the circle of energies that surround him, by drinking a mixture of male and female sexual fluid from a sacrificial jar.[105] Noteworthy here is the gloss given by Jayaratha, the thirteenth-century commentator on the *TĀ*, for the term *siddhi:* he identifies this term with *piṇḍasthairya*, "stability of the body," which is precisely the watchword of the alchemical *RA* (1.14b, 18a, 28b) and the hathayogic works of the Nāth Siddhas. In the same commentary, Jayaratha refers to the fluids produced by sex as "the best of elixirs (*rasāyana*)."[106]

Elsewhere, Abhinavagupta employs alchemical imagery to describe the abstract states of consciousness ideally realized by the practitioner. So, for example, he compares the attainment of absolute consciousness with the transmutation, by mercury, of base metals into gold; and speaks of the burning away of all difference within the "stomach of consciousness" in a way that draws an analogy between digestion in the gross body, the effects of *haṭha yoga* and alchemy on the subtle body, and the gnoseological identification between the finite and absolute self.[107] Elsewhere, he invokes Matsyendra's "fish-belly" technique, stating that the yogin is to "repose devoted to the condition of the belly of the fish."[108]

In this, the Trika Kaula theoreticians, even as they effected their reformation of Hindu tantra, remained in touch with the concrete ground of the tantric enterprise, which was and remains human sexual fluids and their symbolic correlates. The cosmic force that activates and actualizes every facet of tantric practice—that originates from the womb of the Goddess and passes through every link in the chain of transmission, from guru to disciple and thence to his or her disciple, via the inner channels of yogic transformation and through the channels that energize the mystic diagrams that serve as supports for worship and meditation—is ultimately nothing other than a stream (*ogha*) or flow (*srotas*) of sexual fluid. The life and structure of the tantric family or clan (*kula*) is defined by the life- and immortality-giving flow of the clan essence (*kulāmṛta*) that is transmitted, concretely and in the form of sexual fluids, in tantric initiation and worship rituals. This is attested in a wide array of sources. In his *KJñN* (22.2–3), Matsyendra speaks of the transmission of the *kaulāmṛta* through the six *yoginīs*; elsewhere, his entire twenty-first chapter, in which he discusses the *kaula-sadbhāva* ("true essence of the Kaula"), is of the same order: this term as well is used to designate the *yoginī*'s sexual emission.[109] Down to the present day, Assamese tantrikas identify their "lineage nectar" (*kulāmṛta*) with the goddess's menstrual fluid or the commingled sexual fluids of Śiva and the Goddess.[110]

If then the preservation of the universe depends upon—indeed, is nothing other than—the endless cosmic orgasm of the divine, and if the bliss of orgasm is that human experience which is closest to the very being of godhead, then the stuff of orgasm—male semen and the female sexual emission and uterine blood—will, of necessity, play a vital role in the tantric quest for divine autonomy, immortality, and power. No matter how abstract and refined tantric practice has become over the centuries following Abhinavagupta's reformation of the Trika Kaula, sexual fluids remain present, in one or another sublimated form, to every sect or order claiming tantric affiliation. In the idealist and nondualist syntheses of Abhinavagupta and Kṣemarāja, the sublimation of sexual fluids took the (outer) form of a remarkably complex and coherent *semanticization* of ritual (especially in the realm of ritual *mantra*), which was subsequently adopted into the Śrīvidyā cult of the Southern Transmission (*dakṣiṇāmnāya*).[111]

These intellectualized, abstract forms of late "high" Hindu tantrism—which have, of late, defined the field of western scholarship on Tantra—fall outside the purview of the present study.[112] We will rather concentrate on the Siddha perpetuation of the tantric legacy, a tradition whose three components are neatly summarized by the great tantric practitioner-scholar Gopinath Kaviraj: "Some . . . were accomplished (*siddha*) in the alchemical path (*rasa-mārga*), some accomplished through *haṭha yoga*, and still others had perfected themselves through tantric practices or through the use of sexual fluids (*bindu-sādhana*)."[113] Herein lies the "Siddha distinction." Whereas the tantric synthesis generally ignores alchemy and relegates *haṭha yoga* to a secondary role in its hierarchy of practice while placing a very high premium on worship through the use of real or sublimated sexual fluids, the Siddha traditions privilege all three forms of complementary practice. The guiding principle here remains one of controlling a universe that is understood to be a *body*, the body of the divine consort of Śiva, the body of one's own consort, and the feminine in one's own body. In the Siddha play of analogies between microcosm and macrocosm, and the corresponding hierarchies of the interpenetrating realms of universal being, this body is at once a divine, human, and alchemical body, to be perfected through yogic, alchemical, and erotico-mystical practice.

Following Matsyendra's lead is Gorakh who is, in nearly every Nāth Siddha lineage reckoning, called the disciple of Matsyendra/Mīna. While Gorakh certainly embraced and greatly expanded upon the hathayogic pole of Siddha practice, his relationship to those of erotico-mystical ritual and alchemy is more ambiguous. In spite of the fact that the historical Gorakh and Matsyendra lived at least three centuries apart, a rich body of legend describes the freeing of Matsyendra, by Gorakh, from sexual bondage in a Kingdom of Women in Assam. As I will demonstrate in a later chapter, this is a narrativization of the reforms Gorakh effected within the (Nāth) Siddha tradition, which he purged of its erotico-mystical elements in favor of a nearly exclusively hathayogic emphasis.

It nonetheless remains the case that Gorakh is considered to have been the author, if only by attribution, of a distinctly Western Transmission text, entitled the *Gorakṣa Saṁhitā*, that was devoted to precisely this sort of practice. In fact, there exist no fewer than three major works known by the title of *Gorakṣa Saṁhitā*, in which we find all three of the building blocks of the medieval Siddha traditions: alchemy, *haṭha yoga*, and tantric worship involving the use of sexual fluids. The first of the three works, entitled the "Kādi Prakaraṇa" of the *Gorakṣa Saṁhitā*, is a thirteenth-century Śākta work belonging to the canon of the Western Transmission, yet another indication of the interconnectedness of this and Nāth Siddha traditions.[114] (Its ninth chapter is attributed to another Nāth Siddha, Jālandhara. Like the rest of the Kādi Prakaraṇa this chapter is Śākta in its orientation.)[115] This is a work in twenty-seven chapters which, devoted for the most part to tantric worship of the Goddess in a variety of her forms, also lends space to a discussion of *haṭha yoga*, the Siddhas of the Western Transmission, and tantric cosmology.

Another thirteenth-century work, also referred to by certain authors as the *Gorakṣa Saṁhitā*, is one of the major texts of the tantric alchemical tradition. This, by far the most voluminous alchemical work attributed to Gorakh, is variously known as the *Gorakṣa Saṁhitā*, *Bhūtiprakaraṇa* [*BhP*], *Svacchandaśaktyavatāra*, and *Hādibheda*. It is, nonetheless, cast as a dialogue between Śrīkaṇṭha and the goddess Umā, the former being, much like Ādinātha, a pseudonym for Śiva in works of the Western Transmission. I discuss this alchemical work at length later in this chapter. Apart from the *BhP*, a small number of Gorakh's vernacular mystic poems and technical writings in Sanskrit include references to alchemy; curiously, as many of these disparage alchemy as praise it. In the latter category, the sixth Pad of his *bānī*s presents an allegorized description of the yogic body as a goldsmithy cum alchemical laboratory.[116] Another vernacular work attributed to Gorakh, entitled the *Yogadīpikā*, is written in the Old Kannada language. I have not consulted this work; however, a description of it leads me to believe that it is a south Indian version of the *Haṭhayoga Pradīpikā* of Svātmarāma, a fifteenth-century work that borrows heavily from the *Gorakṣa Śataka* and other Sanskrit hathayogic works attributed to Gorakh. Unlike the *HYP*, however, the *Yogadīpikā* contains some alchemical passages.[117]

By far the most important body of teaching attributed to Gorakh, in both the Sanskrit and vernacular media, is that consecrated to *haṭha yoga*, in which field he was India's major systematizer and innovator. Gorakh's major poetic works, anthologized in the *Gorakh Bāni*, include the Sabadī, Pad, Prāṇ Saṅkalī, [Machīndra-] Gorakh Bodh, Gyān Tilak, Ātma Bodh, Caubīs Siddhi, Śiṣyā Darśan, Naravai Bodh, and Kafir Bodh. Another important vernacular work, not included in this anthology, is the *Gorakh*

Upaniṣad.[118] A great number of hathayogic works, written in Sanskrit, are attributed to Gorakh. There is a great deal of overlap between these texts, most of which appear to be elaborations on the so-called *Gorakṣa Śataka*, the "Hundred Stanzas of Gorakṣa" (of which the critical edition contains 201 verses!), which is datable to the thirteenth century.[119] These works include the *Amanaska Yoga*, *Amaraugha Prabodha*, *Amaraughaśāsana*, *Gorakṣa Siddhānta Saṃgraha*, *Gorakṣa Paddhati*, *Mahārthamañjarī*, *Siddha Siddhānta Paddhati*, *Vivekamārtaṇḍa*, *Yogamārtaṇḍa*, *Yogabīja*, and *Yogacintāmaṇi.*[120]

As for the "third," hathayogic *Gorakṣa Saṁhitā*, this is a work that curiously links Gorakh with Dattātreya, who, in western India and Maharashtra in particular, is more of a god (incorporating Brahmā, Viṣṇu, and Śiva—but especially Viṣṇu—in his iconography) than a legendary human figure; and in this he plays a role similar to that of Ādinātha. Yet, there was at least one historical Dattātreya, who authored a number of works on yoga and tantra in the twelfth to thirteenth century. In fact, the fourteenth-century *Śārṅgadhara Paddhati* goes so far as to classify the two major forms of yogic practice, the "six-limbed" practice and the "eight-limbed" practice, as "Gorakhnāthī" and "that of the son of Mṛkaṇḍa" (a reference to Dattātreya, inasmuch as it is this figure who reveals the yogic doctrine of the *Mārkaṇḍeya Purāṇa*) respectively. In the *Gorakh Upaniṣad*, Gorakh terms the former *akula* and the latter *avadhūta.*[121] Indeed, there exists a work entitled the *Dattātreyagorakṣa Saṃvāda* (A Conversation between Dattātreya and Gorakṣa), whose principal subject is yogic practice. This work is known by a number of other names, however. The most common of these is the title *Avadhūta Gītā*, which indeed mentions both Dattātreya and Gorakṣa in its opening verses.[122] However, this dialogue appears to be nothing other than the fifth and final chapter of the hathayogic *Gorakṣa Saṁhitā* (whose third chapter moreover bears a striking resemblance to the *Akulavīra Tantra* of Matsyendranāth). The organization of this third, hathayogic, *Gorakṣa Saṁhitā* also resembles that of the *Siddha Siddhānta Paddhati*, another of Gorakh's seminal hathyogic works. The *Gorakṣa Paddhati*, a manual on *haṭha yoga*, also refers to itself, at one point, as the *Gorakṣa Saṁhitā.*[123] In fact, the alchemical *Gorakṣa Saṁhitā*, i.e., the *BhP* (9.133), states that the *Gorakṣa Saṁhitā* is a work in *five* parts.[124] In the light of the evidence we have passed in review, we must conclude that these were originally independent works which became concatenated into the *Gorakṣa Saṁhitā*, "Gorakṣa's Compendium," a fact that points, if nothing else, to Gorakhnāth's imposing medieval reputation as a Siddha virtuouso.

3. On the "Tantric" Element in Tantric and Siddha Alchemy

A number of scholars have maintained that neither *haṭha yoga* nor alchemy is, properly speaking, a component of Hindu Tantra.[125] To the extent that mainstream tantric literature appears to turn a blind eye toward the two disciplines, or at least ignores the names of their founders or exponents in their elaborate "systematic genealogies," this contention appears to have an element of truth to it. The matter is, however, of a rather more complex order. On the one hand, a number of tantric sources *do* mention alchemy and *haṭha yoga*, either directly or by way of illustrating this or that abstract concept or process. On the other, the alchemical and hathayogic sources themselves often claim to be tantric. Finally, there is the matter of chronology. With the important exception of Matsyendra, who, as we have seen, *is* included in tantric reckonings of lineage founders, nearly all the alchemical and hathayogic teachers and authors postdate the foundational tantric compendia and their postscriptural systematizations.

In his compelling study of Śākta tantrism, Douglas Brooks argues for a polythetic approach to "tantric" phenomena, in which one is to look to family resemblances between the various tantras (texts with the word *Tantra* in their title, sects which claim such texts to be their foundational scriptures, etc.) without taking any single feature or body of features found in such traditions to be normative.[126] It is such an approach that I follow here in my treatment of Hindu alchemy, the discourse of which was as much "in the air" in medieval India as were the antinomian cremation-ground rites of the Kāpālikas and the refined metaphysics of Abhinavagupta and Kṣemarāja.

Here, we will assert that Hindu alchemy is tantric because (a) it says it is; (b) it is tantric in its language and referents; (c) it is tantric in its metaphysics; (d) it is tantric in its practice; (e) it is tantric in its theology; (f) it is tantric in its goals; and (g) alchemical terminology is employed discursively or metaphorically in tantric works of a more general order.

The alchemical classics are revealed by the same gods (Śiva, Bhairava, Śrīkaṇṭha) to the same goddesses (Devī, Bhairavī, Śakti, Caṇḍī[kā]) as are the majority of Hindu tantras. Their form and style are tantric, with most texts consisting of "semidialogues" between god and goddess. Several alchemical preparations bear the names of tantric deities (Nīlakaṇṭha, Ānandabhairava, Svacchandabhairava, Lokanātha, etc.).[127] A great number of alchemical classics contain the term *Tantra* in their titles:[128] others call themselves *Saṁhitā*s, or *-mata*s, also appellations proper to the broader tantric tradition.[129] The content of these works contains references to a number of tantric sects (the Kaulas, Kāpālikas, Paścimāmnāya, etc.), while a number of alchemical authors and Rasa Siddhas (Nāgārjuna, Nandi-[-keśvara], Gorakṣa, Carpaṭi, Manthānabhairava, and Svacchandabhairava) bear the same names as do the divine or legendary founders of other tantric traditions.

Also in the pages of the alchemical sources, we find myriad references to the mystic geography of tantrism, concerning the *śākta pīṭha*s of the Goddess as well as the Himalayan and other mountain shrines generally associated with the cult of Śiva. Tantric *mantra*s, *yantra*s,[130] initiation,[131] forms of worship and devotion to the tantric gods, and "guruism"[132] also figure in the alchemical sources.

Lastly, Hindu alchemy is tantric in its goals and in the means it appropriates to realize those goals. Total autonomy, omniscience, superhuman powers, bodily immortality, and a virtual identification with godhead—although not at the expense of one's autonomy—are the aims of the Hindu alchemist, just as they are of the great majority of nondualist tāntrikas.[133]

In a more general sense, Hindu alchemy shares the same universe as do many of the other medieval Hindu traditions that identified themselves as tantric and which western and Indian scholars alike today identify with tantrism, particularly of the nondualist variety.[134] This is a *divine*, world-affirming[135] universe, the field upon which the godhead fully realizes itself, and offers realization to those humans who propitiate it. It is also an *anthropic*[136] universe, seemingly created for human self-realization, with man the measure of all things and that creature who is specifically adapted to plumbing the depths of its mysteries. The tantric universe is a *pulsating, vibratory* universe,[137] in which matter, souls, and sound are the stuff of the outpouring of godhead into manifestation, with godhead generally identified with Śiva and his self-manifestation or self-reflection taking the form of the Goddess.[138] It is a *bipolar, sexualized* universe,[139] in which all change and transformation are viewed as so many instances of an interpenetration of male and female principles, with metaphysical categories, animals, plants, and minerals all being possessed of a gender marking. It is a vertically *hierarchized* universe, in which that which is higher, closer to the source of all manifestation, is subtler and capable of encompassing, penetrating into, and reabsorbing into itself that which is lower on the great chain of being. It is a *radiating* universe,[140] with the source of the manifest world being located at the center of a vast network of metaphysical categories, divinities, phonemes, etc., all of which are interconnected through a complex interplay of correspondences. And, ultimately, the tantric universe is an *emancipating* universe, a universe that is primordially and virtually free: born of the boundless playing out of divine consciousness, its every constituent part, including the human body and spirit, as well as brute matter, are intrinsically free. Tantrism therefore places a high premium on experience—bodily, practical, concrete experience—which, in conjunction with knowledge, is liberating.[141]

4. Hindu Alchemy: The "Canonical" Works

Generating a description of the Hindu alchemical canon is a perilous task, given the number of Rasa Siddhas whose works are either unknown or not extant on the one hand and the paucity of critical editions of extant alchemical works on the other. Also clouding the picture is the absence of any certitude that the texts which have come down to us are single-author works and not compilations made over a period of several centuries. Much of what follows will therefore be tentative, given the numerous gray or blank areas remaining in our textual "map" of the Hindu alchemical tradition. To this point, the limited historical treatment I have given of certain of these major works has been based, for the most part, on data external to the texts themselves. Here, the analysis will be based on textual and intertextual data. The presentation of the "canon" will follow what I feel to be the most plausible chronological order. In fact, the evidence at our disposal indicates that most of the alchemical classics were compiled over a relatively brief period, with the great majority being generated within a two hundred–year span covering the twelfth and thirteenth centuries.

Just as exegetes evoke the "five attributes" (*pañcalakṣaṇa*) that define a Purāṇa, so we can point to a number of common features, or family resemblances, that unite the major works of the tantric alchemical canon. These include (1) an opening statement concerning the divine origins and greatness of mercury and sulfur, and (2) a praise of the alchemical path as superior to all other Hindu forms of religious practice. Here, bodily liberation (*jīvanmukti*) is compared favorably to the impersonal workings of *mokṣa*, and the complementarity of yogic and alchemical practice is noted. (3) Many works include origin myths of mercury, sulfur, and other of the prime chemical reagents. (4) Many also contain an aphorism in their opening chapter that is quite identical from one text to another: "Swooned, mercury . . . drives away disease; killed, it revives itself; bound, it affords the power of flight." (5) Ritual worship, initiation, and the use of *maṇḍala*s, *mantra*s, etc. as necessary adjuncts to the manipulation of alchemical substances are stressed in most works. (6) The alchemical laboratory and its apparatus (*yantra*s), crucibles (*muṣa*s), and enclosed "fire-pits" for the roasting of mercurial preparations (*puṭa*s), and materiae primae (herbs, minerals, gemstones, metals, animal substances, salts, etc.) are described. Most sources list eight primary (*mahārasa*s) and eight secondary (*uparasa*s) minerals, nine gemstones (*ratna*s), anywhere from six to twelve metals (*lohas*, *dhātus*), and (7) eighteen principal alchemical operations (*saṃskāra*s). Following this, most alchemical works launch into (8) an extended discussion of these operations, by means of which mercury and other minerals and metals are prepared and combined prior to transmutation, (9) followed by a discussion of applications of said preparations to the human body of the alchemist, by which he is rendered immortal. (10) Later works also contain sections on the preparations of various elixirs and aphrodisiacs, to therapeutic ends: this is *rogavāda*, the appropriation of tantric alchemy into Ayurvedic mercury-based pharmacy (*rasa śāstra*).

As is the case with most Tantras, these works are written in a dialogue style, in which Śiva-Bhairava reveals the alchemical gnosis to Devī-Bhairavī. Unlike most Tantras, however, a great emphasis is placed on texts (*śāstra*s, *grantha*s) as opposed to knowledge communicated orally by a master, even if initiation by a guru is described in many of these works. No single alchemical Tantra contains all of these elements; all contain some of them, and some contain additional elements. Not all of the texts I review here are, properly speaking, alchemical tantras; in fact, only five of them—the *Rasārṇava*, *Kākacaṇḍeśvarīmata*, *Rasendra Maṅgala*, *Rasaratnākara*, and *Bhūtiprakaraṇa*—can be said to belong to this category. What distinguishes these from the other major alchemical works is their overriding *dehavāda* emphasis upon bodily immortality as the alchemist's ultimate goal. Here, they may be contrasted with the softer line taken by Māheśvara Siddha works, which may be qualified as *muktivāda* (i.e., using increased longevity as a means to the higher end of gnoseological release into the absolute) on the one hand and, on the other, the emphasis on *dhātuvāda* and the attainment of *siddhi*s found in a number of late works. The alchemical Tantras, whose watchwords are *jīvanmukti* and *kālavañcana* ("skewing Time"), are works of Kaula inspiration, which implicitly follow the doctrines promulgated in such texts as the *KJñN* of Matsyendra, the *KM*, and the *Kulārṇava Tantra*, as well as the old Yāmala texts (*Rudrayāmala*, *Brahmayāmala*, etc.).

Generally speaking, *muktivāda* works take Ayurvedic *rasāyana* as their scientific starting point, are Śaiva Siddhānta in their metaphysical and soteriological orientations, and feed quite directly into later Ayurvedic *rasa śāstra*.[142] Many of the major extant works of Hindu alchemy—the *Rasahṛdaya Tantra*, *Rasopaniṣat*, *Rasendracūḍāmaṇi*, *Rasaprakāśa Sudhākara*, *Rasaratnasamucchaya*, and *Ānandakanda*—fall into this category. That is, the preponderance of data found in these works are *rogavāda* and *muktivāda*, although, as we will see, they are not wholly bereft of references to *dhātuvāda* and *dehavāda* alchemy.

Tantric works emphasizing this-worldly attainments and powers (*dhātuvāda*, *siddhis*) generally take their inspiration from the old "Kriyā Tantras," works on tantric sorcery. None of the major alchemical works falls into this category, although nearly all contain references to sorcery and attendant practices. Two works that may be classified as Siddha alchemical works are the *Mātṛkabheda Tantra* [*MBhT*] and *Khecarī Vidyā* [*KhV*]. The former, rather than being an alchemical Tantra per se, is a Śākta Tantra *tout court*, but one that devotes significant space to alchemy and *haṭha yoga*. As its name indicates, the latter is a work on the hathayogic technique known as *khecarī mudrā;* however, since the term *khecarī* ("one who moves in space," the "aviator") also has a number of tantric and alchemical applications, we include it here.

It has generally been held that the *RM* of Nāgārjuna, by one or another name, is the oldest extant tantric alchemical work. In the preceding chapter, I advanced arguments to refute this misconception. I now reinforce those arguments with additional material from other alchemical texts.

a. The *Rasahṛdaya* (Heart of Mercury) *Tantra* (*RHT*) of Govinda,[143] a work in nineteen chapters dating from the tenth to eleventh century, is very likely the oldest extant Hindu alchemical work. As such, it is unique in a number of ways. To begin, Govinda, unlike all later authors, first (1.2) identifies the combination of sulfur (or mica) and mercury with Viṣṇu and Śiva (Hari-Hara), before making the standard identification (1.33) between sulfur-mica as the menstrual-sexual emission of the Goddess (Gaurī) and mercury as the semen of Śiva. He praises the Rasa Siddhas (1.7), but does not name any of them. Govinda is himself the twenty-fifth Rasa Siddha in the *RM/RRS* [a] list; the *RM* also appropriates his verse 1.2, verbatim, as the opening verse of its final chapter: the *RHT* is therefore older than the *RM*.[144]

Govinda's aphorism (1.3) concerning the miraculous powers of mercury is shorter than those found in most other works and is unusual in that it equates bound mercury with liberation (*mukti*) rather than with the power of flight.[145] This distinction seems to be of a piece with Govinda's general outlook, which clearly follows the soteriology of the Māheśvara Siddhas. Very rarely does Govinda mention *jīvanmukti;* rather, yogic and alchemical practice produce a stable body with which one may accede to the highest end of liberation, i.e., absorption into the absolute, through knowledge of the absolute (*bráhman*).[146]

Govinda lists the usual eighteen *saṃskāra*s (2.1–2) and eight *uparasa*s (9.5), but only six *mahārasa*s (8.4). He lists nine metals (9.5–6). His descriptions of the first eight *saṃskāra*s[147] are very brief, with most of the body of the work being devoted to the preparation of mineral "essences" (*sattva*s) which, combined with mercury, serve to transmute base metals into gold or silver. The final chapter is devoted to the priming of the human body for the ingestion of transmuting mercury, and the preparation of four mercurial elixirs, in the form of pills (*guṭikā*s). Nowhere does Govinda assert that such elixirs lead to bodily immortality: good health, a loving wife, and the birth of sons are as much as he promises.[148] In many ways, the *RHT,* with its sober, taciturn style, is a prolegomenon to the later alchemical tantras, which pick up where it leaves off.

In the final verses of the *RHT,* Govinda praises his king, "Śrī Madana, scion of the Lunar Lineage (*śītāṃśuvaṃśa*) born into the Haihaya clan . . . lord (*nātha*) of the Kirātas" as a master of alchemy (*rasācārya*) whose alchemical gnosis (*rasavidyā*) was not learned, but innate. "I, *bhikṣu* Govinda, having learned much from that king of the Kirātas, am the author of the Tantra called *Rasahṛdaya.*"[149] A number of historians of Indian medicine maintain that Govinda's Madana was a tenth-century king of "Kirāta-deśa," a blanket term, going back to the epics, for the Bhutan-Assam border region; however, a number of Purāṇas locate the Kirātas in the Vindhya mountain region.[150] What Govinda's *RHT* passage in fact states is that Madana is a Somavaṃśin and Haihaya by birth, lord of the Kirātas by princely avocation, and an alchemist by vocation. Now, there did exist, in the ninth through thirteenth centuries A.D., a royal family called the Kalachuris who traced their lineage back through Haihaya and Yadu to the Moon and who therefore considered themselves to be Haihayas and Yādavas of the Lunar Dynasty. The Kalachuris ruled from Tripura (modern Tewar, north of Jabalpur) over a kingdom whose borders more or less correspond to those of modern-day Madhya Pradesh. Their influence, however, extended well to the west (into modern Rajasthan, Maharashtra, Karnataka) and east (Bihar, Orissa) of their boundaries.[151] From the tenth century onwards, there existed, in the same region (Orissa), a religiously latitudinarian royal family known as the Somavaṃśis, who were patrons of Buddhism as well as of Vaiṣṇavism and Śaivism. Finally, two dynasties that ruled in Assam from ca. A.D. 800 to 1100 traced their descent from a king of the "barbarian Cīnas" and the Kirātas.[152] I am therefore inclined to locate Govinda's Somavaṃśi-Haihaya king Madana, lord of the Kirātas, at the eastern extremity (eastern Madhya Pradesh, Orissa) of the Kalachuri sphere of influence (which extended into the western Indian regions I have termed the heartland of tantric alchemy). As for Govinda himself, he could have lived anywhere within the boundaries of this Kalachuri sphere of influence. A tenth- to eleventh-century date for this text is plausible, in the light of the dates of later works that refer back to the *RHT.*

b. The *Rasārṇava* (Flood of Mercury) is the oldest and most important of the alchemical Tantras and may be dated to the eleventh century.[153] It is an anonymous work in eighteen chapters, cast as a dialogue between Bhairava and Devī. It has been attributed by a number of scholars to a certain Bhairavānanda Yogi; "Bhairava," the twenty-ninth Rasa Siddha in the later lists, may be a reference to this text's divine revealer. It is possible that later texts also refer to its author as Manthānabhairava, for reasons that will be discussed momentarily. The *RA* cites no other author or work (with the possible exception of the *Ḍāmara Tantra*)[154] by name. A comparison with the early eleventh-century A.D. *Vimalaprabhā* commentary to the *Kālacakra Tantra* reveals a number of striking similarities in both language and subject matter with the material found in the former work, which appears to be slightly more archaic than that of the *RA.*[155]

Nowhere in the *RA* do we find a comprehensive accounting of the eighteen *saṃskāra*s. In fact, the first eight operations, by which mercury is purified prior to being applied as a transmuting agent to other minerals and metals, are reduced in the *RA* to two: purification (*śodhana*) and rubbing (*mardana*). This is possibly due to the fact that the *RA* followed a rapid Skull-Bearer method (*kāpālika-yoga*)—as opposed to the slower Lunar (*saumya*) method—for these primary operations.[156] The *RA* is far and away the alchemical text that most frequently evokes these *kāpālika* methods, for the liquification of gemstones, the coloration of mercury and metals, etc.[157] Like most alchemical works, the *RA* lists eight primary (7.2) and secondary (7.56) *rasa*s, but lists only six metals (7.97), as opposed to the nine found in most sources. The *RA* (7.57–66) is the earliest text to provide an origin myth for sulfur; only in later texts, however, does one find a mythic account of the origins of mercury. The abundant tantric elements found in the *RA* will be discussed at length in the next chapter.

A number of passages from the *RA* are nearly identical to passages from the *RHT*; these may either be paraphrases of the latter on the part of the former, evidence for the oral transmission of the alchemical gnosis, or indications of the existence of a common source from which both borrowed material.[158] The last appears to be the case, for example, with the description of a preparation that stabilizes and strengthens the body tissues prior to the ingestion of mercury. The *RA* (18.14) copies the *Aṣṭāṅgasaṃgraha* (6.50.245) verbatim, whereas the *RHT* (19.19) appears to paraphrase that work.[159]

As we have already noted on a number of occasions, the *RM* borrows widely from the *RA*.[160] That the contrary is not the case is proved time and again by the fact that the *RM* either unnecessarily embellishes passages from the *RA* or changes the order of passages in ways that do not make the same sense as they do in the *RA*. A prime example of the former phenomenon is the case of the aphorism concerning the powers of mercury. In no other source is the matter stated more succinctly and powerfully than in the *RA* (1.19): "O Goddess! Swooned, mercury, like the breath, drives away disease; killed, it revives itself; and bound, it affords the power of flight." Compare the derivative, embellished, and thereby weakened aphorism of the *RM:* "When bound, [mercury] affords the state of flight; it removes the heap of diseases when swooned; calcinated it is a destroyer of birth and worldly existence; progressed and colored it affords pleasure and liberation."[161] Elsewhere, the *RM*'s list of twenty-seven Rasa Siddhas appears to be an expansion on a group of twenty-four (Rasa) Siddhas mentioned (but not named) in the *RA*.[162]

The latter case in point is demonstrated by the treatment the *RM* gives of the most elaborate alchemical operation found in the entire *RA*. This passage, which constitutes the powerful conclusion of the *RA* (18.208–28), is dramatized in a myth related by Alberuni, in about A.D. 1030, on the subject of the silver threshold of the government house in Dhara (Dhar district, Madhya Pradesh). Alberuni's account is reproduced at the beginning of chapter three of this book; its close similarity to the procedure described in the *RA* is a further indication that this is an eleventh-century text.

In the *RA*, "diamond-bound" mercury, which has proven its efficacy by restoring cripples, freaks, and mutants to wholeness and transmuting ten million times its mass of base metals into gold, is to be employed in the ultimate alchemical Work, the transformation of the entire person of the alchemist into an Alchemical Man. This he will do by plunging himself—

after an appropriate worship ritual—into a cauldron of superheated oil into which pellets of diamond-bound mercury have been placed. At this point, the *RA* explains the principle behind this operation: the five gross elements—"*earth, water, fire, air, and ether*"—of his material body will be serially transformed into their subtle correlates (*tanmātra*s), beginning with that of earth and ending with that of ether. The process is at once a concrete application of the principles of (1) Tantric *bhūtaśuddhi;* (2) "extracting the essence (*pañcāmṛta*)" of the five elements, as described in the *Jayadrathayāmala;*[163] and (3) the basic Siddha principle of telescoping the gross into the subtle as a means to generating a *siddha* body.[164]

Once the alchemist has plunged himself into the cauldron, his laboratory assistant serially adds the alchemical equivalents of the five elements to the mix, culminating with *kha* (ether, but also mica), which is to be placed inside the alchemist's skull (presumably all that remains of his gross body at this point): it is noteworthy here that, as with the hathayogic practice of *khecarī mudrā*, this operation climaxes with ether in the cranial vault.[165] Then, "pumping the bellows [until the mix has] the look of molten gold, [the assistant] should add an alkaline substance (*kṣāra*). No sooner has this been done than he [the Alchemical Man] rises up with a mighty roar: '*Huṃ!*'" Then follows a description of the Man's alchemical apotheosis, in which he sports in the world of the Siddhas with a hundred thousand Siddha maidens.[166]

The *RM*'s treatment of the same operation is punctuated by breaks, inconsistencies, and asides, which indicate a more or less random appropriation of the *RA* passage. The *RM* concludes its description of the miraculous healing powers of diamond-bound mercury with the statement: "Thereupon, one becomes [takes on] another body: there is no need to speculate on this matter." Then, in a very interesting aside not found in the *RA*, the *RM* continues: "This is the Great Work which is called 'Five Nectars' in either the *Manthānabhairava*, or then again mentioned in the demon Rāvaṇa['s *Kumāra Tantra*].[167] All the manifold [life forms] in these three worlds, including all that moves and all that does not move are [composed of the following]: *Earth, water, fire, air, and ether*." It then abruptly segues back to diamond-bound mercury, which is capable of transmuting ten million times its mass of base metals into gold, at which point it follows the *RA* description of the operation, with minor variations and one important omission: the *RM* leaves out the pentultimate operation of placing *kha* in the skull of the Alchemical Man.[168]

One might think that Nāgārjuna, author of the *RM*, had missed the entire point of this operation—i.e., the creation of an Alchemical Man—were it not for the fact that he refers, in his aside, to the "Great Work called the 'Five Nectars' (*pañcāmṛta*)." This is precisely the term employed in the *Jayadrathayāmala* for the tantric "extraction of the essence" of the five gross corporeal elements as the means to generating a Siddha body possessed of the power of flight. Most fascinating here is Nāgārjuna's mention of the texts entitled *Manthānabhairava* and "Demon Rāvaṇa." While the latter can only refer to Rāvaṇa's *Kumāra Tantra* (which is based in part upon the tantric sorcery of the *Kriyākālaguṇottara Tantra*),[169] the former gives rise to thought.

There are two candidates for the *Manthānabhairava* to which Nāgārjuna refers. The first, and less likely of the two, is an eponymous alchemical text by this name, which would then account for the name of Manthānabhairava as the thirty-second Rasa Siddha and for the numerous references to Manthānabhairava (especially to an elixir called *manthānabhairava rasa*) in later alchemical works. In fact, all mentions of Manthānabhairava postdate the *RA*, by which logic one might posit that Nāgārjuna is referring to the *RA* as the (work revealed by) Manthānabhairava. However, the preparation called *manthānabhairava rasa*, as it is described in the *RM* itself, as well as in many later works, is nowhere to be found in the *RA*.[170]

Moreover, while the *RA* is obviously Nāgārjuna's source here, at no time does that text refer to this or any other operation as the Great Work called the "Five Nectars." The second, and more likely, source to which Nāgārjuna may be referring is the twelfth-century *Manthānabhairava Tantra*, one of the core texts of the Western Transmission, a source to which the *RC* seems also to refer.[171] (While Nāgārjuna appears to be the sole alchemical author to ever have cited this seminal work of the Western Transmission, the *RA* itself contains at least one passage that indicates its author's familiarity with that tradition's cult of the goddess Kubjikā.[172] We will return to the impact of the Western Transmission on the tantric and Siddha alchemical traditions in the next chapter.)

The question then arises as to whether the citations, in later alchemical works, of Manthānabhairava *all* refer to a Rasa Siddha by that name, or at times to a work of the Western Transmission; and, if the former is the case, whether Manthānabhairava the alchemist is to be identified with the Bhairava who revealed or authored the *RA*.[173]

The *RM* copies or paraphrases the *RA* in scores of other places, most especially in its fourth chapter, in the course of which it samples approximately sixty-four verses from the *RA*, even repeating itself in the same places as those in which the *RA* is repetitive (which only occurs in the *RA*'s final, eighteenth chapter). Ironically, it is in this fourth chapter that we find the "Buddhist" dialogue, set atop Srisailam, between Nāgārjuna, the goddess Prajñāparamitā, and a host of other luminaries, that convinced Ray and others that this was a Mahāyāna text. In fact, the passage we have just compared with *RA* 18.206–228 is cast in the *RM* is a dialogue between Nāgārjuna and Ratnaghośa![174]

c. The *RA* is copied, paraphrased, or cited in a significant number of later works, with a particularly long passage (18.278–337) on the subject of magical waters being borrowed into the *Kākacaṇḍīśvara Kalpa Tantra* (*KCKT*) (8.2–49).[175] This work, which deals mainly with tantric healing through the use of botanicals, has little or no relationship to the *Kākacaṇḍeśvarīmata* (Doctrine of the Fierce Crow[-faced] Goddess) (*KCM*),[176] an alchemical text in which tantric elements abound. Here too, a number of nearly identical passages in the *RA* and the *KCM* would appear to indicate borrowing from an unknown common source.[177]

As its title indicates, the *KCM* is Śākta in its sectarian orientation. More exactly, Kākacaṇḍeśvarī's corvocephaly is of a piece with such Kaula cults of Kālī as the Kaula Mata and the cult of Guhyakālī, which has been popular in Nepal since at least the eighth century. In both of these cults, zoocephalic or avicephalic goddesses have figured prominently.[178] The Śāktism of the *KCM* is explicit from the outset: while it is the god Bhairava who is doing the revealing, he is nonetheless ringed, atop Mount Kailash, by a circle of "*yoginīs*," named Kāpālī, Kālarātrī, Kākacaṇḍā, Ambikā, Karālī, Kālakarṇī, and Kākacaṇḍeśvarī, who are accompanied by Gaṇanāyaka (Gaṇeśa). In the course of this work, Bhairava refers to Kākacaṇḍeśvarī by a number of names, including Kākacamuṇḍā, Bhairavī, and Cāṇḍālī. Bhairava himself is called Śiva, Sadāśiva, Īśvara, and Sarvajña; and a reference is made in the text to the worship of Baṭukanātha (the "Boy Master") Bhairava.[179] Like the *RA*, the *KCM* contains an abundance of references to worship, mantras, and sexual practices that place it squarely within the tantric tradition. Which tantric tradition is another question, however; the *KCM* appears to be as much inspired by the old Kriyā Tantras as it is by the alchemical tradition.

The opening verse of the *KCM* resembles those of the *Kulānanda Tantra* of Matsyendra and the Buddhist *Lalitāvistara*.[180] Following this and a very powerful opening statement (second only to that found in chapter one of the *RA*) on the inability of the various philosophies and religions to alleviate human suffering, the *KCM* comes directly to its raison d'être, the method or expedient of the "fluid" or "power substance" (*dravyopāya*):[181] "Without the power substance, there can be no realization (*siddhi*), and no enjoyment or pleasure. Without the power substance, men become disembodied ghosts (*preta*s) when they die. They who employed inferior substances [i.e., who followed inferior doctrines] in life roam about blindly in the world of the dead."

Following this introduction, however, the *KCM* suddenly becomes very much a Kriyā Tantra, plunging directly into a very long description of a number of pills (*guṭikā*s) which render the user highly attractive to divine females (nymphs, *yoginī*s, Gandharva maidens, and even Bhairavī herself) and eminently capable of satisfying their sexual desires. In this, it closely resembles discussions of magical "attraction" (*ākarṣaṇa*) and "the acquiring of a heavenly nymph" (*yakṣiṇī-sādhana*, *strīvaśyam*) found in works on tantric sorcery. The highly evocative names of these *guṭikā*s are found in a number of later texts; the earlier *RA* describes one of these, the *amarasundarī* ("Immortal Beauty") pill in some detail. Of much greater interest to the *RA*, however, is a pill that affords magical flight (*khecarī guṭikā*); and the *KCM* follows its instructions for the preparation of this and other aphrodisiacs with its own discussion of the same.[182] From here, the *KCM* abruptly changes its orientation once again and launches into a long discussion of gold making (*dhātuvāda*) through the use of mercury that has been treated with mica, herbs, and sexual fluids before returning, inexorably, to its discussion of aphrodisiacs.[183] Next, it lists the best nights of the year for meeting divine maidens (*devakanyā*), discusses the miraculous panacea called "rock water" (*śailodaka*), and describes the use of orpiment (*haritāla*) and other mineral and plant substances in the preparation of elixirs.[184]

To this point in the text, it would be extremely difficult for an alchemist to carry out any of the operations described in the *KCM* for the simple reason that none of the basic principles of alchemy have been systematically explained: terminology, *materiae primae*, apparatus, procedures are all taken for granted. Now, over halfway through the work, the author seems to have second thoughts and undertakes a systematic exposition of the eighteen *saṃskāra*s and a number of other fundamentals of his discipline. The *saṃskāra* list is unusual inasmuch as neither transmutation nor bodily transubstantiation is enumerated; in their place, it names two operations not counted as *saṃskāra*s in other works: *vidhāna* ("apportioning") and *māraṇa* ("killing"). Following this, it singles out eight of the eighteen operations as the "Eight Works." Its enumeration of these resembles that found in *RA* 10.10–12.[185] In its expanded discussion of these eight procedures, the *KCM* describes the "class of enemies" (*arivarga*), i.e., minerals that attack and "kill" each of the eight metals. Similar classifications are found in the later *RC* (4.50; 14.14 [*ariloha*]) and *ĀK* (7.28).[186] Next follows a discussion of the purification of the secondary *rasa*s, of which six are listed: there is no systematic description of the primary *rasa*s.[187] At this point, a commentary is inserted into the text of the *KCM*,[188] which continues intermittently until the conclusion of the work: a similar *ṭippaṇa* is inserted at a similar point in the *RM*.

Devotional praises of mercury and sulfur (or mica) in combination follow, a commonplace that most alchemical tantras place in their opening chapter.[189] A brief description of the four colors of mica is innovative inasmuch as it classifies the four colors (*varṇa*s) of mica according to "caste" (*varṇa*): white mica is brahman, red is *kṣatriya*, yellow is *vaiśya*, and black is *śūdra*. A number of other works classify mercury in this way; the *KCM* is the sole early text to do so for mica.[190]

Hereafter, the *KCM* once more becomes a work on tantric sorcery and healing. A section on "skewing Time" (*kāla-vañcana*) describes a number of means by which to predict the future and revive the dead or dying. The use of a mixture of male and female sexual fluids (*kuṇḍagolaka*) constitutes a portion of a discussion on a rite through which the *yogin* may gain supernatural powers and immortality. (The *MBhT* also gives a prominent place to the *kuṇḍagolaka* and other such cocktails; the *RA* and *RM* also use the term, but desexualize it into a combination of the herbal essences of the *cāṇḍālī* and *rākṣasī* plants).[191] The *KCM* states that this rite renders the practitioner a *kavi*;[192] we will return to Siddha uses of this term in chapter ten.

The work concludes with a long section on tantric healing through the use of herbs and *mantra*s. One such *mantra* contains a long evocation of *ṛṣi*s (Kaśyapa, Kāpaṭu), gods (Sūrya), kings (Sugrīvarāja, the monkey ally of Rāma), *bhūta*s, and all manner of other creatures (water-goers, sky-goers . . . *piśāca*s, *ḍākinī*s, etc.).[193] In every manuscript version of the work I have consulted, these final folios are written in a curious mixture of Sanskrit and a vernacular in which many Hindustani words are recognizable (*cāval*, *ser*, *suhāg*, *āṭāī*, *lasanu* [= *lesūn*?], *thambhana hoi*, etc.). Given the heterogeneous nature of this work, it is extremely difficult to date. While the concluding portion (which is likely a commentary by a later hand) is certainly quite recent, the *KCM*'s treatment of much of the alchemical and other material appears to be quite archaic. In any case, some version of the *KCM* was already extant in the twelfth century, as it is cited in three twelfth- to thirteenth-century works on tantric sorcery: the *Dattātreya Tantra* (1.5), the *RRĀ* (5.1.7), and the *KPT* (1.9, which merely copies the *RRĀ*), all of which refer to it as the *Kālacaṇḍeśvaramata*. At the same time, an apparent reference it makes to a fourteenth- to fifteenth-century work entitled the *Rasasāra* and the presence of quite modern vernacular terms in its conclusion make it clear that this is a text that was reworked over a period of several centuries, prior to taking its definitive form.[194]

d. Like the *RHT* the *Rasopaniṣat* (*RU*)[195] is a Māheśvara Siddha work, concentrating more on transmutational and therapeutic alchemy than on the goal of *jīvanmukti* through the use of alchemical elixirs. It is unique in comparing mercury to the *ātman*, the individual soul (15.50), and in its praise of liberation (*mukti*) as the highest goal (1.5). Cast in the form of a dialogue between Mahādeva and Pārvatī, it is datable to the twelfth to thirteenth century. It is a southwest Indian work, composed in Kerala.[196] It purports to be an abridgment of a work entitled *Mahodadhi;*[197] both it and the *Mahodadhi* are named in the *BPh* (1.114), also a twelfth- to thirteenth-century work. A number of other textual sources are cited in the same chapter (1.14): these are found in no other work.[198] It describes a preparation discovered by Śrīman Nāgārjuna-muni (16.10): chapter colophons to the thirteenth- to fourteenth-century RM call that text the work of Śrīman Nāgārjuna. Elsewhere, the *RU* paraphrases a passage from the *RA*, in which mercury is compared to a wild elephant in rut, which can only be brought under control by the "elephant goad of mercury" (*rasāṅkuśa*). In the case of the *RA*, the elephant goad is a *mantra* identified with the alchemical goddess Rasāṅkuśī; in the *RU*, it is simply stated that mercury can be stabilized only through decoction (*ghanāt*). The "elephant goad" is a commonplace tantric *mantra*, whose use makes sense in the context of the *RA;* borrowed as it is into the nontantric RU, the metaphor loses most of its impact.[199] Rather than the usual eight, the *RU* (4.4–6) names only seven primary and secondary minerals and seven metals. Its presentation of the alchemical *saṃskāra*s is also highly idiosyncratic, with only six of its *saṃskāra*s corresponding to the standard terminology employed for the alchemical operations. Another six operations, which appear to correspond to more familiar *saṃskāra*s, are presented under the heading of *kūrpa*, a term found nowhere else in the alchemical canon.[200] The *RU* makes no mention of the final *saṃskāra* of transubstantiation. All of these idiosyncracies arise from the fact that this is a work that is relatively early and rather peripheral, both in geographic and sectarian terms, to tantric alchemy.

e. As already stated a number of times, the most problematic element in the *Bhūtiprakaraṇa* (*BhP*) (Production of Supernatural Powers)[201] is its title. To this point I have generally referred to this work as "the so-called alchemical *Gorakṣa Saṁhitā*"; this I have done because the sole edition of this work was published under that title, by Janardana Pandeya, in 1977. In fact, the chapter colophons to Pandeya's edition read: "here ends . . . the *Śiva Sūtra*, contained in the Bhūti-prakaraṇa of the *Gorakṣa Saṁhitā* in 100,000 verses, brought down [to earth] by Svacchanda-Śakti." This is in fact an abridgment of the colophon to what I have termed the "Śākta *Gorakṣa Saṁhitā*," a work that is nearly identical to the Western Transmission work known as the *Śrīmatottara Tantra*. The colophon to this work reads: "here ends . . . that section of the *Kula-kauliṇī-mata* (in 90 million verses, brought down [to earth] at the *yoginī*s' secret Vidyāpīṭha by Śrīkaṇṭha) known as the *Kādi* section, which is included in the latter portion of the 100,000 verse *Gorakṣa Saṁhitā* which was brought to earth by Śvacchanda-śakti, who had received its seventy million-million [verses] from the most excellent Mahā-manthāna [-bhairava]."[202] Here, we are in the presence of textual attribution carried to an exponential level. The *BhP* bears little or no connection to the Śākta work of the same name, save for the fact that the two are revealed by the same form of Śiva (Śrīkaṇṭha).

It is, like nearly every alchemical work, a Śaiva treatise (*Śiva Sūtra*); however, this mention is missing from chapter colophons of most of the manuscript versions that I have consulted. As for the claim that this work is a portion of the "*Gorakṣa Saṁhitā* in 100,000 verses," a single verse (9.136), found at the end of Pandeya's manuscript, states that "the Nāth made this [work] manifest for the benefit of king Siṁha," and quotes "the immortal Nāth [named] Gorakṣa," and but does not make it clear that Gorakṣa is the author of the work. These verses, moreover, are not found in every manuscript of this work.[203] A rare alchemical reference to Gorakh is found in the ca. sixteenth-century *Rasakāmadhenu* (2.362–63), which cites a work entitled the *Gorakṣamata* (The Doctrine of Gorakṣa) in its description of the alchemical uses of a flower called *haṃsapada:* this passage, however, is nowhere to be found in the *BhP.*[204]

The Svacchanda Śakti who is said to have brought the *Gorakṣa Saṁhitā* down to earth is referred to but once in the work itself; however, a number of references to male Svacchanda deities and Svacchanda *mantra*s indicate that this work belongs to the Svacchandabhairava canon (the cult of Svacchandabhairava was especially important in Kashmir, and the *SvT* was the principal work of the so-called Mantra Pīṭha).[205] The title of this work, then, is *Bhūtiprakaraṇa*, and any connection between it and the two other so-called *Gorakṣa Saṁhitā*s is, as has so often been the case in the annals of tantrism, a case of ex post facto attribution or "postscriptural systematization." On the other hand, an attribution of this work to a Rasa Siddha named Svacchandabhairava ought not to be rejected out of hand: in its opening chapter, the *BhP* intimates that it is an abridgment of a much longer Rasa Tantra revealed by Svacchanda.[206]

This is a work in nine chapters, presented in the form of a dialogue between Śrīkaṇṭha and Umā. The latter's name is significant in this work, given that it refers to sulfur as *umāyoni* ("Umā's womb"). Also original, in certain manuscript versions, is the use of the term *śarvaja* ("born from [Rudra,] the Arrow").[207] The mercurial Śiva is also referred to as Pāradeśvara (5.27) and Raseśvara (5.289). The three Trika goddesses, Parā, Aparā, and Parāparā, are also mentioned (1.106), as are the divine Mothers (*mātṛkā*s) (6.281). The alchemist is to worship Bhairava and the circle of *yoginī*s, as well as Gaṇeśa, the regents of the cardinal directions, and brahmin maidens (3.7–8). Ritual sex is also prescribed.[208]

The *BhP* makes vague references to a number of tantric works and corpora. It mentions the three *srota*s of the tantric corpus, as well as (a work entitled?) the *Uttarottara Mātṛtantra*.[209] In addition to the Svacchanda formulae, it describes a number of other *mantra*s, including one that appears to refer to Matsyendra.[210] It mentions the alchemist Nandi (9.134) and, in at least one manuscript, also makes mention of the [Rasa-] *Ratnākara* (*RRĀ*) (however, the *RRĀ* [4.4.100] names Gorakṣanāth and his disciple Gahaṇināth).[211] It also cites the *Rasopaniṣat* and the *Mahodadhi*, both of which it attributes to the goddess Umā, and goes on to give titles of nonextant alchemical works authored by a number of divine alchemical Siddhas (of which two—Śukra and Bṛhaspati—are also mentioned in the *RU*).[212] It is cited, under the title of *Svacchandaśaktyavatāra*, in the fourteenth-century *Rasarājalakṣmī* of Viṣṇudeva.[213] These data would place the *BhP* in the twelfth to thirteenth century, which squares with an apparent reference to it by Somadeva, when he cites Śrīkaṇṭha in his thirteenth-century *RC* (7.1). Its sole geographical references are to the Vindhya range (6.60), to a site "to the southeast of the Himalayas" (2.56), and to a (probably mythic) location called "Virgin Island" (*kumārīdvīpa*), where divine herbs abound (7.113).

In nearly every respect, the *BhP* is a garden-variety alchemical tantra. Its oft-repeated goals are *siddhi*s, Śivahood, and sporting in the heavens with divine maidens;[214] and its means to that end are a blend of alchemy, tantric worship, and devotion to mercurial Śiva *liṅga*s and the Siddhas.[215]

Significant in this regard is its quite frequent reference to mercury as *dravya*, the fluid or power substance, without which the use of *mantras* and other forms of worship are vain. In this, the *BhP* resembles the *KCM*, which it also follows in its numerous preparations in which menstrual blood is used.[216] It also resembles the latter work in its frequent use of vernacular terms, of which one, *khānepāne* (4.77), used as a synonym for *siddhi*, is also found in the *RM*, Matsyendra's *Akulavīra Tantra*, and the *Dattātreya Tantra*.[217] Its aphorism on the powers of swooned, killed, and bound mercury (1.51) is a paraphrase of that found in the *RA*.

The *BhP* devotes much of its seventh chapter to alchemical uses of the sixty-four divine herbs (*divyauṣadhi*), which it identifies, after an alchemical commonplace, with the sixty-four *yoginīs*. These are said to grow in those places where Śiva and the Goddess had sexual intercourse and are to be culled and used at certain specific times of the lunar month and the solar year.[218] Its description of the construction and layout of the alchemical laboratory and the qualities of laboratory assistants generally follow those found in the *RA*.[219] The eight primary and secondary minerals (2.19, 28) and eight metals (2.31), as well as the eighteen alchemical *saṃskāras* (3.4–6), listed in the *BhP* correspond to those found in most alchemical sources.

f. The *Rasendracūḍāmaṇi* (Crest-jewel of the Lord of Rasas) (*RC*) of Somadeva, a work in sixteen chapters, cites a great number of tenth- to thirteenth-century alchemical authors: Manthānabhairava, Nandi, Nāgārjuna, Bhairavācārya, Govinda, Bhāskara, Bhāluki, Srīkaṇṭha, etc.[220] The *RC* is mentioned in the thirteenth-century *RRĀ* (1.10.51–61) and *RPS* (7.37; 9.11), and copied extensively by the thirteenth- to fourteenth-century *RRS*: it therefore dates from the twelfth or thirteenth century. Somadeva calls himself the lord of Karavāla Bhairavapura, a name that corresponds to no known Indian toponym, either medieval or modern; however, Somadeva's mention of both Nāgārjuna and Bhāskara, as well as a familiarity with Mount Abu "in the Gujarat region" (11.111) and the local Saurashtran term for a specific type of clay (11.49) indicate that he was from Gujarat.[221]

Somadeva states, on a number of occasions, that he is one of the greatest alchemists on the face of the earth, and that certain techniques are known to none save Śiva, Nandikeśvara, and himself. In spite of his self-assurance, Somadeva, like many before and after him, copies or paraphrases large portions of earlier works, especially the *RA*. Chapter one closely follows the first chapter of the *RA* in structure and content, from its evocation of the Kaulas (1.6–7, 11–15) and its discussion of "eating the flesh of the cow and drinking liquor" (1.8–10) to its paraphrase of that work's aphorism on the powers of swooned, bound, and killed mercury (1.28) and its discussion of the devotional cult of mercury (1.30–51). Chapter two's discussion of initiation, including instructions for the establishment of images of Rasabhairava and Rasāṅkuśī in the midst of an alchemical *maṇḍala* (2.4–50) closely follows *RA* 2.4–8, 44–76. No fewer than forty verses in chapters ten through fourteen are borrowed from the seventh chapter of the *RA*.[222]

Somadeva is, nonetheless, original on a number of counts. His is the earliest work to contain the origin myth of mercury, as well as the description of a fantastic procedure for the extraction of mercury from its subterranean "wells" (15.4–22). He is the first alchemical author to identify the nine gemstones (12.1) with the nine heavenly bodies (*graha*s), and the first to describe five types of alchemical transmutation, which correspond to the five elements (4.107–11). Curiously, he devotes very little attention to the ninth through sixteenth *saṃskāra*s, preferring to concentrate on the ultimate operations of transmutation (*vedha*) and transubstantiation, which he terms *sevana* (15.28). Apart from the anonymous author of the *RA*, Somadeva is the most stylish of the alchemical authors. His work bears the stamp of a powerful personality.

g. The *Rasaprakāśa Sudhākara* (Effulgence of Mercury, Wellspring of Nectar) (RPS) of Yaśodhara Bhaṭṭa is a work in thirteen chapters devoted to medicinal uses of mercurials and other alchemical preparations. Yaśodhara's name figures in all the Rasa Siddha lists,[223] and he mentions the twelfth- to thirteenth-century Somadeva (9.12) and opium: therefore his is a thirteenth-century work.[224] Yaśodhara states that he is a resident of the Saurashtran town of Jīrṇābhidha, which likely corresponds to the modern toponym of Junagadh.[225] In the opening verses of his work (1.1–4), he evokes a series of deities—Śāradā, i.e., Sarasvatī; Gaṇapati, i.e., Gaṇeśa; and Harihara. This last name is of course a reference to the conjoined Viṣṇu-Śiva, a god whose name is also evoked in the opening verses of the *RHT* (1.2). Given that Yaśodhara identifies his father as a Vaiṣṇava named Padmanābha ("Lotus-Navel," i.e., Viṣṇu) of the Gauḍīya (Śrīgauḍa) brahmin lineage,[226] we can be nearly certain that the author of the *RPS* was a Vaiṣṇava, rather than a Śaiva or Śākta alchemist. He refers to himself as a *kavi* and a *kavivara* (13.14–15).[227]

In spite of Yaśodhara's probable Vaiṣṇavism, his account of the divine origin of mercury (1.5–12) is based on the standard Śaiva myth of the birth of Skanda. Enumerations of the eighteen alchemical *saṃskāra*s (1.30–164) and the eight principal (5.2–3) and secondary (6.1) *rasa*s are unexceptional. Chapter eight includes descriptions of the preparations called *svacchanda-bhairava rasa* (8.132–33) and *manthānabhairava rasa* (8.173–74). In chapter nine, Yaśodhara's enumeration of the sixty-four divine herbs (*divyauṣadhī*s) is based, by his own admission (9.11), on Somadeva's *RC*. An unusually long list of forty *yantra*s is presented in chapter ten; chapter eleven is devoted to gold making. Chapters twelve and thirteen are devoted to Ayurvedic techniques of *vājīkaraṇa*. In addition to Somadeva, Yaśodhara mentions Bhairava (7.26), Nāgārjuna (5.107), and Nandi (6.73).

h. Because of the corrupt nature of the manuscript he consulted, P. C. Ray mistook the *RM* for the *Rasaratnākara* (Mine of Gemstones and Rasas) (*RRĀ*), which he attributed to Nāgārjuna. As already noted, the thirteenth-century *RRĀ* was authored by Nityanātha Siddha, who says as much (1.1.25) and who names Nāgārjuna in an opening verse of his work (1.1.17a). In the same passage, he also mentions the *Rasārṇava* of "Śambhu."[228] It is also in the *RRĀ* (3.1.66–70) that we find an alternate (to the *RM/RRS* [a]) list of Rasa Siddhas, a list that notably includes Carpaṭi (whose name is absent from the *RM/RRS* [a] list); the *RRĀ* (1.1.17b) also cites a work by Carpaṭi, entitled *Svargavaidya-kāpālika*.[229] The *RRĀ* is a later work than the *KCM* as well as the *RC*, both of which it cites;[230] but is earlier than the *RAK*, which cites it,[231] and the *RRS* and *ĀK*, which borrow from it extensively.

I have already indicated the ubiquity of Nityanātha Siddha, "son of Pārvatī," as the tantric author of works on alchemy, *haṭha yoga*, and tantric sorcery, and as a name figuring in both Rasa Siddha (*RRS*) and yogic Siddha (*HYP*) lists. I have also surmised that Nityanātha Siddha may have been a Nāth Siddha polymath, after the fashion of the founder Gorakhnāth, whom he names in *RRĀ* 4.4.100. (He also names Gahananātha,[232] who, if he is the same figure as the Gahaṇinātha who was Gorakh's disciple—and Jñāneśvara's guru's guru—in Maharashtran Nāth Siddha lineages, offers further proof that this is a late thirteenth-century Nāth Siddha text, likely from Maharashtra). The contents of the *RRĀ*, while they betray the author's interest and expertise in the fields of tantric alchemy and sorcery, as well as Ayurvedic therapy, make no reference to hathayogic techniques. Nityanāth sets forth the agenda to his very prolix work in his opening verses (*RRĀ* 1.1.4b–6a): "This treatise in five sections (*khaṇḍa*s) is offered for the benefit of practitioners; [for the benefit of] Ayurvedic physicians (*vaidya*s) in the [first] Rasa division; [that of] the afflicted in the [second] Rasendra [division]; theoreticians in the [third] Vāda division;

[and] the aged in the [fourth] Rasāyana [division]. Supernatural power of an alchemical order (*rasa-siddhi*) is proffered for the sake of [tantric] advisors in the [fifth] Mantra division."[233]

The Rasa and Vāda divisions of the *RRĀ*, composed of ten and twenty chapters or "teachings" (*upadeśas*) respectively, treat for the most part of the operations proper to transmutational (*dhātuvāda*) alchemy, while the Rasendra division, seventy-one chapters in length,[234] treats of therapeutic (*rogavāda*) alchemy. The Rasāyana division, eight chapters in length, is a discussion of elixir (*dehavāda*) alchemy, save its concluding chapter, which is a panegyric of the alchemical wonderland of Śrī Parvata (Srisailam) and the alchemical practices specific to that site.

Much of the final Siddha or Mantra division of the *RRĀ* appears to have been borrowed, more or less piecemeal, into the *KPT* of Siddha Nāgārjuna. This is made manifestly clear in *KPT* 1.13a, which states: "This is called the Mantra division (*mantra-khaṇḍa*) [which is offered] for the welfare of practitioners." The same half verse is found in the Mantra Khaṇḍa of the *RRĀ* (5.1.11a), where the statement makes perfect sense. The twenty-seven chapters of the Mantra division become condensed into twenty chapters in the *KPT*; however, the chapter order of the two is quite identical. Even if it is divided into fewer chapters, the *KPT* is substantially longer than the Mantra Khaṇḍa of the *RRĀ*, again indicating that it is a later expansion Nityanātha's work.[235] Given that the *RM* cites the *KPT*, we must conclude that it too is a later work than the *RRĀ*: therefore, the *Rasa Maṅgala* named in *RRĀ* 1.1.16b cannot be the same work as the *RM*.

Nityanātha Siddha makes a number of statements that are more or less unique to this alchemical source. He mentions both the necessity of belonging to an order (*sampradāya*), and states that his work is a blend of his guru's teachings and his own practical experience (1.1.21a, 22a). Elsewhere, he states that the alchemical teachings were received directly, by the Siddhas, from Śiva's mouth; this mystical technique has been kept hidden in the writings of their order, which he has himself surveyed (3.1.9–10). Then follows an oft-repeated aphorism, of which Nityanātha appears to be the original source: "Neither sequence (oral teachings) without written sources nor written sources without sequence [are acceptable]. Knowing the written sources to be conjoined with sequence (oral teachings), the person who then practices [alchemy] partakes of the *siddhis*."[236]

Nityanātha's discussion of Srisailam (4.8.1–185) is by far his most innovative contribution to the alchemical literature: that this is the Śaiva center in western Andhra Pradesh is clearly proven by references to the *jyotirliṅga* of Mallikārjuna (4.8.2, 5, 129, 135, 173) that is the heart of the cultus there. His catalog of alchemical wonders at a number of sites (a grove called Kadalī Vana, pools, wells, etc.) is by far the most comprehensive of its genre. Elsewhere (1.1.12a–13a), he expands on an aphorism first introduced in *RA* 10.29 and compares various types of mercury with the gods Brahmā, Viṣṇu (Janārdana), Rudra, Maheśvara, and Sadāśiva. These last two names for Śiva would appear to indicate that Nityanātha's pantheon was that of orthodox Śaiva Siddhānta; yet his alchemy, concerned with *jīvanmukti* as an end in itself rather than a means to the orthodox end of *mokṣa*, betrays a more heterodox orientation. Elsewhere, he also mentions Manthānabhairava (4.3.197). Explicit references to the perfection of the human body as the alchemist's highest goal (4.1.2), to sexual relations with menstruating women as a suggested adjunct to work in the laboratory (4.1.4a; 4.3.197–199), and to cremation ground rites (4.4.113) reinforce this emphasis, as does the entirety of the Mantra or Siddha Khaṇḍa, which is wholly devoted to the subject of tantric sorcery.

Nityanātha appears to follow the lead of the *RA* in his discussions of alchemical worship and initiation, the ideal guru, disciple, and female laboratory assistant, etc.: he is in turn copied by Vāgbhaṭṭa II, author of the *RRS*. The *RRĀ*'s rendering of the classical aphorism concerning the powers of swooned, killed, and bound mercury (1.1.24) may be the source from which the *RM* borrows most directly; the *RM* also appears to follow Nityanātha who, in the final verses of this chapter, discusses the *doṣa*s of mercury and suggested quantities of mercury to be employed in the alchemical operations (1.1.25b–33a).

The *RRĀ* lists no fewer than twelve metals (1.8.1–2), among which it includes three alloys and iron rust. On the basis of Nityanātha's name, evocations of Gorakhnāth and Gahaṇināth, his emphasis on the practitioner's adherence to a *sampradāya*, his inclusion in the *HYP*, and the other yogic and tantric works attributed to him, I am inclined to think that Nityanāth was a Nāth Siddha who lived slightly later than Gorakhnāth but earlier than the *BhP* that is attributed to the latter.[237]

i. The *Mātṛkabheda Tantra* (*MBhT*) is, on at least two counts, a singular work in the annals of tantric alchemy. On the one hand it is, in the fullest sense of the term, a Siddha alchemical work, combining the standard theoretical, yogic, ritual, and behavioral components of practice with alchemy.[238] On the other, it is the sole Hindu work containing significant alchemical data to be a clearly eastern Indian product. Most manuscripts of the *MBhT* are found in Bengal, and a list of sacred waters found in the text (4.28) mentions only Himalayan and eastern Indian toponyms.[239] Its title and strong emphasis on the cult of the Goddess make this a Śākta-Śaiva Tantra.

The *MBhT*, a work in fourteen chapters, is cast as a dialogue between Śaṅkara and the goddess Caṇḍikā. Of its twelve chapters, three (chapters five, eight, and nine) are devoted, in the main, to alchemy. Here, however, the use of mercurials is not presented as an end in itself, but rather as a means to the higher end of ritual devotion to Śiva and the Goddess. At the heart of this devotion is the worship of Śiva in the form of a mercurial *liṅga*, the mercury of which has been stabilized and calcinated with menstrual blood. No alchemical Tantra is as attentive to the miraculous powers of uterine or menstrual blood as the *MBhT*. It classifies this fluid (*dravya*) into six types—according to the age, marital status, and sexual experience of the woman in question—and invokes its use in a number of practices, both ritual and alchemical.[240]

The use the *MBhT* makes of the term *dravya*—to refer to both sexual emissions and mercury as "power substances"—parallels usages we have already noted in the *RA*, *KCM*, and *BhP*. Chapter four of the *MBhT* is devoted to the worship of Camuṇḍā Kālikā, whose name evokes that of Kākacamuṇḍā, one of the names by which Kākacaṇḍeśvarī is identified: there is, moreover, a certain symmetry between the Caṇḍikā of the *MBhT* and the Kāka-caṇḍ-eśvarī of the *KCM*. The *MBhT* is thoroughly conversant with the subtle body of *haṭha yoga* and includes extended discussions of the *cakra*s, the "nine doors" (9.20), and the *kuṇḍalinī*. Here, the *MBhT* follows mainstream tantric discourse when it states that the alcohol, flesh, fish, etc. ritually consumed by the practitioner are offerings to the Goddess who, dwelling within the subtle body in the form of the *kuṇḍalinī*, rises up to the practitioner's tongue, in order to enjoy them. The *mūlādhāra cakra*, in which the *kuṇḍalinī* dwells, is identified with the Goddess's *pīṭha* of Kāmarūpa.[241]

Worship of Śiva in the form of a *liṅga* is central to this work, with the mercurial *liṅga* being the optimum type. Neither worship, nor ritual, nor alchemy is effective without the use of *mantra*s, to which the *MBhT* devotes much attention.[242] The work also discusses the importance of the guru, the establishment of lakes, reservoirs, and temples, and various rules of worship—the standard subject matter of a Tantra. The practitioner who follows its instructions gains *siddhi*s and becomes a "Siddha who is the manifest equal of Śiva."[243] The *MBhT* mentions the eighteen Purāṇas, and cites the *Kālī Tantra*, *Nityā[ṣoḍaśika] Tantra* (= *Vāmakeśvara Tantra*, which it also cites), the *Guptasādhana Tantra*, *Vīra Tantra*, and *Ṭoḍala Tantra*.[244] Commentaries on the *Vāmakeśvara Tantra*, by Jayaratha and Śivānanda, date from the thirteenth century;[245] the *Ṭoḍala Tantra* is also likely a thirteenth-century work, making the *MBhT* a relatively late text, probably dating from the latter part of the thirteenth century.

j. It has already been observed, at some great length, what the *Rasendra Maṅgala* (Auspicious Ornament of Mercury) is not: it is neither particularly ancient nor original, freely copying as it does from the *RA* and a number of other tantric alchemical works. It is, nonetheless, an important alchemical Tantra and one that, like the *KCM*, may have certain archaic elements embedded in the thirteenth- to fourteenth-century recension that has come down to us. The two manuscript versions of the *RM* that I have consulted both provide, in their opening verses (1.3–5), a "table of contents" which indicates that this is a work in eight chapters, which treat of the following subjects: (1) operations relative to the primary and secondary minerals and the metals; (2) the "killing" of gemstones and the liquification of all elements; (3) the binding of mercury; (4) mercurial pills (*guṭikā*); (5) humoral therapy; (6) unguents (*añjana*) to enhance the visual and olfactory senses; (7) poisons (*viṣa*); and (8) the host (*gaṇa*), a possible reference to a Śaiva goal of becoming a lord of Śiva's host. However, the same manuscripts contain only the first four of these chapters, together with an auto-commentary which does not discuss the subject matter of chapters five through eight as indicated in the table of contents.[246]

The RM borrows freely from the *RA* and cites the *Manthānabhairava [Tantra]*. It also cites the *Kakṣapuṭa Tantra* which is,[247] as noted, an expansion on the Mantra Khaṇḍa of the thirteenth-century *RRĀ* of Nityanātha. It is cited in the mid-fourteenth-century *Rasarājalakṣmī* of Viṣṇudeva or Viṭṭhala:[248] the *RM* is therefore a work of the late thirteenth or early fourteenth century. While its elaborate mise-en-scène of Nāgārjuna, Prajñāparamitā, Ratnaghośa and others atop Srisailam was sufficient to hoodwink Ray and a number of other scholars, the author of the *RM* may not have intended deceit. For we read in the second verse of this work that "the therapist who carries out his treatment after hearing the *RM* will undoubtedly meet with success. So said Nāgārjuna himself."[249] Moreover, the *RM* lists "Nāgārjuna" as the eighteenth Rasa Siddha.

Now, the chapter colophons to this work call it the "*Rasendramaṅgala* of Śrī Nāgārjuna." The question therefore arises: to which Nāgārjuna is the Nāgārjuna who wrote this work referring? He may, on the one hand, be referring to himself in the third person, in which case he would have done well to include a section on *bhūta-vidyā* in his work, to sort out his multiple-Nāgārjuna personality disorder. On the other, the Nāgārjuna he quotes and places in dialogue with other Buddhist luminaries may be the legendary seventh-century alchemist whose biography was conflated, by Hsuan-tsang and others, with that of the ca. second-century Mādhyamika philosopher. Finally, the Nāgārjuna who authored the *RM* may be referring to an alchemist Nāgārjuna who lived and taught only slightly prior to his time or, indeed, who was his own guru. Here, it is useful to recall that Gauraṇa maintains, in his A.D. 1400 Telugu *Navanātha Carita*, that Nāgārjuna[-nāth] "gave his own (*ātmīya*) name to his disciple, who was thenceforth known as Nāgārjuna Siddha or Siddha Nāgārjuna." It is this figure who, in Gauraṇa's account, attempts to transform Srisailam into a heap of gold. In the *RM*, this is precisely what Nāgārjuna promises to do for the goddess Prajñāparamitā.[250] However, the author of the *RM* is not called Siddha Nāgārjuna, but simply Śrī Nāgārjuna. Contrariwise, the author of the *KPT* is known as Siddha Nāgārjuna, and the *RM* evokes the *KPT* at one point. The *KPT* is, as noted, more a work on tantric sorcery than on tantric alchemy; it would appear from the "table of contents" to the *RM* that its latter chapters deal precisely with the subject of tantric sorcery (chapters on *añjana* and *viṣa* are found in every Kriyā Tantra).

I have already noted that the twelfth- to thirteenth-century *Yogaratnamālā* (*YRM*) may have been authored by the same Nāgārjuna as was the *KPT* (which nonetheless copies from the thirteenth-century *RRĀ*); and I have indicated, on the basis of its use of vernacular language and the authorship of its commentary, that the *YRM* is a Gujarati work.[251] I have also noted that the *KPT* refers to both Śrīparvata and Pattan, with the latter name corresponding to a number of Gujarati toponyms. We also know that in about A.D. 1030, Alberuni had heard of an alchemist named Nāgārjuna who had been based at the Gujarati site of "Fort Daihak" some one hundred years prior to his time. If, then, we maintain that the author of the *RM* is referring to a historical Nāgārjuna who was only slightly prior to his time, or who was indeed his own guru, this "Nāgārjuna in the text" may have been the twelfth- to thirteenth-century author of the *YRM* (and the thirteenth-century *KPT*?), who came to Srisailam from Gujarat, where he became the guru of the Nāgārjuna who authored the *RM*. Whatever the case, it is impossible to identify the author of the *RM* or his teacher with the Nāgārjuna referred to by Alberuni, who could not have lived later than the tenth century. On the other hand, "Nāgārjuna" may have been—as was the case with Matsyendra—a title applied to alchemists who had reached a certain level of expertise, in which case we should not be surprised to be confronted by a host (*gaṇa*, the title of chapter eight of the *RM*) of Nāgārjunas! In any case, the premise for all of these speculations—i.e., that the Nāgārjuna in the text of the *RM* was a historical figure—may itself be groundless.

Following its table of contents, the *RM* launches into a praise of mercury, stating that "through the use of the mercurial method (*rasendra-yogāt*), one becomes a superior *yogin* on this earth, surpassing even the Lord [Śiva] (*nātha-atitulya*)": Śiva is called "Lord" (*nātha*) in a number of passages in this work.[252] Hereafter, the work lists the impurities present in mercury and gives an incomplete list of the alchemical operations, which it calls the "eighteen Works" (*karmāṇyaṣṭādaśa*), and gives the suggested quantities of mercury to be used in these operations.[253]

Chapter two begins with a description of the "Kāpālika method" for the liquification of gemstones, a technique this work borrows directly from the *RA*.[254] The same chapter concludes with another seminal teaching, cribbed from the *RA* (7.151): "killed metals become adequate for internal use."[255] This is precisely the subject of the third chapter, i.e., therapeutic uses of herbal and mercurial preparations and elixirs, most of which bear the names of Śaiva or Śākta deities.[256] Chapter three concludes with a long section on eye medicines (*añjana*), for which, it will be recalled, a ca. fifth-century Nāgārjuna was renowned.[257]

It is in the very long chapter four of the *RM* that we find nearly all of the "Buddhist legend" and the borrowings from the *RA* discussed above.[258] This chapter, on the subject of mercurial *guṭikā*s, gives a description of the same "Immortal Beauty" pill referred to in the *RA* and *KCM;* the *RM* preparation differs slightly from that of the two other texts.[259] It is also in this chapter that we find a list of the eight primary *rasa*s, although lists of the secondary *rasa*s and metals are lacking.[260] A long section in this chapter, devoted to the use of "leech-bound" mercury (i.e., treated mercury whose consistency is that of a leech), placed in the vagina as a female aphrodisiac, appears to be an expansion on a similar discussion found in the *KCM*.[261] The latter portion of this chapter has already been discussed at some length. Following the *RA*, it stipulates that mercury that has been calcinated six times in sulfur is optimal for transmutation and transubstantiation.[262] Like the *KCM*, the *KJñN*, and most other Siddha works, it devotes some space to "skewing Time" (*kāla-vañcana*).[263] It makes mention of the tantric worship of a virgin and of the *dravya* "power-substance" to be employed therein.[264]

Following chapter four in the Paris-Bikaner manuscripts of this work are several folios which neither correspond in their contents to any of the final four chapters of the work nor have a name given to them in the final colophon of these manuscripts. Contained in this "appendix" are an auto-commentary (*ṭippaṇa*),[265] a verse borrowed from the *RHT* (1.2), and the list of the twenty-seven Rasa Siddhas which is borrowed directly into the *RRS*. As noted above, this auto-commentary is similar to that found in the *KCM* and is basically a companion to the work as a whole, giving the five names for mercury (including *śarvaja*,[266] a term also found in the *BhP*, but nowhere else), types of female laboratory assistants, etc. Until the critical edition of this work appears, the authenticity of this final section is open to doubt.

k. The *Rasaratnasamucchaya* (Amassing of Rasas and Gemstones) (*RRS*) of Vāgbhaṭṭa II is a thirteenth- to fourteenth-century work in thirty chapters, of which fourteen (1–11, 28–30) are alchemical or iatrochemical and sixteen (12–27) are Ayurvedic. In spite of its great prestige this is, at least in its alchemical content, a highly derivative text. Its first chapter is, for the most part, a patchwork of passages cribbed from the *RA*, *RM*, and especially the *RHT*.[267] Of its remaining alchemical chapters, much of their content is a transparent adaptation of the *RC* of Somadeva and the *RRĀ* of Nityanātha.[268] Its mention of the Yādava king Siṅghaṇa (d. A.D. 1220) and of opium support a mid-thirteenth-century date; if, as some commentators maintain, it borrows eleven verses (5.132–142) from the ca. A.D. 1375 *Rasaratnapradīpa* of Rāmarāja, then it is a late fourteenth-century work.[269]

l. The *Ānandakanda* (*ĀK*) (The Root of Bliss), the most encyclopedic work of the entire Hindu alchemical canon, is a massive text, over six thousand verses in length. In its colophons, it calls itself the work of Bhairava; the apparent referent here is the tantric god, given that the entirety of the text is cast as a dialogue between Bhairava and Bhairavī. The *ĀK* is divided into two sections, curiously called "recreations" or "places of repose" (*viśrāntis*), which are subdivided into a total of thirty-six chapters and an appendix. The second section, entitled "work" (*kriyā*) is essentially devoted to the chemistry of metals and gemstones. The first section, entitled "nectar making" (*amṛtikaraṇa*), may be termed a Siddha alchemical text, containing as it does chapters on both alchemical and hathayogic (chapters 20 and 21) techniques for the realization of bodily immortality, a chapter (12) on the alchemical wonders of Srisailam, discussions of initiation, etc. As already noted, it is in this work that the sole attempt is made to fuse the Nāth Siddhas together with the Rasa Siddhas: this is, from a history of religions standpoint, the *ĀK*'s greatest innovation.

In spite of its dual emphasis on alchemy and *haṭha yoga*, the *ĀK* is, properly speaking, less a work on Siddha alchemy than an *encyclopedic* work, which incorporates and synthesizes (i.e., copies and paraphrases) all that falls within its fourteenth-century purview. So it is that the *ĀK*'s anonymous author also incorporates extended discussions of Ayurvedic elixir therapy, seasonal dietary regimens, and a number of other ancillary topics into his work.

It has generally been maintained, mainly on the strength of the fact that its three original manuscript sources are housed in south Indian collections, that the *ĀK* is a south Indian work.[270] This is further supported by the inclusion, in the *ĀK*'s Siddha lists, of names whose origins are clearly south Indian (Mūlanātha, Revaṇa, Koṅkaṇeśvara, etc.). If this is a south Indian work, however, it likely emerged from the Deccan plateau rather than either of the southern coastal regions: the seasonal cycles it describes in chapter nineteen correspond to a temperate and continental (versus a tropical and coastal) climate. It is also possible that this chapter, like so much of the rest of this work, is a wholesale borrowing from external (and northern) sources.

The *ĀK* is most ingenious in its ability to inflate the content of passages it borrows from other alchemical works, most especially the *RA*, *RRĀ*, *RC*, and *RRS*. Of these, the *RRĀ* is the *ĀK*'s prime source. So, for example, the *ĀK* chapter (1.12.1–200) on Srisailam is borrowed nearly piecemeal from *RRĀ* 4.8.1–185.[271] It contains the standard origin myth of sulfur (1.13.3–24) as well as of mercury (1.1.8–23: an expansion on that found in *RRS* 1.60–66); its mythic description of the extraction of mercury (1.1.53–62) from its well in "Cinnabar-Land" also expands on the *RRS* (1.85–88) account of the same. Instructions for the worship of Rasabhairava, Rasāṅkuśī, the ten Dūtīs, the eight Vidyeśvaras, the *yoginī*s, and Kubjikā (1.2.165) rely heavily on the *rasamaṇḍala* of the *RA* (2.53–72).

Whereas most alchemical works list six to nine metals, the *ĀK* lists twelve (2.1.9); it lists twenty-three, rather than the standard eight *uparasa*s (2.1.4–8). Its list of the "eighteen" *saṃskāra*s does not include "body work" (*śarīra yoga*); appended to it are a list of subsidiary operations. The *ĀK*'s (2.9.1–97) discussion of the sixty-four divine herbs (*divyauṣadhī*s) is borrowed directly from the *RC* (6.1–72). Its discussions of the use of *mantra*, *yantra*, *nyāsa*, etc. are likewise more prolix than those found in other alchemical sources. Its chapters on *haṭha yoga* make no mention of Gorakhnāth or any other Siddha; the content of these chapters is, however, clearly inspired by the *Gorakṣa Śataka* and the other works of "six-limbed" yoga that it spawned.[272] Its description of the meditation hut (*kuṭī*) is similar to that of Ayurvedic rejuvenation therapy, inasmuch as it is a threefold structure (1.21.4–5). As in many other alchemical sources, the *ĀK* lists its Rasa (and Nāth) Siddhas in a worship context: they are the recipients of water offerings in the "conventional initiation" (*samayā dīkṣā*) section of the work.[273] Graphic representations of the nine Nāths and sixteen Siddhas are also to be figured, together with the eight *Puranic* (and not Tantric) Bhairavas, the sixty-four *yoginī*s, and other deities, on the outer walls of the meditation hut (1.21.71–74).

m. The small gem entitled *Khecarī Vidyā* (*KhV*) (The Aviator's Science; or The Arcane Science of Flight) is, in spite of its relatively late date, a paradigmatic text of the Siddha alchemical tradition. Unlike the *ĀK*—whose encyclopedic content encompasses alchemy, *haṭha yoga*, and nearly everything else under the medieval sun—the *KhV* never strays from its single object. The object in question, the *siddhi* of human flight, is treated in an extensive and generally derivative way: the *KhV* draws, for the most part, on preexisting hathayogic traditions. What is original about the *KhV* is its triadic focus, on hathayogic, erotico-mystical, and alchemical techniques for the realization of its end, a focus I have previously qualified as the "Siddha distinction."

The *KhV*, a work in four chapters and 285 verses attributed to Ādinātha, generally calls itself, in its manuscript colophons, a portion of a work entitled the *Mahākālayogaśāstra.* Two late medieval commentators, Brahmānanda and Nārāyaṇa, refer to a work of the same title as a treatise on *haṭha yoga:* they are presumably referring as well to the *KhV.*[274] This notwithstanding, every manuscript of this work that I have found calls itself the *KhV.*[275] The sole works that the *KhV* itself cites are called "*Mahākāla*" and "Mārtaṇḍaṃ Viveka." The latter of these is the *Yogamārtaṇḍa* or *Vivekamārtaṇḍa* of Gorakhnāth, a work that is, in the main, an expansion on the *Gorakṣa Śataka.* As for the former, if it is not the *Mahākālayogaśāstra* itself, it may be the *Mahākāla Saṃhitā*, a "Kāpālika" work also attributed to "Ādinātha"![276] There exist south Indian recensions of the *KhV*, which comprise only the first chapter of northern versions; this first chapter is moreover often reproduced as the second chapter of the *Yogakuṇḍalī Upaniṣad.* Elsewhere, three verses of the *KhV* are reproduced in the fifteenth-century *HYP* (3.33–35),[277] in the light of which evidence we may conclude that the *KhV* is a fourteenth-century north Indian work.

The *KhV* begins with a praise of itself (1.1–28), followed by an account of the *khecari mantra* (1.29–40). The balance of the first chapter is devoted to a discussion of the mechanical preparations for and hathayogic practice of the so-called *khecarī mudrā* (1.41–74).[278] The second and longest chapter is an extended description of the *siddhi*s, as well as of the subtle body—the *cakra*s, *nāḍī*s, *kalā*s, etc. A portion of this chapter (2.81–97) describes the effects of hathayogic practice on the humors (*doṣa*s) of Ayurvedic theory. Chapter three discusses the raising of the *kuṇḍalinī*, her union, in the cranial vault, with Śiva, who is figured as an internal *liṅga*, and the realization, on the part of the practitioner, of bodily liberation. This is described in terms of the reintegration, or telescoping back into their subtler essences, of the five elements (3.49–52).

It is, however, by virtue of its short final chapter that the *KhV* stands as a paradigmatic Siddha alchemical text. This emphasis is clearly stated in the chapter's opening verse: "I will now speak of the 'divine herbal medicines' (*divyānyauṣadhāni*). Without herbal medicines, absolutely no *siddhi*s can be realized." A short way into its discussion of these "herbal medicines," however, the *KhV* recommends the consumption of "mercury, sulfur, orpiment, and realgar," the mineral mainstays of elixir alchemy. The work concludes (4.13) with the following statement: "Having risen at daybreak, one should eat a decoction of mercury, the sap of the silk-cotton tree, and sulfur, [blended] together with the three sweets [honey, sugar, and butter]. In the space of six months, one becomes unaging and immortal." This is precisely the regime of the Yogis described by François Bernier, a regime which, taken in the morning, "restored the body to perfect health."[279]

SIX

Tantra in the Rasārṇava

1. Chapter One of the *Rasārṇava:* The Text in Its Tantric Context

As we have already noted, the use of alchemical imagery was, for several centuries, a pervasive fixture of both Hindu and Buddhist tantrism. This chapter looks at this phenomenon from another perspective and examines what the alchemists themselves had to say about Kaula and Śākta tantrism. No alchemical source has more to say on tantric theory and practice in general, and the Kaulas in particular, than does the eleventh-century *RA*, decidedly the greatest work of tantric alchemy.

More than any other, this source attests to the highly cosmopolitan nature of the alchemical tradition. Written in a quite grammatical Sanskrit, this text, while it was likely authored in western India, appears to be, like many of the alchemical classics, the production of a quite homogeneous—albeit geographically widespread—tradition. This homogeneity may be attributed in part to the sociology of alchemical knowledge to which I alluded in previous chapters: the authors of these texts were most probably court-based brahmin physicians to Hindu, Buddhist, or Muslim rulers.[1]

What sets the *RA* apart from all other alchemical works, indeed, from the great majority of the Hindu Tantras in general, is the rhetorical flourish its author gives to its opening chapter. I therefore reproduce, as much for their style as for their content, a number of excerpts from this introductory diatribe, in which the alchemical gnosis is favorably compared and contrasted to the other philosophical and religious schools and movements of the day. Our author begins to delineate his position in the fourth verse of this chapter. The Goddess (Devī), Bhairava's interlocutor, addressing him for the first time, says, "O God among gods, O Great God, O incinerator of Time and Love, O leader [*śāsaka*] of the Kaula, Mahākaula, Siddhakaula, etc. lineages!"[2] This introduction immediately reminds us of the sectarian pedigree of Matsyendra: a member of the Siddha Kaula and heir to the

Mahākaulas, he was the founder of the Yoginī Kaula: the author of the *RA* is thereby claiming a similar pedigree for his work.[3] He nuances his position, however, in a number of later verses, in which he unambiguously condemns what he considers to be excessive practices on the part of some tantric groups.

So, for example, in verse 10 he states that "if liberation is to be identified with the excitation of the female genitalia, would not even donkeys be liberated? Indeed, why are rams and bulls not liberated?"[4] And two verses later: "If liberation came from utilizing one's semen, urine, and excrements, which of the races of dogs and swine would not be liberated?"[5] And in verse 24: "For those people who have lost their powers of reason through indulgence in liquor, flesh, sexual intercourse, and the male and female organs, the mercurial science is exceedingly difficult to realize."[6]

The two verses that immediately follow (1.25–26) are placed in counterpoint to all that has preceded: "However (*tu*), mercury is not perfected by those who lack the teaching of the [true] lineage (*kula*) and who have no desire for the true doctrine. They, O Goddess, are [like men] drinking a mirage.[7] He who eats cow meat [and] who drinks the liquor of immortality, him I consider to be one of the *kula* [and] a knower of *rasa*. Other *rasa* experts are inferior."[8]

At first blush, we would appear to be in the presence of a text that contradicts itself. The truth is of a somewhat more subtle order, however. The attacks on the excessive indulgence in erotico-mystical practices and the fire *makāra*s are just that: Śiva's alchemical revelation is, generally speaking, a "post-Trika reformation" one. Following the lead of Matsyendra and perhaps Abhinavagupta in toning down the more extreme mortuary and erotic elements of earlier tantrism, this alchemical Tantra presents itself as a "meta-Śākta-Śaiva" work, superior not only to orthodox Śaiva Siddhānta, but also to the practices of the earlier Kula and prereform Kaulism.

As noted in a previous chapter, the author of the *RA* does consider the alchemical school to constitute a lineage, a line of transmission (*kula*) with a *kula*-teaching of its own. [9] Because the lineage nectar of the alchemical lineage (*sampradāya*) is,[10] like that of other tantric sects, transmitted through female sexual emissions (called *siddhadravya* in the *RA*), he also prescribes sexual intercourse and erotico-mystical worship as means to alchemical transformation (with an exception made for yogins, who are admonished to remain celibate in their preparation of mercury).[11] Elsewhere, a female "laboratory assistant" (and, especially, her sexual and menstrual fluids) is crucial to the alchemist's practice.[12] However, "the fluid" (*dravya*) is to be withheld from "other women" (*paradārāt*).[13]

It is, however, with our author's mention of the heterodox tantric matters of eating cow meat (*gomāṃsa*) and drinking the liquor of immortality (*amaravāruṇi*) that the light truly dawns. Such expressions are commonplaces of the "code language" of *haṭha yoga*. As a commentator explains on the subject of an identical passage in the fifteenth-century *HYP*, these two terms actually refer to the exalted practice of *khecarī mudrā*, whereby the yogin internally absorbs his own semen, which has been transmuted into nectar through yogic practice.[14] Neither meat nor alcohol is actually being consumed; here, the reference is to the hathayogic complement to alchemical operations, a complementarity that is the hallmark of "the [alchemical] Work in two parts."[15]

The tantric alchemist tempers his tantrism and sublimates certain Kaula erotico-mystical practices with hathayogic and laboratory techniques (even if many of these are called *kāpālika* techniques).[16] This sublimation, of the male and female sexual essences so vital to the *yoginī* cults of the Vidyā Pīṭha, into mineral essences to be manipulated by the alchemist, is clearly stated by Śiva: "You, O Goddess, are the mother of all beings, and I am the eternal father, and that which was generated from the great sexual union of us two, that is *rasa*."[17]

The hathayogic component of tantric alchemy will concern us throughout much of the balance of this book; let us first, however, take a longer look at those elements of the *RA* which may be designated as properly "tantric." As I will presently demonstrate, the *RA* remains mainstream in its tantrism, in its use of *mantra*, *yantra*, initiation, worship, etc. At the same time, it purports to be superior to both the orthodox Śiva Siddhānta and the more heterodox Kaula forms of Tantra in the results it promises. For, whereas the former can offer liberation only at death and the latter liberation only in life, tantric alchemy offers certain, verifiable bodily immortality in life, an immortality whose effects are enduring.[18]

The opening benediction of the *RA* sets the tone of the entire work: "He in whom everything [dwells], from whom everything [is issued], who is everything and everywhere, who is all-encompassing and eternal, salutations to that universal soul!"[19] Following the Goddess's salutation, Śiva's first words speak to the goals of every nondualist tantric practitioner, regardless of sectarian affiliation: "Eternal youth, immortality of the body, and the attainment of an identity of nature with Śiva, that is, liberation in the body (*jīvanmukti*), which is difficult even for the gods to attain."[20] From here, the god launches into a condemnation of all other forms of religious practice, reserving his greatest scorn for the six major schools of philosophy—the philosophical foundations of nontantric Hinduism—which equate liberation with release from the body (i.e., which assume that liberation is realized only after death):[21]

> The liberation that occurs when one drops dead[22] is indeed a worthless liberation. [For in that case] a donkey is also liberated when he drops dead. Liberation is indeed viewed in the six schools as [occurring] when one drops dead, but that [kind of] liberation is not immediately perceptible, in the way that a myrobalan fruit in the hand [is perceptible] (*karāmalakavat*).[23]

The concrete emphasis of the alchemical quest is hereafter emphasized repeatedly:

> Liberation [arises] from gnosis (*jñāna*), gnosis [arises] from the maintenance of the vital breaths. Therefore, where there is stability, mercury is empowered and the body is stabilized. Through the use of mercury one rapidly obtains a body that is unaging and immortal, and concentration of the mind.[24] He who eats calcinated mercury (*mṛtasūtaka*) truly obtains both transcendent and mundane knowledge, and his *mantra*s are effective.[25]

Supernatural powers and bodily immortality, the goals of the tantric practitioner, cannot, however, be realized through alchemy alone. The absolute, Śiva, too plays an active role in alchemical transformation: "So long, however, as Śiva does not descend to block the impurity that impedes the soul's liberation, and so long as one's fetters to this world remain uncut, there is no way that true discrimination can arise through the use of calcinated mercury."[26] Divine grace implies its human complement of devotion (*bhakti*), which is also present in the alchemical synthesis, even if such is unusual to tantrism, which places a greater emphasis on ritualized forms of worship (*pūjā*, *upāsana*) than it does upon devotionalism.[27]

To which gods does the alchemist offer his devotion and worship? Not surprisingly, the divine revealers of the *RA* single themselves out, at the conclusion of the first chapter of the work, as the prime objects of the alchemist's worship: these are Rasa-Bhairava, the "Mercurial Bhairava,"[28] and Rasāṅkuśī-Bhairavī, "Bhairavī, the Elephant Goad of Mercury."[29] Bhairava is, of course, one of the tantric names for Śiva, and Bhairavī is his female consort. Therefore, the alchemist is to worship a mercurial *liṅga*, the phallic emblem of Śiva, visualizing it as embodying the eighteen-armed Rasa-Bhairava and his consort Rasāṅkuśī-Bhairavī. Of course, this mercurial *liṅga*, the support for such worship, is composed the stuff of Śiva himself, i.e., of *rasa*, mercury.[30] The alchemist's Rasa-Bhairava is an ectype of the eighteen-armed Svacchanda Bhairava, the deity of the *Svacchanda Tantra* (*SvT*).[31]

It is on the subject of this icon and its mercurial content that the *RA* and a number of other alchemical works wax the most eloquent in praises that bear all the marks of Hindu devotionalism. The most propitious days for worship are the eighth and fourteenth days of the bright lunar fortnight; in addition to worship on these fixed dates, the observance of a special "alchemical celebration" (*rasotsava*) also produces miraculous results.[32] Viewing, touching, eating, recalling, worshipping, and making an offering to mercury yield six types of fruits. The merit one gains from viewing all of the *liṅga*s in the world (including Kedārnāth) is gained from the mere viewing of mercury. By worshipping Śiva in the form of calcinated mercury, with sandalwood, camphor, and saffron, one attains Śiva's heaven, Śivaloka. Eating mercury destroys the triad of sins (in word, deed, and thought), afflictions, and morbid states. The combined fruits that one might gain from worshipping one thousand of Śiva's self-generated (*svayambhū*) *liṅga*s is reaped 100,000-fold by worshipping the *rasa-liṅga* of Śiva.[33] But woe to those ignorant persons who do have no faith in mercury, or who speak ill of it: they will suffer 1,000 rebirths as dogs, 300,000 as cats, 100,000 as donkeys, 100,000 as crows, 100,000 as worms, 100,000 as wild cocks, and 100,000 as vultures![34] It is to this cult of mercury that a number of authors refer when they identify *rasacikitsā* "chemiatry," i.e., the worship of chemicals.[35]

In addition to such external forms of devotional worship, the *RA* also discusses external worship of a distinctly tantric stamp, as well as internal worship, mainly in the context of alchemical initiation, *dīkṣā*.[36]

2. Alchemical Maṇḍalas in Chapter Two of the *Rasārṇava*

We must not hastily conclude from so much sound and fury on the matter of the *rasaliṅga* that Śiva in his mercurial and phallic form was the sole god in the alchemical universe. If the alchemical tradition was a tantric one, then it too should have had a number, nay a pantheon, of supporting deities in its micro- and macrocosms, and this it in fact does, as the second and third chapters of the *RA* reveal with a multitude of details.

As in nearly every Hindu tantric sect, all the gods of the alchemical pantheon are either forms of Śiva, his divine consort the Goddess, or one of their divine attendants. Because the specific names of these deities evoked in the alchemical sources are so many indications of the various sectarian ties of the alchemical school, it behooves us to dwell on these for a moment. The *RA* compares mercury, inasmuch as it incorporates the five elements, with the five-faced Sadāśiva.[37] As already noted, however, Rasa-Bhairava, the supreme divinity of the *RA*, is an ectype of Svacchanda Bhairava (whose cult is mentioned explicitly in the *BhP*).[38] Indeed, the *RA*'s iconography of Rasa-Bhairava, including his enthronement upon the *mahāpreta* Sadāśiva strongly indicates that the cult of Svacchanda Bhairava is its implicit model. As noted in the last chapter, however, the *RA* and such texts as the *BhP*, *MBhT*, and *KCM* are also possessed of an important Śākta component, referring on numerous occasions to the circle of the Mother Goddesses and Yoginīs and the erotico-mystical ritual associated with this configuration. The worship of the Yoginīs and tantric forms of the Goddess are also evoked at a number of points in the *RA*.[39]

A highly refined current of nondualist Śākta tantrism was the Trika Kaula of the Eastern Transmission, the *pūrvāmnaya*, so called for its cultic focus on a triad (*tri-*) of goddesses named Parā, Aparā, and Parāparā.[40] No doubt taking its lead from the Trika, the *RA* incorporates these three goddesses, together with a fourth, Mālinī,[41] into a complex *maṇḍala*, which it instructs the alchemist to construct for the external and internal tantric worship of Rasabhairava and the goddess Rasāṅkuśī.[42] This diagram, whose concrete support consists of a square stone slab measuring ten hand widths on each side, serves a dual purpose. It is to be used both for the consecration of the newly constructed alchemical laboratory and for the sake of gaining alchemical *siddhi*s.[43] Its form is that of a lotus composed of two concentric sets of petals ringing a central pericarp, with the whole surrounded by the standard four-sided, four-gated *bhūpura* enclosure. In the lotus's pericarp, as well as on each of its petals and at the articulations of the *bhūpura*, are placed the entire host of the *RA*'s alchemical pantheon, into the heart of which we now descend.

The alchemist begins his construction of this diagram, at the heart of his laboratory, with the installation of a *rasaliṅga*, composed of mercury (*rasa*). Simultaneously with his installation of this concrete image, he uses the "Elephant Goad of Mercury" *mantra* to establish the alchemical god

Rasabhairava in sexual union with his consort Rasāṅkuśī within his own body.[44] Following the installation of this divine pair, the alchemist constructs his *maṇḍala*, mentally and concretely, from the outside in,[45] starting at the *bhūpura*. On either side of each of the four gateways of this enclosure, he installs and worships eight demonic and semidivine Śaiva guardians, while at each of its eight cardinal points within the enclosure, he installs and worships an array of seven Puranic gods together with the goddess Umā.[46] Working inwards, he installs and worships, on the petals of an outer lotus, the ten female attendants (*dūtī*s), whose names are nothing other female adjectival forms of alchemical processes and potencies.[47] On the petals of the same lotus he worships the eight principal mineral reagents (*mahārasas*)—all "male" in gender—that are employed, in combination with mercury, in the processes of transmutation.[48] On the petals of an inner lotus, he installs eight Rudras—who are to be identified with the eight "Lords of Wisdom."[49] On the pericarp of this lotus are placed the four *śakti*s—Mālinī, Parā, Aparā, and Parāparā—who are identified, respectively, with the four alchemical energies (*śakti*s): the energy of gold, of sulfur (*balā* [for *vali*?]), of diamond, and of magnetite.[50] In the midst of this group of four and at the center of the *maṇḍala* is Rasabhairava. Seated upon the shoulders of a *preta*, he engages in sexual intercourse with the goddess Rasāṅkuśī, who is seated on his lap.[51] Both of these deities are described in detail. Rasabhairava is crystalline, eighteen-armed, five-faced, and three-eyed, with flaming hair, tongues, eyes, etc., and a crescent moon in his piled-up ascetic's chignon.[52] He wears a tiger skin and has a serpent for his sacred thread. As for Rasāṅkuśī, her complexion is the color of molten gold, and she is clad in yellow-colored clothing. She has one face, three eyes, and four arms, which bear the elephant goad (*aṅkuśa*), rosary, and noose and show the gesture of protection. She is to be worshipped with the five Vidyā seed *mantra*s (*bīja*s).[53]

This diagram, with its "superenthroned" divinities, is our key to the theological and sectarian stance of the *RA*'s author.[54] In such a system, that which is closer to the center of the *maṇḍala* is closest to the ultimate reality of the divinity at the heart of the *maṇḍala*, from whom all radiates outwards, while that which is further from the center is lower, in terms of the order of the divine revelation it represents. Working from the outside in, the eight divinities of classical Hinduism are far removed from the center of this tantric system and therefore from the immediate concerns of the alchemist. On and around the two concentric rings of lotus petals, the ten female attendants (*dūtī*s) are a probable evocation of the Vidyā Pīṭha's old and terrible cremation ground–based cult of the *yoginī*s that was reformed by Matsyendra's Yoginī Kaula cult.[55] The basic configuration of the inner lotus is that of the old Śaiva Siddhānta system, surmounted by that of the Trika goddesses; these are, in turn, superseded by the supreme divinities of the alchemical system, who are iconographic ectypes of Svacchandabhairava and Bālā Tripurasundarī, respectively.

So it is that the eight Rudras located on the inner lotus are identified with the eight Vidyeśvaras ("Lords of Wisdom") who ring Sadāśiva in the worship *maṇḍala* of the Saiddhāntika *pūjā* and who stand as mediating categories, in the dualist Śaiva Siddhānta, between the "pure" and "impure" worlds, and as beings through whom the lower order of beings may attain to higher evolutionary stages.[56] As for Sadāśiva himself, he has become demoted, as he is in the iconography of Svacchandabhairava, to the function of a mere vehicle: he is the *preta* upon whose shoulders Rasabhairava is installed.[57] In a later description, in which the *RA* (2.110–16) elaborates on the mystic body of Rasabhairava himself, we find another adaptation of *SvT* traditions. Here, the *RA* identifies various members of Rasa Bhairava's body (knees, loins, heart, mouth) with the five faces of Sadāśiva, of which the last, Īśāna, is located between the deity's eyebrows. Upon his forehead is a half moon; above this is a dot or drop (*bindu*), surmounted by the *nāda*. Higher still, located at the fontanelle, is the goddess Śakti. Above her is the goddess Unmanā ("Beyond Mind"), above whom is the triadic void or ether (*triśūnya*). This configuration is identical to those found in *SvT* and *Netra Tantra* descriptions of the yogic meditative utterance (*uccāra*) of the syllable Oṃ.[58] In yet another description of its principal deity—in this case, his thirty-two-syllabled *aghora* mantra—the *RA* (2.68) further identifies Rasa Bhairava with Svacchanda Bhairava and his cult.[59] As for Rasabhairava's consort, Rasāṅkuśī, she is patterned not after Svacchandabhairava's *śakti* Aghoreśvarī, but rather after Bālā Trīpurasundarī of the Śrīvidyā Kaula.[60] One might choose to see in these iconographic data a reflection of sectarian developments occurring within the Śaiva fold, in tenth- to eleventh-century Kashmir, where the cult of Svacchandabhairava was the dominant Śaiva *cult*, as it continues to be today. During the same period, the dominant Śaiva *doctrine* in Kashmir was the Śaiva Siddhānta, whose particular dualistic interpretation of the *SvT* was countered by later Trika nondualism, in the form of a (later authoritative) commentary on the text by Abhinavagupta's pupil Kṣemarāja (fl. ca. A.D. 1000–50). The new nondualism also entered the Śrividyā Kaula cult of the goddess Tripurasundarī, which became popular in Kashmir during the eleventh century. By the twelfth century, this cult had spread south to the Tamil country, where it continues to thrive.[61] Our author, who probably lived midway between Kashmir and Tamil Nadu (i.e., in the region of Maharashtra) in the eleventh century, was therefore adapting the prevailing Śaiva cults and doctrines of his day into an alchemical "superenthronement" of the images of Rasabhairava and his consort Rasāṅkuśī over those of the supreme deities of other tantric sects and cults.

3. Mantra and Initiation in Chapters Two and Three of the *Rasārṇava*

Following its description of the *rasamaṇḍala*, the *RA* turns to a detailed discussion of *mantra*, of those "tools for thought" by which the tantric practitioner, like the Vedic ritualist before him, empowers himself to manipulate the divinities whose acoustic being is nothing other than the aggregate of the phonemes of the Sanskrit alphabet. In a universe that is vibratory in nature, it is through these primal vibrations that one may most efficiently return to the absolute source of all vibration. Mantras are thus indispensable for the alchemist who, like every other tantric practitioner, has for his ultimate goal the conscious realization of a transcendent self (i.e., identification of oneself with the Self of godhead).

At the culmination of its description of its alchemical *maṇḍala*, the RA identifies the *mantra* of Rasesvara, of (Śiva) the "Lord of Mercury" as the thirty-two-syllabled *aghora mantra* of Svacchanda Bhairava "with attributes."[62] The mantra of the goddess Rasāṅkuśī, the *rasāṅkuśa mantra* is given in encoded form.[63] The *RA* also instructs the alchemist to make use of a number of other garden-variety tantric *mantra*s: these include the *praṇava* (*Oṃ*),[64] the *so'haṃ haṃsa*,[65] the *aghora*, the *mṛtyuñjaya*,[66] the seventeen-syllable *kālī mantra*,[67] the *kālapāśa*,[68] *mahāpāśupatāstra*,[69] etc. These are to be variously used before, during, and after every alchemical operation to ensure success.

Other *mantra*s, perhaps peculiar to this work, are the *mālā* ("garland") and *mūla* ("root") *mantra*s which, like the Raseśvara *mantra*, combine seed *mantra*s with evocations of Bhairava-Śiva.[70] These latter mantras are employed in the practice of *mantra-nyāsa*, the imposition of *mantra*s—each of which is identified with one or another tantric deity—upon the practitioner's own body, by which process that body is divinized.[71] This divinization of the body is crucial to two components of tantric practice. These are initiation (*dīkṣā*), by which a teacher renders a disciple capable of entering upon the tantric path; and worship, because all tantric worship assumes an identification of self with the divine, in order that one may worship one's self as the divinity. In both cases, this imposition of *mantras* effects the transformation of the body, purging it of its gross elements and filling the void left by their implosion with divine essences, in the form of phonemes.[72]

In the latter of these practices, this procedure is doubled by the simultaneous preparation of a concrete worship site, in this case the alchemical laboratory. This practice, called *bhūtaśuddhi*, "purification of the elements," is a commonplace of tantric propitiation.[73] We now turn to this practice, as it is delineated in the rather obscure language of chapter three of the *RA*. Here, Bhairava begins his exposition by saying that he will now describe "another acoustic image" (*punaranyaṃ mantramūrtim*) of the goddess Rasāṅkuśī.[74] He begins his discussion by speaking of the fifth element, space or ether which is called the fifth "house." This he distinguishes from the four other houses, which are "placed in front" (*pradhāna*); that is, they are arranged like the arms of a cross, with the empty fifth house standing as a central "courtyard." Because the element ether is the substrate of sound, this fifth house is also the "house of the *haṃsa* [*mantra*]," in which "the *siddhi*s, five *makāra*s, etc. stand." It is within this space that the practitioner will install the goddess Rasāṅkuśi, in the form of *mantra*s.[75]

With this, the *kālapāśa* ("noose of Time") mantra of the "house of the *haṃsa*" is given: *oṃ śiva hrīṃ kroṃ haṃsa*. The practitioner is then instructed to repeat this *mantra*—called the "mercurial goad" (*rasāṅkuśa*)—one hundred thousand times as the "doorkeeper" (*pratīhara*) at the beginning of the worship. This recitation of "doorkeeper" *mantra*s at the opening of a worship is standard in Śākta-Śaiva tantrism.[76]

Next, "using that same [*kālapāśa*] mantra, he should take up the dung of a young calf, and using that alone, O Goddess, he should take up the ashes of a funeral pyre,"[77] to ritually prepare the "most excellent worship site in which Lord Mercury (Rasendra) dwells" and empower the alchemical apparatus he will use in his experimentation.[78] He then sweeps the site with a brush he has empowered by installing and worshipping Kubjikā—the goddess of the Western Transmission—in it (with the thirty-two-syllabled *kubjika mantra*) together with her full sequence of subordinates. These subordinates, which are so many seed mantras, are termed the four Siddhas, the eighteen Puruṣas, the five elements, and the six Yoginīs.[79] Here, we appear to be in the presence of a number of elements proper to the *paści-*

māmnāya. Kubjikā is, of course, the cult Goddess of the Western Transmission. So too are the six *yoginīs*: chapter 15 of the *KM* and chapter 24 of the *ṢSS* are entitled "Ṣaḍyoginyaḥ,"[80] and there is in this tradition a fixation on the number six that one finds nowhere else in the Hindu corpus. As for the four Siddhas, these are to be identified either with the *gurucatuṣka*, the "Four Gurus" (Mitranātha, Oḍḍīśanātha, Ṣausṭhanātha, and Caryanātha) of Western Transmission tradition[81] or with the four *yuganātha*s, the Lords of the Ages (Khagendranātha, Kūrmanātha, Meṣanātha, and Macchandanātha) of the Siddha Cakra of earlier Kaula tradition.[82] The eighteen Puruṣas mentioned in the *RA* evoke the eighteen Nāthas of the *Kubjikānityāhnikatilaka* and *Saṃvartārthaprakāśa*, figures whom the *ṢSS* specifies are *puruṣa*s, i.e., human males, as opposed to the divine (three or) four Siddhas, of whom they are the sons and disciples. These eighteen are said to be "distinguished in couples"; that is, they are a redoubling of the Nine Nāths who were intermediaries between the divine and the human in the Western Transmission.[83]

Following his installation of Kubjikā, the alchemist of the *RA* "besmears" the site with the Caṇḍaghaṇṭā ("The Goddess of Furious Bells," a tantric name of Durgā), the *mantra* of the Goddess in the eastern house; takes up cow dung in order to smear the site with the Caṇḍabhairavī ("The Furious Goddess of Terror"), the *mantra* of the Goddess in the southern house; and sprinkles water over it with the Caṇḍakāpālinī ("The Furious Goddess of the Skull),"[84] the *mantra* of the Goddess in the northern house. Thereafter, he installs the seventeen-syllabled Kālī *mantra* in the stone mortar, the thirty-two-syllabled Aghora *mantra* in the pestle, etc.[85] While it is difficult to say whether the author of the *RA* was attempting, in this passage, to systematize the tantric *āmnāya*s or *pīṭha*s in his placement of the goddesses of the four houses around the central *haṃsa* house, we can maintain without hesitation that his was a syncretistic endeavor. Chapter three contains *mantra*s from Mantra Pīṭha (Aghora), Paścimāmnāya (Kubjikā), Uttarāmnāya (seventeen-syllabled Kālī), and Śrīvidyā (Tripurābhairavī) worship traditions.[86]

Now that the alchemist's body and laboratory have been ritually purified, the narrator Bhairava turns to the alchemical apparatus, consecrating each with a particular *mantra*, until all that the alchemist will employ in his ritual manipulations of elements has been purified and transformed.[87] From this point on, all of these mundane instruments, chemicals, herbal preparations have been transformed into so many tools (*yantras*) with which the alchemist may master the one divine energy that surges through both the universe and his own body. He is now prepared to embark upon the alchemical life-cycle rites (*saṃskāra*s) that will ultimately render him a second Śiva.

It would appear from the above discussions that the matter of initiation (*dīkṣā*) into alchemical practice is quite entirely omitted from the opening chapters of the *RA*. Yet we find that the second chapter of the work is entitled "rules for initiation" (*dīkṣā-vidhāna*) and that verses 36 to 83 of this chapter give a lacunary account of *dīkṣā*.[88] Many if not most of the standard elements of *dīkṣā* are present: a description of a suitable site for initiation, i.e., upon which to build an alchemical laboratory (2.37–43); a description of said initiation hall/laboratory (2.44–47a); information on the auspicious time for initiation (2.37b-48a); the preparatory *nityapūjā* by the teacher including the visualization and worship of the supreme deities in the midst of the elaborate alchemical *maṇḍala* discussed above (2.48b-74); "terrible offerings" (*aghorabali*) to demonic beings who would otherwise obstruct the ritual (2.75–76); worship of the "elephant goad" or *rasāṅkuśī* (2.77a); oblatory offerings (2.77b-78a); establishment of the consecration vase (2.28b-79); annointment (*abhiśeka*) of the initiate with water impregnated with *mantra*s and poured from that vase (2.80–81); teaching the *mantra* to the initiate (2.82a); and the celebratory all-night *cakrapūjā* for Kumārīs, Yoginīs, and Sādhakas (following Kaula, but not orthodox Siddhānta traditions; 82b-83). What is missing in this account is the *dīkṣā*, or initiation proper (as opposed to *abhiśeka*, annointment, by which one is empowered to give initiation to others), that intervenes, between the *nityapūjā* and the *abhiśeka* ritual, in standard tantric procedure. Nowhere in this portion of the chapter do we find explicit references either to *dīkṣā* in fire in which the initiate's *karma*s are destroyed with oblations into a consecrated fire or to the internal, yogic "initiation by penetration" (*vedhamayī dīkṣā*) of the Kaulas.[89]

What reasons might we adduce for the relative paucity of material in the *RA* on the transformative heart of *dīkṣā*? It may be that the concrete details of initiation were too secret to be committed to writing and were passed on via oral tradition. Alternatively, it may be that the alchemical practices themselves were considered to be the realization and culmination of the process set in motion by *dīkṣā*. This latter explanation is supported in a quite explicit way in a number of nonalchemical sources, which identify mercurial transformations with *dīkṣā* itself. So the tenth- to fourteenth-century *Kulārṇava Tantra*,[90] a seminal Kaula source, states that "just as iron, penetrated by mercury, attains the state of gold, so the soul, penetrated by initiation (*dīkṣā*), attains the state of Śiva."

In a sense, the relative paucity of material on *dīkṣā* in the alchemical sources may be explained by the fact that alchemical transmutation (*vedha*) served as the original model for tantric initiation, especially that most prestigious form called the "initiation of penetration," *vedha*[-*mayī*] *dīkṣā*.[91] Similarly, the purificatory *mantra*s of the broader tantric discipline (*bhūta-śuddhi*, etc.) are also rendered redundant, inasmuch as purification is a concrete enterprise in alchemy.[92] Lastly, the all-important *yantra*s and *maṇḍala*s used as supports for tantric meditation are themselves abstractions of alchemical apparatus.[93] In the alchemical (and to a lesser extent the hatha-yogic) sphere, purification, identification with the divine, and initiation are so many techniques for the concrete transformation of the "power substances" that are the human and divine—and mineral, in the case of alchemy—sexual fluids. Much of the balance of this study is devoted to delineating the myriad ways in which the language of such transformations was a *common* language, shared by the interpenetrating alchemical, hatha-yogic, Siddha, and tantric syntheses of medieval India.

SEVEN

Corresponding Hierarchies: The Substance of the Alchemical Body

1. *Rasa* and *Rasāyana* in Indian Systems of Thought

Rasa (from the same Indo-European root as the English word *resin*) has one of the broadest semantic fields of any term in the Sanskrit language. Originally employed in the Vedas[1] to signify the waters and liquids in general—vital fluids, animal juices, and vegetable saps—applications of the term *rasa* have proliferated over the millennia to embrace such fields as Ayurvedic medicine, *haṭha yoga*, alchemy, and Indian aesthetics. More generally, *rasa* was and remains the "fluid essence" of Indian thought. If the universe is a great pulsating flow of essence and manifestation, *rasa* is the fluid "stuff" of that flow.

Already in Vedic speculation, *rasa* was homologized with water (*āp*), semen (*retas*), the vital fluid (*ojas*), herbal remedies (*oṣadhi, auṣadhi*), nectar (*amṛta*), and *soma* as the moon, the Moon god (also named Candra), and the mythic liquor of immortality.[2] In its most general sense, *rasa* was, in the sacrificial system of the Vedas, a term that could be applied to any oblation offered into fire (*agni*). The essence of said *rasa* was thence conveyed, via the wind (*vāyu*), up to heaven where it was enjoyed by the gods.[3]

This triad, of *rasa-agni-vāyu*, is one that has been reappropriated and reformulated throughout the sweep of Indian history. With the internalization of the sacrifice, the major conceptual and practical breakthrough of the *Āraṇyaka*s and *Upaniṣad*s, *rasa* became identified with the "body as oblation" whose fluid essences were cooked and transformed over the well-tempered fires of ascetic ardor (*tapas*), fires that were fanned by the winds of the vital breaths (*prāṇa*).[4] Once the bodily microcosm was transformed into the seat of the sacrifice (to the detriment of external sacrifice, which had been on the wane ever since the seventh century B.C in India), interest in the internal workings of the body became greatly expanded. Speculation and research took two directions, the one mystical and the other medical.

On the one hand, we find in the late classical Upaniṣads the origins of the mystic subtle physiology of the human body. In these works, we find early vague references to yogic techniques by which to generate transformative inner heat in tandem with the meditative, gnoseological realization (*jñāna*) of the identity of individual soul (*ātman*) with universal soul (*bráhman*). Together, these practices served to burn away and thereby negate the accumulated fruits of prior acts (*karma-phalam*), thereby affording liberation (*mokṣa*) from the cycle of rebirths (*saṃsāra*). In this context, *rasa* was the term employed by the *Maitrī Upaniṣad* to designate the highest emanate of the highest *guṇa*, the strand known as *sattvā*, "essence" or "purity."[5]

Early on, the internal dynamics of *haṭha yoga* came to be viewed as so many interactions between lunar (*candra*), solar (*sūrya*), and vital (*prāṇa*) principles, a transparent variation on the Vedic triad of *rasa-agni-vāyu*. In later hathayogic sources, as well as in more general tantric works on yogic and psychological integration as the technical means (*sādhana*) to the realization of total autonomy, we encounter the important notion of *samarasa*. Literally, "of even *rasa*" or "of the same *rasa*," the term implies, according to the numerous systems in which it is employed, a state of "fluid equilibrium," a condition of stasis in which the emanatory and resorptive impulses of the Absolute are balanced within the human microcosm.[6] In the hathayogic system of the Nāth Siddhas, the *rasa*s in question are portrayed as male and female "drops" (*bindu*), which are lunar and solar, seminal and sanguineous, Śiva and Śakti, respectively. Realizing a state of equilibrium between the two members of this pair is tantamount to the formation of a "great drop" (*mahābindu*), a yogic zygote of sorts, from which the new, liberated, all-powerful, and immortal self of the *jīvanmukta* emerges.[7]

Coeval with these original Upanisadic syntheses was the scientific discipline of traditional Indian medicine, Āyurveda. It was in this field that an important new application of the term *rasa* was promulgated at a very early date. Here, the term *rasa* came to be applied to the product of the first stage of the digestion process: *rasa* was chyle, food that had been moistened and broken down by saliva prior to swallowing. In a more extended sense, *rasa* retained its signifaction, in Ayurvedic usage, as bodily fluid.[8] This was an echo both of Vedic identifications of *rasa* with the waters and of emerging metaphysical systems that identified each of the five elements with a sensory organ and field of sensory activity. In Sāṁkhya, the element water, *rasa*, was identified with the sense of taste. This notion gave rise, in Āyurveda, to the system of the six *rasa*s or tastes—sweet, acid, saline, hot and pungent, bitter, and astringent—with each of the tastes arising from a mixture of water together with the other four gross elements, in varying proportions.[9] Emerging out of this Ayurvedic matrix, India's classic theory of aesthetics, i.e., of taste (*rasa*)—through which the cultivated spectator reinterpreted the raw emotions (*bhāva*s) portrayed in drama, dance, and literature into their corresponding cultivated *rasa*s—was developed some centuries later.[10]

Drawing on the Vedic tradition which maintained that it was water which upheld all plant and animal life, Ayurvedic theory takes *rasa* to be the support of all of the bodily constituents (*dhātu*s). As we saw in chapter two, digestion is conceived in Āyurveda as the serial "cooking" (*pacana*) of the bodily constituents on the constituent fires (*dhātvagni*s),[11] with the end product of this process being semen in men and uterine blood in women. These in turn combine in conception to give rise to the human embryo.

Rasāyana (the "way of *rasa*"), the seventh branch (*aṅga*) of Indian medicine, is the most holistic and prestigious of all Ayurvedic systems of healing, taking the body to be an integrated whole, the microcosmic reflection of the universal macrocosm. Its prestige also lies in the results it promises: *rasāyana* is rejuvenation therapy which, combining clinical practice with the internal use of elixirs, affords long life, whence the classical statement of the *Caraka Saṁhitā* (6.1.7–8): "Long life, heightened memory and intelligence, freedom from disease, a healthy glow, good complexion, a deep, powerful voice, great bodily and sensory powers, the capacity to see one's pronouncements realized, respectability, beauty—all these does one obtain from *rasāyana*. It is called *rasāyana* because it is a means to replenishing the *rasa* and other *dhātu*s of the body."[12]

In the same Ayurvedic context, the *rasāyana*s, in the plural, are the elixirs the physician employs in *rasāyana* therapy;[13] and it was out of this background that the term *rasāyana* emerged as a blanket Sanskrit term for alchemy. Here, the "way of *rasa*" was a mercurial path since *rasa*, the semen or fluid essence of Śiva, was identified with mercury, the transmuting element par excellence. While we do not know at what time this absolutely crucial identification—of the vital sexual fluid (*rasa*) of the phallic god with quicksilver, the fluid metal—came about, we can be sure of another, prior, "alchemical" use of the term *rasāyana*. This was the compound *rasa-rasāyana*, which was employed, in Hindu and Buddhist sources alike, as far back as the second century A.D., to signify the supernatural power (*siddhi*) of alchemical transmutation and bodily transubstantiation. One finds no description whatsoever of a practical method (*sādhana*) for the realization of this *siddhi* in these early sources. Here, *rasa-rasāyana* was but one of eight magical powers (listed together, for example, with *pādalepa*, the smearing of the feet with a cream that produced the power of flight) fantasized by Buddhists and Hindus in the first centuries of the common era.[14]

It is only later, with the alchemical Tantras of the tenth century and after, that laboratory methods for transmutation first come to be discussed systematically, under the heading of *rasāyana*. It is also in this later period that we find references to alchemical practitioners as Rasa Siddhas and to the alchemical doctrine that Mādhava terms "Raseśvara Darśana." What rendered this later form of Indian alchemy tantric was the pivotal notion that alchemical mercury was nothing other than divine semen, and that its principal reagents (sulfur, *gandhaka;* mica, *abhraka*) were the uterine blood and sexual emissions of the Goddess.[15] Working from these basic identifications, the tantric alchemists were able to construct an integrated conceptual framework for their art, a framework that mirrored the general worldview of Hindu tantrism.

Once again, bodily fluids, and the *rasa-agni* polarity of the archaic triad we have already referred to on several occasions (reproduced here as fluid mercury and fiery sulfur) stand as the basic categories of this new synthesis. So it is that Śiva states in the *RA* that "because [mercury] is the *rasa* [vital fluid] of my body, one is to call it *rasa* [mercury]." A more elaborate etymology is found in the *RRS:* "Because of its power to assimilate (*rasanāt*) all other metals, it is known as *rasa.* Or, indeed, it is considered *rasa* because it is effective (*rasyate*) in the destruction of aging, disease, and death."[16]

The term *rasa* may also be employed in the plural in Hindu alchemy, in which case the notion of "essential element" becomes operative.[17] Here, the sixteen principal mineral reagents are generally divided into eight *mahārasa*s and eight *uparasa*s, primary and secondary *rasa*s that are so called because they participate in the transformative powers of mercury, the *rasa* par excellence.[18] It is in this context that the *RC* can portray mercury as Lord Rasa (*raseśvara*) who leads the [*mahā-*]*rasa*s and *uparasa*s to victory in battle against disease and death.[19] This same source also provides an Ayurvedic usage of the compound *rasa-rasāyana*, which it uses to designate a mercurial elixir that is highly effective both therapeutically and alchemically (a usage not far removed from that of *rasāyana* in a number of alchemical sources).

While *rasāyana* has been used as a generic term for alchemy in India since the tenth century, the means and ends of the discipline are more properly identified by two other terms. These are *dhātuvāda*,[20] "the doctrine of elements" and *dehavāda*, "the doctrine of the body." These two branches of tantric alchemy form a unified whole: *dhātuvāda* alchemy, which concerns itself with the transmutation of base metals into gold, is the necessary propaedeutic to *dehavāda* alchemy, the alchemy of elixirs of bodily immortality. Their complementarity is underscored in a classic passage from the *RA*: "As in metal, so in the body. Mercury ought always to be employed in this way. When it penetrates a metal and the body, [mercury] behaves in an identical way. First test mercury on a metal, then use it on the body."[21] The *RRĀ* explains *rasendra*, the "lord of *rasa*s" (one of the five names for mercury), in similar fashion: "It is called *rasendra* because through its proper use, both metals and the body become possessed of *rasa*."[22] In the end, all is but a continuity of the same fluid (*rasa*): divine semen transmutes base metals into gold and transforms human semen into nectar by which the mortal practitioner is rendered an immortal superman, a second Śiva,[23] whose bodily secretions, like Śiva's own, transmute base metals into gold.

For reasons unknown to us—although we may hazard a guess that mercury poisoning had a part to play—there was, in the north Indian heartland at any rate, a gradual shift of emphasis, from the thirteenth century onwards, away from the goal of bodily immortality and towards a more therapeutic use of mercurials and other "elixir" preparations. Here, *rasa śāstra* ("mercurial science") came to apply the scientific—and some of the mystic—discoveries and techniques of tantric alchemy to the Ayurvedic discipline. So it is that the internal application of mercury and other mineral and metallic *rasa*s would come to constitute a subdivision of Ayurvedic *rasāyana*. It is in this subordinate form, as Ayurvedic pharmacy, that tantric alchemy—which gave up nearly all pretension, by the fourteenth century, to being a path to immortality—has persisted over the centuries and continues to thrive down to the present day throughout India.[24] Siddha alchemy, with its persistent emphasis on bodily transformation and immortality through the combined disciplines of yoga and alchemy, has remained more faithful to the original spirit and goals of tantric alchemy than has *rasa śāstra*.

2. Myths of the Origins of Minerals from Divine Bodily Fluids

The most concrete point of intersection between the yogic and alchemical traditions in India lies in the identification of mercury (*rasa*, *pārada*, *sūta*) with the semen of Śiva, and of sulfur (*gandhaka*), red arsenic (*manaḥśilā*) or mica (*abhraka*) with the menstrual blood (*khapuṣpa*, *rajas*, *śoṇita*, *ārtava*) or sexual emission (*vīrya*) of the Goddess. This identification of bodily fluids or compounds with the metals did not originate with the yogic or alchemical traditions. The moon is identified in the Vedas with the draft of immortality, i.e., *soma* or *amṛta*, as well as with the vital fluids of living beings (*rasa*):[25] this last term comes to be employed to signify mercury in alchemical traditions. The divine origins of gold, the subtlest of the metals (*dhātus*), is described in the *Śatapatha Brāhmaṇa*, which states that it arose from the seed of Viśvarūpa, whose body, after he was slain by Indra, was shattered into fragments by Tvaṣṭṛ, the divine smith of the Vedas: "From his seed his form [*rūpa*] flowed and became gold."[26] In the same early source we find a reference to gold refined and produced from the body of Prajāpati through the heat of his austerities.[27] Brahmā, a later form of Prajāpati, is born from a primal union of water and the seed of Agni, called the Golden Egg (*hiraṇyagarbha*).[28] And of course, the statement "gold is immortality" becomes a leitmotif of the brahmanic sacrifice.[29]

In these prealchemical traditions, gold is considered to be the ultimate product of a long period of germination or gestation within the womb of the earth. This notion, also held by the Roman Seneca (ca. A.D. 60) and, much later, by Arabic (the eleventh-century Avicenna) and Chinese thinkers,[30] is already voiced, in India, in the pre-second century A.D. *Rāmāyaṇa*.[31] In this source, the six-headed child god Skanda-Kārttikeya is born from the seed of Agni (Fire) who ejaculates into every opening of the goddess Earth when he sees the goddess Gaṅgā "in her magnificent splendor." Earth generates an embryo, which becomes the metals gold and silver; and from the splendor of these metals the divine child arises. From the various rays emitted by this effulgent child, as well as from various residues produced in his childbirth—afterbirths of sorts—are produced the metals copper, iron, tin, and lead. Taken together, these are the classic "six metals" of Indian tradition, first listed in the *Yajur Veda*.[32]

This myth is important for two reasons. First, metals are treated in it as living substances, with distinctions between animal, vegetable, and mineral blurred: "bodies" of whatever composition or configuration may interact with and even be generated from one another. In this case, fire, fluid, and earth give birth to a god, the six metals, and the natural coloring of certain trees and plants. Here, it is the emanatory dynamic of the proto-Vedānta metaphysics of the Upaniṣads—a system that is very similar to the emanation and participation of Neoplatonist thought—that facilitates such analogies between the animal, vegetable, and mineral kingdoms. The universe in all its parts is a single organic entity, with all that exists on the great chain of being the internal flux of a divinely constituted whole, to which all emanated form necessarily returns in the fullness of time. As such, all in the universe is shot through, "like the scent in a flower,"[33] with the divine essence. Moreover, since all exists on the same continuum of this divine outpouring, all is comparable, even identifiable. The corresponding hierarchies of the elements, body fluids, metals, tastes, *cakra*s, etc. are not discrete and distinct from one another; rather, they are so many expressions of a single unified whole. Thus they are interchangeable, even interpenetrating. In such a quite nearly "pantheistic" context, metals are not merely comparable to body fluids, they *are* body fluids.[34]

The second point that arrests our attention in this origin myth of gold is the god who issues from it: this is a very early account of the birth of Skanda-Kārttikeya.[35] This is a myth that comes to constitute a permanent fixture in every Śaiva Purāṇa, where Skanda (also known as Kārttikeya, Murugan, Subrahmanian, Kumāra, etc.) is depicted as arising from the seed Śiva emits into the mouth of Agni (fire) and thence into a bed of reeds on the shore of the Ganges, where he is suckled by the six daughters of Dakṣa, the Kṛttikās (whence his name Kārttikeya and his six heads), in preparation for his victorious battle against the demon Tāraka. In a wide array of other Śaiva myths, Śiva's seed is said to be fluid gold.[36]

Once this central metaphor was established—i.e., that gold (and, as we will see shortly, mercury and sulfur) were the quintessential reproductive fluids of the great tantric gods—the floodgates were thrown open, as it were, to similar myths of the origins of the lesser elements. So, we learn that diamond (*vajra*) arose from drops of *amṛta* that fell from the gods' mouths to earth after they had churned the Ocean of Milk (*RA* 6.65–66). Tourmaline gems (*vaikrānta*) are the drops of blood the Buffalo Demon shed when he was slain by Durgā (*RA* 6.123–25; *RRS* 2.56–57). Blue vitriol or copper sulfate (*sasyaka*) is the poison and nectar vomited by Garuḍa after his theft of Soma (*RA* 7.39; *RC* 10.71–72; *RRS* 2.119);[37] and copper pyrites (*mākṣika*) the blood that flowed from a wound in Kṛṣṇa's foot (*RA* 7.3–4). Natural gold (*prākṛta-svarṇa*) arose from the abstract quality of activity (*rajoguṇa*) that set the universe in motion; another form of "natural" gold (*svahaja-svarṇa*) is the golden placenta—deposited atop Mount Meru—from which the god Brahmā, the golden embryo, was born at the beginning of our cosmic eon.[38]

The ca. sixteenth-century *Rasakāmadhenu* (Wish-fulfilling Cow of Mercury) identifies the six metals with (the seminal emissions of) six gods: gold arises from Agni, silver from the moon (Candra), copper from the sun (Sūrya), tin from Indra, lead from the serpent king Vāsuki, and iron from Yama, lord of the dead.[39] Other sources, such as the twelfth-century *Lohasarvasvam* and the late nineteenth-century *Rasendra Bhāskara*, trace the origins of a great number of other elements and metals back to the bodies, blood, semen, sweat, and tears of a still wider array of gods and demons.[40] Nāth Siddha sources identify the indestructible body of the Siddha with mercury[41] and a hierarchy of holy men with the hierarchy of metals.[42]

3. Blood and Semen

By far the richest and most elaborate homologies drawn between human and divine body fluids on the one hand and elements from the mineral world on the other are that between mercury and the semen of the phallic god Śiva and that between sulfur and the uterine or menstrual blood of his consort, the Goddess. It is in the context of the myth of the divine birth of Skanda, once again, that we find the myth of the origin of mercury, in the *RC* (15.4–12), *RRS* (1.23–29), *ĀK* (1.8–15), and a number of other alchemical sources.[43] The novel element in these accounts is that it is mercury rather than gold that is produced from that portion of the semen emitted by Śiva which did not contribute directly to the generation of Skanda.

As in the gold origin myth, Agni has a role to play in the alchemical account of the origin of mercury, as it is he who drops from his mouth the semen that becomes the transmuting element:

> In a hidden cave of the Himalayas, Śiva and the Goddess were engaged in love-play when the gods came to plead that they produce Skanda in order that the demon Tāraka, who was threatening the entire universe, might be destroyed.[44] The god Agni [Fire], having taken the form of a pigeon, peeked in through the round window of the apartment within which they had closed themselves in order to generate a son. Upon seeing Agni, Śiva, filled with shame, shed his seed. That seed, of blinding brilliance, fell into the mouth of Fire. Fire, unable to bear the heat of that seed, spit it into the waters of the goddess Gaṅgā [the Ganges river]. She too, overcome by the intensity of that semen, pushed it with her waves to her shores, where a child, Skanda, was born.

> In those places where Agni dropped that seed from his mouth[45] [on his way to the Ganges], it burrowed into the ground to form five wells of mercury, 100 *yojanas* [about 900 miles] in depth. It is there that that semen is found today, in the form of mercury.[46]

It is by drinking this elixir that the gods themselves enjoy immortality. Jealous of humans who might do the same and so threaten their hegemony, the gods requested that Śiva adulterate it with impurities, and so it is that the mercury found on earth comes in a variety of colors. The mercury of the eastern well is white, that of the western well yellow, and that of the southern well, controlled by Nāgas, is blue. The well at the center of this pentadic mercurial *maṇḍala* contains "mixed" mercury, called *miśraka*, which is said to be *mayūra*, variegated like the throat or tail feathers of a peacock. Of the five wells in which this mercury is said to have established itself, however, the *RRS* and *ĀK* single out the northern well, in which mercury is red and pure, as superior to the other four.[47]

This northern well is implicitly identified with Darada-deśa (Dardistan, located to the north of Kashmir),[48] a likely overland source of mercury for India in the age of tantric alchemy. The name of this land evokes the prime Sanskrit term for cinnabar,[49] which is *darada*. So too does the color assigned to the mercury of this well, given that cinnabar (a compound in which one atom of mercury is chemically bonded to one atom of sulfur), the most common naturally occurring mercurial ore, is red in color.

Sulfur too has its origin myth, which parallels that of mercury inasmuch as it is the sexual essence of the Goddess that gives rise to this primary alchemical reagent, the female counterpart to male mercury.[50] This myth is framed in the Puranic account of the churning of the Ocean of Milk, from which the gods gained (through the intervention of Dhanvantari, the divine physician and revealer of Āyurveda) the *amṛta* that rendered them immortal and capable of defeating the antigods, the *asuras*, in their sempiternal war for universal supremacy.[51]

> Once, when the Goddess was sporting together with the female Wizards (*vidyādharīs*), Siddha-maidens, Goddesses, and celestial nymphs in the Ocean of Milk off the coast of White Island, blood issued from her body. That wonderfully scented blood was captivating. Because it stained her clothes, she left these on the shore, and bathed to purify herself. When she wished to return to the town, her clothes were no

longer lying in that place, the tide having carried them out into the middle of the Ocean of Milk.

During the churning of the Ocean of Milk, that blood rose to the surface, together with the nectar (*amṛta*). All the gods and the antigods were pleased with the aroma (*gandha*) that wafted on her blood. The gods and antigods thereby said, "May this be called *gandhaka* ("aromatic": sulphur). May it be used in the calcination and fixing of mercury. May those qualities that are found in mercury also be found in this sulphur." Thus [sulphur] is called *gandhaka* here on earth.

This myth appears to have both an alchemical and a geological explanation. First, the opening verses of the *Mātṛkabheda Tantra* (1.9–14) seem to evoke the myth of the origin of sulfur in a description of an alchemical operation that involves the heating of sewn cloth and menstrual blood together in a vessel of milk.[52] Elsewhere, this account has been interpreted as a mythic description of a submarine volcanic eruption, from which submarine deposits of sulfur would have formed. Similarly, the Puranic mythology of the submarine mare (*baḍavā*), and the doomsday fire (*bāḍava*) that issues from her mouth, may refer to the phenomenon of submarine gas vents or fire jets. As such, *bāḍava* would be the oceanic equivalent of naturally occurring terrestrial gas vents (*jvālamukhī*), which are considered in India to be geothermic manifestations of the Goddess. The most popular pilgrimage site in all of Himachal Pradesh is Jvālamukhī, a blue flame that burns within a natural freshwater spring, identified with the tongue of the Goddess. It has also long been an important center for the Nāth Siddhas.[53]

In the light of these glosses on this myth and the hard fact that India possesses no measurable deposits of mercurial ores, the following statement, from the *Shorter Oxford Economic Atlas*, appears to be significant: "almost all the world's mercury is obtained from the red sulphide mineral cinnabar, HgS, but a little of the metal occurs naturally as small globules associated with cinnabar in certain rocks in the neighborhood of old volcanic regions where the minerals were deposited from hot aqueous solutions during volcanic activity. Many hot springs in such regions are still depositing some cinnabar."[54]

This statement implies that there may have been and continue to be traces of mercury in regions of geothermal activity in India. This would explain, for example, the purported existence of a "mercurial pool" located in the vicinity of a hot sulfur spring in the region of Kedārnāth, an ancient Śaiva pilgrimage site in the Garhwal Himalayas. In the light of these data, the myth of the origin of sulfur may be read as a reference to those sites at which alchemists garnered the *materia prima* of their art.

Cinnabar, mercuric sulfide—composed of mercurial semen and sulfurous uterine blood—is a mineral hierophany of the sexual union of Śiva and the Goddess, a union that, according to Hindu tradition, creates and sustains the universe. Indeed, the Tamil, Malayalam, and Sinhalese term for cinnabar is *liṅgam*, a clear evocation of its sexual valence.[55] Now, cinnabar is also one of the eight amalgamated elements (*aṣṭabandha*) used in the installation of divine idols, and it is here that the obligatory installation of a mercurial *liṅga* at the heart of the alchemical laboratory becomes most meaningful. Here, the *rasaliṅga* is formed of either an amalgam of gold[56] and mercury, or of sulfur and mercury,[57] i.e., of synthetic cinnabar. Elsewhere, the *RA* (11.4) compares the mortar in which mercury is pounded to the *yoni*-shaped chasing (*pīṭha*) in which the image of a Śiva-*liṅga* is set, and the mercury in question to the *liṅga* itself. In another passage (11.102), the same text notes that mercury that has been calcinated in a particular mixture of gemstones, minerals, and herbs becomes phallomorphic (*liṅgākāra*). This appears to be the north Indian cognate to the production, in south Indian alchemy, of "mercurial phalluses," called *gulikā*s (the equivalent of the Sanskrit *guṭikā*, "pill").[58]

Here as well, the *MBhT* substitutes human menstrual blood for its divine mineral equivalent, as if to emphasize the sexual symbolism of this operation: "Place tamarind (*ciñcinī*, the botanical equivalent of the goddess Kubjikā) and mercury together on the support. Mix these together . . . so that the mixture resembles mud . . . Having shaped it into a *liṅga*, one should then harden it [in the following way]. One should tie it up inside cloth that [has been soaked] with menstrual blood [and place it] over a fire [fueled by] cow dung. Some heating will be necessary in order that it become hard."[59]

The red color of compounds of mercury and sulfur inspires all manner of homologization in Hindu traditions. Indeed, the compound cinnabar is naturally red in color; sulfur and mercury both redden when heated, the latter taking on the ruby (*māṇikya*) red color of the rising sun when oxidized at a temperature of 300° C.[60] This redness, identified with that of blood, has long been associated with the life force or vital energy in both India and China. The ancient Chinese used both cinnabar and red minium (oxide of lead) to color the bones of the dead, as a means of ensuring them an eternal afterlife. Here, the "element metal" cinnabar, identified with living blood, was long employed as an elixir of immortality for the living as well.[61]

In India, where gold and other metals are also employed in the cult of the dead,[62] vermilion (*sindūra:* red mercuric oxide or synthetic cinnabar) has long been employed as a substitute for or a complement to blood offerings.[63] Of course, blood is also closely identified with fertility and procreation, and so it is in India that married women wear vermilion in the part of their hair as a sign of connubial felicity. The term *saubhāgyam* refers both to this happy state and to the lead peroxide or vermilion that is the mark thereof: here, the term *hiṅgula* (another common term for cinnabar) may also be employed.[64] Also in India, red arsenic (*manaḥśilā*) is identified with the uterine blood of the Goddess: this is especially the case at the "seat" (*pīṭha*)[65] of the goddess called Kāmākhyā (Gauhati, Assam), at which site the goddess's *yoni* (in the widespread Puranic myth of the dismemberment of the goddess Satī) is said to have taken the form of a great block of red arsenic where it fell to earth.[66]

In the more abstract schemata of *yonipūjā*, the tantric worship of the female sexual organ, the *yoni* is represented as a downturned triangle, at the heart of which is, once again, Kāmarūpa, the abode of the goddess Kāmākhyā, who is identified with the *kuṇḍalinī* and with feminine materiality (*prakṛti*) in the form of menstrual flux (*puṣparūpiṇī*). At the *pīṭha* of Kāmākhyā itself, Assamese tantrics identify their "lineage nectar" (*kulāmṛta*) with the Goddess's menstrual fluid (or the commingled sexual fluids of Śiva and the Goddess); it is at the time of the Goddess's menses, in August-September, when the water that oozes from this stone becomes reddish in color, that their annual gathering takes place.[67]

The powers of the Goddess's menstrual blood are directly linked to its redness. Persons suffering from leucodermia (*pāṇḍuroga*) come to Kāmākhyā to smear their bodies with the Goddess's menstrual blood, thus "coloring" themselves with the ooze of her red mineral hierophany. The ocher dye (*geruā*) with which the Nāth Siddhas color their traditional garb (*kanthā*) is said to originate from the blood of the goddess Pārvatī, who resorted to self-mutilation to dye the robe of Gorakhnāth. Cloth dyed in this color is considered by the Nāth Siddhas to aid in yogic semen retention (*vīryastambha śakti*).[68] This red mineral manifestation of the Goddess at Kāmākhyā is also capable, according to the *Kālikā Purāṇa*, of transmuting base metals into gold. According to medieval legend, a sealed cave, containing a pot of mercury (*rasakumbha*) the drink of which confers immortality, is located in its vicinity.[69]

As we have noted, accounts of such conjoined mineral manifestations of Śiva and the Goddess in the form of mercurial "wells" and sulfurous or arsenious phenomena may have their basis in geological fact. Of the five sacred "alchemical" sites of India, three—Hiṅglāj Devī, Gaurī Kuṇḍ (near Kedārnāth), and Kāmākhyā—combine a mineral manifestation of the Goddess with a mercurial pool or source. The two other sites, Girnar (Junagadh district, Gujarat) and Srisailam (Kurnool district, Andhra Pradesh) appear to lack the feminine complement to masculine mercury. Hiṅglāj Devī is, in a sense, a geographical and mythological mirror to Kāmākhyā. Located at the westernmost fringe of the Indian subcontinent, on the edge of Baluchistan, this shrine is said to be that site at which the goddess Satī's fontanelle, her *brahmarandhra*, fell. Like Kāmākhyā, Hiṅglāj features a number of caves and wells, of which one, known for its geothermic activities, is called Candrakūpa, "Moon Well." Hiṅglāj is clearly named for cinnabar (*hiṅgula-ja*); and one of the many local names by which she is known is "Red Goddess."

The keepsake which pilgrims take with them from Hiṅglāj Devī is not, however, a piece of cinnabar, but rather a lump (or lumps, polished and strung together in a rosary) of nummelite, a type of yellow limestone, called *thumrā*. These lumps are variously described as the petrified seed of the Creator or a combination of cereal grains (*khichri*, a rough rice and lentil dish favored by Śiva) and the blood of a demon. As we will later show, rice often doubles for semen in yogic legend, so the combination of semen and blood is indeed present in the *thumrā* of the Hiṅglāj Devī pilgrimage. Indeed, it is with a large *thumrā* stone that Nāth Siddhas at the Gorakhpur monastery ensured easy delivery to women in the former half of this century: the stones were washed in water and the liquid then given to the women to drink.[70]

Elsewhere, a number of "womb-caves" of the Goddess, which are legion throughout south and east Asia, are considered sacred by Hindus, Buddhists, and Taoists alike. One such cave, called Ca-ri, in extreme southeastern Tibet, has long been revered by Hindus and Buddhists as the abode of Śiva Maheśvara and the Goddess (or, in Tibetan Buddhism, of Cakrasaṃvara and Vajravarāhī). This cave, entered through a narrow fissure identified as the Goddess's *yoni*, is said to contain a lake of *sindūra* (red mercuric oxide), identified with the commingled sexual fluids of divinities inhabiting the "womb-cave" of the Goddess. We will return to the symbolism of this cave in the next chapter.[71]

In the alchemical laboratory, such homologies come to be practically applied through techniques that involve the commingling of human, divine, and mineral blood and semen. Here, the point of convergence between these interpenetrating systems is the person of the alchemist's female laboratory assistant, who is described in the *RA* and a number of other sources. This assistant may be of four types: *kākiṇī* (a woman who menstruates in the dark half of the lunar month, i.e., when the moon is on the wane), *kīkaṇī* (who menstruates in the middle of the lunar month), *kāñcikācinī* (who menstruates in the bright half of the lunar month), or *padminī* (who menstruates either on the full moon or the new moon).[72] The names for this assistant (*kākiṇī* means "cowrie maiden"; *padminī* means "lotus maiden") appear to be direct references to her sexual organ, which is also described in these texts, in ideal terms, as "resembling an *aśvattha* (*Ficus religiosus*) leaf."[73] In fact, everything about the alchemist's female assistant is ideal: she is young, beautiful, raven-haired, doe-eyed, perfectly proportioned, fair of speech and light of laughter, gentle when she kisses and embraces, a lover of dairy products, and a devotee of Śiva.[74]

It is, however, her sexual organ as well as the menstrual blood that flows from it that seems to be at the center of interest here, and this for a very concrete reason, which the *RRS* (6.34) explains. "She who menstruates [literally, "she who flowers," *puṣpavatī*] in the dark half of the lunar month is most excellent for the fixation of mercury [*rasabandha*] in alchemical practice." In what way is the assistant useful to the alchemist's craft? "For twenty-one days, she is to eat sulfur [mixed with clarified butter] . . . Her menstrual blood [then] becomes efficacious in the fixation and calcination of mercury."[75] Other sources instruct the alchemist to place said mercury, wrapped in a piece of cloth, deep in his wife's vulva, to the same end; or to macerate sulfur in a woman's menstrual blood in order to increase its potency.[76]

The *BhP*, which terms sulfur *umāyoni-saṃsarga* ("that which issued from the vulva of [the Goddess] Umā"), states that mercury can be bound and made complete (*saṃskṛta*) only by entering into that *yoni*, i.e., sulfur. Reproductive symbolism is explicit here: mercury, of which one name is *sūta* ("that which is born, generated"), and which transmutes through the agency of *bīja*s ("seeds") of noble metals in combination with sulfur or mica, here enters into the womb of the Goddess (sulfur) to become activated.[77] Alternatively, the same source states that the alchemist may bind or stabilize mercury by placing it in his urethra (*pu[ṃ]randhre*) "together with the menstrual blood of Gaurī." Here, Gaurī may be taken as a name for the Goddess, in which case it is sulfur that is being manipulated here; or it may be taken adjectivally to stand for any "fair woman," in which case it is human menstrual blood that he is commingling with his own seed (*tadbījena*), in all probability through the yogic technique of urethral suction (*vajrolī mudrā*).[78] In this latter case, we are once more in the presence of the "power substances" of early tantric practice. A reference in this source (*BhP* 1.77) to the *khecarī-cakra* ("sky-going circle") of ritualized tantric sex, as well as to the *kuṇḍagola[ka]* as an elixir in other alchemical sources, further documents this connection between ritual and alchemical uses of the products of human and divine sexual intercourse.[79]

At the end of such processes, which serve to stabilize and fortify mercury, this divine semen in its mineral form may at last be ingested by the alchemist in the ultimate *saṃskāra* of *śarīra yoga*, transubstantiation. Here, the *RA* stipulates that sexual intercourse is essential to the activation of the mercury the alchemist has ingested (and adds that said mercury turns him into a sexual animal, whence, no doubt, this text's insistence on his female laboratory assistant's many charms).[80]

This remarkable interplay—between human sexual fluids and their divine and mineral counterparts—spills over into the genre of courtly literature as well, as in the ca. A.D. 1540 *Padmāvat* of Muhammad Jayasī,[81] who allegorically portrays the star-crossed love of his hero and heroine in alchemical terms. Here King Ratansen, who has taken up the celibate life of a Nāth Siddha, is first questioned by the pining Padmavatī's female companions:

> Where did you lose the fair plant [*biravā lonā:* Padmavatī] that makes the silver and the gold? Are you unable to blend yellow arsenic [Padmavatī] with mercury [Ratansen]? Why have you forsaken sulfur [Padmavatī] for the cold fare [of the celibate yogin]?"[82] [Ratansen replies, as if to Padmavatī herself]: ". . . If I were but able to blend the mercury with the yellow arsenic [i.e., to abandon my vow of celibacy], I would give up my life just to see the sulfur . . . I who was [transparent, i.e., dispassionate as] mica, having been turned over the fire [of love], am become [red, impassioned as] cinnabar. My brass body can become yellow gold, if you but choose to make it so . . . If the mercury cannot swallow the sulfur, how shall I call my life yellow arsenic?"[83]

Here, the ingestion of the mineral equivalent of sexual fluids stands as a metaphor for the consummation of love. In the alchemical sources, such emissions, both divine and human, are taken to be elixirs of immortality. So the *RA* states: "Until such time as one eats Śiva's seed, that is, mercury, where is his liberation, where is the maintenance of his body?"[84] The *RHT* elaborates: "A divine body is afforded through the union of the [sexual] emissions of Śiva and the Goddess."[85] And, in yet another source, "a woman's flower mixed with semen, eaten for a year" is proposed as an elixir.[86] Here, the flower (*puṣpa*) in question is menstrual blood (especially that of a virgin, a woman who has yet to be deflowered),[87] and we should not fail to note here that sulfur in its purest form is known in this tradition, as it is in the west, as "flowers of sulfur" (*puṣpita gandhaka*).[88]

Such analogies carry over into the vegetable kingdom as well, in which the "divine herbs" (*divyauṣadhi*) are said to grow in those places in which Śiva and the Goddess once made love.[89] A case in point is the *cāṇḍālī* plant, undoubtedly named for those outcaste women whose menstrual blood has perennially been prized by tantrics for its transformative powers. The root of the *cāṇḍālī* exudes a red milk (*kṣīra*) that is used, like sulfur and menstrual blood, for the fixing of mercury.[90] Elsewhere, Alberuni's celebrated account of Vyāḍi's discovery of the alchemical elixir portrays this alchemist as searching in vain for an essential ingredient called *raktamālā*, which he assumes to be red myrobalan, a plant with red, bloodlike sap. It is only when he bumps his head and bleeds into his alchemical cauldron that his elixir "takes." The same source relates an account of a Siddha who employs the red milk of the plant called *thohar* to transmute the body of a shepherd and his dog into gold.[91]

A moment ago, I mentioned the practice known as *vajrolī mudrā*, through which the male practitioner enabled himself to tap directly into the fluid "power substance" naturally occurring in his tantric consort, the *yoginī*. In technical terms, *vajrolī mudrā* is urethral suction or, more prosaically, the "fountain pen technique," by which the male practitioner, having ejaculated into his female partner, withdraws his own semen, now catalyzed through its interaction with her sexual essence or uterine blood, back into his own body. In so doing, he also draws back into himself, along with his own refined seed, a certain quantity of that female essence which may in turn serve to catalyze the yogic processes (the raising of the *kuṇḍalinī*, etc.) by which his semen becomes transmuted into nectar.

A number of sources note that the woman may do the same as the man, i.e., retain his seed within herself to thereby catalyze her own yogic transformations.[92] Such techniques on the part of the woman, which are described only in the hathayogic sources, appear to be redundant when viewed from the erotico-mystical perspective of a number of Kaula traditions. It is a basic assumption among these traditions that the fluid lineage or clan nectar, the subtle fluid essence of liberating consciousness, is naturally present in women, and it is precisely for this reason that the male tantric practitioner engages in sexual intercourse with her. This was the basic doctrine of Matsyendranāth's venerable Yoginī Kaula: women, because they are embodiments of the Goddess and because it is through their "wombs" that the lineage is perpetuated, have something that men do not; it is therefore necessary for males to tap into the female in order that that boundless source of energy be activated within them. This fluid power substance (*dravya*) or lineage nectar (*kulāmṛta*), also simply known by the term "true being" (*sadbhāva*)—the purest substance found in the human body—is unique to women in their multiple roles as sexual consorts, practitioners of yoga, and biological mothers.[93]

All three roles are present in the fluid exchange involved in the practice of *vajrolī mudrā*. When the *sadbhāva* of a tantric consort is conjoined with the semen of her male partner, a "great fluid" (*mahārasa*) is produced, out of which a perfect yogic child (*yoginībhu*) is born. Because women are naturally endowed with a greater abundance of vital breath (*prāṇa*) than men, the raising of the *kuṇḍalinī* is easier, even natural, for them; thus, when her partner emits his seed into her womb, it commingles with her vital breath and, transformed through her yogic energy, becomes pure *mahārasa*. In erotico-mystical practice, *it is originally in the female partner that the pure substance [the* mahārasa*] resides.* It is this that is transmitted to the male partner and is returned to the female in an endlessly renewed exchange effected through the "two mouths"—i.e., the sexual organs of the partners: "This knowledge beyond duality . . . is rightly said to be transmitted from mouth to mouth . . . it goes from the chief mouth [that of the *yoginī*] to [the adept's] own mouth and vice versa. Bestower of immortality and youth, it is named *kula*, supreme."[94] This practice becomes internalized in certain hathayogic sources, in which one internally drinks the "brilliant white-red" nectar.[95]

The common end result of both the yogic and the erotico-mystical techniques is identical to that obtained through the ingestion of the alchemical cognates to these male and female power substances: white hair and wrinkles disappear, and one becomes rejuvenated.[96] Indeed, mercury is made to double for male seed in certain preparatory techniques for *vajrolī mudrā*, as described by a contemporary practitioner, the Aghori Vimalananda:

> To learn Vajroli you must first thoroughly clean out your body . . . The urinary passage is cleansed by sucking water through the penis into the bladder and through the ureters into the kidneys and then releasing it . . . After you have been able to suck up water through the penis and hold a bladder full of water for three hours, you proceed to use milk, to cool the genital organs. Then . . . clarified butter to lubricate. Honey next; it is very sticky and hard to make flow upward. Finally you do it with mercury, which is extremely heavy . . . When you can hold a bladder full of mercury for three hours without spilling a single drop, you have reached the level of the first qualification [for Vajroli]. A woman prepares for Vajroli in exactly the same way.[97]

Let us consider for a moment the etymology of this rather obscure term *vajrolī mudrā*. While we can be certain that *mudrā* means "seal" and that *vajra* means "penis," the *-olī* suffix (which also appears in the names of the related practices of *amarolī* and *sahajolī mudrās*) is more problematic. In at least one other context, *-olī* appears to have the sense of "sphere" or "ball": one manuscript of the *SSP* (1.73) calls the developing embryo *garbh-olī*.[98] By extension, the *-olī* suffix may refer to the spherical form of the womb of the consort, which would give a reading of "the seal of the penis in the womb."

In the concomitant hathayogic techniques associated with urethral suction, the upward rise of the combined sexual fluids culled by the male practitioner through *vajrolī mudrā* does not culminate in his lower abdomen. Urethral suction is but the beginning of a process, which in fact raises these combined sexual essences, via the medial channel of the *suṣumṇā nāḍī*, all the way up to the cranial vault. In this light, the fluid essence of the subtle body travels along a single channel, which runs from the tip of the penis to the top of the head. We are aided in our considerations of this technique by descriptions from two Buddhist sources, the fifth-century A.D. *Mahāyānasūtrālaṃkāra Sūtra*[99] and a Tibetan Buddhist alchemical source,[100] which describe what we have been calling *vajrolī mudrā* as *maithunasya parāvṛtti*, "retroverting [the product] of intercourse," and *bcud len*, the "extraction of the essence," respectively. Here, a drop of fluid containing the combined male and female essences is carried upward along the *suṣumṇā* to the cranial vault. In these two Buddhist contexts, the practitioner's realization is of a gnoseological order: concomitant to the raising of this drop, he comes to realize for himself the nondifference of *saṃsāra* and *nirvāṇa*, of suffering existence and the extinction of suffering, and thereby experiences the great bliss (*mahāsukha*).[101]

These Buddhist examples find their direct homologue in the Hindu tantric notion of *samarasa* or *sāmarasya*, in which the process initiated by *vajrolī mudrā* is brought to culmination in the yogin's cranial vault.[102] While the term becomes exalted to the point of being identified with *samādhi* and other enstatic, beatific states, the concrete and original sense of the term appears to be that employed by the Nāth Siddhas, for whom *samarasa* is the commingling of two drops (*bindu*s). One of these, solar and red[103] is identified with Śakti, while the other, lunar and white, is identified with Śiva; combined into a great drop (*mahābindu*) of "white-red nectar," they form a yogic zygote of sorts.[104]

A south Indian alchemical source, the *Koṅgana 3000*, identifies the male drop (which it calls *bindu*) with Śiva and mercury, and the female drop (which it calls *nāda*) with Śakti and sulfur, which, when combined, produce bodily immortality in a process called *kalpasādhanai:* this is the homologue of the Nāth Siddhas' *kāyakalpa*, a general term meaning "bodily regeneration."[105] It may be that the *HYP* (4.96) is referring to the same yogic union, in similar alchemical terms, when it states that "the mercurial mind, when calcinated by the *nāda* of sulfur, becomes bound and immobilized."

The fruit of this union, of the yogin's commingled male and female essences, is nothing less than the new, supernatural, immortal self that will now emerge from the "husk" of the gross body, as the result of this yogic process.[106] This is the *siddha-* or *vajra-deha*, the yogin's perfected or diamond body, his innate immortal essence which he has now restored to its pristine perfection by burning away the gross and refining the subtle elements within himself. This is a body possessed of all the yogic *siddhi*s, including the ability to transmute base metals into gold with one's excrements, spittle, etc.[107] It is this new self that is the subject of the first of the *bānī*s of Gorakhnāth: "In the empty vault [of the cranium] a child is making sounds. How can one give him a name?"[108] Such a child of yoga is to be placed in parallel with the *yoginībhu* mentioned a moment ago; it also evokes the transformation, even the procreation, of a disciple by his guru through initiation, a process I discuss in the penultimate chapter of this book.

4. A Cosmopolitan Alchemical Theme

These multifarious identifications and interactions between human and mineral equivalents of divine sexual fluids are brought to their analogical conclusions in a truly astonishing set of instructions for the extraction of mercury from its mercurial well in Darada country:[109]

> Upon seeing a well-adorned maiden who, having bathed after first coming into season, [rides by] mounted upon a horse, mercury, which is found in wells, [becomes] possessed of a desire to seize her, [and] rushes up out [of its well]. Upon seeing it, she gallops away. The mercury pursues her for the distance of one *yojana* [eight to nine miles]. [When] that [mercury which is] born of Śiva then quickly returns to the well, it is caught in troughs dug in its path. That mercury, because of its heaviness, fell from the mouth of Agni in Darada-deśa. That mercury, absorbed into the surface of the earth there, came to remain in that country. By placing that [mercury-rich] ore in a *pātana-yantra*, one kills the mercury.

What makes this description of the extraction of mercury from its northern well all the more astonishing is the fact that this is an account that is found in at least two other alchemical traditions. One of these is a seventeenth-century Chinese encyclopedia, the *Ho han sans ts'ai t'ou hui*, whose section entitled *yin-shui* ("silver water, quicksilver"), gives the same information, but locates its mercurial well "in the land of Fou-lin"—i.e., Syria—"far to the west."[110] This detail is corroborated by the earliest extant source that we have for this account: Syriac recensions of the alchemical works of Pseudo-Zosimus, dated to the fourth to fifth century A.D., describe how mercury is induced to rise up out of its well when a beautiful naked maiden walks past it and then runs quickly away. Young men attack the flowing metal with hatchets and cut it up into bars.[111] This account is further corroborated by the Syrian toponym Bir es Zeibaq, which means "Well of Quicksilver."[112]

The implications of these three parallel accounts are staggering. First, they attest to the very cosmopolitan nature of the world's classical alchemical traditions. We can well imagine that the Silk Road, which was India's pipeline for the raw materials of alchemy, would also have served as a conduit for alchemical knowledge and legend, of the sort alluded to here, between the Mediterranean world and east and south Asia. More than this, we may glimpse, behind the language of this extraction technique, references to another very cosmopolitan tradition—that of the unicorn. The presence of a virgin, a horse, and the theme of capturing an elusive "game" are all present in the alchemical account. While the western unicorn legend was very probably born out of the Indian myth of Ṛṣyaśṛṅga,[113] it is only in the west that the hunting of the unicorn—with the aid of a virgin, who tamed it by grasping its horn—and the transmutative properties of its horn are brought to the fore.[114]

This same theme is treated in Persian alchemical legend as well, in an account of a wondrous creature called the Physician of the Sea.[115] The Physician of the Sea is described as having a golden stone set into its forehead which, when removed, transmutes base metals into gold and cures all diseases. The Jabirian corpus of Persian alchemy, generally dated to the ninth to tenth century, describes the capture of one of these fishlike creatures which, upon being netted and brought aboard a ship off the coast of an island called Sindiyyat,[116] shows itself, after the fashion of a mermaid, to be a beautiful woman. She remains on ship, bears a son by one of the sailors, and later jumps back into the sea, where she becomes a great sea monster who swallows the entire ocean during a great storm.

These legends present more problems than can possibly be treated here. Not the least of these is the direction of transmission of alchemical legend, lore, techniques, and raw materials throughout the first fifteen centuries of the common era. As Joseph Needham has demonstrated, China stands, according the best evidence, as the primal source for the world's transmutational and elixir alchemy. According to Needham's historical reconstruction, the first-century A.D. Chinese technique of *kim* or *chin*, "aurifaction," would have been carried west to the Mediterranean world in perhaps the third century A.D.. This Chinese term would then have been transliterated, by Pseudo-Zosimus, as *chymeia* or *chemeia*, later arabicized into *al-chymeia*, and introduced into European traditions as *alchymia*, alchemy.[117] If Needham is correct, then Syria, which received its alchemy from China in the third century A.D., would have "exported" its legendary extraction technique back to the east, via our thirteenth-century Indian sources, to China in the seventeenth century.

It is impossible to say with any certainty that this was in fact the route that this tradition took. It is equally impossible to determine the ways in which the many alchemical exchanges of this long period, effected along the Silk Road, may have occurred. Another detail of the Indian alchemical account is, however, tantalizing in this regard. One of the regions in which both the western Ptolemy and the Indian Purāṇas located the Daradas (called Daradrai by Ptolemy) was the Indus River region. In his version of the Indo-Persian account related above, Somadeva calls this country Pārada-deśa, "Mercury Land," rather than Darada-deśa. The Pāradas were also located, by ancient and medieval Indian and western sources, in this same general region as the Daradas, i.e., to the northwest or west of India, in either Afghanistan or Baluchistan.[118] Now, the Indus River valley is also that region from which there have been unearthed a great wealth of clay seals, many of which are figured with what have to be the world's most ancient images of unicorns (as distinguished from rhinoceri, which are also represented). But unicorns are not all that this region has in common with the ancient and medieval west. The goddess Hiṅglāj, whose shrine stands astride the coastal range dividing the Indus River plains and the highlands of Baluchistan, also appears to be possessed of a venerable pedigree. In fact, she is referred to by her many Muslim devotees as Bībī Nānī, the "lady grandmother," a denomination which evokes a wide array of cognate names for other ancient mother goddesses, most particularly the Persian Anahitā, the Nanaea of the apocryphal Book of Maccabees (2 Mac 1:13–15), the Chaldean Nāna, and others.[119]

While there is no well of mercury per se at Hiṅglāj, the principal feature of her pilgrimage is Candrakūpa, the "Moon Well," a place of impressive geothermic activity, whose waters do indeed periodically gush up out of its depths and which also is said to belch fire. Pilgrims who come here drop pellets of bread into this pool and interpret their destiny in terms of the eruptions that follow. Similar descriptions—of an Indian "Well of Proof" whose waters contained realgar and were considered to possess magical properties and of a nearby fiery crater that gave off a lead-colored flame but which never overflowed—are found in the third-century A.D. *Life of Apollonius* of Philostratus.[120] The site also features rock-hewn images of the sun and moon, the description and location of which correspond, most intriguingly, to data found in the fourth-century B.C. *Indika* of Ctesias, a work that was written during a protracted stay in the Persian Achaemenian court of Artaxes Mnemon II. Sun and moon are, as well, absolutely pivotal images in the hathayogic system of the Nāth Siddhas, who are the perennial pilgrim's guides to and custodians of Hiṅglāj and whose illustrious founders are said to have come from points as far west as Khorasan, in eastern Iran. We may therefore see in the isolated shrine of Hiṅglāj—which remained, at least down into the middle of the present century, only accessible by a twenty-day camel journey—a possible crossroads for the exchange of alchemical knowledge and imagery in the ancient and medieval world.[121]

It is possible to dig down to a still deeper mythological stratum and see in these accounts variations on the quite widespread Indo-European theme of a well whose fiery liquid contents erupt in pursuit of a woman but are eventually channeled and thereby neutralized. If this is an Indo-European mytheme (the myth is attested in Rome as well as Ireland and India), it would necessarily date from the third millennium B.C. or earlier.[122] In this case, Pseudo-Zosimus's alchemical gloss would have been a much later addition.

5. Pentads in Metallic and Yogic Hierarchies of the Elements

The *RA* (12.83) states that "Sadāśiva exists [in the state of] mercury, [which is] composed of the five elements."[123] One scholar has analyzed this statement in the following highly literal terms: "cinnabar is mined from the earth, on roasting yields mercury, which is a liquid metal, which boils to form a gas."[124] While this explanation makes perfect sense, it is probably not what the author of the *RA* had in mind when he composed this verse: he was rather referring to the five elements as the warp and weft of a nature that was the self-manifestation of the god Śiva, the Absolute.

Drawing on a map of reality whose first grid may well have been the Vedic fire altar, the alchemical and other later Hindu traditions, both esoteric and exoteric, assumed the cosmos to be pentadic in its structure but unified in its essence. However many constituent parts the universe had, these were always reducible to familiar sets of five, fives that radiated outward from a common divine center of gravity like so many spokes on a wheel. Sāṃkhya and Vedānta, the most perennial and pervasive metaphysical systems of India, emerged in the same Upanisadic period as did the earliest traditions of Āyurveda. Indeed, some scholars argue that Āyurveda was the source—rather than a reflection—of a number of Upanisadic (and Buddhist) doctrines and theories. Also in this period there appeared, in such classical Upaniṣads as the sixth-century B.C. *Kāṭhaka* (6.16–17), early rudimentary descriptions of the physiology of the subtle body.

These three systems—the Upanisadic, the Ayurvedic, and the yogic—as well as the alchemical synthesis that would follow some centuries later—were all hierarchical systems. More than this, Indian thinkers were quick to tabulate all manner of correspondences between these systems, between wholes as well as parts. We may take, by way of example, the hierarchy of the five gross elements in Sāṃkhya and the parallel case of the five metals in alchemy.[125] In both systems, that which is higher on the hierarchy emanates, differentiates, or penetrates (*vyāpana*) into that which is lower, and is likewise capable of resorbing (*laya*) that which is lower back into itself. That which is higher is subtler than—and therefore capable of encompassing, even imploding—that which is lower back into itself without being modified.[126] Thus, each of the higher elements telescopes into itself the cumulation of all elements lower than it, together with their characteristic properties and qualities.

In Samkhyan metaphysics, the interfaces of the five lowest differentiates of Spirit (*puruṣa*) with materiality (*prakṛti*) are the five gross elements (*mahābhūta*s) that make up the material world as perceived by the five senses: these are, in descending order, ether, air, fire, water, and earth.[127] The hathayogic subtle body respects the same hierarchy as it incorporates these five elements into the five lower *cakra*s, which are aligned along the spinal column from the perineum up to the throat. In Āyurveda as well, the body is imagined to be composed of the five elements: the element earth corresponds to that which is solid in the body, water to bodily fluids, fire to body heat, air to breath, and ether to the bodily orifices.[128]

Also in Āyurveda, the process of digestion involves the progressive refinement of food from chyle (*rasa*) to semen (*śukra*) through seven intervening stages, which are called *dhātu*s.[129] It is semen, the end product of digestion, that becomes the raw fuel that the techniques of *haṭha yoga* progressively refine into nectar (*amṛta*). *Dhātu* is also the term employed in the alchemical tradition for certain of its basic elements: the *dhātu*s are the metals.[130] Like the elements in Sāṃkhya, the metals may be reckoned as five in number; this figure is often rounded up to six or seven (the same as the number of *dhātu*s in Āyurveda and the *cakra*s in yoga) through the addition of iron and one or another alloy. In the *RA*, six metals are listed: gold, silver, copper, tin, lead, and iron. These metals already appear, in a hierarchized schema, in the *Chāndogya Upaniṣad*.[131]

The most explicit connections between these parallel systems are those made between the five *mahābhūta*s of Sāṃkhya and the five *cakra*s of *haṭha yoga* on the one hand and the five metals of alchemy on the other. In this latter case,

> the absorption of herbs takes place in lead. Lead is absorbed in tin, tin in copper, copper in silver, silver in gold, and gold in mercury.

> Mercury that has been calcinated in sulfur is capable of integrating the body and is capable of "cooking" all the elements. In the same way that earth is absorbed into water, water is absorbed into fire, fire into air, air into ether, ether into the soul (*ātman*), and the soul into the Absolute (*bráhman*). Therefore, just as earth and the other elements associated with it, by virtue of being gross (*sthūla*) are absorbed into water, they and all that follow [water, on the hierarchy of elements] are absorbed into the most subtle (*sūkṣma*) element, which is Bráhman. In the same way, wood and other herbal elements are absorbed into the more subtle element lead, such that they and all that follow [lead, on the hierarchy of metals] are absorbed into mercury.[132]

The south Indian discipline of Siddha medicine goes one step further and expressly identifies the five elements with five metals. Here, gold is identified with earth, lead with water, copper with fire, iron with air, and zinc with ether.[133]

In *haṭha yoga*, the raising of the yogin's energy, figured as the female *kuṇḍalinī* serpent, through the system of the *cakras*, also effects a resorption of gross into subtler elements. Thus, when the *kuṇḍalinī* rises from the *mūlādhāra cakra* (located at the level of the perineum and identified with earth) to the *svādhiṣṭhāna* (located at the level of the sexual organs and identified with water), the element earth becomes resorbed into and encompassed by the element water. Likewise, water is resorbed into fire in the third *cakra*, the *maṇipura* (at the level of the navel); fire into air in the *anāhata cakra* (at the level of the heart); and air into ether in the *viśuddhi cakra* (located in the throat).[134] As in Sāṃkhya, *haṭha yoga*, and the other hierarchical systems, so too in alchemy: that which is higher encompasses, absorbs, that which is lower. By way of demonstration, I cite the ca. tenth-century *RHT*:[135] "Woody plants are absorbed into lead, lead into tin, and tin likewise into copper. Copper [is absorbed] into silver, silver into gold, and gold is absorbed into mercury."[136]

Earlier in this chapter, I identified a set of pentads unique to the alchemical tradition itself. When mercury first comes into the world, it divides itself into five parts, burrowing down into five deep wells, in each of five color-coded directions: the mercury in the northern well is red, while that in the eastern well is white, southern blue, western yellow, and the center variegated, like a "peacock's tail." The five classic names or varieties (*bhedas*) of mercury correspond to these five wells: mercury originating from the northern well is *rasa;* that from the eastern well is *pārada* ("that which gives [-*da*] the far shore [*para-*] [of immortality]"), that from the southern well is *rasendra* ("lord of *rasas*"), that from the western well is *sūta* ("that which was engendered [by Śiva]") and that from the central well is *miśraka* ("mixed; that which mixes with all other *rasas*").[137]

A number of sources hierarchically order these naturally occurring forms of mercury in the mineral world. This they do by assigning a "caste" (albeit in an idiosyncratic way) to the mercury of each of the four directions: white *pārada*, located to the east, is identified with the brahmin caste; blue-black *rasendra*, to the south, is *kṣatriya;* yellow *sūta*, to the west, is *vaiśya;* and red *rasa* to the north is *śūdra*. No value is given for the central well, which is said, in this text, to be the source of the mercury found in all the other wells.[138] The *KCM* assigns castes to four types of mica (*abhraka*); the *RA* does the same for four types of diamond (*vajra*).[139]

Mercury is again cast in the hierarchical mold of the five gross elements when the alchemical texts discuss the five "[modes of] going away" (*gatis*) of mercury.[140] The *gatis* are in fact the five ways in which mercury is lost through physical or chemical reaction.[141] The first of these, *mala-ga* ("dross-gone") is mercury that is lost in solid form; *jala-ga* ("water-gone") is mercury lost in liquid form; *haṃsa-ga* ("goose-gone") is mercury lost into air, through evaporation; and *dhūmra-ga* ("smoke-gone") is mercury lost through fire. The final *gati* of mercury is *jīva-ga*,[142] "soul-gone" mercury, which is the loss of mercury's vital essence into ether, space. Whereas the first four *gatis* of mercury may be remedied through laboratory procedures, the fifth and "invisible" loss of mercury can be countered only through the use of the invisible and mystic techniques of *mantradhyāna*, mantric meditation.[143] It is this subtlest form of mercury, which dwells "within the pericarp [of the lotus] of the ether (*vyoma*) of the heart," which the *RA* instructs the alchemist to recall in order that he may be cleansed of all sins of present and past lives.[144]

The same hierarchical principle applies in discussions of the ways in which mercury transmutes (*vedha*) metals. Here too, the hierarchy of the five elements is fully respected: *lepa* [-vedha] ([transmutation through] "smearing") corresponds to the solid element earth, *kṣepa* ("casting, [into molten metal]") to the liquid element water, *kunta* ("dart[ing]" to air, *dhūmra* ("smok[ing]") to fire, and *śabda* ("speech, speaking") to ether.[145] This last form of transmutation occurs when the alchemist, holding a mercurial pill in his mouth, blows upon a base metal.[146] The parallels between these two hierarchized mercurial pentads, that of *gati* and of *vedha*, is especially clear with respect to the last two members of each of the hierarchies. In both cases, the fourth member is *dhūmra*, smoke, while the fifth element, corresponding to the element ether, sound, and hearing, involves mystic speech (*śabda*). It is in this context that the alchemical use of *mantras*, detailed in the last chapter, is to be understood.

The alchemical tradition knows of a great number of other pentads which, while not arranged hierarchically, nevertheless bear witness, by the simple fact that they are presented as groups of five, to the pervasiveness of Samkhyan metaphysics. These include the five gemstones (*ratnas*), the five salts (*lavaṇas*), the five greater and lesser poisons (*viṣas*), the five animal oils (*vasās*), urines (*mūtras*), biles (*pittas*), excrements (*viṭas*), as well as the classes (*vargas*) of the five white, red, and yellow substances.[147] Here too, alchemy is a particular case of a general rule: other realms of tantra know of the five faces of Śiva, the five *makāras*,[148] the five *amṛtas*,[149] the five principal *pīṭhas*,[150] the five clans (*kulas*), the five transmissions (*āmnāyas*),[151] the five primordial Nāth Siddhas,[152] the five colors, tastes, and dispositions,[153] and so on.

6. Bird and Serpent

In general, it is the upper and lower poles of a hierarchical system that define the nature of the entire range of interrelationships that obtain between that system's constituent elements.[154] So it is that we should expect to find the mineral or metallic equivalents of ether and earth, the highest and lowest of the five elements, playing salient roles within the alchemical system. It is not, however, gold, the highest of the metal *dhātus*, that doubles for the element ether in tantric alchemy, but rather mica (called *abhraka*, *gagana*, *vyoma* or *kha*),[155] one of the three major mineral manifestations of the Goddess. Mica is already identified with the Goddess's sexual emission in the *RA* (6.1–3) and *RRS* (2.2), and a short account of its origin is found in the *Rasakāmadhenu:*[156] "One day the hillborn Goddess saw the mind-boggling Hara; the 'semen' (*vīrya*) she shed produced brilliant mica." The *Rasendra Bhāskara* reproduces this account with minor emendations, adding that "because it fell from the firmament (*gaganāt*) it is also called *gagana;* because it wandered (*abhramāt*) through the clouds (*abhra*), it is called *abhraka*."[157] These are the two principal Sanskrit terms for mica.

Another name for mica, the Goddess's sexual emission, is *vyoma*. Now, *vyoma* is also, at least from the time of the *Suśruta Saṁhitā*,[158] a term used for the element ether, which is identified, in Sāṃkhya, as the substrate of the sound *tanmātra* as well as of the sense of hearing. Like *vyoma*, *gagana* and *kha* are also terms that signify both mica and ether. Located as it is at the summit of the hierarchy of the five elements, ether is, both temporally and logically, the first of the elements that emanates from the second *guṇa*, *rajas*. As such, it constitutes a turning point in the play of nature (*prakṛti*):[159] it is the most subtle differentiate to be found in the visible world and the least subtle differentiate to be found in the invisible world.

It is fitting that ether should be identified, through the term *vyoma*, with the sexual essence of the Goddess. In Sāṃkhya, and even more so in a number of tantric classifications of the *tattva*s—cosmic essences and metaphysical categories—the pivot between pure essence and impure creation is the *māyā tattva*, which is identified with the creative power and activity (*rajas*,[160] the second of the three *guṇa*s) of the female principle, the Goddess, who is the manifestation, or act of reflection, of Śiva, consciousness. The position of ether is therefore an elevated one and is translated, in the subtle physiology of *haṭha yoga*, into the identification of the cranial vault—called the "sphere of the void" (*śūnya-maṇḍala*)—with *vyoma[n]*, *gagana*, and *kha*, i.e., ether.

Here, however, ether is as much an extremely subtle element located *conceptually* at the acme of a hierarchy as it is a locus of empty space, a cavity, hollow, or void (which one is to fill with the "stuff" of mystic experience)[161] located *spatially* at the summit of the subtle body. It is in both of these senses that ether is associated with *haṃsa*, a term translated as "swan," "goose," or "migratory bird." Since the time of the Vedas, the *haṃsa* has been the bird of predilection for authors wishing to discuss the movements of the vital breath (*prāṇa*, a term etymologically related to *ātman*, soul or spirit). Indeed, the *Ṛg Veda* (4.40.5) itself calls the ether (*kha*) the "seat" of the *haṃsa*, and a series of later sources, continuing down to the Tantras, identifies inbreathing and outbreathing with the syllables *haṃ* and *saḥ*.

Haṃsa is at once the sound that the breath makes when one inhales and exhales and the vibratory resonance (*nāda*) of the Absolute that the practitioner hears internally in the course of the spiritual exercises that lead to *samādhi*, total yogic integration.[162] In the subtle body, the *haṃsa* is identified with the empty (*śūnya*) medial channel through which the vital energy, breath, and consciousness descend in the individuation of the Absolute into an individual being.[163] In all of these traditions, breathing is tantamount to identifying the individual soul with the absolute: *haṃso 'ham* is a palindrome that can be read either as "the goose! the goose!" or "I am That," i.e., "I, *ātman*, am That, *bráhman*." The cosmic goose, honking in the void, thus becomes a metaphor for the resorption—of individual breath, sound, and soul—into the Absolute.

The void, the empty space of the heart, *suṣumṇā nāḍī*, or cranial vault, is also termed *kha*—hole, cavity, empty space—whence statements in hathayogic sources concerning the free-floating state of the meditative mind, intellect, or consciousness in the ether: this is *khecara*, "moving in the ether."[164] This principle becomes concretized on an alchemical level as well. Mercury, when bound, is said to become *khecari*, possessed of the power of flight, a power it transmits to the alchemist who holds a capsule of said mercury in his mouth.[165] If, however, it is heated before it has been properly prepared, or too rapidly, it can be lost to evaporation. Here, it is said that until its wings have been clipped (*pakṣa-ccheda*)[166] through various stabilizing techniques, unrefined mercury becomes subject to flight, i.e., evaporation (*pātana*), and may be "gone like a goose" (*haṃsaga*).[167] Here, mercury behaves like the *haṃsa* of the vital breaths: unless these are tethered by yogic discipline, the breath will eventually fly up out of the body to be lost forever, and the person will die. The ideal thus becomes one of fettering[168] that modality of the yogic or alchemical subject which has a tendency to volatilize; by so doing, the wholly integrated subject may enjoy the power of controlled flight, rather than disintegrating, i.e., losing parts of itself that would otherwise fly off. This is the difference between *khecara*, "moving in the ether," and *haṃsaga*, being "gone like a goose." Here again, the original inspiration appears to be Upanisadic. Referring to the soul, the *Kāṭhaka Upaniṣad* (2.21) states: "seated, he travels afar, and recumbent goes everywhere."

As we have shown, *vyoma*, as both mica and ether, is identified with the Goddess's sexual emission. Mercury, when it is identified with the soul (*jīva*), when it transmutes through speech of which the substrate is ether (*śabda-vedha*), and when it becomes possessed of the power of flight (*khecar-a[tā]*), is itself associated with ether.[169] In this way, both mercury and mica, the sexual emissions of Śiva and the Goddess, located at the summit of the alchemical hierarchy, are likened to the ethereal goose.

Śiva's seed is further associated with another sort of bird—as well as with a serpent—in Somadeva's account of the origin of mercury, which varies significantly from the chronologically later *RRS* account presented earlier in this chapter.[170] Like the *RRS*, the *RC* states that Śiva first cast the semen he had shed into the mouth of Agni (Fire), who had taken the form of a pigeon. Somadeva then goes on to say that

> those *dhātus*, in overflowing abundance, were indeed the same as nectar.[171] That which dripped from Śiva's hand truly became mercury (*pārada*). From the dross [of those *dhātus*] born from the immortal and unaging supreme god, there arose the metals (*dhātus*), eight in number. And that *rasa* which fell from the mouth of Agni [who had taken the form of a pigeon] was indeed used by the Lord of Serpents, who wished to leave behind old age and death. But that [mercury] which, while being drunk [by the snake] fell to the ground, did—due to its heaviness—fall through the ground into one hundred *yojana*-deep wells.

This interaction—between a bird (Agni, in the form of a pigeon, from whose mouth drops of divine semen/nectar/mercury fall) and a snake (the Lord of Serpents, who drinks up what has fallen in order to gain immortality)—harks back to mythic themes from both the Vedas[172] and ancient Mesopotamia.[173] In these archaic accounts, a bird is identified with the theft of an elixir of eternal life, of which a serpent (who recovers its youth every time it sheds its skin) would once have been the custodian. The counterpart—or more exactly the archenemy—of this bird who flies through the ether of the heavens to perch atop the tree of life, to name but one tree, is the serpent who lives at the foot of the same tree. This theme is, moreover, the starting point for a multitude of Indian variants on the epic myth of the bird-god Garuḍa's battles with the serpent descendants of Kadru.[174] So it is that we find in the alchemical appropriation of certain perennial themes from Hindu mythology, as well as metaphysical categories from Sāṃkhya, a return to one of the most ancient "creative oppositions" known to humanity.

Indeed, there is much of the serpent in Hindu imagery of death and eternal life. As early as the *Bṛhadāraṇyaka Upaniṣad* (4.4.7), the immortal self is said to discard its mortal body "like a snake sheds its slough." The slough that a snake periodically sheds is an important image in alchemy as well. Here, mercury in its unrefined state is said to be covered with seven "sloughs" or "sheaths" (*kañcukas*). These are coatings of various base metals and other impurities, which float on the surface of mercury (whose specific gravity is greater than that of all the metals, save gold), and which are said to be the creations of jealous gods who feared that mercury would render human alchemists their equals. Mercury, the semen of absolute godhead, must be purged of these coatings if it is to be used with success in alchemical operations.[175]

No doubt working from the Upanisadic image evoked above, a number of Śaiva schools and sects came to apply the notion of the *kañcuka*s to a much broader range of ideas. In a number of these systems, a group of five *kañcuka*s ("sheaths") become an important metaphysical construct employed to explain the difference between God in his transcendence and God in his immanence, between essence and existence, the unity of the divine, infinite self and a plurality of finite selves. Such is especially the case in the orthodox Śaiva Siddhānta, according to whose *Kiraṇāgama* creatures are provided with the five *kañcuka*s while in the "bosom of Māyā," the material cause of the impure worlds. These impure worlds are said to owe their existence to Ananta (or Ananteśa) the first of the eight Vidyeśvaras. Now, Ananta is one of the names of the Hindu cosmic serpent, whose relationship to the *kañcuka*s is an obvious and immediate one. This being the case, the intermediate role of the Vidyeśvaras appears to double that of the *kañcuka*s themselves: they constitute the gray area between divinity and humanity, essence and manifestation.[176]

Abhinavagupta, in his discussion of the untraceable boundary between Śiva and his creation, may well have had the mercurial *kañcuka*s in mind when he wrote the following passage, so close are the conceptual parallels between the chemistry of mercury and the metaphysics of gnoseology here:

> The God, whose nature is a free consciousness, whose characteristic is the supreme light, due to his own intrinsic nature and as a result of his enjoyment of the sport of concealing his own nature, becomes the atomic, finite self, of which there are many. He himself, as a result of his own freedom, binds himself here by means of actions whose nature are composed of imagined differentiations. Such is the power of the God's freedom that, even though he has become the finite self, he once more truly attains his own true form in all its purity.

Here, the dividing line between the impure path (*aśuddhādhvan:* the twenty-five Samkhyan *tattva*s of the manifest world) and the pure path (*śuddhādhvan:* the five transcendent categories of the Trika Kaula) is composed of the intervening six *kañcuka*s. Taken together, these are the thirty-six (25 + 6 + 5) categories of Kaula metaphysics.[177]

A final alchemical parallel, which also brings us back to the important place of the feminine in the alternation of the divine between self-concealment and self-discovery, may be elicited here. In describing the mercury produced from Śiva's semen, the *BhP* states that this next combined with the substance emitted from the Goddess's sexual organ to produce four colors and two types of mercury. Mercury, the mineral form of the body of the wholly transcendent Śiva, is mediated in the world by the Goddess, whose interposition, in the form of her sexual emission, renders said mercury impure.[178]

In alchemy, the image of the serpent is not limited to the mercurial *kañcukas*. It is also widely employed as a signifier for the lower end of a system that is crowned by an ethereal bird: the lowest metal on the alchemical hierarchy is lead, most commonly called *nāga*, "serpent" or *sīsa[ka]*, an allomorph of the name of the cosmic serpent Śeṣa; or, more rarely, *ahirāja*, "serpent king."[179] The *Rasakāmadhenu* (2.1.4) and *Rasendra Bhāskara* (4.108) state that lead arose from the semen of Vāsuki, the king of a mythic race of serpents known for the great wealth it possessed in its subterranean treasure hoards. This bird-serpent opposition is made most explicit in the ca. sixteenth century *Rasakāmadhenu*, which identifies gold, at the summit of the hierarchy of metals, with semen shed by Agni, and lead, at the base of the system, with the seed of Vāsuki. Let us also recall here the *Rāmāyaṇa* myth, related at the beginning of this chapter, in which lead and tin (often used interchangeably) are said to arise from the residue (*mala*) or afterbirth of the generation of gold.[180]

This further recalls the serpent Śeṣa ("Remains," "Residue")[181] who upholds the golden egg of the universe on his many hoods and whose coiled body is composed of the dregs, the calcinated residue of past creations. Of what sort of residue is Śeṣa composed? According to the Purāṇas, the cosmic dissolution or reabsorption (*pralaya*) that occurs at the end of a great age (*mahāyuga*) of some 4,320,000 human years is a two-phase process. The first of these is a universal conflagration, in which Śiva, in his destructive Kālāgnirudra form,[182] incinerates all the gross, inert matter located inside the cosmic egg (while preserving the subtle souls of liberated beings in the ether of the highest levels of the cosmic egg, well above the conflagration). Then follows a great rain and flood, the true dis-solution, which extinguishes the fire and immerses the world in a great ocean.[183] There remains a calcinated or ashen residue from the fire, however, which sinks to the bottom of the ocean of dissolution, to coalesce into the serpent Śeṣa, at the bottom of the cosmic egg.

At the end of a cosmic eon (*kalpa*), of one thousand *mahāyugas* in length, the entire cosmic egg—and not merely the lower levels of its interior—is consumed, and it is upon the chaotic waters of the ensuing flood that the *mahāyogin* Viṣṇu Nārāyaṇa, the "Abode of Mankind," sleeps, in a state of total yogic integration (*samādhi*) for a kalpic night.[184] (Here, Viṣṇu's yogic sleep is the divine model for the *samādhi* of the human yogin who has withdrawn all breath, seed, and consciousness to concentrate these into a single point of pure being-consciousness-bliss. In Viṣṇu's case, all that is subtle and eternal in the universe has been withdrawn into that single point.)[185] What of the gross matter of the previous *kalpa*? It too is preserved, once again in the ever-recyclable serpent body of Śeṣa, who serves, this time, as Viṣṇu's couch, upon which he sleeps away the kalpic night in yogic enstasis. In this way, Śeṣa, the cosmic serpent who ever renews himself from one cycle to another, remains the same serpent even as he is reconstituted from a new mixture of recycled elements. As such, his body is an endless source of raw material for renewed creations. For this reason, he is also called Ananta, "Endless."[186]

The serpent at the base of a system is a commonplace of Hindu cosmology and metaphysics. In both sacred and profane constructions in India, a spike is symbolically driven into the head of this serpent, a head that upholds the world, to ensure a solid foundation.[187] Elsewhere, the semilegendary figures who laid down the foundations of Indian medicine (Caraka), yoga (Patañjali), and alchemy (Nāgārjuna) are all said to be incarnations of great serpents.[188]

Similarly, the ashes that compose the body of the serpent Śeṣa also bear a Vedic pedigree. In the logic of sacrifice, there can be no "first sacrifice"; rather, every "new" sacrifice, ignited with the embers of the sacrifice which preceded it, is a reenactment of that prior sacrifice: this holds as well for the primal sacrifice of the Purusa—recounted in *Ṛg Veda* 10.90—in which we find that the "primal" sacrifice out of which the universe was created itself arose out of preexisting sacrificial materials! Ashes of prior sacrifices are the seeds of future sacrifices, and so it is that the erotic ascetic Śiva can call the ashes of cosmic dissolution that he smears upon his body his "seed."[189] Similarly, when the Vedic sacrificer used a fire drill and block to create a spark with which to ignite a sacrificial fire, it was presumed that the fire produced was latent in the wood of the fire block. In the language of *haṭha yoga*, the *kuṇḍalinī* serpent is described in the same way: until she is awoken, she is fire that is latent in the fire block; once awoken, she is the spark that bursts into manifestation through the "churning" of yogic practice.[190]

Just as "serpentine" lead, at the base of the alchemical hierarchy of metals, must, of teleological necessity, fully actualize its potential by ultimately becoming alchemical gold, so too the sleeping *kuṇḍalinī* must awaken to remount the hierarchy of emanated being and reunite with the absolute in the "place of the ether," the human cranial vault. The temporal endpoints of these processes—of the ripening of metals and the yogic transformation of the subtle body—are spatially located within the hierarchized systems for which they serve as fundaments. So it is that we find, in the coils of these symbolic serpents, the nexus of a Hindu time-space continuum. With this, we turn to the structure of these parallel and interpenetrating systems.

EIGHT

Homologous Structures of the Alchemical Body

1. The Two *Kuṇḍalinīs*

Nāgārjuna's name, in its Tibetan inscription (*klu sgrubs*), evokes terms that signify, in that language, "confused mass," "a mass in the spiral form of a conch shell," "abyss," "abdominal cavity" (*kloṅ*), and "valley floor" (*kluṅ*).[1] These associations, of a founding alchemical wizard, a serpent, the abdominal cavity, and the base of an enclosed environment, evoke the perennial hathyogic image of yet another serpent. This is the female *kuṇḍalinī*, who is explicitly identified with the serpent at the base of the cosmic egg, Śeṣa or, alternatively, Ananta, "the endless one."[2]

In every human body, the female *kuṇḍalinī* serpent sleeps coiled in the place of the "fire of time" (*kālāgni*),[3] with her mouth closed over an internal *liṅga* in the lower abdomen.[4] It is only in the body of a yogin that she is ever awakened, and her awakening corresponds precisely to the initiation of the yogin's progressive withdrawal into total yogic integration (*samādhi*) or fluid equilibrium (*samarasa*). On a more concrete level, it is the rise of the *kuṇḍalinī* that brings about the transmutation of raw semen into nectar in the cranial vault, a locus associated with the ethereal goose. In the last chapter, I evoked the identification of the *haṃsa* of the cranial vault with the subtlest channel of the subtle body, the medial *suṣumṇā nāḍi*. Like the subtlest of minerals, mercury, the *suṣumṇā* can also double as both a bird and a serpent:[5] thus this channel is identified, as well, with the *kuṇḍalinī* serpent who, when awakened, pierces its opening at the base of the spinal column "like a key in the lock of a door-panel," to rush upwards to the cranial vault.[6]

The *kuṇḍalinī* in the body of the yogin is an incarnation of the feminine in this tradition and thereby incarnates all the perils and joys that women can represent for men. She is divine energy (*śakti*) and female materiality (*pṛakṛti*), but she is also a tigress who can drain a man of all his energy and seed.[7] She is twofold, and it is in this perspective that yogic sources speak of this internal female serpent by another name: she is *bhogavatī*, a term that at once bespeaks her enjoyment (*bhoga*, from *bhuj*, "partake, enjoy"), her coiled form (*bhoga* from *bhuj*, "coil, curl"), and her female sex (*-vatī* is a feminine ending). As *bhogavatī*, she is the serpentine female principle within the subtle body.[8]

It is when her name is interpreted in terms of *bhoga* as pleasure that this female serpent's twofold role is brought to the fore in the tantric context. The *kuṇḍalinī* as *bhogavatī* is a female who both *takes* pleasure and *gives* pleasure. In tantric metaphysics, it is the *kuṇḍalinī*'s coiled body itself that is the turning point between emanation and participation, emission and resorption.[9] At ground zero of the self-emission of the absolute into phenomenal being is the *kuṇḍalinī* who takes pleasure as she allows the microcosmic life force to drain away into her sleeping mouth. Her sleep is the sleep of dumb matter, and her head or mouth the sole obstruction to the opening of the upward path to her own return, from existence to essence as it were. Her awakening blows open the "door to the absolute" (*brahmadvāra*) at the base of the medial channel, and her rise along the length of this channel effects the return—on the part of the yogin in whose body she has been awakened—to the wholeness, being-consciousness-bliss, and absolute godhead that is his true nature. Here too, we can glimpse the *kuṇḍalinī*'s role as the microcosmic homologue of Śeṣa, the cosmic serpent and endpoint of a prior creation and the starting point of a future creation, who is located as well at the base of a self-enclosed system.

We can also see, however, why the *kuṇḍalinī* is, unlike Śeṣa, a *female* serpent. When she slumbers, "as if stupefied by a poison," in a man's abdomen, the *kuṇḍalinī* is identified with human mortality, with death-laden existence, and the bondage of the ignorant,[10] which is figured by the incessant drain of semen that she, as woman, effects in man. In this role, the sleeping *kuṇḍalinī* is identified with the fire of time (*kālāgni*) because the mortal who allows her to drain away his semen is doomed to be consumed by the fire of time and die. Such is the fate of a number of yogins of Nāth legend. Most famous among these is Matsyendranāth, who, having had his yogic energy and life force drained away by years of debauchery in a Kingdom of Women, is fated to die within three days if Gorakhnāth cannot reawaken him, i.e., awaken his sleeping *kuṇḍalinī*.

It is when the *kuṇḍalinī* is awakened that she becomes capable of *giving* pleasure—and here too, it is appropriate that she be figured as a female serpent. Her awakening is the beginning of the return or resorption, on a microcosmic level, of the phenomenal world back into the absolute from which it was originally emitted. The yogin, in rousing her from her slumber, finds in the rising *kuṇḍalinī* a vehicle by which to raise himself from mundane existence to the god-consciousness that renders him a second Śiva.

Indeed, the final aim of the yogin, like that of any tantric practitioner, is twofold.[11] On the one hand, he strives toward liberation (*mokṣa*, *mukti*) from conditioned mortal existence; at the same time, however, he also seeks to realize for himself the enjoyment (*bhoga*, *bhukti*) that the absolute, Śiva, knows in his very being.[12] This pleasure that Śiva, the absolute, takes in his manifold creations, his self-realizations, is often cast as his sexual union with his female, manifest aspect, i.e., with the Goddess, who is identified with *vimarśa* (reflective consciousness), *māyā* (creativity), *śakti* (energy), and the *kuṇḍalinī*. It is a pleasure of the same order as that enjoyed by Śiva in his union with the Goddess that the yogin comes to know in awakening and raising his *kuṇḍalinī*. It is in this light that the *kuṇḍalinī* becomes identified, in tantric practice, with both the male practitioner's sexual partner and a goddess to whom he makes sacrificial offerings. As the *MBhT* explains, the practitioner's *bhoga* takes the form of the pleasure he enjoys in his imbibing the *makāra*s that precede sexual intercourse with his partner. The wine that he drinks and the flesh and fish he eats become offerings into the mouth of the *kuṇḍalinī*, who rises up to his tongue to consume them. His *bhoga*, when accompanied by the proper *mantra*s, becomes an inner sacrifice to the Goddess, with whom he thus shares his pleasure. Like his human partner, she becomes his lover, and because she is the Goddess, his savior as well. The *bhoga* offered into her mouth becomes nectar, and her rise transforms his very being.[13] Riding the *kuṇḍalinī* upwards on a wave of mutual pleasure, against the grain of the entropic processes of aging and death, the yogin comes to experience liberation and bliss. Ultimately, he becomes "a second Śiva," in eternal embrace with the Goddess.

How does the yogin awaken the slumbering *kuṇḍalinī* to reverse the order of nature on a microcosmic level? By assuming a number of postures (*āsana*s), by breath control (*prāṇāyāma*), and by means of a number of internal blocks (*bandha*s) and seals (*mudrā*s) that fan the fire of yoga (*yogāgni*), the fire that consumes the fire of time (whence its synonyms *kālāgnirudra* and *yamāntaka*). So, for example the *HYP* states that the "Matsyendra *āsana* . . . arouses the *kuṇḍalinī*"; that the *mahā-mudrā* causes the "*kuṇḍalinī* [to] suddenly become straight just as a coiled snake when struck by a rod straightens itself out like a stick"; and that the *mūlā bandha* "awakens the *kuṇḍalinī*, who straightens, entering the medial channel, like a snake entering a hole."[14] The *kuṇḍalinī*'s awakening marks the beginning of the yogin's own withdrawal into his yogic sleep or trance, into the total integration that is *samādhi*. In this light, we can see that in the universal scheme of things, the great yogin, be he named Śiva or Viṣṇu, ultimately "awakens"—pours himself out into mundane being of which the sleeping *kuṇḍalinī* is the end- or turning-point—in order that human yogins might find a way to genuinely "fall asleep," i.e., enter into the yogic sleep of *samādhi*. On the microcosmic level, this yogic reintegration affords liberation and bliss; on the macrocosmic level, it is nothing other than the *pralaya*, the universal resorption of all mundane existence into the primal and primordial essence that is the Absolute, God.

These two poles of the *kuṇḍalinī*'s mode of being—sleeping and waking, taking and giving pleasure, allowing the body to be consumed by the fire of time and consuming the fire of time—these mundane and transcendent poles are identified as her "poison" and her "nectar."[15] The *kuṇḍalinī* is poison when she remains asleep in the lower abdomen; she is nectar precisely when she rises up through the medial channel of the subtle body to reunite with Śiva, the Absolute, in the yogin's cranial vault.[16] In the hatha-yogic sources, this union is in fact accompanied by an outpouring of nectar, which renders the yogin immortal.

This connection between poison, nectar, and yogic prowess has its reflection in Hindu mythology, in which the serpent king Vāsuki serves as churning rope in the mythic churning of the Ocean of Milk. This churning (which produced sulfur in the alchemical myth related in the last chapter) is best known for its production of the nectar (*amṛta*) of divine immortality. Another byproduct of this process is, however, the production of the most virulent of poisons in the universe (*kālakuṭa*, *halāhala*), which arose from the Vāsuki's venom.[17] This poison, churned out of the ocean, would have consumed the entire universe had Śiva, whose yogic austerities rendered him powerful enough to do so, not swallowed it. It is the trace of this feat that accounts for the dark blue mark found on Śiva's throat in Hindu iconography, and his epithet of "Blue-Throat," Nīlakaṇṭha.[18] Lastly, mercury, Śiva's semen, is a poison for the uninitiated who would presume to partake of it without the proper preparations; for the initiated alchemist, however, it is the nectar of immortality. This coincidence of opposites is divinized in the Tibetan Buddhist homologue of Yamāntaka—that is, of Śiva as "the Death of Death." This is the Tibetan divinity named "Quicksilver" (i.e., mercury) who, although he is a "black poison-faced divinity," is also the "black master of life."[19]

The twofold *kuṇḍalinī*, who incarnates the two prevailing Hindu attitudes toward the manifest world, a world which it always views as feminine—i.e., the Vedantic view of the world as imprisoning *māyā* and the tantric view of the Goddess as a limitless source of energy, *śakti*—is but one of a wide variety of redoubled images proper to the yogic and alchemical body. This dual role of feminine energy—of the Goddess embodied in the world, in a human woman, or in the internal *kuṇḍalinī*—is clearly expressed in a verse from the *Spanda Kārikā* of Abhinavagupta's ninth-century forerunner, the philosopher Vasugupta: "It is Śiva's śakti, that is, his power to act, who, dwelling within limited creatures, causes bondage; When she is known as herself the path, she is the one who makes perfection (*siddhi*) possible."[20] In the balance of this chapter, I examine a number of such phenomena in these interpenetrating symbol systems, in images that range from human mouths to wells to rivers to forests, cities, and even entire kingdoms! Throughout, it will be shown that each image at once points to the imminence of death, the great equalizer, and to its opposite—immortality, the cheating of death (*kālavañcana*)—on the part of the Siddha who knows how to reverse, on the mesocosmic level of his subtle body or alchemical laboratory, the being-towards-death that is the erstwhile fate of all creatures who are bound to this world.

2. Charting the Subtle Body: The Legends of Matsyendranāth

a. Fish Belly

Like the supreme yogic god Śiva, the hathayogin is himself capable—through his raising of the *kuṇḍalinī*—of transmuting poisons into nectar. More properly speaking, that which is poison for mere mortals is, for the yogin who has realized, through his practice, a divine "identity in difference" view of reality, identical to nectar, *amṛta*.[21] Numerous Nāth Siddhas are known for their ability to control (and charm) serpents, yet another metaphor for their mastery of the female *kuṇḍalinī*, and for their ability to treat poisons as elixirs.[22] Likewise, mercury, which is a poison for the uninitiated, becomes an elixir of immortality for the alchemist who knows its secrets.[23] In this section, I interpret a number of yogic metaphors for the mastery of the forces that sleep in the lower part of the body, forces that, when awakened, transform the yogin's being completely.

A moment ago, I evoked Matsyendranāth, the original *guru* of the Nāth Siddhas, who was rescued from death in a Kingdom of Women by his more disciplined pupil Gorakhnāth. It is on this mythic ground that Matsyendra the guru becomes Matsyendra the disciple: after Gorakh has rescued Matsyendra from the Kingdom of Women, he must give his teacher a "refresher course" in *haṭha yoga*. Indeed, it is a leitmotif of Nāth legend that Matsyendra, the teacher of Gorakh, is much more susceptible to the lures of the fair sex, to the world of appearances (*māyā*), than is his pupil, who must constantly awaken him to the reality behind appearances. To be sure, the erotic rituals of the Yoginī Kaula sect of which Matsyendra was the purported founder lie behind much of this mythic imagery. So it is that the yoginīs of Kāmarūpa, from whom Matsyendra received his tantric revelation, become the "Plantain Forest" women who ensnare him, in an important myth cycle of Gorakh and Matsyendra.[24]

In a curious way, Matsyendra is doubly connected, by his name, to the lower half of the yogic body, the place of the sleeping *kuṇḍalinī*. However, just as the *kuṇḍalinī* sleeps at a turning point in the play of divine manifestation and resorption, so too, the symbol system constructed around Matsyendra's name is an ambivalent one. An extensive body of medieval sources connect Matsyendra to his doctrine of the fish belly through a mythic gloss of his name. Matsyendranātha means "He Whose Lord is the Lord of Fishes" (or the pleonastic "Lord Lord of Fishes"), and his connection with fish is explained through a myth in which the Goddess, seated on or near the shore of Candradvīpa ("Moon Island"), has asked Śiva to teach her the most secret of all esoteric knowledge, things he has never told her before.[25] This Śiva agrees to do, but he has barely launched into what will turn out to be the essence of the Hindu tantric teachings than does the Goddess fall asleep. Śiva's words do not, however, go unheeded. Matsyendra, who has been swallowed by a fish (whence his name in these sources), draws up to the shoreline and overhears everything. It is in this way that the "historical" Matsyendra[26] becomes both the link between the divine and human in the transmission of the tantras and the founder of numerous sectarian traditions.[27] In a number of these sources, Matsyendra is further identified with, or called the father (or son or brother or nephew or daughter) of, Mīnanātha, a name which also means "Lord of Fishes."[28]

The earliest mythic account of Matsyendra, that found in the *KJñN* (16.27–56) itself, tells a somewhat different story. This source, which calls him Macchaghna, "Killer of Fishes"[29]—an indication that he was a fisherman—makes no reference to his overhearing Śiva's teachings from the belly of a fish. Rather, it relates that Śiva has committed the *kulāgama* to writing, the which his son Kārttikeya has thrown, in a rage, into the sea. These teachings are then swallowed by a great fish. The god Bhairava takes the form of Matsyendra the fisherman to recover the teachings out of the fish's belly, at a site called Candradvīpa.[30] Later, it is stated that this teaching (*śāstra*) was brought down at Candradvīpa;[31] earlier in the text, however, it is stated that it was brought down by Śiva and the Goddess, at Kāmarūpa.[32]

As a killer of fishes and the founding guru of a tantric lineage and tradiion, Matsyendra may be further linked with another tantric founder. This is the ca. ninth-century Buddhist Siddhācārya Luī-pā (or Lo-yi-pā, Lū-yi-pā, Lū-hi-pāda, Lū-yi-shabs). The original Siddhācārya of the Tibetan *Grub thob*[33] lists and author of two Bengali *caryā* songs (nos. 1 and 29), Luī-pā's name means "Venerable Red-Fish." In Nepal, Luī-pā appears to be further conflated with a Buddhist divinity. Here, a famous red image of the bodhisattva Avalokiteśvara has been worshipped in the village of Bunga and the city of Patan since the seventh century. Since the sixteenth century, this same image has been identified with Rato Macchandernāth, the "red Matsyendranāth"; and, indeed, an old Newari *bhajan*, still sung in Kathmandu, refers to this deity as "Luīpāda-nāth."[34] While scholars generally agree that this is a late and spurious identification, there are a number of piscine elements to the names and roles of this Buddhist divinity that deserve further attention. First, "Luī" is a vernacularization of *lohita/rohita*, i.e., "red": Luī-pā's fish is a red fish, which squares with the color of the Patan image.[35] Second, Avalokiteśvara has, in at least one case, been represented in a piscine mode: at Ratnagiri (Cuttack district, Orissa), the bust of a mutilated Avalokiteśvara image was found to be superimposed upon the image of a large fish, "so as to convert the Bodhisattva into Matsya, the first Avatāra of Viṣṇu." The Hindu Matsyendranāth has himself been portrayed in a manner similar to that of Viṣṇu's fish incarnation, emerging out of the mouth of a fish.[36]

Of much greater interest to us is the identification we find of Matsyendra or Luī-pā's name with the term *matsyodara*, which simply means "fish belly." Tibetan translations of Luī-pā's name, found in the *Tanjur*, include *ña'i-rgyu-ma-za-ba*, which means "one who eats the intestines of a fish"; and *ña-lto-pa*, which restored into Sanskrit yields, precisely, *matsyodara*, "fish belly."[37] Abhinavagupta, who praises Macchanda in an opening verse

(1.7) of his monumental *Tantrāloka*, cryptically refers to *matsyodara* in a later passage of the same work: "On the level of the highest *kuṇḍalinī* is the Emissional Power which is beautiful because it contains within itself the vibration, there the yogin should repose devoted to *the condition of belly of the fish*."[38]

What this term means is stated in elliptic fashion in the thirteenth-century *Amaraugha Prabodha* of Gorakhanāth, who further intimates that this doctrine constituted the very first revealed teachings of Śiva, which that god gave to an audience consisting of Mīnanāth and the Goddess, i.e on the shore of Candradvīpa. Here, Gorakhnāth states: "Holding the breath [when it is] restrained by force (*haṭhāt*) is [called] swallowing into the fish-belly (*mīnodare*). He [who is] blessed with detachment is not conscious until he releases it [i.e., his breath]."[39] What I wish to argue here is that Matsyendra's doctrine of the fish belly—a revolutionary doctrine indeed, given the perennial importance that has been attached to it in Hindu tantrism over the past one thousand years—is about diaphragmatic retention and its effects on the body and consciousness of the yogic practitioner.

This meaning is greatly expanded in the unexpected context of a description of the holy city of Benares given in a number of Śaiva Purāṇas. As any armchair traveler knows, the city of Benares is situated on a wide bend in the holy Ganges River, at the last point at which the river turns north, as if to return to its Himalayan source. It is also a city that is said in certain sources to resemble a fish in shape.[40] Though not because of its piscine outline, the beauty and holiness of Benares are such that Śiva, in a distant mythic past, chose to make Benares, or Kāśī, his home whenever he was not meditating atop Mount Kailash.[41] For Hindu pilgrims from time immemorial, it is not the beauty of the site, but rather the liberating effects of bathing in the waters of the Ganges there—the salvific powers of which are enhanced by Śiva's presence—that has been the prime reason for undertaking a journey to that fabled city.

The Ganges (Gaṅgā) is, however, but one of a triad of holy rivers—and of river goddesses—its two sister rivers being the Yamuna (which joins the Ganges at Prayāg, the modern Allahabad), and the Sarasvati. There is a mystery to this last river, the earliest river to be identified with a goddess in the Vedic literature: rising in the highlands of southwestern Rajasthan, it is a river that "disappears" into the plains of Kacch before ever reaching the sea—and it is this hidden nature of the Sarasvati that is brought to the fore in the Puranic descriptions of *matsyodarī-yoga*, the "fish-belly conjunction" of Benares.

Before we can explain this phenomenon, however, we must first briefly review a commonplace of yogic physiology, according to which the three principal subtle channels (*nāḍīs*) of the life force are identified with these three major rivers (*nadīs*): the solar *piṅgalā* is the Yamuna River, the lunar *iḍā* is the Ganges, and the medial, "empty" *suṣumṇā* is the "fiery," "hidden" Sarasvati.[42] In the practice of breath control, *prāṇāyāma*, it is by pumping up and thereby emptying the two peripheral subtle channels, the *iḍā* and the *piṅgalā*, that the theretofore empty *suṣumṇā* suddenly becomes filled with the subtle breath or life force (*prāṇa*) to become the yogin's internal upward-tending channel to liberation. This yogic homologue to these three river systems of India is so obvious as to not require explanation here.

Benares, the greatest pilgrimage site (*tīrtha*) of India, is said to contain all of the rivers and all of the *tīrtha*s of India within its precincts. It is in this context that the geography of the city, as well as seasonal floods there, contributed to the unusual riverine phenomenon known as the "fish-belly conjunction," down to at least the sixteenth century. Prior to its urbanization over the past two centuries, the inner limits of riverine Benares were constituted by a string of inland pools, tanks, and lakes. One of these was named Matsyodarī, the "[Lake of the] Fish Belly." In particularly heavy rainy seasons, these reservoirs would flood into one another to form a single channel—also called the Matsyodarī—that ran for no less than three miles between the river known as the Varaṇā, the tributary to the Ganges forming the city's northern border, and the stream known as the Asi, which flowed into the Ganges at the southern end of the city.[43] According to folk etymology, the classic name of Benares—Vārāṇasī—derives from the fact that that city-state lay between the Varaṇā and Asi rivers. For certain cartographers of the subtle body, the symbolism was clear:[44] "The two vessels called the *iḍā* and the *piṅgalā* are the real *varaṇā-asi*. The space between them is called *Vārāṇasī*. There it is said that [Śiva] Viśvanāth dwells . . . From the right side of the *ājñā* [*cakra*] and going to the left nostril flows the *iḍā*. It is here called Varaṇā, the upward-flowing [Ganges] . . . Rising from the left side of the *ājñā* lotus[45] and going to the right nostril, this upward-flowing *piṅgalā* has been called of yore the Asi."

This schematization flows directly into the rainy-season phenomenon I have been describing: when the seasonal Matsyodarī opened its periodic channel, the normal flow of Benares's rivers became reversed: the Ganges would actually back up into its tributary, the Varaṇā, and flow therefrom into the seasonal Matsyodarī channel; the Matsyodarī would in turn drain into the Asi, out of the mouth of which the Ganges would empty back into "itself." The waters of the Ganges that were so channeled therefore ran against the river's normal flow, along the underbelly of the piscine outline of Benares—within which the permanent Matsyodarī Lake was located—whence the designations of *matsyodarī* for the periodic stream itself, and *matsyodarī-yoga*, the "fish-belly conjunction," for those periods in which it appeared (and for the site at which the overflow of Matsyodarī Lake ran into the waters of the flooding Ganges).

This anomaly, of a periodic backflooding of the Ganges, is given a yogic gloss in the ca. tenth-century *Liṅga Purāṇa*, a gloss that will at once explain the great yogin Matsyendranāth's piscine associations:

> *Piṅgalā* is the name by which the fiery *nāḍī* is praised, and it is known to be that dried up stream (the Asi) [which runs by the place] where [the tank named] "the trembling sun"[46] stands. *Iḍā* is the name by which the lunar *nāḍī* is praised. It is known to be the Varaṇā [River], where the [Viṣṇu] Keśava [temple] is situated. That *nāḍī* [which runs] between the two is glorified as the *suṣumṇā* and known as Matsyodarī; it is praised as "[a stream] running in both directions" (*viṣuvam*).[47] There where [two currents] come together at the Fish-Belly Pool, a bath yields liberation . . . It is an extraordinary conjunction when the Ganges runs into the Fish-Belly channel to the west of Kapileśvara. A bath at that juncture yields [the fruits of] a thousand horse sacrifices . . . That place is indeed praised as the fluvial *brahma*-syllable.[48]

In a passage from the somewhat later Kāśī Khaṇḍa of the *Skanda Purāṇa*, the Matsyodarī is said to be *bahir-antaścarā*, "flowing both inside and outside" (i.e., surrounding Benares, via the Ganges' normal outer channel as well as that of the inner Matsyodarī), and taking the path of retraction (*saṁhāra-mārga*).[49] With this, we now hold all the necessary elements for a symbolic interpretation of the term "fish-belly conjunction," *matsyodarī-yoga*. The belly of the fish, and that "path of retraction" at which a reversal of the normal flow occurs, is, assuredly, the opening of the medial channel, the *suṣumṇā nāḍī*[50] at the base of the subtle body. The two peripheral channels (the *iḍā* and *piṅgalā*) are the Varaṇā (Ganges) and Asi (Yamuna) rivers, whose flow is reversed such that the "empty" medial channel, the *suṣumṇā* (the Sarasvati River; and in Benares, the Matsyodarī), may be opened and filled with the reversed, upward flow of semen, life force, breath, and mind, which yields liberation and immortality. In this schema, the backward-flowing Ganges itself doubles as the "disappearing" Sarasvati River, which "reappears" in a feat of yogic reversal when it becomes the Matsyodarī, the fish-belly channel.[51]

Matsyodarī-yoga, the "fish-belly conjunction," is, however, more than a mere macrocosmic reproduction of a structure of the subtle body. It also refers to a particular yogic practice, specifically to that practice to which Gorakhnāth alludes in the *Amaraugha Prabodha* passage quoted above. "Holding the breath when it is restrained by force (*haṭhāt*) . . . in the fish belly (*mīnodare*)" is a description of that most fundamental aspect of breath control called *kumbhaka*, the "potlike" diaphragmatic retention of the breaths.[52] Here, the *iḍā* and *piṅgalā* channels are "pumped like bellows," by means of breath control, until the *suṣumṇā* channel suddenly opens. At this point, the two peripheral channels empty and lie "swooned." What follows is automatic: the vital breath that rushes into the *suṣumṇā* rises upward, against the normal downward flow of all bodily fluids, affords yogic liberation.[53] In Puranic mythology, it is precisely by bathing during the period of the "fish-belly conjunction" that the god Bhairava was liberated from the skull of Brahmā that had clung to his hand for twelve years. Having thus completed his "skull bearer's vow" (*kāpālika vrata*), Bhairava established himself as the guardian deity of Benares, at a temple on the bank of the Kapālamocana ("Liberation from the Skull") tank.[54] This god's mythic liberation from his terrible vow is tantamount to the wholly unconditioned state of Śivahood enjoyed by the yogin at the culmination of his practice of "swallowing into the fish belly."

Matsyendra's doctrine of the fish belly would therefore have been, if nothing else, a teaching on *haṭha yoga*. This is supported by the fact that Gorakhnāth, in the opening verses of his twelfth- to thirteenth-century *Gorakṣa Śataka*, invokes Mīnanāth as his guru.[55] Now, while it has been maintained that six-*cakra* yoga was an innovation of the Western Transmission, it would appear that Matsyendra's doctrine of the fish belly (*kumbhaka* as the culmination of breath control), together with a significant number of other references to the subtle body and hathayogic practice found in the *KJñN*, would make him the founding guru of this discipline, or at least of one of its major canons.[56] Abhinavagupta may also be singling Macchanda out for praise on these grounds;[57] it is also possible, however, that the image of the fish belly also had a sexual connotation in Kaula erotico-mystical practice.

Such is certainly the case in the religious belief and practice of the Bāuls, a Bengal-based syncretic sect whose ties to the Nāth Siddhas are numerous and well-documented. As June McDaniel has demonstrated, the Bāuls portray

> Īśvara or the man of the heart [as] a fish (*mīn-rūpa*). This fish [which] swims in the "high tide" of [a woman's] menstrual flow . . . is caught by the enjoyer (*rasika*), the Bāul who is full of love. This is the "tide time in the river," the overflowing of *rasa* [sexual fluids]. He catches the fish and causes it to move in an upward direction. The fish must be caught at the right time, or the waters dry and he is gone . . . The right time is once a month, a Mahayoga. It includes the new moon, the period regarded by the Bāuls as the time before the fish emerges; this is the time of lust (*kāma*). When the fish is present, it is the time of the menstrual flow designated as full moon. The third day [of a woman's menses] is the time to catch the fish; he is not present before that, and there is the danger of the black crocodile of desire.[58]

In this context, we may read *matsyodarī-yoga* as a temporal conjunction in the menstrual cycle of a *yoginī*. Matsyendra the fisherman catches his "fish" of the Kaula revelation at that precise moment and thereby becomes the revealer of the Yoginī Kaula.

b. Moon Island

With this, we exhaust the symbolism of the yogic fish belly; in so doing, however, we bump up against another riddle of tantric parlance. Here, we must consider that in the times of the fish-belly conjunction, the city of Benares, surrounded by the Gaṅgā, Varaṇā, Matsyodarī, and Asi rivers, became an *island*.[59] Here, we are reminded of Moon Island, off the shore of which Matsyendra, in the belly of a fish, overheard Śiva's original tantric teachings. This island has never ceased to tantalize scholars who have attempted, without success, to localize the toponym *Candra-dvīpa* somewhere on the India subcontinent[60] and to explain its implicit identification, in a number of tantric sources, with *Candra-giri* ("Moon Hill") or *Candra-parvata* ("Moon Mountain").

Here again, it may be argued, on the basis of data found in the tantric texts themselves, that Moon Mountain and Moon Island (for what is an island if not a mountain with its feet in the water?)[61] are, like the Fish Belly, locations that appear within the subtle body when a certain body of practice is carried to its conclusion. That this is an inner landscape of the subtle body is already borne out by the *KJñN*'s statement that, by using the net of yogic energy (*śakti-jālam*), Matsyendra the fisherman pulled his fish (containing the *kula* teachings) out of the seven oceans (i.e., the seven *cakra*s),[62] an impossible act in the "real world."

In this case, the mountain or island in question is located either in the cranial vault or the abdominal cavity, but in either case on the left side of the body, i.e., that half of the body through which the lunar *iḍā nāḍī* passes. The *KJñN* itself, which maintains in its chapter colophons[63] that its teachings were brought down (*avatārita*) at Moon Island, offers a certain body of evidence to this effect when it describes the oozing of nectar, via the *brahmarandhra* (the "cleft of bráhman," i.e., the fontanelle), as "gladdening the moon" (*candrāhlādakara*) and associates the lunar posture (*candrāsana*) with the hathayogic practice of *khecarī* [*mudrā*], also effected within the cranial vault.[64] In addition, both this source and a number of other hathayogic works of the Nāth Siddhas and the Western Transmission place great emphasis on the "western" or left side of the body as the locus of the most critical transformations occurring within the subtle body.[65]

The teachings of the *KM* were brought down, as well, at Moon Island; however, this text places equal or greater emphasis on Moon Mountain or Moon Hill, which, as indicated, likely refers to the same locus within the subtle body. This appears to be the meaning of a statement found in the first chapter of this work, which states that Moon Mountain is located to the west of Meru, i.e., the subtle spinal column, which culminates in the *brahmarandhra* at the summit of the cranial vault.[66]

This lunar location is found in other Western Transmission sources, which declare that the textual canon was "brought down"—by a figure variously called Śrīnātha, Śrīkaṇṭha, Ādinātha, or Siddhanātha—at a lunar location called Candragiri, Candradvīpa, Candrapurī, or Candrapīṭha.[67] Once again, however, this location appears to be, at least to a certain extent, an internal one. This is borne out by a passage from an A.D. 1395 manuscript of the *Kubjikānityāhnikatilaka*, which maintains that Śrīnātha—with the aid of three Siddhas named Sun, Moon, and Fire—founded that tantric *kula*, "at the beginning of the Kali Yuga," at a site called Candrapurī ("Moon City"), located in the western region of Koṅkana.[68] In spite of this purportedly geographical reference to Koṅkana, the most satisfactory interpretation of this account remains an allegorical one: Moon City is the site, in the left (western) side of the subtle body, in which the hathayogic praxis culminates, through the interaction of the three principle *nāḍī*s figured here as the Siddhas Sun, Moon, and Fire. This is further supported by a passage from the *Ciñcinīmatasārasamucchaya*, a Western Transmission text which identifies the founding Siddhas Mīnanātha with the moon, Meṣapada with the sun, and Kūrmanātha with fire.[69]

In the later works of Gorakhnāth and other synthesizers of the hatha-yogic gnosis, the identification of the cranial vault as the place of the microcosmic moon becomes a commonplace. It is moreover in a work attributed to Gorakhnāth, the *Amaraughaśāsana*, that the left side of the head, or the cavity of the left nostril, is explicitly identified with the circle of the moon.[70] We may imagine that the city of Benares—identified with the *ājñā cakra* of the cranial vault and theoretically situated atop three hilltops on the northern bank of the Ganges River, between the Varaṇā and Asi rivers—could have been identified with both a mountain and an island, after the fashion of Candragiri and Candradvīpa, by medieval cartographers of the subtle body. When, through the practice of diaphragmatic retention, the central *suṣumṇā* channel opened to serve as an upward conduit for the yogic life force, seed, and energy, a lunar site in the left side of the cranial vault called Candragiri, "Moon Hill," would have flooded to become Candradvīpa, "Moon Island," as in the case of Benares during the fish-belly conjunction.[71]

c. The Mare's Mouth

This is not the sole possible gloss of this phenomenon, however. In addition to the microcosmic Moon Island/Moon Mountain located in the left side of the cranial vault, there is another site at which a similar phenomenon appears to occur: this is the inner *liṅga* covered by the mouth of the sleeping *kuṇḍalinī:* located, according to certain sources, in the left side of the abdominal cavity, this is referred to as the *paścima-liṅga*, the "western *liṅga*."[72] In his fourteenth-century *Chos-hbyung* (History of Buddhism), the Tibetan historian Bu-ston, citing an Indian source entitled the *Nāthābhyudaya Tantra*, gives the following account: "A certain fisherman, having been swallowed by a fish, will die and be reborn as the yogin called Dārika. This one will cast wine into the river Ganges and in an hour an island called Bāḍava will appear."[73] The fisherman in the belly of a fish once again evokes Matsyendra; moreover, in a Tibetan list of the eighty-four Mahāsiddhas, Dārika is listed as the disciple of Luī-pā who is, as noted, a possible equivalent of Matsyendra.[74] Dārika may therefore be symbolically identified with Matsyendra himself or with his double, his "son" Mīnanāth (especially since the Tibetan source says the fisherman dies and is reborn as Dārika). The mention of an island suddenly appearing out of the Ganges would also be an apparent reference to *matsyodarī-yoga*, during which times Benares became an island. What, then, of the name *Bāḍava?*

The term *bāḍava*, "that which arises from a mare (*baḍavā*)," has a particular resonance in Hindu mythology or, more properly speaking, Hindu eschatology. Bāḍava is the name of the submarine fire—or, more precisely, of the fiery fluid composed of both fire and *soma*—which originated from Śiva's third eye when he incinerated Kāma, the Hindu Eros. When that fire, once released, threatened to engulf the entire universe, it was placed by Śiva inside the mouth of a "submarine mare" at the bottom of a southern sea, whence it continues to belch flame down to the present day. One day, when it will have burned away, evaporated, all the water in that ocean, it will incinerate the entire universe, reducing all to ashes.[75] Bāḍava is therefore the fire of the cosmic dissolution, *in potentia*, as well as a fire in the mouth of a female creature.

Which brings us back to the sleeping *kuṇḍalinī*, who sleeps (like the Goddess in the myths of Moon Island) in the left (western) side of the subtle body. (The *KJñN* itself, while it mentions a goddess named Kuṇḍalī, makes no explicit mention of the *kuṇḍalinī* in this role.[76] One may, however, see, in its imagery of the *bāḍava*—the fire of universal dissolution or retraction (*saṁhāra*) in the mouth of a submarine mare (*baḍavā*)—a prefiguration of this more common, but later, image of this female serpent power.) Let us recall here that the *kuṇḍalinī*, when she sleeps, is identified with the *kālāgni*, the fire of time that cooks all creatures to death, through the aging process. Let us also bear in mind that the fire of yoga (*yogāgni*) that destroys the fire of time, is identified as *kālāgnirudra*, the "Rudra of the Fire of Time," that is, a fire which is greater than, which consumes, the fire of time.[77] When she sleeps, the *kuṇḍalinī* is associated with the fire of time, a time whose passage is marked by the movements of sun and moon in the subtle body; when she awakens, sun and moon (here the *iḍā* and *piṅgalā nāḍis*) are immobilized, and the *kuṇḍalinī*, doubling as the *suṣumṇā nāḍī*, is said to "consume time."[78]

Therefore, while the *kuṇḍalinī*'s sleep is associated with the fire of time, the loss of the yogic fuel that is semen, and being-towards-death, her potential for reversing such a process likens her more to the mythic *bāḍava* fire at the bottom of the southern sea, a fire that, once it has consumed the waters of the ocean, will become the *kālāgnirudra*, the fire that consumes time. Once again, it is Matsyendra's *KJñN* that offers a primal and fundamental reading of this yogic process. Here, it is said that the universal retraction (*saṁhāra*) will occur when the fire of the *kālāgnirudra*, the Destroyer of the Fire of Time—a fire he identifies with the mouth of the submarine mare (*baḍavāmukha*)—flares upward. This cryptic utterance, made at the beginning of general discussion of "yogic retraction," precisely concerns the awakening of the fire of yoga in the base of the subtle body, an awakening that leads to total yogic resorption in the cranial vault, the microcosmic equivalent of the *pralaya*, the cosmic dissolution. The *bāḍava* is that fire, in potentia, that slumbers in every subtle body: when mastered and channeled upwards, it affords liberation; when allowed to burn normally, it is the fire of time that cooks all beings to death.[79]

It will also be recalled that *matsyodarī-yoga* is at once a description of the yogic practice of diaphragmatic retention (*kumbhaka*),[80] by which the *nāḍī*s peripheral to the medial *suṣumṇā*, the channel of the rising *kuṇḍalinī*, are emptied. This practice not only suddenly fills the *suṣumṇā* with breath; it also fills this channel with semen, and it is here that Dārika's island in the Ganges suddenly comes into view. Earlier, I cited a passage from the Kāśī Khaṇḍa of the *Skanda Purāṇa* that described the Matsyodarī as taking the "path of retraction" (*saṁhāra-mārga*),[81] i.e., as draining the Ganges into a channel that flowed in a direction opposite to its normal flow. Such is also the case with the subtle body: when the *kuṇḍalinī* rises, she also siphons upwards the semen that had previously remained inert and subject to loss in the yogin's abdomen. In this light, we must evoke another yogic commonplace: *kālāgni*, the fire of time, is identified with *adhoretas*, that is with "downward-tending semen," while *kālāgnirudra* is identified with *ūrddhvaretas*, "upward-tending semen."[82]

What happens when the *kuṇḍalinī* rises? A "column" of ambrosial semen is raised, via the *suṣumṇā nāḍī*, to flood the cranial vault. This is the meaning of the island called "Mare's Mouth" that suddenly appears in the Ganges when Dārika throws wine into its waters: when *matsyodarī-yoga* takes place and the normal downward current of bodily entropy is reversed, the upward channeling of seed causes the theretofore submerged *bāḍava* fire to flare up from the base of the subtle body. This reading is supported by a poem of the fifteenth-century mystic poet Kabīr, who instructs the yogin to "reverse the [flow of the] Ganges, and dry up the ocean."[83] When applied to the sacred geography of Benares, the "path of retraction" taken by the Ganges during a fish-belly conjunction transforms the city into an island. When applied to the sacred geography of the *KJñN* and *KM*, the landform of the subtle body that appears through this dynamic is known as Moon Island or Moon Mountain.

Lastly, there is the matter of the wine Dārika throws into the Ganges to trigger this process. Here, we should note that the tantric Buddhist tradition of which Dārika was an exemplar was a form of tantrism which emphasized the symbolic use of the five *makāras*, the "antisacraments" of wine, fish, flesh, parched grain, and sexual intercourse. It now suffices to return to the *MBhT* passage cited above to understand the meaning of Dārika's gesture. The sacramental wine that the tantric practitioner imbibes becomes an offering into the mouth of the *kuṇḍalinī* who, sharing his enjoyment (*bhoga*), awakens to rise and thereby transform him into a second Śiva.[84]

The *bāḍava*, the fire in the mouth of the submarine mare, has a number of other usages in tantric and alchemical geography. A natural gas vent at the important *śākta pīṭha* of Kāmākhyā is called *bāḍava kuṇḍa*, the "pool of the submarine[-mare] fire."[85] This evokes another such vent, also identified with a goddess; this is Jvālamukhī, "She of the Flaming Mouth," in Himachal Pradesh. In a generic sense, *jvālamukhī* can also have the sense of "(mouth of a) volcano," and it is here that we are brought back to the geology of alchemy, according to which mercury and sulfur naturally occur in areas of volcanic and geothermic activity. In fact, the origin myths of mercury and sulfur evoke, for certain modern Indian interpreters, volcanic eruptions. In the latter case, the sulfur that arises from the churning of the ocean of milk would be the mythologization of a submarine volcanic eruption.[86]

If this is in fact the case, then the origin of sulfur—the uterine blood of the Goddess associated with the lower half of the body in which the *kuṇḍalinī* sleeps—is to be identified with a flaring up of a female submarine fire, a *bāḍava*.

d. The "Plantain Forest" in the Midst of "Love's Body"

Gas vents and volcanos that are so many "mouths" of fire or flame in these mythic and geographical contexts evoke other types of mouths from tantric imagery. Apart from the oral orifice in the head, the most celebrated mouth in tantrism is the "lower mouth" (*adhovaktra*) i.e., the vulva (*yoni*) of the *yoginī*. And indeed, the ca. twelfth-century *ṢSS* (2.14), a foundational text of the Western Transmission, identifies the *mūlādhāra cakra* with the submarine fire (*vāḍavānala*), which its commentator locates in the upper part of the *yoni*.[87] Like the *kuṇḍalinī* herself, the vulva is an organ fraught with danger but also the promise of great power and pleasure for the practitioner who can master himself in its presence. Whence the most seminal of all of the *bānī*s of Gorakhnāth, who adds an alchemical nuance to this sexual image: "Penis in the vulva's mouth, mercury in the mouth of fire, he who can retain these [volatile substances of semen and mercury], him I call my guru."[88]

There is a certain irony to this verse, if we recall that in myth, Gorakh's guru Matsyendra was a teacher who was quite incapable of retaining his seed in proximity to beautiful women, to *yoginī*s. This weakness of Matsyendranātha for the fair sex is the subject of a body of legend set in the land of Kāmarūpa, which is itself identified, precisely, with the center of the *adhovaktra*, the lower mouth or vulva of the *yoginī*, but also with the center of a mystic triangle located at the base of the subtle body, in the same region as the *kuṇḍalinī*.[89] Once again, the locus of these myths is not only a geographical site—the region identified with Assam, in which the temple of the goddess Kāmākhyā is found—but also a locus within the subtle body. Here, the geographic symbolism plays itself out on a double register: Kāmarūpa is both that region of eastern India from which the Śaktism identified with the Yoginī Kaula is said to have originated[90] and a portion of the body, subtle or concrete, identified with feminine sexuality. The mythic perils of Matsyendranāth are very likely a reflection of a cleavage within the tantric tradition. While a number of sects, including the Matsyendra's Yoginī Kaula, incorporated sexual intercourse into their practice,[91] others, including the Nāth Siddhas whose main doctrinal exponent was Gorakh, were overtly misogynous, treating sexuality (epitomized by the vulva) as a trap into which the yogin could fall and thereby lose all the benefits of his prior efforts (in the form of his precious semen).[92] As Lillian Silburn explains, this cleavage may be reflected in two understandings of the term *fish belly*, the one sexual and the other hathayogic:

> the yogin resides at the source of the movements of emanation and resorption of the universe, a state praised as *matsyodarīmata* because it is comparable to the stomach of the fish, which continuously contracts and expands automatically. This realm of bliss has some connection with sexual experience for, like the *suṣumṇā*, the organs are subjected to a similar contraction and expansion conductive to an intimate union which, in a yogin, involves a perfect coincidence of Śiva and the energy, of subject and object, of seed and womb. It is from this coincidence that supreme Beatitude and Consciousness originate.[93]

The mythic cycle of the perils of Matsyendra, most fully developed in two ca. seventeenth-century Bengali-language dramas, the *Mīn Cetan* (The Awakening of Mīna) and *Gorakṣa* (or *Gorakha) Vijaya* (Gorakh's Victory),[94] are a garden of yogic verse on human weakness and yogic mastery in the face of female sexuality. These works offer two mythic explanations for Matsyendra's fall. The first is connected to later versions of the myth of the revelations made by Śiva on Moon Island: the Goddess, angry that Matsyendra has overheard a revelation reserved for her, curses him that he too will one day "fall asleep" and forget all he has overheard.[95] A second account casts the Goddess as the "stepmother" of the four original Nāths, whom she tests by tempting them with her sexual charms. When Matsyendra becomes sexually aroused, she curses him to be debauched in the Kingdom of Women.[96] The *YSĀ*[97] explains Matsyendra's fall as a direct upshot of his yogic powers. Wishing to experience the sensual life of a king, Matsyendra performs the act of *parakāyapraveśa*, entering into the body of another person.[98] In this case, however, Matsyendra, debauched by Queen Kamalā, into whose husband's body (King Trivikrama) he has entered, forgets his true yogic self.[99] At this point, the western *YSĀ* account dovetails into the Bengali account of Gorakh's rescue of his guru (called Mīna in the Bengali song cycle) from the Kingdom of Women or, more properly, the Kadalīrājya, the "Kingdom of the Plantain Forest,"[100] which is generally located in Kāmarūpa (Assam) or Siṁhala (Sri Lanka).[101]

The story opens when Gorakh learns, from Kaṇeri (or Kānha), another Nāth Siddha, that his guru is three days away from his death in the Kingdom of Women, where he has been the prisoner of sixteen hundred women.[102] The kingdom of Kadalī, as Gorakh quickly learns, is prohibited to all males, save for the imprisoned "king" Matsyendra, and so it is necessary for Gorakh to find a subterfuge. This he does by taking on the appearance of a woman and engaging himself in a female musical troupe. It is in this disguise that Gorakh comes to the court of Queen Kamalā and her sixteen hundred female subjects, where he finds his guru fallen into a swoon, at death's door.[103]

The music begins, and when Gorakh plays the first beat on his two-headed drum, the drum sings out "Awaken, Matsyendra, Gorakh has come!" Upon hearing this drumbeat (*nāda*),[104] Matsyendra awakens from his stupor. But Gorakh and Matsyendra are not yet out of the woods. Gorakh must now return his guru's strength, his yogic powers to him.[105] This he does by urging him to perfect his body anew: *kāyā sādha, kāyā sādha guru mochandar.*[106]

Ultimately, however, Gorakh must shock Matsyendra back into yogic consciousness. Matsyendra's fall into mundane consciousness is best symbolized by a son, named Binduknāth ("he who is formed of the drop [of yogically transformed semen]"), whom he has fathered on Kamalā while her prisoner in Kadalī. Gorakh kills and skins the boy, scrubs his skin like a washerman to remove all its bodily impurities, and hangs this skin on the roof to dry, like the hide of some skinned beast—all of these metaphors for yogic purification. Matsyendra and Kamalā are horrified at this act, and when they bewail the murder of their son, Gorakh revives 108 Binduknāths! Seeing at last the illusion of the world to which he has become attached through his sexuality, Matsyendra now truly "awakens," and Gorakh leads him out of the Kingdom of Kadalī (not before, however, the women of the kingdom attempt to take Gorakh's life—Gorakh avenges himself by transforming them into bats!).[107]

Let us dwell for a moment on the name of the kingdom into which Matsyendra has fallen into a sexual lethargy as the plaything of some sixteen hundred women: Kadalī Rājya is the Kingdom of the Plantain Forest. Why plantains? Our first clue comes from classical Indian poetics, in which the thighs of a beautiful woman are compared to the smooth, firm trunks of the plantain tree. In this perspective, Matsyendra has been languishing in a forest of beautiful thighs, a fair statement arrived at through simple arithmetic. Moreover, the plantain is that one of nine sacred trees representing the Goddess most closely associated with vegetative power. So it is that plantain fruit, a small banana with seeds in its interior, is used in fertility rites in Bengal, in which men swinging on hooks drop plantain fruits on women below. The imagery here needs no explanation.[108] Elsewhere, "plantain house" (*kadalīgṛha*) is a term employed in Sanskrit drama to designate a pleasure garden in which the king assigned trysts with women to whom he was not yet wedded.[109]

This metaphor is greatly expanded in the south Indian Vīraśaiva poetry of Allama Prabhu or Prabhudeva, who time and again compares the human body, subject to passion and sorrow in a world of death and rebirth, to a plantain forest:[110]

> I see no one who can conquer the body's vast plantain grove: the seven seas of the world encircle it. In life's vast wood the poisonous rain of the five senses pours. Anger's huge tiger roars and roars . . . The child of sin called greed is eating and eating . . . The well of passions cannot be used.[111]

The Plantain Grove, Kadalī Vana, to which Prabhudeva is referring, is first and foremost a geographical location: this is a grove at Srisailam, a cultic center of Vīraśaivism, but also an important center for such sects as the Kāpālikas, Nāth Siddhas, and Rasa Siddhas.[112] Quite unlike the negative portrayal Prabhudeva gives of his metaphorical Plantain Grove, the Kadalī Vana at Srisailam was a source of healing herbs and magically rejuvenating waters. This tradition, however, of such a grove enclosing a pool of healing and life-giving waters is not original to this site or this period: in the third book of the *Mahābhārata*, Bhīma finds such a pool in the midst of a plantain forest located on the flanks of the Himalayas![113]

There are, in fact, a number of medieval literary references which support this reading of the Kadalī Vana toponym. One of these is Malik Muhammad Jayasī's sixteenth-century *Padmāvat*, a beautiful yogic allegory of the wooing of Padmavatī, princess of Siṁhala, by a prince–turned–Nāth Siddha named Ratansen. This source makes more than one reference to a Kadalī Van which, accessible to Siddhas alone, contains a "fountain of life." In this source, variant readings of Kajarī and Kajalī are also given, variants which may be read in three ways. The term is either: (1) *kadalī van*, "plantain forest," a place identified with the sensual life (as in the legends of Matsyendranāth), but also with a grove of yogic realization and immortality (in the *Padmāvat*); (2) *kajalī van*, "forest of black mercuric sulfide," of the mineral hierophany of the sexual essences of Śiva and the Goddess, which does in fact constitute an elixir of immortality; or (3) *kajarī van*, identified with Zulmāt, the name of the land of death and darkness (*kaj-[j]alī* also means "lampblack") to which Iskandar (Alexander the Great) traveled, according to Muslim legend.[114]

I have already discussed the first reading at length, The third reading is treated in the *Padmāvat* with specific reference to Alexander, as well as to the prince–turned–Nāth Siddha named Gopīcand, who, realizing the transience of this world, left his kingdom and went to Kajarī Van, where he realized yogic perfection. Like Prabhudeva, Kabīr identifies the Kajarī Van with the human body that is subjected to the trammels of carnal passions: "This body is a *kajarī ban* and the mind is an elephant gone mad, the jewel of wisdom is the goad but few are the Saints who can apply it!"[115] Another source, the oral epic entitled the *Alhā Khaṇḍ*, has its eponymous hero schooled by Gorakhnāth in the transitory nature of mundane existence and the virtues of the renunciant life. He follows Gorakh into Kajarī Forest, "a mysterious land from which it is said that someday he will return."[116]

The second reading, which combines the first and third (the alchemical *kaj[j]alī* is both black in color and an elixir of immortality), would sound far-fetched, were it not for the fact that the same term is found, in a similar context, in another source. This is the Punjabi legend of the Nāth Siddha named Pūraṇ Bhagat. This yogin has been dismembered (whence his alternate name of Cauraṅginātha, "Four-[dismembered]-limbs Nāth"), thrown down a well, and left for dead by his evil stepmother, whose sexual advances he had refused. He prays to Gorakhnāth, who restores him to wholeness and initiates him into the Nāth order, following which Pūraṇ Bhagat remains in his well for twelve years, at the end of which he attains immortality. Pūraṇ Bhagat's well—also a fountain of life of sorts—is located in Kajalī Van, near Sialkot (Jhelum district), in the Punjab state of Pakistan.[117] The eighth -to twelfth-century *Yoga Vasiṣṭha* generates a polar opposition between the well and the forest that surrounds it: here, the human mind (which is trapped in an existence of its own making) is allegorized as a man who, having inflicted all manner of wounds upon his own body, plunges into a well (the torments of hell); he then leaves the well to enter into the Plantain Forest (the pleasures of heaven).[118]

There are a number of levels upon which one may interpret these juxtapositions, either of a well or fountain of life at the heart of a Plantain Forest identified with bodily proclivities, a Forest of Mercuric Sulfide, identified with bodily immortality, a land of death and darkness, identified with a failure to attain superhuman goals—or a combination of all three. *Kajalī*, which can be black poison for the uninitiated, is an elixir of immortal life for the consummate alchemist. Matsyendra's Kadalī kingdom was undoubtedly a forest of women's thighs, in the midst of which he nearly lost his life—albeit through a form of tantric practice—but where he in the end realized yogic immortality through Gorakh's intervention. Pūraṇ Bhagat too should have died in his empty well in the midst of the Kajalī Forest, but instead realized bodily immortality through his initiation by Gorakh. In the final analysis, the common theme to these evocations of an immortality that one may grasp even in the midst of bodily sufferings is once again a tantric one. A woman's thighs can lead to the death of a yogin, but they can also constitute a "boat to immortality." Just as the *kuṇḍalinī* can both drain a yogin of his semen (in a process called called "eating poison" in one source) and transmute that essence into the draft of immortality, so too the space between a woman's thighs—the Kāmarūpa in the midst of her *yoni*—can arbor a fountain of life for the tantric practitioner who knows his way around.[119]

The tantric hero (*vīra*) of the Kaula traditions was precisely that exceptional individual who was capable of experiencing, to its very limit, the life of the body in ways that would utterly destroy the beastlike noninitiate (*paśu*) for whom every venture into the prohibited world of feminine sexuality was a deadly enterprise. Whereas the latter, bound like a sacrificial victim (*paśu*) to religious and social convention, could only come to know pain and death through the mystico-erotic practices of the tantric sects, the former could use the same to transcend the human condition and experience the bliss of Śivahood. We illustrate the double register, upon which the landscapes of the subtle body have been interpreted, with a chart:

being-towards-death	overcoming death
normal respiration	swallowing into the fish-belly
downward-flowing Ganges	Fish-Belly Conjunction
sleeping *kuṇḍalinī*	rising *kuṇḍalinī*
kālāgni	*kālāgnirudra/yogāgni*
underwater, simmering *bāḍava*	exposed, upward flaring *bāḍava*
saṃsāra	*saṁhāra*
adhoretas	*ūrddhvaretas*
Kāmarūpa/*adhovaktra*	Candradvīpa/*yoginīvaktra*[120]
deadly Plantain Forest	rejuvenating Plantain Forest

3. Lunar, Empty, and Hg Wells in Hindu Tantrism

In the last chapter, we spoke of the creative opposition between a bird in the vault of the "cranial" heavens and a serpent in the hollow of an "abdominal" cave. Apart from their symbolization as bird and snake, these two poles of the Samkhyan hierarchy of elements, the alchemical hierarchy of metals, and the yogic hierarchy of the *cakras* may also be represented as a set of two wells. The image is a powerful one, in any tradition, for what is a well if not a channel between our sunlit world and the dark subterranean regions? Chthonic dragons guarding enchanted wells, wishing wells—common fare in western folklore, they attest to the universality of this theme. In the yogic and alchemical traditions, the first of these two wells is conventional, in the sense that it is upturned and set into the "base" of these parallel structures. The second well, corresponding to the upper end of these parallel hierarchies, is downturned and placed above the second. When the two are brought together into a double-well image, their combination evokes the internal unity of these bipolar systems. The head and torso of the human body, the communicating chambers of a bicameral alchemical apparatus, the vault of heaven reflected in the waters at the bottom of a well:[121] all of these are so many images of the unity in difference (*bhedābheda*) that is the hallmark of nondualist tantric thought. It is within such a symbol system that the locus of ether (*kha*, *ākāśa*, *vyoman*, *śūnya*) in the human body is identified with the cranial vault, which is characterized, in a number of sources, as a downturned well.

The terms *kha* and *ākāśa* at once signify, from the Upaniṣads onwards, "heaven," "cave," "hole," and "[empty] space." According to the *Mahābhārata*, *ākāśa* has the following properties: it is the elemental substrate of sound (*śabda*), it is all-permeating (*vyāpitva*), and it has the nature of a hollow or cavity (*chidratva*).[122] In Ayurvedic physiology as well, the element ether is present in the body in the form of bodily cavities or orifices. In its quality as void or empty space, ether is vital to tantric worship: it is in a clearing within one's own being that one meditatively constructs the divine object of ritual devotion.[123] As I demonstrate, the realization of an analogous void is necessary to the hathayogin, in his quest for the absolute.

Since the time of the Upaniṣads, the seat of the soul has been located in the heart.[124] There, the soul is suspended in the midst of a void that extends outwards for ten finger breadths from the core of the subtle body. The void or ether (*kha*, *ākāśa*) of the heart remains a key notion in Hinduism, down into the Tantras.[125] However, the concept of another "inner void" also emerges in the Upaniṣads to continue down into the tantric period. This is the void of the medial channel of the subtle breath, which bisects the subtle body vertically.[126] This channel, running upward from the *mūlādhāra cakra* through the heart (which bisects the body horizontally), ends in the "cleft of brahman" (*brahmarandhra*), the fontanelle, in the top of the cranial vault. Whence the statement in the *Kāṭhaka Upaniṣad* (6.16): "There are a hundred and one channels of the heart. One of these passes up to the crown of the head. Going up by it, one goes to immortality."

It is this channel, but more especially the upper endpoint of its trajectory, that the Nāth Siddhas and a number of other tantric schools identify with the ether or void, which they also call *kha* or *śūnya*. For the Nāth Siddhas, *śūnya* is at once the highest metaphysical principle (*param tattva*), the cranial vault or fontanelle, and the abode of Śiva.[127] Here, the importance of the ether lies not in what it is but rather in that which it contains in its empty space—and here, once again, yogic and alchemical elixirs become identified with one another, this time through their association with the "wells" in which both are found.

In no other medieval Indian tradition do we find greater importance attached to this image, of the body as a set of wells, than in that of the Nāth Siddhas. Gorakhnāth, who uses the terms *gagan [maṇḍal]*, *śūnya*, and *kha*[128] to speak of the cranial vault, also states, in perhaps his most renowned *bānī:* "In the circle of ether is an inverted well that is the place of nectar. He who has a guru drinks his fill; he who has no guru goes thirsty."[129] Here, Gorakhnāth's well of nectar in the ether is at once the seventh and uppermost *cakra*, the thousand-petaled *sahasrāra* located in the cranial vault, and the moon, repository of immortal *soma*, shining in the heavens. The moon, identified with the god Candra/Soma, has been viewed as a primal source of ambrosia since the time of the *Ṛg Veda.*[130] In Gorakhnāth's *bānī*, the downturned well that quenches mortal man's thirst for the nectar of immortality is identified with the *soma* that is the stuff of the full moon.

Another of Gorakhnāth's poems, contained in the *Gyān Calīsa* (Forty Gnostic Stanzas),[131] combines the image of the well with the attainment of yogic and alchemical *siddhi*s. Here, the yogin who fills the *ākāśa* (the ether of the cranial vault) with water from a subterranean well gains bodily immortality and the power of transmutation. The same symbolism is found in a number of poems of Kabīr, the language and imagery of whose mystic poetry was greatly influenced by the verses of Gorakhnāth. In one of these, Kabīr says: "The well of heaven has its opening below; its bucket is in the underworld (*pātāle*); the *haṃsa* drinks of its water, but few know of its source."[132] In another, he speaks of a land with "an inverted well, with an opening, as narrow as a thread, through which the married soul draws water . . . From the well in the lotus above, the devotee drinks the nectar."[133]

These images are similar to those found in a longer poem by Gorakhnāth, who once again uses the dynamics of drawing water from a well to describe the workings of the subtle body.[134] Here, he compares the human body to a city filled with all manner of hungry and thirsty animals, which are so many allegorical representations of the human condition. So the cows and buffalo of the city, tethered to the stake of illusion, represent the absence of discrimination (*aviveka*), while its dogs are the mind that steals away and conceals true knowledge. In this city, however, is a well whose water slakes these animals' thirst (for liberation). From this well, the women of the city draw water which they carry in pitchers on their heads—and these pitchers thus constitute portable wells. In this way, there are two metaphorical wells in the city, the well set into the earth and that which takes the form of water pots on the women's heads.

On the level of the bodily microcosm, the interpretation is the following: the well set into the earth here is the *mūlādhāra*, the lowest of the *cakra*s from which the yogin's semen, the raw material of his bodily transformation, is raised. As it rises along the length of the medial *suṣumṇā nāḍī*, this semen is transformed into nectar. This process is consummated in the uppermost *sahasrāra cakra*—the thousand-petaled lotus located in the cranial vault, the ethereal sphere of the void—*śūnya* or *gagan maṇḍal*—which is figured in Gorakh's poem by the water pot atop the female water bearers' heads. Just as these female water carriers (who may be further identified with the *kuṇḍalinī*) slake the thirst of the animals in Gorakh's metaphorical city, so the yogin's refined semen, now transformed into nectar, fills the "void city" (*śūnya purī*) of the cranial vault. When allowed to flow back downwards, it floods the yogin's body with its fluid of immortality.[135]

This poem schematically portrays the yogin's body as two vessels, a lower well and an upper water pot, of which the lower is a source of energy and raw materials and the higher the container of the subtle immortalizing essence of those raw materials. In a Nāth Siddha legend as well, a similar identification is made between the body and two superposed water pots carried on a woman's head. In the tale of Guru Gūgā, or Gūgā Pīr, a low-caste woman speaks of her body in terms of these, protesting to Gūgā that she cannot give him water to drink from her earthen pot (because the vessel of her body is impure). Gūgā lets fly an arrow, smashing the two pots simultaneously, to which the woman reacts with the words "Look at the state of my body; thou hast broken my two pitchers."[136] Once again, we find an echo of this imagery in Kabīr (even if he is mocking the Siddhas in the same verse): "Between the sky and the netherworld, in the space between the two gourds [is the Path]: the six *darśana*s tripped and tumbled down along with the eighty-four Siddhas!"[137]

In the raising of vital breath, seed, and energy, it is at the level of the navel that a preponderance of raw semen and thermal yogic energy yield to a preponderance of cool, refined nectar; therefore, it is here that the mouths of the upper and lower "wells" of the yogic body are joined. So it is that we find a metaphorical symmetry between these two poles or "wells" of yogic imagery. Above, male semen, moon, *soma*, nectar, Śiva, fluidity, and coolness are identified with an upper well; and below, female uterine blood, sun, fire, energy, the Goddess, dessication, and heat are localized in a lower well.

This image of the body as a well into which the yogin enters in order to succeed in his *sādhana*s carries over into Nāth Siddha myth and legend as well. The fullest account to bring such imagery into play is the Punjabi legend of Pūraṇ Bhagat, already mentioned above, who is dismembered and thrown into an empty, broken-down well (*jīrṇāndhakūpa*). Gorakhnāth comes to rescue and restore him, after which he returns to the well to perform yogic austerities for twelve years: when he emerges, he has been transformed into a Siddha.[138] Down to the present day, Punjabi women come, on the new moon, to partake of the cool healing waters of Pūraṇ Bhagat's well (which is no longer empty), which are said to cure barrenness.[139]

In a number of versions of the Gopīcand legend cycle, this Nāth Siddha seals his guru Jālandharanāth (or Hāḍi-pā) into a well; upon his release from the well, again after twelve years, Jālandharanāth reduces metal effigies of Gopīcand to ashes.[140] A nineteenth-century hagiography has Mastnāth, another Nāth Siddha, creating a well to save the besieged city of his princely protégé Mān Singh.[141] Gorakhnāth dries up wells in anger, but also fills wells that are empty.[142] Elsewhere, he throws gold bricks or coins into a well near Kāmākhyā, thereby turning its waters to gold. When his teacher, Matsyendranāth, insists that such will upset the order of the world, Gorakhnāth turns the well water into crystal; and this is the origin of crystal in the world.[143]

Nāth Siddha accounts of yogins who create and enter into wells in order to meditate seem to parallel Taoist myths of "old men of the gourd" who suspend a gourd from the roofbeam of their huts and enter into the universe of that gourd in order to attain the Absolute, the Tao. The Taoist alchemical sources dating from the first half of the first millennium A.D. are particularly rich in legends on this subject, such as the following:

> Che Ts'ouen, who came from Lu, was a student of the Great Alchemical Path. After meeting Chang Chen, he became the administrator of Yun-t'ai (i.e. the mountain called Chiang-su). It was his habit to suspend a *hu[-lu]* vessel of about ten liter's volume [from the roof of his house]. This *hu[-lu]* vase transformed itself into Heaven and Earth; it contained sun and moon. Che Ts'ouen passed his nights there, and called himself "Heaven in a [Double-]Gourd" (*hu-t'ien*). The people called him the "Old Man of the Gourd." Following this he realized the Tao [and became an immortal].[144]

As in the Taoist case, entering into a well is, for the Nāth Siddhas, tantamount to entering into yogic practice, in which consciousness, breath, and semen are simultaneously raised into the cranial vault, the abode of Śiva. It also evokes a *regressus ad uterum* from which the yogin, like the Vedic sacrificer in his initiation hut and the Ayurvedic patient in his womb hut, emerges, reborn, as well as the ultimate alchemical operation described in the *RA*, in which the alchemist's own body becomes the *corpus alchymicum* when he plunges into a cauldron of boiling oil.[145] We will return to this image, of a Siddha entering a well that is a mesocosmic double of his own body, in chapter ten.

Wells are generally considered to possess healing properties, the well of Vaidyanāth in Benares—as well as Pūraṇ's Well and wells of Gorakh in Kacch (Gujarat) and other Nāth Siddha holy sites throughout India[146]—being prime examples.[147] Many tantras contain instructions for the dedication of wells to the Goddess; and while the *śākta pīṭha*s are not wells themselves, they are generally located in the proximity of a well or spring.[148] The *HYP* (1.13) instructs yogins to live alone in a small monastery in whose courtyard a well should be located. The alchemist's laboratory should also be equipped with a well in its northeast corner, which is that part of the laboratory in which are also housed his all-important transmuting elements.[149]

Yet another case of such structural homologies between body, alchemical apparatus, and universe is to be found in the tantric geography of the Indian subcontinent. In the last chapter, we briefly passed in review a number of alchemical hierophanies found at such *śākta pīṭha*s as Hiṅglāj in Baluchistan and Kāmākhyā in Assam.[150] In addition to these, such important Śaiva sites as Girnar in Gujarat[151] and Srisailam in Andhra Pradesh[152] are also possessed of alchemical mythologies. The most systematic and striking example of the geographical and geological macrocosm reproducing the alchemical and yogic macrocosm is that found, however, at Kedārnāth, an important and ancient Śiva temple built over a *jyotirliṅga* located in the Chamoli district of northwestern Uttar Pradesh.

The final stage of this pilgrimage, the fifteen kilometers that separate the village of Gaurī Kuṇḍ and the temple of Kedārnāth itself, has been marked, at least as far back as the twelfth century and down to the present day, by a series of natural springs or pools (*kuṇḍs*). Down in the village of Gaurī Kuṇḍ (this being the name of a natural hot-water spring in which pilgrims bathe), a reddish, sulfurous pool close by the side of the Gaurī Temple is known as Ṛtu Kuṇḍ ("the menses pool," where the Goddess takes her menstrual bath), while at the upper end of this final stage and some thousand meters higher in elevation, behind the temple of Śiva Kedārnāth and at the foot of the peak of the same name, is a clear pool called Ret Kuṇḍ ("the semen pool"), which is said, in both Puranic sources and modern pilgrim's guides, to contain the mercury that arose from Śiva's seed, dropped from the mouth of Agni when he transported it to the shore of the Ganges. Slightly higher, just behind the temple is the Amṛt Kuṇḍ, "pool of nectar"; and still higher, some three kilometers to the north of Kedārnāth, is the Brahmaguphā, the "cave of bráhman."

Once again, but this time on a quite massive scale, the alchemical body is reproduced, with Śiva, semen, and mercury located at the upper end of a geographic hierophany and the Goddess, uterine blood, and sulfur at the lower end of the same self-enclosed system. The relative locations of these two pools on the Kedārnāth pilgrimage route also clue us into the fact that the imagery here is hathayogic as well: the pool of blood below and to the south is to be identified with the yogin's lower *cakra*s, the place of the sun and uterine blood; the pool of semen above and to the north is the place of the moon and of semen that has been transmuted into the nectar that rejuvenates the yogin's body and so affords him *jīvanmukti.* Still higher, the pool of nectar and cave of Brahman are further indications that the upper reaches of the Kedārnāth site correspond to the ambrosial climes of the cranial vault and the fontanelle, the cleft of brahman.[153]

It will be recalled that, in the schema of the *śākta pīṭha*s, it is the shrine of Hiṅglāj Devī, located on a mountaintop in southeastern Baluchistan, that is identified as the Goddess's *brahmarandhra.* Like Kedārnāth, the route to Hiṅglāj, too, is spangled with images of the yogic body. The most important of these is the Moon Well, *candrakūpa*, which, at the upper end of the pilgrim's long journey, is a place of great geothermic activity, of fire and water that well up out of the depths of the earth. Both sun and moon are also present here, in the form of massive carvings hewn into the living rock: this may indeed be the earliest such image on the Indian subcontinent, already appearing as it does in the writings of the fourth-century Greek geographer Ctesias.[154]

Yet another yogic schematization of a natural landscape may be found in the description of a Nāth Siddha site called Aṭaka, located in the eastern Iranian region of Khorasan. Here, the intrepid pilgrim passes by a series of six pools until he comes to a cave upon whose door is figured a "fearsome *cakra*." Over the door hangs a sword. Whoever touches this *cakra* "will explode into a thousand pieces," but he who succeeds in passing through this door gains access to the all-transmuting philosopher's stone (*sparśamaṇi*) locked inside and to the Ganges River, which flows through the place. Here, the seven pools of Aṭaka, crowned by a door, a sword, a river, and a philosopher's stone, appear to be so many representations of the yogic body and the raising of the *kuṇḍalinī* up to the seventh *cakra* which, when pierced, yields the nectar of immortality.[155]

Another parallel may be found in the Indo-Tibetan Buddhist tradition, mentioned in the previous chapter, of the cave known as Ca-ri in south-eastern Tibet. This cave, entered through a narrow cleft identified with the Goddess's *yoni*, opens into a series of caves and lakes (inhabited by gods, goddesses, and *ḍākinī*s), which are explicitly identified with the *nāḍī*s and *cakra*s of the Buddhist subtle body. The pilgrim who follows the subterranean passages of this "womb-cave" to their very end is in fact effecting the ascent of the goddess Vajravarāhī's medial channel, from her *yoni* up to her *brahmarandhra*. The pilgrim, borne upward as it were by streams of divine blood, semen, and *sindūra* (mercuric oxide), concretely effects the union of Prajñā and Upāya (the Buddhist homologues of Śiva and Śakti) and supreme realization.[156]

In addition to the important role they play in alchemical geography and the poetry of yogic experience, wells also are vital, as we saw in the last chapter, to myths of the origin of mercury.[157] Also in the last chapter, we reproduced an account, from the *RRS* and other sources, of the extraction of mercury from one such well, in Darada-deśa, by knowers of tantra (*tantrajñās*) and semidivine Wizards (*vidyādharas*). This is the technique by which a maiden on horseback entices mercury to rise up out of its well and pursue her over hill and dale. Once it has been caught in troughs dug to this end, these sources tell us that this mercury is purified in a sublimation apparatus (*pātana yantra*).[158]

The medieval alchemists in fact knew of three types of sublimating apparatus (*yantra*s)[159] for the extraction (*ākṛṣṭi*) of mercury from cinnabar, i.e., the naturally occuring mercuric sulfide (*darada*) in which it is most commonly found: these are the apparatus of upward sublimation (*ūrddhva-pātana*), downward sublimation (*adhopātana*), and transverse sublimation (*tiryakpātana*). In all three apparatus, mercury is made to sublimate and thereby leave behind its residual impurities in the ores in which it naturally occurs (or with which it is amalgamated), and thereafter to recondense through the interposition of cold water.[160]

The upward-sublimation apparatus is composed of two superimposed vessels, whose mouths are sealed together with several layers of mud-smeared cloth stretched across their interface. A slow fire beneath the lower vessel heats a mixture of herbs and powdered mercury ore, mercuric sulfide, most often in the form of cinnabar. The mercury that evaporates upwards condenses on the inner surface of the downturned base of the upper chamber, which is cooled from above by a cloth soaked in cold water (or by a superimposed cold-water recipient). The mercury that has condensed on this downturned inner surface has a smoky luster to it: when rubbed with a cloth, it immediately takes on the properties of fluidity, luster, etc. one associates with pure quicksilver. In the bottom of the lower vessel there remains the dross of this reaction: free sulfur together with other mineral and plant matter, oxidized and devoid of its original mercury content.[161]

Because of the function it serves, this apparatus is known as the *ūrddhvapātana*. This is not, however, the sole name by which it is known: a number of medieval alchemical sources also call it the *ḍamaru yantra* (Śiva's two-headed drum apparatus),[162] the *śāmbhavī mudrā* (the hermetic seal of Śambhu, Śiva),[163] and the *vidyādhara yantra*, the "wizard apparatus."[164] This first term clearly refers to the shape of this apparatus, the second to a technique of *haṭha yoga*, and the third to both such a technique and to the mythic Wizards who were the innovators of a body of techniques that, precisely, fused alchemical and yogic practice into a single Śaiva system.

The structure and dynamics of this *yantra* appear to replicate the dynamics of yogic reversal—known as *ūrddhvaretas* from the time of the *Māhābharata*—as such is described by Gorakhnāth in his poems about wells and water jars. In this case, the upper chamber of the apparatus is the downturned celestial well in the yogin's head, and the lower chamber the matrix of matter and energy—in the "pot" formed by the diaphragm through the hathayogic technique called *kumbhaka*—from which the gross elements are caused to rise through heating. The fire beneath and cool water atop the two chambers complete the parallel. These are the equivalent of the visceral sun and cranial moon, through the balancing of which the yogin comes to enjoy the nectar (mercury, the refined semen of Śiva) that "condenses" to ooze downward from the top of the cranial vault, the lunar circle.

These parallels are made explicit in a number of medieval texts. In the fifteenth-century alchemical *Rasendracintāmaṇi* of Ḍhuṇḍhukanātha, this bicameral alchemical apparatus is termed *śāmbhavi mudrā*. Now, this same term is used, in the *Amanaskayoga* of Gorakṣanātha, to introduce a yogic technique that that text seems to identify with the *vidyādhara yantra:* "Here is the description of the *śāmbhavi mudrā:* The fist [?] above and the gaze (*dṛṣṭi*) below, the cleft (*bheda*) above and the channels (*sirāḥ*) below, one becomes liberated in the body by using the [*vidyā*]*dhāra-yantra*."[165]

Here, the yogin whose "gaze" and "channels" are below is clearly standing on his head: the sole description of a hathayogic technique in which the term *sirāḥ* is employed in the plural is that of the "chin lock," or *jālandhara bandha*, so called in honor of the great Nāth Siddha, but also in reference to the "net[work]" or "ganglia" (*jālam*) of channels which meet in the region of the throat. This practice effects a lock (*bandha*) on these channels and thus seals off the head as the recipient (*dhara*) of the nectar held in the cranial vault and not allowed to fall downward into the fire of the sun in the yogin's lower abdomen: *jālam-dhara bandha*. This upside-down version of that technique is the structural parallel to the *vidyā-dhara yantra:* the two chambers of the alchemical apparatus are the head and torso of the yogin, the mud-smeared layers of cloth stretched across their mouths are the network of channels, and the nectar that is held in the head is the mercury that condenses on the incurved inner surface of the downturned upper chamber.[166] A number of other interpretations of this verse are possible, including a sexual one: the *Yoni Tantra* employs the term *dhāraka* to signify both "vulva" and "vessel."[167]

Most alchemical sources enjoin the practitioner to follow his use of the *ūrddhvapātana yantra* with that of the *adhopātana yantra*, the "apparatus of downward sublimation": after having sublimated mercury three times in the former, one is to do so seven times in the latter.[168] The *adhopātana yantra* is identical to the *ūrddhvapātana* with the difference that in this case, the "cool" chamber is placed rightside-up in a hollow dug into the ground. Its mouth is bonded to that of the "hot" chamber, here placed facedown, with the cooking fire burning atop its upturned base. In this case, one smears the inner surface of this downturned "hot" chamber with an amalgam of mercury and copper. When this is heated, the mercury sublimates and falls down into the "cool" chamber, which is this time filled with water. There, it recondenses into its natural, but purified and stabilized, form.[169]

The *adhopātana yantra* is in fact a closer homologue to the upside-down yogic posture Gorakhnāth describes in his *Amanaskayoga* than is the *vidyādhara* (or *ūrddhvapātana*) itself. In both the alchemical *adhopātana yantra* and the *dhāra yantra* described by Gorakhnāth, the "seminal" fluid, transformed by a heat source located above, drips downward to remain (held there by gravity) in the reversed upper chamber of the apparatus or, in the yogic case, of the cranial vault. This posture also evokes the *viparītakaraṇa*, or "reverse practice" of yoga, which Gorakhnāth praises in his *Gorakṣa Śataka* (133–35) as a foolproof method for retaining in one's head the precious nectar one has so carefully distilled from "raw" semen. Here, the description of the posture itself is clearly the inspiration for that of the *dhārayantra*, in everything but name: "The navel above, the palate below; the sun above and the moon below."[170] Gorakh refers to this posture in one of his *bāni*s, in which he says to hold the *yantra* upside-down (*ulaṭi yantr dhare*) by standing on one's head. These structures and dynamics of the alchemical body become dramatized in a nineteenth-century hagiography of Lallā, or Lal Ded, the fourteenth-century Kashmiri mystic poetess, who demonstrated "true penance" to her guru Śrīkaṇṭha. "She placed an earthen pot on her head and another under her feet; and with the waning of the moon, her body waned till, on the fifteenth night of the dark fortnight (*amāvas*), nothing was left of her except a little quantity of trembling quicksilver. Then, with the waxing moon her body waxed and, on the full-moon night, she was herself again."[171]

This body of Hindu practices, which incorporates alchemical and hathayogic techniques, bears striking similarities to an earlier Taoist tradition, which constitutes a still more graphic projection of alchemical imagery upon the subtle body. This is the practice termed "feeding the vital principle." This technique, described in a fourth-century Chinese source, the *Taishang suling dayou miaojing*, represents the human body as a set of three "cinnabar fields," of which the uppermost, located in the head, contains an ordered hierarchy of nine "palaces." The third and innermost of these palaces, the Palace of the Cinnabar Field, is the culminating point of breath absorption, the Taoist precursor of the Indian *prāṇāyāma*. Immediately behind this is the fourth palace, called the "Palace of Moving Beads," i.e., of quicksilver, fluid mercury. Once again, the question of whether these striking parallels—between this feature of the archaic Taoist body and the "alchemical body" of Hinduism—are reflective of cultural and scientific exchanges between China and India in this period, a period following the export of Indian Buddhism into China, must remain outside the scope of the present study.[172]

The basic structure of the Hindu alchemical *yantra*s, with their downturned upper and upturned lower chambers, may be taken as a model for both the universe and the human body. Another somewhat simpler homology to the *vidyādhara yantra* is the two-chambered *ḍamaru* (indeed, there exists an alchemical *ḍamaru yantra* as well),[173] the "shaman's drum" carried by the god Śiva and his sectarian followers throughout north India and

Nepal, as well as by Tibetan Buddhist monks. This is an instrument made from two conical or hemispherical drums, joined together at their tapered ends, with their heads facing outwards. Held at its tapered middle, the *ḍamaru* is played by turning the wrist back and forth such that a bead or thong, attached by a cord to the tapered portion, strikes the two heads in alternation. The two chambers of the drum—like those of the *vidyādhara yantra*, the upper and lower halves of the human body, and the upturned and downturned wells of the macrocosm—represent the bipolar relationship between feminine and masculine principles common to so many mystic Hindu traditions. These are the states of involvement in and renunciation of the manifest world through which the human yogin alternately passes, in imitation of the divine yogin, whose yogic withdrawal from and return to mundane consciousness mark the successive resorptions (*pralayas*) and emissions (*sṛṣṭis*) of the cosmic eons.

The bead that successively strikes the two ends of the *ḍamaru* to emit the drum's sound (*nāda*) is also identifiable with the mercury that evaporates out of one chamber of these *yantra*s to sublimate in the other. It also represents the yogin's seed (called *bīja*, which is often closely identified, in tantrism, with *nāda*)[174] which rises (*ūrddhvaretas*)[175] with the *kuṇḍalinī* and returns to the lower body when the yogin returns to mundane consciousness and activities at the conclusion of his austerities.

It is another sort of two-headed drum (called a *mṛdāṅga*) that Gorakhnāth carries in the legend already discussed, in which he "awakens" his teacher Matsyendranāth from a life of debauchery in the Kingdom of Women with the first beat (*nāda*) that he strikes on it. Tibetan Buddhism, whose lists of Mahāsiddhas include the names of Gorakh, Mīna, and other illustrious figures who came to be identified with the Nāth Siddhas, also uses the *ḍamaru* in its ritual practice. A number of *ḍamaru*s, used by practitioners of tantric Buddhism in Mongolia and Tibet,[176] are fashioned from two human skulls, joined together near the fontanelle, with a rectangular hole[177] drilled between them which, establishing communication between the two hemispheres, "allows the instrument to breathe and thereby have a better sound." This hole is called the *nāda*.[178] The *ḍamaru* player generally holds a bell (*ghaṇṭa*) in his left hand, which thereby complements the *ḍamaru* held in the right. Taken together, the two are said, in the Vajrayāna context, to symbolize sun and moon, the right and left channels, and skill in means (*upāya*) and wisdom (*prajñā*),[179] the Buddhist homologues to Śiva and Śakti. More than this, the two skulls which make up the drum are ideally those of a sixteen-year-old young man and a sixteen-year-old maiden. Of course, sixteen is a figure signifying wholeness or plenitude in these traditions, but it will be recalled that the origin of this identification goes back to the lunar symbolism of hathayogic practice: sixteen is the number of digits in the full moon that brims with nectar in the fully realized yogin's head.[180]

Another source from the same Vajrayāna tradition reproduces this structural homology of the two chambers as the two peripheral channels. In a *Caryā* song (no. 3), Virūva-pā analogizes the fermentation of wine with the dynamics of yogic breath control:[181]

> The female wine-dealer [*avadhūtī*, the Buddhist *kuṇḍalinī*] is alone, but she seals together the two chambers [the two channels, sun and moon] and introduces the powder for fermenting the wine [*bodhicitta*, semen]. The wine [*vāruṇī*][182] now flows [borne upward on the subtle breaths] straight to the Sahaja [*sahasrāra*] and that brings immortality. On seeing the sign [of the wine] at the tenth door [the *brahmadvāra*, at the upper endpoint of the central channel],[183] the customer [the yogin] comes of himself and drinks the nectar from the lotus of great bliss [*mahāsukha*, the Buddhist *sahasrāra*].

With these astonishing structural homologies, we are brought back to the cranial vault in which we began this section and to the fusion of all the polarities we have been discussing.

4. Mouths and Doors: The *Khecarī Mudrā* in Tantric Practice

The bipolar locations, on a vertical axis, of male mercury and semen above and female sulfur and uterine blood below are but one means to charting the basic structure of a hierarchized tantric universe. However, in a tantric metaphysics that stresses unity-in-difference (*bhedābheda*), or nonduality-in-duality (*dvaitādvaita*), there has as well to be a stress on equipose, equivalence, and equanimity, on the union or coincidence of polar opposites. In practical terms, the factoring of the two into the one has been perennially enacted, in tantra, through sexual union between practitioner and consort. However, every subtle body is, in the traditions under study, intrinsically androgynous, being divided along the vertical axis between male and female halves after the fashion of Ardhanārīśvara, the "half-female" form of Śiva. Following an Indian (if not human) commonplace that a woman's place is on the distaff, the left side of her husband, the image of Śiva Ardhanarīśvara comprises the right half of Śiva's body and the left half of that of Śakti, the Goddess. With this, we are brought back to our discussion of a subtle body whose left or western (*paścima*) side is female (in spite of the fact that the lunar, male *iḍā* channel issues from the left nostril and the solar *piṅgalā* from the right). As I have argued, the subtle landform known as Moon Island is located either in the left side of the lower abdomen or cranial vault.

It is in the cranial vault that the complementary processes of breath, seed, and mind control culminate in the production of nectar, a new yogic body, and the state of total yogic integration that is *samādhi.*[184] The practitioner cannot, however, merely fill his head with transmuted semen and expect instant immortality. In the last chapter, I evoked the yogic and alchemical notions of *khecara*, "moving in the ether," and the erotico-mystical and hathayogic technique of *vajrolī mudrā*, while a moment ago I discussed the image of the cranial vault as an empty space (*kha*, *śūnya*) or well that comes to be filled with nectar through a variety of yogic techniques. At least one hathayogic source designates the practice of *khecarī mudrā*, "the seal of moving in the ether," as the culmination of *vajrolī mudrā* and *samarasa.*[185] The *KhV*, which treats of every imaginable variation upon the theme of *khecara*, includes discussions of the *khecarī mudrā*, the *khecari mantra*, and the *khecari cakra.*[186] We now turn to a closer examination of this body of techniques.

Although a passage in the *Maitrī Upaniṣad* appears to allude to this practice, the classic description of *khecarī mudrā* as a hathayogic practice is found in the *Gorakṣa Śataka:* "The consciousness wanders in the ether (*khe*) because the tongue, having entered into the hollow (*khe*) above the throat moves about. For this reason, the *khecarī mudrā* is revered by all accomplished yogins." In practical terms, *khecarī mudrā* is a technique that enables the yogin to retain in his cranial vault the nectar that he has accumulated there through his practice. Here, rather than allowing that nectar to fall into the fiery sun at the base of his spine, even when "in the embrace of a beautiful woman,"[187] the yogin internally drinks that transmuted semen and is thereby rendered immortal.

The key to the technique of *khecarī mudrā* lies in the left/right division of the human body and the hathayogic notion of *mudrā* itself. In literal terms, the various *mudrā*s are so many "seals," by which the yogin is able to close off or isolate portions of the subtle body, or the body in its entirety, in order to realize the "pneumatic" or "hydraulic"[188] feats of his craft. As does the alchemist with his various apparatus, the yogin must begin his practice by hermetically sealing his body off from the outside environment. This he does by closing the "nine doors," the bodily orifices.[189] Following this, through the practice of breath control, etc., he gradually closes off all of the seventy-two thousand *nāḍī*s, the breath and energy channels in his body, save the medial *suṣumṇā*, through which he will raise his breath, seed, and mind up into his cranial vault.

According to the yogic physiology of the subtle body, the *suṣumṇā* actually branches into two conduits, at the level of the medulla oblongata (*mastaka granthi*). Here, one branch veers slightly to the left,[190] towards the "lunar" side of the body, at which point it connects with the tenth channel, called the *śaṅkhinī*, the "conch."[191] It is this turn, as well as an inner aperture known as the tenth door (*daśama dvāra*), that affords the yogin the possibility of preserving and using to his advantage the nectar he has channeled upward to this point.

In order to effect *khecarī mudrā*, the yogi forces the tip of his tongue[192] back and upwards into the opening at the back of the soft palate. Then, by concentrating his gaze inwardly to a point between the eyebrows, he causes his "capitalized" nectar to flow, via the *śaṅkhinī*, into the throat, where he drinks it. This process was explained to me by a young yogin of the Jūna Ākhāḍa[193] (a suborder of the "militant" Nāga division of the Dasnāmī order, a division that has long been closely related to the Nāth Siddhas), whom I met on the Kedārnāth pilgrimage trail in May 1984. As he described it, all depended on forcing the Goddess (*kuṇḍalinī*) up into the head, from whence the rain of nectar (*amṛtavarṣa*) would flood down into the body through the *mṛtyūñjayā nāḍī*, a synonym for the *śaṅkhinī*.[194]

It is here that yet another sort of doubling occurs in the subtle physiology. First, the *Amaraughaśāsana* explicitly states that the tenth door is twofold (*dvividha*), composed of "the seminal path of immortality, and the path of death."[195] The former of these is the "upper mouth" of the *śaṅkhinī*, located in the cranial vault, within the subtle *rājadanta*, the "royal tooth," which resembles an ivory tusk. It is this tenth door that one causes to open through the practice of *khecarī mudrā*.[196] The latter, the lower mouth of the *śaṅkinī*, is the place where the medial channel issues into the cranial vault: by closing off this aperture, the yogin ensures that the nectar in his cranial vault will not drain back down this channel and fall into the fire of the sun at the base of his subtle body.[197] Not only are there two mouths to the *śaṅkhinī*, but there appear to be two *śaṅkhinī*s as well. On the one hand, the *Gorakṣa Śataka* (v. 31) states that this duct is located at the base (*mūlasthāne*) of the body; on the other, this "conch," spiral or curved in form, is doubled by the two-mouthed *kuṇḍalinī*, who can also at times be referred to as *śaṅkhinī*.[198] Whence Gorakh's succinct statement: "The tongue and penis are [joined by] a single channel. He who retains [his *rasa* within it] tricks Time."[199] With this, all the yogin needs to know is which valves to open and which to close.

The identification of the two-mouthed *śaṅkhinī* with a channel originating in the left side of the cranial vault evokes one of the esoteric classification systems of the postscriptural systematization of the Hindu tantras. This is the *paścimāmnāya* or Western Transmission, a tradition marked by a certain emphasis on *haṭha yoga* and by its cult of the goddess Kubjikā, the "crooked one,"[200] whose teachings were brought into the world on a lunar western mountain (Candragiri) or island (Candradvīpa), associated with the western face (Sadyojāta) of Śiva. As already argued, these "western" venues correspond less to the topography and toponymy of the Indian subcontinent than to the physiology of the subtle body. On the one hand, the western direction, when transposed upon the bodily microcosm, becomes the left side of the body; and indeed, one Nāth Siddha poem refers to a "western door" (*paśchima dvāra*). This corresponds to an internal "western *liṅga*," of which there are two, another case of doubling in the subtle body.[201] In a universe identified with the Goddess's subtle body, microcosm and macrocosm can at times become confused. So, for example, the *MBhT* states that Śrīnātha is situated on the left side (*vāmabhāgasthā*); and in fact, he is the consort of the Goddess at the westernmost *pīṭha* of the subcontinent, at Hiṅglāj, the site identified as the Goddess's fontanelle (*brahmarandhra*).[202]

Two other readings of *paścima* are possible here. Mark Dyczkowski argues that the term is to be taken temporally: the *paścimāmnāya* is the "subsequent" or "latter" transmission, as opposed to the "former" transmission of the *pūrvāmnāya*.[203] Elsewhere, Gorakhnāth identifies the medial *suṣumṇā* channel with the *paścimamārga* or *paścimapatha* in his *Yogabīja*.[204] Now, one could read this latter compound as "western path," and perhaps even as "subsequent [to the emptying of the left and right channels] path." One could also, however, read *paścima* here as "back" as opposed to *pūrva*, "front." In this case, the *paścimadvāra*, *paścimamārga*, and *paścimaliṅga*, would be the "back (i.e., secret, difficult of access) door," the "back way," and the "*liṅga* at the [entrance to the] back [way]."

We now return to the mouths at the ends of the channels we have been discussing. In Abhinavagupta's discussion of the "clan sacrifice" (*kulayāga*), we are told that "knowledge is to be placed in the mouth of a woman and then taken from the mouth of [that same] woman." The woman in question is the tantric practitioner's consort (*dūtī*) in erotic Kaula ritual practice, and her mouth is her sexual organ.[205] Such is also stated clearly in the *Vāmamārga*, a twentieth-century guide to ritualized tantric sex, in which the male adept is enjoined to assimilate himself to Śiva and his partner to the Goddess and offer his father-mouth into her mother-mouth.[206]

There are, in fact, two mouths at play here as well, or rather a single aperture which, located at the apex of a mystic triangle in the *mūlādhāra cakra*, is called the "lower mouth" (*adhovaktra*) when it is turned downwards, at which time it feeds into the (female) sexual organ. When through yogic or erotico-mystical practice the same is turned upwards, however, it is called the "chief mouth" or the "mouth of the *yoginī*" and is identified with the womb of consciousness, the "circle of bliss from which the energy of emission (*visargaśakti*) flows forth as *kuṇḍalinī* . . . the matrix of creation, and the essence of Kaula doctrine."[207] Similarly, the *Manthānabhairava Tantra* of the Western Transmission speaks of an upper and a lower *yoni*, located at the base and the upper end of the medial channel.[208] In the midst of so many mouths, let us recall here that each tantric system had its own variations on the subtleties of the subtle body, making it impossible to generate a single, unified account of the two upper branches of the split *suṣumṇā* channel, the two "conch ducts," the two "tenth doors," the two "western *liṅga*s," the two "*yoni*s," the two "mouths of the *yoginī*," etc.

As in erotico-mystical practice, so too in alchemy, the practitioner must reckon with the body's doors and mouths. So it is that the *MBhT* (9.19) states that the alchemist, once he has ingested edible mercury (together with meat and a woman's milk), must close the nine doors. More often than actually swallowing said mercury, the alchemist will hold it in his mouth, under his tongue or in a hollow he has cut into his palate. But this mercury, held in the alchemist's mouth, is said to possess, at a certain stage of its preparation, a mouth or mouths of its own, with which it swallows, or more literally, "has its mouthful (*grāsa*)" of the elements it causes to dissolve within itself. In these intermediate phases of its preparation, mercury may be either "mouthed" (*sa-mukha*) or "mouthless" (*nir-mukha*).[209]

As we saw earlier in this chapter, hermetically sealing two mouths of a two-chambered apparatus is also vital to the alchemist's craft. Here, while the term *mudrā* may be employed, it is the term [*sam*]*puṭa* that more often comes into play. A *puṭa* is a capsule or envelope, generally having the form of a closed crucible formed by placing two earthen plates face to face and sealing the joint between them with seven layers of mud-smeared cloth.

This container is placed in the midst of a fire pit filled with cow dung cakes, which provide constant and controlled heat, for the roasting of mercury in combination with various metallic and herbal elements.[210]

In fact, when any two halves of a dual, bipolar system (a man and a woman for example) are brought together in tantric sources, it is generally the term *sampuṭa* ("interlocked," "encased") or *sampuṭīkaraṇa* ("interlocking," "encasement") that is employed.[211] Applications of this term extend well beyond the realm of alchemical apparatus to a number of yogic and tantric configurations as well. In tantric initiation, for example, the guru is said at one point to encase himself, or his mouth, in the body or mouth of his initiate.[212] While there can be no doubt that an exchange of substance takes place between the guru and his disciple in tantric initiation, and that the guru symbolically enters into the body of his initiate, the precise nature and location of this mouth-to-mouth transfer is difficult to pinpoint. While phrases like "give me [your] mouth in [my] mouth"[213] would lead one to imagine that the guru actually locks his mouth over that of his initiate, at least one other reading is possible. This latter reading would have the guru entering his disciple's subtle body to place his mouth at the mouth of the *śaṅkhinī nāḍī* and thereby open that "valve" to liberation in the body.[214] Alternatively, the guru, having filled his mouth with the nectar falling from his own *śaṅkhinī nāḍī*, then transfers that nectar directly into the mouth of his disciple. In many forms of tantric initiation, the guru is described as coursing through the body of his initiate, in which he enters into union with the initiate's *śakti* and opens his channels to liberation.[215] I discuss important parallels between the language of initiation of this sort and that of alchemical transmutation in the penultimate chapter of this book.

In the physiology of the subtle body, the two nostrils, as well as the lunar and solar channels that issue in them, are termed *puṭa*s. In hathayogic practice, these two *puṭa*s are said to "swoon" or fall "lifeless" when the seal that joins them together is pierced, by the opening of the medial *suṣumṇā*.[216] Yet another yogic use of this notion may be found in the term "interlocking crow's beak" (*kākacañcu-puṭa*), which is a synonym for *khecarī mudrā*.[217]

As we know, the *khecarī mudrā* of *haṭha yoga* is a technique by which the practitioner ensures himself the benefits of the fluid of immortality he has culled through long yogic practice.[218] While the alchemical sources first treat *khecari* as the power of flight attained by mercury when it reaches a perfected, stable, solid state, they also reserve a yogic application for the term.[219] Mercury is rendered *khecari* by refining, stabilizing, and fortifying it, in the *ūrddhvapātana* and other apparatus, in red "female" sulfur. A pill of *khecari* mercury, held in the yogin's mouth during his *sādhana*s, catalyzes the transmutation of his semen into nectar and greatly multiplies his powers and longevity. This practice, called *guṭikā bandha*, is in fact the ultimate end, the final *saṃskāra* of the alchemist's art: the application of perfected mercury to his own body (*śarīra yoga*). Treated at length in hathayogic and alchemical sources alike, this is the prime alchemical adjunct to yogic practice.[220] We will return to these final ends of yoga and alchemy in chapter ten.

5. Two Architectural Mesocosms

Earlier in this chapter, I showed that the wells of poem and legend into which Nāth Siddhas entered in their meditative practices were the mystic homologues of their own cranial vaults. In Āyurveda, the practice of "entering into the hut" (*kuṭī praveśa*) is cast as a return to the womb. Another mesocosmic world of the same order, which the tantric practitioner may create and inhabit as a means to identifying body and universe, self and absolute, is the alchemical laboratory, appropriately called *rasamaṇḍapa*, the temple or pavilion of mercury.[221]

The alchemist who inaugurates or reconsecrates such a laboratory begins by tracing, in red *sindūra* (mercuric oxide, a mineral representation of the Goddess), upon a raised altar in the center of this structure,[222] an intricate *maṇḍala* upon which all of the alchemical raw materials, processes, etc., of his craft are symbolically represented.[223] At the heart of this *maṇḍala* he establishes a phallic emblem of Śiva composed of mercury (*rasaliṅga*) in amalgam with either gold or sulfur,[224] which he must propitiate daily if he is to hope to meet with success in his practice.[225] This *liṅga* is set into a semicircular silver chasing (*pīṭha*), which may be taken as yet another mineral emblem of the Goddess's sexual organ.[226] Also at the heart of this structure, the alchemist installs a fire pit or basin (*kuṇḍa*) called the *yonicakra* that will serve as a support for his ritual propitiation of the tantric goddesses of his craft.[227] Lastly the alchemist uses his *rasaliṅga* as a support for his meditation (*dhyāna*), projecting upon it an image of Śiva Raseśvara (or Rasabhairava) in sexual union with the goddess Rasabhairavī (or Rasāṅkuśī).[228]

That the union of these divine principles is a creative one is made explicit in descriptions of the layout of the laboratory proper: radiating outward from this divine center, the cardinal directions are identified with a *maṇḍala* of divinities as well as with the practical "rites of passage" (*saṃskāras*) of the alchemist's art. Thus, the eastern wall of the structure is reserved for the storage of herbs and other plant matter: in the Hindu organization of space, the east is the direction whose regent is Indra, the god renowned for the theft of Soma, divine herb of immortality. To the southeast, the direction of Agni, Fire, are located the alchemist's distilling instruments. To the south, the direction of the dead and Yama, lord of the dead, the alchemist stores his oxidizing, "metal-killing" (*lohamāra*) chemicals. To the southwest, the direction of Nirṛti, the dread goddess of disorder, are arranged mortar, pestle, and other grinding and pulverizing instruments. Arrayed along the western wall, the region of Varuṇa, god of the waters, are the alchemist's liquifying apparatus. To the northwest, the direction of Vāyu, Wind, are the bellows of the alchemist's furnace. The north is the quarter of the god Kubera, lord of the Vidyādharas and possessor of fabulous riches and wealth. Here are located coloring (*rañjana*) agents, the reason for this being that half the alchemist's art of aurifaction (or aurifiction, counterfeiting gold) lay in the tinting of base metals with amalgams of gold and mercury.[229] Lastly, the northeast, the direction identified with that form of Śiva known as Īśāna, is consecrated to the use of mercury as agent of transmutation (*rasavedha*).

The layout of the alchemist's temple-laboratory not only follows the logic of the Hindu organization of space, consecrating as it does each quarter of the structure to an activity that corresponds to the regent of that direction; it also follows the serial logic of the alchemical operations, the *saṃskāra*s, which he effects in transforming "raw" unrefined mercury into a "perfected" agent of transmutation and elixir of immortality. All things Hindu begin in the east, the direction of the sunrise, where the day begins. So too, the enumeration of the quadrants of the laboratory begins with this direction, with the herbs that are the raw materials of the alchemist's work and the lowest elements on the hierarchy of "metals,"[230] and at that point at which the alchemical "life-cycle rites" begin. Following the east, this orientational arrangement of the laboratory also reproduces the order of the alchemical *saṃskāra*s, which begin with the distillation, grinding, and killing of mercury and continue with its transformation of other metals through liquification, heating, and coloring, to culminate in their transmutation.

The principal role in this alchemical ordering of space and time is still played by the alchemist who, holding the center stage—in which he, as a tantric practitioner, identifies himself with Śiva in union with the Goddess in the *rasaliṅga* located at the center of his laboratory—orchestrates the alchemical *saṃskāras* that will have, for their final result, the transubstantiation of the body and being of the alchemist himself.

Just as we find a reasoned ordering of time and space in the alchemical mesocosm that is the laboratory, so too do we encounter a wide array of yogic representations of the subtle body, in which that body is projected upon a given mesocosm, or vice versa. A most graphic example of such a projection is the early nineteenth-century Haṃseśvarī (Our Lady of the Cosmic Goose) temple (Hooghly district, West Bengal), whose six stories, labyrinthine floor plan, and maze of ladders reproduce, in explicit fashion, the *nāḍīs* and *cakras* of the subtle body.[231] A similar projection, on a far more massive scale, is that of the *pīṭhas*, the "footstool" pilgrimage sites of the Goddess which, since the earliest Buddhist Tantras, have at once constituted geographic locations on the Indian subcontinent and centers within the subtle body. Thus the four "original" *pīṭhas* of Buddhism—Kāmarūpa, Jālandhara, Pūrṇagiri, and Uḍḍiyāna—are identified with the four *cakras* of the Buddhist subtle body. This number comes to be expanded to 51 (the Sanskrit phonemes) in the *KM* and the *Pīṭhanirṇaya*, 68 in Nāth sources, 134 in the *Ṣaṭsāhasra Saṁhitā*, and so on.[232] At least five sacred Śākta-Śaiva sites—Kāmākhyā, Srisailam, Hiṅglāj Devī, Kedārnāth, and Girnar—have alchemical traditions connected to them; to these may be added Śiva's Mount Kailash, which is described as an alchemical wonderland in the opening lines of the *Rasārṇava*.[233]

We have noted that the Nine Nāths, rather than being historical figures, are in fact symbolizations of various elements of the universal macrocosm—the nine directions, including the zenith or center, and the subtle body (nine of the "ten doors," the principal *nāḍīs*, etc.).[234] This is appropriate inasmuch as there was no medieval sect in India that was as fascinated, even obsessed, with the array of correspondences it discovered between the universal macrocosm and the microcosm of the subtle body. While the Nāth Siddhas mapped out these "static" homologies, in all their many-splendored detail, in such works as the *Siddha Siddhānta Paddhati*, *Gorakh Bodh*, and *Prāṇ Sāṅkalī*, [235] nowhere are they presented more dynamically and dramatically than in Muhammad Jayasī's *Padmāvat*, in which the storming of the fort of Siṁhala is made into an explicit allegory for transformations within the hathayogic body.

Before we enter into the heart of the matter, a word on Siṁhala or Saṅgaldīp itself is in order, appearing as it does in a great number of Nāth Siddha legends. Like Ratansen in the *Padmāvat*, Pūraṇ Bhagat (Caurangī-nāth) is also required to go to this kingdom. However, rather than going to conquer a woman as does Ratansen when he wins Padmavatī, he is sent there by his guru Gorakhnāth to test his powers of yogic resistance against the amorous advances of that country's queen, Sundrān ("Beautiful").[236] Gopīcand, sent, in a similar way, to the "south country" by his guru Jālan-dharnāth, falls into the clutches of a sorceress named Hīrā ("Diamond"): when he rejects her advances, she transforms him into a ram, and Jāland-harnāth has to come and rescue him. According to one source, Gopīcand's own sister Candrāvalī, prior to deciding to follow in her brother's footsteps and become a *yoginī*, is married the king of Siṁhala. We therefore appear to be in the presence of a common motif which is, however, in the Gopī-cand legends, distributed between the Nāth Siddha himself and his sis-ter.[237] In one version of his legend, Pūraṇ Bhagat is said to be the disciple of Matsyendranāth whose own Plantain Forest, it will be recalled, was lo-cated in one version of *his* legend, in Siṁhala! Matsyendra fares less well than do any of the junior Nāth Siddhas of these accounts, but this is likely due to his connections with the Yoginī Kaula.[238] In every case, we may conclude that this southern island-fortress is a mythic multiform of the Plantain Forest already described above, at once a locus of lethal sensuality and rejuvenating yogic liberation. Here, then, is the allegorical ascent of the fortress of Siṁhala. In it, we will recognize a great number of land-scapes within the subtle body, as have been described throughout this chapter.[239]

> [Śiva speaks] "I will tell you of the fortress of Siṁhala: the ascent is of seven storeys.[240] No one who has set his foot on the heavenly way has returned as a living being. The fortress is as bent (*bāṅk*) as is your body: man, as you may see, is an image of it. It is not to be attained by fighting, through the use of force (*haṭh*);[241] those who do attain it are those who have attained the marks [of yoga].[242]
>
> There are nine gates in that fortress and five constables patrol therein. It has a hidden tenth door:[243] inaccessible is the ascent to this and the way is exceedingly crooked (*bāṅkī*).[244] Only he who has obtained the secret (*bhed*) and climbs like an ant can penetrate (*bhedī*) that pass.[245] At the base of the fortress is a deep pool (*kuṇḍ*): in the midst of this there is a path, as I declare to you . . . [246] As the diver plunges into the ocean and only then does the pearl come to his

> hand; so he who seeks out the door of heaven will make the ascent of Siṁhala-dvīpa.
>
> The tenth gate is [as narrow and lofty as] the silhouette of a palm tree: he who has reversed his gaze (*ulaṭi disiti*)[247] can see it. He who advances while restraining (*bandī*) his breath and his mind . . . can go there . . . [248]
>
> Then king [Ratansen] received the *siddhi guṭikā*.[249] Thereupon he realized the *siddhi*[s] . . . When Śiva gave him the *siddhi* [*guṭikā*], a great clamor arose as the yogins assailed the fortress. All the lotus maidens climbed up (on the roofs) to observe. In laying siege to the Simhala fortress, [it was as if] the yogins had raised a grove of meditation huts [in its place].[250]

This dramatic depiction of the subtle body plunges us into the dynamics of yogic and alchemical transformation, which are to be the subject of the following chapter.

NINE

The Dynamics of Transformation in Siddha Alchemy

1. The "Work in Two Parts"

In an earlier chapter, I showed that the tantric universe was a unified system that oscillated between withdrawal (*nivṛtti*) and return (*pravṛtti*) on the part of a cosmic yogin, between effulgence (*prakāśa*) and reflection (*vimarśa*) on the part of supreme consciousness, between emission and resorption, etc. In such a system, the yogic body becomes the stage for the return of the absolute from existence to essence through the descent and ascent of the *kuṇḍalinī*. As has been indicated, the absolute emanates into the manifest universe and human bodies as a means to enjoying its boundless potential. The return, however, to unity and wholeness is, for those human manifestations of this emanatory dynamic, anything but natural, requiring as it does a forceful (*haṭha*) reversal (*ulaṭā*) of what are, in mortal creatures, irreversible tendencies (entropy, aging, disease, death). Thus, while it is the case that the process of return is, from a divine or absolute perspective, internal to the process of emanation, it is nevertheless an arduous task for the individual who would attempt to realize such through his own subtle body.[1] So it is that long before the much-glorified stage of yogic or alchemical reintegration, in which an emanated or differentiated manifest world implodes on itself, into a single essence—a drop, vibration, phoneme, wave, photon, quantum, etc.—a great deal of unglorious preparatory work must be carried out. That work is the subject of this chapter.

The human techniques for reversing the natural tendency (in an emanated universe) towards greater differentiation or entropy and for realizing for oneself the primordial unity of the absolute—with its concommitant bliss (*bhoga*), supernatural powers (*siddhis*), and bodily liberation (*jīvanmukti*)—are the stuff of *haṭha yoga*. However, as the texts themselves tell us time and again, the human microcosm is intimately entwined with the alchemical and hathayogic mesocosm, with the latter two at once constituting parallel and interpenetrating systems. Whence the classic statements of the *RA*: "As in metal, so in the body. . . . By means of the Work, a stable body is attained. Mercury and breath [control] are known as the Work in two parts (*karmayogo dvidhā*)."[2] This statement is echoed in Gorakhnāth's *Amaraugha Prabodha* (v. 5), which describes the twofold *rājayoga* as botanical and spiritual and the twofold *haṭha yoga* as the "practice of breath and seed."[3] The quest of the alchemist and that of the yogin are one and the same. This is the credo of Siddha alchemy.

Not only the ends, but also the means these two interpenetrating systems employ for the realization of their final goal are also strikingly homologous. In the last two chapters, I showed the content and structure of the two systems to be parallel and interpenetrating; in the present chapter, I turn to their common dynamic. Stated in their simplest terms, hathayogic and alchemical techniques for immortality, termed *sādhana*s ("realizations") and *saṃskāra*s ("perfectionings") respectively, comprise four phases: purification, immobilization, reversal, and transformation. Quite often, the language employed to describe these sequential techniques is identical in the two systems; and even when such is not the case, structural homologies abound, with references to digestion, consciousness-raising, flux, phase changes (from the virtual to the actual), and a vertical dynamic pervasive in both systems. These sequences further constitute models of or for a number of sacrificial, medical, and tantric practices and techniques, which I also outline here.

Saṃskāra is a Sanskrit term that has come to cover an extremely wide semantic field in India. Derived from the same prefix + root (*saṃ[s]-kṛ*) as is the word *Sanskrit* itself, its literal sense is to "per-fect," to render whole or complete; more technical definitions include the "production of new qualities" and "that which makes a person or thing fit for a given function."[4] It is in this latter sense that the term *saṃskāra* plays a pivotal role in Hindu alchemy. The *saṃskāras* are those operations that render mercury fit for transformation, for the production of new qualities in the mineral world. From another perspective, the alchemical *saṃskāra*s may be seen as the exalted "rites of passage" of those humans who, applying the element mercury—first "generated" in the form of the "raw" semen of the god Śiva—to metals and thence to their own bodies, transform themselves into equals of the gods (who, out of jealousy, asked Śiva to adulterate mercury with impurities). As in the case of the human rites of passage, the principal aim of the alchemical *saṃskāra*s is to purify a (mercurial) body that has been tainted through the process of birth, of coming into existence. Here it is significant that *sūta*, "that which was generated," is one of the five standard alchemical terms for mercury, Śiva's seed, which lodged itself in the womb of the goddess earth, at the conclusion of the origin myth of mercury.[5]

In alchemy, as in other spheres of Hindu culture, the number attached to the *saṃskāra*s is eighteen, or more properly speaking, sixteen plus two.[6] The first sixteen *saṃskāra*s prepare mercury and other elements for transmutation, while the final two are the issue of all that has preceded: these are the transmutation of base metals into gold (called *vedha*, "penetration") and transubstantiation, the generation of an immortal body, called *śarīra-yoga* ("body Work"), *bhakṣana* ("eating"), *dehavedha* ("penetration of the body"), or simply *sevana* ("use").[7]

In yoga in general, and *haṭha yoga* in particular, the *sādhana*s ("realizations") are so many homologues of the alchemical *saṃskāra*s. As outlined in the introductory chapter, the term *sādhana* is derived, like *siddhi* ("realization," "supernatural power") and *siddha* ("realized individual," "superman") from the verb *sadh*, to "realize, accomplish, perfect." At least one hathayogic source[8] lists seven *sādhana*s together with their results. These are purification (*śodhana*) through the six practices (*ṣaṭkarmāṇi*); solidity (*dṛḍhatā*) through the postures (*āsana*s); immobility (*sthairya*) through the yogic seals (*mudrā*s); composure (*dhairya*) through the retraction of the senses (*pratyāhara*); lightness (*lāghava*) through breath control (*prāṇāyāma*); direct perception (*pratyakṣa*) through meditation (*dhyāna*); and immaculateness (*nirlipta*) and release (*mukti*) through total yogic integration (*samādhi*).

2. The Alchemical *Saṃskāra*s

If we are to demonstrate a more explicit connection between the alchemical *saṃskāra*s and the hathayogic *sādhana*s, we must go beyond these general observations and undertake a point-for-point comparison of the graded practices that define the two disciplines. We begin our comparison here with a summary of the alchemical *saṃskāra*s, in which the sixteen standard *saṃskāra*s are listed with Arabic numerals, supplementary operations with roman numerals, and the effects of such operations with roman letters. Following this summary, the balance of this chapter will consist of a commentary in which a series of yogic (and, where applicable, sacrificial, medical, and tantric) practices will be juxtaposed with homologous alchemical operations—by which it will be shown that Siddha alchemy did in fact constitute a "Work in two parts."

I. *Śodhana* is the "(preliminary) purification" of mercury, its physical cleansing through washing, melting, marinating, and roasting it in various preparations.[9]

II. *Kṣetrīkaraṇa*, "making (oneself master of) the field," is the purification of the human body, through special diets, emetics, etc., such that it becomes capable of absorbing mercurial preparations. Although the ingestion of such preparations constitutes the eighteenth and final *saṃskāra*, the preparation of the body, analogous in certain ways to the preliminary purification of mercury, must be undertaken well in advance of its ingestion. It is for this reason that I introduce it here.

1. *Svedana* is the "sweating," "steaming," or "fomentation" of mercury in a water bath together with plant and mineral substances. This is the first *saṃskāra*, i.e., the first step in the chemical transformation of unrefined mercury into an agent of transmutation. As such, it differs from *śodhana*, in which the mercury ore is first cleansed physically or mechanically, rather than purified chemically.[10]

2. *Mardana* is the "rubbing," "grinding," or "trituration" of steamed mercury in a mortar, together with plant and acidic substances.

3. *Mūrcchana* is the "fainting" or "swooning" of mercury, by which it is ground in a mortar together with vegetable matter, until it loses its natural characteristics (luster, density, volatility, etc.) and form and becomes purged of certain naturally occurring toxins, impurities, and defects.[11] This is to be distinguished from another process of the same name.

III. *Mūrcchana* as a supplementary operation takes mercury that has already been processed, either through the first eight *saṃskāra*s or by other means, and combines it with sulfur to produce a number of medical preparations for Ayurvedic *rasāyana* or *vājīkaraṇa* therapy.[12] For reasons that will be made clear later in this chapter, we pass directly from our discussion of "swooning" to that of two other vital transformations of mercury, known as "binding" and "killing."

a. As a result of the process of swooning, mercury becomes "swooned," *mūrcchita*.

b. *Bandhana* is the "binding" or "fixation" of mercury, which, like swooning, leaves mercury stable and thereby manipulable, in a state in which it is not subject to evaporation, even when heated over fire. Left unbound, mercury remains volatile whenever it is exposed to heat or sunlight. Once purified, it can be "fixed" via any one of the twenty-five or twenty-six alchemical *bandhas*. Each of these *bandhas* has a specific medical application.[13]

c. *Māraṇa*, the "killing" of mercury (or any metal) reduces it to a fine ash or oxide (*bhasma*), such that the human body is able to absorb it when it is taken in medical preparations. Metals other than mercury are generally killed, in preparation for internal use, by heating them together with iron pyrites and mercuric sulfide. When mercury is killed, it loses its fluidity, density, luster, and brilliance. Tantric alchemy attributes fantastic powers of transmutation to said mercury, which it identifies as "killed ash" (*mṛtabhasma*) or "killed mercury" (*mṛtasūtaka*).[14]

4. *Utthāpana* is the "resurrection" of swooned mercury, effected by steaming it with alkalis, salts, and plant matter and by rubbing it in the open air. Through "resurrection," mercury recovers the brilliance, etc. it had lost through *mūrcchana*.

5. *Pātana*, the "sublimation" or "distillation" of mercury refers to the three processes by which mercury is distilled upwards, downwards, or transversally.[15]

6. *Bodhana*, "awakening," or *rodhana*, "countering, coagulation," are alternative terms for the sixth *saṃskāra*, by which mercury, which has become purged of its toxic content but also its strength through the preceding operations, has its "virility" (*vīrya*) restored to it through irrigation in a salt bath. This operation gives mercury a "mouth" (*mukha*) with which to absorb other elements in the *saṃskāras* that follow.[16]

7. *Niyamana*, "regulation" or "restraint," reduces the motility of mercury (which it has recovered through the previous *saṃskāra*), raising its temperature of evaporation and rendering it lustrous in appearance. This is done by soaking mercury in a bath of alkaline and herbal substances and then steaming it.[17]

8. *Dīpana*, "kindling" or "enflaming," further enhances mercury's potency and luster through steaming in an alkaline bath. This operation is said to kindle mercury's desire to "consume" other metals.[18]

d. Taken as a group, the first eight *saṃskāras* serve to purify and detoxify mercury such that it may be used internally in the treatment of diseases.[19] It is here, however, that the great divide—between the medical use of mercurials (*rogavāda*) and the use of the same for the ends of transmutational (*lohavāda*) and elixir alchemy (*dehavāda*)—is drawn. The realization of these higher, tantric aims requires eight additional *saṃskāras*, by means of which mercury truly begins to behave like a living being, hungering after metals to consume, penetrate, and thereby transmute. The transubstantiation of the alchemist's own body, similarly penetrated by mercury, then follows automatically.

Of the remaining *saṃskāra*s, (9) [*gagana*]*grāsa*, (10) *cāraṇa*, (11) *garbhadruti*, and (12) *bāhyadruti* are but phases in a single continuous process, which culminates in (13) *jāraṇa*, "digestion" or "assimilation." These begin with the measuring out (*māna*) of a given quantity (a "seed," consisting of the calcinated ash, or the "essence," *sattva*) of mica or a metal for its consumption (*grāsa*) by mercury. This is followed by the "chewing" (*cāraṇa*, literally "coursing") of the mica or metal by said mercury, followed by either its internal (to the mass of mercury) or external processing and liquification (*garbha-druti* and *bāhya-druti*, respectively),[21] with the end result being in that metal's total digestion or assimilation (*jāraṇa*) into the mercury.

IV. Because it issues from a series of operations, *jāraṇa* may be viewed as the culmination of these alchemical *saṃskāra*s as much as an operation in itself. From this point onwards, it becomes quite artificial to distinguish mercury from the metals to be transmuted. Once mercury has digested a given metal, that metal no longer exists per se; rather, it is alchemically activated mercury itself that will become transmuted into silver or gold.[22]

14. *Rañjana*, "tinting" or "coloration," involves the heating of mercury with "seeds" of gold, silver, copper, sulfur, mica, and salt, such that mercury takes on the natural colors of the minerals it has absorbed or swallowed.[23]

15. *Sāraṇa* (literally, "flowing"), the "potentialization" of mercury in preparation for transmutation, is effected by heating it in oil into which molten "seeds" of metals, diamond, etc. are poured.[24]

16. In *krāmaṇa* ("taking hold, "progression"), mercury is smeared with a mineral and herbal paste and heated in a *puṭa* such that it becomes capable, as a transmuting agent, of penetrating both metals and bodily tissues.[25]

V. The final two *saṃskāra*s, (17) *vedha* ("transmutation") and (18) *śarīrayoga* ("transubstantiation"), together constitute the final end of the alchemist's work. As such, they are as much the issue of the sixteen prior *saṃskāra*s as alchemical operations in themselves.

With these operations, mercury truly confounds itself with the metallic or flesh-and-blood "bodies" in question, ultimately replacing them with a mercurial or alchemical body. If life is, as the Buddha said, to be regarded as a disease or a wound, then it is appropriate to liken mercury to a *healing virus* (from *vir*, the Indo-European root denoting masculinity—as in *semen virile* and, by extension, *virility*) which takes over the body into which it enters, transforming human tissue into alchemical diamond or gold—gold which, in the immortal words of the Brāhmaṇas, "is immortality."[26] In the following chapter, I provide further discussion of these final *saṃskāras*.

3. Purification

It is in the ancient sacrificial tradition that we find the earliest statements concerning the alternation between manifestation and nonmanifestation on the part of the absolute. This is described in terms of an alternation of divine generations and of the transformative, even reanimating properties of fire. The primordial creator (Puruṣa-Prajāpati), having poured himself—indeed, poured his *rasa*—into the manifest world, lies broken and dying. He can be restored to his prior unmanifest wholeness only through the intervention of his son, Agni, who is the sacrificial fire. By piling a fire altar (*agnicayana*) Agni reconstitutes the body of his father and thereby becomes known as "his father's father." It is through this alternation of generations that it is possible for the divine to be at once one and many, transcendent and manifest; and it is only through the offering, on the part of a human sacrificer, of a major sacrifice that this alternation, this resurrection of the father, can be effected. Indeed, it is in this very same sacrificial context that one finds the earliest use of the verb *saṃskṛ*, to refer the restoration to original wholeness of a god whose body has been identified with what Jan Heesterman has termed the "broken world of sacrifice."[27]

Whenever such a sacrifice was to be offered in ancient India, the piece of ground upon which that sacrifice was to take place had to be prepared long in advance of the actual ritual offering. Preparation essentially involved sealing off a theretofore mundane parcel of land through a series of purificatory acts. Here, purification involved plowing and cultivating the land, allowing it to lie fallow, and finally covering it with a layer of sand, which symbolized the semen of the "emptied" Prajāpati. The language here was sexual: the raised altar was the womb (*yoni*) upon which the semen (*retas*) of Prajāpati was spread, thus filling the void that was left when Prajāpati's body had first become dispersed.[28] Only after the sacrificial ground had been renewed in this way could it serve as the mesocosm for a sacralization of cosmos, society, and the sacrificer, through the offering of the sacrifice itself.

It was not sufficient, however, that the sacrificial ground alone be purified in preparation for the sacrifice. A similar sort of preparation had also to be effected upon the person of the sacrificer, the human pivot of the ritual act. Here, it was necessary that the human sacrificer, no doubt in imitation of the primal sacrificer, Puruṣa-Prajāpati, renew his body in order that it be rendered fit to perform the sacrificial act.[29] This act of preparing the sacrificer's body, of transforming it from a mundane human body into a body worthy of communing with the divine through sacrifice, is *dīkṣā* (literally "habilitation"), a term generally translated as "initiation." Here, the mechanics of initiation entail the same dynamic as the preparation of the sacrificial ground: the purification of a mundane body transforms it into a sacrificial body. As with the preparation of the sacrificial ground, the preparation of the sacrificer himself is described in terms of sexual reproduction and animal gestation. Sequestered within the initiation hut, the sacrificer, "cooked" through the inner heat of his austerities (*tapas*) and the external heat of burning fires placed in the hut, symbolically sheds his mundane body. An embryo of his "new" sacrificial body takes form, incubates, and is born out of the "womb" of the hut, three days later.[30]

The symbolism of this homologous preparation through purification, of both sacrificial ground and sacrificial body, is directly appropriated by the three elements of Siddha practice: *haṭha yoga*, alchemy, and tantric ritual. This first groundbreaking phase is called *kṣetrīkaraṇa*, "mastering, preparing the field" in the first two systems, and *bhūtaśuddhi*, "purification of the elements" in the third. This metaphor of the tilled field is altogether natural within an agrarian society and is not original to these three traditions. Classical Sāṁkhya calls the body-mind complex the field (*kṣetra*) and the soul the farmer (*kṣetrajñā*, literally, "knower of the field") who tends said field without himself being affected by it.[31] In Hinayāna Buddhism, the notion of the transfer of merit is explained through the image of the assembled saints, who constitute an excellent field (*khettūpamā*) in which meritorious acts may be sown and thereafter bear fruit for the benefit of others.[32]

It is in the medical tradition that the theories and techniques pertaining to the preparation of the body as field are most fully developed. In its rejuvenation therapy, the term *kṣetrīkaraṇa* refers to the preparation of the body for the medicines that will be absorbed in the treatment per se.[33] This class of treatments—called *saṃśodhana cikitsā*, "purificatory medicine" or *pañcakarmāṇi*, "the five treatments"—combines such clinical treatments as emetics, purgatives, sudation, etc. as means to purifying the body by voiding it of the elements responsible for its humoral imbalance.[34] At the end of these five sequences—each a fortnight in duration and interspersed with five-day rest periods—the rejuvenation therapy proper may begin.

Interfacing as it did with the therapeutic alchemy of Āyurveda, tantric alchemy makes a nearly identical use of the term *kṣetrīkaraṇa*, with its place in the order of operations homologous to that found in Āyurveda. Simultaneous to his preparation of the mercury he will eventually ingest, the alchemist must also prime his body, in order that it be capable of absorbing that potent elixir. Here, *kṣetrīkaraṇa* means observing, over a fifteen-day period, a strict purificatory diet which effects, through the same five treatments as those employed in rejuvenation therapy, the evacuation of every bodily impurity with which the mercury might abreact.[35] As a result of this operation, the body becomes a field in which a mercurial seed (*rasa-bīja*), when ingested, will germinate. The fruit this seed will produce is an immortal, alchemical body. While apparently agricultural, the language here, too, is sexual. The first three *saṃskāra*s of the human rites of passage, which effect the purification of the womb, are called the "perfectionings of the field," the *kṣetra-saṃskāra*s, by which the female womb is prepared to receive the seed (*bīja*) that is male semen.[36]

Here, the planting of a mercurial seed in the body also reminds us of tantric initiation (*dīkṣā*), which may be performed either with or without "seed" (*sabīja* or *nirbīja*).[37] As the *MBhT* describes it, the "seed" is the condensed *mantra*—identified with the semen of Śiva, who is himself identified with the guru here—that the guru plants in the initiate's body. Indeed, no mantra can be effective without a "seed," and no tantric deity exists independent of his or her seed mantra (*bīja*).[38] Like Prajāpati and Agni in Vedic sacrifice, the relationship between the guru who plants the seed and the disciple in whose body he plants it is one of an alternation of generations. So too, the alchemist whose corporeal field has been properly prepared gives birth to a new, immortal self, out of the old, through the mercurial seed he has planted there.[39] Even if the body so produced is most often called a golden, adamantine, or realized body (*svarṇa-deha*, *vajra-deha*, *siddha-deha*), it is in fact a mercurial body, an alchemical body.

Like the Ayurvedic physician and the alchemist, the *haṭha yogin* must also effect a preliminary cleansing (*śodhana*) of his body. This he does through a series of operations known as *bhūtaśuddhi*, the "purification of the elements," or the *ṣaṭkarmāṇi*, the "six practices," in which the inner contours of his body are purified with air, water, and fire.[40] Like the five treatments of Āyurveda, the majority of these practices ranging from nose wash (*neti*) to enema (*vasti*), flush out the body's physical impurities.[41] Such practices, which cleanse the channels of the subtle body, channels through which the five vital breaths must freely circulate, are already anticipated in the preparation of the fire altar mentioned above: the furrows plowed into the site create the channels through which the vital airs circulate in the body of Prajāpati, the sacrifical Man.[42] Given the task he has set himself—to reintegrate bodily microcosm with divine macrocosm—these preliminaries are vital to the yogin's success in all that follows. From the outset, the intrinsically gross human body cannot be charged with the slightest impurity as such would, like a speck of dust on a mirror, skew the perfect interface, reflection, and realization of one world in another.[43]

The term *bhūtaśuddhi* has a much more extended application in the realm of tantrism, where it also forms an important element of worship and initiation.[44] In tantric ritual, *bhūtaśuddhi* refers to the preliminary purification of the divinities residing in each of the five elements (*bhūta*s) that make up the body.[45] Here, *bhūtaśuddhi* is the purification of both a mesocosmic worship site—once again referred to as a "field," *kṣetra*—and the microcosmic body of the worshipper himself (when the two are not identified),[46] a situation that mirrors that of the twofold Vedic preparation of sacrificial ground and the sacrificer's person. Both are dessicated, "blown out," and burned up before being cleansed with water and flooded with "nectar," processes which, identified with the dissolution of the mundane self, constitute the first step towards the creation of a new divinized self. Here, the lower elements of earth, water, fire, and air, are successively imploded into their higher emanates, until there only remains the most sublime element on the pentadic hierarchy. This is ether, the empty space left by this dissolution, within which the tantric practitioner will establish, through visualization techniques and the planting of seed *mantra*s, a new world at the center of which he will construct the body of that divinity with whom he will come to identify himself.[47]

The tantric worshipper or initiate who has transformed his own being through these processes becomes capable, in turn, of transforming other beings, indeed, the entire universe, through his limitless powers. Such is also the case with mercury in the alchemical context. In its mundane form, as it is found in ores and its various compound forms, mercury is incapable of transforming other mineral substances in any way whatsoever and is capable only of poisoning the foolish alchemist who would attempt to ingest it. Like the bodies of the Ayurvedic patient, *haṭha yogin*, and tantric practitioner, and like the sites upon which Vedic and tantric rituals are carried out, the element mercury must be primed, purified, and consecrated before further operations may be undertaken.

It is in this context that the term employed for the alchemical transformations, *saṃskāra*, takes on its greatest fullness of meaning: "*Saṃskāra*: those acts and rites that impart fitness. Fitness is of two kinds. It arises from the removal of taints or by the generation of fresh qualities."[48]

Of the classic enumeration of the eighteen alchemical *saṃskāra*s, the first eight concern nothing more or less than the preliminary preparation of the element mercury for its eventual application to other minerals. Of these, the first two—*svedana* and *mardana*, "sweating" and "rubbing"—deal most directly with mercury's physical or mechanical purification.[49] The "sweating" of mercury immediately reminds us of the initiation of the Vedic sacrificer and the *kuṭī-praveśa* treatment of Ayurvedic rejuvenation therapy. It is by sweating off, purging oneself of one's old body that it becomes possible to take on a new one. The same is the case in *haṭha yoga*. It is only after his effecting of the "six acts" that the practitioner begins to truly transform his body—by sweating, which is viewed as the first stage in the process of yogic transformation. Here, he induces perspiration through a number of techniques of breath control (*prāṇāyāma*), techniques which culminate in diaphragmatic retention (*kumbhaka*). The sweat that is voided through the pores (literally, "hair wells," *roma-kūpa*) has in fact been forced out through the seventy-two thousand *nāḍī*s, thereby purging them of all impurity.[50]

The parallel with the alchemical *saṃskāra*s appears to be deliberate here, since immediately following this, the yogin is instructed to rub (*mardana*) his body with the perspiration that has been so produced. The combination of these two processes renders the body—not unlike mercury at the conclusion of the first two alchemical *saṃskāra*s—firm and light.[51]

4. Immobilization: *Mūrcchana, Bandhana,* and *Māraṇa*

The second verse of Patañjali's *Yogasūtras* defines yoga as "preventing thought from going around in circles." One may indeed consider the entire history of yogic theory and practice to be a footnote on this formula.[52] Reduced to its simplest terms, yoga ("yoking") is concerned with impeding movement, with the immobilization of all that is mobile within the body. This is a point that the *HYP* makes clear in its opening chapter: "The postures, the various [methods of breath control leading to] *kumbhaka*[s], the practices called *mudrā*, then the practices concentrating on [hearing] the *nāda:* this is the sequence [to be observed] in *haṭha* [*yoga*]."[53] One first immobilizes the body through the postures; next, one immobilizes the breaths through diaphragmatic retention; one then immobilizes the seed through the "seals"; and finally one immobilizes the mind through concentration on the subtle inner reverberation of the phonemes.

The theory here is simple: stop this, that stops. But the practice is anything but simple as anyone who has attempted to maintain a yogic posture, sit still, or simply stop thinking for any length of time knows all too well. What a difficult, even heroic undertaking the immobilization of the body constitutes, yet what fantastic results it yields! For immobilization leads to reversal, reversal to transformation, and transformation is tantamount to bodily immortality and, precisely, to the supernatural ability to transform, reverse, or immobilize whatever one desires in the physical world (*siddhi*). Immobilization or stabilization, in the form of swooning, binding (or fixation), and killing, constitute the "hump" that the Siddha alchemist must get over in order for his goals to be realized. All that follows does so more or less automatically, as if a critical mass has been reached and a chain reaction triggered—whence the most frequently recurring passage, in the entire alchemical tradition.

A single summary passage, concerning the matters of immobilization, stability, death, resurrection, and the power of flight, appears, in nearly identical form, in all of the alchemical classics—the *Rasārṇava*, *Rasahṛdaya Tantra*, *Rasendra Maṅgala*, *Bhūtiprakaraṇa*, *Rasendracūḍāmaṇi*, and *Rasaratnasamucchaya*.[54] More remarkable is the fact that this exact same verse, at least in the form in which it is found in the *RA*, also occurs in the fifteenth-century *HYP* of Svātmarāma. In this latter case, however, Svātmarāma is able to employ "alchemical" terminology to make a yogic point. That is, the same verse may be read on two different registers, the one alchemical and the other yogic. In the context of the "Work in two parts" and the vital matter of immobilization, however, the two perspectives ultimately become fused into one.

The verse in question reads, in the *RA* and the *HYP*, as follows: "Swooned, *rasa*, like the breath, drives away diseases, killed it revives itself, bound it affords the power of flight."[55] In the alchemical *RA*, the term *rasa* refers to swooned, bound, and killed mercury, the ingestion of which, in tandem with the practice of breath control, renders the practitioner healthy, immortal, and possessed of the power of flight. The hathayogic

HYP promises the same results, but takes *rasa* to mean semen, the immobilization and retention of which are paramount to the hathayogic discipline, as witnessed in a poem attributed to Gopīcand:[56] "Steady goes the breath, and the mind is steady, steady goes the mind, the semen. Steady the semen, and the body is steady, that's what Gopīcand is sayin'."

A number of other references further elaborate on the interchangeability of mind, breath, and *rasa* in the techniques evoked in the hathayogic and alchemical sources. The *HYP* equates the immobilized mind with bound or fixed mercury and states that the former results in the immobilization of both breath and body and thereby bodily immortality. In like fashion, the *RA* emphasizes the necessity of unwavering mental concentration for success in the performance of alchemical operations.[57] Gorakhnāth, with the directness we have come to expect of his poetry of yogic experience, states the matter clearly and succinctly: "Penis in the vulva's mouth, mercury in the mouth of fire; he who can retain these [semen and mercury], him I call my guru."[58]

Here, it is the same image, of immobilized *rasa*—that is at once calcinated mercury and semen—that comes to be employed, in a wide array of applications, to describe the parallel yet interpenetrating processes of Siddha alchemy. Although swooning is the sole member of the triad—of *mūrcchana*, *bandhana*, and *māraṇa*—to actually constitute an alchemical *saṃskāra* per se (the latter two being the effects of a number of combined operations), all three are nevertheless central to the alchemist's craft. According to a list provided in the *RA*, all seven of the standard forms of alchemical mercury produced through the *saṃskāra*s are either swooned (*mūrcchita*), bound (*baddha*), or killed (*mṛta*).[59] We now turn to a closer examination of this triad, within the Work in two parts.

a. *Mūrcchana*

It will be recalled that alchemical *saṃskāra* known as "swooning," following directly upon the "sweating" and "rubbing" of mercury, causes the liquid metal to lose its luster, lightness, volatility, etc., which are immediately restored to it in the course of a fourth operation, called "resurrection." Recalling the intimate connection between immobilizing the mind, breath, and *rasa* in the Work in two parts, we should expect to find hathayogic *mūrcchana* playing an analogous role. Hathayogic "swooning" is in fact a direct result of *kumbhaka*, of "potlike" diaphragmatic breath retention, the methods for the realization of which it is now time to describe.

The yogin first draws the subtle breath (*prāṇa*) in through the left nostril and thereby into the lunar channel. Having retained it for as long as possible in the abdomen, he exhales it, via the solar channel and through the right nostril. He then inhales through the right nostril, retains the breath in the abdomen as before, and releases it, via the lunar channel, out the left nostril. By continuing this process, pumping the outer *nāḍī*s "like a blacksmith's bellows," the yogin's diaphragm will, at a certain point, remain filled with air, the pressure of which will force open the orifice (known as the "door of brahman," the *brahmadvāra*) of the medial channel.[60] The subsequent inrush of air into the medial channel causes the two peripheral channels to empty. Deflated in this way, they are called "swooned" (*mūrcchā*), and indeed, one of the eight types of *kumbhaka* is itself called *mūrcchā*, "because it causes the [normally volatile] mind to swoon," i.e., to become one-pointed in its concentration.[61]

It is not the swooning of the two peripheral channels that itself "drives away diseases," as *HYP* 4.27 states. It is rather the effect of their emptying—i.e., the opening and filling of the medial channel—that is essential, as this becomes the path by which the *kuṇḍalinī* surges upwards, carrying with her the life force, seed, and "swooned" mind into the cranial vault. Just as the swooning of mercury is, in the alchemical context, a necessary intermediate step to the transformation of metals and the human body, so too in *haṭha yoga*, swooning affords the practitioner mastery over disease and death. The parallel is explained in these very terms by Brahmānanda, in his commentary to this verse: "Through the use of certain herbs, mercury, which is inclined to be volatile, becomes swooned (*mūrcchita*) in the same way that the breath becomes swooned in the culmination of *kumbhaka*, when one has exhaled and stopped inhaling."[62]

b. *Bandhana*

The hathayogic texts recommend a combination of postures, together with a number of respiratory and "hydraulic" techniques, for the immobilization of the breaths and the diaphragmatic retention that trigger the rise of the *kuṇḍalinī* and all that follows. This body of hydraulic techniques is generally subdivided into "hermetic seals" (*mudrā*s such as the *vajrolī* and *khecarī*) and contractions or "locks" (*bandha*s). These sources describe three principal locks which, effected at the levels of the abdomen, thorax, and head, work hydraulically to effect internal changes in pressure, such that breath and seed become immobilized or begin to be drawn upward. These are the: (1) *mūla bandha*, ("root lock"), an inner contraction of the anus which draws the downward-tending *apāna* breath upward through the medial channel; (2) *uḍḍiyāna bandha* ("the lock of the upward-flying [bird]"), a contraction of the abdomen which, by emptying the lungs, drives them and the diaphragm up into the upper thorax and causes the *prāṇa* to "fly up" through the medial channel into the cranial vault;[63] and (3) *jālaṃdhara bandha* ("the lock of the net bearer"), a contraction of the throat by means of which the yogin seals off his head from his torso and constricts the network (*jāla*) of subtle channels and supports, thereby arresting the downward flow of nectar that has accumulated in the cranial vault.[64] The conjoined aim of the three *bandha*s is to gradually restrict the field in which the volatile breath, seed, and mind may move. First forcing them up out of the abdomen, they "lock" them into the torso; they next "contract" them inside the neck and head; and lastly, they "bind" them there.

The alchemical parallel to these hathayogic techniques is introduced by a verse from the *HYP*: "Instability is a natural characteristic of mercury and of the mind. When mercury is bound, when the mind is bound, who in this world does not become realized (*siddhyati*)?"[65] In alchemy per se, there are twenty-six *bandha*s which effect the binding (*bandhana*), fixation, or immobilization of mercury by altering its physical and chemical composition and behavior. Through the *bandha*s, mercury takes on the consistency of a gel, paste, or solid powder, in which states both its temperature of evaporation and its powers as a transmuting agent are augmented. Yoking the alchemical discipline to that of *haṭha yoga* is an evocative description of a general principle for the fixation of mercury: "In the midst of the Ganges and Yamuna rivers there is a *rākṣasa* named Application (*prayoga*). In his presence mercury is immediately bound." Here, Ganges and Yamuna stand for the bright and dark lunar fortnights, respectively, mediated by the full moon night. The nocturnal "application" in question consists of culling a number of powerful herbs which, on the full moon night, stabilize mercury.[66] Here again, we are reminded of the Work in two parts, as well as of the yogic immobilization of the breaths in the lunar and solar (Ganges and Yamuna) channels, which fill out the subtle moon located in the cranial vault.

The same cranial vault is the locus for another sort of bonding of yogic and alchemical method. Here we are referring to the technique known as *guṭikā bandha*, in which the yogin fixes a mercurial pill (*guṭikā*) in a recess of the palate as a means to catalyzing the effects of his yogic practices. This technique will be described at greater length in the next chapter.[67]

Apart from these specialized contexts, both the yogic and alchemical traditions employ metaphorical images of binding or snaring to describe the rigors of their respective and complementary tasks. So, for example, the *RA* (2.90) praises the *mantra* called *rasāṅkuśa*, the "elephant goad," in the following terms. "One who attempts to obtain mercury without knowledge of the elephant goad [*mantra*] is like one who attempts to mount an enraged elephant in the jungle without a goad. He is beset [with tribulations]." Similarly, in one of his *bānīs*, Gorakhnāth states that by immobilizing the breaths, one may bind (*bandhilai*) the elephant of the mind and bring it into its pen.[68] As we have already seen, the fixing of mercury is also referred to as the clipping of its wings (*pakṣaccheda*), by which it is prevented from volatizing and "flying upwards" (evaporating). Similarly, in yogic practice, it is crucial that the "cosmic goose" (*haṃsa*) of the breaths and vital energy be tethered so as not to leave the body.[69]

In India, all of these images—of binding, ensnaring, tethering, and the like—are as old as sympathetic magic and sorcery itself. As far back as the *Ṛg Veda*, we meet gods like Indra who, through the use of magical, invisible cords, defeat their demonic enemies in battle. Indra's greatest victory is won when he "envelops the enveloper," the archdemon Vṛtra (the "Enveloper"), who has trapped the world in his coils of drought and darkness. Once the binder has been bound, the entire universe is set free, released from its bondage.[70] Indra's feat is reproduced, with variations, by Gorakhnāth, who, according to a relatively late Nepali myth, binds nine "serpent clouds." This provokes a drought which only ends when his guru Matsyendranāth comes to Nepal from Assam, and Gorakh rises to salute him.[71]

In the case of the Vedic and post-Vedic Indra, this god seemingly saves the world in order to ensnare it in his own magical web, for Indra's net of magic (*indrajāla*) is also a veil of *māyā* for those lacking the insight to discern, behind a world of appearances, what is really real. All of the gods, in fact, impose their *māyā* upon the world, if only to differentiate themselves from humans who, were they to penetrate the ultimate reality behind the phenomenal worlds, might otherwise stop offering them sacrifices. In more philosophical terms,

> the chief cause of [the individual soul's] bondage in the objective world is . . . Māyā, usually considered to be an aspect of the God(dess)'s eternal Śakti. It finds itself . . . in the traditional series of categories. The Māyā is that power by which the Supreme Being veils itself, so that the *jīva* [the individual soul], enveloped by ignorance

> about its true cosmic nature, falls into the state of an individual subject with limited knowledge. This means that the nature of Māyā is twofold: limitative and dispersive.[72]

Ropes and knots; binding, loosing, and cutting; it is in these terms that India has perennially portrayed the conundrum of existence. Creatures (*paśus*) are bound to a phenomenal world that is a tightly stitched net of magic or a veil of *māyā;* and when this life ends, it is the noose (*pāśa*) carried by Death himself that ensnares them. In such a world of bondage, what term could better describe liberation and salvation than *mokṣa*—which precisely means the loosing or releasing of the knots and webs and snares that fetter all of creation?[73]

Māyā need not, however, be viewed as a net of illusion spread to obscure the numinous absolute. It can also be seen as the self-actualization of the divine creative impulse, as the "measuring out" (*mā*) or manifestation of pure consciousness, which is free to bind itself if it so chooses. In this, the tantric perspective, the phenomenal world, rather than being a straitjacket to the soul, becomes a field of play for the realized (*siddha*) individual. By extension, it is no longer *mokṣa* or release from conditioned existence that is the Siddha's goal, but rather liberation in the body (*jīvanmukti*), in which the individual experiences the world, for himself, in the same way as does the divine absolute.[74] Once one enters into the universe of the Siddhas, the veil of *māyā* becomes as if turned in on itself. How does one escape the trammels of existence? By binding the bondsman, cutting the cords, burning the burner—and even consuming Death, the great Eater. Once bound, normally volatile mercury and breath afford normally earthbound humans the power of flight. The medial channel, when opened, becomes "the eater of Death," and the upward surge of energy that courses through it cuts through the three knots (called *granthis*) which are the sole remaining obstacles to the yogin's immortality and freedom.[75] When the flighty gazelle of the mind is at last snared in net of the unstruck sound, individual consciousness becomes dissolved in the pure universal consciousness of the divine.[76]

The Siddha not only transcends the laws of nature, he also breaks out of the bonds of the human condition: "the yogin is unbindable (*abādhya*) by any incarnate creature. He can neither be bound by [the noose of] Death, nor by *karma*." "The great binding (*mahābandha*) [affords] release (*vimocana*) from the noose of death (*kālapāśa*)."[77] Like the god Indra of yore, the yogin or alchemist binds in order to be released from bondage; now, however, rather than doing battle with enemies from without, he is able to domesticate Death, time, illusion—nay, human finitude—without ever having to leave the inner landscape of his subtle body.

Herein lies the critical importance of the yogic and alchemical *bandhas*: they bind the mechanism of bondage itself, hobbling, binding with its own noose a Time (Kāla) which is identified with death (*kāla*) before actually turning it back on itself. None of the trammels of existence can fetter the Siddha at play in the world, least of all the ultimate sorrow, the sorrow of death. For whenever Death tries to catch a Siddha in his noose, the latter either slips away, thus cheating Death ("skewing time": *kālavañcana*)[78] or actually beats him up. This is a theme found in the legend of Gopīcand, in which Hāḍipā (Jālandharanāth), upon learning that his young disciple has been taken by Yama's minions to the world of the dead, thrashes them and their master so thoroughly that they promise to never meddle with the Nāth Siddhas again.[79] Mayanā, Gopīcand's sorceress mother, following her initiation by Gorakhnāth, holds similar powers over Yama: "If she should die in the day-time, he [Gorakh] would not let the sun go, but would bind him down,—if she should die at home, he would not let Yama go, but bind him down,—if she should die of a cut from a flat sword (*khā'ā* = a large sacrificial knife), he would bind the goddess Caṇḍī [who bears such a weapon] down—Mayanā would [out-]survive even the sun and the moon."[80]

In a later episode of the same legend cycle, Gopīcand has Hāḍipā bound in chains and buried beneath a stable (or at the bottom of a well), under several feet of horse manure. These Hāḍipā tears away by means of a single *mantra*. The chain on his hand becomes transformed into a rosary of beads; the heavy stone placed upon his chest becomes his yogic garb; and the rope with which he was bound becomes his loincloth.[81]

The regalia and sectarian markings worn by the Nāth Siddhas are, in fact, all explicitly symbolic of those various elements of their yogic practice which afford them their fabled mastery over the processes of aging and death. As such, they constitute a mesocosm, a model of and for the microcosm of the subtle body and the macrocosm of the universe. In the words of Bhartṛhari, "the form of the Jog [*yoga*] is the ear-ring, the patched quilt, the wallet, the staff and the horn, the sound of which is emitted in the Universe."[82] Here, the horn is the *siṅgnād*, a piece of gazelle horn into which the Nāth Siddhas blow to produce the *nāda*, the silent sound that serves to bind and control the wavering mind.[83] In the legend of Hāḍipā, the *japamālā* is a rosary of *rudrākṣa* beads used as an aid in mantric recitation; the *mudrā*s are great hoop earrings which, placed in the thick of the ears at initiation, open a subtle channel vital to yogic practice; and the *kantha* is the patchwork tunic traditionally worn by the Nāth Siddhas.[84]

c. *Māraṇa*

Since at least the time of the epics, the final of the four idealized stages of life observed by males in India has been termed *sannyāsa*, because it is marked by the act of "laying together" the sacrificial fires that had defined one's social existence. Abandoning one's sacrificial fires is tantamount to abandoning the world: henceforth, although one remains in the world, one is no longer a part of it.

Of vital importance to the yogic tradition is the fact that the sacrificial fires in question are gathered together within one's body. There, they serve both as a cremation pyre—by which the now-obsolete mundane, social body is shown to have truly died to the world—and, in the postcrematory existence of the *sannyāsin* (the "renouncer"), as the seat of sacrifice, which has now been internalized. It is here, in the inner fires of *tapas*, which fuel the offerings of one's vital breaths in the inner sacrifice known as the *prāṇāgnihotra*, that the practice of yoga very likely had its theoretical origins.[85]

In the experience of the renouncer, the internal processes of yoga do nothing less than sustain him in a life beyond death. It is to this notion that the *HYP* passage we evoked at the beginning of this section alludes: "killed, *rasa*, like breath, revives itself."[86] It is through this paradoxical process that the *haṭha yogin* and alchemist ultimately realize the bodily immortality that is the final end of their practice. The language both traditions employ to describe this process, through which the practitioner, once "slain" (*mṛta*), is able to revive himself by tricking, even killing Death, carries us to the very heart of Siddha mysticism: you have to first die to become immortal. This is the import of one of Gorakhnāth's most celebrated *bānī*s: "Die yogi die, dying is sweet [when you] die that death by which Gorakh, in dying, gained his vision [of the Absolute, immortality]."[87] An alchemical echo is provided in the *Padmāvat*: "The Siddha's immortal body is like mercury. You can break it down, you can kill it, but you can't make it die."[88]

What is it that dies? It is the gross body, a husk that is to be cast off like the slough of a snake. How is this body made to die, in order that the golden, adamantine, or *siddha* body may emerge? As in the processes discussed above, breath control plays an important role here. So too, however, does the generation of yogic heat, of the fire of yoga (*yogāgni*) that burns up the fire of time or death (*kālāgni*). In the former case, it is once again the two peripheral *nāḍī*s whose emptying is likened to a death that generates new life (the filling of the *suṣumṇā*). In the seal called the *mahāvedha* (the "great penetration"), "the breath, overflowing the two *puṭa*s . . . quickly bursts [into the medial channel]. The union (*sambandha*) of moon, sun, and fire which is to occur surely results in immortality. *When the death-like state* (mṛtāvasthā) *arises, how can there be fear of death?*"[89]

Passing through a state of death to bodily immortality is most especially effected through the mediation of fire—here, the inner fire in which the renouncer has immolated his mundane body once he has "laid together" his sacrificial fires. This image is carried over into the hathayogic system, in which the fires of yoga (also called the fire of the absolute, the *brahmāgni*), kindled at the base of the subtle body, renders the medial channel a "cremation ground" (*śmaśāna*).[90] The hallmark of any cremation ground is, of course, its ashes, and it is with ashes that every Śaiva renouncer, from time immemorial, has smeared his body. Internal fires and external ashes are brought together, in the hathayogic context, in two variations on the *vajrolī mudrā*, called the *sahajolī* and *amarolī mudrā*s. In the former, the partners smear their bodies with a mixture of cow-dung ash and water following *vajrolī;* in the latter it is a mixture of "the nectar that flows from the moon" and ash that one smears over one's body.[91] What are the implications of this externalization of an internal process, this wearing of one's yoga on one's sleeve? The answer to this question is quite nearly as old as the Veda itself.

5. Ashes to Nectar

I have already mentioned the primacy given by the *RA* to the eating of killed or oxidized mercury (*mṛtasūtaka*, also called "dead ash," *mṛtabhasma*) for realizing immortality.[92] I have further alluded to the process of digestion (*jāraṇa*) by which such is obtained and to the fabulous properties possessed by said mercury. "Killed" mercury, itself "unresurrectable" (*nir-uttha*)—that is, incapable of returning to its prior, native state—is now capable of reviving other "killed" metals.[93] What is it that makes *rasa* in its ashen (*bhasmībhūta*) state the most optimum form of mercury, both for transmutation and transubstantiation?

Throughout this book, we have emphasized the complementarity of the three primal sacrificial elements of fire, fluid, and air and of their homologues in the bodily microcosm and the alchemical mesocosm. But what happens when these essences, these *doṣa*s, these *guṇa*s, actually combine? What is the composite or compound that is produced? Since the time of the Vedas, the ringing answer to this question has been *ashes.*[94]

Here, we should note a certain symmetry between the *rasa* of Vedic sacrifice and the *rasa* of alchemical practice. In the former case, the raw material of the sacrificial oblation has no true ontic being until it has been cooked, refined, transformed, through exposure to fire. In this context, every natural and cultural process becomes a matter of cooking: in the aging process, one is said to be "cooked by time."[95] Elsewhere, the advance into the Indian subcontinent by Vedic culture was led by Agni, the sacrificial fire that was carried in a firepot, at the vanguard of "civilization"; it is this same sacrificial fire that restores and perfects (*saṃskṛ*) the *rasa* of Prajāpati that flowed from him to create the world. So too, initiation, cremation, and the passage into the renunciant stage of life are all so many cases of cooking "to a turn" that which would otherwise remain unaltered, in a raw, untamed, undomesticated, even uncivilized form.[96] Thus the prince-turned-yogi Gopīcand can state, "I used to be an unfired pot, thrown whichever way [the wheel] turned. When I was made a Jogī my *guru* did the firing."[97]

In the exemplary cooking process that is the sacrifice, the most subtle remainder of the process of combustion, beyond the cooked "leftovers" consumed by humans and the smoke and aroma of the cooked offering enjoyed by the gods, are ashes, *bhasma[n]* (from *bhas,* "consume," but also "shine"). Ashes are the shining remains of what has been consumed; they are the solid essence of the combustion of fluid oblation by purificatory fire. As such, ash is *rasa* in its optimal form—which is exactly what the alchemical tradition tells us in its myth of the origin of mercury (*rasa*). Its original cosmic matter being concealed by the "accidents" (*kañcuka*s) of its outward form, native mercury cannot, in and of itself, afford immortality. It is only after these superfluous accretions have been dispersed, by reducing mercury to ashes through the alchemical *saṃskāra*s, that its inherent basic properties can be actualized. Ash, *bhasma,* is the supreme manifestation of primal matter. It therefore follows that the reduction of mercury, the *rasa* of the absolute, to ash is tantamount to the recovery of a primordial perfection, of the absolute before its fall into nature, into manifestation. Preternatural (prior to nature) its powers are therefore supernatural (transcending nature). At the same time they are, in a cyclic universe, a reminder of the ultimate destiny of the universe when all things will be reduced to dross (the serpent Śeṣa, "Remains," whose body is composed of ash) and only the pure gold remain.[98] Herein lies the root of the Hindu calcinatory gnosis.

It is in the context of early Śaivism that a true "cult" of ashes first becomes incorporated into the Hindu tradition. Ashes, called either *bhasma* or *vibhūti* ("omnipresent," a term synonymous with *siddhi*, or the eight *siddhis* taken as an aggregate), have since at least the time of the Pāśupatas been integral to Śaiva initiation and worship. Initiation involves bathing in ashes (*bhasma-snāna*), while the worship of Bhairava entails smearing cowdung ash on the forehead—in place of the normal blood-red *sindūra*—as well as consuming a pinch of said ash.[99]

In so doing, humans are, of course, merely imitating the supreme god himself, whose own dark body is made luminous by the patina of iridescent ashes with which he besmears himself and the stuff of whose body is in fact ashen. Tradition in fact holds that Śiva first took to wearing ashes following his incineration of Kāma, the Hindu Eros, in an irrefutable proof that the fires of yoga (*yogāgni*) were greater than those of burning passion (*kāmāgni*). Unmoved after having been pierced by Kāma's arrows of lust, Śiva opened his third eye—located at the level of the *ājñā cakra*—and, with the supernatural accumulation of thermal energy that his yoga had afforded him, reduced Love's body to ashes. The fire that burned Kāma was at once the sublimate of Śiva's *rasa* (for Śiva, as a yogin, is *ūrddhvaretas*), his yogic breaths, and the heat of his yogic austerities. The refined essence of these three elements—ashes—were taken by Śiva and smeared over his body together (as we are told in one version of the myth) with mercury, said to be the concrete form taken by his agitation at the sight of Pārvatī in this myth.[100]

In another myth, Śiva shows his superiority over a human ascetic named Maṅkanaka when the latter, having pierced his skin, "bleeds" pure vegetable sap (*śākarasa*). He then dances for joy, proclaiming that his austerities have been successful (*siddha*). When Śiva does likewise, and bleeds pure, snowy-white *bhasma*, the chastened ascetic is obliged to acknowledge the great god's supremacy.[101] Elsewhere, a myth from the *RA* (11.158–61) relates how the demon Ruru, having eaten a *pala* of twelve-times-calcinated mercurial ash (*bhasmasūtaka*), uproots the earth and pulverizes Śiva's Mount Kailash. Śiva "kills" mercury in combination with lead and red arsenic, smears this amalgam on the tips of his trident, and laminates Ruru.

This parallelism, between ash and *rasa*, is explained, in what may be termed a "theology of ashes," at the conclusion of the important myth of Śiva in the Pine Forest. Here, after the phallic god has brought a group of uncomprehending Vedic sages to heel, he explains to them the importance of ashes.

> I am Agni joined with Soma . . . The supreme purification of the universe is to be accomplished with ashes; I fortify my seed with ashes and sprinkle creatures with it . . . By means of ashes, my seed, one is released from all sin . . . Ashes are known as my seed, and I bear my own seed upon my body . . . Let a man smear his body until it is pale with ashes . . . Then he attains the status of Lord of the Host (*gāṇapatyam*) . . . and grasps the supreme ambrosia.[102]

Śiva's subsequent initiation of the Vedic sages culminates in an ashen bath, a *bhasma-snāna*, after the model of Pāśupata initiation rites. The role of ashes in initiation has a much more ancient pedigree, however, as attested in an important myth from the *Mahābhārata*. This is the epic myth of Kāvya Uśanas and his disciple Kaca, a myth which, while it bears a number of common themes with an Indo-Iranian myth, is nonetheless Hindu in the detail that concerns us.[103] Here, Kaca, the son of Bṛhaspati, the chaplain of the gods (and grandson of Aṅgiras, "Ember"), has been sent to Kāvya Uśanas, the chaplain of the Asuras, the antigods, to wrest the secret of immortality from him. Through a number of plot twists, Kaca not only becomes the disciple (for five hundred years) of Kāvya Uśanas, but also the beloved of the latter's daughter, Devayānī. He is hated and feared, however, by the antigods, who see him, quite rightly, as an enemy agent. They therefore kill and feed the boy to wolves, only to see him revived when Kāvya Uśanas pronounces his immortality formula over the boy's scattered remains. The formula once pronounced, the boy bursts out of the bodies of the wolves, killing them as he himself is reconstituted.

The antigods then kill the boy again, but this time they burn his body and place the ashes in Kāvya Uśanas's evening cordial. When the guru calls out to his disciple, the boy answers him from within his belly. Now the only way to save Kaca is to reveal to him the secret of immortality, such that Kaca, once he has been revived by bursting out of Kāvya Uśanas's body, might revive his guru in turn. When Devayānī says, "Do it, Daddy," Kāvya Uśanas has to give in and so initiates his disciple into the secret of immortality. When the formula is spoken, the boy bursts "like a full moon" out of his guru's body; he then revives his guru.

This myth, which brings together the consumption of ashes, the transmission of a secret of immortality, and initiation, also seems to be the prototype for myths of tantric transmission, in which the guru becomes the disciple of his disciple, and the disciple the guru of his guru. It is, as well, a humanization of the myths of the great gods Agni and Prajāpati and an alloform of the legend of Gorakh and his guru Matsyendra. As such, it may well be, as Georges Dumézil maintains, that "within the corporate body of sorcerers, the disciple is just as important as his master as concerns the continued transmission of the . . . supernatural knowledge that is its commonwealth and its justification. Each needs the other."[104]

In this particular myth, Kaca's initiation further serves to render him Kāvya Uśanas's "biological" son. As such, he is, in a sense, Śiva's grandson, given that Kāvya Uśanas himself once entered into the body of Śiva, from which he exited in the form of a figure named Śukra ("Semen") as the result of that god's yogic powers of digestion.[105] Kāvya Uśanas's legacy lives on in medieval alchemical—as well as certain modern medical—traditions, in which the perfected alchemist is called a *kavi* (an alchemical wizard) and the Bengali Ayurvedic physician a *kavirāj*. The successful alchemist is a *kavi* because he, like the asura Kāvya Uśanas (Uśanas, son of a *kavi*), is capable, through his poetic incantations and mystic knowledge, to bend nature to his will and thereby realize wealth, invincibility, and immortality for himself.[106]

The symbolic use of ashes by Śaiva sectarians has become greatly expanded since the age of the initiatory practices we have outlined to this point. So it is that the cremation ground, upon which human corpses are summarily reduced to ashes, was long the preferred haunt of tāntrikas who, in their drug- or austerity-induced trances, saw and danced with the wild and fulminating Kālī and Bhairava. The infernal dance of this divine pair is purificatory, serving as it does to burn away the decaying matter of a dying cosmos—both within themselves, in the bodies consumed there, and in the universal conflagration for which the burning ground is a mesocosm—for it is only when an ash-smeared Śiva incinerates the universe with his ecstatic dance that universal liberation becomes possible.

A body of devotional practices offered, in coastal Andhra Pradesh, to the terrible Śaiva divinity Vīrabhadra, constitutes yet another practical extension of the Śaiva theology of ashes. Here, the "growing" bodies of "ash fruits," formed of a mixture of cow-dung ash and acacia gum, are at once ritual reminders of the postmortem life of the dead, the "fruits" of *karma*, and manifestations of the expansive power of *vibhūti*, which is homologized with semen, blood, and bone in this tradition. These "ash fruits" are called *piṇḍa*s, "balls," which is the same term as is employed for the rice balls offered to the deceased in Hindu funerary rites, for aniconic stone monuments to the dead which go back to the dawn of human civilization, for the embryo in the womb (all signified by the Marathi *piṇḍ*), as well as the Śiva *liṅga* (Marathi *piṇḍī*), the head as sacrificial offering or, conversely, the human torso or body as a whole.[107] It is this final usage of the term *piṇḍ* that is most common among the Nāth Siddhas. The human body is a *piṇḍ*, a "ball," which can be transformed, through initiation, yoga, and alchemy, into an immortal body. In the last chapter, I noted another usage of this minimalist definition of the body as a sphere or globe: this was the suffix *-oli* found in such terms as *garbholi* (the round fetus in the womb), a term that may bear some connection with the Hindi term for hailstone, *olī*. Elsewhere, the insignia of the Nāgā *akhāḍā*s (whose close relationship to the Nāth Siddha orders has been noted) are nothing other than globes (*golā*s) of ash;[108] and the pills of mercurial ash which, held in the mouth, cause a wholly subtle and immortal alchemical body to emerge out of the husk of the gross, biological body are called *gulikā* (or *guṭikā*s), "globules."[109] According to Siddha logic, these are the wombs from which new life will emerge: ashen globules engender immortal globes.

This leitmotif of Siddha theory and practice is epitomized in the legend of the birth of Kāyānāth ("Body-Nāth"), a figure who likely lived in the seventeenth century, in the Jhelum district of present-day Pakistan, historically one of the most important centers of the Nāth *sampradāya*.[110]

> One day, Gorakhnāth held a great feast for his fellow yogins. When the food had been dished out on leaf plates, the place of honor was given to Gorakhnāth's venerable disciple Ratannāth. As fate would have it, there were two plates of food lying before Ratannāth when he sat down. After eating the food from the first plate, Ratannāth then stood before the second plate. Having pronounced a *mantra*, he then caused ashes to flow from his body, after the fashion of Śiva. These he fashioned into a ball, which he placed before the second plate of food. He then announced that that ball of ashes would eat the food sitting in front of it. The other yogins, who had begun to laugh, were quickly silenced when they saw that Ratannāth's yogic energy was causing the ball of ashes to expand. The ball then split open and a laughing, fully-formed boy emerged from it and set about eating the food on the plate before him. It was then decided that this boy should be given a name and initiation into the Nāth order. Gor-

akh named the boy Kāyānāth, son of Ratannāth; and Vicārnāth initiated him. Kāyānāth later became the abbot of the Bhera monastery, performed many miracles, and lived to the age of 101 years before quitting his body.[111]

While the account of Kāyānāth's birth constitutes the richest example of the symbolic use of ashes by the Nāth Siddhas, it is by no means the earliest such legend. No less a figure than Gorakhnāth himself is the product of a similar manipulation of ashes. In a legend known throughout northern India and Nepal, Gorakhnāth is himself the product of ashes and cow dung—whence his name Go-rakh ("Cow-Ash"). As the story goes, a brahmin woman who desires a son is given a pinch of ash by Matsyendra, who instructs her to eat it together with milk, following her purificatory bath after her next menses. Instead of eating the ash, she throws it onto a heap of cow dung behind her hut. Twelve years later, Matsyendra returns and asks for news of his son. When the woman avows that she had discarded the ash, Matsyendra scoops away twelve years of accumulated cow dung to reveal a perfect twelve-year-old child yogin—for the boy has been practicing his *sādhana*s there since birth—whom he names Gorakh and makes his disciple.[112]

Gorakh's ashen dunghill, both a womb (like the wells in which Nāth Siddhas of legend meditated for twelve years) and a tumulus (like the *samādhi*s under which Nāth Siddhas are buried), has its most significant structural parallel in what is perhaps that sect's most important external attribute. This is the *dhūnī* (from *dhū*, "waft") a conical pile of wood ash and cow-dung ash which the wandering yogin heaps up wherever he alights. Its fire warms him, its coals serve to light his chillum pipe, and its ash is both the present or grace (*prasāda*) he bestows upon all who come to visit him and the substance with which he smears his own body in imitation of Śiva.[113] More than a rough and ready hearth, the *dhūnī* is, quite literally, a double of the yogin's subtle body, a body that has already been cooked and transformed through his yogic austerities. The ashes of the *dhūnī* represent the continuity of his unending *sādhana*s and thereby of his immortal subtle body. Long after a yogin has quit his mundane body, his *dhūnī* (maintained and kept burning, in some cases, for centuries), like his *samādhi*, remains as a memorial and testimony to his continuing presence in the world. India is a country dotted with the *samādhi*s and *dhūni*s of its great yogins, whose eternal essence is epitomized through ashes.[114] This is an identification that is borne out in a great number of Nāth legends, which we now pass in review.

Just as his divine guru Śiva had done to him upon his own initiation, Matsyendra, after he has exhumed Gorakh, initiates him with a bath of ashes. Gorakh does the same to his disciples, first "creating" them from ashes and then initiating them with more of the same. The Nāth Siddhas, and Gorakh in particular, are great yogic progenitors, fecundating women with their yogic "seed," which they carry in their wallets (*jholī*) in the form of rice grains, barleycorns, ashes, or water in which their loincloth has been washed. A number of Gorakh's illustrious disciples, including Gūgā Pīr and Carpaṭi, are conceived and born in this way.[115]

Like calcinated mercury, the ashes of a Nāth Siddha are capable of transforming matter in a myriad of other ways. In the legend of Pūraṇ Bhagat, Gorakh turns bullocks into men and women into asses with ashes; with ashes he dries up wells and causes a garden to burst into bloom. In the legend of Gūgā Pīr, Gorakh creates gemstones and caters a wedding with ashes. Pavannāth enriches an old brahmin couple with a gift of ashes that transforms their poverty into wealth. With ashes from his *dhūnī*, Maṇiknāth flattens a wall.[116] Another Nāth Siddha tradition relates the creation of the earth from ashes from the *dhūnī* of the Goddess Śakti. When Śiva promises to marry her, Śakti gives Śiva two handfuls of ash from her *dhūnī*: when these ashes are strewn upon the waters, the earth is created. In a similar account, Viṣṇu creates the earth with ashes from Gorakh's *dhūnī*.

Yet, it is also ashes to which the universe will return, and these are the ashes that form the body of the cosmic serpent Śeṣa. But Śeṣa is also a venomous serpent, whose fiery breath itself reduces all matter to ashes.[117] As such, he is like Śiva who, possessed of an ashen body and wearing ashes on his yogic body, also reduces all matter to ashes in the universal dissolution—a dissolution dramatized in his incineration of Kāma with the yogic fire he emitted from his third eye. Śiva's creative semen becomes destructive when it has become transformed, yogically, through the raising of the internal *kuṇḍalinī* serpent, into fire; yet it is also by virtue of his yogic practice that he is immune to the calcinating poison spat by the great serpent Vāsuki, which, when he drinks it in the myth of the churning of the Ocean of Milk, turns his throat blue.

The symmetry that emerges out of this data parallels that of the discourse of binding and piercing: just as the Siddha, by virtue of has having bound and pierced the volatile elements of his alchemical body, himself becomes unbindable and impenetrable and all-binding and all-penetrating; so the same Siddha, by virtue of having calcinated and reduced his alchemical body to ashes, himself becomes uncalcinable and all-calcinating, an ashen, ash-smeared, ash-producing, alchemical touchstone.

6. Reversal and Transformation

Our discussion of the transformative powers of the ashes of death has carried us somewhat far afield of our survey of the serial progression of the alchemical operations in their relationship to the theory and practice of *haṭha yoga*. In order that we might return to this progression, let us recall here that while swooning (*mūrcchana*), the third alchemical *saṃskāra*, is a prelude to the powerful and transformative operations of binding (*bandhana*) and killing (*māraṇa*), it also precedes *saṃskāra*s four through eighteen, as those operations are described in the alchemical sources.

With *saṃskāra*s four through eight, we find ourselves in the presence of what appears to be a series of priming techniques not unlike those of yogic *prāṇāyāma* or the alternating ascent and descent of the *kuṇḍalinī*. Following its swooning, mercury is first resurrected (*utthāpana*), after which it is made to fall (*pātana*). Next, it is awakened (*bodhana*) or suppressed (*rodhana*), then restrained (*niyamana*), and lastly kindled (*dīpana*).

As in alchemy, *utthāpana* is a term employed in hathayogic discourse to designate an important "phase change." The *kuṇḍalinī*, when she is awakened from her sleep, rises up (*ut-thā*) along the length of the medial channel. Because the raising of the *kuṇḍalinī* is a repeated practice, she quite naturally falls down again (*pat*) to the base of the subtle body after the yogin has reemerged from his state of yogic withdrawal. As shown in the last chapter, the *kuṇḍalinī* can be made to fall or fly upwards as well, after the fashion of the alchemical *pātana* apparatus.[118] The experienced yogin may, of course, raise and lower his vital breath, energy, seed, and consciousness at will, which translates into so many withdrawals from and returns to mundane consciousness. When he finally chooses to opt out of mundane existence altogether, he definitively halts the downward flow and enters into *samādhi*.

More common than the term *utthāpana* in hathayogic parlance is the term *bodhana*, the awakening of the *kuṇḍalinī*.[119] Now, it happens that alchemical sources alternate between the terms *bodhana* and *rodhana* to designate this sixth operation, in which wholly stabilized mercury is naturally activated through combination with female sulfur. The same alternation is found in the *Kaulāvalīnirṇaya*, a sixteenth-century ritual compilation, which terms the *bindu* of the subtle body, located above the sixth, the *ājñā cakra*, as either Bodhinī ("she who awakens") or Rodhinī ("she who obstructs").

In order to understand this terminology, we must recall that the emanation of the Kaula universe is, on the microcosmic level, phonematic as well as material. All that exists is ultimately acoustic, vibratory in nature, an emanate or devolute of the primeval sonic vibration that gave rise to all creation, the mantra *Oṃ*. When projected upon the subtle body, this acoustic emanation takes the form of the fifty-one phonemes (*mātṛkā*s, "matrices" of subtle sound) of the Sanskrit alphabet, which are situated on the petals of the *cakra*s (styled as lotuses) of the subtle body. When the yogin raises the inner *kuṇḍalinī*, he is in effect telescoping these phonemes back into their higher emanates, causing the last and "lowest" phonemes, the final letters of the alphabet, to be absorbed into ever more subtle phonemes, culminating in the vowels and the phonemes *ha* and *kṣa*. These two ultimate phonemes are located on the two petals of the sixth *cakra*, the *ājñā*, which is situated behind the meeting point of the two eyebrows. The hierarchy of sound does not end here, however, since manifest sound is but the emanate of a subtler, nonmanifest vibration. Beyond the *ājñā*, therefore, exist a number of levels of increasingly subtle substrates of sound, through which manifest sound is made to shade into nonmanifest sound. These shadings, located, in the subtle body, between the *ājñā* and the crown of the head (or even beyond, i.e., outside the contours of the body, in a number of systems), generally include *nāda* (resonance), *bindu* (drop), and *bīja* (seed).[120]

This brings us back to the *bodhinī/rodhinī* alternation, which presumably occurs because the mundane mind (*manas*) becomes obstructed, held back at this point in tantric meditation: but this suppression (*rodhana*) of the fickle mind is nothing other than the first awakening (*bodhana*) of divine consciousness.[121] The hathayogic use of the latter term has been described: after a period of sleep, the *kuṇḍalinī* awakens to rise along the medial channel and thereby transform the yogin's body and being. The former is also an important term in the yogic practice of the Krama Kaula, in which *rodhana* designates "coagulation." When the yogin penetrates the void, he falls prey to the residues of prior thoughts, acts, events, and impressions. The yogin coagulates (*rodhana*) these residues into a single mass which he then melts down or liquidates (*dravaṇa*) through meditation on the circle of Kālīs. Through successive coagulations and liquifications these are ultimately annihilated, permitting the mystic to penetrate the ineffable void.[122] With this, there comes the dawning of the light of pure consciousness, a possible parallel to the eighth alchemical operation, *dīpana*.

While most of the parallels between these four preparatory alchemical *saṃskāra*s on the one hand and yogic and tantric precept and practice on the other are nonexplicit and tenuous at best, we find ourselves on firmer ground in the case of *jāraṇa*, the thirteenth *saṃskāra*. *Jāraṇa*, it will be recalled, consists of the stadial consumption or digestion of ever-increasing quantities of mica or sulfur by mercury, until said mercury becomes bound (*baddha*) or killed (*mṛta*).[123] This is a progressive operation, in which mercury, by taking increasingly large mouthfuls (*grāsa*) of mica, in six successive operations, becomes calcinated. At each stage in this process, the mercury in question becomes physically altered: in the first stage, in which it consumes one sixty-fourth of its mass of mica, mercury becomes rodlike (*daṇḍa*[*vat*]). It next takes on the consistency of a leech, then that of crow droppings, whey, and butter. With its sixth and final "mouthful," in which mercury swallows one-half its mass of mica, it becomes a spherical solid.[124]

This six-step process, by which mercury is bound, is followed by another six-step process, in which the proportions of mica or sulfur swallowed by mercury greatly increase. It is this latter process that constitutes *jāraṇa* proper. After praying to Lord Śiva that he "swallow my mouthful,"[125] the alchemist causes mercury to absorb a mass of mica equal to its own. Next, mercury is made to swallow twice its mass of mica, and so on until the proportions ultimately reach 1:6, with mercury absorbing six times its mass of mica. In this final and optimal phase mercury, said to be "six-times killed," is possessed of fantastic powers of transmutation.[126] More superior yet is a sequence called *khecari jāraṇa*, in which mercury is made to absorb vast quantities of powdered gemstones, the densest substances known to man. At the conclusion of this process, mercury takes the shape of a *liṅga*. The alchemist who ingests said mercury is immediately transported to the realms of the gods, Siddhas, and Vidyādharas.[127] Modern researchers in *rasa śāstra* lament the fact that a certain step in the technique of *jāraṇa* has been lost, and with it the ability to transmute base metals into gold and afford immortality and eternal youth.[128]

We may adduce three hathayogic parallels to alchemical *jāraṇa*, i.e., absorption or digestion. The first and most obvious of these is the six-stage process of the piercing of the *cakra*s. When the yogin raises his seed, breath, and energy through the six *cakra*s, he does nothing less than effect the reabsorption, on a microcosmic level, of the five sense-capacities, action-capacities, and subtle and gross elements back into their ethereal essence. So it is that the element earth, predominant in the lowest *cakra*, the *mūlādhāra*, becomes absorbed into the element water at the level of the second *cakra*, the *svādhiṣṭhāna*. Water is absorbed back into fire at the third *cakra*, the *maṇipura;* fire into air at the fourth, or *anāhata cakra;* and air into ether at the fifth *cakra*, the *viśuddhi*. All are telescoped, swallowed back, into the mind (*manas*) which, identified with the sixth *cakra*, the *ājñā*, will, in the final phases of this process, itself be absorbed into its source and essence, the pure Śiva-consciousness located in the thousand-petaled *cakra* of the cranial vault.

This process is said, in a *bānī* of Gorakhnāth, to effect the absorption or digestion (*jaranā*) of the celibate yogin's seed back into its ambrosial essence, by which he himself is rendered immortal. He who is unable to retain his seed, however, is condemned to death.[129] As we have already shown, it is not semen alone that is raised and transformed through the six-stage piercing of the *cakras*. The rise of the *kuṇḍalinī* is also a telescoping of sound back into its primal unmanifest substrate. It is this dynamic that grounds the practice of *mantra yoga*, the acoustic complement to the hydraulic techniques of *haṭha yoga*. This process, characterized by ever-deepening states of yogic absorption, is qualitatively measured in terms of the audition of increasingly subtle sounds (*nāda*).

An important turning point in this process, known as "reversing the *nāda*,"[130] occurs when the external voicing of *mantras* yields to the audition of unvoiced *mantras* called the "unstruck sound" (*anāhata nāda*).[131] So it is that as the yogin's consciousness is raised through the final phases of yogic practice, the *anāhata nāda*, which begins to reverberate at the level of the heart, undergoes a series of qualitative transformations, successively resounding like the roar of the ocean, of clouds, the sound of the kettledrum, conch, bell, horn, flute, lute, and finally, the buzzing of bees.[132] These transformations, to ever subtler levels of sound, effect the total absorption of the yogin's mind. Becoming one with its object of knowledge—i.e., the Śiva-consciousness that is the substrate of all sound and being—it becomes fused with this object of knowledge and telescoped, absorbed, dissolved into it.[133] These homologies, between *haṭha yoga*, *mantra yoga*, and alchemy, are seemingly taken for granted in a passage from the *HYP* (4.96), which states that "the mind is like mercury which, bound (*baddham*) and freed from its transitory nature through its assimilation (*jāraṇa*) of the sulfur of mantric vibration (*nāda*), wanders about in the ether."[134] A similar use of terminology may be found in the alchemical *RRS*, which designates the ultimate phase of alchemical *jāraṇa*, by which a mercurial compound is roasted in a *puṭa* with six times its mass of sulfur, as *sabīja-bandha* ("binding with seed").[135]

In addition to such qualitative measures of absorption as the inaudible sounds heard by the yogin in his practice, there also exists a set of quantitative measures of the same, which moreover appear to bear a direct relationship to an alchemical progression of a similar order. These are related to the *āsana*s, the yogic postures, through which the yogin not only immobilizes his body, but also his breath, seed, and mental activities.[136] Maintaining a yogic posture alone requires tremendous powers of concentration, and so we should not be surprised to find a quantitative measure of immobility combined with breath retention to be a yardstick for yogic integration. Here it is the four-second *mātra* ("measure of time") or *pala* (the equivalent of six *mātra*s, i.e., 24 seconds) that is of critical interest. As one retains a yogic posture and one's breath for an increasing number of *pala*s, ever-dilating durations of time, one acquires ever more fantastic *siddhi*s. After twenty-four years—i.e., $60 \times 24 \times 365 \times 24$ *pala*s, the highest multiple in this progression—of total yogic absorption, one outsurvives the universal dissolution, in which even the gods Brahmā, Viṣṇu, and Śiva perish.[137]

This notion of a "geometric progression" of a durational order has its alchemical parallel, in which the consumption of an increasing number of *pala*s ("straws," here a unit of weight equivalent to 82.624 grams) of mercury that has undergone the process of *jāraṇa* with mica yields a dilating life span, such that the consumption of ten *pala*s renders the alchemist a second Śiva.[138] When *rasa* and breath control constitute the Work in two parts, a time-mass continuum of this order is quite natural. The impacts of these two allied practices on the human body are also identical: one can neither be consumed by old age (*ajara*) nor by death (*amara*). We will discuss other important progressions of the same order in the next chapter.

7. The Legends of Gopīcand and Caurangināth: Alchemical Allegories?

According to legend, countless Nath Siddhas have closed themselves into wells or caves for twelve-year periods to emerge with transformed bodies; six months of yogic or alchemical austerities are said, in guides to hathayogic practice, to produce the same result.[139] Elsewhere, we have already seen how Dharamnāth was able to incinerate the (since then) lost city of Pattan and a good part of the Sind by simply remaining motionless, standing on his head atop a betel-nut or sopari stone for twelve years.[140]

There exist, however, a number of legends of the Nāth Siddhas in which yogic immobility is raised to a higher level than the mere retention of some fixed posture. These are the many accounts of dismemberment, inhumation, or exile that, in a sense, set the Nāth Siddhas apart from other yogic traditions. Shashibhushan Dasgupta refers to these in his discussion of the "general air of supernaturalism" proper to Nath Siddha traditions. Others, such as Eliade and Van Kooij, find in these accounts traces of the shamanic origins of Nāth Siddha practices.

While many of these feats—like those of the Taoist magicians and immortals in China—may indeed be typologized as shamanic, following the "morphology" of this phenomenon so beautifully developed by Mircea Eliade,[141] they also betray an alchemical stamp. Mercury and its compounds in flux are never anthropomorphized in the Indian alchemical texts (where they are either deified or zoomorphized) as they are in western alchemical traditions, in which the *corpus alchymicum* of the "Ethiopian" or "Son of God" is dismembered, crushed, cooked, etc. to be resuscitated in a new divine form. It is rather in the legends of the Nāth Siddhas that such allegorical dismemberments and tortures occur; and while the origins of these accounts may be as old as religion itself, the "gloss" they receive in Nāth Siddha mythology appears to be both alchemical and yogic.

Of all the legend cycles of the Nāth Siddhas, the song cycles concerning Gopīcand are the among the richest in this sort of imagery.[142] The outline of this legend is as follows: Mayanā[matī], the mother of Gopīcand and a "sorceress" disciple of Gorakh, loses her husband Maṇikcand to Yama (i.e., he dies). When she is unable to wrest her husband back from Death, she is "given" a son to replace him, as it were, by Gorakh. She learns, however, that her son will not survive his adolescence if he does not become a yogin. The intrigue of the cycle lies in the ends to which Mayanā goes to bring her son under the tutelage of a guru—who in this case is Hāḍi-pā, or Jālandharanāth.[143]

The origins of Jālandhara go back to the original cosmogony, as related in the Bengali *Gorakṣa Vijay* and *Mīn Cetan*. Out of a void (*śūnya*) there appears, like a bubble, the Egg of Brahman. The unmanifest Nirañjana then manifests itself as Ādinātha who, from his *tapas*, creates the goddess Ketakī,[144] out of whom arise, from her mouth, the god Brahmā; from her forehead, the god Viṣṇu; and from her *yoni*, the god Śiva. To test these three, Ādinātha takes the form of a decayed corpse, rotting in the wash of a river. Only Śiva is willing to perform Ādinātha's funeral rites: in so doing, he uses Viṣṇu as his firewood and Brahmā as his fire. From the burning corpse of Ādinātha arise the five original Nāth Siddhas: Mīna, from his navel, Gorakh from his matted hair, Jālandhara (Hāḍi-pā) from his bones (*hāḍa*), Kānha-pā (Kaṇerīnāth) from his ears (*kāṇa*), and Cauraṇgī from his limbs (*aṅga*). Śiva then takes Ādinātha's Ketakī as his consort: she becomes the goddess Gaurī. Gaurī then decides to test these four sons' (Cauraṅgī is left out of this episode) yogic constancy.[145] All fail except Gorakh, who looks upon her as his mother—and as a reward is "reborn," as his own son, from water wrung from his *karpaṭi* (loincloth) and drunk by the Goddess: this son is Carpaṭi. Matsyendra is cursed to be debauched by sixteen hundred women in the forest or kingdom of Kadalī; Kānha-pā is exiled to a country called Ḍāhuka; and Hāḍi-pā is turned into a low-caste sweeper (Hāḍi). Such is the mythic origin of Gopīcand's guru.

Mayanā learns that it is only by taking yogic initiation from a Hāḍi that Gopīcand can be saved. But the young prince appears to be more troubled by his sorceress mother and the prospect of exchanging his kingship for servitude to a sweeper than he is by the hearsay that he should otherwise die young. He therefore puts his mother through a series of terrible ordeals, which are so many tests of her yogic power:

> She was thrown into fire, but even her garment was not stained with smoke; she was drowned in water bound within a bag, but mother Gaṅgā herself came forward to welcome her into her [Gaṅgā's] bosom; she walked on a bridge made of hair; she walked on the edge of a razor; she was shut up for seven full days and nights within a boiler containing boiling oil, which was being heated from below constantly;[146] she crossed all the rivers in the boat made of the husk of a corn, but nothing could bring about her death, neither was any part of her body damaged in any way. Mayanā herself declared to her son Gopīcand, "By the practice of mystic knowledge one becomes immortal . . . just like the current of the tide-wave running backward . . . When the creation will sink below and finally dissolve, and the earth will be not and there will remain only all-pervading water, the sun and the moon will set forever and the whole universe will be destroyed—I shall float on for ever—I shall have no death."[147]

(As we shall see, the *RA*, in its concluding verses, promises just such an end for the Rasa Siddha who has perfected his craft: he will live on, above the terrible ocean of existence and beyond the cosmic dissolution, in the world of the divine Siddhas.)[148]

Gopīcand is eventually persuaded to become Hāḍi's disciple. In order to test his sincerity, however, Hāḍi sells him—for twelve cowries worth of cannabis—into bondage in the house of a sorceress named Hīrā (Diamond), in the "southern land," for twelve years. During this time, Hāḍi sits at the bottom of the sea, beneath fourteen fathoms of water. Hīrā transforms Gopīcand into a ram and later sends him to hell, which Hāḍi harrows to save him. At the end of this period, Hāḍi completes Gopīcand's initiation; then, judging that he has made improper use of his yogic powers, nullifies them. A furious Gopīcand has Hāḍi sealed, with horse dung, into the bottom of a well.

Twelve years later, Kānha-pā, also a disciple of Hāḍi, is informed by Gorakh that his guru has been buried in a well by Gopīcand. Kānha-pā, through a subterfuge, manages to exhume Hāḍi. Knowing that Hāḍi's accumulated yogic energy, to say nothing of his wrath at being buried in such a way by his disciple, might well destroy Gopīcand entirely, Kānha-pā makes three effigies of Gopīcand: one of iron, one of silver, and one of gold.[149] When Hāḍi is called up out of the well, his angry gaze reduces the three effigies to ashes. His fury sufficiently diffused at this point, Hāḍi is presented with the real Gopīcand, whose yogic powers he then restores.[150]

These themes, of dismemberment and restoration, and of twelve-year periods of forced meditation, are quite common to Nath Siddha legend. Gorakhnāth explains in a poem that he was born, after twelve years passed inside the womb of a barren woman, with both arms and legs cut off: the commentator to this passage glosses this as birth, through yoga, of a new body from which the net (arms and legs) of *māyā* has been cut away.[151] In another account, Gorakh awakens after twelve years of "death" (*mūvā*).[152] In still another legend, Gorakh hangs himself upside down from a tree over a raging fire, until the odor of his burning flesh attracts the attention of the god Brahmā, who grants him a boon.[153]

While still a novice, Gorakh plucks out the pupil of his eye, which he barters for food to feed his guru Matsyendra: Matsyendra restores his eye, through the use of a *mantra*.[154] This is, of course, the same Matsyendra whose own recumbent and lifeless body is diced up by Queen Kamalā, when he has entered into the body of her husband. Śiva has these pieces brought to his abode on Mount Kailash, where he safeguards them until Gorakh's return, twelve years later. Matsyendra's soul is then restored to his reconstituted body.[155] More often than reconstituting Matsyendra, however, Gorakh is busy dismembering Matsyendra's various sons—generally to awaken Matsyendra from his attachment to phenomenal existence. On one occasion it is Matsyendra's son Mīnā that Gorakh beats against a stone like a washerwoman until he is dead.[156] In another legend, Gorakh kills and skins Matsyendra's two sons Nemī and Pārśva—whose names are identical to those of two founders of the Jain religion—and later revives them.[157] Elsewhere, he transforms certain of his disciples such that one half of their bodies becomes gold and one half iron.[158]

These supernatural, fantastic, and clearly shamanic elements, a staple of Nāth Siddha legend, are nowhere as evident as in the best known and perhaps the oldest of such accounts, the legend of Cauraṅgi ("Four-Limbs") or Pūraṇ Bhagat. This latter name, by which he is known in the longest recension of his legend, from the Punjab,[159] may be read as "Total Devotee" (*pūrṇa bhakta*). Its second member may, however, be read in another way: among many tribal and popular traditions *bhagat* is a term employed for a shaman, soothsayer, sorcerer, exorcist, or a person who communes with the dead. Elsewhere, the term is applied to oracular devotees of the Goddess. When one considers that the Mongol term *böge/bö'e/beki* means "male shaman," this alternate reading for Pūraṇ Bhagat's name (i.e., "Total Shaman") ought not to be rejected out of hand.[160]

While Cauraṅgi is generally held to be the son of King Śālivāhana (Sāl Vāhan, Salwān, Sulivān, Sulwahan in vernacular transcriptions), a Punjabi recension of his legend first calls him King Śaṅkh. Finally, one source maintains that Cauraṅgināth was born of Śiva's seed.[161] Pūraṇ Bhagat is the son of Śaṅkh/Salwān's first queen Acchrān, and it is not until the age of twelve that has his first audience with the junior queen, Lūṇā (or Lūṇān/Nūṇān/Noṇān).[162] This queen, who is in reality a terrible witch,[163] falls in love with her adolescent stepson and attempts to seduce him. When he refuses her advances, she, like Potiphar's wife in the biblical story of Joseph, denounces him to the king, claiming that he had seduced her.[164]

To say that death has no fury like a woman scorned would be a great understatement in Lūṇā's case. At her urging, the king orders that Pūraṇ Bhagat be bound (*bandhke*) hand and foot and that his head be cut off and kebab'ed.[165] When the boy is brought before the king, he takes a vow of truth: let the king plunge him into a cauldron of boiling oil; his innocence will be proven if no part of his body, not even one of his fingers, be burnt.

Lūṇā lights the fire and puts on the cauldron, and Pūraṇ Bhagat is plunged into the boiling oil for four hours, from which he emerges unscathed.[166] Lūṇā nevertheless has her way, and an outcaste is ordered to cut off Pūraṇ Bhagat's hands, gouge out his eyes, and throw him down a well.[167] The outcaste, pitying the young prince, spares him, and instead slays a fawn and brings its eyes and blood to Lūṇā; she, however, tests this blood by plunging a pearl into it and sees that it is not that of her stepson.[168] The outcaste, fearing for his own life, goes to the forest where Pūraṇ Bhagat has hidden. In order to spare him, Pūraṇ Bhagat has him do Lūṇā's bidding. His arms and legs are cut off, his eyes gouged out, and his body thrown down a dry, broken-down well (*jīrṇāndhakūpa*). Also at Pūraṇ Bhagat's request, he returns to the city to tell Acchrān that her son will return after twelve years.[169] Acchrān, turned out of the city by the king, comes to the well in which Pūraṇ Bhagat has been thrown. He cries up to her "Set my elephant free, mother, to go to the Kajali Forest . . ."[170]

Twelve years pass, until one day Gorakh and his retinue of yogins come to Pūraṇ Bhagat's well on their way from their monastery at Ṭilla to Sialkot. There they find the young man and draw him out with a single thread of spun cotton. Gorakh then restores his eyes and, sprinkling nectar (*amṛta*) over him, his limbs.[171] Twenty-four years later, Gorakh returns again to the well and finds that Pūraṇ Bhagat has remained inside, in the practice of yoga. When Pūraṇ Bhagat asks Gorakh to initiate him into the Nāth order, Gorakh first tests his mettle by sending him to beg alms from Sundrān ("Beautiful"), the queen of Siṁhala. There, after an episode evocative of the experiences of Gopīcand and Matsyendra in that land, but in which Pūraṇ Bhagat remains celibate and free (and Queen Sundrān kills herself), Gorakh and his disciple Kānīpā (Kānha-pā) initiate him with ashes and earrings (*mundrān*).[172]

Now a full-fledged yogin, Pūraṇ Bhagat returns to Sialkot, his childhood home, where his mere presence causes his garden to burst into bloom. He restores his mother Acchrān's sight and forgives Salwān and Lūṇā. To the latter he gives grains of *dhāk* and rice from his yogin's wallet, promising that by swallowing them whole, she will conceive and bear a son, Rasālū.[173]

Apart from their clearly "shamanic" motifs, the accounts we have passed in review may in certain cases be also be read as so many alchemical allegories.[174] Dismemberment, binding, sealing under the earth with horse dung, boiling in oil, and birth from a burning corpse evoke the alchemical operations of *mardana*, *bandhana*, *sampuṭa*, *sāraṇa*, *utthāpana*, and *māraṇa*. Hāḍi-pā's incineration of metallic effigies of Gopīcand, Gorakh's transformation of the stuff of his disciples' bodies into bonded gold and iron, the names Hīrā ("Diamond") and Kajalī Van, and an array of other elements also appear to betray an alchemical matrix.

It is, however, the legend of Pūraṇ Bhagat that arguably may most be qualified as a medieval Indian alchemical allegory. Like mercury, its hero is born of Śiva's seed; his stepmother Lūṇā (*lavaṇa*, corrosive "salt")[175] causes him to be dismembered (*mardana*, *māraṇa*), after first boiling him in oil (*sāraṇa*). The well he is thrown into is *jīrṇāndha*, which evokes the closed (*andha*) crucible in which mercury is calcinated (*jīrṇa*, the past passive participal form of the same root *jṛ* that generates *jāraṇa*) or bound (*baddha*). This well is moreover identified with Kajalī Van, the "forest of black mercuric sulfide" (*kajjalī*).[176] After twelve years, he is drawn out of his well and restored through the magical techniques of Gorakhnāth, who restores him to wholeness with *amṛta*. The legend ends with Pūraṇ Bhagat offering Lūṇā grains (*guṭikās*) to eat, by which she conceives Rasālu, "the mercurial one" (*rasa*).[177]

8. The Man with the Golden Finger and Gorakh's Smithy

Such legends of bodily dismemberment and restoration as that of Pūraṇ Bhagat are not wholly unique to the Nāth Siddha tradition. A number of similar accounts, apparently of Rasa Siddha inspiration, are recounted by the eleventh-century Muslim savant Alberuni. One is "a tale about . . . the city of Valabhī":

> A man of the rank of a *Siddha* asked a herdsman with reference to a plant called Thohar, of the species of the Lactaria, from which milk flows when its leaves are torn off, whether he had ever seen Lactaria from which blood flows instead of milk. When the herdsman declared that he had, he gave him some drink-money that he should show it to him, which he did. When the man now saw the plant, he set fire to it, and threw the dog of the herdsman into the flame. Enraged thereby, the herdsman caught the man, and did with him the same as he had done to his dog. Then he waited till the fire was extinguished, and found both the man and the dog, but turned to gold. He took the dog with him, but left the man on the spot. Now some peasant happened to find it. He cut off a finger, and went to a fruit-

seller who was called Ranka, i.e. the poor, because he was an utter pauper and evidently near bankruptcy. After the peasant had bought from him what he wanted, he returned to the golden man, and then found that in the place where the cut off finger had been, a new finger had grown.[178]

In another such account, the body of an alchemist, aided by the king of Malwa, becomes transformed through a series of alchemical *saṃskāras*. This account, related above in chapter three, ends with the king withholding the final "packet" of alchemical preparations, with the result that the alchemist, rather than arising out of the cauldron as a perfect, invincible immortal, is transformed into a anthropomorphic lump of silver.[179]

What is remarkable about this latter account, apart from its content, is that it appears to correspond quite directly to the alchemical operation with which the *RA* closes, at the end of its eighteenth chapter. This procedure, related above in chapter five, culminates when the Alchemical Man emits the *mantra* "Hum!" and arises out of the cauldron with a massive body that shines like the sun and is possessed of all the *siddhi*s.

If such homologous operations are only implicit in the Gopīcand and Pūraṇ Bhagat legends, they are made explicit in a poem in which Gorakhnāth compares his subtle body to goldsmithy:[180]

> I take the gold [the void essence] in the goldsmithy [the cranial vault]—I am a goldsmith by trade. Pumping the bellows [of my breaths], and stabilizing my mercury, I have fixed it and then mixed it together with mica.
>
> I the goldsmith am in my gold. The root *cakra* [*mūlādhāra*] is my firepot. I forge it on the anvil of vibration [*nāda*], using my drop [*bindu*] hammer to press out the gold.
>
> In an ever-verdant forest my poisoned charcoal [burns, with its fire] blowing upward naturally, through the bellows' twin jet.[181]
>
> Harmonizing [the jets of] sun and moon [*iḍā* and *piṅgalā*, upbreath and downbreath] I stop the breath [*kumbhaka*], and breath is merged into breath.
>
> With one *rattī* [grain] of work, you can steal away a *māṣā* [lentil's weight][182]—and I am the *rattī* that does the stealing. Stealing the *māṣā*, I remain within the *māṣā:* by gathering up [gold] in this way, it is I who am gathered into myself.[183]
>
> Gold above, gold beneath, gold in the midst of gold.[184] He who

makes the triadic void his dwelling-place has a body that is neither pure nor impure.[185]

That which is beyond mind [*unmani*] is the balance beam. Mind is the weighing pan, and six lentil's-weight of breath are in the pan. While Gorakhnāth was sitting here seeking after gold, gold came in [to his smithy] of its own accord."[186]

TEN

Penetration, Perfection, and Immortality

. . . the tiny points of light that appear all over the Himalayas
when the holy men light their fires . . . [1]

Whereas Indian medical tradition defines *rasāyana* as the regeneration or reconstitution of the body, through the restoration of the vital bodily fluids (*rasa*s), to a youthful state of health and virility,[2] the alchemical usage of the term is a more ambitious one. In alchemy, the *rasa* in question is mercury, which substitutes itself for human bodily fluids and thereby transforms a body of flesh and blood into a golden (*svarṇa*),[3] adamantine (*vajra*),[4] or perfected (*siddha*) body. As shown in chapter five, the Siddha path consists of three complementary approaches to the attainment of such a body: the erotico-mystical, the hathayogic, and the alchemical.[5] These approaches are complementary inasmuch as all play on the correspondence between human and divine vital fluids (*rasa*s) on the one hand and, on the other, the dynamic of "piercing" or "penetration" (*vedha*), which effects the transformation of the body in question through all three of these complementary techniques. This same term, *vedha*, is employed in (1) a form of tantric initiation involving a transmission of vital fluids from teacher to disciple, (2) the hathayogic piercing of the *cakra*s as well as in a particular technique (called *mahāvedha*, the "great penetration") employed to that end, and (3) the alchemical transmutation of base metals into gold. In fact, the alchemical use of this term makes little sense—for why should transmutation be referred to as "piercing"?—until it is viewed in the light of these parallel and complementary practices.[6] I begin this chapter by showing the ways in which the notion of "perfection through penetration" was meaningful in the tantric context and conclude by delineating the various registers upon which said perfection manifested itself—in the form of supernatural powers (*siddhi*s), bodily immortality (*jīvanmukti*), and apotheosis in the form of accession to the higher spheres of the superhuman Siddhas.

1. Initiation in Medieval Indian Literature

The encounter (or high-impact collision) between representatives of religious and temporal authority and power is a favorite literary theme in India, where kings have been running into one or another sort of holy man, both inside and outside of texts, for millennia. One of the best-known myths of classical and modern Hinduism is the account of Hariścandra, king of Ayodhya, the Job of Hinduism, and the trials he suffers at the hands of Viśvāmitra, who had earlier been the officiating priest at his royal consecration. Following the ritual services he has rendered, Viśvāmitra the priest (even though he was himself a prince by birth) has the right to demand a fee (*dakṣiṇa*) from Hariścandra. According to brahmanic ideology, this fee is Viśvāmitra's due not only because he has performed a service for his king, but also—and most important—because temporal rule is, fundamentally, a brahman prerogative that brahmans, in a mythic past, delegated to their kṣatriya juniors.[7] This they did, we are told, in order that brahmans might concern themselves with the more elevated matters of *dharma* and *mokṣa*, leaving for kings the dirty work of governing, dispensing justice, waging wars, fathering princes, etc. Brahmans retained, however, their authority over kṣatriyas in their role as the advisors, the mentors (*mantrins*) of their kings, by playing a sacerdotal role in rituals vital to the harmonious continuation of the latter's rule and, most important, by deigning to perform the ceremony of royal consecration, of which a crucial moment was the ritual "punishment" (*daṇḍa*), by a brahman priest, with a rod (called *daṇḍa* in the hands of the king, but called a *sphya* in the sacerdotal context) of the otherwise unpunishable (*adaṇḍya*) king.[8] And, following his consecration—the delegation by his brahman initiators of their own sovereignty to him—the king also found himself in their debt in the matter of the fee that was their due. In effect, the king wrote his brahman priests a blank check in these situations, and it is the amount of this check that sets up the dramatic tension in the myth of Hariścandra.

In this Puranic myth,[9] Viśvāmitra, who is furious at Hariścandra for a number of reasons, exacts his revenge by ruining Hariścandra financially. The *dakṣiṇa* that Viśvāmitra demands of Hariścandra is astronomical, an amount far greater than even a king can possibly pay. The righteous Hariścandra attempts to acquit himself of his debt by giving his entire kingdom to Viśvāmitra, yet this is not enough. He then sells his wife and son into slavery, but Viśvāmitra is still unsatisfied. Lastly, he sells himself into slavery and, after a dozen years of terrible suffering and depradation, has his kingdom and family restored to him by the god Dharma—who has been disguised as Hariścandra's employer, an untouchable disposer of corpses on the Benares cremation ground. The happy ending has the royal family and its entire capital city elevated, apotheosized as it were, to an atmospheric level—with Viśvāmitra's blessing.

This is the ca. fourth-century A.D. Puranic myth of Hariścandra,[10] in which an old and uneasy alliance between the sacred authority of the brahman priesthood and the temporal power of kṣatriya royal sovereignty is the source of narrative tension. But India is changing. The Gupta empire, the last Hindu empire of India, collapses in the seventh century. A troubled "middle ages" follows, during which much of north India falls under the yoke of foreign, non-Hindu rulers. The old order is crumbling, and the ritual order ensured by the old brahmanic system is beginning to look antiquated. New forms of religious order and authority (monastic orders) as well as new religious sects appear to fill the power vacuum or to aid Hinduism in going underground in times of Muslim rule.

When paradigms shift, so too do paradigmatic narratives. A tenth-century play by Kṣemīśvara, the *Caṇḍakauśika*[11] (Wrath of Viśvāmitra), is a case in point. The core of this dramatic narrative is the same as that of the Puranic myth: Hariścandra, suffering the fury of Viśvāmitra, has been relegated to a position of abject slavery in Benares. What is novel in Kṣemīśvara's otherwise rather dreary adaptation is the sectarian guise of Hariścandra's savior. Rather than having Dharma, the Hindu god of Universal Order disguised as the untouchable lord of the Benares cremation ground (a figure nowadays called the *ḍom-rāj*), Kṣemīśvara has the god parade as a Kāpālika.[12] He bears all the markings of a tāntrika: he is ash smeared, decked out with human bones and skulls, "having the appearance of Śiva Bhūtanātha." He reads Hariścandra's mind, controls "vampires," and possesses alchemical preparations which afford him immortality (*rasāyana*), the power to transmute (*dhātuvāda*), and the power of flight (*pādalepa*), and possesses an eye unguent (*añjana*) that permits him to see underground to find buried treasure.[13] This Kāpālika, portrayed most sympathetically by Kṣemīśvara, having introduced himself to Hariścandra, departs and then returns in a twinkling with a vampire in tow; on the vampire's shoulders is an immense mineral treasure, discovered with the aid of the Kāpālika's can-see-underground-with-it unguent, which Hariścandra may now use to pay off his debts to the irrascible Viśvāmitra.[14]

Kṣemīśvara's adaptation of the original Purānic account is truly remarkable when we consider the sort of people the Kāpālikas were made out to be by their orthodox critics. The Kāpālikas, fornicators with menstruating women, cremation-ground consumers of human flesh, worshippers of the female sexual organ, brahman murderers, were the Hell's Angels of medieval India. This drama is therefore a watershed of sorts in the history of the literature on brahman-kṣatriya relations in classical India. What Hariścandra cannot pay the brahmanic priest Viśvāmitra retail the Kāpālika wizard can, through his supernatural powers, get him wholesale. We may therefore take Kṣemīśvara's superimposition—of a Kāpālika guise upon a god of moral order—to be an indication of just how tattered that old order was looking to certain elements of Hindu society. We may further see in this tenth-century adaptation an indication that tantric practitioners were replacing old-order brahman priests (even if Viśvāmitra was originally the most heterodox of all the brahmanic sages) in the role of advisors to kṣatriya kings.

The new partnership that was being forged—between Hindu princes and representatives of one or another of the Śaiva orders—such as the Kāpālika described by Kṣemīśvara—is, through some one thousand years of Indian literature, described from a number of perspectives. At times, the new world order curiously resembles the old, with tāntrikas asserting their hegemony over their princely patrons with threats and violence. In nearly every case, narrative depictions of the tāntrika-prince relationship sparkle with the serendipity of the medieval literary style, with vampires, wizards, mysterious ascetics, hidden treasure, and the supernatural intervening time and again. Behind all the glitter, however, one important leitmotif emerges: this is the theme of a yogic or tantric initiation of the king by a Śaiva guru.

We take our second medieval example from the eleventh-century Kashmiri classic, Somadeva's *Vetālapañcaviṃśati* (Twenty-five Tales of the Vampire). These tales, inserted within the massive *Kathāsaritsāgara* (Ocean of Rivers of Story), are themselves framed by a narrative that begins when a king named Trivikramasena discovers that each of the fruits a mysterious ascetic has been bringing him every day for ten years has a precious jewel inside of it. When he questions the ascetic as to his reasons for such largesse, the mystery man, named Kṣāntaśīla, replies that he needs the king to help him perform a secret cremation-ground rite. On the appointed night (the dark of the moon), the king comes to the cremation ground, where Kṣāntaśīla bids that he bring him the corpse of a man hung in a sisoo tree a short way to the south. The king cuts down the corpse which, as it turns out, is possessed by a loquacious vampire who narrates twenty-five stories ending in riddles which the king must solve lest his head burst into a thousand pieces. At the end of the final story, the vampire informs the king that Kṣāntaśīla's true intention has been to offer him, the king, as a human sacrifice to the vampire storyteller, in order to win for himself, Kṣāntaśīla, lordship over the Vidyādharas, the Wizards of medieval Indian tradition. Kṣāntaśīla, who bears all the markings of a terrible Kāpālika, has the tables turned on him by the king, who cuts off his head, the which he then offers, together with the heart, to the vampire. Śiva descends, and in a deus ex machina scenario reminiscent of the Puranic Hariścandra myth, grants Trivikramasena dominion over the earth as well as the Vidyādharas.

This story takes up all of the major elements of the *Caṇḍakauśika* drama, but with all the pieces turned around. Viśvāmitra, the wrathful exemplar of the priestly function who empties Hariścandra's royal treasury in order to better abuse him is here replaced by the evil Kāpālika Kṣāntaśīla who fills Trivikramasena's treasury in order to later abuse him. The good Kāpālika of the *Caṇḍakauśika* is here replaced by the vampire who had been his treasure-bearing coolie; and the vampire of the eponymous tales in a sense effects Trivikramasena's initiation—in this case to lordship over the denizens of an atmospheric realm, the Vidyādharas.

An interesting feature of the Vampire Tales narrative is the need, on the part of a renouncer, of a royal hero in order to accomplish his ends. A similar theme, of a symbiotic relationship between a tāntrika and a heroic prince, is found in an episode from Bāṇabhaṭṭa's seventh-century *Harṣacarita* which describes the meeting between king Puṣpabhūti and Bhairavācārya, a powerful south Indian ascetic, who is decked out in Kāpālika garb and wears great crystal *kuṇḍala* earrings. One day, Bhairavācārya asks the king to come and assist him in the completion of a powerful rite, the goal of which is to gain control over a vampire and become lord of the Vidyādharas. Once again, the setting is a cremation ground under the dark of the moon. Once again, a corpse and all manner of tantric paraphernalia are brought into play. When the terrible vampire arises out of the corpse's mouth, the king's swordsmanship saves the day, and Bhairavācārya becomes a Vidyādhara. Here, the same elements are present, but once again, in a slightly different order. Now it is the vampire who is evil and the Kāpālika who is good rather than the other way around; now the king aids the Kāpālika, rather than the vampire aiding the king, to become the lord of the Vidyādharas. What remains constant is the ritual structure, the transformative late-night cremation-ground rite which effects a breakthrough to another world and superhuman powers.

Another, less obvious, literary account of power politics between tāntrikas and kings is Kalhaṇa's chronicle of the fall of the tenth-century Kashmiri king Cakravarman. Whereas Kalhaṇa wrote his *Rājataraṅginī* in the twelfth century, the amount of detail he gives concerning a piece of palace intrigue—which had occurred some two hundred years earlier—leads one to believe that the story was grounded in something more than Kalhaṇa's imagination. While Sir Aurel Stein, who translated this work at the turn of the century, stated that Kalhaṇa's "amusing anecdote look[ed] to be authentic,"[15] we might also choose to see in it an allegorization of a piece of tantric sorcery.

In the spring of A.D. 936, Cakravarman, with the help of a group feudal landholders called the Ḍāmaras, breaks the back of a military caste called the Tantrins, who had been the praetorian guard of his rival for the throne. Cakravarman has perhaps not seen the last of the Tantrins however; moreover, these Tantrins have much of the tāntrika about them, as the principal episode in Cakravarman's one-year reign[16] would appear to indicate. One night, the king is entertained in his court by an "outcaste" Ḍom (the same Ḍom as the untouchable *ḍom-rāj* of the Benares cremation grounds) singer named Raṅga and his two dancing daughters Haṃsī ("Goosie") and Nāgalatā ("Serpentina"). These last two quickly steal the show, enchanting the king with an open display of their feminine charms, which are described by a court rogue (a description which Stein leaves out of his translation):

> O Lord! The music, as if enchanted by these two lovely dames, has become as alluring as a liquor poured into a crystal glass! It seems as if the moon, bewildered by the shining teeth of these singing girls, is passionately kissing the gleaming columns of the ivory hall! Seeing that we are speaking of her, one of them has shot a glance of smiling indignation our way. The one singing with lowered gaze and trembling earrings, who looks so beautiful, is passionately acting out the reverse (*viparīta*) posture of love.

There is more going on here than dirty dancing, especially if we look at this scene and what follows in the light of tantric imagery. First, the two dancing girls, daughters of the Ḍom Raṅga, are *Ḍombī*s, the most prized of partners in ritualized tantric sex, sex in which the reverse *viparīta* posture is the rule. Their names are revealing as well: as we have seen, in the subtle body, it is both a coiled serpent (the *kuṇḍalinī*) and a goose (the *haṃsa*) that rise from the level of the sexual organs up to the cranial vault to afford the practitioner immortality. In her rise through the yogic *cakra*s, the *kuṇḍalinī* serpent is said to dance with the yogin. And, at the end of her rise, it is the yogin's own sexual fluid which, carried upward through her body, is transformed into immortalizing nectar. As a conduit for the yogin's semen, the female *kuṇḍalinī* may be likened to the female sexual organ: indeed, she is sometimes called *ḍombī*, and the Ḍombī, as the tantrika's favorite sexual partner, was most prized for the transformative powers of her menstrual blood.[17]

For the same reason that there could be nothing more defiling to an orthodox Hindu than the menstrual blood of an outcaste woman, the heterodox tāntrikas valued the same as the most powerful fluid in the universe. For the uninitiated, however, the stuff was dynamite, as Cakravarman quickly learns. Following the night of the big dance, he becomes the Ḍombīs' sexual plaything. He makes them his queens, and they and their outcaste relatives take over the royal court, polluting the entire kingdom in the process. High offices are bestowed upon those who eat polluted leavings (*ucchiṣṭa*) off the Ḍombīs' plates,[18] and Ḍom ministers proudly wear the girls' menses-stained undergarments over their courtly attire. Cakravarman, his mind totally gone, rapes a brahman woman and treacherously puts to death a number of his Ḍāmara allies. Shortly thereafter, Ḍāmaras set upon him one night in the royal latrine and flay his body as it lies upon the swelling breasts of his Ḍombī concubine.

Now, we can read this account, with Stein, as an "amusing anecdote," or perhaps glimpse in it, once again, a piece of tantric power politics (on the part of the Tantrins?), the destruction of a king through a sort of loaded tantric initiation. Here, the closest parallel would be the Vampire Tales, in which the tāntrika is the heavy—with the difference that here there is no vampire to save poor king Cakravarman.

A final group of accounts, all of which are structurally similar, are much more straightforward, as they dramatize a king's tantric initiation, by a Śaiva ascetic of the Nāth order or one of its forerunners, in terms reminiscent of the *Caṇḍakauśika* or even of the ancient royal consecration of kings by brahman priests. The most elaborate of these accounts is that of Deorāj, founder of the Rāwal dynasty, which is found in the bardic chronicles of the Rāwal kings of Jaisalmer.[19] Here, as we saw in a previous chapter, Deorāj (b. A.D. 836), the future founder of the Rāwal dynasty, is visited by a Jogi named Rita who bestows upon him the title of *Sid[dha]* and then goes off, leaving him his *rasa kumbha* or elixir vessel. Deorāj uses the gold produced by this vessel to raise an army and the walls of a fortified city. Rita returns and exacts that Deorāj become his disciple and, as a token of his submission and fealty, adopt the external signs of his order. He places the earrings (*mudrā*) in Deorāj's ears, the little horn (*siṅgnād*) around his neck, and loincloth (*laṅgoṭī*) about his loins. Attired in this way, Deorāj goes about exclaiming "*alakh! alakh!*" Then, having exacted that these sectarian rites of initiation should be continued to the latest posterity, Rita disappears.

Two elements of this account are to be retained. The first is that we have returned here to the ancient brahmanic ideology in which the king is a junior partner in power to his priestly initiator, who grants him his royal power in exchange for a token of his submission in initiation. The second is that his priest, Rita, is a Jogi, a yogin, probably of the Pāśupata order (or some other forerunner of the Nāth *sampradāya*). He bears all the marks of these Śaiva orders: his tattered cloak, great earrings (also worn by the Kāpālika Bhairavācārya in the *Harṣacarita* account), little horn, the words *alakh! alakh!* ("attributeless! attributeless!") are all particular to the Nāth *sampradāya.*

Medieval and modern legend and history abound with accounts of just this sort of alliance—sealed through initiation—between a tāntrika (sometimes identified as a Nāth Siddha) and a fledgling prince. As recently as the early nineteenth century, just such a pact was struck between a Nāth Siddha and the Marwar prince Mān Singh;[20] a number of accords of the same order were made between Nāth Siddhas and princes, in earlier centuries, well to the north of Rajasthan, in Garhwal (Uttar Pradesh) and Nepal. In fact, nearly all of the exemplary Nāth Siddhas of legend are born into princely families, before being saved—from rivals, enemies, evil stepmothers, death—by a powerful yogin, usually Gorakh, who then initiates him into that order. As we have seen, initiation involves the piercing of the ears with the great *kuṇḍala* or *mudrā* earrings that are the hallmark of the Nāth sect, the placing of the little horn, the giving of the *mantra*, etc.

There is another feature of the Nāth Siddhas' tantric kingmaking that should also be noted here. This is a facet of the initiation rite which, although it is evoked in only a few legendary accounts, plays a much more important role in instructions for tantric initiation (*dīkṣā*) as such are found in a number of classic tantric texts. The most comprehensive mythologization of this ritual is found in a chronicle of the Gurkha (named after Gorakh for reasons that will be made clear) dynasty of Nepal. One day, young Pṛthivīnārāyaṇ Śāh, who would later lead the Gurkhas in their successful conquest of the Kathmandu Valley in 1768, chances upon Gorakhnāth, who is meditating in a cave. Gorakh sends Pṛthivīnārāyaṇ Śāh back to his palace to bring him a present (*prasād*) of yogurt, from his mother. When the boy returns, Gorakh instructs him to hold the yogurt out to him in his cupped hands. Gorakh then draws that yogurt into his mouth, attempts to spit it back out into Pṛthivīnārāyaṇ Śāh's hand, and tells him to eat it.[21] Pṛthivīnārāyaṇ Śāh however opens his hands and lets the yogurt fall on his feet. Gorakh then explains to the boy that had he eaten his *prāsād*, the yogurt he had spat out, he would have become a universal emperor. But because he has let the yogurt fall on his feet, he will only conquer the earth as far as his feet will carry him. Pṛthivīnārāyaṇ Śāh's feet soon carry him to the Kathmandu Valley where, through a second intervention by Gorakh, his Gurkhas win a great battle and become the rulers of Nepal. The great guru's intercession is commemorated, down to the present day, on the Nepali one rupee coin, upon which is written, verso, "Long live Gorakhnāth!"[22]

This spitting incident is not unique to the biography of Pṛthivīnārāyaṇ Śāh. Alberuni's eleventh-century account of India includes an episode from the career of the Mahāsiddha alchemist Vyāḍi that is quite similar. Here, Vyāḍi has, at long last, discovered the alchemical elixir and is flying through the air over the royal capital of Ujjain. Looking below, he sees King Vikramāditya standing at the gate of his palace. "Open thy mouth for my saliva" he calls down to the king. The king instead steps out of the way and the saliva falls on the threshold, which is immediately transformed into gold.[23] Similarly, Bāppā Rāwal's guru Hārīta Rāśi, having risen into the air, attempts to spit into his mouth in order to complete his initiation. Like Pṛthivīnārāyaṇ Śāh and Vikramāditya, Bāppā Rāwal allows his guru's expectorate to fall at (or on) his feet, and thereby receives something less than the intended effects of his guru's gift.[24] Yet another such account, concerning the site of Hiṅglāj Devī in Baluchistan, is all the more surprising, because it is reported by the Muslim "Jogis" of the Sind. Jogi Maula Baksh relates the story:[25]

> One day Shah Abdul Latif Bhitai, the Sind's great mystic poet, met Jogi Madan Vaniyo who taught him ablutions of the spirit and took him to the goddess Hinglaj. *Shah saw the Jogis feed Nani Hinglaj milk that she promptly vomited out.* Nani ignored him the first time, but the third time she obediently drank the milk. Taken aback by Shah's success, the Jogis decided that night that they would devour Shah so that his powers, as evinced by his success with Nani, would pass on to

them. Shah overheard their plan and prayed to God for help. So Shah was swallowed by the earth instead and the good earth brought him to the safe haven of Bhit where he started to preach mysticism.

The only way we can make sense of these accounts is by interpreting them in the light of a tantric initiation ritual that was current in the period in which the Nāth Siddhas were enjoying their heyday in northern India. We now turn to this ritual.

2. *Vedhamayī Dīkṣā:* Initiation by Penetration

Four tenth- to fourteenth-century tantric sources—the *Tantrāloka*[26] of Abhinavagupta, the *Kulārṇava Tantra*,[27] the *Śāradatilaka* of Lakṣmaṇadeśikendra,[28] and the "Śākta" *Gorakṣa Saṁhitā*[29]—describe an initiation known as *vedhamayī dīksā*, "initiation having the form of penetration." This initiation basically consists of the penetration, by the guru's *śakti*, of the subtle body of the initiand. Abhinavagupta[30] states that initiation by penetration may take six forms, of which one is called *binduvedha* (penetration of "virile potency," but also, of a "drop," *bindu*, of semen). In all of these variant forms, the guru, having entered the body of his disciple (whose *kuṇḍalinī* has been awakened) unites with that *kuṇḍalinī* within the disciple's body and subsequent raises it from the disciple's lower abdomen up to his cranial vault. The form the guru takes as he courses through his disciple's body may be that of a drop (*bindu*) of seed or of speech. In many descriptions of this operation, the guru is said to exit the disciple's body through the mouth and thus return back into his own body through his own mouth.[31] By means of this initiation, the guru reveals the supreme Śiva to his disciple;[32] the disciple whose bonds have been cut thereby becomes "a manifest Śiva."[33]

What these various sources appear to be describing is a "procreative" transfer of yogic seed between guru and disciple, a transfer that is characterized, in *binduvedha*, by a powerful seminal flow, in both guru and disciple, that spreads through their bodies and rises to the cranial vault of both.[34] In a Buddhist account of the Mahāsiddha lineage of Nāgārjuna, found in Nepal and edited by Giuseppe Tucci in 1930, a description of the Siddha initiation ritual climaxes when, the guru, having meditated on the heart of the disciple, transfers from his own mouth into the mouth of his disciple "that which is contained in the *vajra* vessel" (i.e., "transformed" sexual fluid), and "having pronounced 108 mantras, [says] 'put your mouth in my mouth.'"[35] In the Hindu *Śārada Tilaka*, the guru is said to transfer, through the mouth of his initiate, "that which has oozed inside his mouth" (*vidruvaktrāntare*), after which said fluid is returned back into the mouth of the guru.[36] Elsewhere, the *Yogakuṇḍalī Upaniṣad* describes the yogin's "pure phlegm, whose white color is that of the moon . . . [which] when churned by the breath and the energy of the *kuṇḍalinī*, becomes a rich flow of nectar."[37] Initiation into the Śaiva Aghori sect is effected when the guru places a drop of his semen upon the initiate's tongue.[38] Finally, in a verse perhaps inspired by the *KJñN*,[39] the *TĀ* (29.127–32) prescribes the mouth-to-mouth transfer of sexual fluids for the attainment of *siddhi*s.[40]

In the light of this data, we may conclude that the yogurt that Gorakh "reverses" and offers to spit into prince Pṛthivīnārāyaṇ Śāh's mouth, the transmuting spittle that lands on king Vikramāditya's threshold and on Bāppā Rāwal's feet, the reverse sexual posture that the dancing Ḍombī girl (whose name evokes the *kuṇḍalinī* serpent through which the transformations proper to yoga and initiation take place) adopts in her seduction of King Cakravarman—may all be read as so many thinly veiled accounts of initiations by penetration, in which a guru attempts to transform his disciple into a realized (*siddha*) being, by injecting him with sublimated semen.

Let us, however, go deeper into this matter of the apparent fluid transfer that takes place within the context of the so-called initiation by penetration, an initiation which, as we have seen, has the power to transform a boy into a king and a disciple into a "second Śiva." Here, the term *vedha[na]*, "penetration," will guide us as we attempt to penetrate the plays of correspondences proper to Siddha alchemy and to navigate the labyrinthine internal landscapes of the subtle body.

The noun *vedha*, derived from *vidh*, the weak form of the Vedic root *vyadh*, "pierce," makes its first appearance in the medical literature, where it has the sense of "puncturing, wounding, a wound." *Vedha*, with or without its *-na* suffix, retains this sense of piercing or penetration throughout the medieval traditions that concern us. In addition to these usages, vernacular Middle Indo-Aryan forms of these terms introduce a *ba-/va-* alternation, generating such terms as *bedha* and *bedhana*. These are in turn conflated, particularly in hathayogic sources, with the terms *bheda* and *bhedana*, nominalizations of the Sanskrit root *bhid*, "split, cleave, pierce."

In addition to the use of this term for the form of initiation described in the literary sources we have passed in review, the term *vedha[na]* is also employed in the vocabulary of Hindu alchemy and *haṭha yoga*. In all three instances, an active agent penetrates and thereby fundamentally transforms its passive counterpart. As we will see, the dynamics of the processes designated by these three uses of the same term are quite identical. More than this, the texts which describe these various penetrations explicitly parallel or identify these processes or techniques with one another.

I have already broached the matter of *vedhamayī dīkṣā*, "initiation by penetration." Let us now return to the *Kulārṇava Tantra*, which, immediately following its treatment of this and other forms of initiation, makes the following statement: "Just as penetration by mercury brings about aurifaction (*suvarṇatām*) [in metals], so the soul, penetrated through initiation (*dīkṣā*), attains Siva-hood (*śivatvam*)."[41] This identification was a commonplace of medieval Indian thought, as evidenced in the echoes we find of this statement in a wide array of nonalchemical sources, ranging from the Buddhist *Sādhanamālā* to the Vīraśaiva *Bāsava Purāṇa* to the *TĀ* and *Parāparaprakāśika* of the Trika Kaula, to the *Amanaska Yoga* of Gorakhnāth.[42] This direct comparison, even identification, of initiation by penetration with a form of alchemical penetration, through the metaphor of physical transmogrification (into gold/into Śiva), leads us into the heart of the second field of application of the term *vedha:* Hindu alchemy.

3. Penetration, Transmutation, and Transubstantiation in Siddha Alchemy

The *Kulārṇava Tantra* dates from the same period (tenth through twelfth centuries) as the *RHT*, in which we find one of the earliest uses of the term *vedha[na]* in the sense of "transmutation through penetration [by mercury]." As is common practice in the alchemical literature, the *RHT* lists *vedha[na]* as the seventeenth and penultimate *saṃskāra*. As we have seen, the preceding eight alchemical *saṃskāra*s involve the progressive envelopment by—and absorption of a given metal or mineral—into mercury. At this point, a threshold of critical mass and energy is reached, which automatically triggers *vedha[na]*, the "piercing" or transmutation of said metal by mercury, such that the mercury-metal amalgam is immediately transformed into silver or gold. Mercury that is capable of transmuting base metals into noble silver or gold may thereafter be taken internally. This is the eighteenth and final *saṃskāra*, known as *śarīra-yoga*, "body Work" or "transubstantiation." In this final operation, the alchemist will generally hold in his mouth a solid "pill" (*guṭikā*) of mercury, which will gradually penetrate his body and so transmute it into an immortal golden, diamond, or perfected body.

This transposition of *vedhana*, penetration/transmutation, from metallic to human bodies, is directly addressed, in the terms with which we are already familiar, in the eleventh-century *RA:* "As in metal, so in the body. Mercury ought always to be employed in this way. When it penetrates (*praviśan*) a metal and the body, [mercury] behaves in an identical way. First test [mercury] on a metal, then use it in the body."[43] The use of the term *śarīra-yoga* for the application of perfected, tested mercury to the body is not fortuitous here: in both alchemical and hathayogic sources, the complementarity of the two disciplines is stressed time and again. Whence the statement in the opening of the *RA* (1.18b): "Mercury and breath [control] are known as the Work in two parts."[44]

As already noted many times, the goal of the practitioner, in both Hindu alchemy and *haṭha yoga*, is the attainment of both supernatural powers and bodily immortality. Nowhere are these concrete goals identified more explicitly than in alchemical depictions of *vedhana*. Thus, the *RA* (14.25–36) states:

> A mercurial pill [*guṭikā*] capable of transmuting one hundred times its mass of base metals into gold [*śata-vedha*], when held in the mouth for one month, yields a life span of 4,320,000 years. One thousand–*vedha* mercury, held in the mouth for two months, permits one to lives as long as the sun, moon, and stars. Ten thousand–*vedha* mercury, held in the mouth for three months, yields a lifetime of Indra. One hundred thousand–*vedha* mercury, held for four months, yields a lifetime of Brahmā; one million–*vedha* divine mercury, held for seven months, places one on an equal footing [*pada*] with Īśvara. Smoke-sight-*vedha* mercury, held in the mouth for eight months, renders one Svayambhu Maheśvara. One becomes the creator, destroyer, and enjoyer [of the universe], a maker of curses and boons, omniscient, omnipotent, of subtle and immaculate beauty. Such a man acts at will, creates and destroys at will, moves at will, and himself becomes the universal body [Viśvarūpa] worshipped by all of the gods, including Brahmā, Viṣṇu, and Maheśvara.

Progressions of this sort, in which perfected mercury's powers to transmute base metals into ever-increasing amounts of gold and transubstantiate the human body into ever-more exalted Siddha or divine bodies, are legion in the alchemical sources. Thus, for example, an adamantine pill, formed of a combination of mercury, gold, the "three fruits," the "three hot substances," and "rock water"[45] and plunged in successive oil baths (*sāraṇa*s), has the following effects on base metals and the human body. After one such oil bath, this pill, held in the mouth, yields a life span of a thousand years; after two oil baths, it transmutes ten thousand times its mass of base metals into gold and affords a life span of ten thousand years; after three, the figures reach one hundred thousand; after four, ten million (and the power of flight for the alchemist); after five, one hundred million. After six oil baths, this pill transmutes one billion times its mass in base metals into gold and affords the alchemist a life span of the same duration as the sun and moon and eternal force and virility. After a seventh operation, this pill is given the name of *khecarī* (the "aviator"): "this was proclaimed by Bhairava himself." He who eats a grain of this each day for one month becomes a diamond-bodied Siddha, sporting according to his whim with the other heavenly hosts, and attains Śivahood.[46]

Progressions of a similar order are found in two sources, the one alchemical (*RA*) and the other hathayogic (*Amanaska Yoga* 1.45–98), in which a measure called a *pala* is employed as a means for calibrating the *siddhi*s realized by the practitioner. In the *RA* (18.56–60) account of this progression, the nature and quality of the *siddhi*s realized by the alchemist vary according to the number of *pala*s of mercury that has been calcinated in mica one consumes. Eating one *pala*[47] renders one invulnerable to disease; two *pala*s produce an increase in semen; three *pala*s confer heightened powers; eating four *pala*s cures baldness; with five *pala*s, all wrinkles disappear; six *pala*s afford a telegraphic memory; seven *pala*s destroy eye diseases; eight *pala*s endow one with a bird's-eye view (*tārkṣyadṛṣṭi*) and a life span and powers equal to those of the god Brahmā; nine *pala*s make one the equal of the gods; ten *pala*s make one a second Śiva.[48]

In the *Amanaska Yoga* discussion of what it calls "salvific" or "stellar yoga,"[49] the length of time one holds one's breath (called the "time of absorption": *laya-kāla*) determines the degree of success (*siddhi*) one realizes, in a mounting progression. Here, the term *pala* is used as a measure of time, rather than of mass.[50] *Laya* for one full breath establishes the life force (*prāṇa*) in the body; for four breaths, the replenishment of the seven bodily constituents (*dhātu*s); for one *pala*, reduction of in and out breaths. When the breath is restrained for twelve minutes, the *kuṇḍalinī* straightens; after ninety-six minutes, a trance state is reached in which one has a vision of the "drop of light" (*tejobindu*); after three hours, one's food intake and production of excrements are greatly reduced; after six hours, the light of one's soul shines forth; after twelve hours, the light of the ether principle (*ākāśa-tattva*) shines forth; after a day, one gains supernatural olfactory powers; after two days, the supernatural gustatory powers; after three days, "television" (*dūradarśana*); after four days, the sense of touch at a distance (*dūra-sparśana*); after five days, the sense of hearing at a distance (*dūraśravaṇa*);[51] after six days, the arising of the *mahābuddhi;* after seven days, the mystic knowledge of the entire universe; after eight days, the cessation of all hunger and thirst; after nine days, supernatural speech (*vāksiddhi*); after ten days, visions of hidden wonders; after eleven days, mind travel; after twelve days, the power to move over the earth at will (*bhucaratvam*); after thirteen days, the power of flight (*khecaratvam*); after fourteen days, the power to render oneself infinitesimally small *aṇimā*); after sixteen days, the power to render oneself infinitely great (*mahimā*); after eighteen days, infinite gravity (*garimā*); after twenty days, the unbearable lightness of being (*laghimā*); after twenty-two days, the attainment of all one desires (*prāpti*); after twenty-four days, the fulfillment of all desires (*prakāmya*); after twenty-six days, supremacy (*īśitvā*); after twenty-eight days, one bends the universe to one's will (*vaśitvā*);[52] after a month, the dawning of release (*mokṣa*); after nine months, a diamond body and mastery over the element earth; after eighteen months, mastery over the element water; after three years, mastery over the element fire; after six years, mastery over the element air; after twelve years, mastery over the element ether. He who practices uninterrupted breath retention for twenty-four years gains dominion over the goddess Śakti and the entire universe and enjoys the *siddhi* of "Love's Body" (*kāmarūpa*). Such a yogin, established in the *mahātattva*,[53] retains his integrity and inviolability even after the universal resorption (*pralaya*) of the gods Brahmā, Viṣṇu, and Śiva.

The *pala* measure constitutes what we may characterize as a middle-range case of the Hindu time-space continuum: the *pala* is at once a measure of time (24 seconds) and of mass (82.624 grams). This continuum is operative at the two endpoints of the scale as well. At the infinitesimal end of the spectrum is the *paramāṇu*, "subatom," whose theoretical mass is approximately 0.00000017 grams,[54] but which is also a "space of time," i.e., the time it takes for a beam of sunlight to travel across an atom having said mass. In its discussion of time and space, the *Bhāgavata Purāṇa* joins the infinitesimal to the infinite: "The subatom [*parama-aṇu*] is indeed [a measure of] time, i.e., the time [it takes the sun] to pass through that which has the [spatial] measure of a subatom." A homologous case is the greatest indivisible measure of space, which is also the "supergreat" (*paramo mahān*) measure of time.[55] Following the logic of this statement, a cosmic eon (*kalpa*) is the time it takes a theoretical light beam generated by the transcendent absolute (having the form of the sun, in the mundane world) to pass across the entire expanse of bounded space. The "two infinites" of Blaise Pascal, as well as the time-space continuum and light-years of modern astrophysics and Douglas Adams's "Restaurant at the End of the Universe" all appear to have been theoretically anticipated by medieval Indians, whose universe was at once spatial and temporal.[56]

There is yet another model for measuring time in the Hindu, and particularly the yogic, context. This is the unit of breath called a *mātra* or *pala*[57] which, as we have seen in the context of *laya-kāla*, the "time of breath retention," deploys into life spans equivalent to the duration of the universe. Here, we encounter a direct link between breathing and the duration of life. Four "measures" (*mātra*) of breath equal one *pala* (twenty-four seconds); sixty *palas* equal one *ghaṭikā* (twenty-four minutes), and sixty *ghaṭikās* one day and night. Fifteen days and nights constitute a lunar fortnight, of which two make a human month. Six such months equal a solar semester (*ayana*), of which two make up a human year. One hundred such years are the allotted life span of a human being. Nearly every creature is allotted an optimal life span of one hundred years. However, in the case of the ancestors, one "year" is the equivalent of 30 human years (thus the ancestors live 3,000 human years); and a "year" of the gods 360 human years. Twelve thousand divine years equal a *mahāyuga*, of which one thousand equal a day of Brahmā—who, like the mayfly, lives but for a day; i.e., a "day of Brahmā" is the equivalent of his hundred-year life span.[58] A day of Brahmā is the equivalent of a *kalpa*, a cosmic eon, of which one hundred constitute a *mahākalpa*, or great eon, a life span of Viṣṇu, out of whose navel Brahmā arises at the beginning of each *kalpa*. For the Śaivas, however, a life span of Viṣṇu is nothing more than an in breath and out breath of the supreme god Śiva. In this perspective, all of time, from the infinitesimal to the infinite, is a continuum of breath. Extending one's breath is therefore tantamount to extending one's life span.[59]

4. *Cakra* Piercing and Ear Piercing in Nāth Siddha Practice

Another conceptual model for effecting the yogin's return to and identification with the Absolute brings us back to the transformative dynamics of penetration. According to the metaphysical teachings of Gorakhnāth, all that exists in the universe, from the most inert inorganic matter to the abstract godhead, is ultimately composed of the same substance—i.e., the five elements.[60] Sentient beings, and especially humans, consist of so many "overlays" of these elements, ranging from earth to ether. Yogic practice, like the ritual technique of *bhūtaśuddhi*, therefore consists of imploding lower elements into hierarchically superior elements until all has been absorbed into the empty space of the subtle ether. This vacuum of nothingness in the heart of being—Gorakhnāth's child crying in the ether—is a "clearing" of pure potential out of which supernatural powers, immortality, and a divine or *siddha* body may emerge.[61] This "immanentism," the notion that at the core of every being lies its perfect essence, is given an alchemical gloss in another of Gorakhnāth's mystic verses: "Just as within every stone lies the indestructible touchstone, so within every metal there is gold."[62]

Of course, the prime technique for imploding the lower constituents of one's being into the higher is, in the hathayogic tradition, the piercing (*vedha*, *bhedana*) of the *cakra*s, through breath control and retention. As noted in the *laya-kāla* progression described in the *Amanaska Yoga*, retaining the breath for one *pala* reduces up and down breathing. Diaphragmatic retention follows, and after twelve minutes (i.e., thirty *pala*s) the *kuṇḍalinī* awakens, straightens, and begins her rise through the *cakra*s, piercing them as she mounts toward the cranial vault. An important technique to this yogic end, called *mahāvedha*, the "great penetration," is described in the *Gorakṣa Paddhati*:[63] "With one-pointed mind, the yogin should inhale and retain the subtle breath within his body. Then he should halt the course of the breaths, through the use of the throat lock. Placing the two palms flat on the ground, he should slowly strike the ground with the buttocks. Thereupon the breath, overflowing the two outer channels, bursts into the medial channel . . . This . . . surely generates immortality . . . This is *mahāvedha*, the practice of which confers the great *siddhi*s."

On a conceptual level, the piercing of the *cakra*s effects a stadial resorption or implosion of the lower elements into their higher emanates. Thus, when the second *cakra* (the *svādhiṣṭhāna*) is pierced, the element earth—whose support is the lowest, the *mūlādhāra cakra*—becomes imploded into the element water, the second element on the hierarchy, and so on, until nothing remains but ether in the cranial vault. It is not a coincidence here that the term *kha* at once means "empty space," "ether," "the absolute," and "zero" in the Sanskrit language.[64] The cranial vault, the locus of the ether—both the site at which Siddha techniques for penetration end and that at which mundane existence first begins, when the absolute first penetrates the human microcosm[65]—is the zero point at which the two infinities meet, the point at which "black holes" issue into "white holes."[66] This is precisely the "end" of the *RA*'s process for the creation of the Alchemical Man, which was outlined in an earlier chapter: when all that remains of the practitioner is the fifth element, ether, in the cranial vault, he arises—out of the cauldron in which his lower being had been dissolved and imploded into its higher emanates—as a massive, powerful, perfected Siddha.[67]

Parallels of this sort, between the alchemical and hathayogic techniques of the Siddha alchemist, extend to the ability to transmute: the highest form of transmutation, *śabda-vedha*, is effected when the perfected alchemist, holding a mercurial pill in his mouth, exhales over base metals. Elsewhere, the yogic and alchemical Siddha is capable of using his bodily secretions to "pierce" and transmute base metals into gold.[68] Penetration is not, however, solely a matter of breath, or of the implosion of the hierarchized five elements. As we have already seen in the context of initiation by penetration, there is also a fluid component to this transformative process. Here, the technique of *mahāvedha* just reviewed is but a particular instance of the more general phenomenon of penetration or piercing that occurs within the yogic body when the breath, energy, and seed of the yogin—embodied in the female *kuṇḍalinī* serpent—pierce the six *cakra*s. This piercing of the *cakra*s—called *cakra-vedhana* or *cakra-bhedana*—is also a sexual penetration of sorts, albeit with sexual polarities reversed, given that it is a female *kuṇḍalinī* who awakens, stiffens, rises, even rushes upwards towards the cranial vault, the cavity that is the place of the passive male Śiva. As the *kuṇḍalinī* pierces each of the *cakra*s, great quantities of heat are produced, which refine and gradually transmute the seed that is the stuff of her body: it is this transmuted semen that becomes the nectar that immortalizes the yogin who holds it in his cranium.

Just as in the alchemical case, in which the practitioner holds a pill of refined mercury in the mouth, so in the yogic case, in which his head is filled with nectar: it is refined, perfected semen (of the god Śiva, of the initiating guru, or of the yogin himself) that transmutes his mortal, gross body into an immortal, perfected one. Here, *vedha* refers as well to the transformation of the practitioner himself. We have already seen that the alchemist, like the tantric initiate, becomes a second Śiva. Similar claims are made for the "transmuted" yogin, especially in the mystic verses attributed to Gorakhnāth and others of his sect. So Gorakh says, "Now that you've pierced [*bedhyā*] the lotuses six, go and drink that nectar mix/ . . .

Semen is yoga, semen is what pleases; semen averts the sixty-four diseases/ The rare dude who pierces semen's mystery, he's the creator, he's the divinity."[69]

Gorakhnāth, the author of the hathayogic *Gorakṣa Paddhati* and the mystic *bānīs* just quoted, is also the purported author of the alchemical *BhP*, which in its colophon calls itself a portion of the *Gorakṣa Saṁhitā;* in the Śākta work of the same name, the initiation of penetration is also described.[70] We therefore find in three works attributed to this great medieval Siddha references to all three uses of the term *vedha[na]*—the alchemical, the yogic, and the tantric—I have been discussing here. This is also the same Gorakh who, in the Nepali royal chronicle we summarized earlier, initiated the young Pṛthivinarāyaṇ Śāh by spitting yogurt he had "reversed" in his subtle yogic body into the young boy's hands. Elsewhere, in the legend of his own birth and initiation, Gorakh is portrayed as the first human to have had his ears pierced (or punched, or split, or bored: *phaṭ*) by his guru, Matsyendranāth. Armed with this knowledge, it becomes possible for us to reproduce the symbolic context that made initiation in the narratives I have reviewed the transformative act that it was.

In a number of these accounts, a boy becomes transformed into a king when he is initiated by a Siddha who either spits in his mouth or bores his ears or both. In the first instance, as we have seen, the guru enters and thereby transforms his disciple's body through the initiation rite known as *vedhamayī dīkṣā*, initiation by penetration. But in the latter practice as well, something is being penetrated or pierced. This is the thick cartilage of the initiate's ear. This practice of ear splitting, a hallmark of the Nāth Siddhas, has also earned them the appellation of "Split-Eared Yogis," the Kānphaṭa Yogis. As we saw, however, in Bāṇabhaṭṭa's seventh-century description of the Kāpālika Bhairavācārya, the *kuṇḍala* or *mudrā* worn through the thick of the ear was an external sign of Śaivite sectarian affiliation even before the emergence of the Nāth Siddhas.

What initiation by penetration and ear boring have in common is that both open up channels in the subtle body, channels which must be opened if the practitioner is to succeed in his hathayogic practice. When the guru enters into his disciple's body in the form of a drop of saliva, semen, or sound, it is he who first pierces (*bhed*) the disciple's six *cakras*, before exiting from the latter's mouth back into his own mouth. So too, ear boring, besides opening a hole in the disciple's ear, also opens, as if by synecdoche, a subtle channel inside the head of the initiate.[71] Once open, this channel too becomes a conduit to yogic powers and bodily immortality. In certain sources, it is further maintained that the guru actually penetrates, puts his mouth in the mouth of his disciple, somewhere inside the latter's left inner ear, at the opening of the channel called the "conch" (*śaṅkhinīnāḍī*).[72]

When we look closer, we find that the subtle body has at least ten "mouths" (*mukha*s: a better translation would be aperture or orifice), that the *kuṇḍalinī* serpent has two mouths, and that mercury itself becomes possessed of a mouth when it reaches an optimum level of transmutation. This multitude of mouths gives rise to all manner of complication in descriptions of processes within the subtle body, as well as to all manner of variations on the initiation process, some of which, of an overtly sexual order, remind us of the perils of poor Cakravarman at the hands (or should we say mouths) of the Ḍombī temptresses Goosie and Serpentina.[73]

But so it always is with these Siddha and tantric traditions. It is precisely this simultaneous play upon multiple levels of correspondence that makes these systems work. Each instance of penetration recalls another analogous instance, such that initiation, transmutation, and yogic integration all become a single process; every mouth refers to other mouths. These parallel processes come to exert a cumulative effect as well, with one simultaneously catalyzing and being catalyzed by all the others. Thus, for example, the yogin who combines the internal piercing of his *cakra*s with the practice of holding an all-penetrating mercurial pill in his mouth (*guṭikā bandha*) and/or the sexual penetration of *vajrolī mudrā* becomes capable of alchemically penetrating all matter with his bodily secretions, thereby transforming minerals to gold and boys to princes or human replicas of Śiva. Once inside the system, the various permutations on the process are mutually reinforcing.

The Siddha or tantric initiation rites behind the narratives that were passed in review in the first part of this chapter were the medieval cognates of the Vedic royal consecration of old. In the medieval cases, the institution of priesthood remains, with the Vedic sacrificial priest being replaced by a tantric guru. The ritual reiteration of the priesthood's seniority and superiority vis-à-vis royalty is also retained. However, instead of the rather tame procedure of tapping an unpunishable (*adaṇḍya*) king on the shoulder with the rod of punishment (*daṇḍa*), the tantric initiator actually renders himself the biological father of his royal disciple, using tantric techniques to transform the latter's mundane body into a perfected, tantric one and thereby afford him dominion over this world and worlds beyond. For the Siddha, transforming a boy into a king is, in such a situation, child's play.[74]

5. Kavi, Siddha, Vidyādhara

What is the appearance of one who has transformed himself into an alchemical Siddha? As described in the *RA* (12.366–68),

> he is the darling of fair-eyed vixens, slender-waisted with a compact, rock-hard body, as inflamed as a rutting bull elephant, as alluring as Love himself. The beau of lustful women, his body is a bolt of lightning flashing amidst the storm clouds of his curling jet black hair. As immaculate as the chaplain of the gods (Bṛhaspati), he is an alchemical wizard (*kavi*) and wonder-worker. He moves with the imposing gait of a great bull; his voice is deep and mellifluous. Like the divine elephant Airavant, he surges ever forward into the world, indefatigable. Radiant as a lotus pond, he outlives even the sun, moon, and stars of this world. A consummate logician and expert in all the sciences, he is a protector of the precepts of virtuous men because he knows, by his power of inference, what is righteous and proper. The heroic [*vīra*] equal of Viṣṇu and Śiva,[75] he is as enduring as the sun, moon, and sea.

A number of terms (*siddha, kavi, vīra*) and allusions found in this passage summarize both the historical origins and the ultimate goals of the Siddha alchemist. The last of these, *vīra*, is a reference to the broader tantric tradition within which the Siddha theoreticians often situated themselves. The tantric "hero" is a practitioner who, through his initiation, practice, and gnoseological transformation, has transcended the bounded, duality-ridden world of lower creatures (*paśu*s) of this world. The very same heterodox practices with which the tantric practitioner reaffirms his transcendence and absolute freedom—caste-free sexual intercourse, the consumption of forbidden power substances—are those which otherwise condemn the unwashed masses to hell.[76] As we have noted, intercourse with Siddha maidens, *yoginī*s, even goddesses, is a desideratum for the Siddha practitioner and a recurring theme in every tantric alchemical work.[77]

More specific to these Siddha traditions is the goal of becoming a *kavi*, a wizard. As indicated in the opening chapter of this book, the sense of the term, as it is employed here and in alchemical works, differs from the more broadly accepted usage of "poet." The Vedic *kavi*s, of which the Asura chaplain Kāvya Uśanas was the paragon, were not only wordsmiths (poets) but also death-defying, wonder-working wizards. It is this sense of the term that is intended here and in a number of Siddha works that evoke the *kavi*. Here, it should also be recalled that the "old" supernatural power of *rasa-rasāyana* was one that was to be wrested from the subterranean Asuras. This is precisely what the young Kaca did when he won the formula for immortality from Kāvya Uśanas, who was, by virtue of his knowledge of healing and incantations of immortality, the Asuras' greatest wizard. The Ayurvedic healers of Bengal continue to be called *kavirāja*s down to the present day.[78] This goal or supernatural power of *kavi*-hood, shared by alchemical and hathayogic sources alike, is evoked in the *KJñN*, *KCM*, *RA*, *Gorakṣa Sataka*, *KhV*, and *Śiva Saṁhitā*.[79] The successful alchemist is a *kavi* because he, like the Asura Kāvya Uśanas (Uśanas, son of a *kavi*) or the Vedic singer of hymns, is capable, through his mystic omniscience, to shape his own universal order, bend nature to his will, and thereby realize wealth, invincibility, and immortality for himself.[80]

The *RA* compares the purity of the perfected Siddha to that of Bṛhaspati, the chaplain of the gods and divine counterpart of Kāvya Uśanas, a comparison that leads us from the "subterranean" or "nocturnal" powers of the *kavi* to those more closely identified with the light-filled worlds of the gods and demigods. It is here that the notion of bodily transubstantiation, from human practitioner to *divine* Siddha or Vidyādhara, comes to the fore. Here, the intermingling, in the Siddha lists reviewed in chapter four, of gods, demigods, and perfected humans, is reflective of the essential transformation realized by the Siddha alchemist. By becoming an immortal, invincible "second Śiva," he literally enters the ranks of the semidivine Siddhas and Vidyādharas, if not of the gods themselves.

There is ample evidence for the fact that cults of Siddhas and Vidyādharas predated the emergence of those human practitioners and religious orders who called themselves "Siddhas."[81] In essence, the genius of these orders and their authors was to appropriate for themselves these preexisting traditions and incorporate them into their own syntheses. This is transparently the case with Matsyendranāth, revered as the Siddha founder of a number of tantric cults, whose *KJñN* is replete with references to Siddhas both human and divine. It is to the latter that he clearly refers when he states that "the planets, serpents, gods, *yoginī*s, and Siddhas, *all of them worshipped*, themselves worship the eight Mother Goddesses."[82] Human Siddhas are evoked a few verses later, when Matsyendra speaks of the assembly (*paṅkti*) of gurus, Siddhas, and *yoginī*s.[83] The four lineage Siddhas (*kula-siddha*s) are semidivine intermediaries who have revealed the mystic doctrine to the world in the four cosmic ages: their worship, described in the final verses of the work, was adapted into Kaula ritual.[84] Of course, the revealer of this doctrine in the present age is none other than Macchanda/ Matsyendra himself, making him the ideal model for all humans who would raise themselves up to the level of divine Siddha.[85]

Matsyendra twice mentions Vidyādharīs (the female counterpart of the Vidyādharas) in his *KJñN;* in both cases he describes techniques for attracting and sexually exciting Vidyādharīs and other female demigods. His sole mention of the Vidyādharas places them in the company of a number of male demigods, all of whom the practitioner is to visualize within his body.[86]

I have already reviewed a number of cases in which the matter of becoming a Siddha or Vidyādhara, or gaining mastery over these aerial spirits, was broached in early Śaiva literature. In the *Caṇḍakauśika* of Kṣemīśvara, the final apotheosis of Hariścandra, superintended by the god Dharma in the form of a Kāpālika alchemist, is effected through an aerial car, brought to him by the Vidyādharas.[87] In Bāṇabhaṭṭa's *Harṣacarita,* the Pāśupata Bhairavācarya's goal is to transform himself into the lord of the Vidyādharas.[88] So too, a Śaiva "Great Vow-Taker" seeks to become a Vidyādhara in the *Kathāsaritsāgara* tale of Devadatta the gambler.[89]

This theme, of transforming oneself into a Siddha or Vidyādhara, is also a standard fixture of the alchemical literature. So we read in the twelfth-century *RM* that one who has succeeded in fully transmuting his body—by jumping into a cauldron of boiling oil, mercury, and other alchemical ingredients—swoons and then recovers to find himself transformed into the three-eyed, four-armed Gaṇanātha (lord of Siva's host). The Siddhas and Vidyādharas come en masse to view the transformed alchemist, and together with these denizens of the atmospheric region he flies through the air and is brought before Maheśvara (Śiva), whom he worships.[90] In the origin myth of sulfur, presented in the same source, the Goddess is depicted as sporting with Vidyādharīs, Siddha maidens, and a host of other semidivine women.[91] According to the *MBhT,* the practitioner who follows its instructions gains *siddhi*s and becomes a "Siddha who is the manifest equal of Śiva."[92] So too, the *Śiva Saṁhitā,* a relatively late Nāth Siddha guide to *haṭha yoga,* ends with the promise that the yogin may see the (divine) Siddhas and gain control over the Vidyādharas through his practice.[93] Finally, the *ĀK* concludes its description of the "lithe virgin on horseback" technique[94] for the extraction of mercury with the following statement: "Mercury is found in all of those places that the Siddhas and Vidyādharas caused it to fall [by using that technique]."[95]

It is in the alchemical *RA* that we find the most extended references to the matter of becoming a Siddha. In its discussion of "revivifying water" (*sañjīvanījalam*), it relates that the alchemist who has drunk three measures of this water swoons and then awakens to find himself transformed and possessed of supernatural powers. He is able to "see into cracks in the earth [to find buried treasure] throughout the seven underworlds [haunts of the Asuras]; he is invulnerable to the onslaughts of gods and antigods alike." After further treating this water with mercury, realgar, and the three noble metals, "he suddenly disappears [from human sight] and becomes the lord of the Vidyādharas, surrounded by a circle of Siddha maidens for a period of fourteen *kalpa*s."[96] The same work concludes its description of *khecari jāraṇa* ("calcination of flying [mercury]") by stating that the alchemist who ingests said mercury by means of this technique is immediately uplifted into the presence of the gods, Siddhas, and Vidyādharas, with whom he flies through the air at will.[97] The work concludes on a similar note:[98]

> He mounts into an aerial car made of divine gold studded with divine gemstones and rubies and filled with flowered garlands and banners and the roar of conches and musical instruments. Thereupon, a divine maiden, a singer of nymphen melodies and an alluring dancer, decked out in divine finery and garlands—a lusty beauty and a veritable image of Love in a female form—comes to him and takes the consummate practitioner to dwell in the world of the Siddhas. Then, after having bathed, wined and dined him, and clothed him in divine finery, the love-starved Siddha maiden sports with him for hundreds and thousands of years.

The passage and the entire work end on the statement, "When all the fixed and moving beings in the universe have been annihilated in that terrible flood [of universal dissolution], the Siddha is absorbed into the same place as are the gods."[99] The place in question here is, according to the most widely held Hindu beliefs concerning the fate of the universe, one of the two highest "worlds" or "heavens" (*tapoloka*, and *siddhaloka* or *brahmaloka*), which together serve as a holding tank of sorts for liberated souls. Suspended high above the general conflagration, they are saved from universal dissolution and, most important, the necessity of reincarnation into a transmigrating body upon the reordering of the cosmic egg, by Brahmā, at the beginning of the next cosmic age. Once one accedes to these sublime levels, one need never return.

6. Mountains of Wisdom

A number of tantric sources classify the Siddhas into three groups: gods, semidivine Vedic sages, and humans who have realized a perfected (*siddha*) body.[100] In other words, a number of the Siddhas found in the lists reviewed in chapter four began their ongoing careers as gods, while others are humans who acceded to a divine station through their practice of Siddha alchemy.

Nāgārjuna, a Rasa Siddha who clearly belongs to the last of these three groups, nonetheless shows divine pretensions when he states in his *RM* that "in the perfection of *rasa,* I shall make the world devoid of poverty and disease."[101] Here, *rasāyana,* in both the medical and alchemical senses of the term, is the only means by which humans may enjoy the immortality that the gods, demigods, and denizens of the underworld possess by their very nature. This appears to be the intended sense of a passage from the venerable *Caraka Saṁhitā* (6.1.78): "Like the ambrosia (*amṛta*) of the immortal gods and the nectar (*sudhā*) of the serpents, so the principle of *rasāyana* was to the great seers of old . . . he who uses *rasāyana* in the prescribed manner not only obtains long life on earth but also, upon death, betakes himself to that light-filled realm within which the divine sages dwell."[102]

There are thus three sorts of elixirs of immortality, the access to which depends upon one's ontological status; those humans, however, who make use of the elixir available to them can hope to accede, after death, to a level of existence normally reserved for a certain class of deities. This notion of an exclusive afterlife in the company of semidivine beings, already glimpsed in this medical source, becomes a central concern of the later Siddha traditions. This is the purport of the *RA*'s final word on alchemy, which seems to imply that in order for the alchemist to fully join the ranks of the Siddhas and Wizards, he must physically enter into his alchemical apparatus. This is a principle also found in a number of Chinese alchemical sources—sources in the light of which this and a number of other elements of Hindu alchemical lore come to stand out in higher relief. First of all, transforming oneself into an immortal by entering into one's alchemical apparatus is a commonplace of Taoist alchemy. In the Chinese case, the apparatus in question, called *hu-lu,* was formed out of two superimposed spherical gourds, a configuration at once identified with the head and torso of the subtle body, a double mountain located to the far east or west of China, and an abode of the Immortals (*hsien*).[103] Entering into one's alchemical apparatus is, in these sources, somewhat less dramatic than the operation described in the *RA:* its results are, however, wholly as transformative as those promised in the Hindu alchemical tradition. Taoist alchemical sources dating from the first half of the first millennium A.D. are particularly rich in legends on this subject, one of which was reproduced in chapter eight, on the subject of a certain Che Ts'ouen. It will be recalled that the vessel this Taoist alchemist suspended from his roof beam, called *hu* or *hu-lu,* was at night transformed into Heaven and Earth. Che Ts'ouen, who passed his nights there, called himself "Heaven in a [Double] Gourd" (*hu-t'ien*); people called him the "Old Man of the Gourd." Following this he realized the Tao (and became an immortal).[104]

In the Chinese sources, these identifications—between a bicameral alchemical apparatus, a configuration within the subtle body, a double mountain, and an abode of the immortals—are made much more explicitly than they are in the Hindu sources reviewed to this point. To be sure, the Hindu use of the term *vidyādhara,* Wizard, applies equally to a bicameral apparatus, a hathayogic technique, and the mountain dwelling alchemists who mastered them. What appears to be lacking in the Hindu material is the explicit identification of these semidivine figures and alchemical apparatus with these sacred mountains themselves, an identification which the Taoists make with especial reference to two immortal abodes. These are the mountains H'un-lun and K'un-lun, located to the far east and west of China respectively. The names of both of these peaks are derived from the same root (*hu*) as the term for the double-chambered gourd of Taoist alchemy: more than this, both of these mythic mountains retain the shape of the alchemical apparatus: H'un-lun has the form of two superimposed spheres, while K'un-lun that of two superimposed cones joined at their apex. These mountains are, moreover, situated within the subtle body of the alchemist, in his lower abdomen and head, respectively. As such, they are further identified as the Gates or Wells of Earth (H'un-lun) and Heaven (K'un-lun).[105]

Now, the Hindus also know of at least one mythic double mountain: this is Meru, the pivot of the Hindu universe, which, located to the north of India, has the form of two cones, the one inverted and the other upright, joined at their tapered ends.[106] Like the Chinese Hun-lun, Meru has its microcosmic homologue as well: it is identified with the spinal column (called the *meru-daṇḍa,* "Meru rod") of the subtle body, along whose vertical axis the nectar of immortality is drawn upwards. General descriptions of Meru locate gods and demigods of the likes of the Vidyādharas and Siddhas on its slopes and describe its summit as an extensive plateau, hemmed in by a ring of peaks so as to have the form of a basin or saucer;[107] the *Caṇḍakauśika* (4.34) states that this mountain abode of the Siddhas may be reached through alchemical practice.

It is perhaps incorrect to state that the Hindus made no explicit identification between their alchemical wizards or immortals, their alchemical apparatus, and their sacred mountains. The Sanskrit term *dhara*, generated from the root *dhṛ*, means, as has already been noted, "bearer" or "recipient." Another sense of *dhṛ*, however, is "to support," a meaning that generates another reading of *dhara:* a mountain (*dhara*) is that which supports (*dhṛ*) the earth or the mineral riches within the earth. In this case, *vidyādhara* may be read as "Mountain of Wisdom," while the Vidyādharas, the Wizards, may be considered to be not only the denizens of such mountains, but also the mountains themselves. What we are suggesting here is that behind the medieval Indian cults of divine Siddhas and Vidyādharas as denizens of mountains there lay a more archaic cult of these mountains themselves as a group of demigods.

A number of works have much to say on this subject. An important example is the great tantric opus entitled the *Svacchanda Tantra*, much of whose cosmology is adapted nearly verbatim by Abhinavagupta in his *TĀ*.[108] Here, in an enumeration of the atmospheric levels located above the terrestrial disk and separated from one another by distances of either one hundred or five hundred *yojana*s, this source describes cloud masses (*megha*) (1) that strike down trees on earth with thunderbolts; (2) that cause rains of fishes, frogs, and turtles to fall; and (3) that cause disease-inducing poison rains to fall (and into which are born the subgroup of embodied beings called the Plagues; in this multitude dwell the divine ghouls who form Skanda's retinue, as well as the Obstructors, who are born of Śiva himself). Still paraphrasing the *Svacchanda Tantra*, Abhinavagupta continues:

> Five hundred *yojana*s higher is [the abode of] the Wind [named] "Lightning-Streak." Here at [the level of] "Lightning-Streak" are stationed . . . the "lowest-level Vidyādharas." These are beings who, when in the [prior] form of human wizards (*vidyāpauruṣe*) carried out cremation ground–related practices. When they died, that *siddhi* [rendered them] Siddhas, stationed in the midst of the "Lightning-Streak" wind . . . [109] Five hundred *yojana*s higher . . . there at Raivata itself are the primal Siddhas (*ādisiddhāḥ*) [named] Yellow Orpiment, Black Antimony, and Mercury Ash.[110]

This passage goes on to describe ever-higher levels, inhabited by superior (*viśeṣa*) Vidyādharas who, together with the celestial musicians, sing the praises of Parameśvara, the highest god; and still higher levels in which the most elevated (*uttama*) Vidyādharas are stationed. We will, however, dwell for a moment upon the particular case of Raivata and the clearly alchemical *siddhi*s and Siddhas with which it is associated. Concerning the latter, I first reproduce the *SvT* passage upon which Abhinavagupta based his description: "On Raivata are indeed stationed those great-souled Siddhas. Having undertaken the practices [dealing] in yellow orpiment, the black antimony [of invisibility], the ash [of transmutation], the shoes [of magical flight], the hairy skin [of the tiger, goat, or dog worn or carried by the Śaiva "Vow-Taker" or renouncer], etc., these great-souled ones became Siddhas, having Love's body (*kāmarūpināḥ*)."[111]

Here we can see that, whereas the *SvT* evokes a certain number of mineral preparations instrumentally—to explain that the Siddhas of Raivata are those beings who, while human, gained the *siddhi*s of invisibility, transmutation, magical flight, etc., through the practices of alchemy and renunciation—Abhinavagupta transforms these alchemical staples into a group of demigods whom he terms the "primal Siddhas." Here we are reminded of the Siddhas named Fire, Sun, and Moon who, according to the *Kubjikānityāhnikatilaka*, aided Śrīnātha in founding the *kula*, "at the beginning of the Kali Yuga," at a site called Candrapurī.[112] In both cases, these founding Siddhas are nothing other than elements of the Siddha gnosis itself which, like the Nine Nāths, are hypostasized into abstract deities. Homologous to this ambiguous treatment of the Siddhas, who are here portrayed as humans and here as atmospheric demigods, is that accorded to the Wizards. In these sources, it is clearly stated that the "lowest level of Vidyādharas" is composed of those beings who, when still human, had been Vidyāpuruṣas ("men of occult wisdom") whose cremation-ground practices had won them an atmospheric station after death.[113] It is to this level that such figures as Bāṇabhaṭṭa's Bhairavācārya would have acceded in the medieval literature.

These descriptions are for us proofs of what we have been arguing throughout this book: that the human practitioners of the Siddha disciplines of alchemy, *haṭha yoga*, and erotico-mystical ritual considered themselves to be divine or semidivine Siddhas *in potentia* and that beyond the supernatural powers and bodily immortality that were their immediate goals lay the higher end of apotheosis to the loftier realms of the Siddhas and Vidyādharas. This archaic component of their practice was the prime ground for their Siddha appellation, in spite of an increasing Śaiva (among the Hindu Siddhas) influence that never ceased to diminish and dilute the Siddha coloring of their gnosis. So it is that we find quite nearly as many references to "becoming a second Śiva" as to becoming an atmospheric Siddha or Vidyādhara; in certain sources, the issue is resolved by transforming those same semidivine Siddhas and Vidyādharas into so many members of Śiva's celestial retinue.

In an earlier chapter, I argued that certain mountaintops, lofty pivots between the worlds of the gods and demigods and the world of men, have been singled out since the medieval period as sites at which to realize the various *siddhi*s that enabled one to become a Siddha. Among these were Srisailam, Kedārnāth, Mount Abu, and Girnar. This brings us back to the passages just cited from the *SvT* and the *TĀ* which, in the midst of their descriptions of atmospheric levels located thousands of miles above the earth's surface (a *yojana* equals approximately nine miles), suddenly present the reader with a terrestrial toponym which they identify, precisely, with the alchemical "primal Siddhas" Yellow Orpiment, Black Collyrium, and Mercury Ash. This is the toponym Raivata which was in fact a medieval name for the cluster of peaks known today as Girnar, in the Junagadh district of Gujarat. In praise of this site, the Jain "Raivatācala Māhātmya" calls it the fifth of the twenty-one Jain *siddhādri*s (Siddha mountains) and states that "[here] sages who have ceased to eat and who pass their days in devotion . . . worship Nemīnāth. Here divine nymphs and numerous heavenly beings—Gandharvas, Siddhas, and Vidyādharas, etc.—always worship Nemīnāth."[114] A number of Purāṇas beginning with the ca. ninth-century *Matsya Purāṇa*[115] also devote long descriptions to the site, which they term Raivataka. Two to three centuries later than the *Matsya*, the *Skanda Purāṇa* devotes fifteen chapters to the wonders this site, which it alternatively calls Raivāta or Vastrāpatha.[116]

We clearly appear to be in the presence, in this wide array of sources, of a direct identification of Girnar as both a terrestrial site to which human experts in the esoteric sciences come to perfect themselves through Siddha techniques and an atmospheric or celestial site at which they dwell in their definitively transformed state of semidivine Siddhas. This pedigree of Girnar goes back further still, mentioned as it is by the seventh-century Hsuan-tsang, who describes a meeting there with "rishis endued with spiritual faculties [*siddhi*s]."[117] It is also present in earlier Hindu texts, but here by yet another name, this being Gomanta.[118] We find this early toponym for Girnar mentioned once in the *Mahābharata*,[119] in the context of the episode of Jarāsandha, a regicide king and very early devotee of Rudra-Śiva, who hailed from the Kathiawad region of present-day Gujarat.[120]

A much more detailed description of the site is given in the ca. fifth-century *Harivaṃśa* "appendix" to the epic, which also relates it to the figure of Jarāsandha.[121] While this appears to be no different from a great number of other praises of heavenly mountains, this text is important for two reasons: on the one hand, the mountain in question is Girnar; on the other, this is perhaps the earliest Hindu source to bring the Siddhas and Vidyādharas "down to earth" and to make them the inhabitants of a lofty peak rather than the atmospheric regions. "The [mountain] called Gomanta, a solitary heavenly peak surrounded by a group of [lesser] peaks, is difficult to scale, even by the Sky-goers . . . its two highest horns have the form of two shining gods . . . [122] The interior of this mountain is frequented by Siddhas, Cāraṇas, and Rakṣasas, and the surface of the peak is ever thronged with hosts of Vidyādharas."[123]

The Girnar peak which the Jains identify as Nemīnāth has long been known to Hindu pilgrims by the name of Dattātreya,[124] the semidivine founder and leader of the Nine Nāths of western Indian, especially Maharashtran tradition. Dattātreya is in fact one of a pair of rocky crags that dominate the formation of Girnar, the other being Gorakh: these twin peaks, having heights of 3,450 and 3,470 feet respectively, are by far the highest and most impressive features of the rim of mountains that form a basin some six miles in circumference. Girnar has furthermore constituted one of the most important centers of Nāth Siddha activity in western India, as evidenced in references to it, from the fourteenth century onwards, in legends concerning their founders.[125] In an earlier chapter I argued, on the subject of these twin peaks, that they were called "Gorakh" and "Dattātreya" not because they featured shrines to these Nāth Siddhas but because they *were* these Siddhas, i.e., that the bedrock of the presence and veneration of "human" Nāth Siddhas at Girnar were the semidivine Siddhas whose ranks the latter succeeded in joining through their practice. The semidivine Siddhas dwelling *inside* Gomanta (within the basin formed by the rim of peaks?) and the Vidyādharas dwelling on its surface (on the outer slopes of those peaks?) preceded the likes of the twelfth- to thirteenth-century Gorakh and Dattātreya, who replaced them, and thereby became the demigods identified with its two highest twin peaks. In this light, it is tantalizing to note that the *Kulārṇava Tantra* (6.66) lists Dattātreya and Raivataka in immediate succession as two of the ten gurus of the Kaula *siddhaugha*.

Data from other regions of the Indian subcontinent appear to support this argument. Gorakh, who is called a Vidyādhara in the "Song of Maṇik Candra" is depicted in the "Legend of Pūraṇ Bhagat" as flying through the air at the head of fifty-two hundred visible and invisible disciples.[126] Popular tradition maintains that the founding Nāth Siddhas are still living in the Himalayas, as the guardian spirits of the Himalayan peaks. In the mountainous Gulmi district of central Nepal, a nondescript "god of the summit" is named "Siddha."[127] In the mountainous Chamba district of the Punjab, generally nameless "Siddhs" are worshipped, in the same fashion as serpents and minor goddesses, in rustic temples; an exception is Gugga Mundalikh Siddh, identified with an eleventh-century historical figure named Gūgā Chauhān and with the Nāth Siddha known as Guru Gūgā or Gūgā Pīr, whose shrine is located at Shālū in Himgari.[128] As noted in chapter four, the "historical" Gorakhnāth is said to have discovered a shrine to the Nepali (Gurkha) deity Gorakh, into whose service he devoted himself. Over time, this mountain godling and the human yogin became fused into a single figure: Gorakhnāth, founder of the Nāth *sampradāya* and the site of Gorakhpur.[129]

In the light of this evidence, we must conclude that such historical Siddhas as Gorakh, Dattātreya, and Nāgārjuna, whose acts and lives defined the religious landscape of a certain Gupta and post-Gupta India, became fused in the Hindu imagination with certain classes of gods and demigods, in whose number the *divine* Siddhas and Vidyādharas must be counted; and that it was at such peaks as Girnar, in western India, the heartland of early Śaivism, that such identifications first emerged.[130] While we cannot say to what extent these figures were and are identified with the sacred peaks themselves, my reading of Vidyādhara as "Mountain of Wisdom" should not be entirely far-fetched, especially in the light of the *Harivaṃśa* description of Gomanta.

This peak, which I have identified with Girnar, is said to be inhabited both inside and out by Siddhas and Vidyādharas. Like many sacred mountains, Girnar is a site riddled with caves, of which at least two are identified with Nāth Siddhas (Bhartṛhari and Dattātreya); and what is a mountain cave, if not the macrocosmic replica of the cranial vault of the meditating yogin, the tumulus (*samādhi*) in which deceased yogins are interred, or the upper chamber of an alchemical apparatus within which the alchemist transforms himself into the *opus alchymicum?* As in the Taoist case, the Möbius universe of the Siddhas is so constructed as to permit its practitioners at once to identify cosmic mountains with their own subtle bodies and to enter into those mountains to realize the final end of their practice, the transformation into the semidivine denizens of those peaks.

So it is that these myriad allusions, found in a wide array of Śaiva, Siddha, tantric, and Jain sources, are so many literary vestiges of an archaic cult of divine Siddhas and Vidyādharas who, like the immortals (*hsien*) of Taoism, came to be joined in their ranks by heroic humans (Pāśupatas, Kāpālikas, Nāth Siddhas, and Rasa Siddhas) who, through their dangerous and difficult trials, transcended their human condition. This is the Siddha foundation of tantrism: the archaic goal of gaining power over divine Siddha and Vidyādhara wizards and nymphs funneled into the tantric cults of the *yoginīs*, which were in turn internalized into the practices of *haṭha yoga* and alchemy as practiced by superhuman Nāth and Rasa Siddhas and the more refined and abstract ritual practices of "high" Tantra.

EPILOGUE

The Siddha Legacy in Modern India

> "My dear chap, I ask you!" said Masood, as if it were my fault. Those sadhus would sometimes come to Dewas and bless the Palace, and demand a hundred rupees each. Malarao would speak as fair as he could and give each of them one rupee. They then cursed the Palace and returned to Ujjain.[1]

The medieval Siddhas of India were self-styled imitators of divine and semidivine Siddhas who, through their conjoined practice of alchemy, *haṭha yoga*, and tantric ritual (erotico-mystical or "sublimated," when it took the form of worship of the divine Siddhas), sought to join the ranks of the latter at the end of their practice (*sādhana*) or at the end of their lives. Over the centuries, the cults of the divine Siddhas and Vidyādharas, denizens of the atmospheric regions or of lofty peaks, have gradually diminished and are today found only in remote mountain regions of the Indian subcontinent. In other parts of India, these demigods have been supplanted by or conflated with such historical figures as Matsyendranāth, Gorakhnāth, Nāgārjuna, or Dattātreya, figures who self-consciously aligned themselves with the former, taking their names as honorary titles or indications of various degrees of realization in their mystic arts.[2]

A case in point is "Gorakhnāth" who, having discovered the shrine of the godling Gorkha (divinity of the Gurkhas of the Himalayan region of Gurkha in Nepal), took the name of Gorakhnāth, i.e., "he whose Lord is Gorakh."[3] Such a conceptual shift—from "shrine served by a holy man" to "shrine of the holy man" himself—was effected in the Indian popular imagination, and in the generation of legends that grew up around this composite figure, in the same way as such has occurred in Europe. A local godling, identified with a spring of healing waters or one or another geographic anomaly gradually becomes transformed into a "saint" whose relics are the source of the magic that cures the sick or drives away plagues.[4]

In India, the nocturnal sight of hermits' fires, tiny points of light illuminating the brooding silhouettes of dark mountains, would also have fueled an identification of the semidivine Siddhas with their human emulators.

Today, the majority of those dark hillsides are crisscrossed by metaled roads, over which buses full of pilgrims and tourists travel. The hermits have withdrawn deeper into the mountains or have disappeared altogether from the sight of men. Their departure has left a void in the modern Indian soul, perhaps not unlike that which has marked the American soul since the disappearance of the frontier some one hundred years ago. Something fundamentally real, something whose mere existence has been a millennarian source of spiritual solace, has been lost or is in the process of being lost. How has twentieth-century India reacted to the "disenchantment of the world"?

1. Transmutation in the Twentieth Century

I have met Siddhas who claimed to be alchemists but who would not show me their powers. I met many more who claimed to know alchemists without ever being able to divulge to me their exact whereabouts. There was, however, a well-documented case of transmutation, carried out in 1940 by an Ayurvedic pharmacist in a Benares Hindu University laboratory before a group of scholars. One of the last surviving members of this group, Yadunandan Upadhyaya, gave me an account of the experiment at his Benares home–cum–Ayurvedic dispensary in the spring of 1984:

> Krishna Pal Shastri, a *vaidya* from Jamnagar, in Gujarat, performed the experiment in the laboratory of Benares Hindu University chemistry professor Phaldevasahaya Varma, in the presence of nine or ten Ayurvedic scholars and practitioners and the great industrialist Birla. Shastri hollowed out a soap nut, which he filled with mercury, two or three grams of borax, and a grain of a secret powder. He sealed the nut with a paste of lime and molasses and put it inside a crucible, which he placed on a charcoal fire. He fanned the fire until the nut inside the crucible began to burn. When the smoke cleared, he split the nut open with an iron wedge. Inside was a metal that looked like silver. Half of this metal was taken by Professor Varma and the other half by Mr. Birla. Varma tested it at BHU and Birla at one of his firm's laboratories in Calcutta. In both cases, the metal tested out as pure silver, with only the spectroscopy showing a slight variation from that of natural silver. Sastri had informed those who were pres-

ent that he could also produce gold by the same procedure, by merely substituting ammonium chloride for borax. Later on, at Birla's instigation, he produced gold in this way. He continued to make gold in this way, at the rate of three grams per week, to cover his laboratory and personal expenses.

Marble plaques, in the Viśvanāth Temple on the campus of Benares Hindu University and at the Birla Temple in Delhi, bear witness to Shastri's alchemical feats and state that the gold he manufactured over time totaled seventy thousand rupees in value. I was told by another Banarsi Ayurvedic scholar, Siddhinandan Misra, that Shastri used up all his gold playing the horses and that he died of poisoning by persons attempting to extort his secrets from him.[5] I was unable to corroborate either of these statements.

Similar accounts of alchemical aurifaction have continued to appear periodically in the Indian press. The 8 June 1968 issue of the *Navabhārat Times* ran a story, out of Ahmedabad, concerning an Ayurvedic pharmacist named A. C. Acharya, who had produced pure gold from mercury in four days, at Jamnagar (Gujarat). This story was corroborated by Siddhinandan Misra, who added that the experiment was carried out under the eyes of ten goldsmiths, ten chemists, and six government ministers. *Dharm Yug*'s 7 September 1975 edition states that the "secret ingredient" used in these experiments was "perfected mercury" (*siddhasūta*).[6]

Even if authentic alchemists have become a scarce commodity in twentieth-century India, the Hindu alchemical tradition seems to have left its mark on the Indian psyche in a number of often-unexpected ways. One of these is a tendency to attribute a certain order of *consciousness* to metals. Such a tendency ought perhaps not to surprise us, if we understand tantric thought in the same way as does Sanjukta Gupta when she states that:

> ultimately the conscious bits of the universe, like stones, are also God and hence consciousness, but a consciousness that has decided to conceal itself (*ātmasaṃkoca*). Here we come to the double concealment which God decides on; firstly, He conceals the fact that His true form is identical with the individual soul; and secondly He conceals His true nature as consciousness to manifest Himself as unconscious phenomena. The world of the Tantric, then, is ultimately all God, but it contains a vast range of things, from things as gross as stones to things as subtle as God.[7]

A number of twentieth-century Indian scientists have been sympathetic to this viewpoint. In his renowned *Autobiography of a Yogi*, Yogananda gives an account of the Bengali scientist Jagadis Bose, who demonstrated to him an apparatus he had invented in the 1930s:[8]

> Graphs of my delicate apparatus have proved that trees possess a circulatory system; their sap movements correspond to the blood pressure of animal bodies . . . The more deeply we perceive, the more striking becomes the evidence that a uniform plan links every form in manifold Nature . . . I shall show you experiments on a piece of tin. The life-force in metals responds adversely or beneficially to stimuli. Ink markings will register the various reactions. [Yogānanda then continues, in his own voice:] Deeply engrossed, I watched the graph that recorded the characteristic waves of atomic structure. When the professor applied chloroform to the tin, the vibratory writings stopped. They recommenced as the metal slowly regained its normal state. My companion dispensed a poisonous chemical. Simultaneously with the quivering end of the tin, the needle dramatically wrote in the chart a death notice.

A similar body of assumptions appears to underlie the theories of T. R. Anantharaman, who was, when I interviewed him in December of 1984, the dean of the prestigious Engineering College at Benares Hindu University. In a lecture entitled "Transformations—Metallurgical and Mental," Professor Anantharaman proposes that the four states of human consciousness (matter, life, mind, and supermind) correspond to the four metallurgical phases (gas, liquid, single-phase solid, multiphase solid). Here, the three culminating stages of Pātañjala yoga correspond to phase transformations (nucleation and growth) in the metallurgical solid phase. In such transformations, "embryos" or small nuclei are generated, which are capable of further growth and steady increase in size until transformation occurs. This process of nucleation is to be compared, in yogic practice, to the realization of *samādhi*. In the end, the transformations undergone by the meditating yogin are to be viewed as so many monotectoid transformations, effected on the level of human consciousness.[9]

On a more popular level, we find the pervasive notion in India that the eight metals (*aṣṭadhātu*) are intimately related to the movements and astrological effects of the nine celestial bodies (*navagraha*). By wearing an eight-metal ring, one wards off the baneful influences of such dread planets as Saturn, while enhancing the salutory effects of the auspicious planets. Certain sources identify the Nine Nāths with the eight metals or nine planets; in an interview he granted me in 1984, Mangalraj Joshi, the royal astrologer to King Birendra of Nepal, identified the nine planets with the eight metals.[10]

Of greater and more wide-ranging impact than pseudoscientific theorizing of this order are certain effects the medieval Siddha traditions appear to have had—if only by their transformation or absence—on a number of medical notions and political strategies in late twentieth-century India. These are the subject of the next two sections of this chapter.

2. Impotence: The Ravages of *Gupta Rog*

High in the snow-clad Himalayas, in a cave above Joshimath, lives a five hundred-year-old man whose eyebrows have grown down over his eyes. The four hundred-year-old Sundarnāth Siddha, an expert in the alchemical arts living in the hills above Kathmandu, disappeared and reappeared at will before definitively disappearing in the 1970s.[11] The alchemist Nāgārjuna lived for eight hundred years before giving up his head and life at the request of a young prince. Gorakhnāth, the yogic superman, has stood beside kings and heroes for millenia, abandoning one body for another at will. He and his brother Nāth Siddhas, immortal guardians of the Himalayan peaks, are as old as the mountains themselves. In India, whose recorded traditions of the deeds of gods and humans are among the oldest on the planet, examplary humans have ever rivaled the gods in their longevity and power. Yet this is the same India upon whose sweltering plains "youngmen" are warned in "clinical literature" that they will "look old at the age of 25 [through] the horrors of the wastage of semen . . . Many youngmen have sex many times at night and thus waste this essence of life recklessly. With small production and heavy drainage, supply will exhaust soon and critical consequences will have to be faced."[12]

What connections can we draw between the grandeur and the squalor, between immortality in the highlands and misspent youth in the lowlands of India? A glance at Ayurvedic theories of digestion, metabolism, and the production of sexual fluids provides us with a key to this puzzle. The Upaniṣads inform us that humans are constantly being cooked by the fires of time; and as the myth of King Moon demonstrates, the cooking is never so fierce as when man sheds his seed, his very staff of life.This sentiment is expressed in the beautiful poetry of Tāyumāṉavar, a Tamil Śaiva poet who lived in the first half of the eighteenth century:

> Ecstatically, you think, "sex is bliss."
>
> This embracing becomes more frequent,
> Growing to excess
>
> Like the waning moon,
> Your intellect becomes exhausted.
> And your body shrivels up
> Like a monkey's wrinkled skin.
> You grow old soon [. . .]
>
> When the dark Lord of Death comes,
> Who will protect you,
> O sinful mind?

It would appear that the male sex drive puts males in an impossible bind, in which they find themselves in constant danger of losing their seed, a seed that is accumulated only very slowly and in minuscule quantities through the long process of digestion. According to Ayurvedic theory, this is a seven-step process, in which the food we eat is serially "burned" or refined into *rasa* (chyle), blood, flesh, fat, bone, marrow, and finally, in men, semen (it becomes uterine blood or breast milk in women).[13] Here, it takes some twenty-eight days—a lunar month, and the same time it takes a woman's body to produce an ovum—for the food males ingest to become transformed into semen.[14] Moreover, it requires a prodigious quantity of food to produce a single gram of semen.[15] Ayurvedic theories of conception[16]—according to which male children are produced by a relative preponderance of semen to uterine blood at the moment of conception, while females are produced by an opposite ratio[17]—compound the perils of semen depletion.

These medical notions have given rise, in modern India, to a male concern, if not obsession, with semen retention, in which the garnering and conservation of this, the end product of digestion and the most vital of bodily fluids, is quite nearly synonymous with the maintenance of good health and the prospects for long life. Male virility, indeed, male life expectancy, depends upon a careful conservation of this rare and precious vital fluid which, in addition to being depleted through the inexorable aging process, is in constant danger of being burned up and entirely consumed in a fiery uterine ocean of female sexuality.

The mythic ground for this cultural obsession, or for what Gananath Obeyesekere has termed *cultural diseases* involving the loss of bodily fluids, is the Vedic myth of the origin of royal consumption (*rājayakṣma*), in which the dissipation of semen in sexual intercourse results in the "death" of King Moon.[18] Elsewhere, the yogic sources abound in admonitions to celibacy (*ūrddhvaretas*, "semen held upwards," in the lunar region of the cranial vault), sometimes comparing the vulva to a vampiress that drains a man of his life and virility.[19] A "limit situation" of this attitude was stated with dramatic clarity by the very this-worldy Aghori Vimalananda just over a decade ago:

> You must have heard of women in the Place Pigalle in Paris who can pick up one-franc coins from tables with their vaginas; I have seen this with my own eyes. And I am told that in Laos and Vietnam, some bargirls can smoke cigarettes vaginally . . . A woman who knows Vajroli [here, vaginal suction] can "milk" an unsuspecting man of his semen with her suction. She can make him eject over and over again until there is nothing left to eject, which will sap him of all his *ojas* [human vital fluid, of which there only exist eight drops]. Her glands will be well benefited by this, at his expense.[20]

In a general sense, all women are, according to such popular wisdom, so many vampiresses whose mere presence, even as an image in the male imagination, is sufficient to drain a man of his seed: indeed, this is the cause of male nocturnal emissions (*svapna doṣa*, the "sleep flaw"). The long-term effect of this nefarious influence is death: Hindu India holds widows implicitly guilty for the premature deaths of their husbands, whose very lives they are viewed as having consumed in their insatiable feminine passion.[21] More than once I have been told by Indian men that my bachelorhood (which they have equated with celibacy) was a good thing, because thanks to it I would not die young.

On a more immediate and visible level, the upshot of these concerns is that Indian males, finding themselves constantly beset with the cultural disease of *gupta rog*, the "secret ailment," have been pouring, in ever-increasing numbers, into so-called Ayurvedic *gupta rog* clinics. These are clinics that treat male "sexual disorders," of which the prime symptom, judging from their advertising and literature on the subject, is the birth of daughters. *Putra hogā*, "you will have a son," is the promised cure.[22] In a society in which male children bring wealth into a household (through dowry), while females take it out, chronic "fuel shortages" on the part of males can take on financially catastrophic proportions. As a result, the *gupta rog* clinics do a land-office business throughout India, as evinced in ubiquitous billboard advertising for their remedies.

The economic pressures of a viciously hyperinflated dowry system, compounded with these pervasive notions concerning male and female sexuality, have only increased the perceived, indeed the real, need in India for the remedies sold by the *gupta rog* clinics (the term covers all manner of sexual disorder, including impotence, premature ejaculation, venereal disease, etc.). Within a conceptual context in which women are vampiresses and the loss of seed is tantamount to financial ruin if not death, psychological pressures arising from the urgency of producing male offspring cannot help but have a powerful negative impact on male sexual response. Can there be any outlet for this cultural disease?

3. Omnipotence: India's "Men in Saffron"

For a large segment of the male Indian population, life is in some ways like a bomb with a short fuse, which none save the distant Siddhas and yogins have ever been capable of defusing before an otherwise inevitable explosion. It is in this way that Siddha longevity and male sexual disorders, seemingly situated at opposite poles of the Indian experience, may be viewed as intimately related in Indian thought. Indeed, it is a single millenarian symbol system that joins them together—a system that embraces Ayurvedic rejuvenation therapy (*rasāyana*), the "yoga of violent exertion" (*haṭha yoga*), and elixir alchemy (*dehavāda*). In a sense, this ancient legacy has taken the form of a conundrum (unavoidable aging, loss of virility, death, all identified with failure to retain semen) for which a satisfactory solution is lacking. This false problem of semen depletion may be rooted in a deeper "paradigm depletion." Yet, a solution of sorts has been emerging in India of late, a solution that has the potential to trigger the fall of the "secular state" in the world's largest democracy.

Here, I wish to go one step further, in the certain knowledge that some will find my speculations offensive, and hypothesize that the culturally determined form of impotence known as *gupta rog* is the somatization of a situation of sociopolitical powerlessness or, conversely, that the acceptance of certain forms of sociopolitical powerlessness is in some way related to the cultural disease of *gupta rog*. I have already suggested that this sexual disorder was "sociocultural" inasmuch as it assumed a cause-and-effect relationship between Ayurvedic and yogic notions of physiology and metabolism on the one hand and that form of "impotence" signaled by the birth of daughters as opposed to sons on the other. If it is the case that this disease has arisen out of a fundamental misunderstanding of medical and yogic notions of the digestive and reproductive processes, this does not mean that these venerable traditions have no treatments to offer for those suffering from such ailments. As has been noted, the bodily symptoms of the medical condition I have been discussing are treatable through celibacy, continence, and, should these fail, Ayurvedic therapy and remedies. What of the more pervasive ailment of sociopolitical impotence? Does India know of a cure for this ailment? A growing chorus of "men in saffron," armed with paradigmatic proofs for their treatment, are saying yes, and a growing army of young men are following them, in a quest to recover their social, political, and religious potency. In order to understand the nature of their proofs, we must return to certain of the legends of princes and Nāth Siddhas recounted in the last chapter.

The first of these is the legend of young prince Pṛthivinārāyaṇ Śāh and the yogurt-spouting Gorakhnāth. As we have seen, that legend described the empowerment, through tantric initiation, of an otherwise powerless figure, a petit prince without a kingdom. It is a commonplace of Nāth Siddha legend to "Gorakh-ize" the acts of any powerful member of the sect, regardless of his name. So it is that we find that the Nāth Siddha in Pṛthivinarayaṇ Śāh's life was in fact named Bhagavantnāth, and that the young prince himself was the adult leader, in the mid–eighteenth century, of the diminutive kingdom of Gurkha, which was vying with no fewer than forty-five other kingdoms for control over western Nepal. In 1763, Bhagavantnāth commended himself to the ambitious young prince, quickly became his chief strategist, and set about to vastly strengthening the prince's position by using his tantric charisma to negotiate a series of crucial matrimonial and military alliances between Gurkha and other of the forty-five kingdoms. In 1768, five years of strategy were crowned with success: an army led by Pṛthivinārāyaṇ Śāh and Bhagavantnāth, and composed of their western Nepali allies, conquered the kingdom of Kirtipur, in the Kathmandu Valley, inaugurating the reign of the Gurkha dynasty.

A grateful Pṛthivinārāyaṇ Śāh wished to reward Bhagavantnāth by making him a vassal king; the Yogi refused temporal rule, but allowed that he would be satisfied if he were given Vilās Kumārī, one of the king's daughters, in marriage. This was granted, and Bhagavantnāth received, together with his new bride, a number of major land grants which served to truly solidify the place of the Nāth Siddha order on the religio-political landscape of Nepal. With this, Bhagavantnāth was elevated to the head of his order in Nepal. After his death in 1786 (eleven years after that of Pṛthivinārāyaṇ Śāh), the Nāth Siddhas continued to thrive under the Gurkhas—to the extent that they were frequently called upon by their kings to loan them money, which, thanks to their land revenues, they were able to do and for which they were repaid with interest.[23]

This is not the sole case in which the miraculous transformation of a powerless prince into a victorious king, mythically portrayed as issuing directly from the intervention of (and often initiation by) a Nāth Siddha, turns out to be the result of efforts of a more mundane order. In the preceding chapter, I mentioned the case of Mān Singh, the king of Marwar who gained his throne, in the first years of the nineteenth century, through the miraculous intervention of another Nāth Siddha. According to legend, young prince Mān Singh, whose army was under siege in the fortified city of Jalore by that of his evil cousin Bhīm Singh, was met one night by a mysterious Nāth Siddha named Mastnāth, who had suddenly materialized out of nowhere. Mastnāth led Mān Singh to a "hidden well" within the city walls, within which the prince found provisions enough to feed his starving army. Then, cryptically, Mastnāth predicted that Mān Singh's tormenter Bhīm Singh was not long for this world. Miraculously, Bhīm Singh died that very night.[24]

Colonel James Tod, who toured Rajasthan in the first decades of the nineteenth century and who actually met Mān Singh, tells a slightly different story, based on the testimony of members of the royal household. Mān Singh—who was quite demented by the time Tod met him—did indeed credit the intercession of the high priest of Marwar, whose name was Ayas Dev Nāth or Deonāth, for the twenty-fourth-hour death of his cousin. Others saw matters differently. In the words of Tod, "a dose of poison, it is said, was deemed a necessary adjunct to render efficacious the prayers of the pontiff."

Mān Singh's gratitude knew no limits. He offered Deonāth a share of the throne, which this Nāth Siddha accepted. Over the years that followed, Deonāth himself and the Nāth *sampradāya* in general became fantastically wealthy in the kingdom of Marwar, with Deonāth's income amounting to one tenth of the revenues of the state. The Mahāmandir, centerpiece of the

Nāth Siddha presence in the kingdom, constructed at an expense of over fifty lakhs of rupees to the royal treasury, could house as many as twenty-five hundred persons.[25] In Tod's words once again, "During the few years [that Deonāth] held the keys of his master's conscience, which were conveniently employed to unlock the treasury, he erected no less than eighty-four temples . . . with monasteries adjoining them, for his well-fed lazy . . . disciples." None but Mān Singh was amused, however, and after a meteoric career, Deonāth was gunned down in 1815.[26]

That these two cases were not aberrant is borne out by Peter van der Veer's provocative *Gods on Earth*,[27] a recent study of the social, political, and economic role played by the Hindu religious orders in medieval and modern north India. As van der Veer demonstrates, the "Yogis," Nāgas, and other ascetic orders, prior to the coming of the British and the railroad, used the annual pilgrimage circuit between Hardwar, Bengal, and Jagannath Puri (Orissa) as a trading network, lived in fortified temples, fought as mercenaries in the armies of the highest (at times Muslim) bidder, bankrolled kings and generals in their political conquests, and played an invaluable and extremely lucrative role in long-distance commerce.[28] Indeed, the earliest religious group to take up arms after the Muslim conquest may have been the Nāth Siddhas.[29]

More than this, as Dirk Kolff has demonstrated in his carefully documented *Naukar, Rajput and Sepoy*,[30] putting on the garb of an itinerant yogin seems to have been standard practice for all sorts of mercenaries and traders in precolonial India. Kolff moreover notes that the most commonly recurring time frame for such pseudoascetic peregrinations was a period of twelve years, a figure that, as we have seen, is standard for the completion of yogic *sādhana*s in the traditions under study.[31] In certain cases, historical figures clad themselves in the guise of the yogic god Śiva. So, for example the late thirteenth-century Rānā of Mewar, Rānā Samarṣi, was known as the "Regent of Mahādeva": "a simple necklace of the seeds of the lotus adorned his neck; his hair was braided, and *he [was] addressed as Jogindra, or chief of ascetics*."[32] Alternatively, Śiva himself was portrayed in the role of the yogin–cum–itinerant merchant. A Bhojpuri folk song says of the god that:[33]

> Mahadev has gone to the East to trade
> And four months are passing away.
> Gaura [sic] sits on a chair and watches the road, saying
> When will my ascetic [*tapasi*] come home?

The principal enterprise of many of these itinerant ascetic groups—who were often indistinguishable from tribal confederations or trading cartels in the precolonial period—was the long-distance trade of horses and elephants, etc. Their this-worldly ambitions of wealth and power were, however, rudely brought to a halt by the advent of the British raj and the railroad. Political centralization under foreign rulers who had no use for tantric power brokers to underwrite their authority further undermined their financial, military, and spiritual ambitions. Stripped of their traditional sources of income, power, and prestige, these orders began to lose ground well before the end of the nineteenth century. Over the past hundred years, they have become increasingly sedentary,[34] such that even when the Nāth Siddhas send out itinerant groups of ascetics (called *jhaṇḍīs*) from such centers as Gorakhpur, they have nothing to trade, save for songs glorifying their powerful forebears. Independence has not helped matters; and now, some fifty years into the India's democratic experiment, the Nāth *sampradāya* appears to be on the verge of collapse. The Mahāmandir, the centerpiece of Deonāth's hegemony in Jodhpur, the capital city of old Marwar, has been converted into a public school, the last monk of the once powerful Gorakh Ṭilla monastery of Benares died over a decade ago, and the list goes on.

Or does it? Since at least the 1920s, the monastery of Gorakhpur in northeastern Uttar Pradesh has been the "Rome" of Nāthdom, and its *mahant*, its abbot, the "pope" of the sect. In 1969, Digvijaynāth, this monastery's charismatic but rather ineffectual abbot, died and was replaced by a dynamic figure, already active in regional politics, who took the initiatory name of Avedyanāth. When I visited the Gorakhpur monastery in the winter of 1985, the same Avedyanāth was a most gracious host and helpful informant to me, giving me the run of the monastery and impressing me with his exceptional organizational abilities.

Under Avedyanāth's leadership, the monastery of Gorakhpur has been transformed into a force in the community and even the Gorakhpur district as a whole. But this is small change in comparison to what appears to be the national agenda of Avedyanāth, if not of a much broader confederation of monastic leaders who have been flexing their political muscles of late in India.

On 6 December 1992, a Hindu mob, composed to a great extent of *kār sevaks*, "servants of the cause"—marginalized young men in search of social, political, and religious potency—reduced the 450-year-old Babrī mosque of Ayodhya (Uttar Pradesh) to rubble, claiming that it had been built over the birthplace of the Hindu god Rāma, whose temple the Muslims had torn down to build their mosque. This was anything but a spontaneous demonstration: it was a symbolic gesture and show of strength planned and executed under the leadership of a group known as the Viśva Hindu Pariṣad (VHP), the Hindu World Council. This group, comprised exclusively of members of Hindu renunciant orders, the heirs to the Siddha and other sectarian movements of the Indian middle ages, are a resurgent nationalist Hinduism's "men in saffron." The political cousin of the VHP is the BJP, the Bhāratīya Janatā Party (Indian People's Party), which has, over the past years, appeared to be poised to replace India's secular democracy with a Hindu theocracy. While the national BJP leaders pedal a softer line, this is the outspoken agenda of the VHP, the organizational core of militant Hindu fundamentalism.

Given its reputation as the birthplace of Rāma, the seventh incarnation of the god Viṣṇu, Ayodhya has long been a major religious center in northern India. Its location, in eastern Uttar Pradesh, places it just about 120 miles from Benares, the major Śaiva religious center of north India, and 80 miles from Gorakhpur, the political epicenter of the Nāth Siddha organization. Sitting on the nine-man VHP brain trust is Avedyanāth, who is, in addition to serving as the leader of the Nāth *sampradāya* at Gorakhpur, also the most powerful political figure in that city: he presently represents Gorakhpur district as its member of the Indian parliament in Delhi.

Who is Avedyanāth if not the Gorakhnāth, the Bhagavantnāth, the Deonāth of late twentieth-century India? And if he is indeed nothing other than a modern power broker in a long line of Nāth Siddha power brokers, what compunctions need he have to respect religious or political convention? In addition to his many sacred and secular functions and titles, Avedyanāth is also the chairman of the Rām Janmabhūmi Mukti Samiti, the Committee for the Liberation of the Birthplace of Rāma.[35] As anyone familiar with Hindu sectarian theology knows, this is highly ironic. For, whereas Rāma, the "boy scout" of the Hindu pantheon, is *the* god whose adherents have historically constituted the "right wing" of Hindu religious belief and practice, the Nāth Siddhas have, together with the tāntrikas whose legends and initiatory ideology I have been treating in these pages, long figured among the most "left-handed" (*vāmacāra*) sects of all of Hinduism.

Avedyanāth and the VHP, even if they are championing the symbolically powerful cause of restoring a Hindu site to Hindu hands, are not, in the final analysis, fighting for issues. Rather, they are fighting for power, for a sociopolitical power that is the macrocosmic homologue of the power the tantric practitioner gains over his bodily microcosm, and by extension over the entire universe, through his violent (the *haṭha* in *haṭha yoga*) antinomian practice.[36] The goals of the tantric practitioner were and remain immortality and unalloyed power in the world. Once possessed of this power, the practitioner may use it to blast or bless, to raise untested boys to the throne (Bhagavantnāth and Pṛthivinārāyaṇ Śāh) or to curse entire cities to destruction (as Dharamnāth did to Pattan).[37] The men in saffron have not forgotten these goals, and they seem to be prepared to use certain tried-and-true methods from that past to realize them, in the firm knowledge that such will be mythologized into idealized accounts of transformative initiation rites which naive western orientalists will recount as "amusing anecdotes" to audiences across the world, thereby assuring them of their immortality.

At times I think that a Hindu theocracy could not be more harmful to India than the cynical bureaucracy that the secular democracy has spawned over the past half century. Indeed, such a reversal would just be another epicycle in the broad historical sweep of what Jan Heesterman has termed as India's "inner conflict of tradition," an inner conflict in which two camps inexorably trade places in filling the roles of world maintainers and world renouncers. Here let us recall that Gandhi, political mastermind that he was, won independence for India by playing the role of world renouncer; once that independence was won, his Congress Party activists established themselves in the role of world maintainers. The secular Indian state, corrupted by its own power, seems to be no longer capable of fulfilling this dual role. Has the time then come, once more, for the world-renouncing men in saffron to try their hand at world maintenance? They certainly think so, because the this-worldly ideology of over a thousand years of tantrism tells them so. One need only think of the medieval myths of cooperation between kings and tāntrikas: power and transcendence *are* within reach. Yet, should the men in saffron gain power, they will immediately find themselves faced with the same conundrum as has faced every world renouncer who went the world-maintenance route. As soon as the world renouncer becomes involved in the world, playing the role of royal chaplain, minister, or even surrogate king, he forfeits all claim to transcendence, to the very ground upon which he founded his prior authority. He becomes just another player in the power game, as Pṛthivinārāyaṇ Śāh's Bhagavantnāth perhaps foresaw, but Mān Singh's Deonāth never comprehended.

Between the two extremes I have outlined lie those Siddhas whose approach to life has always featured not a small amount of carefree playfulness. It is this quality that has always impressed me the most among Nāth Siddhas whom I have met: they always seem to be at play—playing with words, playing with other people's minds, playing games with the world. This is an attitude that many before me have noted. For Bernier, the Yogis were people "who scoff at everything, and whom nothing troubles,"[38] while Oman provides turn-of-the-century photographs of Yogis in carefree and uninhibited repose in front of camera, Yogis whose easy and well-adjusted attitude he notes with a mixture of respect and suspicion.[39]

The ideal Nāth Siddha is a god-man who plays with the entire universe, with the lives of the great and small alike, as he pleases. Secure in the knowledge of the identity of microcosm and macrocosm, of the immanence of the Absolute in every creature and stone, he takes the universe to be his plaything, with its every element (nectar and ashes, cloaks and bodies, earrings and the power of flight) interchangeable according to his whim. Like the holder of any sort of power, the Nāth Siddha can use his knowledge for good or for evil; most I have known spend much of their time "getting high" in ways I evoked in chapter four.[40] Their credo is perhaps best encapsulated in a passage from the hagiography of Mastnāth: "Whose friend is a Yogi when he plays? It takes so little to please him. He doesn't give a thought to what's high or what's low. Whatever he wants to do, he just does it . . . The world's four cornerstones are [his] playground; when you're carefree you want for nothing. From a pauper to a king, from a king to a pauper, [he's] never bothered over the difference between the two."[41]

4. Bhandarināth and Me

Soon after I began my fieldwork in India, in the spring of 1984, I met the droll and bearded Bhambhulnāth, the kindly abbot of the Nāth Siddha monastery at Hardwar, to whom I expressed my interest in meeting living alchemists. While he allowed that he didn't know any such persons, he suggested that I should go to Nepal, where the great Nāth Siddha scholar Narharināth, abbot of the Caughera monastery, would be able to give me some pointers. It was October before I finally managed to have an audience with Narharināth, a most impressive figure, who told me he had heard rumors of alchemists living in the region of Mount Abu, in western Rajasthan. I was not to reach Abu until my next research tour of India, in the winter of 1993. There, Samundranāth, the custodian of the Gorakhnāth shrine at Oriya village, told me there were no such people at Abu. However, Inder Dan Detha, a Rajasthani bard (Cāraṇ) and scholar—and part-time resident of Acalgarh at Abu—whom I met in Jodhpur the next month, in March, told me of an encounter he had had with a certain Motināth, whom he had met at the Rāthaḍuṇḍā monastery, in the Meerta City district of eastern Rajasthan, some twenty-five years earlier. Motināth, he said, had had a reputation as an alchemist and was someone who could tell me about the use of mercury and herbs as means to immortality.

So it was that on a hot day in April, I found myself at Rāthaḍuṇḍā talking to the two Nāths—one very senile and the other very stoned—who appeared to constitute the entire population of that monastery. When I asked about Motināth, the younger of the two laughed and said, "He's outside, underneath the new *samādhi*.[42] He gave up his body twenty years ago." So much for my immortal alchemist, I thought. I was, however, intrigued by the Nāth Siddha's aside that at the time he abandoned his body, at an age of about seventy-five, he still had the appearance of a twenty-five-year-old. I then asked whether there were any alchemists living in Rajasthan that he knew of, to which he responded with a loud guffaw. "Alchemists in Rajasthan? Rajasthan's a desert! There's no alchemists here, because there's no herbs here. You've gotta go to the mountains, up to Nepal, up to Hardwar, to find alchemists!" Hardwar was where I had begun my search, some nine years earlier. It seemed I had come full circle in a futile quest for something that no longer existed . . .

One cool premonsoon morning in the Thamel neighborhood of Kathmandu, a month after I had left Rāthaḍuṇḍā, I nearly ran over a Nāth Siddha on my bicycle. There could be no doubt that he was a Nāth: the crystal earrings in the thick of his ears were a dead giveaway. "*Ādeś!*" I cried out to him, as I tumbled down off my bike, "*ādeś!*"[43] Without missing a beat, the Jogi's answer came: "Will you have a vision of the Lord of Serpents?" "A Sampela,"[44] I thought, and more or less knowing what was to follow, said "Sure!" at which point he pulled a wicker basket out from beneath the folds of his capacious saffron tunic, opened the lid—and a cobra that was supposed to rear up and scare the dickens out of me didn't. Prodding and poking, the Sampela tried to coax his serpent into showing more signs of life but, poor guy, it was a cool morning and the snake was still snoozing.

Seizing the moment, I tried to engage the Nāth in some small talk. "What's your name? Where're you from?" "My name's Bhandarināth and *I'm from Hardwar*," he replied. The words of the laughing Nāth of Rāthaḍuṇḍā came rushing back to me. I was in *Nepal*, talking to a Sampela who had come there from *Hardwar*. Had I hit the mother lode? Bhandarināth was typical in many ways. He was on the road most of the year, taking a side trip from the Himalayan high roads to the four *dhams* (Kedārnāth, Badarīnāth, Gaṅgotrī, and Yamunotrī) to visit Kathmandu this time. And by the way, could I give him some money?

At this point, we entered into concerted negotiations. His main concern was money,[45] and mine was information. So back and forth we went. "How much money you gonna give me? A hundred and one rupees would be nice," to which I replied, "Ever meet any alchemists?" I asked him if he knew any Nāth Siddhas who ate herbs and mercury, and he allowed that they all used herbs to improve their quality of life. Then, quickly changing the subject, he told me to pick up a pinch of dirt from the side of the road on which we were standing. I did so, and noted that here, as in many parts of the valley, the soil was very sandy, with a high white mica content. "The seed of Prajāpati[46] and the sexual fluid of the Goddess,"[47] I thought. "I've got a handful of jizz!"

"Now," said Bhandarināth with a theatrical flourish, "put the dirt in my hand and say 'Oṃ jai Paśupatināth!'"[48] He then returned the dirt to my hand and instructed me to repeat the *mantra*. This I did, at which point he told me to open my hand. There, together with the sand and the mica, were grains of unhusked rice! "Shades of Cauraṅginātḥ,"[49] I thought, "more sexual fluids!" I fell all over Bhandarināth, telling him how impressed I was at his piece of magic. Encouraged, he reached into the folds of his still-capacious saffron tunic and pulled out a *jholī*[50] from which he produced a plastic bottle, out of which he spilled two pea-sized pellets into my hand. They appeared to be of mineral composition and were covered with vermilion.

These, Bandarināth assured me, would bring me good health, good life, and success in all that I did, warning me that only I could benefit from their powers: they were nontransferable. Then he asked me to feed him, and I gave him 15 rupees. He said he'd done a lot of talking for 15 rupees, and that 101 was more like what he had in mind. I promised him more the next time I met him. He told me where he was staying, and I promised to come and see him in the coming days. As it turned out, that was the last I saw of Bhandarināth . . .

I raced home on my bicycle, tapping my shirt pocket all the way to be sure that my alchemical (?) booty was still there. As soon as I arrived, I took out a pocketknife and—not without some trepidation—cut into one of the two *guṭikās*[51] Bandarināth had given me. The knife went through the pellet, but not without difficulty, since it was indeed of mineral composition. It was also, clearly, a man-made pill, the product of some chemical operation. My eyes were filled with images of the alchemical Grail. I had passed the test! The Nāth Siddhas on high, approving of my sincerity and diligence, had sent their man to me to deliver the mystic goods!

One of the first things I did upon my return to the west was to take my *guṭikās* to a laboratory for analysis.[52] A week later, the results of the electron-microscopic tests came back. My sample was composed of an amalgam of mineral and vegetable matter. The minerals in question were sulfur (!), silver (!), silicon, phosphorus, potassium, calcium, iron, and chlorine—but no mercury! Was the silver some base metal that had been "digested" and transmuted by mercury, which had left no trace of itself behind? Without a guru, how could I ever know whether this was in fact the philosopher's stone I had cut in half and had fried under an electron microscope or just a medical tablet for chilblains? The second *guṭikā* was still intact.

Our research continues . . .

NOTES

Preface

1. Thomas Pynchon, *Gravity's Rainbow* (London: Picador, 1975), p. 590. According to our best evidence, the vast majority of practitioners of tantric alchemy and *haṭha yoga* have always been males. So it is that I employ the masculine pronoun *he*, rather than *she* or *s/he* when referring to such practitioners.

2. Cf. the *akam* genre of classical Tamil love poetry, whose "five landscapes" are discussed in A. K. Ramanujan, *The Inner Landscape: Love Poems from a Classical Tamil Anthology* (Bloomington: Indiana University Press, 1975), pp. 105–8.

3. Sudhir Kakar, *The Inner World: A Psychoanalytic Study of Childhood and Society in India* (New York: Oxford University Press, 1978); Ashis Nandy, *The Intimate Enemy: Loss and Recovery of Self under Colonialism* (Delhi: Oxford University Press, 1983). Given that many of the interpretive connections made between *les mots et les choses* in this book are my own, some may be moved to turn their analytical lights on my own psychological profile as well.

4. *La poétique de l'espace* (Paris: Presses Universitaires, 1974). A recent western study of an eastern tradition, which I feel to be most respectful of the phenomenological approach, a book which moreover devotes many of its pages to charting mystic landscapes, is Norman Girardot's admirable *Myth and Meaning in Early Taoism* (Berkeley: University of California Press, 1983).

5. Even if, as Gadamer and others have demonstrated, such is patently impossible: one always comes to a text with a forejudgment of its meaning. This includes, for the alchemical portion of the books, the models of the modern science of chemistry. Many are the historians who have treated tantric alchemy as a protochemistry or iatrochemistry and who have, working from this methodological assumption, projected the writings of the alchemical tradition upon a modern chemical grid. Such attempts are, I believe, tentative at best, given our uncertainty of the modern equivalents of medieval (and often local) terminology. This is especially the case with botanical names, in which the sources abound. Similarly, modern interpretations of the subtle body of *haṭha yoga* which would see in the medieval texts proofs

for the advanced state of Indian knowledge of physiology and psychology force the textual data into impossible and highly prejudicial directions.

6. On the theological uses of anagogy, as a complication of analogy and allegory, in the medieval west, see Marie-Dominique Chénu, *Nature, Man and Society in the Twelfth Century*, tr. and ed. Jerome Taylor and Lester K. Little (Chicago: University of Chicago Press, 1969; reprint Chicago: Midway Books, 1979), pp. 123–24.

7. Symbolic language is employed with such great success in these traditions because the name of a thing bears the efficacity of a given object: Jean Filliozat, "Taoïsme et yoga," *Journal Asiatique* 257 (1969): 63.

8. Douglas Renfrew Brooks, *The Secret of the Three Cities: An Introduction to Hindu Śākta Tantrism* (Chicago: University of Chicago Press, 1990), p. 209.

9. Betty Jo Teeter Dobbs, *The Foundations of Newton's Alchemy or "The Hunting of the Greene Lyon"* (London: Cambridge University Press, 1975), p. xi.

10. *RRĀ* 3.11b–12a: na krameṇa vinā śāstraṃ na śāstreṇa vinā kramaḥ/śāstraṃ kramayutaṃ jñātvā karoti sa siddhibhāk//. Cf. *BhP* 3.96; 4.139; 9.140b–141a; and *RRS* 6.2.

11. Mircea Eliade, *Forgerons et alchimistes*, 2d rev. ed. (Paris: Flammarion, 1977); idem, *Yoga: Immortality and Freedom*, 2d ed., tr. Willard R. Trask (Princeton, N.J.: Bollingen, 1973).

12. "Why Gurus Are Heavy," *Numen* 33 (1984):40–73.

Chapter One

1. Reproduced with translation and notes in B. N. Goswamy and J. S. Grewal, *The Mughals and the Jogis of Jakhbar: Some Madad-i-Ma'ash and Other Documents* (Simla: Indian Institute of Advanced Study, 1967), pp. 120–24. Jakhbar monastery is located in the Gurdaspur district of the Punjab.

2. The root *tan* is a cognate of the English *tension* and *tensile*, in which the senses of stretching and weaving are also present. On *tantra* as ritual framework, see Brian K. Smith, *Reflections on Resemblance, Ritual, and Religion* (Oxford University Press, 1989), p. 126, citing *Āśvalayana Śrauta Sūtra* 1.1.3.

3. In order to avoid confusion between Tantra as written work and tantra as religious phenomenon, I follow general modern usage and refer to the latter as "tantrism." I further adjectivize "tantra" into "tantric" to speak, for example, of tantric ritual. I often refer to tantric practitioners as *tāntrika*s, following Sanskrit usage.

4. This and all the other terms discussed here are generated from the verbal root *sādh/sadh* (weak form *sidh*), which means "to realize, succeed."

5. On the uses of this appellation, see below chap. 4, nn. 112–14.

6. To these groups we might also add the Burmese *Zawgyi*s (= *Yogi*s) or *Weikza*s

(= Vidyā[puruṣas?]), a group of more or less suicidal mercury-drinking Theravāda Buddhist monks: Patrick Pranke, "On Becoming a Buddhist Wizard," in Don Lopez, ed., *Buddhism in Practice* (Princeton: Princeton University Press, 1995), pp. 343–58; Maung Htin Aung, *Folk Elements in Burmese Buddhism* (London: Oxford University Press, 1962; reprint Westport, Conn.: Greenwood Press, 1978), pp. 41–50; Melford Spiro, *Buddhism and Society: A Great Tradition and Its Burmese Vicissitudes* (New York: Harper & Row, 1970), pp. 163–71; and Joseph Needham et al., *Science and Civilisation in Ancient China*, 6 vols. in 17 tomes (Cambridge: Cambridge University Press, 1954–88), vol. 5, pt. 3 (1976), "Chemistry and Chemical Technology: Spagyrical Discovery and Invention: Historical Survey, from Cinnabar Elixirs to Synthetic Insulin," p. 166.

7. They are also called *Nāth Yogis*, the *Nāth Sampradāya*, *Kānphaṭa* ("Split Eared") *Yogis*, *Jogis*, and *Gorakhnāthis* in modern northern India.

8. Most fully initiated members of the Nāth Siddha order are given names, upon initiation, that end in the suffix *-nāth*. Throughout this book, however, I often shorten the names of these figures, and call Gorakhnāth "Gorakh," Matsyendranāth "Matsyendra," etc. Furthermore, in those cases in which I retain the suffix, I generally transliterate it as *-nāth*, following modern usage, rather than *-nātha*, the Sanskritic ending. Only in those cases in which I am referring to a given Nāth Siddha as the author of a Sanskrit-language work do I retain the *-nātha* suffix (as in "the *Rasaratnākara* of Nityanātha").

9. On the overlap between the terms *tantra* and *śākta* (applied to those sects whose immediate object of devotion was the Goddess, *Śakti*), see *HT*, pp. 5–7. Most Hindu tantric sects were in fact Śākta-Śaiva, worshipping the Goddess as a more accessible form of Śiva than the god himself.

10. For the hundreds of references to the semidivine Siddhas and Vidyādharas in Somadeva's monumental 11th c. *Kathāsaritsāgara*, see the index to *Ocean*, vol. 10, pp. 302, 351 [s.v. "Siddhas, independent superhumans" and "Vidyādharas, independent superhumans"].

11. So, for example, according to a Bengali recension of the *Rāmāyaṇa*, the paradise land of Uttarakuru was reached by crossing a river called Śailoda ("Rock Water"), whose touch turns men into stone. On either bank of that river grow reeds called *kichaka*, which carry Siddhas to the opposite bank and back. This is a country where the Siddhas live together with divine nymphs in forests whose trees and flowers, composed of precious stones, exude a miraculous resin that is nothing other than the nectar of immortality itself. On this, see *Encyclopedia of Religion and Ethics*, 12 vols., ed. James Hastings (New York: Scribner's, 1908), s.v. "Abode of the Blest (Hindu)," by H. Jacobi. On "rock-water," see below, chap. 4, n. 189.

12. See below, chap. 10, nn. 82–85.

13. *Paraśurāmakalpasūtra* 4.10 (ed. A. M. Sastri and S. Y. Dave, Gaekwad's Oriental Series, no. 22 [Baroda: Oriental Institute, 1950], p. 149). Significant here is the redundancy in the term employed for the second category of Siddhas, mediating between the divine (*divya*) and the human (*mānava*): these are the perfected (*siddha*) Siddhas. The *Lalitā Sahasranāma* (cited in Bagchi, introduction to *Kaulajñānanirṇaya*, p. 20) delineates the same divisions. The earliest enumeration of the three *ogha*s may be that of the *Kulārṇava Tantra* (6.63–68), which divides the founding Kaula gurus along these lines (*Kulārṇava Tantra*, ed. Taranatha Vidyaratna with an introduction by Arthur Avalon [John Woodroffe][Madras: Ganesh and Company, 1965; reprint Delhi: Motilal Banarsidass, 1975]): see below, chap. 4, n. 62. The *Tantrarāja Tantra* (2.2–5) divides a group of nine Nāthas (identified with bodily orifices) into three groups of the same three "streams": in John Woodroffe, *Tantrarāja Tantra: A Short Analysis*, 3d ed. (Madras: Ganesh and Co, 1971), p. 19. Janardana Pandeya, in his introduction (p. *ja*) to the second volume of his edition of the *Gorakṣa Saṁhitā*, 2 vols. (Sarasvatibhavana Granthamala, vols. 110, 111 [Benares: Sampurnananda Sanskrit Visvavidyalaya, 1976, 1977]), divides certain of the Rasa Siddhas into these three categories. Four of the eight directions in the Kaula "Circle of Siddhas" (Siddha Cakra) are assigned to the Siddhas (south) and the Siddhaugha (west), Mānavaugha (northwest), and Divyaugha (southwest): Mark S. G. Dyczkowski, *The Canon of the Śaivāgama and the Kubjikā Tantras of the Western Kaula Tradition* (Albany, N.Y.: SUNY Press, 1988), p. 81. See also ibid., p. 90, on the three *ogha*s in the *Ciñcinīmatasārasamucchaya*, a text of the Western Transmission.

14. *Atharva Veda* 1.4.4; 3.31.10; 10.2.17; and 19.53.1. *Rasa* and the waters are further identified with notion of "healing remedy" (*bheṣaja*), which becomes the foundation of traditional Indian medicine (*āyurveda*) and elixir therapy (*rasāyana*). See below, chap. 7, sec. 1.

15. The foundational works of Indian medicine (Āyurveda), the *Caraka* and *Suśruta Saṁhitā*s, date from this period: see below, chap. 2, n. 15. See bibliography for editions.

16. The earliest excavated Śiva *liṅga* is the Guḍimallam image from Andhra Pradesh. On its dating, see Gritli v. Mitterwallner, "Evolution of the *Liṅga*" (who dates the image to the first century B.C.) and Doris Meth Srinivasan, "Significance and Scope of Pre-Kuśāṇa Śaivite Iconography" (who dates it to the fourth to third centuries B.C.), both in Michael Meister, ed., *Discourses on Śiva: Proceedings of a Symposium on the Nature of Religious Imagery* (Philadelphia: University of Pennsylvania Press, 1984), pp. 18–19, 34, and plate 18.

17. Alexis Sanderson, "Purity and power among the Brahmins of Kashmir," in *The Category of the Person: Anthropology, Philosophy, History*, ed. Michael Carrithers, Steven Collins, and Steven Lukes (Cambridge: Cambridge University Press, 1985),

p. 199. The perspective of all Hindu tantric texts of which I am aware is that of the male practitioner. Miranda Shaw (*Passionate Enlightenment: Women in Tantric Buddhism* [Princeton: Princeton University Press, 1994]) has recently advanced the theory that it is the female practitioner's perspective that originally predominated in Buddhist tantric practice. While I find her arguments improbable, I leave it to my colleagues in Buddhist studies to confirm or disprove her hypothesis.

18. For further discussion, see below, chap. 5, sec. 2.

19. Whence the maxim "privately a *śākta*, outwardly a *śaiva*, and a *vaiṣṇava* in court; bearing various outward appearances, the followers of the *kula*-system spread over the earth": *Yoni Tantra* 4.20, cited in *The Yonitantra*, critically edited with an introduction by J. A. Schoterman (Delhi: Manohar, 1980), p. 16.

20. This relationship was first charted in the *Sāṃkhya Kārikas* (39, 42) and commentaries. For a discussion, see Lakshmi Kapani, *La notion de saṃskāra*, 2 vols. (Paris: De Boccard, 1991, 1993), vol. 2, pp. 422–28.

21. For further discussion of the origins and history of *haṭha yoga*, see below, chap. 5, nn. 83–92, and chap. 8, sec. 2a.

22. *RA* 17.165a.

23. Whereas Śiva is the name that takes precedence over all other names (Mahādeva, Bhairava, etc.) for this male divinity, there is no such order of precedence for the Goddess's many names (Durgā, Pārvatī, Śakti, Caṇḍī, Kālī, Devī, etc.). I therefore generally refer to her as the Goddess (which is also a literal translation of the name Devī).

24. Bhudeb Mookerji, *Rasa-jala-nidhi or Ocean of Indian Chemistry and Alchemy*, 5 vols. (Calcutta: K. C. Neogi, 1926–38), vol. 1, p. xiv.

25. *RA* 1.19. For variant readings, from other alchemical sources, see below, chap. 5, n. 161, and chap. 9, nn. 54–55.

26. *Śatapatha Brāhmaṇa* 7.4.1.15. The all-absorbing capacities of mercury are those of any element at the summit (although it is more accurate to say the center) of a Hindu hierarchy (on this see David N. Gellner, *Monk, Householder, and Tantric Priest: Newar Buddhism and its Hierarchy of Ritual* [New Delhi: Cambridge University Press, 1992], pp. 45–48). Concomitant to this ability is also the inherent power of expansivity, the power to become all-encompassing. This is precisely the nature of *bráhman*, the Absolute of Vedānta metaphysics: the verbal root of *bráhman* is *bṛh*, "to magically expand." This is what mercury does when it transforms millions of times its own mass of base metals into gold.

27. The two important modern exceptions to this rule are the Śrī Vidyā tradition of Tamil Nadu and the tantric form of Hinduism that continues to predominate in Nepal.

28. See below, chap. 10, sec. 1, and chap. 11, sec. 3.

29. This scorn and mistrust carries down to nineteenth-century Britain, in which, according to the ethnographer H. A. Rose (*A Glossary of the Tribes and Castes of the Punjab and Northwest Frontier Province*, 3 vols. [Lahore: Superintendent, Government Printing, Punjab, 1911–19], vol. 2, p. 407), certain elements of the Rāwal branch of the Nāth Siddhas had made their way to Europe, where they were notorious purveyors of quack medicines and cures! On the modern-day Indian confusion between the magicians and tāntrikas, see Lee Siegel, *Net of Magic: Wonders and Deceptions in India* (Chicago: University of Chicago Press, 1991).

30. Joseph Needham et al. *Science and Civilisation in China* vol. 5, pt. 4 (1980): "Chemistry and Chemical Technology: Spagyrical Discovery and Invention—Apparatus, Theories and Gifts," pp. 497–98.

31. François Bernier's *Voyages* were originally published in Amsterdam, in two volumes, in 1699, by David-Paul Marret. The present passage is translated from a modern edition of the work, *Voyage dans les Etats du Grand Mogol*, with an introduction by France Bhattacharya (Paris: Fayard, 1981), p. 245.

32. *RV* 7.59.12. Cf. *RV* 3.3.7; 9.100.1; 2.38.5; 7.90.6; *Atharva Veda* 18.3.62; *Śatapatha Brāhmaṇa* 2.6.1.12; and Wendy Doniger O'Flaherty, *Tales of Sex and Violence: Folklore, Sacrifice, and Danger in the Jaiminīya Brāhmaṇa* (Chicago: University of Chicago Press, 1985), p. 20.

33. *RV* 4.26–27. For Indo-European and ancient Near Eastern parallels, see David M. Knipe, "The Heroic Theft: Myths from Ṛgveda IV and the Ancient Near East," *History of Religions* 6 (1967): 328–60.

34. Charles Malamoud, "Le corps contractuel des dieux: remarques sur le rite védique du *tānūnaptra*," in *Cuire le monde*, p. 238.

35. Charles Malamoud, "Les dieux n'ont pas d'ombre: remarques sur la langue secrète des dieux dans l'Inde ancien," in *Cuire le monde*, p. 250. On the brahmanic definition of sacrifice, see idem., "Cuire le monde," in ibid., p. 47, citing *Āpastambha Yajña Paribhāṣa Sūtra* 1 and *Kātyāyana Śrauta Sūtra* 1.2.1.

36. *Śatapatha Brāhmaṇa* 10.1.5.4, with the commentary of Sāyaṇa who states that one hundred years is how long *amṛta* keeps the gods immortal! Cf. *RV* 10.161.3b; *Atharva Veda* 2.29.2.

37. Charles Malamoud, "La théologie de la dette dans le brahmanisme," in *Cuire le monde*, pp. 125–27.

38. *Compact Edition of the Oxford English Dictionary*, s.v. "mortgage."

39. *RV* 8.48.3a, 4b, 12a, translated in Wendy Doniger O'Flaherty, *The Rig Veda* (Harmondsworth: Penguin, 1981), pp. 134–35.

40. *Śatapatha Brāhmaṇa* 9.5.1.7–8,11.

41. *RV* 9.86.39; 10.107.2. Later, the mediating "drop" is dropped, and the iden-

tity of (King) Soma and moon is made: *Śatapatha Brāhmaṇa* 10.4.2.1; 11.2.5.3. See below, chap. 2, sec. 2 and 4, and chap. 7, n. 2.

42. *Śatapatha Brāhmaṇa* 6.1.2.4.

43. *Śatapatha Brāhmaṇa* 6.2.2.6.

44. *RV* 1.23.19a; 10.137.6; *Atharva Veda* 1.4.4. See also Kenneth Zysk, *Religious Healing in the Veda*, Transactions of the American Philosophical Society, vol. 75, part 7 (Philadelphia: The Society, 1985), pp. 90, 92.

45. See below, chap. 2, n. 1.

46. On this verse, see Louis Renou, "Études védiques," *Journal Asiatique* 243 (1955), p. 437, n. 2. Cf. *Jaiminīya Brāhmaṇa* 3.335; and *Kāṭhaka Saṁhitā* 8.5 and 12.13, discussed in Stephanie W. Jamison, *The Ravenous Hyenas and the Wounded Sun: Myth and Ritual in Ancient India* (Ithaca, N.Y.: Cornell University Press, 1991), pp. 191–93. These homologizations are assumed by the *Rāmāyaṇa*, in its account of the birth of Skanda: see below chap. 7, sec. 2.

47. *Yajur Veda* 7.4.1.10.

48. *Prāṇa*, breath or "life force" is further identified with the soul (*ātman*), a term etymologically linked to the German *atmen sich* and the Latin *animus*. It may further be equated with "spirit," which is present in "re-spir-ation." Breath is further identified with the universal self or soul, *bráhman*, in *Kauṣītaki Upaniṣad* 2.1.

49. Zysk, *Religious Healing*, pp. 8, 241. Cf. Louis Renou, *Etudes védiques et paninéennes*, 17 vols. (Paris: de Boccard, 1955–69), vol. 2, p. 66, note (quoted in André Padoux, *Vāc: The Concept of the Word in Selected Hindu Tantras* [Albany, N.Y.: SUNY Press, 1989], p. 6) "In fact, the creation of the cosmos is similar to that of a work of art, either being the *kavi*'s deed." An equally important link between the *Atharva Veda* and the medical and alchemical traditions lies in one of the terms employed by the former to designate the physician. The image of the *kavi*, the inspired poet of the Veda, stands behind both the Ayurvedic physician (called *kavi-rāja* in Bengal) and the alchemical wizard (*kavi*) who ultimately creates his own universe. See below, chap. 9, nn. 105–6 and chap. 10, nn. 78–80.

50. Surendranath Dasgupta, *A History of Indian Philosophy*, 5 vols. (Cambridge: Cambridge University Press, 1922; reprint Delhi: Motilal Banarsidass, 1975), vol. 2, p. 284 and n. 1. According to the *Taittirīya Saṁhitā* (6.4.9), the itinerant physician was impure; Brahmans therefore were not to take up medicine as a profession. According to the *RV* (1.180.2), the divine physicians, the Aśvins, are drinkers of "mead" (*madhu*) rather than *soma:* Jean Filliozat, *La doctrine classique de la médecine indienne: ses origines et ses parallèles grecs*, 2d ed. (Paris: Ecole Française d'Extrême Orient, 1975), pp. 15–16.

51. *Caraka Saṁhitā* 1.30.20. Cf. Dasgupta, *History*, vol. 2, pp. 273–84.

Chapter Two

1. Smith, *Reflections*, pp. 46, 203, 224.

2. The term *mesocosm* was coined by Paul Mus (who further uses the terms "protocosm" for "microcosm" and "metacosm" for "macrocosm" in his study of Indian Buddhism) in his lengthy foreword to *Barabudur* (Hanoi: Imprimerie d'Extrême Orient, 1935), p. 100. Mus's terminology has been further expanded by John S. Strong (*The Legend of King Aśoka: A Study and Translation of the "Aśokāvadāna"* [Princeton: Princeton University Press, 1983], pp. 104, 118–20, 131–33). On this see my "*Dakkhina* and *Agnicayana:* An Extended Application of Paul Mus's Typology," *History of Religions* 26:2 (November 1986), pp. 191–95.

3. On this fascination with number, see Charles Malamoud, "Exégèse de rites, exégèse de textes," in *Cuire le monde*, p. 282 and throughout.

4. By "bipolar" I mean two polar opposites which, in spite of, or indeed because of, their opposition, interact dynamically. Male and female are bipolar, as are moon and sun, semen and blood, etc. See *HTSL*, pp. 1–2.

5. *Śatapatha Brāhmaṇa* 7.2.1.4: *Taittirīya Brāhmaṇa* 1.5.9.4.

6. Mus, *Barabudur*, pp. 53, 59, 203–4.

7. *Bṛhadāraṇyaka Upaniṣad* 1.4.1–6.

8. *Chāndogya Upaniṣad* 6.8.7; *Haṭhayogapradīpikā* 4.50, 56 (*Haṭhayogapradīpikā of Svātmarāman*, with the commentary of Brahmānanda, ed. and tr. Srinivasa Iyengar [Madras: Adyar, 1972]). For an early mythological account of the "bottling up" of the absolute *bráhman* within the human body, wherein it becomes identified as the *ātman*, see *Aitareya Āraṇyaka* 2.4.1–3.

9. On the *kalā*s, see below, sec. 4 of the present chap.

10. Sanjukta Gupta, "The *Maṇḍala* as an Image of Man," in Richard Gombrich ed., *Indian Ritual and its Exegesis*. Delhi: Oxford University Press, 1988, p. 35. On the five elements, see below, sec. 3 of the present chap. and chap. 7, sec. 5.

11. Cited in Jean Filliozat, "La discipline psychosomatique du yoga et ses fondaments théoriques," *Annuaire du Collège de France* (1965–66), p. 384.

12. *RV* 10.16.1. See also Gopinath Kaviraj, *Bhāratīy Saṃskṛti aur Sādhanā* (Patna: Bihar Rashtrabhasha Parishad, 1977–79), vol. 2, p. 281; and Malamoud, "Cuire le monde," in *Cuire le monde*, p. 52 n. 52, citing the *Yājñavalkya Smṛti* (3.84).

13. Robert C. Lester, *Theravada Buddhism in Southeast Asia* (Ann Arbor: University of Michigan Press, 1973), pp. 23–24, 53; Caroline A. F. Rhys-Davids, "Original Buddhism and Amṛta," *Mélanges chinois et bouddhiques* [Brussels] 6 (1938–39), p. 378. On the medical language of the later Śaiva *Pāśupata Sūtra*s (ca. 1st c. A.D.), see Nagendranath Bhattacharyya, *History of the Tantric Religion (A Historical, Ritualistic and Philosophical Study)*. Delhi: Munshiram Manoharlal, 1982, pp. 16, 201–2.

14. On Buddhist terminology in Caraka, see Priyavrat Sharma, *Āyurved ka vaijñānik itihās*, 2d ed., Jaikrishnadas Ayurveda Series, no. 1 (Benares: Chowkhambha Orientalia, 1982) p. 102. It is widely held that the replacement of surgery (*śālākya*) by pharmacy (*rasa śāstra*) in Indian medicine was also due to Buddhist influence: see below, chap. 3, n. 21.

15. Dasgupta, *History* 2:393–99. The dating of the foundational Ayurvedic texts continues to be a matter of some discussion. The Chronology Committee of the National Institute of Sciences of India dates the composition of the *Caraka Saṁhitā* to ca. A.D. 100, and that of the *Suśruta Saṁhitā* to the 3d–4th centuries A.D.: D. M. Bose, ed., *A Concise History of Science in India* (New Delhi: Indian National Science Academy, 1971), p. 223.

16. *Caraka Saṁhitā* 4.1.1–156. For a discussion, see Dasgupta, *History* 1:212–19.

17. Jean Filliozat, "Les mechanismes psychiques d'après les textes de yoga," *Annuaire du Collège de France* (Paris: 1970–71), p. 416.

18. Ibid., p. 416.

19. *Caraka Saṁhitā* 4.5.5.

20. *Caraka Saṁhitā* 4.4.13.

21. A very early use of the term *dhātu* is *Atharva Veda* 11.3.78. Cf. the ca. 11th c. A.D. *Śārada Tilaka* (6.7) [*Śārdatilakam of Lakṣmaṇadeśikendra with the Padārthadarśa Commentary by Rāghavabhaṭṭa*. edited by Mukunda Jha Bakshi, 3d ed. [Varanasi: Chowkhamba Sanskrit Series Office, 1986]), a tantric ritual guide, which identifies the seven *dhātu*s with the seven mother goddesses (*mātṛkā*s). On digestion in general, see *Caraka Saṁhitā* 6.15.3–38, especially vv. 32–35.

22. C. Dwarkanath (*Introduction to Kāyachikitsā* [Bombay: Popular Book Depot, 1959], pp. 318, 320) defines *rasa* as plasma, including interstitial fluid and lymph; and the *dhātu*s as "intermediary metabolites," intended for the maintenance of stable formed tissue. See below, chap. 7, sec. 1, for an extended discussion of the term *rasa*.

23. In digestion the lower *dhātu*s nourish the higher ones either directly or indirectly with *rasa* irrigating each of the higher *dhātu*s consecutively. This latter (and later) conceptualization holds that each of the last six *dhātu*s are nourished "directly" by the food one eats through its own particular channel, via the *rasa dhātu* (*Caraka Saṁhitā* 4.28.4, with the commentaries of Cakrapaṇidatta and Śivadāsa Sena, discussed in Dwarkanath, *Kāyachikitsā*, pp. 319–26). Cf. *Caraka Saṁhitā* 6.15.15–16; *Śārṅgadhara Saṁhitā* 1.5.11–12; and *Yājñavalkya Smṛti* 3.84.

24. *Caraka Saṁhitā* 6.15.17; *MBhT* 2.5–6.

25. Jan Gonda (*Triads in the Veda*, p. 210, cited in Georges Dumézil, *Les dieux*

souverains des Indo–Européens, 3d ed. [Paris: Gallimard, 1986], p. 253) calls *doṣa*s "morbific entities." A more general translation for this term, which would take into account its uses in other spheres of Indian discourse, is "break in continuity."

26. Edeltraud Harzer, s.v. "Sāṃkhya" in *Encyclopedia of Religions*, ed. Mircea Eliade (Chicago: University of Chicago Press, 1986).

27. *Caraka Saṁhitā* 1.12.13; *Suśrūta Saṁhitā* 4.33.3. The earliest mention of the *tridoṣa* is useful to the dating the emergence of Āyurveda per se in India. Whereas wind and bile are already mentioned in the Vedas, the term for phlegm (*śleṣma*) does not appear until the ca. 1000 B.C. *Śatapatha Brāhmaṇa*. Following this, it is not until the ca. 313 B.C. *vārttika* of Kātyāyana on Pāṇini (*Aṣṭādhyāyī* 5.1.38) that the three are mentioned together in a compound (*vātapittaśleṣman*). One may thus surmise that the definitive formation of Ayurvedic medical theory occurred between 1000 and 313 B.C.: Filliozat, *Doctrine classique*, pp. 154–59.

28. The *dhātu*s are the material causes for health, while the *doṣa*s are the dynamic causes: Dasgupta, *History*, 2:334.

29. Louis Renou and Jean Filliozat, *L'Inde classique: manuel des études indiennes* (Paris: Imprimerie Nationale, 1947–53), vol. 2, pp. 152–53. On the symbolic role of the five breaths, from the *Chāndogya Upaniṣad* (3.13; 5.19) to tantric Buddhism, see Alex Wayman, *Yoga of the Guhyasamājatantra: The Arcane Lore of Forty Verses* (New York: Samuel Weiser, 1977), pp. 70–71.

30. The higher *dhātu*s are heavier than the lower: *Caraka Saṁhitā* 1.27.337.

31. Francis Zimmerman, "Ṛtu-Sātmya: Le cycle des saisons et le principe d'appropriation," *Puruṣārtha* 2 (1975), pp. 87–105.

32. *Gopatha Brāhmaṇa* cited in Sharma, *Āyurved*, p. 501.

33. Zimmerman, "Ṛtu-Sātmya," pp. 87–92. Also in the *Atharva Veda* (8.1.11–12), Time is identified with the sacrificial fire that can cook and mature (when it is the *Jātavedas* or *Vaiśvānara*) or consume and devour (when it is the *Kravyāda* fire).

34. In the "complete" system, the *six* Indian seasons correspond to the six "tastes" (*rasa*s), each of which is most appropriate to one of the seasons: Zimmerman, "Ṛtu-Sātmya," pp. 94–95, 100–104.

35. The effect on the macrocosm of wind, the third element in the triad, is termed *vikṣepa*, "dispersion." An explicit paralleling of sun, moon, and wind with their macrocosmic functions and the three *doṣa*s is found in *Suśruta Saṁhitā* 1.21.8.

36. January 14, called *makara saṃkrānti*, is the sole fixed solar date of the lunisolar Indian calendar: Jean-Luc Chambard, "Les trois grands dieux aux enfers: Tradition orale et cycle des fêtes hindoues dans un village de l'Inde centrale (M. P.)," in Catherine Champion, ed., *Littérature populaire et tradition orale en Inde* (*Puruṣārtha* 17) (Paris: Éditions de l'E.H.E.S.S, 1994), appendix 2. According to Chambard's informants, the twenty-four-day discrepancy between the solstice date (December

21) and January 14 is due to the 23.27° angle between the equator and the ecliptic in central India.

37. *Hārīta Saṁhitā* 4.20–30 (*La Hārītasaṁhitā: texte médical sanskrit*, ed. and tr. Alix Raison [Pondicherry: Institut Français d'Indologie, 1974]). Cf. Zimmerman, "Ṛtu-Sātmya," p. 94.

38. *Caraka Saṁhitā* 6.8.2–11; *Suśrūta Saṁhitā* 6.41.4–5.

39. *Raghuvaṁśa* 19.37–47, cited in Zimmermann, "Ṛtu-Sātmya," p. 96.

40. *Taittirīya Saṁhitā* 2.3.5.1–3; *Maitrāyaṇī Saṁhitā* 21.7; *Kāṭhaka Saṁhitā* 11.3. The myth has its origins in *RV* 10.85.2.

41. Rohiṇī may alternatively be identified with the sun: Filliozat, *Doctrine classique*, p. 85.

42. *Aṣṭāṅga Saṃgraha* 6.49.245 (*Śrīmadvāgbhaṭṭaviracita Aṣṭāṅgasaṃgraha*, ed. with a Hindi translation by Kaviraj Atrideva Gupta, 2 vols. [Bombay: Nirnay Sagar Press, n.d.]). This verse is directly borrowed into the *RA* 18.14; similar formulas are found in *Caraka Saṁhitā* 6.7.69; *Bṛhat Saṁhitā* 75.3; and *RHT* 19.19. For a discussion, see Siddhinandan Misra, *Āyurvedīya Rasaśāstra* (Benares: Chowkhambha, 1981), pp. 19–20. The classic account of the Ayurvedic healing of *rājayakṣma* is found in *Caraka Saṁhitā* 6.8.1–191. Cf. Palmyr Cordier's translation, with synoptic passages from the works of Bhela, Vṛnda, and Cakrapāṇi, in "Histoire de la médecine indienne. La phtisie pulmonaire," *Annales d'hygiène et de médecine coloniales* 15 (1912), pp. 255–66 and 535–48.

43. *Suśruta Saṁhitā* 1.14.14–15; but see 6.15.32 for a figure of six to seven days.

44. According to popular traditions in Rajasthan and elsewhere in India, it takes forty days and forty drops of blood to produce one drop of semen: G. Morris Carstairs, *The Twice-Born: Study of a Community of High-Caste Hindus* (London: Hogarth Press, 1961), pp. 83–84. Cf. *SSP* 1.73 (in Kalyani Mallik, ed., *Siddha Siddhānta Paddhati and Other Works of the Nātha Yogīs* [Poona: Oriental Book House, 1954]).

45. On the use of the terms *saumya* and *āgneya* for the male and female sexual fluids in conception, see *Suśrūta Saṁhitā* 3.3.3.

46. *Vāja* is the Sanskrit cognate of the English (and Latinate) "vigor." It is also related etymologically to the Sanskrit *ojas* (Monier Monier-Williams, *A Sanskrit-English Dictionary* [London: Oxford University Press, 1899; reprint Delhi: Motilal Banarsidass, 1984], s.v. "vāja"), the so-called eighth *dhātu* (*Atharva Veda* 2.18.1, with the commentary of Sāyaṇa) which is nothing other than the fluid of life itself, of which eight drops are located in the heart: *Caraka Saṁhitā* 1.17.74–75; 1.30.7.

47. E. Anantacharya, *Rasayana and Ayurveda* (Vishakapatnam: World Teacher Publications, 1935, 1982), pp. 12–14, summarizing discussion from the *Caraka* and *Suśruta Saṁhitās*.

48. *Caraka Saṁhitā* 6.1.16–24; *Suśruta Saṁhita* 4.29.10–12; and the A.D. 1131 *Manasollāsa* (2.14–51). Dalhaṇa's commentary to *Suśruta Saṁhitā* 3.3.4 provides a discussion of the three-chambered female reproductive system. For further discussion, see Arion Roşu, "Yoga et alchimie," *Zeitschrift der Deutschen Morgenländischen Gesellschaft* 132 (1982), p. 374; and *idem.*, "Consideration sur une technique du *Rasāyana* ayurvédique," *Indo-Iranian Journal* 17 (1975), 7–28, which indicates parallels with the Vedic initiation hut (*dīkṣāśāla*) and similar Taoist structures. Archaeologically excavated pre–4th c. A.D. Buddhist ascetics' cells in the Barābar, Nāgārjuni, and Guntupalli Caves clearly reproduce such a double-womb structure: Alexander Cunningham, *Archaeological Survey of India, Four Reports Made during the Years 1862–63–64–65* (Simla: Government Central Press, 1871), plate 19 and pp. 44–53; Debala Mitra, *Buddhist Monuments* (Calcutta: Sahitya Samsad, 1971), pp. 44–46 and figs. 14–15.

49. See *Gorakṣa Śataka* (verse 133 of *Das Gorakṣaśataka*, ed. by Karl A. Nowotny [Wetterschlick b. Bonn: Richard Schwarzbold, 1976]): nābhideśe vasati eko bhāskaro dahanātmakaḥ/ amṛtātmā sthito nityan tālumūle ca candramāḥ.

50. Aghehananda Bharati, *The Tantric Tradition* (London: Rider and Co., 1965; New York: Grove Press, 1975), p. 264, citing Vansidhar Sukul Vaidyaraj, *Vāmamārg* (Allahabad: Kalyan Mandir, 1951), p. 111.

51. Lawrence Babb, *The Divine Hierarchy: Popular Hinduism in Central India* (New York: Columbia University Press, 1975), pp. 128–40. Babb bases his analysis on fieldwork he carried out in village Madhya Pradesh (Chattisgarh district). On the "meteorological" origins of Goddess worship in the Vedic literature, see A. L. Basham, "Notes on the Origins of Śāktism and Tantrism," in *Religion and Society in Ancient India: Sudhakar Chattopadhyaya Commemoration Volume* (Calcutta: Roy and Chowdhury, 1984), pp. 148–53. I am grateful to Douglas Brooks for bringing this article to my attention.

52. *Bṛhadāraṇyaka Upaniṣad* 6.2.13–16; *Chāndogya Upaniṣad* 5.10.1–7; *Praśna Upaniṣad* 1.9–10; *Kauṣītaki Upaniṣad* 1.2–3; *Śatapatha Brāhmaṇa* 2.1.3.1–9.

53. Śaṅkara'a *Commentary on the Chāndogya Upaniṣad* (5.10.4), translated in Michel Hulin, *La face cachée du temps: L'imaginaire de l'au-delà* (Paris: Fayard, 1985), p. 369, who also refers to Śaṅkara's *Commentary on the Brahma-Sūtras* (3.1.6).

54. Śaṅkara's *Commentary on the Chāndogya Upaniṣad* (5.10.6), ibid., pp. 369–70.

55. See below, sec. 4 and nn. 88–96.

56. On the evolution from three to five, see David M. Knipe, "One Fire, Three Fires, Five Fires: Vedic Symbols in Transformation," *History of Religions* 12 (1972), pp. 28–41.

57. *Śatapatha Brāhmaṇa* 6.1.2.19; 10.1.3.1–4. Already in the *Atharva Veda*

(3.27.1–6) five "world protectors" (*lokapāla*), the gods of the cardinal directions, are identified with five colors and five elements.

58. It is found, for example, in the alchemical *Rasendra Maṅgala* (1.9): *pañcatvaṃ gati.*

59. Eliade, *Yoga: Immortality and Freedom*, p. 32; and Haraprasad Shastri, ed. *Advayavajrasaṃgraha*, Gaekwad's Oriental Series, no. 40 (Baroda: Oriental Institute, 1927), p. xxviii.

60. Giuseppe Tucci, *Tibetan Painted Scrolls*, 3 vols. (Rome: Libreria dello Stato, 1949), vol. 1, pp. 233, 243.

61. Louis de la Vallée Poussin, "Le Bouddhisme et le Yoga de Patañjali," *Mélanges chinois et bouddhiques* [Brussels], vol. 5 (1936–37), pp. 224–27.

62. See *Kāṭhaka Upaniṣad* 3.10–11 and 6.7–8, and its discussion by Madeleine Biardeau in *Asian Mythologies*, s.v. "Purāṇic Cosmogony," p. 44.

63. Gerald James Larson, *Classical Sāṃkhya: An Interpretation of its History and Meaning*, 2d ed. (Delhi: Motilal Banarsidass, 1979), pp. 171–76.

64. Ibid., p. 236.

65. There is a dynamic relationship that obtains between the *tanmātra*s and the *mahābhūta*s: sound generates ether; touch, catalyzed by ether, generates air; color, catalyzed by air, generates fire, etc. On this, see Priyanaranjan Ray, *History of Chemistry in Ancient and Medieval India Incorporating the History of Hindu Chemistry by Acharya Prafulla Chandra Ray* (Calcutta: Indian Chemical Society, 1956), p. 264.

66. T. A. Gopinath Rao, *Elements of Hindu Iconography*, 2 vols. in four tomes (Madras: Law Road Printing House, 1914–16), vol. 2, part 2, p. 374.

67. Shashibhushan Dasgupta, *An Introduction to Tantric Buddhism*, 2d ed. (Calcutta: University of Calcutta Press, 1958), pp. 19, 25, 29–33.

68. Bhattacharyya, *History*, p. 224.

69. A transcendant sixth, Vajrasattva, was equated with pure consciousness and Ādi Buddha, the "primal" Buddha: ibid., pp. 232–33.

70. Dasgupta, *Introduction*, pp. 85–86. For an expansion of this discussion, see also Tucci, *Tibetan Painted Scrolls*, 1:235–39.

71. Ibid., p. 239.

72. *Taittirīya Saṁhitā* 7.1.6.2, cited in Filliozat, *Doctrine classique*, p. 85.

73. *Śatapatha Brāhmaṇa* 1.6.4.5; *Bṛhadāraṇyaka Upaniṣad* 1.5.14. Sixteen (or seventeen) is also the number of priestly technicians employed in a *soma* sacrifice (Jan Heesterman, *The Inner Conflict of Tradition* [Chicago: University of Chicago Press, 1985], p. 210 n. 33). Elsewhere, the *soma* plant is said to be sixteen petaled: Shashibhushan Dasgupta, *Obscure Religious Cults*, 3d ed. (Calcutta: Firma KLM Limited, 1976), p. 251.

74. *Bṛhadāraṇyaka Upaniṣad* 1.5.15–16. On such "participation in number" see Betty Heimann, *Facets of Indian Thought* (London: Allen and Unwin, 1964), pp. 95–99, "The Discovery of Zero and Its Philosophical Implications in India." See above, n. 3.

75. Monier-Williams, *Sanskrit-English Dictionary*, s.v. "kalā." This carries over into the hathayogic physiology, in which the *ādhāras*, the "supports" of the subtle body, are sixteen in number: *SSP* 2.10–25; *HYP* 3.73.

76. Dasgupta, *History*, 2:317.

77. *Aitareya Brāhmaṇa* 1.3.

78. *Śatapatha Brāhmaṇa* 10.4.1.17. Prajāpati is also called *ṣoḍaśin*, "having sixteen parts," in *Yajur Veda* 8.36. The person (*puruṣa*) is said to consist of sixteen parts, of which the sixteenth is immortal, in the *Chāndogya Upaniṣad* (6.7.1–3) and *Praśna Upaniṣad* (6.2).

79. *Mahābhārata* 12.224.43; 12.298.15. It is in this context that the use of the term *soma* for the herbal medicines ingested in the *kuṭīpraveśa* technique takes on its greatest fullness of meaning: *Suśruta Saṁhitā* 4.29.4–10. On the duration of the menstrual cycle, see *Yājñavalkya Smṛti* 79, quoted in the 13th c. *Smṛticandrikā of Devaṇṇabhaṭṭa*, Āhnika Kāṇḍa (an English translation with notes) by J. R. Gharpure, 1st ed. (Bombay: V. J. Gharpure, 1946), pp. 25–26. Cf. *Manu Smṛti* 3.46 (*Manu Smṛti*, with the commentary of Kullūka Bhaṭṭa, ed. Gopala Sastri Nene, Kashi Sanskrit Series, no. 114 [Benares: Chowkhamba Sanskrit Series Office, 1970]).

80. Jan Gonda, *Medieval Religious Literature in Sanskrit*. History of Indian Literature, II, 1 (Wiesbaden: Harassowitz, 1977), p. 171.

81. The association with Śiva is especially powerful if the new moon (*amāvāsyā*) falls on a Monday, in which case he is called *sompati*, "lord of the moon": Babb, *Divine Hierarchy*, pp. 109–10. A north Indian guide to the "sixteen Mondays vow" is the anonymous *Solah Somvār tathā Somvār aur Saumya Pradoṣ Vrat Kathā* (Hardwar: Ranadhir Booksales, n.d.).

82. *RV* 8.47.17, in Monier-Williams, *Sanskrit–English Dictionary*, s.v. "kalā."

83. The classical study of this subject is Jan Gonda, "The Number Sixteen," in idem., *Change and Continuity in Indian Tradition* (The Hague: Mouton, 1965), pp. 115–30.

84. Heesterman, *Inner Conflict*, p. 210, n. 33.

85. *Jaiminīya Upaniṣad Brāhmaṇa* 3.38.8.

86. *Mahānirvāṇa Tantra* 10.127 (Arthur Avalon, *Tantra of the Great Liberation* [London: Luzac & Co., 1913; reprint New York: Dover Publications, 1972]), cited in Gonda, "Sixteen," p. 116.

87. *Mahābhārata* 12.293.4–8.

88. This is stated most graphically in the five-fires doctrine of the *Chāndogya Upaniṣad* (5.4.1–5.9.2), which constitutes the earliest systematic Indian statement on the cycle of death and rebirth in its relationship to the cycle of the year and the food chain.

89. In this regard, the *Mahābhārata* (12.293.3–7) statement that the other fifteen digits of the moon are merely "vestures" (*kośa*s) of the immortal digit is a significant one. For a discussion of the fifteen fiery and one lunar *kalā*s in the microcosm and macrocosm, see Ramlal Srivastav, ed., *Yogavāṇī: "Gorakh" Viśeṣāṅk* (Gorakhpur: Gorakhnath Mandir, 1977), p. 40.

90. The *SSP* (1.64) lists seventeen (16 + 1) digits, of which the last is alternately called *amṛta* or *nivṛtti*. Cf. *Amaraughaśāsana*, p. 12.

91. The *SSP* (1.65) lists thirteen (12 + 1) solar digits.

92. *Gorakh Bānī* Sabadī 89. Cf. the *Gyān Chautīsā* (v. 2) which, after evoking the sixteen lunar and twelve solar *kalā*s, speaks of the four remaining digits as the immortal abode of the *gurudev*. The *SSP* (1.66) however, enumerates eleven (10 + 1) fiery digits in the body. In basic tantric worship practice as well, fire is said to be composed of ten *kalā*s: *HT*, p. 146. The *Kulārṇava Tantra* (6.37–40) lists and names sixteen lunar, twelve solar, and ten fiery *kalā*s, which it identifies with the phonemes.

93. This process is also cast, in yogic parlance, as a raising of the yogin's female energy (*śakti*), of the indwelling Goddess herself, towards union with her beloved Śiva who, identified with the absolute *bráhman*, resides in the moon of the cranial vault. The mounting of the Goddess (*śakti-cālana*) is also described as the awakening and raising of a female serpent, named *kuṇḍalinī*, from the lower abdomen to the head. In Buddhist Siddha sources, this female energy is termed *avadhūtī*, *cāṇḍālī*, or *ḍombī*, all names for "outcaste" women: Kaviraj, *Bhāratīy*, 2:262.

94. *Śvetāśvatara Upaniṣad* 2.12. *Kālāgnirudra* literally means "Rudra [i.e., the destroyer] of the fire of time."

95. The number is variable: certain systems describe a system of nine, twelve, or even twenty-seven *cakra*s, of which six extend beyond the top of the head into space: "The System of Cakras According to Gorakṣanātha," in Gopinath Kaviraj, *Aspects of Indian Thought* (Calcutta: University of Burdwan, 1966), pp. 229–37.

96. *HYP* 3.4.

97. *Asian Mythologies*, s.v. "Purāṇic Cosmogony." See below, chap. 7 nn. 181–86.

98. In this perspective, *kalā* is at once the inactive aspect of the goddess Śakti as principle of manifestation and the active aspect of the god Śiva as principle of nonmanifestation: Padoux, *Vāc*, p. 89; Gopinath Kaviraj, *Tāntrik Sādhanā aur Saṃskṛti* (Patna: Bihar Rastrabhasa Parisad, 1979), pp. 209–10.

99. Dasgupta, *Obscure*, p. 243.

100. *Gorakh Bānī* Sabadī 219; Pad 56.2. Cf. *HYP* 3.3; *KJñN* 6.16, 28; 14.23, 26; 17.17.

101. Harvey Alper, "The Cosmos as Śiva's Language Game: Mantra According to Kṣemarāja's *Śivasūtravimarṣinī*," in idem., *Mantra* (Albany: SUNY Press, 1989), pp. 264, 274, 289 n. 44.

102. The matter is much more complex than this, bringing into play the *bindu* ("drop" of energy, sound, and light) and *bija* ("seed"), which are identified in a number of ways with Śiva and Śakti, according to the textual sources. On the interrelationship of *nāda*, *bindu*, and *bīja* in phonematic emanation, see *HT*, p. 94, and Padoux, *Vāc*, pp. 96–121, esp. p. 116. In the tantric "initiation of penetration" (*vedhamayī dīkṣā*), the guru completes his acoustic penetration of his initiate by telescoping the final letters of the Sanskrit alphabet into the *bindu*. This he unites with the *kalā*, which he in turn unites with the *nāda: Śārada Tilaka* 5.137. See below, chap. 10, sec. 2.

103. Paul Eduardo Muller-Ortega, *The Triadic Heart of Śiva: Kaula Tantricism of Abhinavagupta in the Non-dual Shaivism of Kashmir* (Albany: SUNY Press, 1989), pp. 152–54. The sixteen vowels, especially the *visarga*, are identified with Śiva, the consonants with Śakti: Padoux, *Vāc*, p. 417.

104. Padoux, *Vāc*, p. 79.

105. Pratapaditya Pal, *Hindu Religion and Iconology According to the Tantrasāra* (Los Angeles: Vichitra Press, 1981), pp. 18–19.

106. *Mahābhārata* 12.328.13.

107. Dasgupta, *Obscure*, p. 47.

108. Padoux, *Vāc*, p. 91, n. 12. On the creation of new "niches" to accomodate an ever-expanding metaphysics, see *HTSL*, p. 14; Dyczkowski, *Canon*, p. 125. In a veritable explosion, the number of *kalā*s is quadrupled in some sources to sixty-four, itself a widely employed tantric "round number." A Nāth Siddha text speaks of the sixty-four lunar digits, which have as their homologues sixty-four locations within the body: Sarasvati Sahagal, *Gorakh Darśan* (Hyderabad: Madhu Printers, 1979), p. 123. The sixty-four practical, mechanical, and fine arts, have also been referred to as *kalā*s since at least the time of the Tantras.

109. Raj Bali Pandey, *Hindu Saṁskāras* (*Socio-Religious Study of the Hindu Sacraments*), 2d ed. (Delhi: Motilal Banarsidass, 1969), pp. 17–23.

110. The end result of the alchemical *saṃskāra*s can be "sixteen-*varṇa* gold," the Indian homologue of twenty-four-carat gold: *Rasahṛdaya Tantra* (*Śrīmadgovindabhagavatpādaviracita Rashṛdayatantram* with the commentary of Caturbhuja Misra, tr. into Hindi by Daultarama Rasasastri (Benares: Chaukhamba Orientalia, 1989) translator's introduction, p. xxxi. This carries over into the Indian monetary system. Since at least the time of the *Manu Smṛti* (8.136) and down to the middle of

the twentieth century, a basic monetary subunit has been the sixteenth fraction of a whole: Gonda, "Sixteen," p. 117. Just as the ancient *kārśāpaṇa* was divided into sixteen *māṣa[ka]*s, so the pre-1947 Indian rupee was divided into sixteen annas, whence expressions referring to gold or river water as "sixteen annas pure": Milton Singer, ed., *Krishna: Myths, Rites, and Attitudes* (Chicago: University of Chicago Press, 1966), p. 84; Briggs, *Gorakhnāth*, p. 130. Cf. *BhP* 6.408b–409a, which refers to mercury that has been combined with sixteen "seeds" of other elements and becomes capable of producing gold.

111. *BhP* 6.485; 7.11.

112. The *mātra* (twenty-four seconds) is defined in Brahmānanda's commentary to *HYP* 2.12. *Prāṇāyāma* begins with the holding of the breath for 12½ *mātra*s, with all further yogic practice merely being so many multiples of this basic unit, culminating in *samādhi*, total yogic integration, when the breath is held for twelve days. A similar geometrical progression, working from a basic unit, occurs in the alchemical domain as well: see below, chap. 10, sec. 3.

113. Basava, *vacana* no. 537, translated in A. K. Ramanujan, "The Myths of Bhakti: Images of Śiva in Śaiva Poetry," in Meister, ed., *Discourses on Śiva*, p. 213. Cf. Anne-Marie Gaston, *Śiva in Dance, Myth and Iconography* (Delhi: Oxford University Press, 1982), p. 164; and Stella Kramrisch, *The Presence of Śiva* (Princeton: Princeton University Press, 1981), pp. 275–78.

114. Monier-Williams, *Sanskrit–English Dictionary*, s.v. "ātman." See above, chap. 1, n. 48.

Chapter Three

1. Aung, *Folk Elements*, pp. 68–69. On the Zawgyis and Weikzas, see ibid., pp. 41–54 and Needham, *Science and Civilisation*, vol. 2, "History of Scientific Thought" (1956), p. 174; and vol. 5, pt. 3, p. 166. See also above, chap. 1, n. 6.

2. *Bāṇa's Kādambarī (Pūrvabhāga Complete)*, ed. by M. R. Kale, 4th revised ed. (Delhi: Motilal Banarsidass, 1968), pp. 338–39. Cf. *Kādambarī: A Classical Sanskrit Story of Magical Transformations*, tr. with an introduction by Gwendolyn Layne (New York: Garland Publishing, 1991), pp. 225–26.

3. *Alberuni's India*, ed. with notes by Edward Sachau, 2 vols. (London: Kegan Paul, Trench, and Trubner, Inc., 1910; reprint Delhi: Munshiram Manoharlal, 1983), vol. 1, pp. 191–92. Variants on this myth are found in both Telugu and Cambodian sources: the 15th c. Telegu *Bhojarājīyamu* of Ananta names the alchemist Sarpaṭi [Carpaṭi]: Arion Roşu, "Alchemy and Sacred Geography in the Medieval Deccan," *Journal of the European Ayurvedic Society* 2 (1992), p. 155. The Cambodian source calls the alchemist a "brahmin" and the king the "leprous king of Angkor Thom": Jean Filliozat, "Al-Biruni and Indian Alchemy," in Debiprasad

Chattopadhyaya, ed. *Studies in the History of Science in India*, 2 vols. (New Delhi: Educational Enterprises, 1982), vol. 1, p. 342, citing G. Porée and E. Maspero, *Moeurs et coutumes des Khmers* (Paris: 1938), p. 73.

4. The Nāth Siddha Gopīcand's capital city is called Dhāra (Dhārānagar) in Richard Carnac Temple, *Legends of the Panjāb*, 3 vols. (London: Turner and Company, 1884–86; reprint Patiala: Department of Languages, Punjab, 1963), vol. 2, p. 63 (legend no. 18, v. 680).

5. Needham, *Science and Civilisation in China* vol. 5, pt. 4 (1980), pp. 497–98. Less than forty years after Marco Polo, the Muslim traveler Ibn Battûta describes yogis, encountered near Gwalior and in coastal Tamil Nadu, who specialized in the preparation of mineral pills: Ibn Battûta, *Voyages*, 3 vols., tr. into the French by C. Defremery and B. R. Sanguinetti with an introduction and notes by Stéphane Yerasimos (Paris: Maspero, 1982), vol. 3, pp. 171, 275.

6. Bernier, *Voyage dans les Etats du Grand Mogol*, p. 245. This detail, of Yogis being great eaters, seems to run against the accepted image of such persons as ascetic in their eating habits. Yet, such seems not to be the case with these Yogis, who have no use for self-mortification. On eating sulfur at daybreak, see *Khecarī Vidyā* [*KhV*] 4.13 (NNA MSS no. 5–6568). All *KhV* references are to this manuscript. Elsewhere, as I show in chap. 9, mercury's powers of "consumption" are also prodigious.

7. One of Oman's later works is entitled *Cults, Customs, and Superstitions of India* (London: 1908).

8. John Campbell Oman, *The Mystics, Ascetics and Saints of India* (London: 1903; reprint Delhi: Oriental Publishers, 1973), pp. 60–61. I have modernized some of Oman's language. For other accounts of alchemists, see ibid., pp. 56–59.

9. The ca. 1st c. A.D. *Arthaśāstra* (2.12.2; 2.13.3) of Kauṭilya appears to refer to the amalgamation of gold with mercury in mining, metallurgy, and coinage, when it uses the terms *rasaviddha* and *rasapāka:* R. P. Kangle, *The Kauṭilya Arthaśāstra*, 2 vols. (Bombay: University of Bombay, 1960), vol. 1, pp. 121–22 and notes; vol. 2, pp. 55–56. *Rasa* may, however, mean "smelted ore" rather than "mercury" in this case: Subarayappa, "Chemical Practice," in Bose, *Concise History*, p. 305. In his 6th c. *Bṛhat Saṁhitā*, a work devoted mainly to astrology, Varāhamihira (75.3) mentions an aphrodisiac preparation containing mercury (*pārada*) and other minerals.

10. *Caraka Saṁhitā* 6.7.70–71.

11. *Suśruta Saṁhitā* 4.25.39; 5.3.14; 6.35.7. Sharma (*Āyurved*, pp. 76, 89, 113) maintains that the "original" *Suśruta* is more ancient than the *Caraka*, but that Nāgārjuna's 6th–9th c. recension (and addition of a sixth section, called the "Uttaratantra") of the *Suśruta* is later than the final recension of the *Caraka*. Cf. Majumdar, "Medicine," in Bose, *Concise History*, p. 223.

12. *Aṣṭāṅga Saṃgraha* 6.49.245. The *Aṣṭāṅga Hṛdaya* (6.13.36) prescribes the use of mercury for *timira roga*. Arion Roşu (*Gustave Lietard et Palmyr Cordier: Travaux sur l'histoire de la médecine indienne*, Publications de l'Institut de Civilisation Indienne, no. 56 [Paris: De Boccard, 1989], p. lxxxix n. 148), who takes his citations from Kunte's 1912 Bombay (4th) edition of the *AH*, and Athavale's 1980 Poona edition of the *AS* respectively, notes the following classic references to mercury in these works: *AS* 6.30.80 = *AH* 6.13.36; 6.32.31; 6.25.61b–62a; and *AS* 6.49.392 = *AH* 6.39.162. On the dates of Vāgbhaṭṭa the Elder, and the closely related *Aṣṭāṅga Saṃgraha* and *Aṣṭāṅga Hṛdaya*, see Sharma, *Āyurved*, pp. 172–90.

13. Even prior to the medieval emergence of *rasa śāstra*, Āyurveda had its own form of elixir or rejuvenation therapy, called *rasāyana*, with which it claimed to be able to prolong life for one hundred, even five hundred years. Unlike *dehavāda* and *rasa śāstra*, however, *rasāyana* preparations are nearly exclusively herbal: Subbarayappa, "Chemical Practice," in Bose, *Concise History*, p. 316; and Roşu, "Yoga et alchimie," pp. 365–66.

14. The earliest list of the eight *siddhi*s is found in the pre–3d. c. A.D. Buddhist *Subāhuparipṛcchaśāstra* (par. 199, translated by W. Wassiljew, in *Der Buddhismus, seine Dogmen, Geschichte und Literatur* [Saint Petersburg, 1860], vol. 1, p. 218). Variant lists are found in the 3d–11th c. A.D. Buddhist *Sādhanamālā* (ed. Benoytosh Bhattacharya, Gaekwad's Oriental Series, 51 [Baroda: 1928, vol. 2, pp. lxxxv, 350 [vv. 3–5], and 509 [vv. 14–16], as well as in the 9th–10th c. A.D. Hindu *KJñN* (*Kaulajñānanirṇaya and Some Minor Texts of the School of Matysyendranātha*, ed. by Prabodh Chandra Bagchi, Calcutta Sanskrit Series, no. 3 [Calcutta: Metropolitan, 1934]) of Matsyendranāth (5.3–4), and the slightly later Hindu alchemical Tantra, the *KCM* (NNA MSS no. 5–3969, fol. 2b.3–4). Unless otherwise indicated, all *KCM* references are to this manuscript. All of these three lists include the *siddhi* of *rasa-rasāyana*. A parallel list, from a Tibetan Buddhist source, the *Dragpa jets'en*, is found in Stephan Beyer, *The Cult of Tārā* (Berkeley: University of California Press, 1973), p. 252. The eight *siddhi*s are defined in Benoytosh Bhattacharya, *An Introduction to Buddhist Esoterism* (Oxford: Oxford University Press, 1932), pp. 85–86. Three of the eight are found in the 6th c. A.D. *Aṣṭāṅga Saṃgraha* of Vāgbhaṭṭa the Elder: Sharma, *Āyurved*, p. 179.

15. Perhaps the earliest occurance of the term may be construed from the *Mahābhārata* (1.165.10) description of Vasiṣṭha's wish-fulfilling cow, which in addition to milk gives "the six flavors and the fluid ambrosial elixir" (*ṣaḍrasaṃ cāmṛtarasaṃ rasāyanam*). Cf. *Rāmāyaṇa* 4.27.3. An alternative Hindu enumeration of the eight *siddhi*s, which differs entirely from the eight "magical" *siddhi*s, is first found in *Āpastambha Dharma Sūtra* 2.9.23.6–7. A *siddhi* not generally included in such Hindu listings is the power to transmute base metals into gold with one's bodily

secretions. An early mention is verse 74 of the *Yogatattva Upaniṣad* (tr. in Jean Varenne, *Upanishads du yoga* [Paris: Gallimard, 1971]), p. 81.

16. The ninth-century Jain author Ugrāditya devotes the twenty-fourth and penultimate chapter of his medical work, the *Kalyāṇakāraka*, to *rasa-rasāyana:* Bhagiratha Prasada Tripathi's foreword to *Gorakṣa Saṁhitā* (*Part Two*), ed. Pandeya, p. 1. Cf. Sharma, *Āyurved*, pp. 194–95, 225.

17. The *Chou I Tshan Thung Chhi* (A.D. 142), attributed to Wei Po-Yang, is the earliest Chinese canon of theoretical alchemy: Needham, *Science and Civilisation*, vol. 5, pt. 4 (1980), p. 248. See below, sec. 3.

18. *RA* 18.211–21. This alchemical operation is discussed in chap. 5, sec. 4b.

19. *RA* 18.211.

20. *RA* 17.165a, 166a. The latter part of the Sanskrit phrase translated here reads: pūrvaṃ lohe parīkṣeta tato dehe prayojayet.

21. So, for example, Nāgārjuna, the 6th–9th c. final redactor of the *Suśruta Saṁhitā*, removed *śalyatantra* from the canon: for a survey of the question, see Arion Roşu, "Le renouveau contemporain de l'Āyurveda," *Wiener Zeitschrift für die Kunde Südasiens* 26 (1982), p. 65; and Misra, *Āyurvedīya*, pp. 9–10, 18; and Sharma, *Āyurved*, p. 540.

22. On *rasa śāstra*, which Prafulla Chandra Ray and others have termed "iatrochemistry," see Subbarayappa, "Chemical Practice," in Bose, *Concise History*, p. 314. Cf. Roşu, "Yoga et alchimie," p. 365.

23. On *rasacikitsā*, see Roşu, "Renouveau," pp. 65–66; and Majumdar, "Medicine," in Bose, ed. *Concise History*, p. 233. Both of these scholars relate *rasacikitsā* to the south Indian school of Siddha medicine. See below, chap. 4, nn. 112–14 for a discussion of the medieval Māheśvara Siddhas, who were the likely pioneers of this tradition.

24. In the words of Alberuni, "The greediness of the ignorant Hindu princes for gold-making does not know any limit": Sachau, *Alberuni's India*, 1:193.

25. The complementarity of mercurial alchemy and breath control is already present in the *RA* (1.18) and other texts from the tantric period. It is the greatly increased emphasis on the latter that distinguishes Siddha alchemy from tantric alchemy. On this comparison, see Needham, *Science and Civilisation*, vol. 5, pt. 5 (1983), "Spagyrical Discovery and Invention: Physiological Alchemy," p. 257.

26. *Sarvadarśana-saṃgraha of Sāyaṇa-Mādhava*, ed. with commentary by Vasudev Shastri Abhyankar, Government Oriental Series, Class A, no. 1 (Poona: Bhandarkar Oriental Research Institute, 1924; reprint 1978), p. 202; English translation in *The Sarva-darśana-saṃgraha or Review of the Different Systems of Hindu Philosophy by Madhava Āchārya*, tr. E. B. Cowell and A. E. Gough (London: Kegan Paul, Trench & Trubner, 1882; 7th reprint ed. Benares: Chaukhamba Amarabharati,

1978), p. 137. Mādhava quotes the *RHT, RA, RRS*, a lost work entitled *Rasasiddhānta*, and that of an author named Sarvajñā Rāmeśvara.

27. See Dasgupta, *Obscure*, pp. 254–55.

28. The *Rasaratnākara* of Nityanātha and the *Bhūtiprakaraṇa* of Gorakṣanātha: see below, chap. 5, secs. 4f and 4h.

29. *Amarakośa* 1.1.11: vidyādharāpsaro yakṣarakṣo gandharvakiṃnarāḥ/piśāco guhyakaḥ siddho bhūto 'mi devayonayaḥ (*Śrīmad Amarasiṁhaviracitaṃ nāmaliṅgānuśāsanam Amarakośa*, 2d ed., ed. with Hindi and Sanskrit commentaries by Brahmananda Tripathi, Chaukhamba Surbharati Granthamala, no. 52 [Benares: Chaukhamba Surbharati Prakashan, 1982]). The *Bhāgavata Purāṇa* (5.24.4) locates the Siddhas and Vidyādharas at the highest atmospheric level, immediately below the spheres of the sun and Rāhu, the "descending node" of the moon. In the Buddhist *Mañjuśrī Mūlakalpa*, the bodhisattva Vajrapāṇi, the foremost of the Vidyādharas, is iconographically placed to the left of Śākyamuni: David Snellgrove, *Buddhist Himalaya: Travels and Studies in Quest of the Origins and Nature of Tibetan Religion* (Oxford: Cassirer, 1957), p. 287. See also above, chap. 1, n. 10.

30. See above, chap. 1, n. 13.

31. Translation in Swami Hariharananda Aranya, *Yoga Philosophy of Patañjali*, with the commentary of Vyāsa (Calcutta: University of Calcutta, 1981), pp. 333–34.

32. Priyavrat Sharma, *Indian Medicine in the Classical Age*, Chowkhamba Sanskrit Studies, vol. 85 (Benares: Chowkhamba Sanskrit Series Office, 1972), p. 99. As an Ayurvedic category, *bhūtavidyā* is limited mainly to mental disorders and complications in childbirth, both of which arise from demonic influences.

33. The classic work on the subject is Jean Filliozat, *Étude de démonologie indienne: le Kumāratantra de Rāvaṇa et les textes parallèles indiens, tibétains, chinois, cambodgien et arabe*, Cahiers de la Société Asiatique, 1è série, vol. 4 (Paris: Imprimerie Nationale, 1937). This work is an expansion of an earlier article by Filliozat, "Le Kumāratantra de Rāvaṇa," *Journal Asiatique* 226 (1935):1–66. The *Kumāra Tantra* as an independent work is certainly pre–11th century; much of the material in it draws on the *Atharva Veda*, the epics, and the *Caraka* and *Suśruta Saṁhitā*s.

34. A Sittar alchemical work, the *Bogar 7000* (probably of late date) names Rāvaṇa's son Indrajit as an alchemist: personal communication from N. Sethu Raghunathan, Madurai, February 1985.

35. *Auṣadhibhiḥ asura-bhavaneṣu rasāyaneti:* Vyāsa's commentary on *Yoga Sūtra* 4.1 (this verse has a parallel in the Buddhist *Abhidhammakośa* [7.122]). It has been argued that *Yoga Sūtra* 4.1 was a late non-Patanjalian addition made some time after the 4th c. A.D. On this, see Roşu, "Yoga et alchimie," pp. 369, 371; Vallée Poussin, "Le Bouddhisme et le Yoga de Patañjali," p. 241.

36. upasamprāptaḥ kamanīyābhir asurakanyābhir upanītaṃ rasāyanam: *Sāṃkhya Yogadarśana or Yogadarśana of Patañjali*, ed. Gosvami Damodara Sastri et al. (Benares: Chaukhambha Sanskrit Sansthan, 1990), p. 392. The ca. A.D. 1040 king Bhoja of Dhāra is the first commentator to gloss *auṣadhi* as "such elixirs as mercury, etc." (*pāradādi rasāyanādi*): for a discussion of these commentaries on *Yoga Sūtra* 4.1, see Roşu, "Yoga et alchimie," pp. 370–72. See also *RA* 12.102–3 on the method used by these semidivine and demonic females to recover said fluids; and *KCM* (fol. 6b.4–7a.1) on alchemical means of gaining access to such creatures.

37. For a discussion, see Roşu, "Yoga et alchimie," pp. 376–78. The *Bhāgavata Purāṇa* is dated to the 6th–12th centuries A.D.

38. V. R. Madhavan, *Siddha Medical Manuscripts in Tamil* (Madras: International Institute of Tamil Studies, 1984), p. 27. While *asura*s (antigods, "Titans"), *bhūta*s (beings, bogeymen), and *rākṣasa*s (brahmin ghouls; technically, Rāvaṇa was one of these) are all different types of demons according to Hindu demonology (see *Amarakośa* 1.1.11), they are often conflated in both popular and literary discourse.

39. See for example the rich epic mythology of Kāvya Uśanas, the chaplain of the Asuras, whose sorcery was more powerful than the sacrificial knowledge of Bṛhaspati, chaplain of the gods. On this, as well as the semantic field of the term *kavi*, from which Kāvya Uśanas' name as well as terms for "(alchemical) wizard" are generated, see below, chap. 9, sec. 5 and chap. 10, sec. 5.

40. *RA* 2.10–11.

41. Hasan Mujtaba and Nafisa Shah, "Taming of the Serpent," *Newsline* (Pakistan), August 1992, p. 82. Gūgā Chauhan, also known by the names of Guru Gūgā (or Gogā), Gūgā Pīr, Gūgā Vīr, or Zahīr Pīr, is counted by the Nāth Siddhas as one of their own. While his principal shrine is located in Rajasthan, Gūgā is also revered throughout north India, in Pakistan, and the Deccan. On his cult and legend, see Pushpa Bhati, *Rājasthān ke Lok Devtā evaṃ Lok Sāhity* (Bikaner: Kavita Prakashan, 1991), pp. 89–97; Jacky Assayag, "Pouvoir contre 'puissances': Bref essai de démonologie hindou-musulmane," *L'Homme* 131 (July–Nov. 1994), p. 47; E. C. Lapoint, "The Epic of Gūgā: A North Indian Oral Tradition," in S. Vatuk, ed., *American Studies in the Anthropology of India* (New Delhi: Manohar, 1978), pp. 281–308; and Stuart H. Blackburn, Peter J. Claus, Joyce B. Fluekiger, and Susan Wadley, eds., *Oral Epics in India* (Berkeley: University of California Press, 1989), pp. 26–27, 224–27.

42. On the hathayogic symbolism of this passage, see above, chap. 2, nn. 95–96; on a similar Nāth Siddha tradition, a legend involving Jālandharanāth and Gopīcand, see below, chap. 9, nn. 149–50.

43. On this great Serpent, called Śeṣa or Ananta, see below, chap. 7, sec. 6; and chap. 8, sec. 1.

44. N. Dutt, "Notes on the Nāgārjunikoṇḍa Inscriptions," *Indian Historical Quarterly* 7:3 (Sept. 1931), p. 639; Rahula Sankrtyayana," (Recherches Bouddhiques II) L'Origine du Vajrayāna et les quatre-vingt siddhas," *Journal Asiatique* 225:2 (Oct.–Dec. 1934), p. 212.

45. āryaka nāmā Gopāla-dārakaḥ siddhādeśena samādiṣṭo rājā bhaviṣyati: *Mṛcchakaṭikā*, Act 2 (*Mṛcchakaṭikā of Śrī Śūdraka*, ed. by Jagdish Chandra Mishra [Benares: Chaukhamba Surbharati, 1985], p. 117). For discussions, see P. Lal, *Great Sanskrit Plays in Modern Translation* (New York: New Directions, 1964), p. 79; Divakar Pandey, *Gorakhnāth evam unkī Paramparā kā Sāhity* (Gorakhpur: Gorakhpur University, 1980), p. 67; and Sankrtyayana, "Recherches," p. 213.

46. *Vāsavadattā*, vv. 78–79, 87 (in Fitz-Edward Hall, *The Vāsavadattā of Subandhu* [Calcutta: Asiatic Society of Bengal, 1859]).

47. The two may have been separate toponyms, for mountains in the same region. The Srisailam of the *Māhabhārata* and other Hindu sources would be none other than the site of one of the twelve self-generated (*svayambhu*) liṅgas of Śiva and modern-day Hindu religious center in the Kurnool district of Andhra Pradesh, while the Buddhist Śrīparvata would correspond to the modern Nāgārjunikoṇḍa, some sixty miles to the east. On this question, see Arion Roşu, "A la recherche d'un *tīrtha* énigmatique du Deccan médiéval," *Bulletin de l'Ecole Française d'Extrême Orient* 60 (1969), p. 46. See below, chap. 4, sec. 5a.

48. *Mahābhārata* 3.83.16–21; David Lorenzen, *The Kāpālikas and Kālamukhas: Two Lost Śaivite Sects* (New Delhi: Thomson Press, 1972), p. 51. Other early Sanskrit references to Srisailam are the *Suśrūta Saṁhitā* (4.29.27), the 6th c. A.D. *Bṛhat Saṁhitā* of Varāhamihira (16.3), and the *Padma Purāṇa:* Roşu, "A la recherche," p. 39; and idem, "Alchemy and Sacred Geography," p. 153.

49. "Brahmi Inscriptions at Nāgārjunikoṇḍa," *South Indian Epigraphy. Annual Report for the Year Ending 31st March 1927* (Madras: Archaeological Survey of India, 1927), pp. 73–74 (Brahmi inscription no. 214). See also Etienne Lamotte, *Histoire du Bouddhisme indien, des origines à l'ère Śaka* (Louvain: Université de Louvain, 1958), pp. 377, 382, 583, 589.

50. According to Kaviraj (*Bhāratīy*, vol. 1, pp. 411–12, citing *Vinaya Piṭaka* 2.35), the Buddhists of Śrīparvata knew of the *ṛddhi*s of "transmutation" and "transubstantiation."

51. The Siddhāthakas were one of four Śrīparvata-based schools to form the Andhra contingent of the 3d c. A.D. Mahāsaṅghika heresy. The Mahāsaṅghikas were branded heretical because they maintained that *nirvāṇa* was, rather than the extinction of suffering as taught by the Buddha, a "positive faultless state": Dutt, "Notes," p. 650, citing *Kathavatthu* 9.2, 19.6.

52. Roşu, "A la recherche," pp. 47–48; idem., "Alchemy," p. 153. I cannot say

whether the Siddhas of whom Śiva is made the Lord here were of the divine or the human variety. The Śaivas who apparently eased the Buddhists out of the Andhra country included the Pāśupata sect (Bāṇa's alchemist is called a "Mahā-pāśupata"). These would later be followed by the Kāpālikas and Vīraśaivas: see below, chap. 4, n. 163.

53. Tirumūlar, *Tirumantiram* 1463 (1490) quoted in Kamil V. Zvelebil, *The Poets of the Powers* (London: Rider and Company, 1973), p. 27.

54. Thiru N. Kardaswamy, *History of Siddha Medicine* (Madras: 1979), p. 311, calls Tirumūlar the disciple of Nandhi Devar, whom he says later incarnated himself as the 12th c. Vīraśaiva saint (and alchemist, in some sources) Allama Prabhu (ibid., p. 354). A certain Nandi is cited in three post–12th c. works, the *Rasendracūḍāmaṇi*, the *Rasaprakāśasudhākara*, and the *Rasaratnasamucchaya:* see below, chap. 5, nn. 16, 211, 220. A certain Nandikeśvara is termed an "authority on alchemy" (*rasādhikārika*) in a 9th c. work; the Jain ayurvedic writer Ugrāditya (see above, n. 16) calls his guru Śrī Nandī: Sharma, *Āyurved,* pp. 194–95, 225, 480. Nandi is called the "god of alchemy" in *Kāvyamīmāṁsa* 6: idem, *Indian Medicine in the Classical Age,* p. 42.

55. Eighteen independent lists of the eighteen Sittars are culled from manuscripts by V. R. Madhavan in his *Siddha Medical Manuscripts in Tamil,* pp. 20–26.

56. Zvelebil, *Poets of the Powers,* p. 36 and n. 44; and Renou and Filliozat, *L'Inde classique,* vol. 2, p. 163. Sittar medical works are older.

57. Moti Chandra, *Sārthavāh* (Patna: Bihar Rashtrabhasha Parishad, 1953), p. 188, quoted in Sharma, *Āyurved,* p. 480 n. 1.

58. There, at the Dhandhayuthapani shrine, associated with Bogar, worshippers obtain a sacred ash which has curative powers: A. Shanmuga Velan, *Siddhar's Science of Longevity and Kalpa Medicine of India* (Madras: Sakthi Nilayam, 1963), p. 49. Bogar is also said to have created the famous image of Murugan at his Hill Temple at Palani from an alloy of nine poisonous metalloids: Manuel Moreno, "*Pañcāmirtam:* God's Washings as Food," in *The Eternal Food* ed. Ravindra Khare (Albany: SUNY Press, 1992), p. 159.

59. On Koṅganar, see below, chap. 4, sec. 2.

60. Bogar's principal work, the *Sattakāntam,* which is certainly much later than the dates of the Bogar of legend, has him travel to Rome, Jerusalem, and Mecca as well: Filliozat ("Taoïsme et yoga," p. 78 [citing Paramananda Mariadassou, *Medecine traditionelle de l'Inde,* 4 vols. (Pondicherry: Sainte Anne, 1934–38), vol. 3, p. 6 n. 2]) and P. C. Bagchi ("Compte-rendu de Benoytosh Bhattacharyya, édition de la *Sādhanamālā,*" *Indian Historical Quarterly* 6 [1930], pp. 584–87) consider Bogar to have been a south Indian who went to China; Needham (*Science and Civilisation,*

vol. 5, pt. 5 [1983], p. 285) and Shanmuga Velan (*Siddhar Science*, p. 18) see him as a Chinese (Taoist) philosopher who came to south India to study medicine.

61. Maritime trade between China and ports on India's west coast (Muzuris and Broach) was under way by the end of the 4th c. A.D.: Needham, *Science and Civilisation*, vol. 1 (1954), pp. 171, 174, 178–79; vol. 5, pt. 4 (1980), pp. 354, 406–7; and vol. 5, pt. 5 (1983), p. 282.

62. Indeed, the very term "alchemy" is likely derived from the Chinese root *kim/chim* ("aurifaction") or the term *chin i* ("potable gold"): Needham, *Science and Civilisation*, vol. 5, pt. 4 (1980), pp. 351–53, 355. For a history of Taoist alchemy in this period, ibid., pp. 213–59; 320–31.

63. It should be noted that mercury naturally occurs, in traces, in areas of geothermic activity, where (often sulfurous) hot springs throw up small quantities of cinnabar from deep in the earth: *Shorter Oxford Economic Atlas of the World*, 2d ed. (London: Oxford University Press, 1959), p. 88. Such traces may have sufficed, prior to the importing of foreign mercury, for the fledgling alchemists of the Indian subcontinent. See below, chap. 7, sec. 3, for the symbolic importance of this geothermal and geological phenomenon.

64. Filliozat, "Taoïsme et yoga," p. 46, citing I-Ching, *Ta Tang Hsi-yu chiu fa kao seng chuan*, ed. and tr. Edouard Chavannes, *Mémoire composé de la grande dynastie T'ang sur les religieux éminents qui allèrent chercher la Loi dans les pays d'Occident* (Paris: Ernest Leroux, 1894), pp. 23–24; and Arthur Waley, "Notes on Chinese Alchemy," *Bulletin of the School of Oriental Studies* 6:1 (1930), pp. 22–24.

65. Needham, *Science and Civilisation*, vol. 1 (1954), p. 212; ibid., vol. 5, pt. 3 (1976), p. 160. The case of Nārāyaṇasvāmin is found in the A.D. 863 *Yu-yang Tsa Tsu* of Tuan Chêng-Shih: ibid., vol. 5, pt. 4, p. 197.

66. Bhattacharyya, *History*, p. 99; Prabodh Chandra Bagchi, "On Foreign Element in the Tantra," *Studies in the Tantras* (Calcutta: University of Calcutta, 1975), pp. 48–49.

67. *Su yu ki: Buddhist Records of the Western World, Translated from the Chinese of Hiuen Tsiang* (A.D. *629*) by Samuel Beal, 2 vols. (London: Trubner & Co., 1884; reprint ed. Delhi: Munshiram Manoharlal, 1969), 2:212–16. For a discussion, see Thomas Watters, *On Yuan Chwang's Travels in India, 629–645* A.D., 2 vols. (London: Royal Asiatic Society, 1904–05), 2:200–8. On Hsuan-tsang's role in the translation of the *Tao te ching*, see Filliozat, "Taoïsme et yoga," p. 41.

68. Bāṇabhaṭṭa also describes a prince who, "mad for the elixir of life," is dying from the medicines given him to counter the disease of royal consumption (*rājayakṣma*); and a young physician named Rasāyana who, although he had mastered Āyurveda in its entirety, takes his own life when he is unable to heal an ailing

king: *Harṣacaritra* 6.224 and 5.178 (*The Harṣacarita of Bāṇabhaṭṭa with Exhaustive Notes [Ucchvāsas I–VIII]*, ed. Pandurang Vamana Kane [Bombay: n.p., 1918; reprint Delhi: Motilal Banarsidass, 1973]).

69. I-Ching, *A Record of the Buddhist Religion as Practiced in India and the Malay Archipelago* (A.D. *671–695*), tr. J. Takakusu (London: Clarendon Press, 1896; reprint ed. Delhi: Munshiram Manoharlal, 1966), pp. 134–35.

70. The two pilgrims were named Hui-sêng and Sung yün. The date was A.D. 520: Needham, *Science and Civilisation*, vol. 1 (1954), pp. 207, 209; and vol. 5, pt. 4 (1980), p. 354.

71. China also imported Indian medicine at the same time as it did Buddhism: a text entitled *Buddha-vaidyarāja-śāstra* was translated into Chinese in A.D. 230: Needham, *Science and Civilisation*, vol. 5, part 4 (1980), p. 336. Manuscript fragments on Hindu sorcery of the "Kakṣapuṭa" variety, dating from the Tang period (A.D. 618–906) and found in Kucha, in Chinese Turkestan, indicate that the Chinese were interested in this Indian tradition as well: Filliozat, "Taoïsme et yoga," p. 76. On the *Kakṣapuṭa Tantra*, a 13th c. Hindu work attributed to Siddha Nāgārjuna, see below, chap. 5, sec. 5j and nn. 60–61.

72. In the 5th c. A.D. *Mahāyānasūtrālaṃkāra Śāstra*, for example: Needham, *Science and Civilisation*, vol. 2 (1956), p. 428; and vol. 5, pt. 5 (1983), pp. 270, 274–75.

73. For a full discussion of these practices and their Taoist symbolism, see below, chap. 7, nn. 87, 92–101. Cf. Needham, *Science and Civilisation*, vol. 2 (1956), pp. 148–50, and vol. 5, pt. 5, pp. 269–75. The Ayurvedic rejuvenation (*rasāyana*) technique of *kuṭī-praveśa*, "entering the hut," has a close Taoist parallel. See above, chap. 2, n. 48; below, chap. 10, nn. 103–5; and David Gordon White, *Myths of the Dog-Man* (Chicago: University of Chicago Press, 1991), pp. 163, 176.

74. Needham, *Science and Civilisation*, vol. 2 (1956), pp. 425, 427; vol. 5, pt. 5 (1983), p. 283.

75. Indeed, the Persian traders who did much of the actual transporting of goods along the Silk Road, especially between the 5th c. and 10th c., were popularly regarded as alchemists in the Chinese capital of Chang-an, due to the magical powders and precious stones in which they traded: Needham, *Science and Civilisation*, vol. 2 (1956), p. 187.

76. Sharma, *Āyurved*, pp. 179, 470, 473. Nāgārjuna's connection with Tārā may derive from the fact that she was identified, at some level, with Prajñāparamitā, the deified "Perfection of Wisdom," the eponymous *sūtra* of which he wrote the definitive commentary: *Tārā-Tantram* with an introduction by A. K. Maitra (reprint ed. Delhi: Bani Prakashan, 1983), p. 19. For a general discussion, see Bharati, *Tantric Tradition*, pp. 58–84.

77. For Tārā, see p. 172 of Hall's edition of the *Vāsavadattā*, cited in Beyer, *Cult of Tārā*, p. 7; *pārada [-piṇḍa]* is mentioned in verse 181.

78. Cited in Sharma, *Āyurved*, pp. 178–79, 470. Varāhamihira's *Bṛhat Saṁhitā*, a northwestern text, is the source of Vāgbhaṭṭa's early reference to mercury. See above, n. 9.

79. Two images of "To-lo" (Tārā) are reported by Hsuan-tsang in the early 7th c.: Beal, tr., *Buddhist Records*, vol. 2, pp. 103, 174. Patna had overland trade links with Kathmandu (Alastair Lamb, *British India and Tibet, 1766–1910*, 2d ed. [London: Routledge and Kegan Paul, 1986], pp. 3–4, also a locus of Tārā worship in the early 7th c. (Beyer, *Tārā*, p. 5), and with Takṣaśila and Khotan, the great hubs of the Silk Road in the northwest.

80. The king of Kāñci erected a temple to the "Chinese goddess" in about A.D. 720: Needham, *Science and Civilisation*, vol. 5, pt. 5 (1983), p. 286. Kāñci, the modern Conjeevaram, located forty-three miles south of Madras, was the capital of the Cola empire. Buddhism flowered there briefly, in the period under study here: Lamotte, *Histoire*, p. 383.

81. *Kalyāṇ Śakti Aṅk* (Gorakhpur: Gita Press, 1934), p. 227. This was, moreover, a period in which a great number of royal ambassadors were sent by sea from south India to China: one was sent from Kāñci, in 720 A.D.: Needham, *Science and Civilisation*, vol. 5, part 5 (1983), p. 286.

82. Ernst Obermiller, *History of Buddhism (Chos-hbyung) by Bu-ston*, 2 vols. (Heidelberg: Harrassowitz, 1931–32; reprint Delhi: Sri Satguru Publications, 1986), vol. 2, p. 122; Misra, *Āyurvedīya*, p. 8; Dutt, "Notes," p. 637, citing *Pag Sam Jon Zang by Sumpa Khan-po Yese Pal Jor*, 2 vols., ed. Sarat Chandra Das (Calcutta: Presidency Jail Press, 1908), vol. 1, pp. 85–86.

83. Lucette Boulnois, *Poudre d'or et monnaies d'argent au Tibet* (Paris: Editions du C.N.R.S., 1983), p. 124.

84. Needham, *Science and Civilisation*, vol. 2 (1956), p. 132. Cinnabar also occurs naturally on islands in the Bay of Bengal, perhaps the Andamans, according to the *Suleiman Saudagar*, a 9th c. travel account cited in Fitz-Edward Hall, *Bibliography* (p. 363) summarized in the commentary to the *RRS* [*Śrīvāgbhaṭācāryaviracitaḥ Rasaratnasamucchaya*, ed. with Hindi commentary by Dharmananda Sharma (Delhi: Motilal Banarsidass, 1962)] p. 208).

85. F. E. Treloar, "The Use of Mercury in Metal Ritual Objects as a Symbol of Śiva," *Artibus Asiae* 34 (1972), p. 239.

86. Sharma, commentary to *RRS*, pp. 186, 208–9; Sharma *Āyurved*, p. 477; and George Watt, *Dictionary of the Economic Products of India*, 6 vols. (Calcutta: Superintendent of Government Printing, 1889–96), 2d reprint, in 10 vols. (Delhi: Periodical Exports, 1972), vol. 5, p. 232.

87. Needham, *Science and Civilisation*, vol. 5, pt. 5 (1983), pp. 280–86.

88. There was in fact an ancient overland trade route which linked Szechuan with India, via Yunnan, Burma, and Assam, and a highly syncretistic alchemical tradition arose in Burma in about the 5th c.: Needham, *Science and Civilisation*, vol. 2 (1956), p. 174; vol. 5, pt. 3, p. 166.

89. *Sādhanamālā*, ed. Bhattacarya, vol. 1, pp. 193–94; vol. 2, pp. 265–66. Both of these passages are followed by the colophon: "extracted from the land of the Bhoṭas [Tibet] by the Arya-nāgārjuna-pādas." Cf. ibid., vol. 2, pp. xlv–xlvi, for a discussion.

90. While the Dragon Kaju was not founded until the early 12th c., the Nyingma sect to which the "ancient" divinity Quicksilver belongs dates from the origins of Tibetan Buddhism itself: Beyer, *Tārā*, pp. 42–43, 54; Michael Lee Walter, *The Role of Alchemy and Medicine in Indo–Tibetan Tantrism* (Ph.D. thesis, Indiana University, 1980), pp. 44, 58–60, 90, 215, 216. For a brief survey of the Nyingma alchemical systems attributed to the 8th c. founders of Tibetan Buddhism, Vimalamitra and Padmasambhava (but which in fact date from the 12–13th centuries), see ibid., pp. 28–29, 182, and idem, "Preliminary Results from a Study of Two Rasāyana Systems in Indo-Tibetan Esoterism," in *Tibetan Studies in Honor of Hugh Richardson*, ed. Michael Aris and Aung San Sun Kyi (Warminster, Eng.: Aris and Phillips, 1979), pp. 319–24.

91. Sharma, *Āyurved*, p. 470. Tārā was introduced into Tibet by the Nepalese princess Tr'itsün, the daughter of Aṃśuvarman and wife of the first great Tibetan king Songtsen gampo (A.D. 617–50), who brought a sandalwood image of the goddess to her husband's palace when she married him: Beyer, *Tārā*, p. 5.

92. The Tibetan Buddhists nevertheless had and continue to have their own alchemical tradition. In addition to the alchemical traditions of the Nyingma schools, the early 11th c. *Kālacakra Tantra* contains alchemical data. See below, nn. 122–27.

93. Sharma, *Indian Medicine*, pp. 38–42; Sharma's commentary to the *RRS*, p. 207; Needham, *Science and Civilisation*, vol. 5, part 5 (1983), pp. 187, 217; D. C. Sircar, *Cosmography and Geography in Early Indian Literature* (Calcutta: Indian Studies: Past and Present, 1967), pp. 74, 89, 106, 108, 128; André Wink, *Al-hind: The Making of the Indo-Islamic World*, vol. 1: Early Medieval India and the Expansion of Islam, Seventh to Eleventh Centuries (Delhi: Oxford University Press, 1990), p. 232; and Watt, *Dictionary*, pp. 232–33. On mentions of the countries of Pārada-deśa and Hiṅgula-deśa in the age of Pāṇini, see Sharma's commentary to *RRS* 1.68–75 (p. 12). Kauṭilya, who hailed from present-day Pakistan, knew of *hiṅgula: Arthaśāstra* 2.13.23.

94. Sharma, commentary to *RRS*, p. 199; Watt, *Dictionary*, 5:233. See also Ching-lang Hou, *Monnaies d'offrande et la notion de Trésorerie dans la religion chinoise* (Paris: Mémoires de l'Institut des Hautes Etudes Chinoises, 1975), p. 124. The richest modern-day deposits in the entire region are found in Khaydarkan (*Shorter Oxford Economic Atlas*, p. 88), in the central Asian republic of Kyrgyzstan, which would correspond to the mercury-rich region of Farghāna mentioned in the *Hudūd al-'Alam* 25.45–49 (*Hudūd al-'Alam*, "The Regions of the World": A Persian Geography 372 A.H.–982 A.H., tr. and explained by V. Minorsky [1937; reprint ed. Karachi: Indus Publications, 1980], p. 116).

95. Giuseppe Tucci, "Animadversiones Indicae," *Journal of the Royal Asiatic Society of Bengal* n.s. 26 (1930), p. 147.

96. The Tibetan *Tanjur* contains fifty-nine works by "Nāgārjuna" on Buddhist Tantra (listed in Bhattacharya, *Sādhanamālā*, vol. 2, pp. cvi–cviii); Palmyr Cordier lists twelve magico-medical and nonmedical works, in Sanskrit and Tibetan, authored by Nāgārjuna (*Nāgārjuna et l'Uttaratantra de la Suçrutasamhitā* [Antananarivo: private printing, 1896], pp. 2–3). To these may be added the works of the Mādhyamika philosopher Nāgārjuna, as well as numerous other works attributed to "Nāgārjuna" by other authors.

97. Bhaiṣajya-Nāgārjuna or Bhadant Nāgārjuna, the Keralan author of a medical work entitled *Rasavaiśeṣika Sūtra* (Renou and Filliozat, *l'Inde classique*, vol. 2, p. 168).

98. Śrī Nāgārjuna Muni, who, according to the ca. 12th c. *Rasopaniṣat* (16.10), discovered a method for whitening copper without sulfur.

99. Albert Grünwedel, "Die Geschichten der vierundachtzig Zauberer (Mahāsiddhas) aus dem tibetischen übersetzt," *Baessler-Archiv* 5 (1916), pp. 137–228, cited in Toni Schmidt, "Fünfundachtzig Mahāsiddhas," *Ethnos* 2–3 (1955), p. 120.

100. Max Walleser, "The Life of Nāgārjuna from Tibetan and Chinese Sources," in Bruno Schindler, ed., *Asia Major, Hirth Anniversary Volume* (London: 1923), p. 424.

101. Buddhist legend knows of two Nāgārjunas who would have preceded the historical figure I am now discussing. One is Menander's ca. 140 B.C. interlocutor in the *Milinda Panha*, the "Questions of King Milinda"; the other is a bodhisattva who incarnated himself as the king of Kashmir in about the same period, according to the 12th c. *Rājataraṃgiṇī* of Kalhaṇa (1.173, 177).

102. According to the 5th c. Chinese pilgrim to India Fa-hsien, Nāgārjuna also received the *Avataṁsaka* (or *Paramārtha*) *Sūtra*s from the Nāgas. On the Chinese traditions, beginning with Kumārajīva's 5th c. biography of Nāgārjuna, see K. Venkata Ramanan, *Nāgārjuna's Philosophy: As Presented in the Mahā-Prajñāparamitā-*

Śāstra (Delhi: Motilal Banarsidass, 1975), p. 27; and Cordier, *Nāgārjuna et l'Uttaratantra*, p. 2. The term *mahānāga* has an esoteric meaning: Tucci, "Animadversiones Indicae," p. 140.

103. The source of the Tibetan legend is the A.D. 1322 *Chos hbyung* (History of Buddhism) of Bu-ston: Obermiller, *History*, vol. 2, p. 124. Cf. Bhattacharyya *History*, p. 239. The *Chos hbyung* also relates the legend of the gold-making elixir obtained by Nāgārjuna from the intermediate continent. See above, n. 82.

104. The Śātavāhana king whom these sources call Śātavāhana or Śadvaha-rāja was named Gautamaputra Śātakarṇi. Nāgārjuna's "Epistle to a Dear Friend" (*Suhṛllehika*) was written to this figure: Venkata Ramanan, *Nāgārjuna's Philosophy*, pp. 27–28. Cf. Krishna Gairola, "Les conditions sociales et religieuses à l'époque de Śātavāhana dans l'Inde (Ie siècle av. J.-C.–IIe siècle ap. J.-C.)," *Journal Asiatique* 243 (1955), pp. 281–95.

105. *Harṣacarita* 8.283–84. Bāṇabhaṭṭa also states in two places (*Harṣacarita* 415 and *Kādambarī* 393) that the tribal peoples of the Vindhya mountains painted their swords with mercury (*pārada*): Sharma, *Indian Medicine*, p. 217.

106. Needham, *Science and Civilisation*, vol. 5, pt. 3 (1976), "Spagyrical Discovery and Invention: Historical Survey from Cinnabar Elixirs to Synthetic Insulin," p. 162.

107. But Fa-hsien merely reports an account he heard secondhand of the Bhramaragiri monastery, which he never himself saw: Watters, *On Yuan-Chwang's Travels*, 2:208. Cf. Gairola, "Conditions sociales," pp. 289–90. From the 2d through 6th centuries, the Andhra Vaitulyakas popularized the cult of Prajñāparamitā—so closely associated with the philosopher Nāgārjuna—in this region: Bhattacharyya, *History*, p. 222.

108. The meeting occurred near a city called Narasiṁha, on the banks of the Chenab River: Watters, *On Yuan–Chwang's Travels*, vol. 1, pp. 286–87.

109. The sole extant manuscript of this work is its Chinese translation, the *Ta chih Tu Lun*, completed by Kumārajīva in A.D. 406. See Etienne Lamotte, ed. and tr., *Traité de la grande vertu de sagesse de Nāgārjuna (Mahāprajñāparamitā śāstra)*, 4 vols. (Louvain: Institut Orientaliste, 1949–76), vol. 1, pp. 382–83; and Needham, *Science and Civilisation*, vol. 5, pt. 3 (1976), pp. 161, 164.

110. *Mahāyāna Saṃgraha Bhāṣya*, 221–22. The *Abhidharma Mahāvibhāṣa* recounts a myth of gold making by the 3d c. B.C. Candragupta Maurya and his minister "Chaṇakya," i.e., Kauṭilya, the author of the *Arthaśāstra!*: Needham, *Science and Civilisation*, vol. 5, pt. 3 (1976), p. 164.

111. Bhattacharya, *Sādhanamālā*, vol. 2, pp. xliii–xlvi. On Nalanda as a purported Buddhist seat of alchemical learning, see below, chap. 4, n. 120. This Nāgār-

juna may also have been the eye doctor mentioned in Chinese sources as early as the 8th c., and reported by Vṛnda to have inscribed the instructions for an eye medicine on a pillar at the Buddhist center of Pāṭaliputra (Patna): see below, n. 146.

112. Indeed, Alex Wayman refers to the tantric commentarial tradition (on the *Guhyasamājatantra*), founded by Nāgārjuna, who authored the *Piṇḍīkṛta-sādhana*, the *Pañcakrama*, and the *Aṣṭādaśa-paṭala-vistara-vyākhyā*, as the "Arya School." He dates this tantric Nāgārjuna, the guru of Aryadeva, to the latter half of the 8th c.: Alex Wayman, *Yoga of the Guhyasamājatantra: Arcane Lore of the Forty Verses* (New York: Samuel Weiser, 1980), pp. 84, 91, 96.

113. Bhattacharya, *Sādhanamālā*, vol. 2, p. xiv; Dutt, "Notes," p. 638.

114. Tucci, "Animadversiones Indicae," p. 145.

115. This vague reference may have been inserted to square with another tradition which held that Nāgārjuna was first initiated into the tantric or "diamond" path (*vajrayāna*) by the bodhisattva Vajrasattva, at a place called the Iron Tower in south India: Dasgupta, *Obscure*, p. 17.

116. The earliest such prophecy is found in the Sanskrit *Mahāmegha Sūtra*, which was first translated into the Chinese between A.D. 414 and 421 (a relatively early Tibetan translation of this passage, much less confused than those which follow, is found in the *Kanjur* [8.2]). An expanded version is found in the *Laṅkāvatāra Sūtra* appendix known as the "Sagathakam," which first appears in Chinese translation in A.D. 513. The final chapter of the *Mañjuśrīmūlakalpa*, which is styled after the Sagathakam prophecy, is datable to about the 11th c. A.D. This is followed by the Tibetan prophecies found in Bu-ston's *Chos hbyung* (1322) and Tāranātha's *Dam-pa'i-chos-rin-po-che* (1608). This last source further conflates all that had preceded it with both a Sanskrit work entitled the *Mahāsiddha-vṛttānta* and the *Grub thob*. On these sources, see especially Tucci, "Animadversiones Indicae," pp. 138–48; Dutt, "Notes," pp. 636, 639; Ariane MacDonald, *Le maṇḍala du Mañjuśrīmūlakalpa* (Paris: Maisonneuve, 1962), pp. 2–3, 20; Watters, *On Yuan-Chwang's Travels*, vol. 2, pp. 200–4; Obermuller, *History*, vol. 2, pp. 110, 120–28; and *Tāranātha's History of Buddhism in India*, ed. Debiprasad Chattopadhyaya, tr. Lama Chimpa Alaka Chattopadhyaya (Simla: Indian Institute of Advanced Study, 1970), pp. 102–10.

117. *Caryāpada* 22, cited in Dasgupta, *Obscure*, p. 39. On these songs, see below, chap. 4, sec. 1.

118. For a list of these works, see Bhattacharya, ed., *Sādhanamālā*, vol. 2, p. cvi. On the dating of the translation of medical and magical works into Tibetan and their incorporation into the *Tanjur*, see Palmyr Cordier, *Vāgbhaṭa et l'Aṣṭāṅgahṛdayasaṁhitā* (Besançon: private printing, 1896), p. 11. One of the works of Nāgārjuna

found in the *Tanjur* (Derge 1609; Peking 2480) is entitled *Kakṣapuṭa:* this work, however, is distinct from a ca. 13th c. Hindu work by the same title, which does in fact contain some alchemical data. See below, chap. 5, secs. 5h and 5j.

119. Chattopadhyaya, *Tāranātha's History,* pp. 106, 110, 243; Dasgupta, *Introduction,* p. 54.

120. On this, see David Seyfort Ruegg, "Sur les rapports entre le Bouddhisme et le 'substrat religieux' indien et tibetain," *Journal Asiatique* 252 (1964), pp. 82–88. Apart from Harṣa, the religious syncretism and tolerance of the Chandela kings of Khajuraho, as well as the Vijayanagara kings, is well documented: for references, see Roşu, "A la recherche," p. 48.

121. James B. Robinson, *Buddha's Lions: The Lives of the Eighty-Four Siddhas* (Berkeley: Dharma Publishing, 1979), pp. 88–89, 206, 256–57. Vyāḍi's *Rasasiddhiśāstra* (Derge 4313) and *Dhātuvādaśāstra* are found together with the *Sarveśvararasāyana* in the Āyurveda section of the *Tanjur;* a work entitled *Dhātuvāda* is included in the Tantra section: Edward Todd Fenner, *Rasāyan Siddhi: Medicine and Alchemy in Buddhist Tantras* (Ph.D. thesis, University of Wisconsin, 1979), p. 23; and Misra, *Āyurvedīya,* p. 21.

122. The *Kālacakra Tantra* was composed in north India by a native of Java in the late 10th to early 11th c., after which it was carried to Tibet. Internal evidence indicates that the *Vimalaprabhā* commentary was composed by the same person or people as compiled the *Kālacakra Tantra,* in either 1012 or 1027: John Newman, "A Brief History of the Kālacakra," in *The Wheel of Time: The Kālacakra in Context* (Madison, Wis.: Deer Park Books, 1985), n. 13 to p. 85, and personal communication, Charlottesville, Virginia, February 1995. The only other alchemical system that we may qualify as Buddhist is the Burmese *zawgyi* or *weikza* system, but this, although practiced by Buddhist monks, has a decidedly Taoist stamp to it: see above, chap. 1, n. 6; and above, n. 1 to the present chap.

123. *Vimalaprabhā* 5.230, and Fenner, *Rasāyan Siddhi,* pp. 80, 183–84. Mundane mercurial alchemy, whose goals are gold making and the accumulation of power, remains acceptable to the Tibetans, but because the practitioner is dependent upon external elements rather than his own contemplative procedure, it is deemed a lower form of practice: Beyer, *Tārā,* p. 261. In chap. nine of his 14th c. *Rasasāra* the Hindu alchemist Govindācārya speaks of his indebtedness to the Tibetan Buddhists, who he says taught him the art of *raṅgākṛṣṭi* or *raṅgadruti:* Jan G. Meulenbeld, *History of Indian Medical Literature* (Leiden: Brill, 1996) [draft of 10 May 1994], p. 879.

124. Compare the *Vimalaprabhā* (5.206) aphorism on the powers of bound and killed mercury to that of *RA* 1.19; *Vimalaprabhā* 5.204 on testing mercury on metals before consuming it to the classic *RA* (17.265) statement; the *Vimalaprabhā*

(5.213–15) description of an alchemical mandala to that of the *RA* (2.49–82); and the *Vimalaprabhā* (5.202b) on a corrosive mineral water called *kartarī* with a discussion of the same in *RA* 12.205b–206. The *Vimalaprabhā* (2.108–111) discussion of the dynamics of *prāṇāyāma* closely resembles early Hindu *haṭha yoga.* Cf. Fenner, *Rasāyan Siddhi*, p. 77. If anything, the *Vimalaprabhā* data is slightly more archaic than that of the *RA:* it lists only seven *mahārasa*s and six *uparasa*s in contradistinction to the two eightfold categories of the latter Hindu work.

125. Walter, *Role of Alchemy*, p. 28. Another 14th c. Tibetan work, brought to my attention by David Germano, is the *Tshig Don mDzod* (Precious words and meanings) of kLong Chen Rab 'Byams Pa (1308–63). This work, citing the *Thal 'Gyur* (Direct consequence), discusses *bcud len* in terms similar to those found in Bo dong—i.e., in the form of both "inner" and "outer" alchemy—in II.3.i.-b.2.i.a.2.i, "The meditative session which eliminates attachment to food."

126. Bo dong's discussion of "outer" and "inner" alchemy is found in his 14th c. *bCud len gyi man ngag bshad pa* in *Encyclopedia Tibetica: The Collected Works of Bo doṅ Paṇ-chen phyogs-las-ram-rgyal* ed. S. T. Kazi (New Delhi: Tibet House, 1970), vol. 2, pp. 507–601. Yet another variety of *rasāyana* is a Tibetan Buddhist practice known by the Mongolian name of *tuiurgnikji*, which involves the preparation of holy water: J. Deniker, introduction to *Gods of Northern Buddhism*, by Alice Getty, p. xi, cited in Dasgupta, *Obscure*, p. 39.

127. See also Robert Thurman, tr., *The Tibetan Book of the Dead: Liberation through Understanding in the Between* (New York: Bantam Books, 1994), p. 146, on the eighty-four Mahāsiddhas as persons who transmuted "demon blood and other bodily substances" into the elixir of immortality. Certain elements of "outer alchemy" have persisted in Tibet, down to the present day. In a discussion of the extraction of the essence (*chu leṇ:* i.e., *bcud len*), the present-day Tibetan Buddhist teacher Nankhai Norbu indicates that a specially prepared mercury pill is the "medicine" to be used for overcoming hunger in the "Dharmakāya-style" *chu-len* of Dzog-chen practice: *The Teachings of Namkhai Norbu, 1982* (typescript), pp. 89, 93. I am grateful to David Germano for sharing this source with me.

128. Light metaphysics is absolutely essential to the early Buddhist system of the *Guhyasamāja Tantra.* On this, see Wayman, *Yoga*, pp. 77–83 and throughout. Cf. Walter, *Role of Alchemy*, pp. 28–29, who notes the parallels between Nying-ma and Nāth Siddha practice.

129. This is the case only in the very important and influential philosophical summa of Abhinavagupta: on this see Alexis Sanderson, "Meaning in Tantric Ritual," in Anne-Marie Blondeau, ed., *Le Rituel*, vol. 3. (Paris: Ecole Pratique des Hautes Etudes, 5è section, 1996), pp. 15–95.

130. Here, I am using the Weberian—rather than a theological—reading of

the term *soteriology:* for a discussion see Gellner, *Monk, Householder, and Tantric Priest,* p. 6.

131. Ancient pilgrimage sites, located at points of contact with China, in eastern and (perhaps) northwestern India, the four *pīṭhas* are mentioned in the *Sādhanamālā* (ed. Bhattacharya, vol. 2, p. 453). They are quickly internalized to become part of the yogic landscape of the subtle body in Buddhism (*Caryāpada* 2.4; 4.3, in Per Kværne, *An Anthology of Buddhist Tantric Songs: A Study of the Caryāgīti* [Oslo: Universitetsforlaget, 1977; reprint Bangkok: White Orchid, 1986], pp. 76) and later Hinduism (*ṢSS,* 1.55–61; 4.118–32, in J. A. Schoterman, *The Ṣaṭsāhasrasaṁhitā, Chapters 1–5* [Leiden: Brill, 1982], pp. 64, 141).

132. In particular, the Vidyāpīṭha doctrines and practice of the Hindu Kāpālikas were closely paralleled by the Highest Yoga (*yogānuttara*) Tantras and the Kāpālika Yoginī cult of esoteric Buddhism: Alexis Sanderson, "Śaivism and the Tantric Tradition" in *The World's Religions,* ed. Stewart Sutherland et al. (London: Routledge and Kegan Paul, 1988), pp. 678–79.

133. This reading of *rasāyana* as the "coming forth (i.e., the extraction) of the elixir" corresponds quite exactly to the Tibetan *bcud len.* I am grateful to Chris Wilkinson for this suggestion. See below, chap. 5, n. 84.

134. See below, chap. 5, n. 83.

135. Schoterman, *Ṣaṭsāhasrasaṁhitā,* p. 6; Dyczkowski, *Canon,* p. 48. The references to the *Kubjikāmata* are too vague to be verified. For an extended discussion, see below, chap. 5, nn. 85–92.

136. The Siddhas and Siddhaugha are worshipped in the Siddha Cakra which dates from well before the 11th c.: Dyczkowski, *Canon,* p. 81. See above, chap. 1, n. 13.

137. Haraprasad Shastri, *A Catalogue of Palm-Leaf and Selected Paper Manuscripts Belonging to the Durbar Library, Nepal,* 2 vols. (Calcutta: n.p., 1905, 1915), vol. 1, pp. lxi, lxiv, lxx, 57, 99–100, 111, 258; vol. 2, p. 80; and Schoterman, *Ṣaṭsāhasrasaṁhitā,* pp. 5–6, 11–12, 36–39, on the major works of this tradition, all of which date from the 14th c. or before: the *Kubjikāmata, Ciñcinimata, Manthānabhairava Tantra, Kubjikānityāhnikatilaka, Śrīmatottara Tantra,* and the *ṢSS.* Closely identified with the latter two works are the figures of Manthānabhairava and Gorakṣanātha; mentioned in the *Kubjikānityāhnikatilaka* (NNA MSS no. 3–383; cited in Bagchi, *KJñN,* p. 68) is a certain Matsyendranātha. Matsyendra appears to identify himself with Siddhanātha in the *Jñānakārika* (2.1; in Bagchi, *KJñN,* p. 116); and in the *Nārada Purāṇa* (Uttara khaṇḍa 69.25, cited in *NSC,* p. 23), where it is said that Matsyendra resides in Kāmarūpa as Siddhanātha: Kāmarūpa is sometimes identified with the site of Candradvīpa (Bagchi, introduction to *KJñN,* pp. 29–32).

138. Schoterman, *Ṣaṭsāhasrasaṁhitā,* pp. 36–39. A manuscript of the *Kubjikāni-*

tyāhnikatilaka, in Newari script, is dated to A.D. 1197 by Shastri (*Catalogue,* 1:lxiv, 111–12) and to A.D. 1395 by Bagchi (*KJñN,* p. 67). Further evidence for the antiquity of the southwestern Indian origins of this cult is found in an inscription, dated to A.D. 1030: Saletore, "Kanaphaṭa Jogis," pp. 18–19.

139. The *Grub thob brgyad cu rtsa bzhi lo rgyus* is found in vol. 86, pt. 1 of the *Tanjur:* Palmyr Cordier, *Catalogue du fonds tibétain de la Bibliothèque Nationale,* vol. 3, Index du Bstan-hgyur (Tibétain 180–332) (Paris: Bibliothèque Nationale, 1915), p. 247. Cf. Tucci, "Animadversiones Indicae," p. 142; and idem., *Tibetan Painted Scrolls,* vol. 1, pp. 226–27. On the mid–14th c. dating of the Tibetan translation, see Simon Digby, "To Ride a Tiger or a Wall? Strategies of Prestige in Indian Sufi Legend," in Winand Caellewaert and Rupert Snell, eds., *According to Tradition: Hagiographical Writing in India* (Wiesbaden: Harrassowitz, 1994), p. 105.

140. Keith Dowman (*Masters of Mahāmūdra: Songs and Histories of the Eighty-Four Buddhist Siddhas* [Albany, N.Y.: SUNY Press, 1985], p. 386), maintains that the "Acts" were narrated, and not authored by Abhayadatta; they were translated into Tibetan by sMon grub shes rab. The *Tanjur* also contains lists of the works of the eighty-four Siddhas. Variants of Kubjika's name are Kucipa, Cubji, Kusūlī, and Kubjipa: Dowman, *Masters,* p. 206.

141. The Hindu and Jain Vidyādharas had their Buddhist homologues in the Vidyārājas: Ruegg, "Sur les rapports," p. 83. We have noted Nāgārjuna's connection with Tārā: as the leader of the Mahāvidyā goddesses, she is called "Vidyārajñī": Bhattacharyya, *History,* p. 225. The Vidyādharas (*rig 'dzin*) serve as intermediaries for the preparation of the elixir in Tibetan sources as well: Walter, *Role of Alchemy,* pp. 36–37 and n. 77.

142. My use of Max Weber's terminology is intentional here. After the death of the founder of a given social or religious group, a founder whose personal *charisma* held the group together, that group's structural cohesiveness must be *routinized,* i.e., reordered along pragmatic lines, if the group is to survive (unless, of course, a charismatic figure replaces the charismatic founder, which is a rare scenario).

143. Two complementary processes may have been operative here. On the one hand, such names as "Matsyendra" may have been titles bestowed upon persons who had reached a sublime level of initiation (Tucci, "Animadversiones Indicae," pp. 133–34; cf. John K. Locke, *Karunamaya: The Cult of Avalokitesvara–Matsyendranath in the Valley of Nepal* [Kathmandu: Sahayogi Press, 1980], pp. 422–27 and notes). On the other, post–13th c. ascetics may simply have claimed to actually have been the "original" Gorakhnāth, etc. Simon Digby terms this "charismatic impersonation" and makes a cogent argument for its prevalence in what may be the most widely circulated unpublished manuscript in the field of South Asian studies: "Encounters with Jogīs in Indian Sūfī Hagiography," typescript of

paper read at the School of Oriental and African Studies, London, 27 January 1970, p. 32.

144. *Yogaśataka: texte médicale attribué à Nāgārjuna*, ed. and tr. Jean Filliozat (Pondicherry: Institut Français d'Indologie, 1979), pp. vi, 105; idem., *Doctrine classique*, pp. 10–11; and Palmyr Cordier, "Récentes découvertes de mss. médicaux sanscrits dans l'Inde (1898–1902)," *Le Muséon*, n.s. 4 (1903), pp. 336–39. If one accepts that the *Yogaśataka* is mentioned in all but name by the late 7th c. Chinese pilgrim I-Ching (Sharma, *Āyurved*, p. 195), then this is a 7th c. work. More tenable is the hypothesis that this was the same Nāgārjuna who, in about the 9th c., edited the *Suśruta Saṁhitā* and added to it the final "Uttara" section. A Tibetan translation of this work is found in the *Tanjur*.

145. A rare reference to mercury is found in *Suśruta Saṁhitā* 6.35.7. Palmyr Cordier offers a compendium of convincing textual references to support the case that this editor was indeed named Nāgārjuna: *Nāgārjuna et l'Uttaratantra*, pp. 1–6; and "Récentes découvertes," pp. 332–33. Cf. Sharma, *Āyurved*, pp. 76–77, for other "alchemical" or "tantric" *Suśruta* passages attributable to Nāgārjuna.

146. *Siddhayoga* 16.149: nāgārjuneṇa likhitā stambhe pāṭaliputrake. Prafulla Chandra Ray (*A History of Hindu Chemistry from the Earliest Times to the Middle of the 16th Century* A.D., 2 vols. [Calcutta: Prithwis Chandra Ray, 1904–09], vol. 1, pp. xxxii, liii, xcii) asserts that *kajjali* was the active ingredient in this preparation. Cf. Sharma, *Āyurved*, pp. 195, 330. Chinese references to an eye specialist named Nāgārjuna begin to appear in the latter half of the 8th c.: Needham, *Science and Civilisation*, vol. 5, pt. 3 (1976), p. 163.

147. Sharma, *Āyurved*, pp. 229, 290–91, 479. Cakrapāṇidatta, like Vṛnda, also quotes extensively from the *Yogaśataka:* Cordier, "Récentes découvertes," p. 338.

148. Sharma, *Āyurved*, p. 291. Following Cakrapāṇidatta, Vaṅgasena would, in his *Cikitsāsārasaṃgraha*, introduce further innovations in mercury-based *rasa śāstra;* but by this time, the tantric alchemical tradition was well established: ibid., p. 295.

149. Ayurvedic works attributed to Nāgārjuna include the *Jīvasūtra*, *Yogasāra*, *Sārasaṃgraha*, *Bheṣajakalpa*, and the *Ārogyamañjari:* Bhattacharyya, *History*, p. 20; Ray, *History*, vol. 1, p. xcii; Jean Filliozat, "Liste des manuscrits de la Collection Palmyr Cordier conservés à la Bibliothèque Nationale," *Journal Asiatique* 224 (1934), pp. 155–73. The *Jīvasūtra* and the *Bheṣajakalpa* are preserved in Tibetan translation only: Sharma, *Āyurved*, p. 195.

150. See below, chap. 5, n. 4.

Chapter Four

1. There is an important distinction between "clan" and "lineage": members of the former claim descent from a divine ancestor; those of the latter claim a human

as their founder. On this, see Daniel Gold, *The Lord as Guru* (New York: Oxford University Press, 1987), pp. 18, 93–110.

2. Sanderson, "Śaivism," p. 668. The Siddha lists "front-loaded" certain elements of the old Siddha cults into their idealized genealogies: Dyczkowski, *Canon*, pp. 79–82. See above, chapter 1, n. 13, and chap. 3, n. 136.

3. *HTSL*, p. 40. This is particularly the case with the *āmnāya* classification of Kaula traditions, as set forth in the Nepali *Ciñcinīmatasārasamucchaya:* Dyczkowski, *Canon*, pp. 66–68.

4. Wendy Doniger O'Flaherty, *Dreams, Illusion and Other Realities* (Chicago: University of Chicago Press, 1984), p. 203, evoking comments made by Diana Eck in a panel discussion of the American Academy of Religion, New York, 21 December 1983. Cf. Douglas Brooks's discussion (*Secret*, p. 63) of the structure and function of the *śrīcakra* or *śrīyantra*, the greatest of all tantric cosmographs.

5. The texts of the Vidyā Pīṭha are divided into the *yāmala*s, the "Union Tantras" and the *śaktitantra*s, the "Power Tantras"; this latter group forms the textual base for the Trika synthesis: Sanderson, "Śaivism," pp. 668–72. The four literary *pīṭha*s are also identified with the four primordial *pīṭha*s of early Hindu and Buddhist tantrism (Jālandhara, Uḍḍiyāna, Pūrṇagiri, and Kāmarūpa, mentioned in *KJñN* 8.20–22, which substitutes Arbuda for Pūrṇagiri), with four *cakra*s of the subtle body, four colors, etc.: Dyczkowski, *Canon*, pp. 49–55.

6. Abhinavagupta makes no mention of the *āmnāya* system; it is, however, mentioned in the *Kubjikāmata* (*KM*), the root tantra of the Western Transmission (Dyczkowski, *Canon*, p. 66) and the 10th–14th c. *Kulārṇava Tantra* (3.7–10). See below, chap. 5, n. 93

7. It is also along the lines of the *āmnāya* system that Alexis Sanderson organizes his excellent survey, "Śaivism and the Tantric Traditions" (especially pp. 680–90). But see Dyczkowski (*Canon*, p. 87) and Goudriaan (*HTSL*, p. 14), who characterize this classification as "empty": it is, however, to the artificiality of assigning of geographical coordinates to the four schools that these authors are referring. A fifth ("upper") *āmnāya* would later be added: *HTSL*, p. 17.

8. Scholars have been attempting for decades to make *guru-paramparā*s out of these lists; such may be possible for certain figures: see, for example Sankrtyayana, "Recherches Bouddhiques," interleaf following p. 218; Bhattacharya, *Sādhanamālā*, vol. 2, pp. xlii–cix; and Tucci, "Animadversiones Indicae," p. 142.

9. Tucci, *Tibetan Painted Scrolls*, vol. 1, p. 226.

10. Hazariprasad Dvivedi (*Nāth Sampradāy*, 3d ed. [Allahabad: Lokabharati Prakasan, 1982], pp. 26–35) reproduces a number of these lists, noting that a total of 148 distinct figures can be generated from them.

11. See above, chap. 3, n. 139. A similar list, dating from A.D. 1513, is found in

the Bhaktapur (Nepal) Museum; another has been found in Java, Indonesia: Locke, *Karunamaya*, p. 422.

12. Sankrtyayana, "Recherches Bouddhiques," p. 220; Dharmavir Bharati, *Siddh Sāhity*, 2d ed. (Allahabad: Kitab Mahal, 1955, 1968), p. 31. On the history of this work, see A. I. Vostrikov, *Tibetan Historical Literature*, tr. from the Russian by Harish Chandra Gupta (Calcutta: R. D. Press, 1970), p. 66. This text also lists the caste and country of the Siddhas.

13. The doctrines exposed in these texts correspond to those of the late Vajrayāna traditions of the Yoginī-tantras or Yogānuttaratantras: personal communication from Alexis Sanderson, 6 July 1992. See above, chap. 3, n. 132.

14. On the dating of this collection, see Dušan Zbavitel, *Bengali Literature*, History of Indian Literature, vol. 9, fasc. 3 (Leiden: Brill, 1976), pp. 124–25, who also notes that these poems, while tantric, are neither specifically Buddhist nor Hindu. Kværne, *Anthology*, has produced a historical study and quadrilingual (proto-Bengali, Sanskrit, Tibetan, English) edition of this fascinating collection.

15. P. C. Bagchi ("The Cult of the Buddhist Siddhācāryas," *Cultural Heritage of India*, vol. 4, p. 275) indicates that the enlarged Tibetan translation of these songs is found in volumes 47–48 of the *Tanjur*. In addition to these, the *Tanjur* contains Tibetan translations, from the Sanskrit, of a number of other works attributed to these figures.

16. The *RA* (14.40) evokes, without naming them, *twenty-four* [Rasa] Siddhas, which I take to be an indication of its relative antiquity. See below, chap. 5, n. 162.

17. Bibliothèque Nationale (Paris), Fonds Cordier, Sanscrit MSS no. 1222, fol. 30a.9–30b.2. Meulenbeld (*History*, draft of 10 May 1994, p. 971) maintains that these verses, forming as they do a portion of the *ṭippaṇa* (commentary) on the work (which begins at fol. 30a.3 of the present manuscript), are posterior to the *RM* proper, and borrowed by the commentator, from the *RRS*.

18. This author is so named in order to distinguish him from the Vāgbhaṭṭa the Elder and Vāgbhaṭṭa the Younger, who authored the Ayurvedic *Aṣṭāṅgasaṃgraha* and *Aṣṭāṅgahṛdaya*, respectively: Sharma, *Āyurved*, pp. 481–82 (who calls the author of the *RRS* "Rasa-Vāgbhaṭṭa").

19. *RRĀ* 3.1.66–69, in *Śrīpārvatīputranityanāthasiddhaviracita Rasaratnākarāntargataścaturtho* [*sic*] *Ṛddhikhaṇḍaḥ-Vādikhaṇḍaḥ*, ed. Jivaram Kalidas Shastri, Rasashala Granthamala, no. 9 (Gondal: Rasashala Aushadhashram, 1940).

20. Dharmananda Sharma's edition of the *RRS* lists fifteen additional Rasa Siddhas in 1.2–7; whereas Janardana Pandeya, the editor of the *Gorakṣa Saṁhitā* (introduction to vol. 2, p. *cha*), presents a list of sixty-seven Rasa Siddhas which he claims to be from the *RRS*, but of which only the first thirty-three are identical to those listed in Sharma's edition of the *RRS* (1.2–6a), with the last thirty-four being

unique to Pandeya's unspecified source. I have not been able to locate an edition of the *RRS* (there are several) in which such a list appears.

21. One modern author emends the first names on this list into an alchemical guru-disciple lineage (*raseśvara paramparā*), with certain variations: (1) Ādināth; (2) Candrasena; (3) Nityānanda; (4) Gorakhnāth; (5) Kapāli; (6) Bhāluki; (7) and Māṇḍavya: Gananath Sen, *Āyurveda Paricaya* (Shantiniketan: Visva Vidya Samgraha, 1942), pp. 12–13, 174.

22. This and the three italicized names that follow correspond to a Tibetan *guru-paramparā*, found in the *Grub thob*, in which (17) Nāgārjuna is the guru of (19) Nāgabodhi as well as of (16) Vyāḍi, Kubjika, and Paṅkaja. Vyāḍi is, in turn, the guru of (15) Kambala: Tucci, "Animadversiones Indicae," p. 142.

23. This is the sole Rasa Siddha on whose name the *RRĀ* and the *RRS* 6.51–53 do not agree.

24. Meulenbeld, *History* (draft of 10 May 1994), p. 835. The only names listed by Caturbhujamiśra that do not figure in the *HYP* list are: Gaja, Khaṇḍin (but see Khaṇḍa, no. 22 in the *RM/RRS* [a] list), and Nāgadeva.

25. The numbering of Siddhas 28 through 33 in *RRS* (a) 1.5–7 is identical to that found in *RRS* (c) 1.5–10.

26. The list is found in the seventh chapter of the *Varṇaratnākara*, ed. S. K. Chatterji and Babua Misra, Bibliotheca Indica, no. 262 (Calcutta: Bibliotheca Indica, 1940), pp. 57–58. The *Varṇaratnākara* is the oldest known text written in the Maithili language. It was composed by Kaviśekharācārya Jyotīśvara, the court poet to King Harisiṁha Deva of Simraungaḍh (Mithila, a kingdom whose ancient borders would fall between modern-day Bihar and Nepal), who reigned from A.D. 1300 to 1321: Dasgupta, *Obscure*, p. 202, n. 1. See below, n. 50.

27. An edited version of this work exists: *Ānandakanda*, ed. Sri S. V. Radhakrishna Sastri. Tanjore Sarasvati Mahal Series, 15 (Tanjore: TMSSM Library, 1952). The same work constitutes MSS no. 830 (Āyurveda, no. 2) of the Śrī Bhuvaneśvarī Pīṭh Auṣadhāśrama (Gondal, Gujarat) collection, now held at Gujarat Ayurved University, Jamnagar.

28. Under the patronage of King Mān Singh, the Nāth Siddhas of Jodhpur, drawing on Maharashtran sources, also generated lists of eighty-four Siddhas: P. N. Joshi, *Mahārāṣṭra ke Nāthpanthīya Kaviyoṃ kā Hindī Kāvya* (Mathura: Jawahar Pustakalaya, 1976), pp. 216–22, cited in Pandey, *Gorakhnāth*, pp. 104–5. Gorakhnāth heads an Oriyan list of sixty-four Siddhas: ibid., p. 105.

29. "Sidh Vandanāṃ" is the first poem in the anthology *Nāth siddhoṃ kī bāṇiyāṃ*, ed. with an introduction by Hazariprasad Dvivedi, 2d ed. (Benares: Kasi Nagaripracarini Sabha, 1978), pp. 1–2. One also finds evocations of the nine Nāths together with the eighty-four Siddhas in Muhammad Jāyasī's 16th c. *Padmāvat* (Bhar-

ati, *Siddh Sāhity*, p. 28) and in a modern work by the great Nepali Nāth Siddha scholar Narharināth, entitled *Nav Nāth Caurāsī Siddh* (Benares: Rastriya Press, 1968). Worship of the nine Nāths, the eighty-four Siddhas and the Śrīvidyā goddess Bālāsundarī concludes the Nāth Siddha initiation ceremony: George Weston Briggs, *Gorakhnāth and the Kānphaṭa Yogis* (Calcutta: Y.M.C.A. Press, 1938; reprint Delhi: Motilal Banarsidass, 1982), p. 33.

30. Cauraṅgi is the ninth Nāth and Cauraṅgī the first Siddha in the *ĀK* list.

31. Saletore, "Kanaphaṭa Jogis," p. 19.

32. Revaṇa is listed with eight other familiar Nāths in the *YSĀ* (ed. Sivanath Yogi, tr. Candranath Yogi [Ahmedabad: Sivanath Yogi, 1924]: on this work, see below, n. 183), pp. 116–35. He figures in modern-day Maharashtran religious posters of the Nine Nāths. On the Vīraśaiva Revaṇa Siddha, see *Śūnyasampādane*, ed. and tr. S. C. Nandimath, L. M. A. Menezes, R. C. Hiremath, et al. 5 vols. (Dharwar: Karnataka University Press, 1965–72), vol. 5, p. 374; and Jan Gonda, *Medieval*, p. 227.

33. *HTSL*, p. 12.

34. A bibliography of Tamil medical-alchemical works, prepared in 1826 by Whitelaw Ainslie, was published by D. V. Subba Reddy in *Madras Medical Journal* 2:3 (July 1972), pp. 150–55.

35. These names are culled from lists found in Madhavan, *Siddha Medical Manuscripts*, pp. 20–26. I have Sanskritized the Tamil orthography of these names. On this last group, see Ramana Shastri, "Doctrinal Culture," p. 305, on the eighteen "Māheśvara Siddhas of the Śuddha Marga."

36. This list is taken from Shastri's Sanskrit introduction to the *ĀK* (pp. 8–9), to which the editor refers as "those renowned as the 18 Siddhas, of which Agastya was the first, among the Draviḍas."

37. See above, chap. 3, n. 59.

38. His name is rendered Satnāth or Satyanāth: he is one of the Siddhas referred to in the "Siddhamata-nirvāhaṇam" chapter (49) of the 14th–15th c. *Śaṅkaravijaya* of Ānandagiri (*Śrīśaṅkaravijaya of Anantānandagiri*, ed. N. Veezhinathan, with an introduction by T. M. P. Mahadevan [Madras: University of Madras, 1971]). On the Satyanāthī (or Satnāthī) panth, see Dvivedi, *Nāth Sampradāy*, pp. 12, 178–80. On his identification with Brahmā, ibid., and *Gorakh Upaniṣad* (in Mallik, *SSP*, p. 73). On his alchemical works, and the spread of the Satnāthī panth to Uttar Pradesh (Srinagar, Pauri Garhwal district) and Karnataka (Dharwar), see *NSC*, p. 219. The Nāth monastery at Mṛgasthali, above the Paśupatināth temple in Kathmandu, belongs to this suborder, as does the monastery at Puri (Orissa): Pandey, *Gorakhnāth*, p. 65.

39. The nine-plus-sixteen configuration is a commonplace of such Western Transmission sources as the *Manthānabhairava Tantra: HTSL*, p. 56. The number sixteen here is linked to the sixteen *akṣara*s of the Nine Nāths, who are one with the sixteen *nityā* divinities (*ṣoḍaśanityātmā*): *Tantrarāja Tantra* 2.16. Chapters 42 and 43 of the *ṢSS* are entitled "Śrī Ādināthavaktrāvatāra" and "Śrīmūlanāthāvatāra," respectively: Schoterman, *Ṣaṭsāhasrasaṁhitā*, p. 15.

40. *Bhāradvāja Saṁhitā*, cited without reference in Pandey, *Gorakhnāth*, p. 109. The *KJñN* (8.18) names a Koṅkaṇāī-pāda. See below, n. 54.

41. On the *Ciñcinimatasārasamucchaya*, see Shastri, *Catalogue*, vol. 1, p. lxi. Cf. Dyczkowski, *Canon*, pp. 67, 69, 90, 138 n. 23, and 191 n. 222; and Schoterman, *Ṣaṭsāhasrasaṁhitā*, p. 39.

42. The *Kubjikānityāhnikatilaka* presents, in addition to the given names of its teachers, their *caryā-* name, their *pūjā-* name, their *gupta-* name, their *kīrti-* name, as well as additional names based on fanciful etymologies. Here, Matsyendra is one of the seven names of the fifth (in a series of nine, followed by a series of sixteen) teachers, whose given name is Viṣṇuśarman: Bagchi, *KJñN*, p. 68.

43. Sanderson, "Purity and Power," p. 214 n. 110. See below, chap. 5, n. 93.

44. *TĀ* 1.7 (vol. 1, p. 25). For editions, see bibliography. On the identification of Macchanda Vibhu with Matsyendra, see Pandey, *Gorakhnāth*, p. 21. In his commentary to this verse, Jayaratha states that "he [Macchanda] is also renowned for having brought down the entire *kula-śāstra*."

45. Sanderson, "Trika Śaivism," in *Encyclopedia of Religion*, vol. 13, p. 15.

46. Dyczkowski, *Canon*, pp. 69, 79–82; *HTSL*, p. 54. On the name of the "northern" Matsyendra's consort, Koṅkaṇā, see Sanderson, "Śaivism," p. 681.

47. Dyczkowski, *Canon*, p. 89.

48. These are summarized in Locke, *Karunamaya*, pp. 291–300.

49. Another geographical explanation for this toponym may be found in the Goan site of Candranāth Hill in the Salsete *tāluka* of Goa, on the Konkan coast of India, upon whose summit the Śaiva temples of Candreśvara and Bhūtanāth are situated. The custodians of these temples were Nāth Siddhas—according to their current *pūjārī*—until a recent date. On these "lunar" toponyms, see above, chap. 3, nn. 137–38; and below, chap. 5, n. 81.

50. In the course of the 12th c., Jaiṭugi (1191–1210), the Yādava king of Devagiri; the western Cālukya king Someśvara III Bhūloka Malla (1127–38), to whom the *Manasollāsa*, which contains long passages on *dhātuvāda* and *rasāyana*, is attributed; and the 12th c. Kālacuriya king Tribhuvanamalla Bijjana, who had close connections with Basava, the founder of Vīraśaivism, all claimed to have reduced Nepal to vassal status. The Māllas of Bhaktapur imported brahmins from Bengal to

serve as temple priests: Sylvain Lévi, *Le Népal*, 3 vols. (Paris: Ernest Leroux, 1905; reprint Paris: Toit du Monde & Errance, 1985), vol. 1, p. 364; Sharma, *Āyurved*, p. 311; Bagchi, "Further Notes," *Studies*, p. 19. Harisiṁhadeva, the Maithili king who commissioned the *Varṇaratnākara* (see above n. 26) in the early 14th c., was obliged to seek refuge in Nepal when his kingdom was destroyed by Muslims. His widow and court found refuge in Bhaktapur with Rudra Mālla, where they exerted a profound influence on the political and cultural history of the Kathmandu Valley in the late Mālla period. Harisiṁhadeva traced his dynastic roots back to Karnataka: Locke, *Karunamaya*, p. 422 n. 42.

51. In terms of mythic geography, the *liṅga* at Paśupatināth, the national temple of Nepal, is said to have the same origin as that of Gokarṇeśvara, located on the coast of northern Karnataka; the Godavari River of Maharashtra state is said to have a branch in Nepal; the Deccan forest of Śleṣmāntaka is transferred to the Kathmandu Valley. In terms of religious institutions, south Indian Śaivite brahmins and tāntrikas controlled Paśupatināth throughout much of the Mālla period. Lévi surmises that it was the Pāśupata "Yogis" who originally transformed Paśupatināth from an indigenous deity into a form of Śiva: Lévi, *Le Népal*, vol. 1, pp. 364–65. Cf. Axel Michaels, "On 12th–13th Century Relations between Nepal and South India," *Journal of the Nepal Research Center* 7 (1985), pp. 69–72.

52. On the Caryā songs, see Locke, *Karunamaya*, p. 426; on Kubjikā, Mark Dyczkowski, "Kuṇḍalinī, the Erotic Goddess: Sexual Potency, Transformation and Reversal in the Heterodox Theophanies of the Kubjikā Tantras," American Academy of Religion Annual Meeting, San Francisco, 23 Nov. 1992, p. 2 n. 3. I am grateful to Dyczkowski for providing me with a typescript of his lecture.

53. This passage is found in the fourteenth chapter of the *Kubjikāmata* (London, Wellcome MSS no. g501, fol. 69a lines 4–7; fol. 69b, lines 2–3).

54. *Manthānabhairava Tantra*, cited in *HTSL*, p. 55; Schoterman, *ṢSS*, pp. 32, 37–38.

55. The nine Nāths (divided into *divya-*, *siddha-*, *and mānava-oghas*) are identified with the bodily orifices in the *Tantrarāja Tantra* 2.2–5 (in Woodroffe, *Tantrarāja*, p. 19), which also (2.58–72) lists nine types of consecrations (*abhiṣekas*), in which nine gemstones, which correspond to the eight bodily *dhātus*, are placed in medicated water: ibid., p. 20. The *RC* (12.1) identifies the nine gemstones with the nine heavenly bodies. See below, chap. 8, n. 234.

56. The *Tantra Mahārṇava* is quoted without reference by the 17th–18th c. *Gorakṣa Siddhānta Saṃgraha* (ed. Janardana Pandeya, Sarasvatibhavana Granthamala, no. 110 [Benares: Varanaseya Sanskrit Visvavidyalaya Press, 1973], pp. 44–45). I base my dating of this anonymous work on a citation in it (p. 10) of the *Śaktisaṅgama Tantra*, which has been dated to the 16th–17th c. by Goudriaan (*HTSL*, p.

69). Ādinātha's role here closely parallels that of Ādi Buddha, who is identified with Vajrasattva in Buddhist tantra: Dasgupta, *Obscure*, p. 195.

57. The *Tantra Mahārṇava* passage is cited in Dasgupta, *Obscure*, p. 206. Cf. Schoterman, *ṢSS*, p. 15; and Dyczkowski, "Kuṇḍalinī," p. 13.

58. Such is explicitly stated in the opening verses of the *Ṣoḍaśanityātantra* (1.7b–8a: reproduced in Shastri, *Catalogue*, vol. 2, p. 148); and *Tārā Tantra* 1.24b–26, where they are called the Kaula gurus. The names of the Nāthas in this and other lists often end in *-ānanda*, rather than *-nātha:* this is peculiar to the Western Transmission, whose initiates received names with just such endings: Dyczkowski, "Kuṇḍalinī," p. 1.

59. Schoterman, *ṢSS*, pp. 6, 32, 35–38. On this, see also Dyczkowski, *Canon*, p. 87; *HTSL*, p. 37; and Bagchi, *KJñN*, p. 21. On Tamil traditions of *nine* Sittars, see Madhavan, *Siddha Medical Manuscripts*, p. 22.

60. *Gorakh Upaniṣad* reproduced in Mallik, *SSP*, pp. 72–75. A similar list is found in the *Śrīnāthakathāsāra* of Dwarkanāth (ed. Narharinath [Benares: n.p., 1951]), p. 4; and Shastri, *Catalogue*, vol. 2, p. 149.

61. In his commentary to *TĀ* 1.6, Jayaratha quotes an unnamed earlier source which in fact makes this identification (vol. 1, p. 24). For an expanded discussion of this complex matter, see below, n. 143; and chap. 8, nn. 33–37.

62. A number of these variant lists are found in Pandey, *Gorakhnāth*, pp. 105–8; Dasgupta, *Obscure*, pp. 206–7. Cf. Dvivedi's valiant attempts (*Nāth Sampradāy*, p. 169; *Nāth Siddhoṃ*, p. 14) to generate a single genealogy from these numerous lists. Kalyani Mallik has attempted to correlate Siddhācārya and Nāth Siddha lineages in the same fashion: Pandey, *Gorakhnāth*, p. 104. See below, n. 160.

63. The Bengali drama, variously known as the *Gorakṣa Vijaya* or *Mīn Cetan*, gives this data: Dasgupta, *Obscure*, p. 209. No manuscript of this Bengali work, variously attributed to Sheikh Faysullā, Kabīndradās, Śyāmdās Sen, and Bhīmsena Rāy, predates the 17th c., although it is clearly the product of earlier folk traditions: Zbavitel, *Bengali Literature*, pp. 189–90. The earliest literary work by this name is the Sanskrit-Maithili play composed between 1412 and 1428 by Vidyāpati (Harimohan Misra, ed., *Kavikokil Vidyāpati-kṛt Gorakṣavijay* [Patna: Bihar-Rashtrabhasha-Parishad, 1974]) at the behest of Śivasiṁha, king of Mithila and descendant of Harisiṁha Deva, the king for whom the *Varṇaratnākara* was composed early in the 14th c.: Mataprasad Gupta, *Prācīn Bhāṣā nāṭak Saṅgrah* (Agra: Agra University Press, 1970), pp. 29–37. Nepali popular dramas treating similar themes also predate the Bengali works: Bagchi, introduction to *KJñN*, p. 13. An edition of the Bengali drama (*Gorkha-bijay* of Bhīmsen Rāy) is by Pancanand Mandal (Calcutta: Visvabharati Granthalaya, 1949).

64. *YSĀ*, p. 14. This work is attributed to Jñāneśvara: see below, n. 183. Cf.

Dasgupta, *Obscure*, p. 207 n. 3; and Pandey, *Gorakhnāth*, p. 106. Unique to this Maharashtran tradition is an identification of these nine Nāths with "nine Nārāyaṇas" of the Avadhūta *sampradāya* founded by Dattātreya. Jñāneśvara's commentary on the *Bhāgavad Gītā*, the *Jñāneśvarī*, in which identical data is found in 18.1733–42, is dated to A.D. 1290.

65. *Navanāthacaritra* of Gauraṇa, ed. K. Ramakrishnaiah (Madras: Madras University Press, 1970), cited in Roşu, "Alchemy and Sacred Geography," p. 154; and Ashok Prabhakar Kamat, *Mahārāṣtra ke Nāthpanthīya Kaviyoṃ kā Hindi Kāvya* (Mathura: Jawahar Pustakalaya, 1976), p. 26. A similar list is found in the *Bhāradvāja Saṁhitā:* Pandey, *Gorakhnāth*, p. 109.

66. Rose, *Glossary*, vol. 2, p. 393, reproduced with modifications in Briggs, *Gorakhnāth*, p. 77, as chart D. This lineage account is found in the *Tahqīqāt-i-Ciśtī:* Raya Bahadur Munshi Haradayal Singh, *Riporṭ Mardumaśumārī Rāja Mārvāḍ Bābat san[vat] 1891 Īsvī, Tīsarāhissā*, 2 vols. (Jodhpur: Vidyasal, 1895), vol. 2, p. 231.

67. Additional partial or impressionistic lists of the Nine Nāths are also found in the *Agni* and *Brahmāvaivarta Purāṇa*s, as well as a work entitled the *Kedārakhaṇḍa* (not to be confused with the opening section of the *Skanda Purāṇa*): Pandey, *Gorakhnāth*, p. 109.

68. Śārṅgadhara is the name of the author[s] of the 14th c. *Śārṅgadhara Paddhati* and *Śārṅgadhara Saṁhitā*, both of which contain alchemical data, and of which the former also contains data on *haṭha yoga* (and mentions Gorakṣa in v. 4372). For editions, see bibliography. Śārṅganātha is, together with Gorakh and Matsyendra, considered to be a founding guru of the old Nāth monastery at Kadri, in Karnataka: see below, n. 74.

69. See especially Briggs, *Gorakhnāth*, pp. 62–77, and chart A (interleaf between pp. 74–75), which presents twelve alternative listings of the twelve subdivisions of the sect. Cf. Singh, *Riporṭ*, p. 240; and Dvivedi, *Nāth Sampradāy*, pp. 12–15; 165–68.

70. Briggs, *Gorakhnāth*, p. 65, who notes that Bhartṛhari's guru is considered by some to have been Jālandharī-pā.

71. Padu Kala is located on the main road between Pushkar and Meerta City, approximately 40 km northwest of Pushkar. Nārāyaṇ Nāth's leadership is contested by the two Nāths presently living at the Rāthāḍuṇḍā monastery, 15 km to the south, who claim the rightful succession. Inside the temple containing ten of the *samādhi*s in question was also a moldering stack of papers, which Nārāyaṇ Nāth maintained contained the records of the Vairāg Panth, a claim I was unable to verify. According to Briggs (*Gorakhnāth*, pp. 122–24), the seat of this suborder is at Pae dhuni, in Bombay.

72. Saletore, "Kanaphaṭa Jogis," pp. 17–19. Cf. Briggs, *Gorakhnāth*, p. 58. Kar-

ṇerī or Kaṇerī-nāth is so named because he originally hailed from (Vijayanagara in) Karnataka or Kanara: Dvivedi, *Nāth Sampradāy*, p. 78.

73. See above, chap. 3, n. 138.

74. Bhasker Anand Saletore, *Ancient Karnataka*, 2 vols. (Poona: Oriental Books Agency, 1936), vol. 1, pp. 94, 377–84; and idem, "Kanaphaṭa Jogis," p. 18 and n. 3. A similar identification, of a Nāth Siddha (Matsyendra) with Avalokiteśvara, is found in the cult of Lokeśvara-Rato Macchendranāth in the Kathmandu Valley.

75. Pietro della Valle, *Travels*, vol. 2, pp. 345–46, quoted in Bhasker Anand Saletore, *Social and Political Life in the Vijayanagara Empire (A.D. 1346–A.D. 1646)*, 2 vols. (Madras: B. G. Paul & Co., 1934), p. 53.

76. *Jñāneśvarī* 18.1733–42. The succession he traces is: Matsyendra—Gorakh—Gahaṇīnāth—Nivṛttināth—Jñāneśvara. Jñāneśvara's grandfather, Tryambaka Pant, who purportedly encountered Dattātreya on Girnar, was a contemporary of Gorakṣa: Pandey, *Gorakhnāth*, p. 20.

77. Pandey, *Gorakhnāth*, p. 20, and Kamat, *Mahārāṣṭra*, p. 288.

78. Listed are Jālandhara, Govindacandra, Kānha, Nāgārjuna, Kaṇerī, Goḍacūlī, and Luī-pā: Pandey, *Gorakhnāth*, p. 20.

79. Saletore, "Kanaphaṭa Jogis," pp. 20–21.

80. Charlotte Vaudeville, *Kabir Granthavali (Doha)*, Publications de l'Institut Français d'Indologie, no. 12.(Pondicherry: Institut Français d'Indologie, 1957), p. v; Bharati, *Siddh Sāhity*, pp. 333–34. On the ca. 14th c. "canonization" and "anthologization" of a corpus of vernacular poetry attributed to Gorakh and many of the other historical nine Nāths, see below, chap. 5, sec. 2.

81. *Śārṅgadhara Paddhati*, vv. 4372–4419 (pp. 662–69 of Peterson's edition). Cf. Sharma, *Āyurved*, pp. 197–98.

82. Nowotny, *Gorakṣaśataka*, p. 19.

83. Locke, *Karunamaya*, p. 433. The A.D. 1382 inscription is from Itum Baha; and the 1391 inscription from the "Gorakhnāth" cave in Pharphing, fifteen miles south of Kathmandu. This latter inscription commemorates Acintanāth's establishment of an image of Gorakh's feet, for worship in the cave. The feet and inscription are currently found outside the cave, inside of which an image of the Tibetan lama Rinpoche now presides. Acintanāth's name curiously resembles that of Gorakṣa's and Cauraṅgi's guru in the *Grub thob:* Mīna-pā is alternately referred to as Acinta-pā: Dowman, *Masters*, p. 81; Bagchi, *KJñN*, p. 23.

84. The inscription commemorates the installation of five *liṅga*s, together with images of "Gorakṣaka," Bhairava, Añjaneya (Hanumān), Sarasvatī, and Siddhi Vināyaka (Gaṇeśa): Briggs, *Gorakhnāth*, p. 247.

85. *Pāśupata-Sūtras* (1.2–38), with the commentary of Kauṇḍinya, ed. R. Anan-

thakrishna Sastri (Trivandrum: 1940), cited in Gonda, *Medieval*, p. 218. The Pāśupata use of the term *yoga* is glossed by Kauṇḍinya as *ātmeśvarasaṁyoga:* ibid., p. 217 n. 16.

86. Gonda, *Medieval*, pp. 165–66.

87. The scriptures of the Śaiva Siddhāntins, which were compiled in north (Madhya Pradesh, Kashmir) and south (Tamil Nadu) India between the 7th and 10th centuries, are called the Āgamas, which traditionally dealt with four subjects: *jñāna* ("knowledge"), *yoga* (internalized worship), *kriyā* ("ritual," external worship), and *caryā* ("conduct, behavior"). In fact, most of the content of the *āgama*s deals with the last two (and the definition of *kriyā* has in fact been altered from "magic, sorcery" to its present meaning). The Śaiva Āgamas are subdivided into four classes (Śaiva, Pāśupata, Soma, and Lākula), with the Śaiva group being further subdivided into left-hand, right-hand, and Siddhānta. The pre–A.D. 924 *Kiraṇāgama* does, however, contain a section on "sixfold" yoga that appears to anticipate teachings of Gorakhnāth: Gonda, *Medieval*, pp. 164–67, 180–81, 189.

88. Dvivedi, *Nāth Sampradāy*, p. 11. Briggs (*Gorakhnāth*, p. 63) gives a figure of eighteen, rather than twelve, original Śaivite sects.

89. *Śabara Tantra*, quoted in *Gorakṣa Siddhānta Saṃgraha*, p. 14. Cf. Pandey, *Gorakhnāth*, p. 107.

90. Briggs, *Gorakhnāth*, p. 63; Dvivedi, *Nāth Sampradāy*, pp. 11, 180.

91. It is significant that all but four of the twelve celestial images (*jyotirliṅga*s) of Śiva are located in northwestern India. The exceptions are Mallikārjuna, at Srisailam; Viśvanātha at Benares; Vaidyanātha in eastern Bihar; and Rameśvara [-nātha] at Ramesvaram. The 2d c. B.C.–2d c. A.D. Kushanas who, based in the Kabul Valley, ruled over much of northwestern India, including the Punjab and western Rajasthan, were the earliest imperial devotees of Śiva, to whose name they adjoined the epithet Mahādeva or Maheśvara.

92. This modern list, enumerated by a disciple of Gambhīrnāth, a former abbot of the Gorakhpur monastery, is found in Dvivedi, *Nāth Sampradāy*, p. 12. Seven alternative modern lists are given by Pradip Kumar Bandyopadhyay, *Nātha Cult and Mahānād* (Delhi: B. R. Publishing Company, 1992), pp. 71–73. Cf. Briggs (*Gorakhnāth*, pp. 62–75), who attempts a historical reconstruction of the twelve *panth*s (of which there are actually at least thirty).

93. Briggs (*Gorakhnāth*, pp. 34–38) indicates that the organization of the Nāth *sampradāya* is ideally quite centralized, but that such is not the case in practice. Avedyanāth, the current abbot of the Gorakhpur monastery, is a *primus inter pares*, both on institutional grounds and by virtue of his dynamism and powerful personality. See below, chap. 11, sec. 3.

94. Even if the *Nāth sampradāya* has always been a loose confederation of monas-

tic orders and lineages, certain of its member groups have, at different periods in history, been highly successful in organizing themselves into economic, political, and military powerhouses, using their itinerancy to develop wide-ranging networks of trading and fighting men who were at times capable of removing kings from their thrones and replacing them with princes of their own choosing. See below, chap. 11, sec. 3.

95. In addition to the lineage found in the A.D. 1030 Siddheśvara inscription noted above, oral and written traditions concerning the Jūṇa Ākhāḍa establishment at Ayodhya known as "Siddhagiri's monastery" indicate a lineage comprising abbots whose names end in *-nāth* prior to A.D. 1300, after which their names end in *-giri*, the traditional Dasnāmi suffix: Peter Van der Veer, *Gods on Earth: The Management of Religious Experience and Identity in a North Indian Pilgrimage Centre*, London School of Economics Monographs on Social Anthropology, 59 (London: Athlone Press, 1988), p. 146.

96. According to Pitambaradatta Barthwal (cited in Bharati, *Siddh Sāhity*, p. 323), *Nāth* was a title, meaning guru or lama in Bengali Vajrayāna or "Vajranāthī" Buddhist traditions, whence allusions to *nāth* in Saraha-pā and Kāṅha-pā as "one whose mind is unwavering" (*Dohakośa*, pp. 31, 44, 46).

97. Bharati, *Siddh Sāhity*, p. 325. See below, n. 213.

98. The Nimnāthis and Pārasnāthis, both Jain subdivisions, claim descent from two sons of Matsyendra. A number of subdivisions are now in the hands of Muslims (Zāfir Pīrs, Rāwals or Nāgnāthis) or foreigners (Dhajjannāthis). The Sepalas, Sapelas, or Samperas are (generally low-caste) snake charmers. Together with the Bāmārg ("left-handed," possibly an offshoot of the Kāpālikas) subdivision, they claim descent from Kāṇipā: Briggs, *Gorakhnāth*, pp. 63, 66, 69, 71, 72, 74. Cf. Dvivedi, *Nāth Sampradāy*, pp. 163–64, 178. See below, chap. 8, n. 193, on the relationship between the Nāth Siddhas and the Dasnāmī Nāgas, and chap. 11, sec. 4, for my encounter with a Sapela.

99. On this, see, for example, Pitambaradatta Barthwal, *Yog-Pravāh* (Benares: Kashi Vidyapith, 1946), p. 56, on the subject of Jñāneśvara's guru, Gahaṇīnāth. Dvivedi (*Nāth Siddhoṃ*, p. 15) notes that the so-called "Śaiva" lineages have generally been more tantric in their orientation than the "Gorakhnāthis," whose practices reflect their founder's hathayogic legacy.

100. See Briggs (*Gorakhnāth*, chart A, interleaf following p. 74) for twelve variant lists of the twelve *panth*s; ibid., pp. 62–77, on their tangled lineages; and Dvivedi, *Nāth Sampradāy*, pp. 166–67, who indicates the four different orders who claim descent from Hetunāth and the five orders who claim descent from Colīnāth (Ghoḍā Colī). The nature of the confusion and competition that arises from too many groups and too few "slots" is illustrated by the reaction of the Nāth Siddhas

of the Rāthāḍuṇḍā monastery when I told them I had just come from the residence of Nārāyaṇ Nāth at Padu Kala, Rāthāḍuṇḍā's rival for the seat of the Vairāg *panth:* "He's nobody."

101. In the middle of the 11th c., Alberuni describes "Jogis" with pierced or bored ears and ochre robes: Singh, *Riporṭ*, vol. 2, p. 235. Under the heading of "Jogi," Singh lists six different groups for the case of 19th c. Rajasthan: 1) Nāths or Kānphaṭas; 2) Masāniya Jogīs; 3) Kālavelīs; 4) Aughars; 5) Aghoris; and 6) Rāwals (ibid., p. 241).

102. Some hold that *Jogi* and, in Bengal, *Kāpālika* are the names of scheduled castes precisely because they descend from *yogin*s, perhaps Nāth Siddhas, who broke their vows of celibacy. Indeed, this applies to the majority of 20th c. Nāth society: i.e., most Nāths are noncelibate householders. For (dated) census figures, see Briggs, *Gorakhnāth*, pp. 4–6, 53, where he notes that the 1881 census counted 350,000 "Jugīs" in Bengal. The 1895 census *Riporṭ* (Singh, vol. 2, p. 235) of Marwar counts 30,213 Jogis, of which 16,427 are male and 13,786 are female.

103. Briggs, *Gorakhnāth*, pp. 63, 67, and passim; Dvivedi, *Nāth Sampradāy*, pp. 163–64, 178. Certain Nāths who trace their lineage back to Kānha-pā wear their *kuṇḍala*s through the lobes, rather than the thick cartilage of their ears: ibid., p. 5. Occasionally one can, by looking at a list, discern changes within a lineage or a monastery. So, for example, the *pothīratan* lineage shows a shift from Kānphaṭa to Aughar leadership in the succession Macchandar—Gorakṣa—Ratannāth—Dharmadās (after which all gurus in the lineage have names with the Aughar suffix of *-dās*): Pandey, *Gorakhnāth*, p. 107, citing Rangeya Raghava, *Gorakhnāth aur unkā Yug*, pp. 18–19.

104. These include the periodical *Yog Vāṇī*, as well as special editions of the same publication, on Gorakhnāth, the vernacular poetry (*bāṇī*s) of Gorakh, Nāth Siddha hagiography, etc. See bibliography under Srivastav.

105. *Yogabīja* 8, 81, 189 and *Gorakṣasiddhānta Saṃgraha*, p. 12. For other references, see Dvivedi, *Nāth Sampradāy*, pp. 1–3.

106. Aughars suffix their names with *-dās*. Members of the Pā *panth*s, who trace their descent back to Jālandharī-pā, suffix their names with *-pā* and are for the most part Aughars (but do not use the suffix *-dās*). Members of the Kanthaḍi subsect suffix their names with *-kanthaḍ:* Briggs, *Gorakhnāth*, pp. 33, 67; Locke, *Karunamaya* p. 431.

107. Briggs, *Gorakhnāth*, pp. 44–61, and Nowotny, introduction to *Gorakṣaśataka*, p. 53.

108. *RA* 1.4; *KJñN* 16.48.

109. Daulat Ram Shastri, foreword to Siddhinandan Misra's edition of the *RHT*, p. 11. Modern university-level instruction in *rasa śāstra* does not fit the traditional

guru-disciple model of instruction. Such south Indian traditions as those of the Sittars of Tamil Nadu and the *aṣṭavaidya* brahmins of Kerala (on which see Francis Zimmerman's excellent *Le discours des remèdes au pays des épices: Enquête sur la médecine hindoue* [Paris: Payot, 1989]) are medical rather than alchemical.

110. *RA* 2.2, 91. Cf. *RRĀ* 1.1.21a, 22a. Kāyastha Cāmuṇḍa, the 15th c. author of the *Rasasaṅketakālikā*, twice mentions the *sampradāya* of his guru (4.85, 91).

111. *RA* 1.27a: na garbhaḥ sampradāyātha raso garbho vidhīyate.

112. So, for example, the *RA* (2.39) advises the alchemist to establish his laboratory in a country where the people are Māheśvaras, i.e., followers of Śiva.

113. An alchemical author patronized by Bukku I was Viṣṇudeva, author of the *Rasasindhu* and *Rasarājalakṣmi:* Meulenbeld, *History* (draft of 10 May 1994), p. 943. Neither he nor his works are mentioned by Mādhava.

114. See, for example *RU* 1.5 and 15.50 and *RHT* 1.15–17, 20–26, 31–32. See below, chap. 5, nn. 146 and 196.

115. Dasgupta, *Obscure*, pp. 192–93, 254–55. It is related in the "Prabhuliṅgalīlā," of the *Bhaviṣya Purāṇa* (cited in Gopinath Kaviraj, *Tāntrik Vāṅmay meṃ Śākta Dṛṣṭi* [Patna: Bihar Rastrabhasa Parisad, 1963], p. 272).

116. *Śūnyasampādane* 21.1–9 (vol. 5, pp. 388–95). The same source (p. 374) relates a similar hostile encounter between Gorakh and Revaṇa, in which the latter's *siddhi*s prove to be stronger than those of the former. See below, n. 167 and chap. 8, nn. 110–12.

117. Raman Sastri's analysis ("Doctrinal Culture," pp. 300–8) totally confuses matters by attempting to identify the "Māheśvara Siddhas of the Suddha Marga" with the Tamil Sittars. Far more useful discussions are Dasgupta, *Obscure*, pp. 192–93, 254–55; and the editor's introduction to the *RU* (with Hindi translation and commentary of Badrinarayan Sarma, 2 vols. [Ajmer: Krsna Gopal Ayurved Bhavan, 1959], vol. 1, p. 12).

118. Roşu ("Alchemy and Sacred Geography," p. 153), who notes that "according to certain archaeologists, these sanctuaries may have been founded by *siddha* ascetics who were practitioners of alchemy (*rasavāda*)." In the balance of this article, however, Roşu tends to discount such claims.

119. *Viṣṇudharmottara Purāṇa* 3.40.1–9, translated in Shiva Sheikhar Misra, *Fine Arts and Technical Sciences in Ancient India with Special Reference to Someśvara's Mānasollāsa* (Benares: Krishnadas Academy, 1982), p. 101. I have been told that such preparations are still in use, in Rajasthan, where they are called *candralepa* ("mooncoating"), and in Karnataka, where the carving style is called *hemarapanth*.

120. Sharma, *Āyurved* (pp. 471 [photo], 473), maintains that there was an alchemical laboratory at Nalanda, noting the remains of an oven found in the ruins there as evidence. However, Satya Prakash (*Prācīn Bhārat meṃ Rasāyan kā Vikās*

[Allahabad: Prayag Visvavidyalaya, 1960], pp. 835–37), who analyzed the chemical content of a number of metal objects found at Nalanda, found no trace of mercury in any of them.

121. Personal communication from Dr. Surya Kumar Yogi, Menal, Rajasthan, March 1985.

122. Treloar, "Use of Mercury," pp. 232–33. The ruins of the Chandi Bukit Batu Pahat temple are located in Kedah, Malaysia.

123. Ray, *History*, vol. 2, pp. xxxviii–xliii. It should be noted that in 1903, shortly after the publication of Ray's first volume, Palmyr Cordier ("Récentes découvertes," pp. 347–48) described this text under its proper name of *Rasendramaṅgala*, noting that it was "quite identical to the *Rasaratnākara* recently used by Prof. P. C. Ray."

124. Lévi, "Kaniṣka," p. 106; Filliozat, *Doctrine classique*, p. 10; Eliade, *Yoga: Immortality and Freedom*, p. 416.

125. Dominik Wujastyk, "An Alchemical Ghost: The Rasaratnākara by Nāgārjuna." *Ambix* 31:2 (July 1984), pp. 70–83.

126. See below, chap. 5, sec. 4j.

127. See above, chap. 3, secs. 2 and 3, for the historical background to the *RM*'s dramatization.

128. Ray, *History*, vol. 2, pp. xli–xlii. He further claims (ibid., p. liii), on the basis of a manuscript colophon, that Govinda, the author of the *RHT*, "was evidently a Buddhist" in spite of the fact that this text, too, is thoroughly Hindu.

129. Ibid., pp. xlii–xlvi. Ray's note, in which he speaks of his indebtedness "for the passages cited here" to Shastri, "who has wended his way through the bulky MS," does not state where in the *Kubjikāmata* Shastri allegedly found these passages: they are certainly not in his *Catalogue* (vol. 1, pp. lxxviii–lxxx), which Ray also cites. Ray's attribution of the description of six-times killed mercury to the *Kubjikāmata* is repeated by Mircea Eliade (*Forgerons et alchimistes*, revised ed. [Paris: Flammarion, 1977], pp. 112–13) and White ("Why Gurus Are Heavy," *Numen*, 33 [1984], p. 52). His misconception, that many of the early alchemical tantras were Buddhist, is followed by O. P. Jaggi, *Yogic and Tantric Medicine* (Delhi: Atma Ram and Sons, 1973), pp. 133–34.

130. Here, it is worthwhile to note that a later Indian historian of alchemy, Bhudeb Mookerji, states in the introduction to volume one of his five-volume *Rasa-jala-nidhi*, that "it is earnestly hoped that Dr. Sir P. C. Ray will live to bring out a revised edition of his book, which contains so many misinterpretations . . . due, no doubt, to a hasty and superficial study of the subject."

131. Here, Sharma (*Āyurved*, p. 474) miscites pp. 125–26 of the 1956 revised one-volume edition of Ray's *History*, which are a discussion of Tamil Sittar alchemy. Khilji's sustained invasion of Bengal began in A.D. 1202.

132. Sachau, *Alberuni's India*, vol. 1, p. 22. That Alberuni did not consider alchemy to be a science, but rather a popular superstition is made abundantly clear: ibid., vol. 1, p. 193.

133. As I have argued (see above, chap. 3, nn. 122–24), the early 11th c. *Vimalaprabhā* commentary to the *Kālacakra Tantra* contains alchemical data that is quite identical to that of the Hindu *RA*, which belongs to the same century.

134. See below, chap. 5, nn. 22–26.

135. Sharma, *Āyurved*, pp. 310–11, 402–3.

136. *Śārṅgadhara Saṁhitā*, ed. and tr. K. R. Srikanta Murty (Benares: Chaukhambha, 1984), pp. xiii–xiv.

137. Carl Ernst, "The Arabic Version of 'The Pool of the Water of Life' (Amṛtakuṇḍa)," has identified forty-five manuscripts of the Arabic translation of this work and notes that there exist two Persian translations, two Turkish translations, and one Urdu translation of this work. One manuscript makes reference to historical events transpiring in the early 13th c.: personal communication from Carl Ernst, Chapel Hill, N.C. November 1994. See below, n. 153.

138. Needham, *Science and Civilisation*, vol. 5, part 5 (1983), p. 285; Dvivedi, *Nāth Sampradāy*, p. 22. For other cases of Hindu-Muslim mystic syncretism in Bengal, see Dasgupta, *Obscure*, pp. 157–87, on the Bāuls of Bengal. See Zbavitel, *Bengali Literature*, pp. 189–90 on the dating of this literary work in Bengali.

139. Krsna Kumar Bali, *Ṭillā Gorakṣanāth* (Haridwar: Pir Kala Nath Trust, 1983), p. 17 and throughout. Cf. Bharati, *Siddh Sāhity*, pp. 325–26.

140. Thus Bandyopadhyay (*Nāth Cult*, p. 43) states (misquoting Sukumar Sen, *History of Bengali Literature*, with a foreword by Jawaharlal Nehru [New Delhi: Sahitya Academy, 1960], p. 42) that "there is no doubt that the Nāth cult originated in Eastern India, probably in Bengal, *long before the fourteenth century when we first get a reference*." For an informed discussion of such theories and their pitfalls, see Bharati, *Siddh Sāhity*, pp. 323–24. Cf. Pandey, *Gorakhnāth*, pp. 18–19.

141. Bharati, *Siddh Sāhity*, pp. 335–38. See Vaudeville (*Kabir Granthavali* (*Doha*), pp. viii–ix; xviii–xx) for the specific terms *śūnya* and *sahaja*.

142. Chattopadhyaya, ed., *Tāranātha's History*, p. vii.

143. See above, chap. 3, n. 143, and below, chap. 8, nn. 33–37. Luī-pā is the author of six Buddhist works preserved in the *Tanjur:* Chattopadhyaya, *Tāranātha's History*, p. 393.

144. Chattopadhyaya, *Tāranātha's History*, p. 320. Tāranātha also maintains that Gorakṣa was born as a Buddhist by the name of Anaṅgavajra, and was the son of the Pāla king Gopāla.

145. See above, n. 63.

146. He calls Jālandharī-pā his guru in song no. 36; he refers to *kuṇḍala*s (which

he identifies as the sun and moon, i.e., the two peripheral channels of the subtle body) and the unstruck sound in song no. 11: Kværne, *Buddhist Tantric Songs*, pp. 119, 215.

147. Dvivedi, *Nāth Sampradāy*, p. 7; Rose, *Glossary*, vol. 2, p. 390; Moti Singh, *Nirguṇ Sāhity: Sāṃskṛtik Pṛṣṭhabhūmi* (Benares: Nagaripracarini Sabha, 1963), p. 52.

148. Dowman, *Masters*, pp. 81–90. Tāranātha's is a case of mistaken identity: Nowotny, *Gorakṣaśataka*, pp. 24–25; and Chattopadhyaya, *Tāranātha's History*, p. 227. Cauraṅgi gives the same account of himself in verses 1–2 of the ca. 14th c. *Prāṇ Sāṅkalī* (in Dvivedi, *Nāth Siddhoṃ*, p. 19); but the *Grub thob* myth is clearly the source of later Hindu legends of Pūraṇ Bhagat of the Punjab: ibid., p. 227; and Nowotny, *Gorakṣaśataka*, pp. 24–25. While the Tibetan sources make Cauraṅgi and Gorakṣa Pāla princes of Bengal, the vernacular Indian traditions make Cauraṇgi the son of king Śālivāhana of Sialkot (Jhelum dist., Punjab, Pakistan). The accuracy of this tradition is attested by a reference Gahaṇīnāth (13th c.) makes to Gorakh as the guru of Pīpā: in the 19th c. Punjabi songs of Pūraṇ Bhagat, Pīpā is the adoptive father of Loṇa, the "Potiphar's wife" of this story: Dasgupta, *Obscure*, p. 388; Temple, *Legends*, vol. 2, pp. 388–89. See below, chap. 9, sec. 7, for an extended discussion of this legend.

149. This is Rahul Sankrtyayana's theory ("Recherches Bouddhiques," p. 228). On the Jogi and Kāpālika subcastes, see Dasgupta, *Obscure*, pp. 368–69; and Briggs, *Gorakhnāth*, pp. 4–6, 53. As far as conversion to Islam from Hinduism is concerned, it has been hypothesized that renouncers who were dispossessed by their religious orders for having broken their vows of celibacy were eventually driven to embrace Islam. Here, their status changed from dispossessed Hindu (called "Jogi" in this case) to Islamicized *julaha* (Kabīr belonged to this group, which straddled Hinduism and Islam). These Islamicized subcastes were then converted, en masse, by the Nāth Siddhas, which would thus account for the large numbers of householder Nāths: personal communication from Nagendranath Upadhyaya, Benares, March 1985.

150. If at times their work appears to have Hindu overtones, this is because they cribbed much of their material from such Hindu tantric texts as the "Yoginīsaṃcāra" of the *Jayadrathayāmalatantra*, the *Picumata-Brahmayāmalatantra* and the *Tantrasadbhāva*. On this and other resemblances between the esoteric Buddhism of the Highest Yoga Tantras (*yogānuttara tantra*) and the Yoginī cults of the Kāpālika Vidyāpīṭha, see Sanderson, "Śaivism," pp. 678–79.

151. Chattopadhyaya, *History*, p. 227.

152. *Vāyutattvaṃ Bhāvanopadeśa* of Ghorakṣa (*Tanjur*; Derge 2377; Peking 3219) is less than one folio in length. It is a poetical description of a number of hathayogic

phenomena, in the colophon of which the author identifies himself as Ācārya Ghorakha. Curiously, the text that follows (Derge 2378) bears the same title as this one and is attributed to Cauraṅgi, that Siddha with whom Gorakṣa's legend becomes confused in Tibetan hagiography. I am grateful to Steven Weinberger for translating this text from the Tibetan. On the *caryā* songs attributed to Ghorakṣa in the *Tanjur*, see above, n. 15.

153. On this date, see Digby, "Encounters with Jogīs," p. 34.

154. This is a role Gorakṣa continues to play in rural Bengal: for a study, see Sarat Chandra Misra, "On the Cult of Gorakṣanāth in Eastern Bengal," *Journal of the Department of Letters* (University of Calcutta) 14 (1927), pp. 1–41.

155. Pandey, *Gorakhnāth*, p. 60. See above, n. 74, for a possible parallel development at Kadri, in Karnataka.

156. Ernst Bruce Alexander, *Statistical Description and Historical Account of the North-Western Provinces of India* [Gazetteer, Northwest Provinces, vol. 6] (Allahabad: Northwest Provinces and Oudh Government Press, 1881), pp. 371, 436. Cf. Pandey, *Gorakhnāth*, p. 61, citing the *Citrāvalī* of Usmān Kavi without citation. The same author states (ibid.) that "Allah ud-Din Khilaji destroyed the famous temple of Gorakhnāth in the 13th century," which is chronologically impossible. Its destruction by Aurangzeb in the 17th c. (ibid.) is more likely based in historical fact.

157. The ca. 13th c. *MBhT*, a Śākta Tantra and the sole text with any significant alchemical content to have come out of eastern India, makes no mention of any of the Siddhas.

158. Edward C. Dimock, Jr., *The Place of the Hidden Moon: Erotic Mysticism in the Vaiṣṇava-sahajiyā Cult of Bengal* (Chicago: University of Chicago Press, 1966. Reprint Delhi: Motilal Banarsidass, 1991), pp. 249–70.

159. A ground-breaking survey of the often sympathetic relations between the Nāth Siddhas and Sūfis in medieval India is Digby, "Encounters with Jogīs." See also Gold, *Lord as Guru*, pp. 207–8; and Dominique-Sila Khan, "L'Origine ismaélienne du culte hindou de Rāmdeo Pīr," *Revue de l'Histoire des Religions* 210 (1993), pp. 27–47; and idem, "Rāmdeo Pīr and the Kāmaḍiyā Panth," in *Folk, Faith, and Feudalism*, ed. N. K. Singhi and Rajendra Joshi (Jaipur: Rawat Publications, 1995), pp. 295–327.

160. Many vain attempts have been made to generate biographies of the major Nāths out of the mass of legend on their subjects: Dasgupta, *Obscure*, pp. 191–92, 218, 367–98; Dvivedi, *Nāth Sampradāy*, pp. 149–80; idem, *Nāth Siddhoṃ*, pp. 4–21; and Briggs, *Gorakhnāth*, pp. 228–50.

161. The entire Gangetic Plain, from Bengal in the east to Jalandhara (Punjab) in the northwest, was politically unified under the Pāla kings of Bengal between the 8th and 12th centuries: Joseph E. Schwartzberg, ed. *A Historical Atlas of South*

Asia (Chicago: University of Chicago Press, 1978; second impression, with additional material, New York: Oxford University Press, 1992), p. 146, pl. xiv.

162. *Vāsavadattā*, verse 87; and Roşu, "Alchemy and Sacred Geography," p. 153. The *RRĀ* (4.8.1–185: *Śrīnityanāthasiddhaviracita (Rasaratnākarāntargataś caturtha) Rasāyanakhandaḥ*, ed. Yadavji Trikamji Acharya [Benares: Chaukhamba Sanskrit Pustakalaya, 1939]); and the *ĀK* (1.12.1–200) contain long descriptions of Srisailam. See also Arion Roşu, "*Mantra* et *Yantra* dans la médecine et l'alchimie indiennes," *Journal Asiatique*, 274:3–4 (1986), pp. 251, 255.

163. The Kāpālikas, who had important ties with Srisailam, were also especially strong in the south, following the 10th c. Prior to that, they may have been centered in the Himalayan regions, where their practices of ritualized sex strongly influenced the nascent tantric tradition, as documented in the ca. 9th c. *Jayadrathayāmala Tantra:* Gonda, *Medieval*, pp. 165, 216; Lorenzen, s.v. "Śaivism: Pāśupatas," in *Encyclopedia of Religion;* idem, "New Data," in Hiltebeitel, ed., *Criminal Gods*, p. 231; and idem, *Kāpālikas*, pp. 106–8.

164. The oldest existing edifice on the peak of Srisailam itself is the Mallikārjuna temple, which houses the *jyotirliṅga* of the same name. This temple dates from the 13th–14th c.: Roşu, "A la recherche," p. 34. A Mallikārjuna is located at Śrīparvata in the 6th c. *Vāsavadattā:* Hall, *Vāsavadattā*, p. 11.

165. *Mālatī-Mādhava* (*Bhavabhūti's Mālatī-Mādhava, with the Commentary of Jagaddhara*, 3d ed., M. R. Kale, ed. [Delhi: Motilal Banarsidass, 1967]), act 5, vv. 1–2. See also Lorenzen, *Kāpālikas*, p. 95, and below, chap. 5, n. 84.

166. Sastri, "Doctrinal Culture," p. 304; Bhattacharyya, *History*, p. 284. The Tungabhadra, a branch of the Krishna or Kistna River, flows past Alampur (Kurnool district, Andhra Pradesh), the western "gateway" to Srisailam (Roşu, "Alchemy and Sacred Geography," p. 155), and on to the modern Hampi (Bellary district, Karnataka), i.e., the capital of Vijayanagara, whose kings were, in the 14th–17th centuries, great patrons of the Vīraśaivas. Kadri, the great "Yogi" monastery, was also located within the borders of this empire: Saletore, *Social and Political Life*, vol. 2, p. 53. In more common usage, the term *Antarvedī* referred to the Doab, the region lying between the Ganges and Yamuna rivers in modern-day south central Uttar Pradesh: D. C. Sircar, *Studies in the Geography of Ancient and Medieval India* (Delhi: Motilal Banarsidass, 1990), pp. 303–7.

167. This is not the same text as that portion of the *Bhavisya Purāṇa* cited above in n. 116. In the *Śūnyasampādane*, a Vīraśaiva source, Allama Prabhu condemns Gorakh's alchemy in no uncertain terms: Ramanujan, *Speaking of Śiva*, p. 147. While Allama Prabhu lived in the 12th c., this work, which casts him as a contemporary of Gorakh, was compiled during the reign of the Vijayanagara king Devar-

āya II (A.D. 1419–47): *Śūnyasampādane*, foreword to vol. 1, p. ii. See also Dasgupta, *Obscure*, p. 255.

168. Kardaswamy, *History*, p. 354. The *liṅga* at Paśupatināth, the "national shrine" of Kathmandu and Nepal, is also called *paraspati*, transmutational. Tradition holds that a man wearing lead bracelets once purposely embraced the *liṅga*. The bracelets were turned to gold, but the man, who had come to worship out of desire rather than devotion, was physically unable to leave the temple sanctum until he had removed the bracelets: personal communication from Purna Giri, Hardwar, March 1984.

169. Kardaswamy, *History*, p. 330. Korakkar's south Indian *samādhi* is located at Poiyur (Thanjavur district), a village near Nagapattinam on the Tamil coast: ibid., p. 354. A Nāth Siddha establishment is located at the same site: personal communication from N. Sethu Raghunathan, Madurai, January 1985.

170. *Korakkar Malai Vagatam* (Madurai: G. Ramasamkykone Booksellers, 1968), cited in N. Sethu Raghunathan, "Contribution of Yoogi Munivar for Siddha System of Medicine," *Heritage of the Tamils: Siddha Medicine*, ed. S. V. Subrahmanian and V. R. Madhavan (Madras: International Institute of Tamil Studies, 1983), p. 616.

171. Roşu, "Alchemy and Sacred Geography," p. 153. On Nityanātha's probable membership in the Nāth order, see below, chap. 5, n. 41 and sec. 4h.

172. B. Rama Rao and M. V. Reddy, "A Note on Gorakṣanātha and his Work *Yogadīpikā*," *Bulletin of the Indian Institute of the History of Medicine* (Hyderabad) 12 (1982), pp. 34–35. Following this episode, Gauraṇa goes on to relate the battle between the diamond-bodied Gorakh and the divine-bodied Allama Prabhu: see above, n. 115. The so-called *Yogadīpikā*, as these authors describe it, is clearly an Old Kannada version of the *Haṭhayogapradīpikā* of Svātmarāma, with added material on the transmutation of base metals into gold: ibid., p. 37. See below, chap. 5, n. 117.

173. Roşu, "Alchemy and Sacred Geography," p. 154. Another Hindu version of this legend is found in the *Kathāsaritsāgara* (41.57): *Ocean*, vol. 3, pp. 252–56. Cf. Watters, *Yuan-Chwang*, vol. 2, pp. 201–6. See above, chap. 3, nn. 106–107.

174. Watt, *Dictionary*, vol. 5, pp. 232–34. Cf. Roşu, "Alchemy and Sacred Geography," pp. 155–56.

175. The Vijayanagara kings (A.D. 1336–1565), although based at Hampi, were devotees of Śiva Mallikārjuna at Srisailam: Konduri Sarojini Devi, *Religion in the Vijayanagara Empire* (New Delhi: Sterling, 1990), pp. 88–89, 176, 180.

176. Roşu, "A la recherche," pp. 44–46, 52. See above, chap. 3, n. 47.

177. *NSC*, pp. 215, 217; idem. "*Gorakh*" *Viśeṣāṅk*, pp. 266–68. There are prob-

lems of chronology here. Satyanāth is associated with the 16th c. Garhwali king Ajaypal; Ānandagiri, if he is the same hagiographer of Śaṅkara as the Ānandagiri who authored the *Śaṅkaravijaya*, is a 14th–15th c. author; and Śaṅkarācārya himself is an 8th century reformer of Hinduism.

178. *KJñN* 16.5–7; *KM* 2.5–6; *KPT* 15.2 and 16.9 (pp. 356 and 367 of Jivananda Bhattacarya, ed. *Indrajālavidyāsaṃgraha* (Calcutta: V. V. Mukherji, 1925) Cf. Pandey, *Gorakhnāth*, pp. 66–68.

179. Srivastav, ed. "*Gorakh*" *Viśeṣāṅk*, p. 119.

180. Like the Cālukyas of Kalyāṇī (10th–12th c.) before them, the Yādavas of Devagiri (A.D. 1175–1318) ruled an area comprising Maharashtra, Karnataka, and the western Deccan (encompassing the region of the Andhran Srisailam): Schwartzberg, *Historical Atlas*, pp. 147–48, pl. xiv.3).

181. While Bhāskara's is an extremely common name, it may well be that the same Bhāskara who was eulogized by Siddha Nāgārjuna in the opening verse of the 12th–13th c. *Yogaratnamālā*, was also the author of a lost alchemical work entitled the *Rasendra Bhāskara:* Priyavrat Sharma, *Nāgārjuna's Yogaratnamālā with the Commentary of Śvetāmbara Bhikṣu Guṇākara* (Benares: Chaukhambha Orientalia, 1977), pp. 9–11; and idem, *Āyurved*, p. 230.

182. Sharma, *Āyurved*, pp. 310–12, 402–7, 474, 482, 697. A precious document which records the royal patronage of Ayurvedic physicians and alchemists by the early Yādavas is a passage from the *Saṅgītaratnākara* (1.2–13), a treatise on music by Śārṅgadeva, the grandson of Bhāskara: the passage is reproduced in Sharma, *Āyurved*, p. 311.

183. This is the *Yogisampradāyāviṣkṛti* (*YSĀ*). In an introduction to the *YSĀ*, (p. *ca*), Candranath Yogi states that his is an abridged Hindi translation of Jñāneśvara's translation (into "Maharashtran") of a Bengali original written shortly before his time. He gives no explanation for this "Bengali original," which I find implausible, given that the names of the Nāth Siddhas treated in the work correspond to those found in western Marathi rather than Bengali hagiographic traditions. At this point, I am unable to confirm Candranath Yogi's assertion that this is in fact a work (or translation) originally composed by Jñāneśvara; however, apart from some mentioned in a number of appendices, none of the persons figuring in the work appears to be later than Jñāneśvara's late 13th c. dates. The manuscript used by Candranath Yogi is dated to A.D. 1773–74.

184. Pandey, *Gorakhnāth*, p. 65.

185. The *Tantra Mahārṇava* is a work which locates the Nine Nāths at eight of the nine cardinal directions. Nāgārjuna's Godavari location corresponds to the southern quadrant: Dasgupta, *Obscure*, p. 206. See below, chap. 5, n. 82.

186. Kaviraj, *Bhāratīy*, vol. 1, pp. 151, 191–92, 197, 203; Briggs, *Gorakhnāth*, p. 121.

187. Srivastav, "*Gorakh*" *Viśeṣāṅk*, p. 119. The 7th c. Bāṇa mentions that plantain flourishes along the shore of the Godavari: Sharma, *Indian Medicine*, p. 145.

188. Chinese and Persian reports of exceptional Indian waters date back to the middle of the 9th c. Like mercury and sulfur, sal ammoniac occurs naturally in regions of geothermic activity: Needham, *Science and Civilisation*, vol. 5, pt. 4 (1980), pp. 197–98, 435–37.

189. *RA* 12.236–39. Cf. yet another reference to a Srisailam, where "rock" or "peak water"—*śailodaka*—is found, as well as a long list of sources of low-grade "rock water," most of which are in southwestern India (*RA* 12.282–87).

190. *Kadalīmañjunātha Māhātmya* (p. 33), quoted in Pandey, *Gorakhnāth*, p. 66.

191. The reference is found in *RRS* 16.126. See above, nn. 134–35, and chap. 5, n. 269. One could, however, read *RA* 12.236 ("on the southern path, in the direction of Death") as an indication that the author was from somewhere further to the north. However, such is a commonplace way of speaking of India south of the Vindhyas (Yama, Death, is the regent of the southern quarter). Prior to the Yādavas, the Cālukyas of Kalyāṇī ruled this region. While the *Mānasollāsa* (A.D. 1131), written by or for the Cālukya monarch Someśvara III ("Bhūlokamalla"), contains long passages on medicine (1.135–307), sorcery for locating buried treasure (2.332–61), transmutational alchemy (2.377–94) and the testing of gemstones (2.378–536), it shows no direct influence from the *RA*, which dates from a century earlier: *Mānasollāsa of King Bhūlokamalla Someśvara*, 3 vols, ed. G. K. Srigondekar, Gaekwad's Oriental Series, no. 28, 2d ed. (Baroda: Oriental Institute, 1967).

192. Sharma, *Yogaratnamālā*, pp. 8–10, 13; idem, *Āyurved*, pp. 310–11, 402. See below, chap. 5, nn. 60 and 251.

193. Sharma, *Yogaratnamālā*, pp. 14–17.

194. Phyllis Granoff, "Jain Biographies of Nāgārjuna: Notes on the Composing of a Biography in Medieval India," in Phyllis Granoff and Koichi Shinohara, eds., *Monks and Magicians: Religious Biographies in Asia* (Oakville, Ontario: Mosaic Press, 1988), pp. 48–49.

195. The "Śātavāhana" king is an obvious carryover from Buddhist traditions. Paliṭṭanakapura is to be identified with both the modern Palitana and Mount Śatruñjaya, as well as Vallabhi and Pattan, and by extension, Mount Dhāṅk.

196. Summarized in Granoff, "Jain Biographies," pp. 48, 50–51. The *Prabandhacintāmaṇi* calls the elixir "ten-million transmutation mercury" (*koṭavedhī-rasa*); the "grinding of mercury" (*pārada-mardana*) is the second alchemical *saṃskāra:* Dvivedi, *Nāth Sampradāy*, p. 153.

197. See below, chap. 7, n. 69.

198. Granoff, "Jain Biographies," p. 52. Dhank is located sixteen miles (by road) northwest of Upaleta (Rajkot district, Gujarat). Dominik Wujastyk also describes an image of Nāgārjuna—together with that of a figure named "Baroṭ" (who, he was told, wrote Nāgārjuna's biography)—which, located in a private dwelling in the village of Dhank itself, is receiving active worship: letter dated 24 February 1993.

199. According to Shantilal Pranjivan Joshi, who wrote the forward to the 1959 Ajmer edition of the *RU* (p. 11), it was with the alchemical gold produced at Valabhī that the Jains financed the building of the 10th–14th c. Dilwāra temples of Mount Abu, considered by many to be the most beautiful examples of Jain temple architecture in India.

200. Valabhī had been the capital of the Maitraka kings, whose charters date from A.D. 502 to 766. Popular and bardic traditions, which maintain that Valabhī fell in A.D. 524, are chronologically impossible: D. C. Sircar, *The Guhilas of Kiṣkindhā* (Calcutta: Sanskrit College, 1965), pp. 24–25. On Amru ibn Jamāl, see *Historical and Cultural Chronology of Gujarat*, ed. M. R. Majumdar et al., 2 vols. (Baroda: University of Baroda, 1960), vol. 1, p. 226.

201. For a complete rendering of this account, see below, chap. 9, sec. 8.

202. Sachau, *Alberuni's India*, vol. 1, p. 193.

203. Personal communication from Dominik Wujastyk, London, May 1992.

204. Briggs, *Gorakhnāth*, pp. 116–17. This leads into another legend concerning Dharamnāth and Dhinodar hill, the site of an important Nāth monastery to the north of Bhuj, the capital of Kacch: Dalpatram Pranjivan Khakhar, "History of the Kānphaṭas of Kacch, *Indian Antiquary* 7 (1878), pp. 47–53. These accounts further resemble the myth of the fall of Kṛṣṇa's capital, Dvaraka, which was swallowed up by the ocean shortly after the conclusion of the great *Mahābhārata* war: Dvaraka is located across the Gulf of Kacch from Mandavi. The fact that the Kathiawar peninsula and Kacch are both low-lying regions with swampy, shifting coastlines is no doubt also a source for accounts of "fallen" cities of Pattan. See the maps of Gujarat in Schwartzberg, *Atlas*, pp. 8–32, which indicate that the Kacch region has been periodically submerged by the ocean over the past millennia.

205. Walter Ruben, *Eisenschmiede und Dämonen in Indien*, Internationales Archiv für Ethnographie, 37, suppl. (Leiden: Brill, 1939), p. 205, citing *Liṅga Purāṇa* 1.97.1–42.

206. *KPT* 2.40: asya pūrvamevāyutaṃ japtvā tato 'nena mantreṇa pāśānaṃ saptābhimantritaṃ kṛtvā *pattane vā grāme* kṣipet vā tena pāśānena vṛkṣam tāḍayet/ grāma madhye aprārthitaṃ sukhabhogam prāpnoti. Cf. *KPT* 1.33 (in Bhattacarya, ed, *Indrajālavidyāsaṃgraha*, pp. 267, 280).

207. Nāgārjuna's toponym may correspond to Patan, a city in northern Kathiawar that has been continuously inhabited since the period in question and near to which is a mountain (Osam) that has long been a site connected to the practice of Ayurvedic medicine: *Kalyāṇ Śakti Aṅk*, pp. 661, 664. The Pattan that Dharamnāth brought down was located in southern Kacch, over two hundred miles to the southwest. Both toponyms are, however, within Gujarat, as are a number of other toponyms ending in *-patan.*

208. Granoff "Jain Biographies," p. 60, citing Jyoti Prasad Jain, "Jain Authors and Their Works," *Jaina Antiquary* 33 [1980], p. 27. Granoff does not give the title of this work.

209. *Pāduha-doha* no. 126, cited in Srivastav, ed., *"Gorakh" Viśeṣāṅk*, p. 50. Cf. Dasgupta, *Obscure*, pp. 58–60.

210. Elizabeth Sharpe, *An Eight-Hundred Year Old Book of Indian Medicine and Formulas, Translated from the Original Very Old Hindi into Gujarati Character and Thence into English* (London: Luzac & Co, 1937; reprint New Delhi: Asian Educational Services, 1979), p. 6. A 12th–14th c. alchemical text, entitled *Rasaratnasamuccaya,* was the work of the Jain monk Māṇikyadeva Sūri: J. C. Sikdar, ed. and tr., *The Rasa-ratna-samuccaya of Māṇikyadeva Sūri* (Jaipur: Prakrta Bharati Academy, 1986), p. i. It in no way resembles Vāgbhaṭṭa II's alchemical work of the same title.

211. *RC* 2.1; *RPS* 13.15. See below, chap. 5, n. 225.

212. Watt, *Dictionary*, vol. 5, p. 233. The Jamnagar alchemical experiment was described to me by Siddhinandan Misra: personal communication, Benares, March 1985.

213. John Cort, "Twelve Chapters from *The Guidebook to Various Pilgrimage Places*, the *Vividhatīrthakalpa* of Jīnaprabhasūri," in Phyllis Granoff, ed., *The Clever Adulteress and the Hungry Monk: A Treasury of Jain Literature* (New York, Mosaic Press, 1990), pp. 251–58; and *Skanda Purāṇa* 7.2.6.8. Girinārāyaṇa, the Sanskrit name for this site, reflects a link with the cult of Dattātreya as an incarnation of the god Viṣṇu. In the *YSĀ*, the nine Nāths are identified with nine Nārāyaṇas, and led by Dattātreya. The names of the nine Nārāyaṇas are found in the *Bhavisya Purāṇa* (cited in Rajesh Dikshit, *Śrī Navanāth Caritra Sāgar* [Delhi: Dehati Pustak Bhandar, 1969], pp. 13–14); the nine Nāths mentioned there are those currently revered in Maharashtrau traditions.

214. Watters, *Yuan-Chwang's Travels*, vol. 2, pp. 248–49; Bāṇabhaṭṭa, *Harṣacarita* 8.226. The *YSĀ* states that Matsyendra ended his career at Girnar: Mallik, *SSP*, p. 10. The early 19th c. *Nātha Caritra* (ASL MSS no. 1573/1645) of Mān Singh, king of Marwar, devotes no fewer than fourteen chapters (1.2; 2.1–13) to Girnar; most of these concern the travels of Gopīcand to the site and the meetings he had with

Dattātreya, Matsyendra, and other Nāth Siddhas there. Mān Singh was married to a Gujarati princess. See also Kaviraj, *Bhāratīy*, vol. 1, p. 197, on the Aghori Bābā Kinnarām, who had a vision (*darśan*) of Dattātreya on Girnar in 1724.

215. Briggs, *Gorakhnāth*, pp. 110–19; Pandey, *Gorakhnāth*, pp. 63–64.

216. Personal communication, Kathmandu, October 1984. See below, chap. 11, sec. 4, for the fruit of my searches. The geographical remoteness of the sites of Girnar and Abu may also account for their perennial frequentation by Nāth Siddhas and members of other tantric orders whose practices were viewed as abominable by mainstream Hindu society. On the terrible practices of the Aghoris at these two sites, see H. W. Barrow, "On Aghoris and Aghorapanthis," *Anthropological Society of Bombay* 3:4 (1893), pp. 199, 211–14, 246.

217. A number of major Nāth sites are called "[Gorakh] Ṭilla," an alloform of "Ṭileti": the most important of these is found above Jhelum (Jhelum district, Punjab, Pakistan): Briggs, *Gorakhnāth*, pp. 101–3. Formerly, the Nāth Siddhas had an important monastery called Gorakh Ṭilla in Benares: ibid., p. 84.

218. At Mount Abu, "Gopīcand's cave" is located near the top of the central peak (above it is a temple to the goddess Camuṇḍā) of Acalgarh; in the pass between this and the eastern peak is a shrine to Gorakh. At Girnar, it is Bhartṛhari whose cave (an image of Gopīcand is there as well) is located in a dip between the first and second peaks and Gorakh whose *dhūnī* is found atop the central peak.

219. See below, chap. 10, nn. 125–30.

220. Cannabis, called *vijaya* "victory" in a number of tantric texts is, according to the *Tārā Tantra* (3.1–11), essential to ecstasy. The 7th c. south Indian Tirumūlar sings the praises of marijuana in his *Tirumantiram* (Roşu, "Yoga et alchimie," p. 370); and the *kañja* plant (*gañja*, marijuana) is called "Gorakh's root," *korakkar-muli*, in Sittar traditions (Kardaswamy, *History*, p. 354).

221. Briggs, *Gorakhnāth*, p. 72. See above, n. 67.

222. This and a number of other Rajasthani legends that follow were related to Colonel James Tod, author of *Annals and Antiquities of Rajasthan*, ed. with an introduction by William Crooke, 3 vols. (London: H. Milford, 1920; reprint Delhi: Low Cost Publication, 1990). Tod (vol. 1, pp. 258–60) presents the following account as history; Sircar (*Guhilas*, pp. 12–13) demonstrates that it is a legend. Wink (*Al-Hind*, vol. 1, p. 294) maintains that the Guhilots who would become the lords of Mewar originated in Gujarat, noting the existence of a forest named Guhila in that province.

223. The Acalgarh fort at Abu was the old stronghold of the Paramāras of Candravatī and Abu: B. N. Dhoundiyal, *Rajasthan District Gazateers: Sirohi* (Jaipur: Government Central Press, 1967), p. 430. The ruins of Candravatī are situated

about halfway between Ambā Bhavanī and Abu, at about twelve miles' distance from both sites: Alexander Kinloch Forbes, *Rās-mālā: Hindu Annals of Western India, with Particular Reference to Gujarat* (London: Richardson, 1878; reprint New Delhi: Heritage Publishers, 1973), p. 210.

224. Tod, *Annals and Antiquities*, vol. 1, p. 259; and Sircar, *Guhilas*, pp. 12–13. A number of legends connect the aboriginal Bhīls of Rajasthan and Gujarat with the alchemical touchstone. The founder of the Mandalgarh branch of the Cālukya race raised the walls of his fortress (Mandalgarh) with the gold he made from a *pāras patthar* ("touchstone") found by a certain Mandoo, a Bhīl in his service: Tod, *Annals and Antiquities*, vol. 2, p. 545. A similar scenario involving a Bhīl blacksmith's apprentice is found in the *Kathāsaritsāgara* (*Ocean*, vol. 3, p. 161 n. 1).

225. Tod, *Annals and Antiquities*, vol. 1, pp. 255, 259, 265–70; and Sircar, *Guhilas*, pp. 26–27.

226. Here, Bāppā's legend parallels that of Guha. Bāppā's mother is also from the kingdom of Candravatī.

227. *Ekaliṅga Māhātmyam* 19.35–68 (Premlata Sharma, *Ekaliṅgamāhātmyam (Ekliṅg Mandir kā Sthalapurāṇ evaṃ Mewāḍ ke Rāj-Vaṃś kā Itihās* [Delhi: Motilal Banarsidass, 1976], pp. 85–88). This source does not provide the important account of spitting, which is given only in Tod (*Annals and Antiquities*, vol. 1,pp. 264–65), who also indicates that the initiatory thread with which Hārīta Rāśi invested Bāppā Rāwal was called *janeo*, which is a specifically Nāth Siddha term.

228. Gaurishankar H. Ojha, "A Gold Coin of Bāppā Rāwal," *Journal of the Asiatic Society of Bengal*, new series no. 6, vol. 23, Numismatic Supplement no. 40 (1926–27), pp. 14–19.

229. On Hārīta Rāśi's name, see Sircar, *Guhila*, p. 25. Rāśi was also a common suffix to names of Kālamukhas, an early sectarian evolute of the Pāśupatas: A. S. Altekar, "The Rāshtrakūṭas," in G. Yazdani, ed., *The Early History of the Deccan*, 2 vols. (London: Oxford University Press, 1960–61), vol. 2, pp. 705, 707. According to Singh's 19th c. *Riporṭ* (vol. 2, p. 241), the forerunners of the Kānphaṭa Jogis in Rajasthan were called "Rāśī."

230. Briggs, *Gorakhnāth*, p. 247; and Henri Stern, "Le temple d'Ekliṅgjī et le royaume de Mewar (Rajasthan) (rapport au divin, royauté et territoire: sources d'une maîtrise)," in *L'Espace du Temple* [*Puruṣārtha* 10] (1986), p. 30 n. 19.

231. Dvivedi, *Nāth Sampradāy*, pp. 174–75.

232. Briggs, *Gorakhnāth*, p. 66; idem., *The Chamārs* (Oxford: Oxford University Press, 1920), p. 76; Rose, *Glossary*, vol. 2, pp. 407–8; *NSC*, pp. 191–92; Dvivedi, *Nāth Sampradāy*, p. 179. The Pāgalpanthis may be connected, through the persons of Caurañgināth-Pūraṇ Bhagat and Rasālu, with an 11th c. king named Gaj, whose

capital, originally called Gajapurī, had its name changed to Rāwalpiṇḍi (the "Rāwal's body"?): ibid., p. 178. There is also an Indian *jāti* called Rāwal, which probably descends from these western Yogis: Briggs, *Gorakhnāth*, pp. 49, 53, 54.

233. *Gorakh Bānī*, Pad 31. Cf. Briggs, *Gorakhnāth*, p. 66; Dvivedi, *Nāth Sampradāy*, p. 165; and *NSC*, p. 191–92, 226. There is a Nāgnāth temple located at Dwarhat, north of Ranikhet, in the Almora district of western Uttar Pradesh: Kanti Prasad Nautiyal, *The Archaeology of Kumaon* (Varanasi: Chowkhambha, 1969), p. 219.

234. *NSC*, pp. 191, 224; idem., ed. "*Gorakh*" *Viśeṣāṅk*, p. 370; Rose, *Glossary*, vol. 2, p. 396; and Tucci, "Animadversiones Indicae," p. 137. See below, chap. 5, nn. 15–16.

235. On Jvālamukhī-Bāḍava, the "seven-tongued flame," in the *Mahābhārata* (3.80.106), see Surinder Mohan Bhardwaj, *Hindu Places of Pilgrimage in India* (Berkeley: University of California Press, 1973), pp. 44, 47–48. On the *bāḍava* of the subtle body, see below, chap. 8, sec. 2c.

236. The Nāth Siddhas associate the site with Gorakh and Nāgārjuna: Kathleen M. Erndl, *Victory to the Mother: The Hindu Goddess of Northwest India in Myth, Ritual, and Symbol* (New York: Oxford University Press, 1993), pp. 44–48.

237. On the role of the Nāgnāthis on the Hiṅglāj pilgrimage, see Devadatt Sastri, *Āgneyatīrtha Hiṅglāj* (Bombay: Lokaloka Prakashan, 1978) pp. 4, 6–8. The Rāwal "caste" traditionally worships Hiṅglāj Mātā, together with Śiva Mahāḍev, Bhairava, Gorakhnāth, and Macchandranāth: R. E. Enthoven, *The Tribes and Castes of Bombay*, 3 vols. (Bombay: Government Central Press, 1923), vol. 3, pp. 306–8. On the Muslim Jogis of the Sind who continue to go to Hiṅglāj on pilgrimage, see Mujtaba and Shah, "Taming," p. 83.

238. *Yogvāṇī* 2:3 (March 1977), pp. 44–46, cited in Pandey, *Gorakhnāth*, p. 64.

239. Tod, *Annals and Antiquities*, vol. 2, p. 1196.

240. I have summarized Tod's rendering of this account. The name of Tod's "Rita" may be related to the Rītabiknāth "Yogi caste" of the Central Provinces who, Briggs reports (*Gorakhnāth*, p. 50), prepare and sell soap-nut (an ingredient used in an alchemical experiment conducted in the 1940s: see below, chap. 11, sec. 1).

241. See below, chap. 10, nn. 19–21.

Chapter Five

1. Marcel Detienne, *L'invention de la mythologie* (Paris: Gallimard, 1981), pp. 131–43.

2. The majority of these solitary citations are culled from a list found in Sharma (*Āyurved*, pp. 489–94), who inventories alchemical titles together with their alleged authors, without any other descriptive material. He notes that he obtained this list from Siddhinandan Misra, author of *Āyurvedīya Rasaśāstra* and other works, and

suggests that other data are available in the *Rasaratnākara* (there are three distinct works by this title) and the *Rasakaumudī* (of which there are also three), as well as the *Pāradasaṁhitā* and other 20th c. works on *rasa śāstra*.

3. The names Ādinātha, Rudra, Viṣṇu, and Brahmā figure in the *Kulārṇava Tantra* (6.63b–64) list of the twelve deities of the *divyaugha*.

4. Personal communication from N. Sethu Raghunathan, Madurai, January 1985, referring to an appendix to the 14th c. *Śārṅgadhara Saṁhitā*. I am more inclined to attribute these lacunae to the fact that much of what south Indian historiography treats as historical fact (names of authors and texts, etc.) is in fact legend. So, for example, A. Shanmugavelan (*Siddhar Science*, p. 16) maintains that the Vedic sage Agastya (Agathiar) learned the Tamil language from the (Buddhist bodhisattva) Avalogithar in north India, before coming south to found the discipline of Sittar alchemy; the same Agastya would have taught medicine to the elder Vāgbhaṭṭa!

5. Sharma, *Āyurved*, p. 491; Ray, *History*, vol. 2, p. xcvi.

6. Rāvaṇa is mentioned by name in *RM:* Paris MSS no. 1222, fol. 27b, lines 9–10. In the *Rāmāyaṇa*, Candrasena (2) was the name of Rāvaṇa's father-in-law (i.e., the father of Rāvaṇa's wife Mandodarī), a king of Siṁhala-dvīpa (generally identified with Sri Lanka): Singh, *Nirguṇ Sāhity*, p. 63. A Sittar alchemical work names Rāvaṇa's son Indrajit as an alchemist: see above, chap. 3, n. 34. Another of Rāvaṇa's sons, Meghanāda, is named as a Nāth Siddha in a ca. 1400 A.D. Telugu text, the *Navanāthacaritra* of Gauraṇa: see above, chap. 4, n. 65.

7. *RM*, fol. 25a, lines 6–10. Cf. Sharma, *Āyurved*, pp. 185, 493.

8. *RM*, fols. 24b.1, 26b.9. Cf. Cordier, "Récentes découvertes," p. 347.

9. Roşu, "Yoga et alchimie," p. 376; idem, "Mantra," p. 252.

10. *RC* 15.35. Earlier than the Bhāskara who was Nāgārjuna's guru (see above, chap. 4, n. 181), another Bhāskara would have authored a commentary on the *Suśruta Saṁhitā*, entitled the *Suśruta Pañjikā*, in the 12th century: Sharma, *Yogaratnamālā*, pp. 9–11; and idem., *Āyurved*, p. 230, 310–11, 402–5. Somadeva also mentions Dineśvara (15.34), Daṇḍī, and the sage Brahmajyoti, who are mentioned nowhere else.

11. Sharma, *Āyurved*, pp. 489–94. Naravāhana is a title of Kubera, the Hindu god of wealth; Naravāhanadatta is a hero of Somadeva's *Kathāsaritsāgara* who becomes the emperor of the Vidyādharas: *Ocean*, vol. 8, pp. 21–132, and vol. 9, p. 119.

12. These works are the *Rasasiddhiśāstra* (no. 4313 in the Derge *Tanjur*) and the *Rasāyana Śāstroddhṛti*. See above, chap. 3, n. 121.

13. See above, chap. 4, n. 235.

14. The *Carpaṭ Nāth jī ke ślok* is found in Dvivedi, *Nāth Siddhoṃ*, p. 18. A fragment (5 folios, 72 verses) of a vernacular work entitled *Carpaṭ Rasāyan* is held by

the MSL (Hindi MSS no. 669). His lost *Svargavaidyakāpālika* is mentioned in the 13th c. *RRĀ* (1.1.17). A *Carpaṭi Siddhānta* is mentioned in Priyanaranjan Ray, *History*, p. 128. The Nāth Siddhas also attribute two other nonalchemical works—the *Carpaṭamañjarī* (of which a passage is quoted in Barthwal, *Yog-Pravāh*, p. 71) and the *Caturbhavābhivāsanakrama*—to Carpaṭi: *NSC*, p. 199. Three Buddhist works attributed to him—none of which are alchemical—are preserved in the *Tanjur*: Tucci, "Animadversiones Indicae," p. 137; Bagchi, *KJñN*, p. 28; Chattopadhyaya, ed., *Tāranātha's History*, pp. 153–54. On Carpaṭi and Vyāḍi, see Dowman, *Masters*, p. 382.

15. On the Buddhist Siddhācārya Carpaṭi's alchemical legend, see above, chap. 3, n. 121. A Telegu myth involving "Sarpaṭi" is found in the *Bhojarājīyamu* of Ananta: Roşu, "Alchemy and Sacred Geography," pp. 154–55. On the *Prāṇ Saṅgalī*, see *NSC*, p. 194.

16. According to Śaiva Siddhānta metaphysics, Śrīkaṇṭha is the seventh of the eight Vidyeśvaras, emanates or devolutes of Sadāśiva.

17. Sharma, *Āyurved*, p. 697. Chapter colophons to the *Ānandakanda* read: *iti śrī bhairavokte ānandakande*. Dvivedi (*Nāth Sampradāy*, p. 190) names Manthānabhairava as the author of the lost *Rasaratna*. A certain Ma[n]thana-siṁha, physician to the king of Malava, is the author of the ca. 14th c. *Rasanakṣatramālikā*: Ray, *History*, vol. 2, p. lx.

18. Sanderson, "Śaivism," pp. 671, 699. Manthāna (the "Churner") Bhairava, which is the name of a wild ascetic form of Śiva whose cult belongs to the old Vidyā Pīṭha, later replaces the thirteenth and culminating Kālī in the *krama* of Kaula tradition. The northern transmission also had the same tradition of four "Yuga Nāthas" as did Abhinavagupta. It, however, called these the *gurukrama*, the succession of teachers: *HTSL*, pp. 76–77.

19. For manuscripts of this work, see bibliography. This work is cast as a dialogue, in which the alchemical gnosis is revealed to the goddess Kākacaṇḍeśvarī by a form of Śiva who is variously called Īśvara, Sadāśiva, or Bhairava. Another work, entitled the *Kākacaṇḍīśvara Kalpatantra*, ed. Kailashpati Pandey, Kashi Sanskrit Granthamala, 73 (Benares: Chowhkambha Sanskrit Series Office, 1963) is also an alchemical work. This text, substantially shorter than the *Kākacaṇḍeśvarīmata*, may be identical to the *Mahārasāyanavidhi*, referred to by Shastri in his *Catalogue* (vol. 1, p. lviii).

20. *RU* 1.9, 46–58 (which summarizes the chapter contents of the *Mahodadhi*). The *Bhūtiprakaraṇa* (1.114b) states that the *Mahodadhi* (but not the *Rasarājamahodadhi*) is a work in twelve thousand verses, while the *Rasopaniṣat* is a work in six thousand verses. This work goes on (1.115–21) to list a number of divinely au-

thored (by Vīrabhadra, Śukra, Indra, Vināyaka, etc.) alchemical works mentioned in no other source.

21. Misra, *Āyurvedīya*, pp. 39–40; Sharma, *Āyurved*, p. 490. Two procedures, called the "Kāpālika method" and the "sequential Kāpāli method," are described in the *RA* (6.84; 14.85; 16.34, 43) and later works as techniques for the coloration or liquification of gemstones, mercury, and other minerals. A work entitled the *Svargavaidya-kāpālika*, attributed to Carpaṭi by Nityanātha, author of the *RRĀ*, is also a possible source for the name of the Rasa Siddha "Kāpālika." See above, n. 13.

22. Sharma, *Āyurved*, p. 482. Cf. Siddhinandan Misra's foreword to Tripathi's edition of the *RA* (*Rasārṇavam nāma Rasatantram*), p. 13.

23. *Iti īśvarasamvādaṃ rasavādaṃ sudurlabham/ rasārṇavaṃ mahāśāstram . . . mahāsiddhi yogānandena bhāṣitam:* ASL MSS 4256 (dated samvat 1732, i.e., A.D. 1675–76) and erroneously catalogued under the title *Rasarājaśaṅkara*, fol. 105a; ASL MSS 4273, fol. 109 (dated samvat 1684 i.e., A.D. 1627–28); and ASL MSS 4274, fol. 149.

24. Bhairavānanda Yogin is the purported author of the *Dhātukriyā* or *Dhātumañjarī*, a post–16th c. work: Satyaprakash, *Prācīn Bhārat*, p. 625. However, see below, n. 53.

25. iyaṃ hi poṭalī proktā siṅghaṇena mahībhṛtā . . . siṅghaṇasya vinirdiṣṭā bhairavānandayoginā lokanāthoktapoṭalyā upacārā iha smṛtāḥ.

26. See above, chap. 4, nn. 180, 191.

27. The mantras and iconography of this alchemical pair are described in *RA* 2.52–53, 62–72.

28. Like a number of alchemical works with *-kalpa* in their title, the *Rasakalpa* claims to be a portion of the *Rudrayāmala Tantra:* Ray, *History*, vol. 2, p. lvii–lviii. See below, nn. 153, 160.

29. *BhP* 1.111b–112b. See below, n. 202.

30. *BhP* 9.136b: *nāthagorakṣa samprokta.* See below, n. 203.

31. Svacchandabhairava is the deity of the *Svacchanda Bhairava* or *Svacchanda Tantra*, the principal Tantra of the *mantra pīṭha*. Like Manthānabhairava, Svacchandabhairava has an alchemical preparation named after him: the *RM* (fol. 6b.4) and *RPS* (8.132–33) describe a *svacchandabhairava rasa*. Elsewhere, one also finds mineral preparations called *ānandabhairava rasa*, *sannipātabhairava rasa*, and *tripurabhairava rasa*.

32. Letter from Alexis Sanderson dated 6 July 1992, citing *Svacchandatantra* 2.88c–94b, and who also notes that the thirty-two-syllable mantra of Rasabhairava (*RA* 2.68) is a variant of the thirty-two-syllable *aghora* mantra that is the *sakala* form of Svacchandabhairava: (*SvT* 1.41–43). See below, chap. 6, nn. 59, 62.

33. Sharma, *Āyurved*, p. 493.

34. This work is quoted extensively by Kṣemarāja (fl. A.D. 1000–50) in his commentary on chapter nineteen of the *Netra Tantra.*: Dyczkowski, *Canon*, p. 42. A palm-leaf manuscript of this work held in the NNA (MSS no. 3–392 [Śaivatantra 67]) is dated Nepal samvat 304 (= A.D. 1184). See Bagchi, *KJñN* (p. 2), and Gonda, *History* (p. 216), on Śrīkaṇṭha-guru as the great preceptor of the Pāśupatas.

35. Sharma, *Āyurved*, p. 492. Dvivedi (*Nāth Sampradāy*, p. 190) names Manthānabhairava as the author of this work. See below, nn. 170–73.

36. A single alchemical manuscript (no. 1.14.ii.19) entitled *Ghoḍā Colī* is held in the private collection of the Śrī Rāmacaraṇa Prāya Vidyāpīṭh in Jaipur; three one-folio manuscripts of the *Ghoḍācoli Vākya* (MSL MSS nos. 1481, 1482 [a], and 1483 [b]) are held in the Mahārāja Mān Singh Library in Jodhpur. Ghoḍā Colī is listed as a Rasa Siddha in the *ĀK* and as a Mahāsiddha in the *HYP.*

37. Barthwal, *Yog Pravāh*, pp. 68–69; Dvivedi, *Nāth Sampradāy*, p. 167.

38. Kardaswamy, *History*, p. 354. See above, chap. 3, n. 54.

39. See below, n. 235.

40. Pandey, *Gorakhnāth*, p. 118. Another work on tantric sorcery, the *Kāmaratna*, is alternatively attributed to Nityanātha Siddha, "son of Pārvatī," or to Śrīnātha, Siddhanātha (a name sometimes identified with Matsyendranāth), or Nāga Bhaṭṭa: *HTSL*, p. 122.

41. There is confusion over this attribution. The *Gorakṣa Siddhānta Saṃgraha* knows of two texts entitled *SSP*, of which one was authored by Gorakṣanātha and the other by Nityanātha. Nowotny (*Gorakṣaśataka*, pp. 23–24) indicates that Fitz-Edward Hall found a copy of the *SSP* attributed to Nityanātha, but notes that Rajendralal Mitra (*The Yogic Aphorisms of Patañjali* [Calcutta: n.p., 1883, appendix, "A Descriptive List of Works Extant on the Yoga System of Philosophy," S.S. 1181) disagrees. Kaviraj (*Bhāratīy*, vol. 2, p. 275 n. 1) agrees with Hall; while Briggs (*Gorakhnāth*, p. 255), citing Mitra, calls the author Nityānanda Siddha. This last name corresponds to that of one of the Siddhas enumerated in chapter 49 of the *Śaṅkaravijaya* of Ānandagiri, which constitutes a Siddha charter of sorts. On this, see David Gordon White, "The Nath Siddhas," forthcoming in Constantina Rhodes-Bailly, Douglas Renfrew Brooks, William K. Mahony, and Paul Muller-Ortega, eds., *Siddha Yoga: Continuity and Freedom in a Contemporary Spiritual Tradition*, vol. 2 (nn. 29–32).

42. *Ācārya Yaśodhara kṛta Rasaprakāśasudhākara*, with a Hindi translation by Siddhinandan Misra, Jaikrishnadas Ayurveda Series, no. 54 (Benares: Chaukhambha Orientalia, 1984).

43. Edited, together with a 12th c. work, the *Lohasarvasvam* of Sureśvara, by Yadavji Trikamji Acarya (Bombay: Nirnay Sagar Press, 1925).

44. Discussion in Misra, *Āyurvedīya*, p. 39.

45. The latter of these two works is ASL MSS no. 4267. On these texts and the dating of their author to the reign of Bukka I of Vijayanagara, see Meulenbeld, *History* (draft of 10 May 1994), pp. 799–800, 943.

46. ASL MSS no. 4260. For a historical discussion, see Misra, *Āyurvedīya*, p. 42.

47. ASL MSS no. 4222. For a historical discussion, see Sharma, *Āyurved*, p. 409.

48. Ed. Jivaram Kalidas (Bombay: Venkatesvara Steam Press, 1967).

49. Ed. Manirama Sastri (Bikaner: Maniramasarma, 1934).

50. Ed. with notes by Yadavji Trikamji Acarya and Hindi commentary by Indradeo Tripathi, Chaukhamba Ayurveda Granthamala, 10 (Benares: Chaukhamba Amarabharati Prakashan, 1984). For a discussion, see Sharma, *Āyurved*, pp. 336, 484.

51. ASL MSS no. 4348.

52. ASL MSS no. 4258.

53. A portion of the *Dhātukriyā* is reproduced in Priyanaranjan Ray, *History*, pp. 414–42: it appears to be the same text as the *Dhātukalpa*, attributed to Nāgārjuna in manuscript colophons, as are the *Pāradakalpa* and *Gandhakakalpa:* see bibliography and Ray, *History*, vol. 2, pp. lvii–lviii.

54. Sharma, *Āyurved*, p. 485.

55. ASL MSS no. 4280. On the dating of this text, see Meulenbeld, *History* (draft of 10 May 1994), p. 805.

56. Tantric sorcery is the subject of three classes of tantras, according to the *Netra Tantra*'s classificatory scheme of the *śrota*s: these are the Vāma Tantras (on the gaining of *siddhi*s), Garuḍa Tantras (on poisons), and Bhūta Tantras (on possession and exorcism): *HTSL*, pp. 16–17. All such works are placed within the fourth, lower *śrota* of an alternative classificatory schema, found in the *Brahmayāmala Tantra:* Dyczkowski, *Canon*, pp. 39, 42.

57. NNA MSS nos. 3–392 (dated A.D. 1184) and 5–4947 (reel nos. B25/32 and A149/2); Kaiser Library (Kathmandu) MSS no. 297 (reel no. C30/16).

58. ASL MSS no. 4184.

59. ASL MSS no. 3967.

60. The *KPT* has been edited and constitutes the last of the six works anthologized in the *Indrajālavidyāsaṃgraha*, ed. Bhattacarya, pp. 264–390. The *Yogaratnamālā*, a much shorter work, has been edited with an excellent historical introduction by Priyavrata Sharma. Sharma notes parallel verses on p. 13 of his introduction.

61. The *Dattātreya Tantra* has been published as an independent work by Rajesh Dikshit (Delhi: Dehati Pustak Bhandar, n.d.). It is also included in Bhattacarya's

edition of the *Indrajālavidyāsaṃgraha* (pp. 132–79). Compare 1.5a of this work (*uḍḍīśe merutantre ca kālacaṇḍeśvare* tathā) with *RRĀ* 5.1.7 and *KPT* 1.9ab (*uḍḍīśe* vātule tantre ucchiṣṭe siddhiśāvare kiṅkiṇī *merutantre ca kālacaṇḍeśvare* mate).

62. The *Mātṛkabheda Tantra* has been edited by Chintamani Bhattacharya, Calcutta Sanskrit Series, 7 (Calcutta: Metropolitan, 1933, 1958); and translated by Michael Magee [Loknath Maharaj] (Delhi: Indological Book House, 1989).

63. See above, chap. 4, n. 191.

64. Peter Peterson, ed., *The Paddhati of Śārṅgadhara, A Sanskrit Anthology* (Bombay: Central Book Depot, 1888), pp. 659–703. For a historical discussion, see Sharma, *Āyurved*, pp. 197–98; and K. R. Srikanta Murthy's introduction to his edition and English translation of the *Śārṅgadhara Saṁhitā*, which states (p. v) that the alchemical portions of the *Paddhati* were taken from a lost text entitled *Yogarasāyana*.

65. Kaviraj, *Bhāratīy*, vol. 2, p. 292, note 1. On the role of the *Yogaśikhopaniṣad* in later 108 Upaniṣad traditions, see Christian Bouy, *Les Nātha-Yogin et les Upaniṣads*, Publications de l'Institut de Civilisation Indienne, no. 62 (Paris: De Boccard, 1994), pp. 112–13.

66. *Mānasollāsa* 1.2.10–51.

67. Pitambaradatta Barthwal, *Gorakh Bānī* (Allahabad: Hindi Sahitya Sammelan, 1942), who offers tentative Hindi translations. Another edition of this collection, which includes a long and sometimes useful Hindi commentary, was published by the Gorakhnāth Mandir in Gorakhpur in 1979: Ramlal Srivastav, ed., "*Gorakh Bānī*" *Viśeṣāṅk* (*Yog Vāṇī*, special issue no. 1 for 1979) (Gorakhpur: Gorakhnath Mandir, 1979).

68. Dvivedi, *Nath Siddhoṃ*, introduction, pp. 1–2, on the contents of *Gorakh Bānī* (cf. Barthwal's introduction to *Gorakh Bānī*, pp. 11–20), and pp. 2–4, 16, 21, on the contents and dating of the works of the other Nāth Siddhas. Cf. Vaudeville, *Kabir Granthavali* (*Doha*), p. v; Ronald Stuart McGregor, *Hindi Literature from Its Beginnings to the Nineteenth Century* (Wiesbaden: Otto Harrassowitz, 1984), pp. 21–22, 132; and Dasgupta, *Obscure*, p. 373.

69. Dvivedi, *Nāth Siddhoṃ*, p. 56 ("Bhartharī jī kī sabadī," v. 6).

70. Reproduced in Mallik, *SSP*, pp. 82–87. See above, chap. 3, nn. 3, 121.

71. One of the two is edited in Dvivedi, *Nāth Siddhoṃ*, p. 39.

72. Chap. 13 of the *Dattātreya Tantra* is entitled "Rasāyanam" and contains four magical recipes that make use of mercury and sulfur, as well as other mineral, herbal, and animal (herpal) ingredients. Other chapters contain descriptions of "magical" uses of minerals, as for example chap. 8, which explains how to use *kajjalī* on one's eyes to bring a woman under one's power (*strīvaśīkaraṇa* is, moreover, the title of this chapter). See Sharma, *Āyurved*, p. 492. The manuscript of a work en-

titled the *Datta Patala* was in the possession of an old Delhi *vaidya* named Sriram Sharma Shastri. When I met him, in January of 1985, he was attempting to produce alchemical gold by following its instructions.

73. The *Rasadarpaṇa* is cited by the 16th c. *Ṭoḍarānanda:* Sharma, *Āyurved,* pp. 486, 491, 493.

74. The colophon to the NNA MSS no. 1–1473 of the *KM* states that it was *ādyāvatāre;* the same is said of a list of sixty-four *yoginīs* contained in the *Kubjikā-pūjā-paddhati* (fol. 52): Shastri, *Catalogue,* vol. 1, p. 58; and vol. 2, p. 80. Ādinātha is the author of the *Mahākāla Saṁhitā:* Pandey, *Gorakhnāth,* p. 112. The Tārā Khaṇḍa of the *Śaktisaṅgama Tantra* is cast as a dialogue between the goddess Śakti and (Śiva-)Ādinātha: Dvivedi, *Nāth Sampradāy,* p. 4 n. 1.

75. Ādinātha is invoked as a divinity in the opening (1.1) of the *SSP* of Gorakhnāth, and is later (5.5–12) quoted at some length in the same work.

76. Five of these are edited together by Bagchi, in his *Kaulajñānanirṇaya.* They are: *Kaulajñānanirṇaya;* two distinct works entitled *Kulavīra Tantra* (A and B); *Kulānanda Tantra;* and *Jñānakārikā.* A short vernacular work, entitled *Matsyendranāthjī kā pad,* has been edited in Dvivedi, *Nāth Siddhoṃ,* pp. 64–65; and in Mallik, *SSP,* p. 76. The *Yoga Viṣaya,* a Sanskrit work on *haṭha yoga* attributed to Matsyendra, is edited ibid., pp. 45–47. A relatively early work, also attributed to Matsyendra, is the *Candrāvalocana:* it is quoted in the *HYP* (4.16, 54): Bouy, *Nātha-Yogin,* p. 82 n. 345. A very late hathayogic source, entitled the *Matsyendra Saṁhitā,* is found in manuscript form in the MSL and the NNA. Cf. Pandeya, introduction to *Gorakṣa Saṁhitā,* vol. 1, p. *gha.*

77. *RA* 1.4b: kulakaulamahākaulasiddhakaulādi śāsanam (here I emend *nāśanam* of Ray's and Tripathi's editions to *śāsanam,* which is the reading found in the three ASL manuscripts of the work, and which makes more sense). *RA* 18.228a: tasminekārṇave ghore naṣṭasthāvarajaṅgame. Cf. Matsyendra's *Kulānanda Tantra* (in Bagchi, *KJñN,* p. 107, whose opening verse is repeated nearly verbatim by the *KCM* [1.1]).

78. *KJñN* 16.47–49. Cf. Bagchi's interpretation, on p. 35.

79. *Mṛgendrāgama,* Caryāpāda 1.36b–37, 40b–41a (Hélène Brunner-Lachaux, *Mṛgendrāgama, Section des Rites et Section du Comportement avec la Vṛtti de Bhaṭṭanārāyaṇakaṇṭha,* Publications de l'Institut Française d'Indologie, no. 69 [Pondicherry, Institut Français d'Indologie, 1985], pp. 364, 366). In a list of auspicious dream visions, the same source (Kriyāpāda 8.14a–15b) names "seeing white mica . . . the Siddhas . . . [and] coming upon the *siddha*-fluid." This last element is glossed by the commentator as *rasāyana.* See above, chap. 3, n. 133.

80. Tarapada Mukherji, ed., *Gopicandra Nāṭaka* (Calcutta: University of Calcutta, 1970), p. xliv; Bagchi, *KJñN,* p. 1. A ca. 14th c. palm-leaf manuscript in the

Nepal National Archives, entitled *Śrīkāmākhyāguhyasiddhi* purports, in its colophons, to be have been "brought down by Śrī Matsyendra-pāda": ibid., p. 60. This work is cited in the late–13th c. *Kubjikānityāhnikatilaka:* Dyczkowski, *Canon*, pp. 163–64 (n. 23 to part 2). However, as Tucci notes ("Animadversiones," p. 134), Matsyendra may have been an initiatory name given to a number of persons.

81. See chapter colophons to the *KJñN* and *KM*, discussed below, chap. 8, sec. 2b. Like Srisailam, which has been identified with at least three peaks, Candragiri is also a ubiquitous mountain. An inscription from Karnataka locates a Candrapurī in the western ocean (Saletore, "Kanaphaṭa Jogis," pp. 20–21). Candragiri is also the name of a peak situated at the western end of the Kathmandu Valley. Candradvīpa, Candragiri, Candrapurī, and the "western country" (*paścima diśi:* Dvivedi, *Nāth Siddhoṃ*, p. 9 = v. 105) are also mystic locations within the subtle body.

82. Cited in *NSC*, pp. 49, 217; Dvivedi, *Nāth Sampradāy;* and Pandey, *Gorakṣa Saṁhitā*, vol. 1, p. *cha* (who also notes that the *Gorakṣasahasranāmastotra* gives the southern toponym of Vāḍava as Gorakh's birthplace). On this, see also Bagchi, *KJñN*, p. 64.

83. Such early Buddhist works as the *Guhyasamāja Tantra* (with the *Sekoddeśa* and other commentaries) know of six-limbed (*ṣaḍaṅga*) *haṭha yoga*, but only speak of the four specifically Buddhist *cakra*s. In Buddhist systems, the Upanisadic *tarka* ("analytical reasoning") is replaced with *anusmṛti*, "recollection," and in Hindu *haṭha yoga* with the *āsana*s ("postures"). One commentary on chapter 18 of the *Guhyasamāja Tantra*, entitled "Ṣaḍaṅga Yoga," is the work of Nāgārjuna. It is extant in Tibetan: Wayman, *Yoga*, pp. 163–73. The Mahāsiddha authors of the pre–12th c. *Caryāpada*s were also well acquainted with a number of hathayogic techniques, but held to the older four-cakra system. See also *Majjhimanikāya* 12 and 36, as evidence that the Buddha himself was a teacher of *haṭha yoga:* Nowotny, *Gorakṣaśataka*, p. 14. A number of hathayogic techniques are vaguely described in Patañjali's *Yoga Sūtra*s 2.46–50: Vyāsa, in his 5th c. commentary to the *Yoga Sūtra*s, lists a number of postures but gives no account of the *cakra*s. The practice of diaphragmatic retention is alluded to, by the term of *stambha-vṛtti*, in YS 2.50. The ca. 1st c. A.D. *Mṛcchakaṭikā* mentions one yogic posture (1.1: *palaṅkāsana*); none are mentioned in the *Mahābhārata* (E. W. Hopkins, "Yoga Techniques in the Epics," *JAOS* 22 [1901], pp. 345–48, 369, 373). The *MBh* (5.42.33) compares the yogin who cultivates *vīrya* with "a dog that eats its own vomit."

84. nityaṃ nyastaṣaḍaṅgacakranihitaṃ hṛtpadmamadhyoditam/ . . . nāḍīnāmudayakrameṇa jagataḥ pañcāmṛtākarṣaṇādaprāptotpatana: *Mālatī-Mādhava* 5.2. On the importance of this passage for the history of *haṭha yoga*, see Dvivedi, *Nāth Sampradāy*, pp. 82, 84; and Sanderson ("Purity and Power," p. 213 nn. 89, 108), who

notes that this method of extraction is described in minute detail in chapter 3 of the *Jayadrathayāmala* (NNA MSS no. 5–1975, Śaiva tantra 429), fol. 184, v. 5–8. It is unlikely, however, that this source is as old as Bhavabhūti. The process is also described in Matsyendranāth's *KJñN* 11.18. The *RA* (18.217–19) appears to describe a similar process, but on an external, alchemical register. See above, chap. 3, n. 133.

85. Sanderson, "Śaivism," pp. 687–88.

86. This list is also found, with variations, in *KJñN* 5.25b. In 3.6–10, Matsyendra describes a set of nine *cakra*s. These correspond precisely to standard enumerations in later sources.

87. *KJñN* 3.2–3 is adapted, nearly verbatim, by the *HYP* (4.14): Bagchi, *KJñN*, p. vii. On *matsyodara*, see below, chap. 8, sec. 2a.

88. The earliest extant manuscripts of both works are held in the Nepal National Archives. The *KM* (NNA MSS no. 1–285) is dated A.D. 1160; the *KJñN* (NNA MSS no. 2–362 [H]) is dated to the mid–11th c. A.D. (Bagchi, *KJñN*, p. 5).

89. Abhinavagupta (apparently paraphrasing *KJñN* 22.8–9) speaks of his reverence for Macchandanāth in *TĀ* 1.7: "May Macchandanātha be propitious to me, he who tore apart the glowing net made of knots and holes, a batch of bits and pieces unfolding and spreading everywhere" (tr. in Silburn, *Kuṇḍalinī*, p. 121). Cf. *TĀ* 29.32, and Jayaratha's commentary to *TĀ* 1.18; Sanderson, "Śaivism," p. 681; and Goudriaan, *HTSL*, p. 18.

90. He mentions the *KM* in his *Parātriṁśikāvivaraṇa*, p. 184 (cited in Dyczkowski, *Canon*, p. 172, n. 79). See also ibid., pp. 48–49, 65, 84, and Schoterman, *Ṣaṭsāhasrasaṁhitā*, p. 6.

91. The *TĀ* 7.40 cites a work entitled *Yoginīkaula*, on the subject of the distribution of the *śaktitattva* into *pada*s, *mantra*s, *akṣara*s, and *cakra*s.

92. Dyczkowski, *Canon*, p. 65, n. 65. The *KM* also mentions the Siddha Kaula (ibid., p. 171, n. 70) and the Siddha-mārga (London, Wellcome MSS g501, fol. 35.7–8).

93. Sanderson, "Śaivism," p. 681; Dyczkowski, *Canon*, p. 163 (n. 23 to p. 62). The other three are Khaga (Bird), Tortoise (Kūrma), and Meṣa (Ram). Abhinavagupta never employs the term *āmnāya* in his writings; he seems however to assume it: ibid., p. 66.

94. Dyczkowski, *Canon*, p. 81.

95. The Western Transmission subscribed to this same mythic doctrine. On this, the sons of Macchanda (or Mīnanātha), and the *ovalli* system, see Dyczkowski, *Canon*, pp. 62, 70, 163–64, 166, and 191 (nn. 23, 32, and 233 to part 2); and Sanderson, "Śaivism," p. 681.

96. For historical discussions, see Sanderson, "Śaivism," p. 679; idem., "Trika Śaivism," p. 15; Dyczkowski, *Canon*, pp. 65, 80; and *HTSL*, p. 50. See above, chap. 3, n. 132.

97. Sanderson, "Purity and Power," p. 214 n. 110, citing *TĀ* 13.301, 320–21b; and *Mahāmnāyaprakāśa* 1.30.

98. Sanderson, "Trika Śaivism," in *Encyclopedia of Religion*, vol. 13, p. 15. In spite of these reforms, and the broadening of the Trika base in 10th–11th c. Kashmir, it was the dualist orthodox Śaiva Siddhānta doctrines and the cult of Svacchanda-bhairava that remained predominant in the valley: idem., "Kashmir Śaivism," vol. 13, p. 16.

99. On the collection and use of combined sexual emissions (called *kuṇḍagolaka*, etc.) in prereform ritual and worship, see *KJñN* 11.18, 32; 18.7–8; *HTSL*, p. 44; Dyczkowski, *Canon*, p. 80; and Schoterman, *Yonitantra*, pp. 28–29, 32.

100. See *KJñN* 18.6–23 on ritualized sex; 8.31–32 for an explicit discussion of the use of eight types of *vidyā* [goddesses]; 8.30–45 on means to gaining access to the sixty-four *yoginī*s; and 11.1–43 on the offering and consumption of prohibited foods and sexual fluids. See also 14.56 and 17.42. Cf. Sanderson, "Trika Śaivism," *Encyclopedia of Religion*, vol. 13, p. 15.

101. Dyczkowski, *Canon*, pp. 60, 62, 82.

102. Sanderson, "Śaivism," pp. 663, 679–80; idem, "Purity and Power," pp. 191–92; idem, "Trika Śaivism," p. 15. On historical clues for the geographical and temporal parameters of these changes, see also Dyczkowski, *Canon*, pp. 34–35, 48, 55, 86, 92, 189 n. 193. On the Vidyāpīṭha as the most important subdivision within the tantric classificatory system of the four *pīṭha*s, ibid., pp. 49–52.

103. *TĀ* 15.160–70b with Jayaratha's commentary, cited in Sanderson, "Maṇḍala," p. 176, n. 29.

104. *TĀ* 29.127–32. This practice is prescribed for those whose goal is enjoyment (*bubhukṣu*s) as a means to attaining *siddhi;* and for those who have yet to attain self-realization (*aprāptavibodha*). See below, chap. 10, sec. 2.

105. Dyczkowski, *Canon*, p. 80.

106. Jayaratha's commentary to *TĀ* 29.129a. I am grateful to Alexis Sanderson for bringing this reference to my attention.

107. *TĀ* 3.261–64 and 5.151. Cf. idem., *Parātrīśikā-laghuvṛtti* 11–16, with commentary, in Muller-Ortega, *Triadic Heart*, pp. 181, 189, and 195 (English translations) and 283, 286, and 288 (original Sanskrit).

108. *TĀ* 5.58a, translated by Muller-Ortega, *Triadic Heart*, p. 123.

109. On this, see Silburn, *Kuṇḍalinī*, p. 174; and Dyczkowski, *Canon*, p. 82.

110. See below, chap. 7, n. 67.

111. See above, chap. 3, n. 129.

112. Important works include Harvey Alper, ed., *Mantra* (Albany: SUNY Press, 1989) (much of his volume is devoted to the methodological principle of treating tantric *mantra* as a "language game"); Brooks, *Secret* (mainly on the Śrīvidyā tradition); Muller-Ortega, *Triadic Heart;* and Padoux, *Vāc.* On the parallel Vedic intellectualization of concrete sacrifice, see Frits Staal, *Rules Without Meaning* (New York: Peter Lang, 1989), and Jan Heesterman, *The Broken World of Sacrifice* (Chicago: University of Chicago Press, 1993).

113. Gopinath Kaviraj, *Tāntrik Sādhanā aur Siddhānt* (Patna: Bihar Rashtrabhasa Parisad, 1979), p. 392. *Bindu-sādhana* refers to practices involving "drops" (*bindu*) of sexual fluids.

114. This is an abridgement of the *Śrīmatottara Tantra,* which is also closely related to the *Manthānabhairava Tantra,* a work that also refers to itself as Kādi text: see *HTSL,* p. 55, and below, nn. 202, 209.

115. Elsewhere, Jālandhara has no alchemical works to his name, either in Sanskrit or vernacular languages. His anthologized poems are on the subject of *haṭha yoga.* Like a number of other Nāth Siddhas, Jālandhara appears to have been too busy *living* his yoga to have written about it. The rich body of legend surrounding him contains a wide array of yogic and alchemical motifs. Jālandhara has seven Buddhist works attributed to him in the *Tanjur:* Chattopadhyaya, *Tāranātha's History,* p. 417. He is also the author of a Sanskrit work, definitely from within the Nāth Siddha fold, the *Siddhānta Vākya:* Dvivedi, *Nāth Sampradāy,* pp. 6–7. His vernacular poem, "Jalandhrī Pāv jī kī sabadī," is edited in idem., *Nāth Siddhoṃ,* pp. 30–31, and Mallik, *SSP,* pp. 90–91.

116. This poem is translated and discussed below, chap. 9, sec. 8. Gorakh disparages alchemy and other tantric practices that afford *siddhi*s inferior to those procured through yogic practice in *Yogabīja* 174.

117. Rao and Reddy, "A Note on Gorakṣanātha and His Work *Yogadīpikā,*" p. 37. See above, chap. 4, n. 172.

118. The *Gorakh Upaniṣad* is edited in Mallik, *SSP,* pp. 72–75.

119. This work is often referred to simply as the *Haṭha Yoga.* The critical edition was established by Nowotny (*Das Gorakṣaśataka*) in 1976.

120. For a longer listing of these works, see Dvivedi, *Nāth Sampradāy,* pp. 98–99; Briggs, *Gorakhnāth,* pp. 252–53; Pandey, *Gorakhnāth,* pp. 82–83; Nowotny, *Gorakṣaśataka,* pp. 23–24; and Gopinath Kaviraj's introduction to his edition of the *Gorakṣa Siddhānta Saṃgraha* (Benares: Vidya Vilas Press, 1925), pp. *ṭa–ṇa.*

121. *Śārṅgadhara Paddhati* 4372: dvidhā haṭhaḥ syādekastu gorakṣādisusādhitaḥ/ anyo mṛkaṇḍaputrādyaiḥ sādhitoniśamudyataiḥ. Dattātreya's exposition of yoga is found in *Mārkaṇḍeya Purāṇa* 39.1–65; 40.1–41; and 41.1–26. Cf. Mallik, SSP, p. 75.

122. Pandey, *Gorakhnāth*, pp. 89–90. Elsewhere, a manuscript (MSL MSS no. 1557) of the *Dattagorakṣasaṃvāda* claims to be a portion of the *Tantra Mahārṇava*.

123. The sole extant recension of the hathayogic *Gorakṣa Saṁhitā* appears to be a ca. 16th c. manuscript, written in Bengali characters, held in the Nepal National Archives, which was translated into Bengali by Prasannakumara Kaviratna in 1897. For a discussion of the relationships between the these works, see Tucci, "Animadversiones Indicae," pp. 134–36; Bagchi, *KJñN*, p. 64; and Pandey, introduction to *Gorakṣa Saṁhitā*, vol. 1, p. *ṭa*. Chapter 1 of the *Gorakṣa Saṁhitā* parallels chapters 1–3 of the *SSP;* chapter 3 parallels *SSP* 4; and chapter 5 parallels chapter 6 of the *SSP*, which describes the *avadhūta*. Cf. *Gorakṣa Paddhati* 1.4.

124. Meulenbeld (*History*, draft of 10 May 1994, p. 1011 n. 14010) attempts to make sense of this statement by dividing the work as follows: (1) *Kādi-prakaraṇa* (the Śākta work); (2) *Bhūtiprakaraṇa* (the alchemical work); (3) *Yoga-khaṇḍa;* (4) *Nāḍījñānadīpikā;* and (5) the *Avadhūtagītā*.

125. On alchemy, see Bhattacharya, *Sādhanamālā*, vol. 2, p. xxi. On *haṭha yoga*, see *HT*, p. 165. This source (p. 9) nevertheless includes alchemy and *haṭha yoga* in its list of the eighteen "constituents of tantra." The alchemical literature is discussed in the chapter entitled "Tantras of Magic" in the survey of tantric literature produced by these same scholars: *HTSL*, pp. 117–26.

126. Brooks, *Secret*, pp. 52–53.

127. *RRS* 13.61; 16.7, 31.

128. The *Rasārṇava* calls itself a "great Tantra" in 1.57. The full title of the *Rasahṛdaya* is *Rasahṛdaya Tantra;* the *BhP* calls itself the *Bhūti Tantra* (2.101), etc.

129. The alchemical *BhP*, for example, calls itself the *Hādibheda* of the *Gorakṣa Saṁhitā*.

130. A *yantra* is an apparatus which controls or subdues (*yam*) the volatile elements combined in it (another use of *yantra*, as a synonym for *maṇḍala*, diagram, has the same meanings, since by using it as a meditational support, the yogin is able to concentrate and bring his mind under control).

131. *HT*, pp. 78–89.

132. Brooks, *Secret*, p. 134; Gupta,"Pañcarātra," in Alper, *Mantra*, p. 235.

133. Sanderson, "Purity and Power," p. 192.

134. This description therefore excludes the important orthodox Śaiva Siddhānta, which was dualist, nonvibratory, nonbipolar, etc.

135. In opposition to Vedānta, which sees the phenomenal world as *māyā*, illusion that veils ultimate reality: Navjivan Rastogi, *The Krama Tantrism of Kashmir* (Delhi: Motilal Banarsidass, 1979), vol. 1, p. 39, citing the *Mahārthamañjarī* of Maheśvarānanda, p. 14.

136. On the anthropic principle, see John D. Barrow and Frank J. Tipler, *The Anthropic Cosmological Principle* (New York: Oxford University Press, 1986). Cf. S. K. Ramachandra Rao, *Śrī-Cakra* (Delhi: Sri Satguru Publications, 1989), p. 9: "The world is in reality a deliberate mechanism for the objectification of consciousness (*prameya*) while the individual is an equally deliberate mechanism for the subjectification of consciousness (*pramāta*)."

137. Summarized in Padoux, *Vāc*, pp. 51, 79–83.

138. In Trika Kaulism, an optical model is used to express the relationship between Śiva and Śakti: Śiva is pure illuminating consciousness, *prakāśa;* and the goddess reflective consciousness, *vimarśa:* Abhinavagupta, *Parātriṁśikā-vivāraṇa*, p. 90, quoted in Muller-Ortega, *Triadic Heart*, p. 98. See also ibid., pp. 95–99.

139. Brooks, *Secret*, pp. 66, 88–89.

140. Brooks, *Secret*, p. 63; Rao, *Śrī-Cakra*, pp. 7–12.

141. Brooks, *Secret*, pp. 49, 124; Rastogi, *Krama*, p. 38.

142. Another instance of the fundamental cleavage between these two approaches is to be found in the former's system of nine "alchemical" (*rasa-sampradāya* or *kāpālika*) *saṃskāra*s, as opposed to the latter's eighteen "Ayurvedic" (*bhagvān śaṅkara* or *saumya*) *saṃskāra*s: Misra, *Āyurvedīya*, pp. 214–15.

143. This work has been edited twice in this century, by Yadavji Trikamji Acarya (Lahore: Motilal Banarsidass, 1927), and by Daultarama Rasasastri, with an introduction, commentary, and Hindi translation (Benares: Chaukhambha Orientalia, 1989).

144. *RM* fol. 29b.10–30a.1; 30b.1. See below, n. 265.

145. Vāgbhaṭṭa II, author of the *Rasaratnasamucchaya* (1.33), copies this verse verbatim, as he does much of Govinda's first chapter.

146. *RHT* 1.15–32. He mentions *jīvanmukti* in 1.33.

147. The eighteen *saṃskāra*s are discussed in detail in chap. 9, sec. 2.

148. The four elixir pills are: *amarasundarī*, *mṛtasañjīvanī*, *vajriṇī*, and *khecarī*. These and the results they produce are outlined in 19.61–76.

149. *RHT* 19.78–80 of Misra's edition. These concluding verses are not found in the NNA (MSS no. 3-118/ reel no. B165/1) manuscript of this work. On the basis of the word *bhikṣu* in 19.80, Ray (*History* [1956], p. 149) concluded this was a Buddhist work.

150. Sharma, *Āyurved*, p. 480; Misra, *Āyurvedīya*, pp. 34–35; and Romila Thapar, "The Image of the Barbarian in Early India" *Comparative Studies in Society and History* 13:3 (July 1971), p. 424.

151. On the genealogies and history of the Chedi or Kalachuri kings, see Alexander Cunningham, *A Report of a Tour in the Central Provinces in 1873–74 and 1874–*

75, Archaeological Survey of India, vol. 9 (reprint ed. Benares: Indological Book House, 1966), pp. 77–113; R. D. Banerji, *The Haihayas of Tripuri and Their Monuments*, Memoirs of the Archaeological Survey of India, no. 23 (Calcutta: Government of India Central Publication Branch, 1931), pp. 1–116; and Babb, *Divine Hierarchy*, pp. 3–6. Wink (*Al-Hind*, vol. 1, p. 287) surmises that they were driven out of Malava in the 7th–8th centuries by the Pratīhāras.

152. Wink, *Al-Hind*, vol. 1, pp. 258–59. Madana could not have been an important Kalachuri prince, however, since his name occurs nowhere in its royal inscriptions.

153. A later work, entitled the *Rasārṇavakalpa* (*RAK*) claims to be a portion of the older *Rudrayāmala Tantra: HT*, p. 11. This work has been edited and translated into English by Mira Roy and B. V. Subbarayappa as *Rasarṇavakalpa* (*Manifold Powers of the Ocean of Rasa*), (New Delhi: Indian National Science Academy, 1976). *RAK* 78–207 is borrowed from *RA* 12.8–182; other portions of this text bear similarities to the *KCKT*; it has one verse in common with the *RM*: Meulenbeld, *History* (draft of 10 May 1994), p. 873, note 12450; and p. 875.

154. In its two printed editions, RA 3.23a reads "ḍāmarākhyā mahāmantra dhamanīṣu niyojayet." Certain manuscript versions (ASL MSS no. 4256, fol.12a.10) read ḍāmarākhyāṃ mahātantram. . . . There exists a work on tantric sorcery, entitled the *Uḍḍāmara Mahātantra*, which I have not been able to date. A work entitled *Ḍāmara Tantra* has been edited and translated by Ram Kumar Rai (Benares: Prachya Prakashan, 1988).

155. On the dating of the *Vimalaprabhā*, see above, chap. 3, n. 122.

156. Cf. the *KCM*, which singles out eight (of which six figure in the *RA* enumeration) of the eighteen *saṃskāra*s as *aṣṭakarma*, the "eight Works." See above, n. 142, and below, n. 185.

157. Partial lists of the *saṃskāra*s are found in *RA* 10.10 and 11.210–12. According to Siddhinandan Misra (*Āyurvedīya*, p. 214), a number of other alchemical works follow the *kāpālika* method for the purification of mercury. Other *kāpālika* methods are mentioned in *RA* 6.43, 84; 14.85; 16.34; etc. See below, chap. 6, n. 16; and above, n. 142.

158. Quite often, the sole difference between passages found in the two works is in word order. Compare *RHT* 2.3 and *RA* 10.41; *RHT* 12.4 and *RA* 8.36; *RHT* 17.3–5 and *RA* 17.78; and *RHT* 19.2, 9, 18a, 20 and *RA* 18.3, 8, 13a, 15ab.

159. For a discussion, see Misra, *Āyurvedīya*, pp. 19–20.

160. So too does the 12th c. *RAK*, which goes so far as to co-opt the *RA*'s title even as it claims to be a portion of the *Rudrayāmala Tantra*.

161. *RA* 1.19: mūrcchito harate vyādhiṃ mṛto jīvayati svayam/ baddhaḥ khecar-

atāṃ kuryāt raso vāyuśca bhairavi. Cf. *RM* 1.8: baddhaḥ khecaratāṃ padāṃnayed dharate vyādhisamūho mūrchitaḥ/ jaritabhavo janmabhavo vināśanaḥ kramito rañjitaḥ bhuktimuktidaḥ. *RA* 1.19 is copied verbatim by *HYP* 4.27. See below,chap. 9, nn. 54–55.

162. *RA:* 14.40. "The Siddha [who uses] 'diamond-bound' mercury is quite invincible to the gods and demons. He [becomes] the leader of the twenty-four Siddhas (*caturviṃśatisiddhānāṃ nāyaka*), a bestower of all the *siddhis*." The *RM*'s list of twenty-seven Rasa Siddhas, which occurs in its commentary (*ṭippaṇa*), may be borrowed from the *RRS:* see below, n. 265.

163. See above, chap. 3, n. 133 and n. 84 to this chapter.

164. A terse exposition of this theory and attendant practice is found in the *Jñānakārikā* (2.2b–4) attributed to Matsyendranāth (in Bagchi, *KJñN*), p. 116. See also the metaphysics of Gorakhnāth, as presented in Dvivedi, *Nāth Sampradāy*, pp. 102–13.

165. See below, chap. 8, sec. 4.

166. *RA* 18.221–27.

167. *RM* fol. 27b.9–10: pañcāmṛto mahāyogaḥ hyukto manthānabhairave vā rākṣasarāvaṇe vā punastatraiva bhāṣitam.

168. *RM* fol. 28a.3–8.

169. Roşu, *Liétard et Cordier*, introduction, p. c.

170. *RM* fol.7a.1–3 prescribes this *rasa* for ailments involving wind and bile. It is composed of mica, orpiment, copper, iron, *saurabharāja*, and mercury, as well as a number of botanicals. *Manthānabhairavarasa* is also described in the *RPS* (8.173–74) and the *RRS* (14.90–92), which uses more or less the same ingredients and prescribes it for the treatment of coughs. See above, n. 31.

171. Dyczkowski, *Canon*, pp. 97–98. Eagerly awaited is Mark Dyczkowski's critical edition and translation of this monumental work, now under preparation. The *RC* (6.1) cites the *Manthānabhairava Mahāgama* as the source for its discussion of the divine herbs (*divyauṣadhi*). See also above, n. 114.

172. Kubjikā is mentioned in *RA* 3.8, 31, referring to a *mudrā* and a *mantra.*

173. This entire passage opens, in the *RM* (fol. 26b.10), with the statement: "I will now tell . . . what was done by *Mārtaṇḍeya* [or *Mārkaṇḍeya*]." The former would refer either to a divine father of Yama (Mārtaṇḍa); the Vaiṣṇava sage to whom was revealed an eponymous Purāṇa; or to the *Rāja Mārtaṇḍa* of King Bhoja (the narrativization of this operation casts Bhoja as the alchemist's royal assistant in both Alberuni's and the Telugu author Ananta's versions: see above, chap. 3, n. 3). Evidence from the 12th–13th c. *RC* militates against an identification of Manthānabhairava with the Bhairava who revealed or authored the *RA*. This author evokes both a

Bhairavācārya (whom he seems to identify as the author of the *RA*), and Manthānabhairava: *RC* 1.28, 6.1, 12.25, 16.55, 16.72.

174. *RA* 11.198–205, 209, 214, 218; 12.104–9, 348–51; 15.131; 14.3–20; 18.165–69, 174–77, 194, 201–3, and 211–21. The *RM* copies or paraphrases the *RA* in each of the four chapters (with *ṭippaṇa*) contained in the two manuscripts I have consulted (Paris MSS no. 1222 and GAU MSS no. 862/34). The *RA* repeats itself in the following places: 18.165–70 = 18.201–3, 206–7, 218.

175. The *KCKT* (41.6) cites Nāgārjuna and a work entitled *Siddhayoga* (*KCKT* 8.7–15, referring either to Nāgārjuna's *Āścaryayogamālā—Yogaratnamālā*, or to Vṛnda's *Siddhiyoga*). It is likely a 13th c. work, from western India.

176. NNA MSS no. 5–3969 (reel no. A211/19). A partial edition (of selected portions of the first six chapters) of the *KCM* is found in Priyanaranjan Ray, *History*, pp. 345–50.

177. Passages that are nearly identical are *RA* 6.34–38 and *KCM* 6.21–25, 29–30 (numbering here is from Ray's partial edition, p. 350); *RA* 7.10 and *KCM* fol. 19b.4–5; *RA* 10.10–12 and *KCM* fol. 17b.2–3; *RA* 12.280, 293b–294 and *KCM* fol. 13b.3–5; *RA* 12.311, 313–14 and *KCM* fol. 14a.3–4 and 14b.2–3; and *RA* 18.94–95 and KCM fol. 5a.7–8. No manuscript of the *KCM* numbers its chapters or verses.

178. Sanderson, "Śaivism," pp. 682–85. An echo of these cults is found in the *KJñN* 23.2–9.

179. On the worship of Baṭukanātha, see *KCM* fol. 6a.5–6. The *RA* (2.119–21) prescribes the worship of Baṭukeśvara, in the context of a rite intended to pacify demons who might otherwise destroy one's Work. Mercury is referred to as *rasabhairava* in fol. 7b.1: the *RA* calls for the worship of Rasa (the "Mercurial") Bhairava. Sarvajña is likely a distortion of Śarvaja ("Arrow-Born"), a name of Rudra-Śiva used extensively in some manuscript versions of the *BhP.*

180. The *Kulānanda Tantra* passage is found in Bagchi, *KJñN*, p. 107; on the *Lalitāvistara* (v. 44 = KCM 1.1) see Snellgrove, *Indo-Tibetan Buddhism*, vol. 1, p. 302.

181. *KCM* 1.28, 29, 33 (numbering here is from Ray's partial edition, p. 348). Cf. *BhP* 1.1–12. The term *dravya* is employed in the *RA* to signify the sexual fluids (2.121b) offered in tantric worship (*siddhadravya*), as well as all the "secret" fluids (124b–125a), including mercury, used in alchemy. *Dravya-guṇa* is the term employed in modern Āyurveda for pharmacology.

182. The *amarasundarī* is described in *RA* 18.94–95, in KCM fol. 5a.7–5b.6, in *RM* fol. 16a.5, and in *RHT* 19.65–66. The *RA* (18.174–75) also mentions a pill called *vajrāṅgasundarī*, the "Diamond-Limbed Beauty." The *KCM* follows its discussion of these aphrodisiacs (fol. 3a.9–6a.1) with an account of the *khecarī guṭikā* (fol. 6a.2–6b.1), which mainly concerns secretly "sporting" in the sky with *śākinīs*,

bhūtas, *vetālas*, *brahmarākṣas*, women of divine beauty, and the goddess Bhairavī. In the *RA*, the emphasis is on flight and immortality.

183. *KCM* fol. 6b.3–12b.7.

184. *KCM* fol. 12b.7–17a.5.

185. *KCM* fol. 17a.8–17b.3. See above, n. 156.

186. The KCM list of eight metals is quite idiosyncratic: tin, iron, gold (which it calls *niṣka*), lead, white copper (*kāṁsya*), copper, copper or iron pyrites (*mākṣika*), and mercury.

187. The *uparasas* are discussed in *KCM* fol. 20b.5–21a.9.

188. The auto-commentary begins at fol. 20b.2 (cf. *RM*, Paris MSS no. 1222, fol. 30a.3). It is found in every one of the manuscripts of the *KCM*, held both in the ASL and NNA collections, that I have consulted: see below, n. 265.

189. *KCM* fol. 22b.4–23a.3.

190. *KCM* fol. 23a.3–4. On the *varṇa*-classification of mercury by color, see below, chap. 7, n. 138. The *RA* (6.67b–68) classifies diamonds according to caste and gender.

191. *KCM* fol. 24a.4–25a.1. Cf. *RA* 15.131–32, which is paraphrased by *RM* fol. 9b.7–8 and 17b.3.

192. *KCM* fol. 28b.8.

193. *KCM* fol. 29b.3–7. A work entitled *Sugrīva[va]-śaṃkaraṇī-vidyā* (Spell Which Subjugates Sugrīva) is devoted to the exorcism of a host of evil spirits through the intervention of this powerful figure: *HTSL*, p. 124.

194. *KCM* fol. 22a.1. The numerous manuscripts of the *KCM* I have consulted are more or less identical, in spite of the geographical diversity of their provenance. The sole dated manuscript I consulted is ASL MSS no. 3952, dated to A.D. 1679. The *Rasasāra* (ASL MSS no. 4260) of Govindācārya (not the same as the *RHT* author) is a 14th–15th c. text. It is an alchemical tantra, whose content is similar to that of the *RA* and the *KCM*. See above, n. 61.

195. This work has been edited twice in this century: *Rasopaniṣat*, ed. Sambhasiva Sastri (Trivandrum: Superintendent, Government Press, 1928); and *Rasopaniṣat*, 2 vols. ed. with commentary and Hindi translation by Badrinarayan Sarma (Ajmer: Krsna Gopal Ayurved Bhavan, 1959).

196. A detailed description of a site in Kerala is found in *RU* 16.11–13. This is one of a number of Keralan works on therapeutic alchemy. Others include the *Rasavaiśeṣika Sūtra* of Bhadant Nāgārjuna, the *Vaidyamanoramā*, *Dhārākalpa*, and *Sahasrayoga:* Sharma, *Āyurved*, p. 697. The *RU* also details the location of another south Indian site, named Rāśima. This source does, however, list sites in north India: sites at which *vaikṛnta* is found include Mewar, Swat, Nepal, Jammu, and Kashmir: Meulenbeld, *History* (draft of 10 May 1994), p. 936.

197. *RU* 1.9, 56; and in chapter colophons.

198. These are: the *Prabhṛtamata*, *Vātulamata*, *Vaiṣṇavamata*, *Aindramata*, *Śaṅkaramata*, *Bṛhaspatimata*, and *Śaukramata*.

199. *RA* 2.90; *RU* 1.90. On the *aṅkuśā mudrā* as a stabilizing device to be used by the tantric sorcerer for the purposes of subjugation and attraction, see *Vīnāśikhatantra* 84–87 (ed. Teun Goudriaan [Delhi: Motilal Banarsidass, 1985], with Goudriaan's commentary, pp. 54, 56.

200. On the *saṃskāras*, *RU* 1.20–39; on *kūrpa*, *RU* 11.12.

201. *Bhūti* here is a shortening of *vibhūti*, a synonym for the *siddhis* that are the stated goal (along with bodily immortality) of this work: Pandeya's introduction to *Gorakṣa Saṁhitā*, vol. 2, p. *ka*.

202. A more simplified colophon is found in the ASL manuscript (no. 4401) of the work (entitled *Svacchandaśaktyavatāra*): "thus ends the Production of Supernatural Powers [which is contained within] the *Svacchandaśaktyavatāra* ("the work brought down to earth by Śakti") within the *Śatasāhasr[y]a Saṁhitā* ("the compendium of 100,000 verses"). The colophon to the *BhP*, i.e., the so-called *Hādibheda*, follows 9.141 of Pandeya's edition of the *Gorakṣa Saṁhitā* (vol. 2, p. 578). The colophon to ASL MSS 4401 occurs at the end of an additional tenth chapter. The colophon to the *Kādi* or "Śākta" *Gorakṣa Saṁhitā* resembles that of the *Manthānabhairava Tantra*, which also ascribes itself to the Kādi variety: *HTSL*, p. 55.

203. *BhP* 9.135a, 136b, 137a: siṁhabhūpahitārthāya nāthena prakaṭīkṛtaḥ/ . . . nātha gorakṣaḥ samproktaḥ sarasaṃ kālakūṭavat pūrvaṃ vijñāyate saṁyak sākṣād amṛtavadbhavet. These verses are missing from the conclusion of chapter nine in ASL MSS no. 4401 (entitled *Svacchandaśaktyavatāra*). This manuscript, however, contains a long tenth chapter, on tantric sorcery, whose opening verse (10.1) is identical to *RA* 1.1. This chapter does not, however, belong to the rest of the work. It is also missing from MSL MSS no. 1431.

204. *Rasakāmadhenu*, ed. by Yadavji Trikamji Acarya (Bombay, Nirnaysagar Press, 1925; reprint Benares: Chaukhambha Orientalia, 1988).

205. *BhP* 1.78b–79: svacchandakaulave nātha varṣāvidyāmukhena vā/ svāyambhukaulave nātha dīptādyena makhena tu/ ebhir etatkrameṇaiva bhavajaṃ pūjayet sadā. Cf. 8.98 and 9.129. Through the use of mercury, one becomes a second Svacchanda Śiva (5.178; 6.480). Svacchanda (Bhairava) is to be worshipped together with Śakti, "in accordance with the precepts mentioned in the *Svacchanda*" (7.108). The term *kaulave* is employed in the *KJñN* (11.7, 9; 16.24, 62) to connote an "expert in the Kaula practices" (*kaula-vit*), by which the five tantric *makāras* are implied.

206. *BhP* 1.111–12. The "Svacchanda" text mentioned in *BhP* 7.108 is more

likely the Tantra by the same name than a lost eponymous alchemical work. See above, n. 31.

207. On *umāyoni*, see *BhP* 2.6; on *śarvaja* (changed to *sarvajñā* in a number of manuscripts), see ASL MSS no. 4401, chap. 1, v. 10, and throughout.

208. *BhP* 1.77: varṇisvaramahālakṣmī kāmodayamahodayaiḥ/ khecarīcakrayogeṇa mahāmārīmakhena vā. Cf. 6.514. On the *khecarīcakra*, see below, chap. 8, n. 165.

209. *BhP* 1.15a: praviṣṭāḥ sarvaśāstreṣu siddhānte vāmadakṣiṇe. "Uttarottara Mātṛtantra" is a possible reference to the *Śrīmatottara Tantra*, of which the "Śākta" or "Kādi" division of the *Gorakṣa Saṁhitā* is an abridgment: Pandeya, introduction to *Gorakṣa Saṁhitā*, vol. 1, pp. *ṭa–ṇa*. MSL Hindi MSS no. 649, entitled *Gorakṣa Saṁhitā Bhāṣa*, calls the *Gorakṣa Saṁhitā* a portion (*khaṇḍa*) of the *Śrīmatottara*, in its chapter colophons.

210. 4.108: kadalī vanajā bandhyā guḍūcīkandajaṃ rasam/ pāyasaṃ caiva mīnā nāma japāyasi sandhitam. The *aghora mantra* is evoked frequently, as is the *trailokya-ḍāmara* (7.163) and a form of mantric recitation called *svayambhu*. See below, chap. 6, nn. 59, 62, 66.

211. This evocation is found only in the closing verse of chapter nine of ASL MSS no. 4401 (fol. 106b.4–5): ratnākarokti vikhyātaṃ bhūtitantraṃ mahodayam.

212. *BhP* 1.111–23. Cf. *RU* 1.14, 56.

213. Meulenbeld, *History* (draft of 10 May 1994), p. 941. See above, n. 202.

214. *BhP* 1.28; 5.178, 262; 6.222; 7.144, 152, 244; 8.63–65.

215. *BhP* 1.82–89, 5.62.

216. *BhP* 1.5, 8, 11, 25 (in ASL MSS no. 4401). On the use of *dravya* in the *KCM*, see above, n. 181. Cf. *RA* 1.22, which states that mercury renders one's *mantras* effective. On alchemical uses of menstrual blood, see below, chap. 7, sec. 3.

217. The term *khānepāne* is found in *BhP* 4.77; *RM* fol. 27a.9 (*khānipāna*); and *Dattātreya Tantra* 9.13. *Khānapāna* is found in *Akulavīra Tantra* [B], v. 135b (in Bagchi, *KJñN*, p. 106). A general discussion of vernacular terms in the *BhP* is found in Tripathi's foreword to Pandeya's edition of the *Gorakṣa Saṁhitā*, vol. 2, pp. 7–8.

218. *BhP* 7.114–19. The itinerant alchemist is also instructed to go outside of India in his search for divine herbs (7.125).

219. *BhP* 4.118–32. See below, chap. 7, sec. 3; and chap. 8, sec. 5 on the *RA* descriptions. It is worthy of note that two of the qualities which the *BhP* assigns to its laboratory assistants correspond to names of "mystery" Rasa Siddhas from the lists reviewed in the last chapter. *Viśārada* ("expert") is the name of the fourth Rasa Siddha in the early lists; while *śūra* ("Mighty") may lie at the root of the names Śūrasena (no. 9), Śūrānanda, and Śūravida (no. 19).

220. *RC* 6.1; 7.1; 11.88–90; 12.25; 15.32–35; 15.54; 16.72. It also mentions Svacchandabhairava (14.52), a possible reference to the *BhP.*

221. *RC* 2.1; 14.199. See also Siddhinandan Misra's introduction, pp. 12–13. The *RC* also mentions Srisailam (8.23), the Tapti River and Kanauj (10.129), the Vindhya mountains (14.91), and Saurashtra (14.174). The type of earth in question is potash alum, *phiṭkarī* in Sanskrit. Whereas Mount Abu is presently located within the state of Rajasthan, its cultural and political ties have historically been Gujarati. Only the 1987 Bombay edition of the Rasakhaṇḍa of the *RRĀ* contains a reference to the *RC:* Meulenbeld, *History* (draft of 10 May 1994), p. 954.

222. *RC* 14.58; 16.60.

223. Curiously, he is called Yaśodhana in the *RRS* [a] list. On the basis of the *RPS*'s use of the terms *dvīpāntarotthā* and *rasakarpūra*, Jan Meulenbeld (*History,* draft of 10 May 1994 p. 871) maintains that Yaśodhara Bhaṭṭa was a 16th, and not a 13th c. author as previously supposed. His argument is, however, based upon a later identification of the former preparation with *cobacīnī,* a plant of foreign origin introduced into India in the 16th c.

224. *RPS* 8.32, 37; 13.1. Opium, imported to India from the west, is first mentioned in the ca. A.D. 1175–1225 *Gadanigraha* of Soḍhala.

225. *RPS* 13.15. See above, chap. 4, n. 211.

226. *RPS* 13.14. The Gauḍiyas are so called because their lineage originated in Gauḍa, i.e., Bengal-Orissa.

227. Meulenbeld, *History* (draft of 10 May 1994), p. 871. On the alchemical usage of the term *kavi,* see above, chap. 1, n. 49, and below, chap. 10, nn. 78–80.

228. *Rasārṇava* is the reading found in all of the manuscripts of the Rasakhaṇḍa of the *RRĀ* I consulted in the Nepal National Archives (see bibliography); however Tripathi's edition of this work gives a reading of "*rasāyane*" for *RRĀ* 1.1.16a.

229. The *Svargavaidya-Kāpālika* is not extant; however, Carpaṭi figures as a Rasa Siddha in alchemical legend and is the author of a number of extant alchemical manuscripts: see above, chap. 3, n. 121.

230. The *RRĀ* cites the *RC* in 1.10.51–61; and it names the *KCM* in 5.1.7. On the former citation, see above, n. 221.

231. Meulenbeld, *History* (draft of 10 May 1994), p. 955.

232. Meulenbeld, *History* (draft of 10 May 1994), p. 954.

233. The *RRĀ* has never been edited *in toto;* each of its divisions has, however, been edited separately, although many are extremely difficult of access. See bibliography.

234. Meulenbeld, *History* (draft of 10 May 1994), p. 947. According to this author, the Rasendrakhaṇḍa is largely in agreement with the Ayurvedic *Mādhavanidāna* in its etiology, symptomology, and treatment of diseases.

235. Wujastyk, "Alchemical Ghost," p. 75. Wujastyk however errs in identifying the *RRĀ* as an epitome of the *KPT:* this he does on the basis of chapter colophons to two of the manuscripts of the Siddha Khaṇḍa of the *RRĀ* held by the Wellcome Institute, London: ibid., pp. 75, 82. Chapter colophons to the manuscript of the Siddha Khaṇḍa I consulted (NNA MSS no. 5–3092, Āyurveda 266) call it the work of Nityanātha Siddha, son of Pārvatī."

236. *RRĀ* 3.11b–12a. See above, n. 10 to the preface.

237. *RRS* 6.1–60 = *RRĀ* 3.1.10–76.

238. On the "*lakṣaṇa*s" of the Tantras, see *HTSL*, p. 10.

239. Listed are Benares, Kāmarūpa (Assam), Hardwar, Gaṇḍakī (a river in central Nepal; nearby is the Śaiva pilgrimage site of Muktīnāth), Vadarīka (Badarīnāth, in the Garhwal Himalayas), and Gaṅgāsāgara (in the Ganges delta, West Bengal). The *RHT* of Govinda may also have been an eastern Indian work: see above, nn. 151–52.

240. *MBhT* 1.5–16; 5.17–33; 8.30–34. See above, nn. 109–10, on the more or less synonymous *sadbhāva*, *kulāmṛta*, and *kaulāmṛta*.

241. *MBhT* 3.7–8, 18–20; 14.13–14.

242. *MBhT* 7.58–60; 8.18–24; 12.14–17.

243. *MBhT* 7.36.

244. *MBhT* 1.7; 5.4; 7.2–5, 60; 8.18; 10.22; 14.21.

245. André Padoux, "The Body in Tantric Ritual: The Case of the Mudrās," in Teun Goudriaan, ed., *The Sanskrit Tradition and Tantrism* (Leiden: Brill, 1990), p. 66.

246. ASL MSS no. 4281 (of which Paris MSS no. 1222 is a copy, commissioned by Palmyr Cordier, and containing a number of corrections on the Bikaner original); and GAU MSS no. 862. This last manuscript does not contain the commentary found following chapter four in the Bikaner manuscript. The ASL manuscript, from which the Paris manuscript was copied, continues for a few additional lines and ends with the colophon "thus ends the *RM* of Śrīman Nāgārjuna." All manuscripts of the *RM* are four chapters in length: personal communication from Dominik Wujastyk, May 1994.

247. Paris MSS no. 1222, fol. 22a.6. Cf. GAU MSS no. 861, fol. 28a.9–10: vakṣye sarvahitārthaṃ kakṣapuṭaṃ sarvasiddhikaram.

248. Meulenbeld, *History* (draft of 10 May 1994), p. 986.

249. rasendramaṅgalaṃ śrutvā yaścikitsetcikitsakaḥ/ tasya siddhir na sandeho svayaṃ nāgārjuno 'bravīt.

250. *RM* fol. 25a.2–3: parvatāgṛha prāsādā saśailavanakānanāṃ kāñcanamayāṃ kariṣyāmi. On the *Navanātha Carita*, see Roşu, "Alchemy," p. 154, citing P. V. Parabrahma Sastry.

251. See above, n. 60 of this chapter. The "Laghu Vivṛti" commentary on the *YRM* is dated A.D. 1239.

252. *RM* fol. 1b.4; 6a.3.

253. *RM* fol. 1b.7–fol. 2a.1. Here too, it follows the *RA* (10.36–37). The *RC* (15.30) gives the same measures.

254. *RM* fol. 4a.1–4, borrowing from *RA* 6.81–84.

255. *RM* fol. 6a.8: mṛtāni lohāni rasi bhavanti. I am grateful to Damodar Joshi for this interpretation of the term *rasī*, i.e., digestible in the same way as is *rasa*, chyle, the first of the eight *dhātus*: personal communication, Benares, December 1984.

256. Names include *ekaliṅgeśvara-rasa; svacchandabhairava-rasa, manthāna-bhairava-rasa, jvālamukhī-rasa, kumārī-rasa, varāhī-rasa, vaḍavāmukha-rasa*, etc. See above, n. 31.

257. See above, chap. 3, nn. 131, 146. Here, *añjana* is used in the sense of balm, unguent, or ointment, rather than in the sense of a miraculous preparation (usually with a black antimony—*añjana*—base) which affords invisibility and other supernatural powers.

258. Of the thirty-seven folios of the Paris manuscript of the *RM*, fols. 15a to 29b make up chapter four alone.

259. *RM* fol. 16a.5. Cf. *RA* 18.95 and *KCM* fol. 3b.6–9.

260. *RM* fol. 17b.1–2.

261. *RM* fol. 19b.10–21a.10. Cf. *KCM* fol. 12a.3–12b.6.

262. *RM* fol. 21b.5–6. Cf. *RA* 11.70–73.

263. *RM* fol. 24b.6.

264. *RM* fol. 25b.3–4.

265. *RM* fol. 30a.3.

266. *RM* fol. 30b.6. See above, n. 188.

267. *RRS* 1.32–59 = *RHT* 1.3–33.

268. Chaps. 2–5 and 7–8 of the *RRS* are mainly drawn from the *RC* (chaps. 10–12, 14, 3–4, respectively); much of chap. 6 is from *RRĀ* 3.1.1–76. Chap. 9 is mainly inspired by the *RA* and *RC;* chap. 10 samples passages from chaps. 5–9 of the *RC;* chap. 11 draws on the *RA* and the *RRĀ:* Meulenbeld, *History*, draft of 10 May 1994, pp. 979–80. Its two *RRS* Siddha lists (1.2–5 and 6.51–55) are borrowed directly from the appendix to the *RM* and the *RRĀ* (3.166–71).

269. Meulenbeld, *History* (draft of 10 May 1994), p. 979 n. 13681. The *Rasaratnapradīpikā* is ASL MSS no. 4222. Its author, Rāmarāja, who also compiled the *Madanavinodanighaṇṭu* (NNA MSS no. 4–2224, reel no. A1289/4), was a subject of the Pāla king Madanapāla, who ruled in the latter part of the 14th c. On his dates, see Sharma, *Āyurved*, p. 409.

270. See Radhakrishna Sastri's long Sanskrit introduction (pp. 1–14) to his 1952 edition of the *ĀK*; and Misra, *Āyurvedīya*, p. 38. Three copies of the Tanjore manuscript are housed in the Gujarat Ayurved University's collections: GAU MSS nos. 829, 830, and 831.

271. These parallel passages are presented in the form of a chart in Radhakrishna Sastri's introduction to the 1952 edition of the *ĀK* (p. 13).

272. See also *ĀK* 1.3.101–3, on the inner yogic production and consumption of the nectar of immortality. *ĀK* 1.20.22–34 also clearly borrows from *RĀ* 1.8–19.

273. *ĀK* 1.3.9–56. Four other types of initiation are described. These are: *sādhaka-*, *nirvāṇa-*, *ācārya-*, and *siddha-dīkṣā* (*ĀK* 1.3.57–109).

274. Brahmānanda, "Jyotsnā" commentary to *HYP* 1.1. On Nārāyaṇa, who cites this work in his 17th c. commentary on the Yoga Upaniṣads, see Bouy, *Nātha-Yogin*, pp. 68–74. I have not been able to locate an independent text entitled *Mahākāla-yogaśāstra*.

275. All of these manuscripts are held in Jodhpur (MSL MSS 1468, 1469, 1470, and 1471, of which the last dates from samvat 1740 [A.D. 1683–84]) and Kathmandu (reel nos. A-999/7; A-1289-9; C-86/617; E-1145/12; and M-23/10, of which the first dates from samvat 1735, or A.D. 1678–79).

276. The *Yogamārtaṇḍa* is reproduced in Mallik, *SSP*, pp. 56–71. On the *Mahākāla Saṁhitā*, see Pandey, *Gorakhnāth*, p. 112.

277. Bouy, *Nātha-Yogin*, p. 41.

278. This technique will be discussed at length in chap. 8, sec. 4.

279. Bernier, *Voyages*, p. 245.

Chapter Six

1. See K. R. Srikanta Murthy's introduction to his edition of the *Śārṅgadhara Saṁhitā* (p. xiv). Cf. *BhP* 9.135, in which the author calls his royal patron "Siṁha"; and *RHT* 19.78, in which Govinda names his patron as "Madana . . . Lord of the Kirātas." I have translated this chapter of the *RA* in its entirety: "The Ocean of Mercury: An Eleventh Century Alchemical Text," in Donald Lopez, ed. *Indian Religions in Practice* (Princeton: Princeton University Press, 1995).

2. Ray's and Tripathi's editions of the *RA* substitute *nāśana* ("destroying") for *śāsaka* in this half verse (1.4b), which makes little sense in the light of what follows. Moreover, *śāsaka* (or *śāsana*) was the reading I found in the three manuscripts of the *RA* that I consulted while in India (ASL MSS nos. 4256, 4273, 4274).

3. *KJñN* 16.47–49. Cf. *RC* (1.6–7) which gives the "Kaula" etymology of *pārada*, the term for mercury. See above, chap. 5, sec. 5f.

4. An apparent play on words: whereas the first half verse (10a) employs the third person plural of the present indicative of the verb *muc*, "release, liberate"

(*muñcanti*, "they liberate"), this half verse (10b) employs the past passive participle (*mukta*), which must therefore be read in the sense "what ram or bull['s semen would?] not be released?"

5. This is a reference to the use of the so-called *pañcāmṛta*, the "five nectars," which include the male and female sexual emissions, urine, excrement, and marrow: *KJñN* 11.11; and the *Vimalaprabhā* commentary on *Kālacakra Tantra* 2.119, in Fenner, *Rasāyan Siddhi*, p. 138.

6. Elsewhere, the text describes as feeble-minded those unknowing persons who, indulging in liquor and flesh and deluded by Śiva's *māyā*, prattle that "we have gone to the world of Śiva" (1.29) and sends to hell those persons who, knowing *mantra* and Tantra, corrupt the *rasa-yoga* (1.45). These rhetorical verses are reminiscent of those found in the coeval *Akulavīra Tantra* [B] (1.79–86), which mocks the trappings of yoga.

7. *RA* 1.25.

8. *RA* 1.26. Cf. *RC* 1.8–10. Gorakhnāth refers to drinking the liquor of immortality in *Gorakh Bānī* Sabadī 137.

9. Cf. *RA* 2.2, 8, in which the ideal alchemical guru is described as "one who is attached to the *kula* path" (*kula-mārga-rata*) and the ideal pupil as "one who is devoted to honoring the *kula* [divinities]" (*kula-pūjā-rata*). See also *RA* 18.101.

10. *RA* 18.48–55. The *RA* (1.27) refers to mercury itself as the "womb" of the alchemical lineage: for a discussion, see above, chap. 4, n. 111.

11. *RA* 2.121b; 18.115. Cf. *RA* 18.47–52, 132, 144. See above, chap. 5, nn. 109–10.

12. *RA* 2.17–27; 6.90; 15.92, 131; 18.169b. See below, chap. 7, sec. 3. Such an assistant woman is to view herself as the daughter of the goddess Caṇḍī (or Kālikā) and the god Śiva (Sadāśiva, Tripurāntaka): *RA* 2.31, 34–35.

13. *RA* 2.124b–125a; 18.53–54.

14. *HYP* 3.48–49, with the commentary of Brahmānanda. See below, chap. 8, sec. 4, for an extended discussion of this practice.

15. *RA* 1.18. A second, and more concrete interpretation, is one suggested to me by Professor Mukunda Raj Aryal of Tribhuvan University (personal communication, Kathmandu, June 1993). Referring to modern-day techniques of temple roof gilding, which he himself witnessed at Bhaktapur, one of the three royal capitals of the Kathamandu Valley, Aryal noted the use of mercury for the amalgamation of the gold used in such work. When the gilders are actually working with the mercury-gold amalgam, they stuff their mouth's with chunks of raw [buffalo?] meat; and they regularly wash their mouths out with alcohol. These would presumably be techniques for reducing, as much as possible, the likelihood of inhaling or ingesting the mercury being used.

16. *RA* 6.84; 14.85; 16.34.

17. *RA* 1.34; *RRS* 1.79. *Rasa*, while generally referring to mercury alone, can also mean, by extension, "essential compound," e.g., mercuric sulfide, cinnabar, mica, etc.: Roşu, "Yoga et alchimie," p. 363.

18. I am grateful to Alexis Sanderson for this insight, as well as for a great number of other comments contained in a very long letter (of 6 July 1992) in which he responded to an early draft of this chapter. While many of the details (mainly from the *SvT*) concerning tantric iconography and *mantra* found in this chapter come from that letter, I will, out of a concern for brevity, refrain from citing it repeatedly.

19. This passage has a number of parallels in other tantric sources, among which may be counted a passage from Abhinavagupta's *Parātriṁśikāvivaraṇa* (p. 88, quoted [p. 276] and translated [p. 160] in Muller-Ortega, *Triadic*), in which that author identifies the ether of the heart with the eternal absolute. Abhinavagupta is himself commenting on a passage from the *Yogavasiṣṭha:* Padoux, *Vāc*, p. 81, n. 139. Cf. *Amanaska Yoga* 1.23.

20. *RA* 1.8. "Śivahood" (*śivatvam*) in one's own body, a standard goal of tantrism, is also evoked in *RA* 1.31a; 12.337b; 17.25ab; 18.29b, 59ab.

21. Although he does not call it so by name, he is singling out orthodox Śaiva Siddhānta here. See Sanderson's discussion of this school, which dominated Kashmiri religious theory and practice prior to the 9th century: "Śaivism," pp. 690–93.

22. The term used is *piṇḍapāta*, literally, the "fall[ing away] of the body."

23. *RA* 1.9, 13. Cf. *RRS* 1.54; *RHT* 1.28. Here, the author is denigrating the Śaiva Siddhānta view of liberation upon death in favor of the Kaula doctrine of bodily immortality, which is itself inferior to the practical techniques of the alchemists, whose methods and results are proven and tangible.

24. Here I emend *yathā dhyānam* with *samādhanam.*

25. *RA* 1.20–22. This notion, of a stabilizing the body (*piṇḍadhāraṇam: RA* 1.18a), or bodily stability ([*piṇḍa-*]*sthairya*), the watchword of tantric and Siddha alchemy, appears to be appropated by Jayaratha, in his commentary on *TĀ* 29.127–32, in which the mouth-to-mouth exchange of sexual fluids practiced by adepts whose goals are *siddhis*: here, Jayaratha glosses *siddhi* with *piṇḍasthairyādi.*

26. *RA* 1.25. This descent is termed *śaktipāt.* But see the editor's comment (p. 6) on a variant reading, in the *RC*, which would make this a straightforward statement on the reduction (*pāta*) of volatile energy (*śakti*) in mercury. Cf. *RC* 10.54, which states that the grace of Śiva is necessary for the liquefaction of mica.

27. *RA* 1.37–40; 18.193b. Cf. *BhP* 6.217; 7.108; 9.76. On tantric *pūjā*, see *HT*, pp. 121–62. See also below, sec. 3.

28. *RA* 1.59; *RC* 1.4, 2.21. Other clearly alchemical names of Śiva mentioned in other texts are Pāradeśvara, "Lord of Mercury" (*BhP* 5.27); Raseśvara (mentioned

together with Gaurī: 5.289), etc. The *RC* (following 2.50) also singles out the five tantric (as opposed to the eight Puranic) Bhairavas, of which each corresponds to a syllable in the all-powerful *aghora mantra*. Nandikeśvara is singled out as a Śaiva alchemical divinity in a number of sources (e.g., *RC* 14.58); however, this may be a divinization of a Rasa Siddha named Nandi, who is cited throughout the alchemical literature, most especially by Somadeva, author of the *RC* (5.77; 11.89–90; 14.128; 15.29, 35, 66; 16.64). Cf. *BhP* 9.134; *RRS* 1.5.

29. *RA* 1.59; *RC* 1.5, 2.21. A male Rasāṅkuśa[-bhairava] is named as a Rasa Siddha in *RRS* 1.5.

30. *RA* 1.37–44; *RRS* 1.23–28; 6.14–26; *MBhT* 8.1–10; *RC* 1.37–38. See also Treloar, "The Use of Mercury," especially pp. 237–38; and Siddhinandan Misra's introduction to the *RC* (p. 5), in which he discusses the alchemical grounds for the foundation and installation of the *rasaliṅga*. Cf. *MBhT* 7.58–69 and 12.14–18, with notes (pp. 38–39, 59) on the benefits of worshipping *liṅga*s made from the eight metals, mercury, flowers of sulfur, etc. This construction is discussed extensively in chap. 8, sec. 5.

31. See above, chap. 5, nn. 29–32, 205.

32. *RA* 2.105–6, 126–30 Cf. *RC* 2.42; *RRS* 6.57.

33. *RA* 1.37–40, 43. Cf. *RRS* 6.19, in which the figure is raised to ten million. Other Śaiva deities evoked in the *RA* (18.186) are Nandikeśa and Kumāra. On the alchemical significance of the important Śiva *liṅga* of Kedārnāth, see below, chap. 8, n. 153.

34. *RA* 1.48–51.

35. Roşu, "Renouveau," pp. 65–66; and Majumdar, "Medicine," in Bose, ed., *Concise History*, p. 233.

36. *RA* 2.110–18 describes an image of Rasa-Bhairava which the alchemist projects upon on his own subtle body: this corresponds to similar configurations found in a number of tantras (Padoux, *Vāc*, pp. 120–21; Sanderson, "Maṇḍala," pp. 186, 190–92). "Masters of yoga" (*yogindras*) are to be worshipped with *arghya*, flesh, fish, and *yoginīmantras*: *RA* 18.55. Cf. *RRS* 6.56.

37. *RA* 12.83; *BhP* 6.46. The five faces of Sadāśiva (mentioned in *RA* 2.110–11) are supports for that great god, the supreme attributeless divinity of the Śaiva Siddhāntins. On this, see T. A. Gopinath Rao, *Elements of Hindu Iconography*, 2 vols. in 4 tomes (Madras: Law Road Printing House, 1914–16), vol. 2, pp. 367–68, 374; appendix B, pp. 187–91.

38. The *BhP* actually calls this divinity Svacchanda Śiva (5.178), Svacchanda Kaulava (8.98; 9.129: the Svacchanda of the Kaula virtuousi: *kaulavit*), "the slayer of Time" (*kālaghna*), or simply Svacchanda (7.108). The same text (8.98; 9.129)

also mentions Svayambhu Kaulava, a common name of Śiva, or of his phallic emblem the *liṅga* in devotional Śaivism. This term is formed by grafting to the term Kaula the ending *-ve* or *-va:* this is apparently a shortening of *-vit*, "knower, expert, virtuoso," a term used extensively in the *KJñN* (7.30; 11.79; 14.49; 16.24, 62; 18.1; 23.1). The *BhP* (7.108) also describes Svacchanda[-bhairava] in union with his consort Śakti (*śaktisaṃyuktaḥ*).

39. *RA* 2.8, 121a; *BhP* 6.229, 281, 297, 399, 431; Cf. *KJñN* 8.27–45. The *BhP* (7.369) states that offerings to demonic female divinities (*piśācīs*, *rākṣasīs*, *vāmadevīs*), made with inauspicious practices, either Svāyambhuva, *mantra*-based, or Śākta, never succeed.

40. On the highly elaborate Trika cult of these goddesses, see Sanderson, "Śaivism," pp. 673–74, 681–82; and idem, "Maṇḍala," pp. 188–89, 199.

41. *RA* 2.62. Cf. *TĀ* 15.331c–333b. In this role Mālinī "encompasses" the three goddesses. More often, this role is played by either Kālasaṃkarṣiṇī or Mātṛsadbhāva: Alexis Sanderson, "The Visualization of the Deities of the Trika," in André Padoux, ed., *L'image divine: culte et méditation dans l'hindouisme* (Paris: Editions du CNRS, 1990), pp. 45–47. See below, n. 50.

42. *RA* 2.47–73, especially 2.51–63, 69–71. A nearly identical *maṇḍala* is described in *RC* 2.23–35. This *maṇḍala* is graphically reproduced in Roşu, "*Mantra* et *Yantra*" p. 252. Quite different is the *maṇḍala* described in *RRS* 6.40–57, in which it is the minerals themselves, as well as the twenty-eight founding Siddhas of the alchemical tradition, that are worshipped in sequence.

43. *RA* 2.50–51, 72.

44. *RA* 2.52–53. The *RRS* (6.22) is more explicit than the *RA* on the meditative superimposition of these anthropomorphic images upon the *rasaliṅga*.

45. On this practice, of working from the outside in (*laya-krama*), see *HT*, p. 164.

46. *RA* 2.56. Moving clockwise from the east, their names are Śakra (Indra); Skanda; Rudra; Pavana (Agni); Śiva; Pāvaka (Vāyu); Umā; and Vyāpaka ("the Emanator").

47. *RA* 2.57–58a. Their names are Lepikā ("[Transmutation by] Smearing"); Kṣepikā ("[Transmutation by] Casting"); Kṣārikā ("Corroding, Reducing [Metals] to Ashes"); Rañjikā ("Tinting, Coloring" [of Metals]); Lohatī ("Metallica"); Bandhakārī ("Binder [of Mercury]"); Bhucārā ("[The Power of] Moving over the Earth" [at Will]"); Mṛtyunāśinī ("Destroyer of Death"); Vibhutī ("Superhuman Powers"); and Khecarī ("Power of Flight"). In the Vidyā Pīṭha, the *dūtī* is the consecrated consort with whom the tantric practitioner copulates in order to produce the mingled sexual fluids he offered to the gods: Sanderson, "Śaivism," p. 671.

48. *RA* 2.59. Their names are Mākṣika (copper pyrites); Vimala (iron pyrites); Śaila (*śilājatu*, bitumen); Capala (selenium); Rasaka (calamine); Sasyaka (copper sulfate); Gandhaka (sulfur); and Tāla (*haratāla*, orpiment).

49. *RA* 2.60–61. These are the Vidyeśvaras: see below, n. 56.

50. *RA* 2.62. "In the lotus's pericarp [at the heart of the *maṇḍala*], starting from the east are the four *śaktis*." Here, Aparā is described as *vajraśakti* and Parāpara as *kānti:* these epithets are taken up by Somadeva in *RC* 2.23–24, who names the four alchemical Goddesses (*rasa-śaktis*) as Mālinī, Vajriṇī ("Diamond Maiden"), Kāntā ("Magnetite Maiden"), and Abhrā ("Mica Maiden"). Parā and Aparā are also mentioned in this source.

51. *RA* 2.63a, 64b.

52. *RA* 2.63b–64a, 65–66a.

53. *RA* 2.69–72.

54. The classic discussion of the tantric superenthronements is Sanderson, "Maṇḍala," pp. 178–82, 187. I am deeply indebted to this author for his detailed commentary on the superenthronements found in the *RA* passage, which I reproduce here.

55. In *RA* 2.8b, the alchemical disciple is described as one devoted to the worship of the circle of the *yoginīs* and the *kula.* The presence of the eight *mahārasas*, the principal reagents with mercury in the alchemical *saṃskāras*, is troubling. Although these are the "inner circle" of mineral reagents vis-à-vis mercury, they are never divinized and do not seem to fit well into this *maṇḍala.*

56. Rao, *Elements*, vol. 2, pt. 2, pp. 396–97, and Sanskrit appendix B, pp. 187–91. Their names are: Ananteśa, Sūkṣma, Śivottama, Ekanetra, Ekarudra, Trimūrti, Śrikaṇṭha, and Śikhaṇḍi.

57. Svacchandabhairava rides on the shoulders of the *preta* Sadāśiva in the *SvT* (2.81b); Sadāśiva is also the *mahāpreta* who symbolizes the Goddess's lotus seat in her tantric worship: *HT*, p. 144. Cf. *TĀ* 5.322a. Placed before the tantric image of Pañcāli Bhairava in Kathmandu is the recumbent image of a figure called Vetāla, whose name evokes the "vampires" of tantric sorcery who possess corpses (*pretas* in this context) and whose services are sought out by powerful tantric practitioners. The iconography of this recent image appears to reproduce that of Svacchandabhairava. On such vampires, see below, chap. 10, sec. 1.

58. These passages, from book four of the *SvT* and chap. 22 of the *Netra Tantra*, are discussed in Padoux, *Vāc*, pp. 404–11.

59. More specifically, Rasabhairava is identifiable with the *sakala* ("with attributes") form of Svacchandabhairava. See *SvT* 2.88b–94a, for Svacchandabhairava's appearance; and 2.115a, which states that his consort is seated on his lap. For a

discussion of *sakala* and *niṣkala* mantras in nondualist Kashmir Śaivism, see Padoux, "Body," pp. 72–73.

60. *Nityāṣoḍaśikārṇava* 144b, 145a; *Devīrahasya*, p. 100; *Puraścaryārṇava*, p. 806.

61. Sanderson, "Śaivism in Kashmir," in *Encyclopedia of Religion*, vol. 13, pp. 16–17.

62. *RA* 2.68: Oṃ hrīṃ krīṃ raseśvarāya mahākālāya mahābalāyāghorabhairavāya vajravīra krodhakaṅkāla kṣlauḥ kṣlaḥ. The same mantra is found in *SvT* 1.41–43.

63. *RA* 2.72a: pūjayedrasasiddhyārthaṃ vidyayā pañcabījayā. Decoded, Rasāṅkuśī's mantra is "aiṃ hrīṃ śrīṃ klīṃ sauḥ"—which is, like her iconography, modeled after that of Bālā Tripurasundarī (aiṃ klīṃ sauḥ). It also resembles the five *praṇava*s or seed mantras of the Kubjikā cult (aiṃ hrīṃ śrīṃ phreṃ sauḥ). Cf. *RA* 2.84, where the five elements are identified with these same five seed-mantras of the *rasāṅkuśī mudrā;* and in which the *rasāṅkuśa mantra* is praised (2.89–90) and the construction of a circular oblatory basin—homologized with the goddess's sexual organ (*yonicakra*) and with which *mantra*-based worship is also to be performed—is described (2.77–85).

64. *RA* 3.5.

65. *RA* 3.19, which identifies the "eighty-eight thousand" herbal preparations in which the alchemist will later macerate his mercury and other elements with the *kula-khecāri*, the "sky-going lineage." These are all brought together in the *so'haṃ haṃsa* utterance.

66. *RA* 2.76; 18.60b. Cf. *RRS* 6.38; *RC* 2.47.

67. *RA* 3.16.

68. *RA* 3.6.

69. *RA* 3.27.

70. *RA* 2.97–98. These *mantra*s are used here, in conjunction with *mantra-nyāsa*, for predicting the success of a future alchemical operation. Using a hexagonal *maṇḍala* upon whose corners are figured six forms of Bhairava and at whose center is figured Rasabhairava, the practitioner causes girls and boys whom he has brought together to serve as media for posing questions to the divinity: *RA* 2.92–103, discussed in Roşu, "*Mantra* et *Yantra*," pp. 254–55.

71. Padoux, *Vāc*, p. 47; Gonda, *Medieval*, p. 171. The title of chapter three of the *RA* is "mantra-nyāsa."

72. Sanderson, "Maṇḍala," pp. 174–75; Wheelock, "Vedic," in Alper, *Mantra*, pp. 103–4; Muller-Ortega, *Triadic Heart*, pp. 162–81. In the *RC* (2.51), alchemical mantras are to be imposed upon a patient as a means to curing him of disease: Roşu, "*Mantra* et *Yantra*," p. 254.

73. On this, see below, chap. 9, nn. 40–47.

74. *RA* 3.2. Her anthropomorphic image, to be worshipped with the five Vidyā *bīja*s ("seed mantras") has already been discussed in 2.69–73.

75. This is clarified, somewhat, in *RA* (3.4a): "In the same way as a *liṅga*'s chasing (i.e., the yoni in which it is set) defines the *liṅga*'s form, so that which '*liṅga*'s'—i.e., *māyā* (*liṅgimāyā:* alternate reading *liṅgitāyā*, in ASL MSS no. 4256, fol. 11b.3)—is to that which is "*liṅga*'ed." (Or, "that which marks defines that which is marked"). The line of the vulva is called by the name "ether" in the fifth house: *RA* 3.4b. Cf. *RA* 2.114–16, for a list of explanatory synonyms for "ether" as a support for the inner visualization of a tantric deity. On the five houses as the five elements, see Kaviraj, *Bhāratīy* 1:555–56. On the five houses as the five components of the *oṃkāra*, of which the fifth is the subtle *nāda*, see Eck, *Banaras*, p. 115.

76. RA 3.5–7a. Here, I am following the reading of the Kashmir manuscript used by Ray in his critical edition, as well as emendations suggested by Alexis Sanderson (letter of 6 July 1992), who substitutes *kroṃ*—the seed syllable which animates the *mantra* and which is known as the "goad"—for *krīṃ*, which is not a normal seed syllable. On *kroṃ* as the goad (*aṅkuśa*), see *Nityaṣoḍaśikārṇava-ṛjuvimarṣinī*, p. 150, line 9. Bhairava's statement in 3.3a, that "four (houses) are placed in front, while *haṃsa* is the fifth" would also refer to the fact that *haṃsa* is the final element of the *kālapāśa mantra*.

77. Cow dung and ashes are standard exoteric and esoteric purifying agents.

78. *RA* 3.7–8.

79. *RA* 3.9–12. The *kubjika mantra* is mentioned again in *RA* 3.31a.

80. Schoterman, *Ṣaṭsāhasra Saṁhitā*, p. 14.

81. Ibid., p. 37.

82. These four are identified with the four cardinal directions on the inner square of the important Kaula *siddhacakra*, which is graphically reproduced in Dyczkowski, *Canon*, p. 81, and which has been discussed above, chap. 5, nn. 77, 93–94.

83. *ṢSS* 1.2 with Schoterman's commentary (*Ṣaṭsāhasra Saṁhitā*, pp. 32, 36–37). The *KJñN* (16.50) may be referring to the latter group in its mention of the four *kulasiddha*s.

84. Caṇḍakāpālinī is the supreme goddess of the *yāmala*s, the "Union Tantras" of the Vidyā Pīṭha; it is to her that the hathayogic *Gheraṇḍa Saṁhitā* is revealed. Kālī was worshipped as Caṇḍakāpālinī in mainstream Śaiva funerary rites in medieval Kashmir: Sanderson, "Maṇḍala," p. 201 n. 156.

85. *RA* 3.13–16.

86. The *tripurābhairavī mantra* is found in 3.25. My thanks to Alexis Sanderson for clarifying the language of this difficult passage.

87. These include the four-syllabled *haṃso'ham*, identified as the *kulakhecarī* (*RA* 3.19); *rasāṅkuśī* (3.20b); *triśiras* (3.22a); *ḍāmara* (3.23a), etc.

88. In verse 38, the goddess asks Bhairava a question concerning *dīkṣā;* verse 83b begins, "The practitioner who has been so initiated . . ." Cf. *RRS* 6.27–31.

89. Summarized in letter from Alexis Sanderson, dated 6 July 1992.

90. *Kulārṇava Tantra* 14.89.

91. On this, see Gonda, "Dīkṣā," in *Change and Continuity*, pp. 439, 443. See below, chap. 10, sec. 2.

92. John Woodroffe, *Principles of Tantra: The Tantratattva of Śrīyukta Śiva Candra Vidyārṇava Bhaṭṭācārya*, 2 vols. (Madras: Ganesh and Co., 1970), 2:477, cited in Walter, *Alchemy and Medicine*, p. 70 (n. 23 to p. 16): "In order that this unclean body may be purified, it is dried up by means of the Vāyumantra and burnt and reduced to ashes by means of the Agnimantra." See below, chap. 9, sec. 3.

93. T. A. Gopinath Rao, *Elements*, 2:1, pp. 10–11, cited in Gonda, "Dīkṣā," in *Change and Continuity*, p. 430: "ancient and widespread ideas in connection with 'initiation,' 'consecration,' or 'transmutation' have here been embedded in the typically Śaivite pattern of Hinduism and are put into practice in the framework of Hindu ritual, requiring different *kuṇḍa*s (receptacles for fire) and *maṇḍala*s ('mystic drawings')."

Chapter Seven

1. *RV* 1.105.2 describes the exchange of a certain *rasa* between the partners in sexual intercourse.

2. See, for example, *RV* 1.23.19; 9.86.39; *Atharva Veda* 1.4.4; 1.6.2–3; 3.31.6–11; *Śatapatha Brāhmaṇa* 1.6.4.5; 6.2.2.6; 7.3.1.3. See above, chap. 1, nn. 40–45.

3. See, for example, *Śatapatha Brāhmaṇa* 7.3.1.26.

4. As, for example, the *prāṇāgnihotra: Vaikhānasa Smārta Sūtra* 2.18.

5. *Maitrī Upaniṣad* 5.2. The term occurs in an emanatory schema, in which *tamas*, the lowest *guṇa*, differentiates into *rajas*, which in turn differentiates into *sattvā*, which "when impelled, flowed forth as *rasa*."

6. Indeed, *soma* as oblation and *agni* as sacrificial fire are identified with sun and moon in *Śatapatha Brāhmaṇa* 1.6.3.23–25. An alternative reading of *samarasa* is *sāmarasya*.

7. *Gorakṣa Paddhati* 1.71–75, which is quite nearly identical to *Yogamārtaṇḍa* 61–64. The two texts are expansions on the 13th c. *Gorakṣa Śataka*.

8. *Caraka Saṁhitā* 6.7.71.

9. Dasgupta, *History*, vol. 2, pp. 357–59.

10. *Nāṭyaśāstra* 6, cited in G. K. Bhat, *Rasa Theory and Allied Problems* (Baroda: M. S. University of Baroda, 1984), p. 11.

11. A yogic parallel are the seven fires of yoga (*yogāgnis*), which render the body "cooked": *Mārkaṇḍeya Purāṇa*, cited in Kaviraj, *Bhāratīy*, vol. 1, p. 178. Cf. *Gorakh Bānī*, Sabadī 156–57. A late south Indian alchemical source, the *Yogimuni 1000* ([3.10–62], ed. and tr. S. Raghunathan [Madurai: Madurai University, 1982]) describes how the conjunction of the five elements with the *guru* brings about the ripening (*pac*) of the elements and metals into gold. On the wide semantic range of the verb *pac*, see Charles Malamoud, "Cuire le monde," in *Cuire le monde*, pp. 35–71.

12. Cf. *Caraka Saṁhitā* 6.1.78–80 quoted below, chap. 10, n. 102.

13. Misra, *Āyurvedīya*, pp. 517–80.

14. Roşu, "Yoga et alchimie," pp. 376–78. See above, chap. 3, nn. 12, 30–32, 133.

15. *RC* 11.5.

16. *RA* 1.36; *RRS* 1.76.

17. The term *rasa* in the singular also refers to essential compounds, such as cinnabar, mica, pyrites, etc., in their native states: Roşu, "Yoga et alchimie," p. 363. Kauṭilya's ca. 1st c. B.C. (*Arthaśāstra* 2.12.2–4) reference to *rasa* would therefore be to smelted ore (and not to mercury, as some have argued). See also Subbarayappa, "Chemical Practices," in Bose, *Concise History*, p. 305.

18. The *mahārasas* act directly on mercury; the *uparasas* catalyze the effects of the *mahārasas*: Misra, *Āyurvedīya*, p. 342. Mercurial preparations in which plants are used are called *rasauṣadha* and *rasabhasma rasāyana* (*RA* 12.358). A number of "magical waters" are alternatively referred to as *rasas* or *udakas*: *RA* 12.189–292; *RRS* 11.125; *KCKT* 8.18–39; Kardaswamy, *History*, p. 343; Subbarayappa, "Chemical Practices," in Bose, *Concise History*, pp. 336–37; *Vimalaprabhā* 202cd, in Fenner, *Rasāyan Siddhi*, p. 153.

19. *RC* 1.3. Elsewhere (15.2), Somadeva states that the essence of all remedies is to be found in mercury (*sūta*).

20. Prior to the 12th c., this branch of Hindu alchemy was termed *lohavāda*, "the doctrine of metals": personal communication from Damodar Joshi, Benares, September 1985. The modern Hindi term for alchemy, *kīmiyā[garī]*, is a late borrowing from the Persian: Ramcandra Varma, ed., *Saṃkṣipt Hindi Śabd Sāgar* (Benares: Nagaripracarini Sabha, 1981), p. 206.

21. *RA* 17.165–66: yathā lohe tathā dehe kartavyaḥ sūtakaḥ sadā/ samānaṃ kurute devi praviśan dehalohayoḥ/ pūrvaṃ lohe parīkṣeta tato dehe prayojayet.

22. rasībhavanti lohāni dehā api susevanāt rasendrastena vikhyātaḥ: *RRĀ* 2.1.7, cited in Misra, *Āyurvedīya*, p. 173, n. 4; Cf. *RM*, Paris MSS no. 1222, fol. 6a.8; and *RA* 7.151ab. Misra takes *rasī* to mean "oxidized" in the case of metals and "joined with chyle and the other *dhātus*" in the case of the human body.

23. *RA* 16.25b: dvitīya iva Śaṅkaraḥ.

24. On *rasacikitsā*, see Roşu, "Renouveau contemporain," pp. 65–66; and Majumdar, "Medicine," in Bose, ed. *Concise History*, p. 233.

25. *Caraka Saṁhitā* 6.7.1.

26. *Śatapatha Brāhmaṇa* 12.7.1.7: 12.8.1.1, 15.

27. *Śatapatha Brāhmaṇa* 6.1.3.1–5.

28. *Śatapatha Brāhmaṇa* 2.1.1.5; 11.1.6.1–11. In this egg, the silver part of the shell becomes earth and the golden part sky: *Chāndogya Upaniṣad* 3.19.1–2. A Tibetan creation myth reproduces these themes: *Asian Mythologies*, s.v. "Cosmogonic Myths of Tibet."

29. *Śatapatha Brāhmaṇa* 3.5.2.27; *Aitareya Brāhmaṇa* 7.4.6; *Maitrāyaṇī Saṁhitā* 2.2.2.

30. Needham, *Science and Civilisation*, vol. 5, pt. 4 (1980), p. 362. The notion of a "ferment" (Greek: *mátza*) that could be used to effect a "biological" replication of metals is found in the pre–common era *Corpus Hermeticum*, the Greco-Syriac Pseudo-Zosimus (ca. A.D. 300), the Persian Jābir ibn Hāyyan (9th c.) and the European Geber (13th c.): ibid., p. 366.

31. *Rāmāyaṇa* 1.36.10–22. Cf. *Mahābharata* 13.84.68–70. Another such mineral myth is found in the early (pre–8th c. B.C.) *Jaiminīya Brāhmaṇa* (1.223).

32. *Yajur Veda* 18.13, cited in Sharma, *Āyurved*, p. 466. The *RC* (14.5) states that the semen from which *vahni-sambhūta* ("fire-born") gold was produced was that of Śiva, semen which Agni vomited after having swallowed it in the myth of the birth of Skanda. The *RRS* (5.6) agrees, calling such gold (*vahnija-svarṇa*). See below, n. 56, for identifications of gold with female sexual fluids.

33. *Dhyānabindu Upaniṣad* 1.5, in *The Yoga Upaniṣads with the Commentary of Śrī Upaniṣad-Brahmayogin*, ed. A. Mahadeva Sastri, Adyar Library Series, vol. 6 (Madras: Adyar Library and Research Center, 1968), p. 189.

34. As early as the *Atharva Veda* (11.3.7–8), the metals are identified with constituents of the body, according to the brahmanic system of *adhyātman-adhiyajña-adhidaivatā* system of homologies. Here, flesh is identified with the "dark metals" (lead and iron?), blood with copper, ashes with tin, and complexion with gold. See above, chap. 1, n. 46.

35. This is the same god who, in Kaula traditions, throws the Kaula scriptures, revealed by Śiva, into the sea. Matsyendranāth, the "Lord of the Fishes-Nāth," recovers these, and later transmits them to humanity. See below, chap. 8, sec. 2b.

36. Wendy Doniger O'Flaherty summarizes a number of such myths from the epics and Purāṇas, in *Śiva: The Erotic Ascetic* (New York: Oxford University Press, 1981), pp. 105, 107–8.

37. Tamils call copper sulfate *nīlakaṇṭha*, identifying it with the blue of Śiva's

throat after he swallowed the poison that fell into the Ocean of Milk from the mouth of Vāsuki, the serpent churning rope employed by the gods and antigods: personal communication from N. Sethu Raghunathan, Madurai, January 1985.

38. *RC* 14.3–4; reproduced in *RRS* 5.4–5. The latter form of gold is undoubtedly a reference to the myth of the golden embryo, the *hiraṇyagarbha*, of *Śatapatha Brāhmaṇa* 11.1.6.1–11.

39. *Rasakāmadhenu* 2.1.4, cited in Misra, *Āyurvedīya*, p. 496.

40. *The Lohasarvasvam of Śrī Sureśvara* (vv. 9, 72–74, 103–4, and 116), with Hindi commentary by Pavani Prasad Sharma, ed. Brahmashankar Mishra (Benares: Chowkhamba, 1965); and the *Rasendra Bhāskara* (3.86–4.119; 5.6–26; 6.12) of Lakṣminārāyaṇa (Jaipur: n.p., 1896). On the dating of the former text, see Meulenbeld, *History* (draft of May 10, 1994), p. 775.

41. *Padmāvat* 24.2 (= 245). A complete edition of this work, with a Hindi commentary, is Rajnath Sharma, *Jayasī Granthāvalī (Padmāvat—Ṭīkā Sahit)* (Agra: Vinod Pustak Mandir, 1965, pp. 476–81). A partial edition, but with a superior commentary, is *The Padumawāti of Malik Muhammad Jaisī*, edited with a [Hindi] commentary, translation, and critical notes by George Grierson and Sudhakara Dvivedi, Bibliotheca Indica, n.s. 877 (Calcutta: Baptist Mission Press, 1896). Partial English translations, based on Grierson and Dvivedi's edition, are A. G. Shirreff, *Padmāvatī of Malik Muhammad Jaisi*, Bibliotheca Indica, 267 (Calcutta: Royal Asiatic Society of Bengal, 1944); and Lakshmi Dhar, *Padumāvatī: A Linguistic Study of the 16th Century Hindi (Avadhi)* (London: Luzac & Co., Ltd., 1949). This passage is found in Grierson and Dvivedi, *Padumawāti*, p. 530; Sharma, *Jayasī Granthāvalī*, p. 386; and Shirreff, *Padmāvatī*, p. 148.

42. *Gorakh Bānī*, Sabadī 118, attributed to Ratannāth or Ratan Pīr, identifies iron with the Muslim holy man (*pīr*), whose yogic teachings he identifies with copper. Silver is equated with Muhammad and gold with God (*khudai, ṣudai*).

43. These include the *Rasakautuka* (ASL MSS no. 4203: fol. 2b.4–11; fol. 3a.1–5); the *Śivakalpadruma* of Śivanātha (ASL MSS no. 4349: fol. 2a.1–10); the 15th c. *Rasasindhu* of Viṣṇudeva (ASL MSS no. 4267: fol. 1a.9–11); and the 15th c. *Rasasaṅketakālika* of Camuṇḍakāyastha (1.2–4).

44. Mercury is thus a remedy for *tāraka-roga*, the disease of Tāraka: Misra, *Āyurvedīya*, p. 170.

45. The 11th–14th c. *Skanda Purāṇa* (1.29.87) seems to refer to this myth in its account of the birth of Skanda. At one point in this myth, the gods all become pregnant because Agni, who has already swallowed the semen, is the mouth of the gods. Then, "Śiva's semen having torn open their bellies, an ugly mercurial [*pārada*] lake of that [semen], 100 yojanas [in expanse], was formed."

46. A Buddhist version of this myth is found in a 14th c. Tibetan source, the

bCud len gyi man ngag (On the Extraction of the Essence) of Bo dong. This differs from the Hindu myth in that Śiva is made to be a form taken by Vajrasattva to unite with the Goddess; she scatters his seed about to make mercury: *Encyclopedia Tibetica*, vol. 2, pp. 522–23, cited in Fenner, *Rasāyan Siddhi*, pp. 80–81.

47. On the adulteration of the mercury in these wells, see *RRS* 1.80, and *ĀK* 1.15. Other alchemical works containing this origin myth and references to the five wells include the *Rasakautuka* (ASL MSS no. 4203, fols. 2b.4–3a.5), *Śivakalpadruma* of Śivanātha (ASL MSS no. 4349, fols. 2a.1–10), and *Rasasindhu* of Viṣṇudeva (ASL MSS no. 4267, fols. 1a.9–2a.2).

48. On the location of the land of the Daradas see Wink, *Al-Hind*, p. 232; Ray, *History*, vol. 1, p. 43, n. 1; D. C. Sircar, *Studies in the Geography of Ancient and Medieval India*, 2d revised ed. (Delhi: Motilal Banarsidass, 1977), p. 34 and n. 4; p. 68 and n. 9; and Sharma's notes to *RRS*, pp. 207–8. See also above, chap. 3, n. 93.

49. The word *cinnabar* is derived from the Greek *kinnábari*, which has the same (unknown) root as the Persian *zanjifrah: Oxford English Dictionary*, s.v. "cinnabar." Another Sanskrit term for cinnabar is *hiṅgula*, which is identical to the Persian term: Watt, *Dictionary*, 5:232. The nearest source of naturally-occurring ore cinnabar to the Indian subcontinent is Garmśir (Pir Kisri) in Afghanistan (Watt, *Dictionary*, 5:233).

50. Whence the statements of *RA* 7.72 and 11.82: "Sulfur is, by its nature and by its form, the form of mercury (*rasarūpa*)." "None of the *rasa*s or *uparasa*s is superior to sulfur." The former statement is a reference to the Indian distinction between essence and existence as "name" (*nāma*) and "form" (*rūpa*). In fact, all the major iatrochemical preparations of mercury (*kajjalī*, *rasasindhūra*, *rasaparpaṭī*, and *makaradhvaja* are essentially compounds of mercury and sulphur: Bhagwan Dash, *Alchemy and Metallic Medicines in Āyurveda* (New Delhi: Concept Publishing, 1986), p. 102.

51. *RA* 7.57–66; *RRS* 3.2–12; *KCKT* 44.2–3.

52. The problematic term in this passage is *śambala*, which the commentary to recension *ñ* of the *MBhT* glosses as "that which is released monthly by one's wives." This commentary is indicated by Michael Magee in his translation of the work: *Shri Matrika Bheda Tantra*, pp. iii and n. 1 to p. 1.

53. For the theory concerning submarine volcanos, see Sharma's commentary to *RRS*, chap. 11 (p. 210). On the doomsday fire and underwater fire jets or gas vents, see *Kalyāṇ Śakti Aṅk* (Gorakhpur: Gita Press, 1934), p. 640. This image is transferred to the subtle body in *KJñN* 2.1–3; and the "Śākta" *Gorakṣa Saṁhitā* 23.117–18. The *RA* (9.5, 8) describes, in succession, two types of saline reagents (*bīḍa*) called *vaḍavāmukha* and *jvālāmukha*. See below, chap. 8, sec. 2c.

54. *Shorter Oxford Economic Atlas of the World*, prepared by the Economist Intelligence Unit, 2d ed. (London: Oxford University Press, 1959), p. 88. Cf. Sharma's commentary (p. 184) to chap. 11 of the *RRS*. Much of the sulfur in India comes from sulfur springs which are also *pīṭha*s of the Goddess: ibid., pp. 211, 214–15.

55. On the term *liṅgam*, see Watt, *Dictionary*, 5:232, and Bose, *Concise History*, p. 317.

56. Powdered cinnabar may also be used for the tracing of two-dimensional mystic diagrams (*yantra*s, *maṇḍala*s). The preparation of gold and mercury used to form the *rasaliṅga* is described in *RRS* 6.17–18. Here, in contradistinction to the the epic origin myth of the metal, gold is made to be the mineral homologue of the Goddess: see Misra, *Āyurvedīya*, p. 83, quoting an uncited source: "The Goddess in the form of gold, Sadāśiva in the form of mercury, the liṅga made through the union of these is called the *rasaliṅga*." It should be recalled that two forms of natural gold are said, in the *RRS* (5.4–5) to arise from the *rajoguṇa* and from the placental material of the egg of Brahmā, respectively: both of these origins evoke the female element.

57. Subbarayappa, "Chemical Practices," in Bose, *Concise History*, p. 330.

58. This constitutes the tenth of the eighteen branches of Sittar alchemy. The practitioner holds three such *gulikā*s in his hand and mouth and attached around the waist to aid in raising the *kuṇḍalinī*, and transforming the subtle body: C. S. Narayanaswami Aiyar, "Ancient Indian Chemistry and Alchemy of the Chemico-Philosophical Siddhānta System of the Indian Mystics," in *Proceedings and Transactions of the Third All-India Oriental Conference*, Madras, 22–24 Dec. 1924 (Madras: Law Printing House, 1925), pp. 600–8. Purusottamānanda Tīrtha, who runs an Ayurvedic dispensary in Trichur (Tamil Nadu), carries such a *gulikā* on a belt he wears around his waist: personal communication from Catherine Clémentin-Ojha, Paris, February 1992. See below, chap. 9, n. 109 on the term *gulikā/guṭikā*.

59. *MBhT* 8.31–33. The term *svapuṣpa*, used here for "menstrual blood," is defined in *MBhT* 5.31 as the first menstrual blood shed by a woman after her defloration. The *MBhT* (5.27–33) describes the six types of women whose menstrual blood may be employed in tantric ritual. Cf. *RA* 2.25. On *ciñcinī*, see above, chap. 4, n. 41.

60. Needham, *Science and Civilisation*, vol. 5, pt. 4 (1980), p. 456. Yogiraja Vaidyaraja, "Yoga Research on Mercury and the Dhatus," *Cakra, A Journal of Tantra and Yoga* [New Delhi] 4 (March 1972), p. 186. Cf. the "Śākta" *Gorakṣa Saṁhitā* 13.99.

61. S. Madhihassan, *Indian Alchemy or Rasāyana* (New Delhi: Vikas, 1979), pp. 47–48.

62. Gold is to be placed in the tumuli (*samādhi*s) of the Nāth Siddhas: Briggs, *Gorakhnāth*, pp. 40, 42. On similar practices among the Munda-speaking Asurs of

central India, a metal-working tribal people, for whom the soul is composed of iron, see Ruben, *Eisenschmiede*, p. 88.

63. Madhihassan, *Indian Alchemy*, p. 47; Briggs, *Gorakhnāth*, p. 129.

64. Sharma's commentary to *RRS*, p. 208; and *NSC*, p. 295. The tribal Bhīls and Birhors continue the use of blood: Ruben, *Eisenschmiede*, p. 115.

65. The *Kalyāṇ Śakti Aṅk* (p. 648) reproduces an unspecified Puranic passage which states that wherever the body parts of the goddess Satī cut away by Viṣṇu's discus fell, they took the lithic form (*pāśanatām*) of the *siddha pīṭhas.* The most complete discussion of the *pīṭha*s of the Goddess, and the correspondences to Satī's body parts, is D. C. Sircar, *The Śākta Pīṭhas* (Delhi: Motilal Banarsidass, 1973). The Goddess is herself called a stone, or stone or mountain-born (*śailajā*, Pārvatī) and identified with the lithic in a wide array of Hindu contexts: see Madeleine Biardeau, *L'Hindouisme, Anthropologie d'une civilisation* (Paris: Flammarion, 1981), p. 143.

66. On the identification of the Kāmākhyā stone as red arsenic, see Karel R. van Kooij, *Worship of the Goddess According to the Kālikā Purāṇa*, pt. 1, A Translation with an Introduction and Notes of Chapters 54–69 (Leiden: Brill, 1972), p. 26, citing *Kālikā Purāṇa* 64.85–86 and Heinrich Zimmer, "Die Indische Weltmutter," in *Eranos Jahrbuch* (Ancona, Switzerland: Eranos, 1938), pp. 204–5. Dyczkowski ("Kuṇḍalinī," p. 7, note 13) maintains that the stone is black.

67. *The Yonitantra*, ed. J. A. Schoterman (Delhi: Manohar, 1980), p. 24; Bharati, *Tantric Tradition*, p. 259–60; Bhattacharya, *History*, p. 133; Fréderique Apfel-Marglin, *Wives of the God-King* (New York: Oxford University Press, 1985), p. 240; and Dyczkowski, "Kuṇḍalinī," p. 7 n. 13.

68. Dvivedi, *Nāth Sampradāy*, p. 18; *Kalyāṇ Śakti Aṅk*, p. 640; Briggs, *Gorakhnāth*, p. 18; Dikshit, *Navanātha Caritra*, p. 22. Gorakh created mountains of gold, crystal, and ocher (*geru*) as a means to "awakening" his debauched guru Matsyendra, according to the *Nātha Caritra* of Rājā Mān Singh of Jodhpur: *NSC*, p. 30.

69. Van Kooij, *Worship*, p. 26, citing *Kālikā Purāṇa* 64.73 and 76.89. The adjacent mercurial cave is a creation of the 13th c. *Siṁhāsanadvatriṃśika* (Franklin Edgerton, *Vikrama's Adventures or the Thirty-two Tales of the Throne*, 2 vols., Harvard Oriental Series, 26 (Cambridge, Mass.: Harvard University Press, 1926), 1:182–86; 2:166–67). Coloring (*rañjana*) through amalgamation is the greater part of transmutation in a number of alchemical contexts: see below, chap. 9, n. 23.

70. On Hiṅglāj Devī, her geography, pilgrimage, history, and the present-day relationship of the Nāth Siddhas to her cult, see Sastri, *Āgneya Tīrth Hiṅglāj*, throughout; Briggs, *Gorakhnāth*, pp. 89 (on the use of *thumrā*), 103–10; and *Encyclopedia of Religion and Ethics* (New York: Scribner's, 1914), s.v. "Hiṅglāj," by William Crooke.

71. A description of this site is found in a 16th c. Tibetan guide to Ca-ri, written by Padma dkar-po. This is cited at length in R. A. Stein, *Grottes-Matrices et Lieux Saints de la déesse en Asie orientale* (Paris: Ecole Française d'Extrême Orient, 1988), pp. 37–43.

72. *RA* 2.17–19, 25. The *kākiṇī* is again described in 18.165–67, where she is called *kāminī*. She is called *kālinī* in *RRS* 6.34. Cf. *BhP* 4.129–32; and *RM* fols. 35b.3–5; 36a.1–2.

73. *RA* 2.23; *RRS* 6.34. *Kākiṇī* is the name of a female divinity whose worship is described at length in chapters 58–62 of the *Rudrayāmala Tantra.* Here, she is one of six consorts of Śiva [*Śakti*s], who are identified with the six *cakra*s, all of whose names are derived from Sanskrit phonemes: *ḍākinī, rākinī, lākinī, kākinī, śākinī* and *hākinī.* In this context, *kākiṇī* is identified with the *anāhata cakra,* located in the heart (15.54–56).

74. *RA* 2.20–24; *RRS* 6.32–33.

75. *RRS* 6.35; *RA* 14.2. A preparation of zinc carbonate, mercury, and menstrual blood transmutes lead into gold: *RA* 7.31. In fact, the percentage of sulfur in a woman's blood is the highest at the time of her menses: personal communication from Siddhinandan Misra, March 1985. Sulfur, in addition to increasing the potency of mercury, is said in the *RRS* (3.17, 45) to increase the potency of male semen.

76. *KCM* fols. 12a.8–9; 21a.6–7. A procedure similar to the first of these is also prescribed in the eponymous *KCKT.* Here (8.68–70), an alchemical charm for invulnerability in battle is produced by placing equal amounts of gold, silver, and copper in menstrual blood, wrapping the whole with a lotus filament, sprinkling it with cold water, and placing it in the *yantra sthāna.* A nearly identical preparation, called a "tigress pill" (*vyāghrī-guṭikā*), is described in the *RA* (12.348–49) and the *RM* (fol. 16b.4–5). These latter two sources instruct the alchemist to place this preparation inside a woman's vulva, her *guhya-sthāna* (rather than in a *yantra-sthāna*).

77. *BhP* 2.5b–6a; 4.7; 5.1. Cf. *RHT* 3.28b on mercury that is bound when it enters the *yoni* (*yāvadviśati na yonau tāvadbandhaṃ kuto bhajate*).

78. *BhP* 3.29b–30a: purandhre gaurirajasā tadbījena bhavantu tat/ jalajādyamla-saṃyuktaṃ bandhanaṃ yāti sūtakaḥ. Later, the same source prescribes a preparation containing menstrual blood for increasing the powers of mercury to absorb (*grāsa:* literally, "swallow, consume") mica (5.284–87); and for "cutting the wings" (*pakṣaccheda*) of volatile mercury (6.15–17). Here, one is to dry, on a piece of blue cloth, a woman's menstrual blood. Through this cloth, one is to strain human breast milk, the which is then macerated together with male semen.

79. For a discussion of this tantric ritual, see Schoterman, *Yonitantra*, pp. 26–32. *Kuṇḍa[ṃ]golakam* is an elixir in *KCM* (ASL MSS no. 3952, fol. 32a.3–5); a *kuṇḍagola* produced by a Cāṇḍālī or a Rākṣasī is also mentioned in the *RM* (fols. 9b.7–8; 17b.3). Cf. *MBhT* 5.19–21.

80. *RA* 18.47–49, 115–16, 144, 165–72. An alchemical teaching by the Tibetan Vimalamitra (the sixth of the eight teachings of the *Bdud-rtsi-bam-po-brgyad-pa*, called the *Amṛtakuṇḍali* in Sanskrit) enjoins that "there be sexual union during the time of her [the female consort's] menstrual flow (*'dzag pa*)—her great blood (*khrag chen*) together with the yogin's semen will be known as the most excellent sort of *rasāyana*": Walter, *Role of Alchemy*, pp. 144–45, 168, 173.

81. For a historical discussion of the work and its author, as well as a summary of the plot, see McGregor, *Hindi Literature*, pp. 67–70. For full bibliographic details, see above, n. 41.

82. *Biravā lonā* is an imaginary transmuting herb; however Lona (from the Sanskrit *lavaṇa*, "salty, beautiful") is also the name of a powerful witch in north India: see below, chap. 9, n. 163. *Haratāra* (Sanskrit *haratāla*), yellow arsenic or orpiment, has a brilliant orange-yellow color which, like red arsenic or realgar (*manaḥśilā*) lends itself to an identification with female passion and, more specifically, menstrual blood. Mercury "swallows" sulfur in alchemical reactions; the question being asked here is why Ratansen does not allow himself to enjoy the sweetly perfumed body of Padmavatī: see the origin myth of sulfur (*gandhaka*), which, when churned out of the ocean of milk was declared "aromatic": above, n. 51.

83. *Padmāvat* [310–12 = 27.3–5] in Sharma, *Jayasī Granthāvalī*, pp. 476–81; and Dhar, *Padumāvatī*, p. 56. Cf. a description of such color changes in the laboratory, in Dash, *Alchemy*, pp. 141–42. As McGregor (*Hindi Literature*, p. 70) notes, Padmavatī is equated with Gorakhnāth slightly later in this text (27.14). Thus, the consummation of love is also an allegory on a yogin's transformation through initiation.

84. *RA* 1.28. The same source [11.104–7] describes the immediate and long-term effects of eating said mercury.

85. *RHT* 1.33: divyātanurvidheyā haragaurīsṛṣṭisaṃyogāt.

86. *Vimalaprabhā* 2.119, translated in Fenner, *Rasāyan Siddhi*, p. 138. Menstrual blood both transmutes copper into gold and, when eaten, affords immortality, according to *MBhT* 5.27–43, especially 37–42. See also Schoterman, *Yonitantra*, p. 29.

87. *MBhT* 5.28. A number of tantric sources specifically recommend a nonvirgin, ideally a low-caste woman (especially a Cāṇḍālī or Ḍombī), for such practices: Schoterman, *Yonitantra*, pp. 18–21, 24–25, 31–32; and Bhattacharya, *History*, p. 136.

88. Sharma, note to *RRS*, p. 121.

89. *BhP* 7.114–15. Such herbs are to be gathered with devotion to Śiva, and with the *bījas* (seeds, but also seed *mantras*) of Śakti, (pronounced) one by one.

90. *RC* 6.21. On the role of the outcaste Cāṇḍālī or Ḍombī woman in the worship of the female sexual organ, and the subsequent production of the power substance, the *yonitattva*, through sexual intercourse with her, see Schoterman, *Yoni Tantra*, pp. 24–25. *Cāṇḍālī* is also a term for a woman in the first day of her menses (ibid., p. 25), and for the female energy located in the abdomen (Kaviraj, *Bhāratīy*, 2:262–63. A 15th c. Bengali commentary to the Buddhist *Laghu Kālacakra Tantra* states that that part of the female organ which resembles the beak of a bird is called "bird mouth." The canal which carries semen down from the bird mouth is called *cāṇḍālī* when, instead of semen, it carries menstrual flow. *Ḍombī* is that canal which, during the menses, points upward. At the time of the discharge of semen, the same *Ḍombī* becomes *Avadhūtī:* Shastri, *Catalogue*, vol. 2, pp. iv–v.

91. Sachau, *Alberuni's India*, vol. 1, pp. 189–92. See below, chap. 9, n. 178.

92. *HYP* 3.83–91; 99–103; *Yoga Śāstra* of Dattātreya 299–312; *Gorakṣa Paddhati*, appendix to 1.82, pp. 50–55. Alternatively, the practitioner may use his partner's *yonitattva* for purposes of external ritual and worship: Schoterman, *Yonitantra*, p. 28.

93. On these terms, see above, chap. 5, n. 109, and n. 67 of the present chapter. The term *sadbhāva* is found in *KJñN* 21.10.

94. *TĀ* 29.126, 129, translated in Silburn, *Kuṇḍalinī*, pp. 190–91. These multiple roles of the female consort and her sexual essence are discussed in Silburn, *Kuṇḍalinī*, pp. 189–92. Italics are my own.

95. *Śiva Saṁhitā* 4.1–5; *HYP* 3.100, 102.

96. Silburn, *Kuṇḍalinī*, p. 192 (commentary to *TĀ* 29.128–29): "The process of breath and efficience going from the *yoginī*'s mouth to the *siddha* and vice-versa is precisely *samputīkaraṇa* . . . *Prāṇa* and *vīrya* are so intimately mixed as to be transformed into each other and to become one and the same. According to the tradition, the adept is rejuvenated; white hair and wrinkles disappear." In alchemical parlance, elixir mercury is *valipalita vināśana.*

97. Robert Svoboda, *Aghora, at the Left Hand of God* (Albuquerque, N.M.: Brotherhood of Life, Inc., 1986), pp. 280–81, quoting his Aghori teacher Vimalānanda. See ibid., pp. 279–90 for an expanded discussion of *vajrolī mudrā.* Here as well, "heavy" mercury is located at the summit of a hierarchy of fluids: water, milk, clarified butter, honey, and mercury.

98. *Vajra-* and *sahaja-* may also likely refer to the mystic Buddhist traditions known as *vajrayāna* and *sahajayāna. Olī* may be a middle Indo-Aryan shortening

of *-alaya* ("abode, place of"), in which case this term would mean the "seal of the place of the penis." Another possible source of the *-olī* ending is *-ovalli*, which means, in a tantric context, a "current of doctrine": Dyczkowski, *Canon*, p. 81 and n. 233.

99. Needham, *Science and Civilisation*, vol. 5, part 5 (1983), pp. 270–74, who also discusses the Taoist cognate to this: *huan ching*, "making the Yellow River flow backwards." According to Dharmavir Bharati (*Siddh Sāhity*, p. 325), the Nāths borrowed their theory and practice of the *vajrolī mudrā* from the Mahāyāna Buddhists. The practice is referred to in *Gorakh Bānī* Sabadī 141: bajarī kartā amarī rāṣai amarī karaṃtāṃ bāī/bhog karaṃtāṃ je vyaṃd rāṣai te goraṣ ka gurubhai. Cf. Sabadī 142, below, chap. 8, n. 88. Jerzy Kosinski (*The Hermit of 69th Street* [New York: Zebra Books, 1991] p. 69 n. 111) refers to this practice as "acclivity," a term not found in the *Oxford English Dictionary*.

100. *bCud len gyi man ngag* of Bo dong, in *Encyclopedia Tibetica*, vol. 2, pp. 522–23, 556, cited in Fenner, *Rasayan Siddhi*, p. 82.

101. At least two secret Tibetan Buddhist tantric initiations involve these same elements: sexual intercourse (which is literal and not figurative here), the intermingling of sexual fluids (the red drop of the Prajñā-maiden's pudenda (*padma*) and the white drop of the master's *vajra*), the internal raising of these commingled fluids (described as nectar), and the bliss of the realization of Buddha consciousness. The texts of these initiations are translated, with commentary, by David Snellgrove, *Indo-Tibetan Buddhism: Indian Buddhists and Their Tibetan Successors*, 2 vols. (Boston: Shambhala, 1987), vol. 1, pp. 256–64.

102. This term is discussed in *SSP* 5.7; *Akulavīra Tantra* [A] 43; *Gorakṣa Paddhati* 1.75; *Kulānanda Tantra* 4, 58; and a host of other hathayogic and tantric sources. For discussions, see also Srivastav, "*Gorakh Bānī*" *Viśeṣāṅk*, pp. 15, 238; idem, "*Gorakṣa*" *Viśeṣāṅk*, pp. 45–46, 156–57; Dvivedi, *Nāth Sampradāy*, pp. 58–59, 72; Gonda, *Medieval*, p. 224; and Mallik, *SSP*, p. 21.

103. The red *bindu* is said to shine with the same ruddy brilliance as liquid *sindūra*, mercuric oxide: *Yogamārtaṇḍa* 61, in Mallik, *SSP*, p. 61; and *Gorakṣa Śataka* 73. This mixture of red and white fluids may have its origins in the combination of (reddish) *soma* and white milk in Vedic oblations, and a tantric parallel in the ritual consumption of the *yonitattva* together with wine: Schoterman, *Yonitantra*, p. 30.

104. *Gorakṣa Paddhati* 1.71–75 (= *Gorakṣa Śataka* 72–76 = *Yogamārtaṇḍa* 61–64). Verse 64 reads: śukraṃ candreṇa saṃyuktaṃ rajaḥ sūryeṇa saṃyutam/ dvayos samarasaikatvaṃ yo jānāti sa yogavit: "Semen is conjoined with the moon, uterine blood is conjoined with the sun. He who knows *samarasa* to be the unity of the two, he is a knower of yoga." On the *mahābindu*, see *Gorakh Bānī*, Sabadī 237, and

p. 32 of the Gorakhnāth Mandir edition of *Gorakh Bāni*, which equates *mahābindu* with *mahāśūnya*. See also *Dhyānabindu Upaniṣad* 87–88, in Varenne, *Upanishads du yoga*, p. 111; and Filliozat, "Taoïsme et yoga," p. 66.

105. Personal communication from N. Sethu Raghnathan, Madurai, January 1985. The titles of a great number of the Tamil alchemical sources are composed of the name of the author followed by the number of verses in the treatise. Cf. *HYP* 3.100, with Brahmānanda's commentary, on the notion that *nāda* becomes *bindu* in a woman's body—whence the need for a female partner in erotic tantric rites. On *bindu* and *nāda*, see above, chap. 3, n. 102.

106. *Yoga*, literally "union" is, in the mystic parlance of the Nāth Siddhas, the union of sun and moon, fire and fluid, ovum and seed, that which is enjoyed (*upabhogya*) and that which enjoys (*bhoktā*), and ultimately, the commingling of the principles of creation and destruction: Dasgupta, *Obscure*, pp. 235, 238–39.

107. *Śiva Saṁhitā* 3.54; *Yogatattva Upaniṣad* 74; *RA* 11.144; 12.251, 265; 18.28, 83, 163. The yogin, whose own body has been rendered golden or adamantine (Śiv Gorakṣ Bāvanī 38, in *Gorakṣa Stavāñjali*, ed. Yogi Bhambhulnath [Haridwar: Goraksanath Mandir, n.d.], p. 20; *Gorakh Bānī* Pad 13.1; 50.2) becomes polymorphously perverse at this point, capable of transforming base metals into gold (as does mercury), base and noble metals into human bodies, human bodies into metals, stones, animals, etc. The mythology of the Nāth Siddhas is replete with such transformations, often effected by Gorakh.

108. *Gorakh Bānī*, Sabadī 1.1. Kabīr expresses a similar sentiment in *doha* 13.23 in Vaudeville, *Kabir Granthavali (Doha)*, p. 87: "He finds himself face to face with the Lord, and becomes a child (*bālak*) again." For a differing interpretation, see Bharati, *Siddh Sāhity*, pp. 337–38. See above, n. 94, and chap. 10, sec. 2.

109. *RC* 15.13–15; *RRS* 1.85–88; *ĀK* 1.53b–62a; *Rasakautuka*, ASL MSS no. 4203, fol. 4a.6–9; *Śivakalpadruma* of Śivanātha, ASL MSS no. 4349, fol. 2b.1–6.

110. M. F. de Mely, "L'alchimie chez les chinois et l'alchimie grecque," *Journal Asiatique*, 9è série 6 (Sept.–Oct. 1895), pp. 314–40, especially pp. 332–33.

111. Needham, *Science and Civilisation*, vol. 5, pt. 4 (1980), p. 337.

112. De Mely, "L'alchimie chez les chinois," p. 334.

113. *Mahābhārata* 3.110.1–3.113.25.

114. De Mely, "L'alchimie chez les chinois," p. 334. The Renaissance "Hunting of the Greene Lyon," as a metaphor for the quest for the alchemical elixir, may be of a similar origin: Betty Jo Teeter Dobbs, *The Foundations of Newton's Alchemy: "The Hunting of the Greene Lyon"* (London: Cambridge University Press, 1975).

115. This Jabirian account is said to be an elaboration of an Indian legend of Maṇimekhalā, "the jewel engirdled one." Maṇimekhalā's story is referred to in the *Kathāsaritsāgara* of Somadeva (*Ocean*, vol. 9, p. 51). The myth is discussed in Sylvain

Lévi, "Maṇimekhalā, divinité de la mer," in *Mémorial Sylvain Lévi* (Paris: P. Hartmann, 1937), pp. 371–83.

116. Paul Kraus, *Jābir ibn Hayyān: Contribution à l'histoire des idées scientifiques dans l'Islam* (Paris: Les Belles Lettres, 1986), pp. 90–93. Kraus identifies Sindiyyat with an island off the coast of the Sind, in southern Pakistan. He opines (p. 91, n. 4), however, that *Suvarṇa-bhūmi*, the "Golden Land," generally identified with the "greater India" of southeast Asia, perhaps Burma, may be intended here. On this toponym, see Wink, *Al-Hind*, vol. 1, pp. 334–42.

117. Needham, *Science and Civilisation*, vol. 5, pt. 4 (1980), pp. 330–425, especially pp. 339–355.

118. On Darada-deśa, see above, n. 48. On Pārada-deśa, see Sircar, *Studies*, p. 33 and n. 4; p. 68 and n. 9; and p. 70.

119. On possible identifications of Bībī Nānī with other mother goddesses, see William Crooke, "Hiṅglāj," *Encyclopedia of Religion and Ethics*, vol. 6, p. 715.

120. A modern description of the Candrakūpa is found in Sastri, *Āgneya Tīrth Hinglāj*, pp. 29–47. See esp. p. 45. The *Life of Apollonius* is a work of fiction which nonetheless contained numerous geographic and ethnographic details culled by Philostratus from ancient travel accounts. Philostratus localizes his "Well of Truth" somewhere in the Indus River region: *Philostratus, Life of Apollonius*, tr. C. P. Jones and edited, abridged, and introduced by G. W. Bowersock (Harmondsworth: Penguin, 1970), p. 75. See below, chap. 8, sec. 2b, for a discussion of other "lunar" toponyms.

121. On the rock-hewn images of the sun and moon, see Crooke, "Hiṅglāj," p. 45; Briggs, *Gorakhnāth*, p. 106 (reporting an account given by Charles Masson in 1844); and Ctesias, "Indika," in Photios, *Bibliotheca* (46a.13–19), ed. and tr. René Henry, 6 vols. (Paris: Les Belles Lettres, 1959), vol. 1, p. 136.

122. Jaan Puhvel, *Comparative Religion* (Baltimore: Johns Hopkins University Press, 1986), "Fire in Water," pp. 277–83, especially p. 279, on the Irish Nechtan's well. Cf. Georges Dumézil, *Mythe et épopée*, vol. 3, part 1, pp. 22–89, especially pp. 27–31.

123. pañcabhūtātmakaḥ sūtastiṣṭatyeva sadāśiva. Cf. *BhP* 1.32–37. Sadāśiva is, of course, a god who is represented iconographically with five heads: see above, chap. 2, nn. 64–66. Elsewhere, the south Indian tradition of Siddha medicine bases its practice of *pañcikaraṇa* ("the five practices," or simply "doing five"), the purification of the elements used in its therapy, upon the assumption that Śiva and Śakti are present in every element: Kardaswamy, *History*, p. 340.

124. Treloar, "Use of Mercury," p. 238.

125. On this, see David Gordon White, "Why Gurus Are Heavy," *Numen* 33 (1984), pp. 43–44 and notes.

126. The classic theoretical statement is Louis Dumont, *Homo hierarchicus, le système des castes et ses implications* (Paris: Gallimard, 1978), appendix 4, "Vers une théorie de la hiéarchie," pp. 396–403.

127. Each of the five elements is quadrupled within this system: to each of the five *tanmātras* (subtle elements, senses) there corresponds a gross element (*mahābhūta*), a "grasping organ" (*karmendrīya*) and a sensory organ (*jñānendrīya*). On the generation of lower elements from higher in Sāṃkhya, see B. N. Seal, "The Physicochemical Theories of the Ancient Hindus," appendix to Ray, *History* (1956), pp. 264–65.

128. *Caraka Saṁhitā* 4.5.5. The same schema is echoed in the *ṢSS* (4.24) of the Western Transmission tradition: Schoterman, *ṢSS* p. 129. Cf. the slight variations suggested by Jean Filliozat, "Taoïsme et yoga," p. 48.

129. *Dhātu*, "that which supports" (from the Sanskrit root *dhā*, support, ground), is the Ayurvedic term for the constituent parts of the body and the alchemical term for the metals. In both cases, these are the constituent elements of their respective systems, without which the entire (biological or metallic) body would collapse and disintegrate. See above, nn. 11, 20.

130. Prior to the 12th c. alchemical synthesis, the term *loha*, which specifically means iron, was employed as the generic term for metal: personal communication from Damodar Joshi, Benares, September 1984.

131. *RA* 7.97–98. Cf. *Chāndogya Upaniṣad* 4.17.7: "Just as one would mend gold with salt, silver with gold, tin with silver, lead with tin, iron with lead, wood with iron." Enumerations of the metals vary from one source to another, some adding such alloys as brass, bronze, bell metal, etc. to reach totals of as many as twelve (in *ĀK* 2.1.9) metals. See Misra, *Āyurvedīya*, pp. 493–96, for a discussion of the nomenclature of the metals in all the major alchemical texts.

132. Syamasundaracarya Vaisya, *Rasāyan Sār*, 5th ed. (Benares: Syamasundar Rasayansala, 1971), vol. 1, p. 70. Although this is a modern work (the first edition appeared in 1914), its statement of the process of resorption (*layakrama*) respects the classic formulation.

133. In a general sense, this south Indian tradition makes greater use of the system of the five elements, in its formulations of the applications and powers of mercurial medicines, than do the northern traditions. Personal communication from N. Sethu Raghunathan, Madurai, India, January 1985. Cf. Subbarayappa, "Chemical Practices," in Bose, *Concise History*, p. 334.

134. *HT*, p. 176. Cf. *Saṭ-cakra-nirūpaṇa* 4-29, trans. with commentary in John Woodroffe, *The Serpent Power*, 9th ed. (Madras: Ganesh and Co., 1971), pp. 330–87.

135. *RHT* 1.12: kāṣṭhauṣadhyo nage nagaṃ vaṅge vaṅgamapi līyate śulbe / śul-

baṃ tare taraṃ kanake kanakañ ca līyate sūte. An identical passage is *RRS* 1.60. *RA* 7.97 makes the same statement in a more elliptical way: "that which precedes [is higher on the hierarchy] is imperishable [*akṣaya*] with regard to that which is lower." The *Mahābharata* (5.39.65) describes the hierarchy of the five metals in the following terms: "Silver is the dross [*mala*] of gold; copper the dross of silver; tin the dross of copper; lead the dross of tin; and dross [*mala:* here, iron?] the dross of lead." Cf. *Chāndogya Upaniṣad* 4.17.7 for a still earlier formulation.

136. Two modern empirical explanations for the hierarchy of the metals are offered in Misra, *Āyurvedīya*, pp. 494, 498: that which is higher on the hierarchy requires greater heat for its purification than that which is lower; that which is higher on the hierarchy loses less of its mass when heated than that which is lower.

137. *RRS* 1.30–37; *ĀK* 1.18–23. This is an idealized schematization: as noted, the term *pārada* likely derives from the name of the country, located to the west or northwest of India, from which mercury was imported to India: see *RC* 15.14–15. Cf. above, chap. 3, n. 93, and n. 118 of the present chapter.

138. *RPS* 1.17–18; *Rasakautuka* (ASL MSS no. 4203), fol. 3a.5–6; and *Śivakalpadruma* (ASL MSS no. 4349), fols. 6a.12–6b.2. The five states or phases of mercury (*avasthā*) appear not to be arranged hierarchically: *RA* 10.17–18.

139. *KCM* (ASL MSS no. 3952), fol. 30b.3–4; *RA* 6.67–68.

140. The third and fourth members of the hierarchy appear to be reversed in the discussions of the *gati*s and *vedha:* air precedes fire in both cases, in opposition to the Samkhyan ordering of the five elements, in which fire is the third and air the fourth element on the pentadic hierarchy.

141. *RA* 10.13–15; *RRS* 1.82–83.

142. Mercury is identified with the soul (*ātman*) both here (*RRS* 1.83) and in *RU* 15.50. The fifth *gati* of mercury is called *jīva-vat* in *ĀK* 1.40. In the *Caraka Saṁhitā*'s Ayurvedic analysis of semen, only the four lower elements are present (on this, see Sharma's notes to *RRS* 1.81–83, on p. 13 of his edition); it is however united, at conception, with *ākāśa*, ether, which is omnipresent and static in the ovary: *Caraka Saṁhitā* 4.2.4, cited in Dasgupta, *History*, vol. 2, pp. 302, 307.

143. *RRS* 1.83. The *RA* (10.15) stipulates that the fifth *gati*, the *jīva-gati*, of mercury is invisible, while the first four are visible. Sharma, in his notes to *RRS* 1.83 (p. 13), states that, due to its invisibility, the fifth *gati* of mercury is also called *daivī-gati*, its "divine motion." He suggests the use of such "Siddha mantras" as the *aghora*, and the adjunction of yogic practices to halt the loss of mercury through this *gati*, or to render it visible.

144. *RA* 1.41. Another term for mercury is *vyoma-dhāraṇa*, "maintaining mica / ether [in mental concentration]": Monier-Williams, *Sanskrit-English Dictionary*, s.v. "vyoman."

145. *RC* 4.106–11; *RRS* 8.90–94.

146. *RRS* 8.95.

147. *RA* 5.28, 32–41.

148. These are the "M-words" or antisacraments of tantric practice, possibly subversions of the *pañcagavya*, the five pure products of the cow that were the orthodox brahmin's mainstay: *māṃsa*, meat; *matsya*, fish; *mudrā*, parched grain; *madhu*, spiritous liquor; and *maithuna*, sexual intercourse.

149. The five "nectars," here are bodily secretions used in secret tantric ceremonies: blood, semen, urine, feces, and flesh: *KJñN* 11.5, 11.

150. These are the "stools" or "seats," pilgrimage sites of the Goddess. As many as 134 *pīṭha*s are enumerated in certain lists. Five are singled out, however, and are identified here with the five elements. Kāmākhyā (here called Kāmarūpa) is one of these: Schoterman, *ṢSS*, appendix 2, pp. 222–25.

151. On the five *kula*s, see Marie-Therèse de Mallmann, "Divinités hindoues dans le tantrisme bouddhique," *Arts Asiatiques* 10 (1964), pp. 68, 72–74. On the five *āmnāya*s ("transmissions"), emanating out of the five faces of Śiva, see *Kulārṇava Tantra* 3.7–10.

152. The more traditional number is nine: however, the Bengali *Gorakṣa Vijaya* and other traditions speak of the five original Nāths. These are Adināth, the primal Nāth, and four Nāths who arose from his body parts; Gorakhnāth, who arose from his head; Matsyendranāth, who arose from his navel; Kaṇerināth, who arose from his ears; Jālandharanāth, who arose from his bones; and Cauraṅginātḥ, who arose from his limbs: Mukherji, *Gopicandra Nāṭaka*, p. xxxvi.

153. These three groups of five are treated together in a work of the Nāth Siddhas entitled *Goraṣ Ganeṣ Guṣṭi* (in Srivastav, ed., *"Gorakhbānī" Viśeṣāṅk*, pp. 388–90. All three groups are related, serially, to the five elements.

154. Dumont, *Homo hierarchicus*, pp. 104–5, 397. See above, n. 126.

155. *Abhraka* and *gagana* are the two more common terms; the *RA* (6.31) also mentions *vyoma*. The *RC* uses all four terms interchangeably in chapter 16, employing *kha* once, in 16.37. *Kha-puṣpa*, "cavity-" or "hole-flower," is a common term for menstrual blood in tantrism: Bhattacharya, *History*, pp. 132, 136.

156. The *Rasakāmadhenu* passage is reproduced without verse citation in Sharma's commentary to *RRS* 2.1.

157. *Rasendra Bhāskara* 3.42. *Abhra* connotes wetness in such Vedic passages as *Atharva Veda* 1.12.3 (cited in Dasgupta, *History*, vol. 2, p. 331, n. 2).

158. See above, n. 144. *Vyoman* is the "firmament" in *Atharva Veda* 8.18.13. The five *ākāśa*s are identified with the five *vyoma*s in the *SSP* and are discussed by Kaviraj, *Tāntrik Sādhanā*, p. 401.

159. However, *RRS* 5.5 states that natural gold (*prakṛta-svarṇa*) originally arose from the *rajoguṇa*. See also Biardeau, *Hindouïsme*, pp. 106, 110. The pivotal, female, and creative role of ether/empty space is set forth in the *Caraka Saṁhitā* (4.2.4) discussion of conception: see above, n. 142.

160. The association of *rajas*, the *guṇa* of activity, with the Goddess, is supported etymologically. *Rajas* at once means menstrual blood, pollen, redness, and passion, all terms with highly feminine connotations in India.

161. Abhinavagupta lends a pivotal role to the fifth element, which he calls *ākāśa-śakti*, the "power of space." On this, he says that, unlike the powers of the four lower elements, "the power of space plays no role in sustaining the finite subject. For the power of space is inherent in the individual soul as the true subjectivity, at once empty of the objects and providing a place in which objects may be known. This is the Emissional Power in its lowest form" (commentary on *Parātrīśikā Laghuvṛtti* 5–9a, translated in Muller-Ortega, *Triadic Heart*, p. 131). See below, note 176, on the *kañcuka*s.

162. The goose seems to be identified with the breaths even before the syllables of its name come to represent the sound of inbreathing and outbreathing themselves. The original notion would have been that the goose of the breath kept one alive so long as one of its feet remained tethered to the body: its flight, up and out of the body, is death. This is the implication of *Aitareya Āraṇyaka* 2.1.8 (citing *Ṛg Veda* 1.164.38), even if this text does not mention *haṃsa* explicitly.

163. Silburn, *Kuṇḍalinī*, p. 23.

164. *Gorakṣa Śataka* 64–70, especially 67.

165. *RA* 2.89; 11.151. *Khecarī* is also referred to in the context of a thirty-two-syllable Kubjikā *mantra*, in 3.9. A *khecarī* clan lineage (*kula*) is named and its *mantra* discussed in 3.17–20 and 12.59. Certain herbs are also referred to as *khecarī*, because they produce the power of flight in mercury: 12.52–54. One of the *uparasa*s, *kāsīsa* (ferrous sulfate) is called *khecara* in *RC* 11.1 and *RHT* 9.5. It is called *khaga* ("sky-going") in *RA* 7.56. *Khecara* is one of the eight "magical" *siddhi*s listed (along with *rasa-rasāyana*) in the 3d–11th c. A.D. *Sādhanamālā:* Bhattacharya, *Sādhanamālā* 2:lxxxv.

166. *RHT* 4.5; *RC* 16.4, 44, 52–55, 75. Clipping the wings of volatile mercury is the remedy for *cāpalyadoṣa*, the "flaw of instability." This is effected through *niyamana* ("regulation"), the seventh of the eighteen alchemical *saṃskāra*s: Misra, *Āyurvedīya*, p. 195.

167. The play of correspondences is not perfect here, since evaporation can be identified with the element air, rather than ether or space. Both appear to be present here. *Haṃsaga* mercury (*RA* 10.14–15; 11.126–31; 12.68–70; *RRS* 1.81–83 and

pp. 13, 133) is related to the element air, referring as it does to mercury's tendency to evaporate, *haṃsaga*, in the sunshine whose beams are called *haṃsapāda* in *Atharva Veda* 11.4.21—or into the wind as breath, also called *haṃsa* in yoga.

168. On this, see *Cirpatjī kī sabadī* 23, in Mallik, *SSP*, p. 84: "bind the flying *haṃsa*" (*udaina haṃsā lāgai bandh*). Cf. *HYP* 4.92 and *BhP* 5.148, 168–69.

169. Elsewhere, the *Gorakṣa Paddhati* (p. 60 of the Bombay edition, cited in Bharati, *Siddh Sāhity*, p. 340), calls the ether the void (*śūnya*) in which Śiva (whose semen is mercury) dwells.

170. *RC* 15.4–12.

171. Siddhinandan Misra, who translated this text into Hindi, chooses to see in the plural use of the term *dhātu* a reference to the sexual fluids of both Śiva and the Goddess (*śiv-pārvatī ke antim dhātu*): Misra, *RC*, p. 289. Elsewhere (16.8), Somadeva calls mica (*abhraka*) and mercury (*pārada*) the final *dhātu*s of the Goddess and Śiva. Here, these *dhātu*s are "final" in the Ayurvedic sense of the term: as the sexual emissions of the two, they are the final distillates of divine processes of digestion.

172. This is the Vedic myth of Indra's theft of Soma, the divine draft of immortality. In the *Ṛg Veda* (4.26–27), it is Indra who, mounted on an eagle or falcon (*śyena*), steals the *soma* (later identified with lunar nectar and semen) from the atmospheric Gandharvas. In Brahmanic myth (*Taittirīya Saṁhitā* 6.1.6; *Śatapatha Brāhmaṇa* 3.6.6.2), the rivalry is between a serpent named Kadrū and a falcon named Suparṇī. This develops, in later epic myth, into the baroque account of the bird Garuḍa's "theft" of the *soma* from the serpents, or from Indra and the gods: *Rāmāyaṇa* 3.35; *Mahābhārata* 1.20.1–1.30.25.

173. For the Babylonian myth of Etana and the Zu bird, as well as a wide array of Indian and Indo-European parallels to this mythic theme, see David M. Knipe, "The Heroic Theft: Myths from Ṛgveda IV and the Ancient Near East," *History of Religions* 6:4 (May 1967), pp. 328–60. Cf. Jarich G. Oosten, *The War of the Gods: The Social Code in Indo-European Mythology* (London: Routledge & Kegan Paul, 1985), pp. 69–71.

174. *Mahābhārata* 1.20.1–1.30.25.

175. *RRS* 1.80; *ĀK* 1.35–37; *RC* 15.24–25, 43–49; *BhP* 3.22. Misra (*Āyurvedīya*, p. 197) describes this purification in terms of a snake shedding its skin. It is noteworthy that in Ayurvedic embryology, heating in the uterus generates seven layers (*kalā*s) of skin and the seven *dhātu*s around the blood and semen that were originally present at conception: Dasgupta, *History*, vol. 2, pp. 312, 317.

176. On the *kañcuka*s in Śaiva Siddhānta thought, see Gonda, *Medieval*, p. 186; on the Vidyeśvaras, see Rao, *Elements*, vol. 2, part 2, p. 397, and above, chap. 6, n. 56.

177. *TĀ* 13.103–4, translated in Muller-Ortega, *Triadic Heart*, p. 139. Cf. *Parā-*

trīśikā Laghuvṛtti 5–9a, translated ibid., p. 131. Cf. Dasgupta, *Obscure*, p. 219, and Srivastav, ed., *"Gorakṣa" Viśeṣāṅk*, p. 272, for Nāth Siddha interpretations.

178. *BhP* 2.5b–7a: tatrādau tu rasaḥ sūtaḥ śivadehādvinirgataḥ/ tato 'nyattu ghanaṃ khyātamumāyonisamudbhavam/ sitaṃ pītaṃ tathā raktaṃ kṛṣṇañ caiva tu varṇataḥ // vajrākhyañ caiva māṇḍūkaṃ dvividhaṃ tu prakīrtitam.

179. For *ahirāja*, see *RA* 13.370. One type of mica is called *nāga*, "serpent," because of the hissing sounds it makes when heated: *RC* 10.6.

180. The alchemical sources refer repeatedly to lead and tin as *pūta*, "smelly," a fact that may have inspired this mythic representation of them as *mala*, dross. In the gradual transformation of the human body into an alchemical body, the first of an eight-stage process is called "piercing" or "transmuting" the skin (*tvacāvedha*), by which the body is transmuted into lead and tin (*pannaga*): *RA* 18.150.

181. Śeṣa (along with his brothers Ananta, Vāsuki and Takṣaka) is the Lord of Serpents in Hindu mythology. Somadeva's evocation of the Lord of Serpents who drinks the divine semen that has fallen from the mouth of Agni would thus refer to this same figure. On Śeṣa as "remains," see Charles Malamoud, "Observations sur la notion de 'reste' dans le brahmanisme," in *Cuire le monde*, pp. 28–29.

182. Śiva's name here is to be identified with the fire of yoga (*yogāgni*) that destroys the fire of time (*kālāgni*) in the microcosm. The universal resorption is a reabsorption of both matter *and time:* time which generally cooks all creatures is itself cooked by the dissolution. Time yields to eternity, until the universe is re-emitted by the great yogin. The fire of Śiva's yoga is also greater than the fire of desire (*kāmāgni*), as illustrated in the myth of his incineration of Kāma, the Hindu Eros, with fire from his third, yogic, eye.

183. Whence the final verse of the *RA* (18.228), which states that the perfected Siddha dwells eternally in the highest level of the cosmic egg—sometimes known as Siddha-loka—even when all living beings have been annihilated in the terrible flood (of the end of the world).

184. In later sources, particularly Śaiva Purāṇas and Tantras, it is Śiva who is the great yogin, a distinction he has retained down to the present day in India. In this light, the statement that mercury is the exudation or sweat of the sleeping (i.e., yogically withdrawn) Śiva, is a telling one: *RA* 1.36. See above, chap. 2, sec. 5.

185. Puranic cosmogony is in fact an appropriation, run in reverse, of the stages of yogic withdrawal: *Asian Mythologies*, s.v. "Purāṇic Cosmogony."

186. Ibid., and Biardeau, *Hindouïsme*, pp. 121–22. A translation of the *Viṣṇu Purāṇa* (6.3.14–41; 6.4.1–10) treatment of cosmic dissolution is in Dimmitt and Van Buitenen, *Classical Hindu Mythology*, pp. 41–43.

187. Mircea Eliade, *The Sacred and the Profane: The Nature of Religion* (New York: Harcourt Brace Jovanovich, 1959), pp. 54–55; Stella Kramrisch, *The Hindu Temple*,

2 vols. (Calcutta: University of Calcutta, 1946; reprint Benares: Motilal Banarsidass, 1976), vol. 1, p. 62, n. 105.

188. Filliozat, *Doctrine classique*, p. 19. Nāgārjuna is called the son of Vāsuki in a Nāth source: *NSC*, p. 226. A Rajput royal lineage calls itself the *nāgavaṃśī*, "serpent lineage," claiming descent from one or another of the great serpents of Hindu myth: Ruben, *Eisenschmiede*, p. 110.

189. See below, chap. 9, n. 102.

190. Kaviraj, *Bhāratīy*, vol. 1, p. 311; Silburn, *Kuṇḍalinī*, p. 42, citing Abhinavagupta, *Tantrāloka-viveka* 22. Cf. *Śvetāśvatara Upaniṣad* 1.13, in which meditation on the Oṃ causes the subtle mark (*liṅga*) of the divine within all humans to manifest itself.

Chapter Eight

1. Toni Schmidt, "Fünfundachtzig Mahāsiddhas," *Ethnos* 2–3 (1955), p. 120; Rolf Stein, "Jardins en miniature," p. 54. A seemingly identical image appears in the context of the pilgrimage to the shrine of Hiṅglāj Devī, in eastern Baluchistan. This is a *liṅgam-yoni*, the image of the sexual union of Śiva and the Goddess, which is branded on the upper right forearm of Nāth Siddhas travelling to the site. The image, reproduced by Briggs (*Gorakhnāth*, p. 110), is of a scrolled letter U in the hollow of which are nested two concentric circles.

2. *HYP* 3.1.

3. *RHT* 1.7; *MBhT* 3.12–14; *SSP* 3.5; *Gorakṣa Paddhati* 1.60; *BhP* 9.117–19. Cf. Dvivedi, *Nāth Sampradāy*, pp. 187–88; Misra, *Āyurvedīya*, p. 28; Kaviraj, *Bhāratīy*, vol. 1, pp. 555–56; Srivastav, "*Gorakṣa*" *Viśeṣāṅk*, p. 132; idem, "*Gorakh Bānī*" *Viśeṣāṅk*, p. 332; *NSC*, p. 131.

4. *Toḍala Tantra* 9.14b–15b: pṛthvīcakrasya madhye tu svayambhūliṅgamadbhutam/ sārddhatrivalayākārakuṇḍalyā veṣṭitaṃ sadā/ liṅgacchidraṃ svavaktreṇa kuṇḍalyācchādya saṃsthitā. Cf. 9.21. Alternatively, her mouth is said to cover the *brahmadvāra*, the "door of brahman," which is the opening to the lower end of the *suṣumṇā nāḍī*: *Gorakṣa Paddhati* 1.17–19; *Yoga Mārtaṇḍa* 36. Cf. *NSC*, p. 131, which states that she sleeps with her mouth closed around the "western" *liṅga*.

5. Silburn, *Kuṇḍalinī*, pp. 22–23. This discussion, of the place of the *kuṇḍalinī* in the hathayogic system of the Nāth Siddhas, differs significantly from Silburn's descriptions (ibid., pp. 19–24, 63–69) of the two *kuṇḍalinī*s (the *adhaḥ*- and *ūrdhva-kuṇḍalinī*s) or the three aspects of the *kuṇḍalinī* (*śakti*-, *prāṇa*-, and *parā-kuṇḍalinī*s) in the Trika Kaula system of Abhinavagupta and others.

6. *Gorakṣa Paddhati* 1.47–56; *Yoga Mārtaṇḍa* 36–40. The editor of the *Gorakṣa Paddhati*, citing "other sources," reproduces the following verse (numbered 2) on p. 28: "in between the *iḍā* and *piṅgalā* is the child widow, the *kuṇḍalinī*."

7. This is the particular perspective of the Nāth Siddhas who, anti-Śākta to the extreme, deny whenever possible any constructive role to the feminine. This is in marked contrast to the Trika system, for which the *kuṇḍalinī* is the dynamic manifestation of Śiva in the universal macrocosm as well as the human microcosm: Silburn, *Kuṇḍalinī,* p. 24. Gorakhnāth compares women to tigresses and succubi: see below, n. 92.

8. Biardeau, *Hindouïsme,* p. 167. *Bhogavatī* is the name of the city or a sacred *tīrtha* of the serpent race, in the Hindu epics: Monier-Williams, s.v. "[1]bhoga," citing the *Rāmāyaṇa, Mahābhārata,* and *Harivaṃśa.*

9. Padoux, *Vāc,* pp. 81–83. Cf. Sanderson, "Maṇḍala and Āgamic Identity," pp. 178, 185; Brooks, *Secret,* p. 111; Silburn, *Kuṇḍalinī,* pp. 19–24, 52–53, 64–66.

10. Silburn, *Kuṇḍalinī,* p. 27, 42, citing Kṣemarāja's commentary on *Śivasūtra* 2.3. Cf. Kaviraj, *Bhāratīy,* 1:309.

11. On the *bhukti/mukti* dyad see Brooks, *Secret,* pp. 91, 105. Rasik Vihari Joshi ("Notes on Guru, Dīkṣā and Mantra," *Ethnos* 37 [1972], pp. 106–7) discusses *mokṣa* and *bhoga* as two forms of tantric initiation. But see Sanderson's ("Śaivism," pp. 667–68) important nuanced discussion of the mutual exclusivity of *mokṣa* and *bhoga* in early tantrism. *Mokṣa* was the goal of "liberation-seeking" celibate ascetics, while *bhoga,* supernatural experience generally gained through sexual union, was the goal of such "power-seeking" tantric movements as the Mantramārga.

12. See *MBhT* 14.3–10, on *divya-, vīrya-,* and *paśu-bhoga,* also in relation to the *kuṇḍalinī.*

13. *MBhT* 3.1–16; 14.13–14; and Bharati, *Tantric Tradition,* pp. 252, 260.

14. *HYP* 1.27; 3.11; 3.61–69.

15. Silburn, *Kuṇḍalinī,* pp. 15, 27, 52.

16. See Silburn (*Kuṇḍalinī,* pp. 27, 52) for Abhinavagupta's (*TĀ* 3.171) play on the word *viṣ[a]:* when she sleeps, the *kuṇḍalinī* holds the poison that destroys human vitality; when she awakens, this poison transforms itself into all-pervading (*viś*) power.

17. This is the origin myth of poison, in *RRS* 29.1–11.

18. It is this mythic feat and the quest to, once again, become a "second Śiva," that appears to be the raison d'être of the so-called "Poison Tantras" (*viṣatantras*), of which the *Yogaratnāvali* revealed by Śrīkaṇṭha Śiva (ASL MSS no. 4184) is an example.

19. He is further identified with Vajrabhairava. This god's consort is Ekajaṭā: see Beyer, *Tārā* pp. 42–43, 54; and above, chap. 3, nn. 89–90.

20. *Spanda Kārikā* 3.16, trans. in Harvey Alper, "The Cosmos as Śiva's Language-Game," in idem, *Mantra* (Albany: SUNY Press, 1989), p. 280.

21. *TĀ* 3.171.

22. Gūgā Chauhan or Gūgā Pīr, whom the Nāth Siddhas claim to have been one of their number, is renowned for his power over serpents: Rose, pp. 395, 409. Nepali legend maintains that Gorakhnāth held back the "great serpents" of the rains in Nepal for some twelve years, a reference that at once harks back to Vedic myths of Indra taming the rain serpent Vṛtra and to Gorakh's yogic control of the *kuṇḍalinī.*

23. *BhP* 9.118b–119a. On the mythic theme, of a disciple becoming his guru's teacher and the guru becoming his disciple's pupil, in its relationship to the ideology of brahmanic sacrifice, according to which that which precedes (e.g. a prior sacrifice) is necessary to that which follows (e.g. a present sacrifice, lit from the embers of the prior sacrifice); but also that that which precedes can only persist through that which follows (the prior sacrifice is reborn through the present sacrifice), see below, ch. 9, n. 104.

24. According to the *KJñN* (22.10), the Yoginī-Kaula doctrines were found "in every house in Kāmarūpa." Three Padas (2, 43, and 49) of the *Gorakh Bānī* take the form of teachings made to his guru after his rescue from the Kingdom of Women: Srivastav, "*Gorakh Bānī*" *Viṣeśāṅk*, p. 327. So too, in the Bengali *Mīn Cetan–Gorakṣa Vijay* cycle, it is made clear that the yoginīs of this mystic doctrine and the women of the Plantain Forest were one and the same. Indeed, the origin of the "householder Nāths" is also traced back to these yoginīs, who inveigled celibate yogins into moving in with them: Dvivedi, *Nāth Sampradāy*, pp. 22, 56.

25. The opening lines of the 17th c. Bengali work *Mīn Cetan* are the Goddess's question to Śiva: "Why is it, my Lord, that thou art immortal and mortal am I? Advise me the truth, O Lord, so that I also may be immortal for ages" (tuṁhī kene tara gosānī āṁhi kene mari/ hena tattva kaha dev joge joge tari). In answer to her question, Śiva expounds on *haṭha yoga*, in the monologue that Matsyendra overhears: Dasgupta, *Obscure*, p. 228.

26. Matsyendra's name, like that of Nāgārjuna, cannot be attached to a single historical figure. It is rather to be seen as an initiatory title, given to tantric practitioners who had reached a certain advanced level of mastery: Tucci, "Animadversiones Indicae," p. 133.

27. Matsyendra is described as dwelling in the belly of the fish in the c. A.D. 1290 *Jñāneśvarī* (18.1729–35) of the Marathi saint Jñāneśvara: Avedyanāth jī Mahārāj, "Mahāyogī Guru Gorakhnāth evam unkī Tapasthalī," in Baba Cunninathji, ed. *Tan-Prakāś* (Gorakhpur: Gita Press, 1981), p. 186. The same description is given in another Marathi source, the 13th c. *YSĀ.* A similar account is found in the *Skanda Purāṇa* (6.263.33–61). The *Gorakṣa Vijay* and *Mīn Cetan* call him Mīnanāth and say he took the form of a fish to eavesdrop on Śiva, who related his secret teachings to

the Goddess in a raised pavilion amidst the Ocean of Milk: Sen, *History*, p. 44. Another Nāth legend explains Matsyendra's piscine origins. A king named Udhodhar is cremated. His navel will not burn and is cast into a river, where a fish devours it to give birth to Matsyendra: Rose, *Glossary*, p. 393; *Himavatkhaṇḍa* (of the *Skanda Purāṇa*), p. 73 (appendices); and *Nārada Purāṇa*, 2.69.6, cited in *NSC*, p. 22.

28. Jayaratha, in his commentary to *TĀ* 1.6 (vol. 2, p. 24), quotes a source that identifies the Siddha Mīna with Macchanda, in this episode. The relationship between Gorakṣanātha (7) and his guru Mīnanātha (6) in *HYP* 1.5 is symmetrical to that obtaining between the figures Gorakṣa-pā (9) and Mīna-pā (8) in the Tibetan *Grub thob*. This squares, moreover, with the statement made by Gorakṣa in the second verse of his earliest work, the *Gorakṣaśataka*, that his guru was Mīnanātha. It is a later conflation that identifies Matsyendra (the second Siddha, listed after Ādinātha, in the *HYP* list) or Luī-pā (the first Siddha of the *Grub thob* list) with Mīna. The historical Gorakṣa or Gorakhnāth was an early 13th c. figure, whereas Matsyendra, his purported guru, could not have lived later than the 10th c.; it is Mīna who was Gorakh's guru.

29. Matsyendra calls himself *matsyaghna* in *KJñN* 16.37, where he says he is from the *kaivartta* fisher caste (see below, n. 108). He calls himself *māchlī ghana*, "Killer of Fishes," and Machandar Nāth, a vernacularization of his Sanskrit name, in a song entitled *Matsyendranāthjī kā pad*, in Mallik, *SSP*, p. 76. He is also known as Macchaghnapāda, Macchendrapāda, Matsyendrapāda, Mīnapāda, Mīnanātha, Macchendra, Macchendapāda, and Macchindranāthapāda: Bagchi, *KJñN*, p. 6; and Dyczkowski, *Canon*, p. 163 (n. 23 to p. 62). On Matsyendra's ambiguous relationship to Mīna in Nepal, see Locke, *Karunamaya*, p. 427.

30. There are actually two thefts and two recoveries of these scriptures at Candradvīpa, and it is only on the second occasion that Śiva-Bhairava becomes Matsyendra: *KJñN* 16.23–36, 52; 22.10–12. The many variants of this legend are reviewed in Bagchi's introduction (pp. 6–32) to the *KJñN*.

31. *KJñN* 16.21: yadāvatāritaṃ jñānaṃ kāmarūpe tvayā mayā ("[When] the [Kaula] gnosis was brought down at Kāmarūpa by you [and] by me"). Cf. 16.26a. However, 22.10b and 12ab state that "this teaching [is found] in the household of every *yoginī* in Kāmarūpa . . . This great teaching was brought down at Candradvīpa. That [teaching] whose abode was the belly of a fish (*mahāmatsyodarasthitiḥ*) is sung at Kāmākhyā."

32. Kāmarūpa is generally identified with the important *pīṭha* of the Goddess at Kāmākhyā (Gauhati district, Assam). It is also a site within the subtle body, located at the center of a downturned *yoni*, which is itself identified with the sexual organ of the tantric consort, the yoginī. See below, nn. 89–90.

33. The *Grub thob*, a Tibetan translation of Abhayadatta's 11th–12th c. *Caturaśītisiddha Pravṛtti* ("Acts of the Eighty-four Siddhas"), is found in vol. 86, part 1 of the *Tanjur:* see above, chapter 3, nn. 139–40.

34. Locke, *Karunamaya*, pp. 282, 297–300, 433 n. 80.

35. Bagchi, *KJñN*, p. 22. The color of the image is noted in the earliest datable manuscript (11th c.) in which it is mentioned: Locke, *Karunamaya*, p. 300.

36. Marie-Therèse de Mallmann, "Divinités hindoues dans le tantrisme bouddhique," *Arts Asiatiques* 10:1 (1964), p. 71, referring to Archive Photograph no. 1623416/4, cliché no. 53.24, of the Musée Guimet. The depiction of Matsyendra emerging from the mouth of a fish can be cause for confusion, particularly in western India where Dāriyanāth (also known as Jhullelāl, Khwāja Khizr, Amarlāl, Zinda Pīr, etc., according to region) the "lord of the current," is the god of the Indus River: Briggs, *Gorakhnāth*, p. 65. In Pushkar, where there is a temple to this deity and a temple to the major Nāth Siddhas, a Nāth custodian of the latter stated that "Matsyendra was the same as Jhullelāl": personal communication from Dominique-Sila Khan, Pushkar, India, April 1993.

37. Chattopadhyaya, *Tāranātha's History*, p. 153 n. 28, and p. 178 n. 11; Bagchi, *KJñN*, pp. 22–23; Mallik, *SSP*, p. 15; and V. W. Karambelkar, "Matsyendranāth and His Yogini Cult," *Indian Historical Quarterly* 31 (1955), p. 362.

38. *TĀ* 5.57b–58a, translated in Muller-Ortega, *Triadic Heart*, p. 123 (italics my own). Muller-Ortega translates *matsyodaradaśā* as "the condition of the belly of the fish." The term *matsyodarasthitiḥ*, found in *KJñN* 22.12, has the same sense.

39. *Amaraugha Prabodha* 10: bibhrāṇaḥ pavanaṃ haṭhānniyamitaṃ grāso 'sti minodare / kaivalyo bhagavānvimucya sahasā yāvannacetatyasau. This text is found in Mallik, *SSP*, p. 49. Gorakh claims to be quoting a text entitled the *Sampuṭa*. These words, put in the mouth of Śiva and addressed to Pārvatī and Mīnanātha, appear to constitute the beginning of the teachings offered on the shore of Candradvīpa. I am grateful to John Roberts for his aid in translating this passage.

40. Diana Eck, *Banāras: City of Light* (Princeton: Princeton University Press, 1983), p. 118.

41. *Skanda Purāṇa* 2.2.12.21–40, cited in Eck, *Banāras*, p. 94.

42. *Rudrayāmala Tantra* 27.45, which further identifies the three rivers with *pūraka*, *recaka*, and *kumbhaka;* and moon, sun, and fire. It further mentions the *kuṇḍalinī* (as *kuṇḍalī*), as well as the six *cakra*s, which it associates with six Śivas, six Śaktis, and six "shafts" (*ṣaṭśara*): 27.42–56. Cf. Cauraṅgīnāth, "Prāṇ Sāṅkalī," verse 80, in Dvivedi, *Nāth Siddhoṃ*, p. 23. On the geographical disappearance of the Sarasvati River, see *Kalyāṇ Śakti Aṅk*, p. 651, which also mentions that a "Sarasvatī Gaṅgā" exists near Kedārnāth, in the Himalayas (ibid., p. 671): see below, n. 153.

43. In a "normal" monsoon, the Matsyodarī would flood *northward* into a series

of tanks before emptying into the Varaṇā. It was only in exceptionally heavy flooding that the volume of water flowing in the Ganges would back up into its Varaṇā tributary, and in turn into the Matsyodarī channel, reversing its more common northward flow. A small tank, all that remains of the Matsyodarī Lake of old, is today called Macchodarī: Eck, *Banāras*, pp. 116–18. Following James Prinsep's 1822 map of Benares (which she reproduces schematically on p. 47), Eck maintains that the "reversed" southward current of the Ganges-Matsyodarī emptied into the Ganges proper near Benia Tālāb (the "Confluence Pool"), slightly to the north of Daśāśvamedh Ghāṭ. While such may have been the case in the early 19th century, the Puranic sources indicate that this occurred a mile further to the south, via the Asi River. A string of lesser lakes and ponds, located by Prinsep between the 19th-century outlet and the Asi River, could well have served to channel the Matsyodarī down to the Asi in earlier centuries.

44. *Śiva Saṁhitā* 5.100, 104, 109. Cf. Eck, *Banāras*, p. 26.

45. A Hindu commonplace identifies Benares with the two-petaled *ājñā cakra* which, located at a point behind the bridge of the nose, is the final point of convergence of the *iḍā* and *piṅgalā* channels.

46. *Liṅga Purāṇa*, Kapileśvara Māhātmya, Oṃkāranirṇaya, and Guhyayātanavarṇanam, chap. 9 (reproduced in the 12th c. *Kṛtyakalpataru* of Bhaṭṭa Lakṣmīdhara (vol. 8, *Tīrthavivecanakāṇḍa*, ed. K. V. Rangaswamy Aiyangar [Baroda: Oriental Institute, 1942]), pp. 34–35. Lolārka Kuṇḍ lies near the mouth of the Asi River, near the southern edge of Benares: Eck, *Banāras*, pp. 177–78. Lolārka's solar associations make the southern Asi River the obvious macrocosmic homologue of the solar *piṅgalā nāḍī*. This somewhat skews the hathayogic symmetry in another way, however: ideally, the Ganges ought to flow backwards, northwards, and upwards from the sun (Asi) towards the moon (Varaṇā); however, since the Ganges' normal flow is northeasterly at Benares, its backward-flowing stream *must* flow in a southwesterly and "downward" direction, from moon to sun. What is essential here is that *matsyodarī-yoga* is identified with the Ganges running against its normal flow.

47. *Kṛtyakalpataru, Tīrthavivecanakāṇḍa*, p. 35. *Viṣuvam* also means "at the equinox": the flooding that would have precipitated the appearance of this stream could only have occurred during the summer monsoon: it is therefore possible that *matsyodarī yoga* fell on the autumnal equinox, at the culmination of the monsoon season. The *Darśana Upaniṣad* (4.43b–44a) identifies the two "equinoxes" with the concentration of the life force/yogic breaths in the *mūlādhāra* (spring) and the cranial vault (autumn), respectively (in Sastri, ed., *Yoga Upaniṣads*). Once again, the latter "equinox" would correspond to a generalized upward flow of the life force through the medial channel.

48. *Kṛtyakalpataru, Tīrthavivecanakāṇḍa*, p. 59.

49. Quoted from the Kāśī Khaṇḍa of the *Skanda Purāṇa* by Mitramiśra, "Tīrtha Prakāśa," in *Vīramitrodaya*, p. 240 (cited in *Kṛtyakalpataru, Tīrthavivecanakāṇḍa*, p. lxxviii). Cf. Nārāyaṇa Bhaṭṭa's (ca. 1580) *Tristhalīsetu* (p. 140, cited in Kubernath Sukul, *Varanasi Down the Ages* [Bhargava Bhushan Press, 1974], p. 200): "The Matsyodarī *tīrtha* is indeed twofold because it is [both] there in its own place [the Matsyodarī Lake] and outside of it, due to its channel that runs around [Benares]. It is most preeminent when, during the rainy season, the water of the Ganges, whose course is swollen during the rainy season, flows in a reverse direction via the mouth of that channel."

50. Also called the *brahma-mārga*, the "path of brahman," which is an echo of the *Liṅga Purāṇa* (in *Kṛtyakalpataru*, p. 59) reference to *matsyodarī* as the fluvial [form] of the *brahman*-syllable. Gorakhnāth refers to the *suṣumṇā* as the "subterranean Ganges": *Gorakh Bānī* Sabadī 2.

51. On the commonplace identification of *kumbhaka* with the *suṣumṇā* and the Sarasvati River, see *Rudrayāmala Tantra* 27.43–45. A cryptic passage from the third chapter of Durjayacandra's Amitapadā commentary on the Buddhist *Catuṣpīṭhatantra* is adduced by Tucci to explain Jayaratha's gloss—in which he gives *maccha* as a synonym for *pāśa*—on Abhinavagupta's reference to Macchanda in *TĀ* 1.7. The Buddhist commentary gives the compound *makara-mīnaka:* Tucci, "Animadversiones Indicae," p. 134. I maintain that this compound is a reference to the two riverine goddesses, the Gaṅgā and Yamunā, whose marine vehicles are, precisely, the *makara* and *mīna;* and that here too, this pair symbolizes the two peripheral channels of the subtle body, which must be emptied before the *suṣumṇā* can be filled.

52. *Kumbhaka* is compared, in Brahmānanda's commentary on *HYP* 4.27, to the binding of mercury.

53. *HYP* 2.7–9, 35. The *kuṇḍalinī* doubles as the *suṣumṇā nāḍī* and is also called the "infant widow" in *HYP* 3.109–10. A *Matsyodaratantra*, of which the chief subject is the the subtle body of *haṭha yoga*, would appear to take its name from the practices we have been describing: *HTSL*, p. 102.

54. *Tristhalīsetu*, p. 168, cited in Eck, *Banāras*, p. 119.

55. *Gorakṣa Śataka*, v. 2. This mention of Mīnanāth is found in all recensions of this work. Cf. the ordering of Matsyendra, Mīna, and Gorakh in the *Grub thob* and *HYP* Siddha lists. See above, n. 28.

56. See above, chap. 5, nn. 83–92.

57. See above, chap. 5, nn. 93–96.

58. McDaniel, *Madness*, pp. 182–85. The opposition between *mīnaka* (fish) and *makara* (crocodile) in Durjayacandra's *Amitapadā* (see above, n. 51) may also refer to this body of sexual practice.

59. Eck, *Banāras*, p. 117.

60. Bagchi identifies Moon Island with the Chinese "double-mountain" known as K'un-lun, which is itself located within the Taoist subtle body ("The Island of K'un-Lun and Candradvīpa," in *Bhārata-Kaumudī: Studies in Indology in Honor of Dr. Radha Kumud Mookerji*, 2 vols. [Allahabad: Indian Press, 1945, 1947], vol. 1, pp. 47–55). Cf. idem, *KJñN*, pp. 29–32. Dasgupta (*Obscure*, p. 384) locates it on the coastline of the Bakerganj district of Bangladesh. S. M. Ali (*The Geography of the Purāṇas*, 2d ed. [New Delhi: People's Publishing House, 1966, 1973], pp. 77–78 [citing *Vāyu Purāṇa* 45.51–58], 86–87, and fig. 8) locates it to the west of Lake Baikal in central Asia.

61. On the Candragiri toponym in the Kathmandu Valley, see above, chap. 4, n. 49.

62. *KJñN* 16.33–35.

63. Chapter colophons to the *KJñN* call it the revelation of the "Great Yoginī-kaula, brought down to earth by Matsyendrapāda at Moon Island." The same is also stated *in textu* in *KJñN* 22.12.

64. *KJñN* 5.6, 12.

65. *KJñN* 17.23a; 20.11a. For the western *liṅga* in the head, see *Gorakh Bānī*, Sabadī 187a, and the *Rājā Rānī Saṃbād* of Gopīcand, v. 105 (in Dvivedi, *Nāth Siddhoṃ*, p. 9). On the "microcosmic west," see also *Gorakh Bānī*, Sabadīs 41 and 267.

66. *KM* (London, Wellcome MSS g501) fol. 4a.5–7.

67. See above, chap. 3, n. 137.

68. Schoterman, *ṢSS*, pp. 36–39. A manuscript of this work, in Newari script, is dated to A.D. 1197 by Shastri (*Catalogue*, 1:lxiv, 111–12) and to A.D. 1395 by Bagchi (*KJñN*, p. 67).

69. Dyczkowski, *Canon*, p. 68–69. This squares with Bāul tradition, which identifies the fish (above, n. 58) with the moon: "My unknown moon moves through the water in the form of a fish." (McDaniel, *Madness*, p. 184).

70. *Amaraughaśāsana*, p. 10.

71. If, in the subtle physiology of the cranial vault, there exists a corresponding eastern mountain to the western Candraparvata of the KM (see above, note 66), then the three mountains, taken together, represent the so-called *trikuṭa*, the "triple-peaked" configuration located in the same region, which is also identified with the three phonemes of the syllable Oṃ (on this, see Silburn, *Kuṇḍalinī*, p. 132). This would further correspond to the sacred geography of the city of Benares, which is built upon three hills, the which are identified with the three tips of Śiva's trident, called the *triśulabhūmī* in the geography of the subtle body (ibid., p. 58).

72. On the lower western *liṅga*, see *Gorakṣa Śataka* 19. Cf. *SSP* 2.2, which states

that the *kuṇḍalinī* sleeps with her mouth over the *paścima-liṅga*, located in the second cakra, the *svādhiṣṭhāna*. It is out of this vortex that seed is emitted in ejaculation: Srivastav, "*Gorakh*" *Viśeṣāṅk*, p. 131.

73. E. Obermiller, ed. and tr., *History of Buddhism (Chos-hbyung) by Bu-ston*, 2 vols. (Heidelberg: Harrassowitz, 1931–32), vol. 2, "The History of Buddhism in India and Tibet," p. 120 (= fol 109a of Bu-ston's text). Obermiller gives the transcription "Badaha" for the name of this island, a name which makes no sense. The *Nātha-abhyudaya-tantra* cited by Bu-ston is called the *Mahā-kāla-tantra-rāja*, in the *Kanjur*. A microfilm (reel E-1358/7) of a manuscript, in Newari characters, of this work, held in the Nepal National Archives, gives the reading *bāḍāvām* (fol. 55b, line 5). It is with this reading that I emend Obermiller's translation.

74. Tucci, *Tibetan Painted Scrolls*, 1:226–27, citing *Tanjur* 67, p. 34. The "historical" Dārika-pā would have lived in Bengal during the 10th c. reigns of Amrapāla, Hastipāla, and Kṣāntipāla: Chattopadhyaya, *Tāranātha's History*, pp. 178, 311.

75. See O'Flaherty, *Śiva*, pp. 286–92, citing *Mahābhārata* 6.8.26; *Bhāgavata Purāṇa* 4.30.45, for the mythology of the submarine fire and the submarine mare. Cf. *TĀ* 8.98, which locates Vāḍava to the south of Jambudvīpa, between two mountains, named Cakra and Maināka. The southern sea in which the Indian submarine mare/fire is found parallels the Scandinavian Mūspellsheimr, the fire world in the Southern Hemisphere whose raging will be the end of the world: Puhvel, *Comparative Mythology*, p. 219. This is an alloform of the myth of the birth of Skanda and the origin of mercury: see above, chap. 7, sec. 3.

76. A goddess named *Kuṇḍalī*, who appears to be associated with the left side of the body (*vāmākhyā*) is mentioned in *KJñN* 17.23 and 20.11.

77. *Siddha Siddhānta Samgraha* 3.5, cited in Dvivedi, *Nāth Sampradāy*, pp. 187–88; *Gorakṣa Paddhati* 1.60; *BhP* 9.117–19; *Gorakh Bānī*, p. 332. Cf. *MBhT* 3.12–14.

78. *HYP* 4.17. Cf. *HYP* 4.108: "the yogin in *samādhi* is not consumed by time."

79. *KJñN* 2.2b–3: *kālāgnirudrasaṃjñā tu nakhāgre nityasaṃsthitam/ yadā prajvalate ūrddhaṃ saṁhārantu tadā bhavet/ baḍavāmukhamahattvañca pātāle sahasaṃsthitaḥ*. "That which is known as the Destroyer of the Fire of Time is forever located at the tip[s] of the toenail[s]. It is when it flares upwards that the universal retraction occurs. On the universal level [*mahattvam*] this is the mouth of the submarine mare, which is located in the underworld [*pātāle*]." See also Bagchi's commentary, p. 43. A late paper manuscript of the *Gorakṣasahasranāmastotra* found by Bagchi in the Nepal National Archives calls the land of Gorakhnāth's birth "Baḍava": Bagchi, *KJñN*, p. 64.

80. Thus a parallel passage from the ca. 12th c. *Vīnāśikha Tantra* (vv. 70b–71ab):

nirodhe kumbhakaḥ proktaḥ prāṇāyāmaṃ prakīrtitam/ dhyātvā kālāgnibījaṃ tu yugāntānalasaprabham/ nyaset pādatale mantrī jvālāmālākulam mahat.

81. See above, n. 49.

82. Misra, *Āyurvedīya*, p. 28; Kaviraj, *Bhāratīy*, vol. 1, pp. 555–56.

83. *ulaṭī gaṅg samudrahi sokhai:* in *Kabīr Granthāvalī*, ed. Shyam Sundar Das (Benares: Kashi Nagaripracarini Sabha, 1954), p. 141. Cf. a verse from another Kabīr anthology, *Sant Kabīr*, ed. Ramkumar Varma (Allahabad: 1947), p. 20: *ulaṭī gaṅg jamun milāvu/ binu jal saṅgam man mahiṃ nhāvu.* See also *Gorakh Bānī* Sabadī 55, 90, 115.

84. See above, n. 13. On the "five nectars" of early Buddhist tantra, see *Guhyasamāja Tantra* (p. 26 of Bhattacharya's 1931 edition), and *KJñN* 11.15–16.

85. *Kalyāṇ Śakti Aṅk*, p. 640.

86. Sharma's commentary to *RRS*, pp. 39, 184–85; Misra, *Āyurvedīya*, p. 170; *Shorter Oxford Economic Atlas*, p. 88.

87. Dyczkowski, *Canon*, pp. 63–64; Schoterman, *ṢSS*, p. 73.

88. *Gorakh Bānī*, Sabadī 142: bhag muṣī byand, agani muṣī pārā; jo rāṣai so guru hamārā. This is a continuation of Sabadī 141, which is a discussion of *vajrolī* and *amarolī mudrā*s: bajarī karaṃtāṃ amarī rāṣai amarī karaṃtāṃ bāī / bhog karaṃtāṃ je vyand rāṣai te goraṣ kā gurubhai.

89. In the more abstract schemata of *yonipūjā*, the tantric worship of the female sexual organ, the *yoni* is represented as a downturned triangle (Silburn, *Kuṇḍalinī*, p. 43), at the heart of which is, once again, Kāmarūpa, the abode of the goddess Kāmākhyā, who is identified with the *kuṇḍalinī* and with feminine materiality (*prakṛti*) in the form of menstrual flux (*puṣparūpinī*): Schoterman, *Yonitantra*, p. 24; Bharati, *Tantric Tradition*, pp. 259–60; Bhattacharya, *History*, p. 133; and Dyczkowski, "Kuṇḍalinī," p. 7, n. 13. See above, chap. 7, n. 67.

90. In Assam, specifically at Kāmākhyā, whence he is said to have brought it to Nepal: Karambelkar, "Matsyendranāth," p. 365. Cf. *KJñN* 16.46–49; and Jayaratha's commentary to *TĀ* 1.6. (vol. 1, p. 24). As their names indicate, Kāmākhyā and Kāmarūpa are locations identified with eroticism. One account of Matsyendra's birth has him born the son of Pārvatī at Kāmākhyā: *Nārada Purāṇa*, Uttara Khaṇḍa 69.6, cited in *NSC*, p. 50.

91. When Matsyendra (Macchanda) is taken to be the founder of Kaulism, it is his six sons who are noncelibate (*adhoretas*) who are singled out as qualified to be revealers of the Kaula cult: Sanderson, "Śaivism," p. 681. According to the *Candrādityaparamāgama* (cited in Bandhopadhyay, *Nātha Cult*, p. 48), Yoganātha (an incarnation of Śiva) married a maiden named Surati, who was a manifestation of Śakti. They had sixteen sons, beginning with Ādinātha. From them, six house-

holding (i.e., noncelibate) sons were born: Ādinātha, Minanātha, Satyanātha, Sacetanātha, Kapila, and Nānaka. Ten others—Giri, Puri, Vāratyādi, Śaila, Nāga, Sarasvati, Rāmānandi, Śyāmānandi, Sukumāra, and Achyuta—left their homes and wander from place to place. See above, chap. 5, n. 95.

92. See *Gorakh Bānī* Sabadī 177, on the loss of a yogin's semen as the shame of his guru; *Gorakh Bānī* Pad 48.1–3, on the female vulva as a tigress or vampiress. Cf. Kabīr, *Doha* 20.6 (in Vaudeville, *Kabir Granthavali*, p. 98). On the cleavage, within the Nāth Siddhas, between the celibate and hathayogic "Gorakh" and noncelibate, erotico-mystical "Matsyendra" branches, see Bharati, *Siddh-Sāhity*, p. 324. However, Dvivedi (*Nāth Sampradāy*, p. 50) divides the Nāth Siddha lineages between the descendants of the "hathayogic" Gorakh *and* Matsyendra, and the "erotico-mystical" Jālandhara and Kānipā.

93. Silburn, *Kuṇḍalinī*, p. 58.

94. On these works, see Zbavitel, *Bengali Literature*, pp. 189–90. This legend cycle is summarized in Sen, *History of Bengali Literature*, pp. 43–49; Dvivedi, *Nāth Sampradāy*, pp. 43–46; and Cunninath, *Tan-Prakāś*, pp. 197–200. Other versions, which differ little from these accounts, are the Maharashtran *YSĀ;* the *Dharmamaṅgala* of Sahadev Cakravarti (summarized in Dasgupta, *Obscure*, p. 368, n. 1), and the 20th c. *Nātha Caritra*, an adaptation of three works from the Jodhpur library of Mān Singh, the early 19th c. Marwari royal patron of the Nāth Siddhas. There are also vernacular versions of this drama, in Nepali, Maithili, and other medieval languages: Mukherji, *Gopicandra Nāṭaka*, pp. xxxvi, xliv. See above, chap. 5, n. 80.

95. Sen, *History of Bengali Literature*, p. 44.

96. Ibid., p. 45; *NSC*, pp. 95–97; and Pir Premnath, *Śiva-Gorakṣa* (New Delhi: Vijnana Prakashan, 1982), p. 15.

97. Summarized in Dvivedi, *Nāth Sampradāy*, pp. 48–49.

98. Matsyendra's feat of *parakāyapraveśa* (and Gorakh's role) is also chronicled in the 15th–17th c. *Śaṅkara Digvijaya* (9.80–84) of Mādhava. On this feat, see also *NSC*, pp. 27, 57–59; and *KJñN* 10.26–8. The god Rudra is said to have taken the human form of Lakulīśa, the ca. 2d c. A.D. founder of the early Pāśupata sect by entering and reanimating a brahmin's corpse on a cremation ground: Sanderson, "Śaivism," p. 664.

99. Alternatively, Matsyendra's queen dices up the body that the yogin has "left behind," so that he cannot return to it: Camanlal Gautam, *Śrī Gorakhnāth Caritra* (Bareilly: Samskrti Samsthan, 1981), p. 62, 96–97; Dvivedi, *Nāth Sampradāy*, pp. 48–49. In other sources, his lusty queen is named Paramilā, Maṅgalā, or Kamalā: Cunninath, *Tan-Prakāś*, pp. 198–99.

100. Sen, *History*, pp. 45–46; *NSC*, pp. 27, 57–59, 61; Dvivedi, *Nāth Sampradāy*, pp. 48–49. Pir Premnath (*Śiva-Gorakṣa*, p. 15) simply calls this *kadalī van*, the

"plantain forest." The alchemical *BhP* (4.108) seemingly evokes this myth when it states that a "barren woman born in the Plantain Forest (*kadalī vanajā vandhyā*) repeats the name of Mīna in incantation (*jāpayasi*)" when a number of ingredients are mixed together.

101. Cunninath, *Tan-Prakāś*, p. 198. It is also located on the Malabar coast: the site of the old and important Nāth monastery of Kadrī is identified with Kadalī: Narharinath, *Nav Nāth*, p. 7.

102. Dvivedi, *Nāth Sampradāy*, p. 45. *NSC*, pp. 58–59. As a multiple of sixteen, the figure of sixteen hundred, surely symbolic, is given in a number of sources: Cunninath, *Tan-Prakāś*, p. 199; Temple, *Legends of the Panjāb*, vol. 2, p. 6 (v. 50). Pir Premnath (*Śiva-Gorakṣa*, p. 15) places the number at sixteen. Ratansen requests and receives sixteen thousand *paduminī* women in *Padmāvat* 62.6.

103. Gorakh is conquering death with this feat, and, as such, he is specifically said to harrow hell to thrash Yama (the god of Death), who had presumed to take his guru from him: *Gorakṣa Vijaya* pp. 45–48, cited in Dasgupta, *Obscure*, p. 222.

104. Temple, *Legends*, 2:21 (v. 208); Pancanand Mandal, ed. *Gorakha Vijaya* (Calcutta: Visvabharati Granthalaya, 1949), Gautam, *Gorakhnāth Caritra*, pp. 51–55; Dvivedi, *Nāth Sampradāy*, p. 48. See below, nn. 174–78.

105. He must also return Matsyendra's soul to his original body: this he does with the help of a *yakṣiṇī*, who has reconstituted the butchered body of the Nāth, and placed it atop Mount Kailash for safekeeping: Gautam, *Goraknāth Caritra*, pp. 96–97.

106. *Gorakha Vijaya*, pp. 21–22, cited in Dasgupta, *Obscure*, p. 223.

107. Gautam, *Gorakhnāth Caritra*, p. 62; Dvivedi, *Nāth Sampradāy*, p. 46; Dasgupta, *Obscure*, p. 213; Srivastav, *"Gorakh" Viśeṣāṅk*, p. 262. In another legend, Gorakh kills and revives two other of Matsyendra's sons, the "Jain" Nemīnāth and Parśvanāth: Briggs, *Gorakhnāth*, pp. 190, 223; Rose, *Glossary*, 2:394.

108. Jan Gonda, *Viṣṇuism and Śivaism: A Comparison* (London: Athlone, 1970), p. 112. In the case of the group studied in Bengal by Ralph Nicholas ("Ritual Hierarchy and Social Relations in Rural Bengal," *Contributions to Indian Sociology*, n.s. 1 [Dec. 1967], p. 69), the young men who do the swinging are "temporary renouncers" coming from the Mahisya caste, whose original caste name was Kaibarrta, i.e., the same as that of the fisherman Matsyendra in the *KJñN* (16.27–56) myth of the recovery of the Kaula teachings from the Ocean of Milk: see above, n. 29.

109. Dasgupta, *Obscure*, p. 378 n. 2. Dasgupta notes that the term found in the Bengali *Maṅgala-kāvyas* is *kalā-van*. Here, a philological identification of plantains (*kadala*) with lunar digits (*kalā*) is significant one: the full moon would be a bunch of sixteen plantains. In a yogic context in which the moon in the cranial vault fills with semen, the plantain would again bear a sexual significance.

110. *Śūnyasampādane* 21.12 (vol. 5, p. 399).

111. Oddly, it is a rejection of Gorakhnāth's body-oriented yogic practice that the poet, Prabhudeva, is making here. See above, chap. 4, nn. 115–16, 167.

112. See above, chap. 4, nn. 163–64.

113. *Mahābhārata* 3.146.63–64, cited in Grierson and Dvivedi, *Padumawāti*, p. 253. See also Madeleine Biardeau, *Histoires de poteaux: Variations autour de la Déesse hindoue*, Publications de l'Ecole Française d'Extrême Orient, 154 (Paris: Ecole Française d'Extrême Orient, 1989), p. 286. In the epic, Bhīma encounters his "father," Hanumān, who is guarding the forest, a motif found in one of the legends of the Kadalī-rājya. Dvivedi (*Nāth Sampradāy*, pp. 53–54), who lists a number of possible locations for a historical Kingdom of Women which may have lain behind this motif, favors both Garhwal-Kumaon, in the Himalayan foothills of western Uttar Pradesh, and Kāmarūpa, in Assam, as the most likely venues.

114. On these three variant readings, see Grierson and Dvivedi, *Padumawāti*, p. 250. Similarly, Bengali sources on Matsyendra's imprisonment give the variant readings of *kacali* and *kachar* for *kadalī:* Bagchi, introduction to *KJñN*, p. 17. On Alexander's Zulmat, see Shirreff's translation of and notes to *Padmāvatī* 166 [12.5] and 528 [= 42.5] (pp. 91, 288–89); and Sharma, *Jayasī Granthāvalī*, p. 804.

115. Kabīr, *Sākhī* 29.2 (in Vaudeville, *Kabīr*, p. 290). On Gopīcand, see Grierson and Dvivedi, *Padumawāti*, pp. 251–52. See also Shirreff's translation of and notes to *Padmāvatī* 166 [12.5] (p. 91).

116. On the *Alhā Khaṇḍ*, see Stuart H. Blackburn, Peter J. Claus, Joyce B. Fluekiger, and Susan Wadley, eds., *Oral Epics in India* (Berkeley: University of California Press, 1989), pp. 197–202. Both the legends of Ratansen and of Alhā concern 12th c. Rajput princes facing the Turkish conquest of north India, and both hail from the same Hindi-speaking heartland of north central India. The Gopīcand legend flourishes in Bengal as well as across western India: a Rajasthani song cycle of Gopīcand is translated and interpreted by Ann Grodzins Gold, *A Carnival of Parting: The Tales of King Bharthari and King Gopi Chand as Sung and Told by Madhu Natisar Nath of Ghatiyali, Rajasthan* (Berkeley: University of California Press, 1992), pp. 159–310. Cf. idem., "Gender and Illusion in a Rajasthani Yogic Tradition," in *Tale, Text and Time: Interpreting South Asian Expressive Traditions*, ed. Frank Korom, Arjun Appadurai, and Margaret Mills (Philadelphia: University of Pennsylvania Press, 1990), pp. 102–35. A Punjabi version is given in Temple, *Legends*, vol. 2, pp. 1–77 (legend no. 18).

117. On *kajalī ban* in the legend of Pūraṇ Bhagat (who appears to borrow from Kabīr when he tells his mother to "loose his elephant in Kajali Van": see below, chap. 9, n. 170), see Temple, *Legends* 2:426 (legend no. 34, "Pūraṇ Bhagat," v. 604). In a Rajasthani folk cycle, Gopīcand cries out to his guru Jālandharanāth, "Oh ho

ho, Guru Maharaj . . . your eyes are closed over there in Kajali Woods": Gold, "Gender and Illusion," p. 118.

118. *Yogavasiṣṭha* 3.98–99, in Swami Venkatesananda, *Vasiṣṭha's Yoga* (Albany, N.Y., SUNY Press, 1993), pp. 119–20.

119. On eating poison (*viṣāhār*), see *Amaraughaśāsana*, p. 8. On the thighs of a woman as a boat to salvation, cf. the words of the Kāpālika Kapota in the *Kālikā Purāṇa* (49.1–53.217) myth of Tārāvatī, Candraśekhara, Bhairava, and Vetāla, translated in O'Flaherty, *Śiva*, p. 206.

120. With the awakening of the *kuṇḍalinī*, the triangle of the downturned mouth reverses its direction to become an upturned mouth (*ūrddhavaktra*): Silburn, *Kuṇḍalinī*, pp. 27, 34–35 (plates), 173–74, 190; cf. Dyczkowski, *Canon*, p. 64, citing *TĀ* 28.147.

121. On this perennial image in Chinese symbolism of the microcosm and macrocosm, see Rolf Stein, "Jardins en miniature d'Extrême Orient," *Bulletin de l'École Française d'Extrême Orient* 52 (1942), pp. 100–4; and below, chap. 10, sec. 6.

122. *Mahābhārata* 12.255.8, cited in Malamoud, "La brique percée," in *Cuire le monde*, p. 90.

123. Van Kooij, *Worship of the Goddess*, p. 42; Muller-Ortega, *Triadic*, p. 123; and Sanderson, "Maṇḍala," pp. 169–76, especially 174–76.

124. *Bṛhadāraṇyaka Upaniṣad* 4.2.2–3; 4.4.22; *Chāndogya Upaniṣad* 3.14.2–3; 8.1.1–4; *Maitrī Upaniṣad* 7.2. The heart is also said to be the seat of the mind (*manas*) in RV 8.89.5. In the medical tradition, the heart is said to be the seat of consciousness and the site of the "eighth *dhātu*" of the body: this is *ojas*, the fluid that keeps the body alive, of which there are only eight drops: *Caraka Saṁhitā* 1.17.74–75; 1.30.4, 7.

125. A number of tantric sources locate the ether or void in the heart. These include the works of the Trika Kaula reformers (Muller-Ortega, *Triadic*, especially pp. 142–46; and Padoux, *Vāc*, pp. 28, 128 n. 117, 137 n. 140), in which the heart is the locus of the void/ether, because it is here that sound arises in its subtlest form. Ether is the substrate or sound source of the primal vibration (*HYP* 4.101).

126. Silburn, *Kuṇḍalinī*, p. 40 n. 7, citing Kabīr, *Granthāvalī* 31.1–3.

127. Such Upanisadic identifications of the void with the absolute *bráhman* (*kham brahman: Bṛhadāraṇyaka Upaniṣad* 5.1.1) may have facilitated this localization: the cranial vault is the locus of *bráhman*, where the central channel (also called the *brahmamārga*) culminates in the *brahmarandhra*. Abhinavagupta (*TĀ* 3.137–40) terms the *śivavyoman*, the "heaven of Śiva" (*vyoman*, however, also is a term for ether), as the highest of his metaphysical categories and the highest point in the subtle body, identifying it with the seventeenth *kalā* or thirty-seventh *tattvā:* Padoux, *Vāc*, p. 91. See also ibid., pp. 95–96, 281, 424, on the connections between

this metaphysical concept and mantric practice. Nāth Siddha localizations of the void in the cranial vault may be found in *Gorakh Bānī*, Sabadī 1.18, 23, 45, 51, 55, 176, 231, etc.

128. *Gorakṣa Śataka* 67. Detailed discussions of the many uses of the term *śūnya* in the medieval Hindu and Buddhist mysticism of the Bengali Siddhācāryas, Nāth Siddhas, Vīraśaivas, Maharashtran mystics, Kabīr, etc., are Vaudeville, *Kabir Granthavali*, p. xx; Bharati, *Siddh Sāhity*, pp. 336–69; and Shankar Gopal Tulpole, *Mysticism in Medieval India* (Wiesbaden: Harrassowitz, 1984), pp. 196–97.

129. gagan maṃdal maiṃ ūṃdhā kūbā tahāṃ amṛt kā bāsā/ sagurā hoī su bhari bhari pīvai nigurā jāī piyāsā: *Gorakh Bānī*, Sabadī 23. On other uses of *śūnya*, cf. Sabadī 1, 46, 91, 176. Cf. *Śiva Saṁhitā* 4.31.

130. *RV* 1.164.36; 8.69.3; *Atharva Veda* 10.8.9. Cf. *Śatapatha Brāhmaṇa* 1.6.4.5; 6.1.2.4; 7.1.1.10–16; 10.4.2.1; 11.2.5.3; 12.7.3.4. The head is compared to a downturned vessel, filled with *yaśas* that is identified with breath in *Chāndogya Upaniṣad* 2.2.3. The classical study on the early history of such identifications is Jan Gonda, "Soma, Amṛta and the Moon," in *Change and Continuity*, pp. 38–70.

131. *Gyān Calīsa* 24–26, in Srivastav, "*Gorakh Bānī*" *Viśeṣāṅk*, p. 352. This work is not included in Barthwal's edition of the *Gorakh Bāṇi*.

132. *Doha* 5.45, in Vaudeville, *Kabir Granthavali*, p. 16.

133. V. K. Sethi, ed. *Kabir: The Weaver of God's Name* (Beas, Punjab: Radha Soami Satsang Press, 1984), pp. 233, 461. Cf. Das, *Kabīr Granthāvalī* 14.40; "Chalu haṃsa va deś." On Kabīr's language, see ibid., pp. 56, 199.

134. *Gorakh Bānī*, Pad 47.1–8, with Srivastav's commentary, pp. 302–5. Pad 47 is found on pp. 141–42 of Barthwal's edition of the *Gorakh Bāṇī*.

135. Verses 5–8 of Barthwal's edition read as follows:

ūjaḍ ṣeḍā nagar majhārī tali gāgari ūpar panihārī
magarī pari cūlhā dhūndhāī povaṇhārā kau rorī khāī
kāṃmini jalai agīṭhī tāpai bici baisaṃdar tharhar kāṃpai
ek ju raḍhiyā raḍhtī āī bahū bivāī sāsū jāī
nagarī kau pāṇīṃ kūī āvai ulaṭī carcā goraṣ gāvai.

(*Gāgari*, the term employed here for water pot, is defined as a "small metal vessel": *Samkṣipt Hindi Śabd Sāgar*, s.v. "gagarā."

136. Temple, *Legends*, vol. 1, pp. 166–68 (vv. 513–38 of legend no. 6, "The Legend of Gurū Gūgā"). Verses 536–37 read: "hāl dekho mere tan kā / phor do garhe dīe mahāre." On *doghar[ā]*, the practice of carrying two superposed water pots on one's head, see v. 522, and note on p. 167.

137. *Sākhī* 20.5 [= *Doha* 31.11], in Vaudeville, *Kabīr*, p. 262. Already in the Vedas, heaven and earth are viewed as two halves of a single whole, at once joined together and held apart by a pillar (*RV* 1.160.4; 3.31.12–13, etc.): the term *rodasī* is a

dual form ("heaven and earth") that was primordially a singular: Monier-Williams, *Sanskrit-English Dictionary*, s.v. "rodas."

138. The full account is found in Temple, *Legends*, vol. 2, pp. 375–456 and Charles Swynnerton, *Romantic Tales from the Panjāb* (Westminster: Archibald Constable & Co., 1903), pp. 411–41. It is summarized in Briggs, *Gorakhnāth*, pp. 184–85, 197–98. The original myth of this sort may be the Rgvedic account of Trita, who is thrown down a heavenly well (the dark of the moon?) by his treacherous brothers. He performs a mock *soma* sacrifice at the bottom of the well, and the gods come and "flush" him out (the waxing of the moon?): *RV* 1.105.1–28; *Jaiminīya Brāhmaṇa* 1.184; *Mahābhārata* 9.35.3–51, in O'Flaherty, *Tales of Sex and Violence*, pp. 53–57.

139. The well, called Pūraṇ's Well, is located in a village named Puranwāla, five miles outside of Sialkot, in the Punjab (Pakistan): Briggs, *Gorakhnāth*, pp. 98–99, 185; and personal communication from Alain Wattelier (who visited the site in the 1970s), Paris, June 1985.

140. Briggs, *Gorakhnāth*, p. 194. Another Nāth Siddha, Kanthaḍīnāth, also seals himself into a well to mediate: *NSC*, p. 22.

141. Tod, *Annals and Antiquities*, vol. 2, pp. 825–26; *NSC* 286; Sankarnath Yogisvar, *Śrī Mastnāth carit* (*Śrī Mastnāth adbhut līlā prakāś*) (Delhi: Dehati Pustak Bhandar, 1969), p. 136. Through the miracle of this well (related in chap. 20 of Sankarnath's work), Mān Singh acceded to the throne of Marwar in 1804, and it is a historical fact that he established his Nāth Siddha miracle worker as his chief minister: see below, chap. 11, sec. 3.

142. Briggs, *Gorakhnāth*, p. 188.

143. Rose, *Glossary*, vol. 2, p. 394n.

144. Stein, "Jardins en miniature," pp. 57–58, citing the *Yun-ki ts'i-tsein* (quoted without reference in the *P'ei-wen yun-fou*). The gourd doubles for one of the three "fields" or "wells of cinnabar" located in the Taoist body. Cf. idem, "Architecture et pensée en Extrême-Orient," *Arts Asiatiques* 4:3 (1957), pp. 176, 185.

145. On Vedic *dīkṣā*, see *Aitareya Brāhmaṇa* 1.3. On Ayurvedic *kuṭīprāveśa*, "entering the hut," a three-chambered hut that is explicitly identified with the female reproductive organs, see above,chap. 2, nn. 47–48, and *Caraka Saṁhitā* 6.1.16: "The sages knew of two sorts of *rasāyana:* that of entering the hut, and [the practice] of wind and sun (*vātatāpī*)."

146. Dalpatram Pranjivan Khakhar, "History of the Kānphaṭas of Kacch," *Indian Antiquary* 7 (February 1878), p. 47; *Śrīnāth Tīrthāvalī* of Mān Singh (Churu, Rajasthan: n.p., 1951), vv. 5, 42, 283–85.

147. Briggs, *Gorakhnāth*, p. 99; *Kṛtyakalpataru* of Lakṣmīdhara, vol. 8, p. 84.

148. Personal communication from Surya Kumar Yogi, Menal (Rajasthan),

March 1985. For a general discussion, see *MBhT* 11.23–35. On the importance of wells at the *pīṭhas* of Kāmākhyā and Hiṅglāj, see Van Kooij, *Worship*, p. 27; and Briggs, *Gorakhnāth*, p. 108.

149. *RC* 3.1; Misra, *Āyurvedīya*, p. 80.

150. Such mineral theophanies are quite a commonplace at *pīṭhas* of the Goddess—or conversely, many sulfurous pools, in areas of geothermic activity, are considered to be manifestations of the Goddess (Sharma's commentary to the *Rasaratnasamucchaya*, pp. 10–11; 184–85; 210–11). See above, chap. 7, nn. 53, 70–71.

151. Girnar is a site that is shared by Śaiva Hindus and Jains alike. In the case of this *tīrtha*, the alchemical mythology is Jaina, and is found in chap. 4 of the *Vividhatīrthakalpa*, trans. John Cort, "Twelve Chapters from *The Guidebook to Various Pilgrimage Places*, the *Vividhatīrthakalpa* of Jinaprabhasūri," in Phyllis Granoff, ed., *The Clever Adulteress and the Hungry Monk* (New York: Mosaic Press, 1990), pp. 25–90. Cf. Granoff, "Jain Biographies of Nāgārjuna," pp. 48–49, on Jain mythology of the alchemist Nāgārjuna; and Roşu, "Alchemy and Sacred Geography," p. 156.

152. The alchemical wonders of Srisailam are praised at great length in the Rasayāna Khaṇḍa [part 4] of the *Rasaratnākara* of Nityanātha. Chap. 8 of this section is entitled "Śrīparvata Sādhana." Cf. Roşu, ibid., pp. 151–56, who questions the alchemical cachet of Srisailam as described in this and other sources.

153. *Devī Purāṇa*, cited in Lakṣmīdhara, *Kṛtyakalpataru*, vol. 8, p. 231; and *Skanda Purāṇa* 1.27.33–77; 1.29.87. The same pools, etc. are described in the pilgrim's guide I purchased while on the Kedarnāth pilgrimage in May 1984: *Śrī Kedārnāth Māhātmya* (*Yātrā Gāīḍ*, ed. Shersingh Shah (Kedarnath: Shersingh Shah, n.d.), pp. 41–43.

154. Sastri, *Āgneyatīrtha Hiṅglāj*, p. 54. See above, chap. 7, nn. 70, 120. Given the fact that the Ganges and the Yamuna, identified with the *iḍā* and *piṅgalā* channels of the subtle body, rise out of Himalayan glaciers to the east and west of Kedārnāth respectively; and that a "Sarasvatī Gaṅgā" (i.e., *suṣumṇā*) appears near Kedārnāth (*Kalyāṇ Śakti Aṅk*, p. 671), the subtle physiology of the *nāḍīs* is also geographically reproduced here. The sixth cakra, the *ājñā*, located between the eyebrows at that place at which the three major *nāḍīs* are said to meet, is moreover called Kedār in *HYP* 3.24. The Nine Nāths and "Kedār" are identified with the ten doors in *Gorakh Bānī* Pad 9.1. See above, sec. 2b.

155. *Śrīnāth Tirthāvalī*, vv. 267–72. A similar image, that of hitting a brass cup atop seven bamboo poles, is found in the "Marriage of Sakhī Sarwar," legend no. 22 in Temple, *Legends*, vol. 2, p. 127.

156. Stein, *Grottes-Matrices*, pp. 37–43. See also ibid., pp. 15–23 for a survey of Hindu "womb-caves" throughout the Indian subcontinent, including those of Hiṅglāj and Kāmākhyā.

157. The medical and chemical name for mercury is hydrargyrum, from *hydros* + *argentum*, whence the symbol Hg in the periodic table; it is therefore possible to abbreviate "wells of mercury" to "Hg Wells." It will be recalled that an author named H. G. Wells wrote a book entitled *The Food of the Gods*, an apt denomination for the mercury that alchemists ate.

158. See above, chap. 7, sec. 3.

159. A *yantra* (from the root *yam*) is that which controls or subdues. In alchemy, the term is applied to apparatus of the sort we are describing here, which control such volatile elements as mercury and fire. For other uses of the term in tantrism, see above, chap. 6, n. 93.

160. The extraction of mercury from cinnabar, through the use of the *vidyādhara* or *ūrddhvapātana yantra* is described in *RRS* 9.56. The sublimation of mercury, through amalgamation with copper and in combination with various plant substances, also in the *ūrddhvapātana yantra*, is described in *RRS* 11.37. Similar instructions are found in *ĀK* 4.38–43, *RHT* 2.8, *RA* 10.55, and in every other major alchemical work. The *RA* (7.49) also describes a procedure for the purification of cinnabar in the same *yantra:* the resulting essence (*sattva*) of cinnabar has the appearance of mercury (*rasasaṅkāśa*).

161. *RRS* 9.24–25. In some sources, the upper pot is upturned and filled with water, such that mercury condenses on the outside surface of its base: Misra, *Āyurvedīya*, p. 225.

162. *RRS* 9.57.

163. *Rasendracintāmaṇi* 8.3, cited in Prakash, *Prācīn Bhārat*, p. 575.

164. Sharma, identifying the *ūrddhvapātana yantra* with the *vidyādhara* in his commentary to *RRS* 1.88 (p. 14), cites the *Rasapaddhati*. This apparatus is also described in *RC* 4.42; 5.51–52.

165. *Amanaskayoga* 2.15: ūrddhvamuṣṭiradhodṛṣṭir ūrddhvabhedastvadhaḥ śirāḥ /dharāyantravidhānena jīvanmuktaḥ bhaviṣyati. The *śāmbhavī mudrā* is a Kaula technique which would appear to have some connection to the Kubjikā cult of the Western Transmission, in which a "masculinized" form of practice is called *śāmbhava* ("pertaining to Śambhu, Śiva"): Sanderson, "Śaivism," p. 687. *Śāmbhavī-vidyā* is the subject of the *Jñānasaṅkālinītantra* (*HTSL*, p. 102); and *śāmbhavī dīkṣā*, a form of initiation particular to the Nāth Siddhas (Bharati, *Tantric Tradition*, pp. 90–91). *Śāmbhavī* is also synonymous with the medial channel, the *suṣumṇā*, according to *HYP* 3.4; and the hathayogic *śāmbhavī mudrā* is nearly identical with the renowned *khecarī mudrā* (*HYP* 4.38–39). On this, see below, sec. 4 of this chapter.

166. *Gorakṣa Śataka*, v. 62. Other verses (131a, 138c) speak of a pool (*dhāra*) of lunar nectar in the cranial vault, which the yogin is to drink, lest it fall into the sun in the lower abdomen.

167. The *Yonitantra* passage (68a) is translated and discussed by Schoterman on pp. 12–13 of his edition of the text. Elsewhere, the *KCM* (fol. 24a9–24b.1) states that "by using [a device] composed of *dharā*, one attains immortality" (*dharāmāyā pra[yo]gena cāmaratvāpnuyāt*). This verse of the *Amanaskayoga* (ed. Yognath Swami [Poona: Siddh Sahity Samsodhan Prakashan Mandal, 1967]) is singled out by the great tantric scholar Gopinath Kaviraj (foreword, p. 22) as the most singular portion, if not the very heart of this text (editor's preface, pp. 10–11), and the editor and Hindi commentator discusses his difficulty in making sense of it (pp. 11–14). He refers to the *Mahābhārata* (1.179.14–17) account of Arjuna's winning of Draupadī, in which the epic hero pierces the target (*vivyādha lakṣyam*) (called "piercing the fish" [*matsyavedha*] in Hindi) placed atop a pole with an arrow shot from the bow Śiva has previously given him. This he does by looking downward (*adhodṛṣṭiḥ*) into a pool of water (*dhārayantra*) as he clenches his fist around his upward-held bow (*ūrddhvamuṣṭi*): his head is turned downwards (*adhaḥ śiraḥ:* but the text gives *sirāḥ*) as his target (*bheda*) is above. His "piercing of the fish" is at once the hitting of his target, the winning of Draupadī, an inward-looking posture of yoga, or a reverse technique of sexual intercourse. This interpretation has the merit of preserving the orthography *dhāra*, whereas my interpretation requires a reading of *-dhara*.

168. *RRS* 11.38.

169. *RRS* 9.9; 11.39. Cf. Dash, *Alchemy*, pp. 58–62, on the identification of the various *-pātanas* as variant processes, all of which make use of the *vidyādhara yantra*.

170. *Gorakṣa Śataka* 135. Verses 133–34 read: "In the region of the navel dwells the lonely sun, whose essence is fire; located at the base of the palate is the eternal moon, whose essence is nectar. That which rains down from the downturned mouth of the moon is swallowed by the upturned mouth of the sun. The practice [of *viparītakaraṇa*] is to be performed as a means to obtaining the nectar [which would otherwise be lost]." This passage is also found in Gorakhnāth's *Yogamārtaṇḍa*, vv. 121–122a, 123b. This posture is described in both the *HYP* (3.77–79) and *Gorakṣa Paddhati* (pp. 48–49), immediately before their respective treatments of the *vajrolī mudrā*. It is dramatized in a legend from Dhinodar, in Kacch (Gujarat), described above, chap. 5, n. 204.

171. *Gorakh Bānī*, appendix 1 to Barthwal's edition, p. 242. The full verse reads: ulaṭi yantr dhare siṣar āsaṇ kare/ . . . silahaṭ madhye kāṃvarū jītale/ nirmal dhuni gagan māṃhī. The upside-down yantra here is the (normally) downturned triangle of the inner *yoni*, located in the *mūlādhāra cakra*, here identified with the old Buddhist *pīṭha* named Sirihaṭṭa, at the center of which is the *pīṭha* named Kāmarūpa. For a discussion of this element of the subtle body, see above, n. 170. Lallā's story

is told in the *Tārīkh-i hasan* of Pīr Ghulam Hasan: Jayalal Kaul, *Lal Ded* (New Delhi: Sahitya Akademi, 1973), p. 14. I am grateful to Patricia Greer for sharing this reference.

172. Henri Maspero, *Le Taoïsme et les religions chinoises*, with a preface by Maxime Kaltenmark (Paris: Gallimard, 1971), p. 492 and n. 6. Cf. Kristofer Schipper, *Le corps taoïste* (Paris: Fayard, 1982), pp. 137–53. The Palace of the Cinnabar Field is also termed Nihan, the ideogram for which was, in this early period, the same as that for the *nirvāṇa* of import Buddhism. Also qualified as the residence of the Highest One (Maspero, *Le Taoïsme*, p. 493), its resemblance to the *bráhman* of Hinduism and the *śūnya* of Siddha traditions is equally striking.

173. In alchemy as well, there is an apparatus properly known as the *ḍamaru yantra*. This apparatus is nearly identical to and may be used interchangeably with the *urddhvapātana:* see *RRS* 9.57 with Sharma's commentary, p. 143; and *Rasahṛdaya Tantra*, introduction, p. xxiii.

174. The location of a mystic *ḍamaru* in the head would appear to refer to this tantric schema: *Bhūtaśuddhi Tantra* 3.3, in *Tantrasaṁgraha*, 4 vols., ed. Gopinath Kaviraj and Ramaprasad Tripathi (Benares: Sampurnanand Sanskrit Visvavidyalaya, 1973–81), vol. 4, p. 313. See below, chap. 10, sec. 6.

175. Literally, "upward-tending semen," this term is most often translated as "celibacy, chastity." The sense, however, was that the ascetic is holding his semen up and away from his penis, from which it might all too easily slip away from him. Indian popular tradition is filled with accounts of "semen-headed yogis," a reflection of this interpretation: G. Morris Carstairs, *The Twice Born* (London: Hogarth Press, 1958), p. 86.

176. Four such drums (catalogue numbers R.VII-230, R.XII-835, R.XII-836a, and R.XII-798a) are presently housed in the National Museum of Denmark in Copenhagen. I am grateful to Rolf Gilberg, curator of this collection at the National Museum, for his ready cooperation in supplying me with this information.

177. This description of the Tibetan *ḍamaru*, called the "skull drum" (*thod-rna*), is found in Mireille Helffer and Marc Gaborieau, "A propos d'un tambour du Kumaon et de l'ouest du Népal: Remarques sur l'utilisation des tambours-sabliers dans le monde indien, le Népal et le Tibet," in *Studia instrumentorum musicae populares*, Festschrift to E. Emsheimer on the occasion of his 70th birthday (Stockholm: Musikhistorika Museet, 1974), p. 78 and pl. 13.

178. Ibid., p. 75.

179. Ibid., p. 78.

180. Personal communication from Sangye Sonam, a Tibetan monk at Chatral Rinpoche's monastery, Pharphing, Nepal, May 1993. I am grateful to Peter Moran, who served as my interpreter in this interview.

181. *Caryāpada* 3, with the commentary of Munidatta and the translation (compiled in "Yambu," in Nepal) of Kīrticandra, reproduced in Bagchi, "Some Aspects of Buddhist Mysticism in the Caryāpadas," *Studies*, pp. 75, 79, 84–85. I have enhanced and "Hinduized" Bagchi's treatment of this passage.

182. Cf. *HYP* 3.47 which terms a homologous process "drinking the immortal liquor" (*pibedamaravāruṇīm*).

183. See below, sec. 4, for an extended discussion of the "tenth door" of the subtle body.

184. *Yogamārtaṇḍa* 177: "When the upbreath disappears and the mind is absorbed, that is then called the unity of *samarasa, samādhi*."

185. *Gorakṣa Paddhati* 1.68–74. Schoterman (*Yonitantra*, p. 29) suggests that the *vajrolī mudrā* may have been used in lieu of the *khecarī mudrā* in some cases: instead of maintaining the combined *bindu*s in the head through the latter, the practitioner would recover the same fluids through urethral suction and then simply drink them.

186. *Khecaricakra* refers to an elaborate *maṇḍala* of sixty-four *yoginī*s and to the circle in which tāntrikas engage in ritualized sex. On this, see Dyczkowski, "Kuṇḍalinī," p. 6; *BhP* 1.77; *RA* 3.17, 20; and Vidya Dehejia, *Yoginī Cult and Temples: A Tantric Tradition* (New Delhi: National Museum, 1986), pp. 44–45. The contents of the *KhV* have been discussed in detail: see above, chap. 5, sec. 5m.

187. *Maitrī Upaniṣad* (6.19): "By pressing the tip of his tongue against the palate . . . one sees *bráhman* through contemplation." Another early reference is found in *KJñN* 6.18–28. Cf. *Gorakṣa Śataka* 67; *Gorakṣa Paddhati* 1.68; *Yogamārtaṇḍa* 58; *Gorakh Bānī* Sabadī 133; *HYP* 3.41–42.

188. Kakar, *Shamans*, p. 203. See Bharati, *Tantric Tradition*, pp. 242–43, for a general discussion of the multiple meanings of this term.

189. *Atharva Veda* 10.8.43; *Śvetāśvatara Upaniṣad* 3.18. The yogin seals himself off doubly from the outside by enclosing himself in a windowless room to meditate: *Yogatattva Upaniṣad* 32, in Varenne, *Upanishads du yoga*, p. 74. This recalls as well the initiation hut of Vedic *dīkṣā* and the Ayurvedic practice of *kuṭīpraveśa*. See above, chap. 2, nn. 47–48.

190. Kaviraj, *Aspects of Indian Thought*, pp. 236–37; Dasgupta, *History*, 2:253.

191. *Amaraughaśāsana*, pp. 10–11, discussed in Silburn, *Kuṇḍalinī*, pp. 131–32; Dasgupta, *Obscure*, pp. 239–42, citing *Gorakha Vijaya*, ed. Mandal, pp. 141, 143–44. Cf. *Yogaviṣaya* of Matsyendranāth, vv. 30–31, in Mallik, ed. *SSP*, p. 47.

192. In order to do so, he has already cut away the frenum, which anchors the tongue to the lower palate, through a technique described in *HYP* 3.32.

193. On the Jūna Ākhāḍā, see Rajesh Bedi, *Sadhus: The Holy Men at India* (New Delhi: Brijbasi Printers, 1991), p. 79; S. Sinha and B. Saraswati, *Ascetics of Kashi:*

An Anthropological Exploration (Varanasi: N. K. Bose Memorial Foundation, 1978), pp. 93–94.

194. This echoes a statement from the *Yogaviṣaya* attributed to Matsyendranātha (v. 24 in Mallik, ed. *SSP,* p. 47): "When the *nāda* is heard, the *śaṅkhinī* showers the body with nectar." The *śaṅkhinī* runs from a point behind the forehead to the throat: Silburn, *Kuṇḍalinī,* p. 130. Drinking nectar is a commonplace of Nāth mystic poetry: *Gorakh Bānī* Sabadī 67, 171; *SSP* 6.64.

195. *Amaraughaśāsana,* p. 7.

196. Silburn (*Kuṇḍalinī,* p. 131) and Dasgupta (*Obscure,* pp. 239–42 and notes) assume there to be but one "tenth door," an impossibility given the descriptions of this door, which is to be variously opened and closed in different textual descriptions. The mouth of the *śaṅkhinī* is called the tenth door in Gorakhnāth's *Amaraughaśāsana* (p. 11), and *SSP* 2.6. The Nine Nāths and "Kedār" are identified with the ten doors in *Gorakh Bānī* Pad 9.1; the yogin is enjoined to lock this door in Pada 23.1, but to "blast it open" by closing the other nine in *Ātmabodh* (in *"Gorakh Bānī" Viśeṣāṅk,* p. 340). In the legend of Pūraṇ Bhagat, the evil stepmother Lūṇā is identified as the tenth door of the royal palace: Temple, *Legends,* 2:398 (vv. 265–66); in the *Padmāvat,* it is the tenth door by which the fortress of Laṅka (the body) must be stormed: see below, sec. 5 and n. 243; and chap. 9, sec. 7.

197. The clearest discussion of this doubling of the tenth door is found in Kaviraj, *Aspects,* p. 237. On the *śaṅkhinī*'s two mouths, see Mandal, ed., *Gorakha Vijaya,* p. 141, cited in Dasgupta, *Obscure,* p. 240. The Nāth Siddhas generally identify the tenth door with the *brahmarandhra,* by which the fontanelle is intended: *Gorakh Bānī* Sabadī 135 (in which the yogin is said to throw a "door panel" [*kapāṭ*] across this opening). The lower mouth is located in the *tālu-cakra,* the sixth cakra in the nine-cakra system which expands upon the more conventional system of 6 + 1: *SSP* 2.6. Cf. *Gorakh Bānī* Pad 23.1, with commentary; and *Ātmabodh* 2 (in Srivastav, *"Gorakh Bānī" Viśeṣāṅk,* p. 340).

198. *Amaraughaśāsana,* discussed in Silburn, *Kuṇḍalinī,* p. 129: she is so called because when she sleeps, she is coiled three and one half times around the *liṅga* located in the abdominal region. The *SSP* (1.67), also apparently identifying *śaṅkhinī* with *kuṇḍalinī,* states that the *śaṅkhinī* flows in the urethra (*liṅgadvāra*) and via a straight path up into the *brahmarandhra* and thence into all of the ten doors.

199. *Gorakh Bānī* Sabadī 219a. Identical to this is verse 5 of "Mahādev jī kī sabadī" (Dvivedi, *Nāth Siddhoṃ,* p. 66). The same concept is found in the *ṢSS* (chap. 42, in Schoterman, *ṢSS,* p. 87, cited in Dyczkowski, *Canon,* p. 65), which states that the goal of the practitioner is "the union of the two [the highest and the lowest] mouths," identified with the highest and lowest of the seven cakras, as well as with the upper and lower *yoni*s of the Śākta subtle body.

200. Here, a "crooked" goddess may be easily assimilated to a curved duct, and one of the synonyms for both the *śaṅkhinī* and the *kuṇḍalinī* is *baṅka nāla*, "curved duct." This term also has an alchemical application: this is a curved tube which, tapered at one end, is used as a blowpipe for ventilating a flame. Yet, the 14th c. *Gorakh Bodh* (v. 62 in Barthwal's numbering, *Gorakh Bāṇī*, p. 186) distinguishes between *suṣumṇā*, *śaṅkhinī*, and *baṅka nāla*. On the *baṅka nāla* of the subtle body, see also *Yogaviṣaya* v. 22 (in *SSP*, p. 46) and *Gorakh Bānī* Pad 53.3. The alchemical *baṅka nāla* is described in *RA* 4.58 and *RRS* 10.45. Cf. Misra, *Āyurvedīya*, pp. 147–48.

201. For the western *liṅga* in the head, see *Gorakh Bānī* Sabadī 187a and the *Rājā Rānī Saṃbād* of Gopīcand, v. 105 (in *Nāth Siddhoṃ*, p. 9). On the "microcosmic west," see also *Gorakh Bānī*, Sabadī 41 and 267. The *KJñN* (17.23, 20.11) also associates a coiled (*kuṇḍalākṛti, kuṇḍalī*) goddess with the left side. On the lower western *liṅga*, see *Gorakṣa Śataka* 19. Cf. *SSP* 2.2, which states that the *kuṇḍalinī* sleeps with her mouth over the *paścima-liṅga*, located in the second *cakra*, the *svādhiṣṭhāna*. It is out of this vortex that seed is emitted in ejaculation: Srivastav, "*Gorakh*" *Viśeṣāṅk*, p. 131.

202. *MBhT* 7.18; *Śrīnāthakathāsāra* of Dwārkanāth, ed Narharināth Yogi (Benares: n.p. 1951), p. 23.

203. Dyczkowski, "Kuṇḍalinī," p. 3 n. 7.

204. *Yogabīja* 135, 148, 159. Cf. Kaviraj, *Bhāratīy*, vol. 2, p. 285.

205. *TĀ* 29.124–29. On the female sexual organ as the *yoginīvaktra*, the "mouth of the *yoginī*," see *Tantrāloka Varttika*, vol. 2, p. 104, cited in Padoux, *Vāc*, p. 61.

206. *Vāmamārga* (in Hindi), by Pandit Vanisidhar Sukul Vaidyaraj (Allahabad: Kalyan Mandir, 1951), v. 110, English translation in Bharati, *Tantric Tradition*, p. 264. The Hindi reads (ibid.,p. 277): "phir śakti ko gaurī kī apne ko śiv kī bhāvanā kar . . . mātṛmukh meṃ pitṛmukh arpit kare."

207. Silburn, *Kuṇḍalinī*, p. 190, citing *TĀ* 29.124–26, with the commentary of Jayaratha; and Dyczkowski, *Canon*, p. 64, citing *TĀ* 28.147. For further discussion, see Silburn, *Kuṇḍalinī*, pp. 27, 173–74, and plates on pp. 34–35.

208. *Manthānabhairava Tantra*, Kumārikākhaṇḍa 13.110–43, summarized in Dyczkowski, "Kuṇḍalinī," pp. 17–18 n. 27, who remarks that "although one can distinguish two Yonis, there is in fact only one."

209. *RA* 11.17–18, 29–41; *RRS* 8.75–79. The image may be based on moveable Śiva *liṅga*s, over which "mouthed" sheaths could be superimposed: Bagchi, "Further Notes on Tantrik Texts Studied in Ancient Kambuja," *Studies*, p. 21.

210. On the term *mudrā* in alchemical terminology, see Sharpe, *Eight-Hundred Year Old Book*, p. 106. *Puṭa*s are discussed in *RA* 6.101–22; *RRS* 10.47–64, and every

major alchemical work. Their construction and use are summarized in Dash, *Alchemy*, pp. 197–99.

211. Silburn, *Kuṇḍalinī*, pp. 169, 192, in which *sampuṭīkaraṇa* is an exchange of male and female energies that occurs through, but is not limited to, the act of sexual intercourse. The same term applies to the telescoping of elements back into their source, in the ascension of the *kuṇḍalinī* or in the distillation of the 51 phonemes of the Sanskrit language into the bisyllabic *aham*, the universal I (ibid., p. 9). The term *sampuṭa* means "skull" or "cranium" in Hindi: *Saṃkṣipt Hindi Śabd Sāgar*, s.v. "sampuṭa."

212. Kaviraj, *Bhāratīy* 1:276, 282, 287–89; *KM* (London, Wellcome MSS no. g501) fol. 35a.7–8, describing the *kaulaketu* ritual of the Siddha Mārga.

213. Tucci, "Animadversiones Indicae," pp. 154–55. This is a portion of a text describing a tantric Buddhist initiation. Cf. *KM* (London, Wellcome MSS no. g501) fol. 35a.7–8; *KJñN* 18.22–23; and *KPT* (in Bhattacarya, ed. *Indrajāla vidyāsaṃgraha*, p. 265) for similar language.

214. Kaviraj, *Bhāratīy*, 2:293 n. 1: "The mouth of the *śaṅkhinī nāḍī* is, in tantric treatises, precisely the mouth of the guru; it is otherwise designated as Śiva's upper mouth. It is from this site that the teaching of the [initiatory] *tāraka mantra* is transmitted into the disciple's right ear."

215. The *Śārada Tilaka* (5.139) has the guru transfer "that which has oozed inside his mouth" (*vidruvaktrāntara*) into the mouth of his disciple. Often, the guru is said to directly penetrate the heart of his disciple with the divine energy he has stored up inside himself. On this notion, and the similarities and differences between tantric initiation between males and ritualized sex between a male and a female, see Silburn, *Kuṇḍalinī*, pp. 175–76.

216. *Gorakṣa Paddhati*, appendix to 1.62 [p. 32] and 2.16; *HYP* 3.12, 27.

217. *Rudrayāmala Tantra* 17.73, 85–87.

218. *Khecarī mudrā* is also the term employed by a Nāth suborder, the Gūdaras, for the cylinders of wood which they pass through their earlobes. The Gūdaras were founded by a member of the Dasnāmi sect and are not generally considered by Nāth *sampradāyins* to be one of their own: Briggs, *Gorakhnāth*, p. 11. Given the fact that the piercing of the ears opens a channel without which yogic practice cannot be effective, the term is an apt one: on this, see below, chap. 10, sec. 4.

219. *RA* 11.151, 154, 162–63, 219.

220. On *guṭikā bandha*, see *Gorakh Bānī* Sabadī 49; on the *khecarī* and other alchemical *guṭikā*s, see *RA* 12.336–37, *RHT* 19.65–76; *RRS* 11.88; and Brahmānanda's commentary to *HYP* 4.27. On the *siddhi guṭikā*, see *Padmāvat* 222 [= 23.1] (p. 482 of Grierson and Dvivedi, *Padumawāti*; and p. 135 of Shirreff, *Padmāvatī*). On

khecari mercury, see *RA* 2.89; 3.9, 17–20; 11.98–107, 149–53, 162–63; 12.380; on *khecarī śakti*, see *KJñN* 5.4; 6.18–28; 7.14; 20.10; and Dyczkowski, *Canon*, p. 168 n. 52. A folktale from Benares casts Gorakhnāth in the miraculous recovery of thousands of such *guṭikās*: personal communication from Siddhinandan Misra, Benares, March 1985.

221. In the *RRS* (6.13–14), there is a "division of labor" between the practical and the spiritual components of the alchemist's craft. On the one hand, the alchemist carries out his chemical operations in a laboratory (*rasaśāla*); on the other, he effects his daily worship of the alchemical gods in a temple (*rasamaṇḍapa*) built nearby.

222. The *RRS* (6.21) says the *rasaliṅga* is to be located on the eastern side of the alchemical altar (itself located at the center of the *rasamaṇḍapa*). The Chandi Bukit Batu Pahat (Malaysia) alchemical temple site studied by Francis Treloar ("Use of Mercury," pp. 232–40) has its *rasaliṅga* at the center of the structure. The *rasamaṇḍapa* described in the *RA* (2.52) also has the *rasaliṅga* at its center.

223. On this *maṇḍala* in the *RA* and *RC*, see above, chap. 6, sec. 2. The *RC maṇḍala* is graphically reproduced in Roşu, "*Mantra* et *Yantra*," p. 252 (fig. 5). A simpler *maṇḍala* is described in Misra, *Āyurvedīya*, p. 83.

224. See above, chap. 7, sec. 3 and nn. 56–59.

225. *RA* 1.43; 2.52; *RRS* 1.23–28; 6.14–23; *MBhT* 8.1–10; *RC* 1.37–38. See also Treloar, "Use of Mercury," especially pp. 237–38; and Siddhinandan Misra's introduction to the *Rasendracūḍāmaṇi*, p. 5, in which he discusses the alchemical grounds for the foundation and installation of the *rasaliṅga*.

226. Misra, *Āyurvedīya*, p. 85. In his description of the Chandi Bukit Batu Pahat alchemical temple ruin, Treloar states that the mercurial *liṅga* unearthed there was set in a silver semicircle: Treloar, "Use of Mercury," pp. 237–38.

227. *RA* 2.77–82. The *Vimalaprabhā* commentary to the Buddhist *Kālacakra Tantra* (2.213–15) presents a similar iconographic representation of this worship support, for use in the alchemical Jambhala rite: Fenner, *Rasāyan Siddhi*, pp. 160–63.

228. *RA* 3.63–73; *RRS* 6.22–23. For the iconography of these images, see above, chap. 6, nn. 61–63.

229. See below, chap. 9, n. 23.

230. *RHT* 1.12. See above, chap. 7 sec. 5.

231. Bhattacharya, *History*, pp. 376–78.

232. The classic source on the *pīṭhas*, which includes a critical edition of the 16th c. Bengali *Pīṭhanirṇaya*, is Sircar, *Śākta Pīṭhas*, passim; for a lively rejoinder, however, see Pal, *Hindu Religion*, pp. 24–27. The Nāth Siddha reckoning is found in *Gorakh Bānī* Sabadī 163. Much of the latter part of the *ṢSS* (especially 4.1–11) is

devoted to the Goddess's tour of her footstools, across an Indian subcontinent that is situated, in its entirety, within her body: Schoterman, *ṢSS*, p. 148.

233. For the alchemical lore relative to Hiṅglāj and Kāmākhyā, see above, chap. 7 nn. 65–70. Kedār has been discussed above, n. 153. Alchemical descriptions of Srisailam are found in *RRĀ* 4.8.1–185. The *RA* description of Kailash is in 1.2–3.

234. On the symbolism of the Nine Nāths, see Dasgupta, *Obscure*, p. 206, citing the *Gorakṣa Siddhānta Saṃgraha*, pp. 44–45; the *Tantrarāja Tantra* (2.2–5, in Woodroffe, *Tantrarāja Tantra*, p. 19); and Schoterman, *ṢSS*, pp. 31–39. See above, chap. 4, nn. 53–60.

235. The *Gorakh Bodh*, a vernacular work cast in the form of a conversation between Gorakhnāth and his guru Matsyendranāth, is a veritable "skeleton key" to the "intentional language" of the Nāth Siddhas concerning the bodily microcosm. Cf. the *Prāṇ Sāṅkalī* of Cauraṅgīnāth, vv. 206–341 (in Dvivedi, *Nāth Siddhoṃ*, pp. 19–28); and in Sanskrit, the third chapter of Gorakhnāth's *SSP.*

236. Temple, *Legends*, 2:441; Swynnerton, *Romantic Tales*, pp. 426–33.

237. Dvivedi, *Nāth Sampradāy*, pp. 185–86; Grierson and Dvivedi, *Padumawāti*, p. 251–52. Jayasī himself speaks of Siṁhala and Laṅka as two different places (Shirreff's notes to *Padmāvatī* 2.16), even if he clearly knows Siṁhala or Saṅgaldīp to be an island situated to the south of India. There is, however, much more of fairyland than hard geography to Jayasī's Siṁhala, just as there is to the Kingdom of Women into which Matsyendra falls in the myths we related above.

238. It is Pūraṇ Bhagat (Cauraṅginātb) himself who claims Matsyendra for his guru: *Prāṇ Saṅkali* vv. 207, 221, 307, in *NSB*, pp. 19, 20, 26. On the localization of Matsyendra's "Plaintain Forest" in Sri Lanka, see Cunninath, *Tan-Prakāś*, p. 198; Temple, *Legends*, 2:19 (v. 194); and above, n. 101. *Gorakh Bānī* Pad 1.1–4 presents Matsyendra's imprisonment in the Kingdom of Women as the result of his Kaula propensities. The text of the poem consists of Gorakh's arguments against sexual intercourse as a component of tantric practice.

239. *Padmāvat* 219–22 [= 22.8–10; 23.1], in Grierson and Dvivedi, *Padumawāti*, pp. 478–82; Sharma, *Jayasī Granthāvalī*, pp. 347–55; and Shirreff, *Padmāvatī*, pp. 134–35. A similar description is in 2.16–18. This translation relies to some extent on Shirreff's translation; it relies more heavily, however, on Dvivedi's and Sharma's superior Hindi *ṭīkā* and commentary. Words in parentheses correspond to Shirreff's annotations; words in square brackets are my own additions.

240. The six *cakra*s and the *sahasrāra:* see above, chap. 2, n. 95. Similar imagery is found in such popular traditions as the legend of the marriage of a Muslim fakir named Sakhī Sarwar. In a preliminary test, Sakhī Sarwar is made to hit with an arrow a brass cup that has been perched atop seven superimposed bamboo poles: "Marriage of Sakhī Sarwar," legend no. 22 in Temple, *Legends*, vol. 2, p. 127.

241. *Haṭh*, the modern Indo-Aryan form of *haṭha*, as in *haṭha yoga*.

242. *Cīṅhe* (pl.), "marks," "signs," are the emblems a yogin wears (earrings, horn, wallet, etc.: see chap. 9, nn. 82–84) which are so many marks of his initiation into a given—in this case the Nāth Siddha—order.

243. The nine gates and the tenth door are the bodily orifices and the inner *brahmarandhra* or *śaṅkhinī nāḍī* (also known as the *baṅka nāla*); the five constables are the five breaths: see above, chap. 2, n. 29.

244. *Bāṅk[ī]*, an alloform of *baṅka*, as in the bent tube, the *baṅka nāla*, another name for the *śaṅkhinī nāḍī*, associated with the *daśama dvāra*, the tenth door, located in the head. The reference to the body as "bent" or "crooked" at the beginning of this description would also refer to the crooked body of the *śaṅkhinī*, which doubles as the *kuṇḍalinī*. See above, n. 200.

245. *Bhed*, "penetrate" has the extended meaning of "secret," as such are generally impenetrable until one has a clue with which to unlock them. This is the standard hathayogic term used for the "piercing" of the *cakra*s by the *kuṇḍalinī*. In alchemical parlance, this term comes to be closely identified with *vedh*, "pierce, penetrate," which is the term employed to signify transmutation, in which mercury is said to penetrate and thereby transform base metals into gold and mortals into immortals.

246. Cf. the "pools" in the ascent of Kedārnāth (above, sec. 3, nn. 109–11); and the channeling of the Ganges associated with *matsyodarī*. The path rising out of the pool at the base of the fortress (the *mūlādhāra cakra*, where the *kuṇḍalinī* sleeps) is clearly the medial *suṣumṇā nāḍī*: see above, n. 153.

247. Cf. the discussion of the reverse (*viparīta*) yogic posture and the alchemical *vidyādhara* and other *yantra*s: above, nn. 120–21.

248. The idea here is that one must dive down into the pool at the base of the fortress (the *mūlādhāra*) in order to gain access to the path (the *suṣumṇā nāḍī*) that rises out of its depths. As I show in chap. 9, sec. 46, such can only be effected by restraining or binding (*bandh*) mind, breath, and seed.

249. See above, n. 220.

250. At once a reference to the opening of the lotuses that are the *cakra*s when they are pierced and the initiatory role of the *padminī*, the Lotus Maiden, in tantric initiation: see below, chap. 10, sec. 2.

Chapter Nine

1. Padoux, *Vāc*, pp. 82, 124–26; Silburn, *Kuṇḍalinī*, pp. 19–24, 52–53, 64–66. The human body is the turning point of another important medieval metaphysical system. This is the Neoplatonist emanation and participation of John Scot's "Division of Nature," in which the return towards cosmic wholeness begins, after the

Fall, through the sexual union of Adam and Eve: Mircea Eliade, *The Two and the One*, trans. J. M. Cohen (Chicago: University of Chicago Press, 1979), p. 104.

2. *RA* 17.165a; 1.18ab. Cf. *RU* 15.50 (cited in Misra, *Āyurvedīya*, p. 31 n. 2), which describes the knower of mercury (*rasavid*) and the knower of the soul (*ātmavid*) as the two "subtle seers" (*sūkṣmadarśinau*). One may choose to see a precursor to this twofold method in the *Caraka Saṁhitā*'s (6.1.16) reference to the two complementary elixir therapies (*rasāyanas*), i.e., *kuṭīpraveśa* and *vātātapika*, "[the practice of] wind and sun": Roşu, "Consideration," p. 7. On *kuṭīpraveśa*, see above, chap. 2, nn. 47–48.

3. auṣadhyo 'dhyātmakaśceti rājayogo dvidhā kvacit / haṭho 'pi dvividhaḥ kvāpi vāyubinduniṣevanāt. Cf. *RA* 4.23, which calls for the conjoined use of botanicals and *mantras*.

4. Śabara's commentary to *Jaiminīya Sūtra* 3.1.3 and *Tantravārttika*, p. 1078, cited in Pandey, *Hindu Saṃskāras*, p. 16, who also gives many specialized uses of the term. Cf. *Caraka Saṁhitā* 1.26.30. See also Kapani, *Notion de saṃskāra*, passim.

5. See *RA* 1.36 on *sūta; RRS* 1.79–80 on divine jealousy as ground for the alchemical *saṃskāras*; and Pandeya's introduction to the *BhP* (*Gorakṣa Saṁhitā*, vol. 2, p. *gha*), for a commentary. See *Manu Smṛti* 2.27 and *Yājñavalkya Smṛti* 1.13 on the rites of passage. Cf. Kapani's discussion: *Notion de saṃskāra*, vol. 1, pp. 89–94. See above, chap. 7, sec. 2, on origin myths of metals, in which gold is accompanied by various metallic "afterbirths."

6. The figure of eighteen alchemical *saṃskāras* is reached by taking the classic number of sixteen *saṃskāras* (cf. Siddhinandan Misra's commentary to the discussion of the *saṃskāras* in the *RC* preceding 4.85, on p. 54.) and adding to these the resulting processes of transmutation and bodily transubstantiation. The *Vaikhānasa Smārta Sūtra* is a source that lists eighteen life-cycle *saṃskāras*: Kapani, *Notion de saṃskāra*, vol. 1, p. 86; for a figure of sixteen, see *Mṛgendrāgama*, Kriyā 6.9–11 (cited in Gonda, *Medieval*, p. 171). See above, chap. 2, sec. 4.

7. The eighteen *saṃskāras* are listed in *RHT* 2.1–2. Succinct descriptions are found in *RC* 4.85–106. This material is copied, for the most part, by the *RRS* (8.62–88), which also lists them in 11.15–16. A synoptic table of the *saṃskāras*, taken from fifteen major alchemical sources, is given in Misra, *Āyurvedīya*, pp. 212–13. An adequate English-language description of the mechanics of the eighteen *saṃskāras* is given by Subbarayappa, "Chemical Practice," in Bose, *Concise History*, pp. 320–22. Subbarayappa's informant was Dr. Damodar Joshi, of the Rasaśāstra Department of the Ayurvedic College of Benares Hindu University. Dr. Joshi was also my principal informant on such matters, during my stay in Benares, from August to January 1984 and in March 1985.

8. *Gheraṇḍa Saṁhitā* 1.9–11.

9. Misra, *Āyurvedīya*, pp. 94–96, 198–99; and Dash, *Alchemy*, pp. 91–92, 185–86.

10. On this distinction, see Misra, *Āyurvedīya*, p. 211.

11. The process of *mūrcchana* is described in *RRS* 11.35. The properties of swooned mercury are described in *RA* 11.199.

12. On this distinction, see Dash, *Alchemy*, pp. 92–93; and Misra, *Āyurvedīya*, p. 248.

13. The *RRS* is the most systematic source on *bandhana*, which it defines (8.66; 11.60); it also gives a list (11.61–64) and practical descriptions (11.65–112) of the twenty-five means for fixing mercury. Cf. Misra, *Āyurvedīya*, pp. 309–21.

14. Specific procedures for the killing of mercury are given in *RRS* 11.113–21; 30.1–21. The powers and properties of killed mercury (*bhasmasūta*, *mṛtasūtaka*) are given in *RA* 1.22 and 11.200; and *RM* fol. 9a.2–3. The *RA* (12.82) and *RC* (1.26) stipulate that mercury, as the semen of Śiva, is not truly killed when reduced to ashes, but merely "greatly swooned." On the killing of other metals, see Subbarayappa, "Chemical Practice," in Bose, *Concise History*, pp. 325–26, citing *RRS* 5.13 and *RHT* 9.16.

15. This process has been discussed at length in chap. 8, sec. 3.

16. *RRS* 11.47–48. The salt in question, called *ambuja* ("water-born") or *saindhava* ("from the Sindhu [Indus River] region"), is said to have arisen from a combination of "male and female sexual emissions and the menstrual blood of a forbidden woman": Sharma's commentary to *RRS* 11.48 (p. 167), citing the *Rasāvatara*.

17. *RRS* 11.49. Cf. Dash, *Alchemy*, pp. 63–64.

18. *RRS* 11.51–52. Cf. Misra, *Āyurvedīya*, p. 235.

19. *RRS* 11.59. Cf. Dash, *Alchemy*, p. 65. The first eight *saṃskāra*s are treated summarily in *RHT* 2.1–20.

20. *RRS* 8.72.

21. *RRS* 8.80–85. Dash, *Alchemy*, pp. 65–73. The *RHT* devotes all of its third chapter to *grāsa*, its fourth chapter to *cāraṇa*, its fifth chapter to *garbhadruti*, and its fifteenth chapter to *bāhyadruti*.

22. The alchemist knows he has reached the stage of *jāraṇa* when the mercury no longer increases in weight after absorbing a given mineral substance: *ibid.*, p. 73. Chapter six of the *RHT* is devoted to *jāraṇa*.

23. *RRS* 8.87; *RHT* 8.1–19. Indeed, the coloring of metals with mercury colored in this way may have been the greater part of so-called transmutation in this tradition: Subbarayappa, "Chemical Practice," in Bose, *Concise History*, p. 320.

24. *RRS* 8.88; *RHT* 16.1–36.

25. *RA* 11.216–17; *RHT* 17.1–8. Neither the *RC* nor the *RRS* contains descriptions of *krāmaṇa*.

26. *Śatapatha Brāhmaṇa* 3.8.2.27: *amṛtam āyur hiraṇyam*, literally "gold is non-death; gold is longevity." Cf. *Śatapatha Brāhmaṇa* 7.4.1.15–17 and 13.4.1.7.

27. *Śatapatha Brāhmaṇa* 6.1.2.13–26 and 7.3.1.16, discussed in Malamoud, "Briques et mots: Obervations sur le corps des dieux dans l'Inde vedique," in *Cuire le monde*, pp. 262–63; and Kapani, *Notion de saṃskāra*, vol. 1, pp. 58–71. Cf. White, "*Dakkhina* and *Agnicayana*," pp. 192–94, 212–13.

28. *Śatapatha Brāhmaṇa* 7.2.2.7–19; 7.2.4.1–26; 7.3.1.9–11; and *Āpastamba Śrauta Sūtra* 16.19.11–13, discussed in Charles Malamoud, "Cosmologie prescriptive: Observations sur le monde et le non-monde dans l'Inde ancienne," in *Le temps de la réflexion* 10 (1989), pp. 320–21; idem, "Village et forêt," in *Cuire le monde*, p. 101 n. 35; and Kapani, *Notion de saṃskāra*, vol. 1, pp. 63–65.

29. Malamoud, "Cuire le monde," in *Cuire le monde*, pp. 60–62.

30. *Aitareya Brāhmaṇa* 1.3. *Dīkṣā* is defined as *tattva-śuddhi*, "purification of the constituent elements," in Kaviraj, *Bhāratīy*, 1:282.

31. *Maitrī Upaniṣad* 2.5; *Manu Smṛti* 8.96; 12.12,14; *Yājñavalkya Smṛti* 3.178; *Bhagavad Gītā* 13.1–2; *Caraka Saṁhitā* 4.1.65. Cf. Dasgupta, *History*, 1:214. *Kṣetra* refers to the lower evolutes of Prakṛti, feminine materiality, while *kṣetrajñā* is to be identified with male Puruṣa, spirit.

32. White, "*Dakkhina* and *Agnicayana*," pp. 205–6.

33. Personal communication from Siddhinandan Misra, Benares, March 1985. See also Misra, *Āyurvedīya*, p. 326, and above, chap. 2, sec. 2.

34. Zimmerman, "Ṛtu-Sātmya," pp. 97–99. Cf. Sharma, *Āyurved*, pp. 276–77, 495–503.

35. *RA* 18.2–19; *RRS* 11.66. The alchemist's preparation in fact begins with his initiation, by a guru, into the alchemical arts. Once again, parallels—between human birth and the *saṃskāra*s as rites of passage, and the alchemical *saṃskāra*s—are explicit: Pandeya's introduction to *BhP* (*Gorakṣa Saṁhitā*, vol. 2), p. *ña*.

36. *Āyurveda Prakāśa* 1.489, cited in Misra, *Āyurvedīya*, p. 327. In preparing it for its ingestion, one is to nourish mercury itself with *bījas* of gold and silver: *RA* 8.16–22. Cf. *KCM* (London, Wellcome MSS no. g473) fol. 45.4–9, in which menstrual blood is used as an adjunct. On the *kṣetrasaṃskāra*s (*garbhādāna*, *puṃsavana*, and *sīmantonnayana*), see *Manu Smṛti* 9.33, 36–38. In legal terminology, the surrogate male who fathers a child on a widow (*kṣetra*) who has lost her husband (*kṣetrin*) is called the "inseminator" (*bījin*): *Gautama Dharma Sūtra* 28.30, cited in Kane, *History of Dharmaśāstra* vol. 2, pt. 1, p. 599, quoted in Gail Hinich Sutherland, "*Bīja* (Seed) and *Kṣetra* (Field): Male Surrogacy or *Niyoga* in the Mahābhārata," *Contributions to Indian Sociology*, n.s. 24 (1990), p. 78.

37. Joshi, "Notes," pp. 106–7; *HT*, p. 85; Kaviraj, *Bhāratīy*, 1:279.

38. *MBhT* 10.3–4. The unity of Śiva and Śakti is portrayed as that of seed (*bīja*) and sprout (*aṅkura*) in a number of sources: Narharinath, *Nav Nāth Caurāsī Siddh* (Benares: Rashtriya Press, 1968), p. 25 (v. 3). Cf. *Kāmakalāvilāsa*, quoted in Woodroffe, *Serpent Power*, p. 132.

39. There is a certain symmetry here between the father-son relationship of Agni-Prajāpati and the guru-disciple relationship of Gorakh-Matsyendra: see below, n. 74 of the present chapter.

40. *HYP* 2.23. Cf. Renou and Filliozat, *L'Inde classique*, vol. 2, p. 52.

41. *HYP* 2.22–38. This identification, of *ṣaṭkrīya* as the means to bodily *bhūtaśuddhi*, was confirmed for me in a personal communication from Mahant Avedyanāth, Gorakhpur, January 1985.

42. *Śatapatha Brāhmaṇa* 7.2.2.18–20; 7.2.4.10.

43. This is clearly stated in *Padmāvat* 22.8 (= 219), in Grierson and Dvivedi, *Padumawāti*, p. 479, and Shirreff, *Padmāvatī*, p. 134: "Now that you are a Siddha, you have obtained a state of purity (*śudhi*). The mirror (*darpaṇ*) of your body has been cleared of dust." Cf. *Śvetāśvatara Upaniṣad* 2.14.

44. *HT*, p. 81. Two texts entitled *Bhūtaśuddhi Tantra* may be found, in edited form, in the *Tantrasaṃgraha*, vol. 3, pp. 565–625; and vol. 4, pp. 308–16.

45. Jaggi, *Yogic and Tantric Medicine*, p. 117. The term may originally have referred to the casting out of "beings" or "spirits" inhabiting the area upon which the ritual was to be performed. *Bhūta* at once means "element" and "spirit": Van Kooij, *Worship*, p. 21. Cf. *BhP* 7.368–74.

46. Descriptions of outer and inner *bhūtaśuddhi* are found in *Kālikā Purāṇa* 52.18–19; 53.13–14; 57.93–108 (in B. N. Shastri, *Kālikāpurāṇa* [text, introduction, and translation into English], 2 vols. [Delhi: Nag Publishers, 1991], vol. 2, pp. 751, 756, 816–19). (The same passages, with different chapter and verse numbering, are translated in Van Kooij, *Worship*, pp. 45, 166). Cf. *HT*, pp. 136, 140, 143; Sanderson, "Maṇḍala," pp. 174–75; and Woodroffe *Principles of Tantra*, 2:477 (cited in Walter, *Role of Alchemy*, p. 70).

47. *Kālikā Purāṇa* 55.21–35 (in Van Kooij, *Worship*, pp. 45–46) gives a detailed description of the divinity who is to be projected upon this empty space. Cf. *Mahānirvāṇa Tantra* (ed. Woodroffe), pp. 76–77; Bharati, *Tantric Tradition*, p. 246; Gupta, *HT*, pp. 136, 140, 143; Sanderson, "Maṇḍala," pp. 174–75; and Wheelock, "Mantra in Vedic and Tantric Ritual," in Alper, ed., *Mantra*, p. 121. Compare *RA* 18.208–210. On a Theravāda Buddhist precursor of this technique, see Paul Mus, "La notion de temps réversible dans la mythologie bouddhique," *École Pratique des Hautes Etudes. Annuaire 1938–1939* (Melun: Imprimerie Administrative, 1938), pp. 30–31.

48. *Tantravārttika*, p. 1078, cited in Pandey, *Hindu Saṃskāras*, p. 16. Cf. Kapani, *Notion de saṃskāra*, vol. 1, pp. 89–94.

49. *Śodhana* is derived from the same root as *śuddhi*, in *bhūtaśuddhi*. Apart from the first eight *saṃskāras*, relatively pure mercury may be obtained through extraction from cinnabar (in the *vidyādhara yantra*, through the process of distillation, *pātana:* see above, chap. 8, sec. 3), and a number of simpler methods. *Svedana* is described in *RA* 10.41; *RHT* 2.3; *RC* 15.36; and *RRS* 8.62; 11.29.

50. *HYP* 2.12, 19. This process is widely reported in sources (quoted at length in Brahmānanda's commentary on 2.12) that range from the *Yājñavalkya Smṛti* to the *Liṅga Purāṇa*. Cf. *Caraka Saṁhitā* 6.15.29–30 (cited in Dasgupta, *History* 2:326) on the body's natural voiding of waste products through the bodily orifices and pores. The *KJñN* (14.32) calls the first of a list of five sets of Kaula schools "Starting at the Pores" (*romakūpādi*).

51. *HYP* 2.13.

52. *Yoga Sūtra* 1.2 reads *yogaś cittāvṛtti nirodhaḥ*, of which the most generally accepted and elegant translation is "yoga is the suppression of the states of consciousness."

53. *HYP* 1.56.

54. The most succinct rendering is found in *RA* 1.19: for variant readings in other works, see above, chap. 5, nn. 145, 161, 218, 222, 237.

55. The verse is found in *HYP* 4.27, in which the Sanskrit reads: mūrcchito harate vyādhīn mṛto jīvayati svayam/ baddhaḥ khecaratāṃ dhatte raso vāyuśca pārvati. Cf. *RA* 1.19: mūrcchito harate vyādhiṃ mṛto jīvayati svayam/ baddhaḥ khecaratāṃ kuryāt raso vāyuśca bhairavi.

56. *Rājā rānī saṃbād*, v. 18 in Dvivedi, *Nāth Siddoṃ*, p. 9. Statements of this kind are legion in the hathayogic sources. Cf. *HYP* 2.2 and 4.28 for a more sober formulation.

57. *HYP* 4.26, 28; *RA* 2.117–18. Cf. *RA* 1.20–22, the verses immediately following the classic statement of 1.19.

58. *Gorakh Bānī* Sabadī 142. Cf. Sabadī 238 and *RA* 2.117–18.

59. *RA* 11.197. The seven forms—*mūrcchita*, *mṛtasūta*, *jalūkabandha*, *mūttibandha*, *paṭṭabandha*, *bhasmasūta*, and *khoṭa[bandha]*—are described in 11.198–208. *RA* 10.29 establishes a metaphorical, if not literal, identification between various forms of treated mercury and Hindu divinities: "Through the power of the Work (*karmayogabalāt*) mercury takes the form of Brahmā when it is purified (*āroṭa*); (Viṣṇu) Janārdana when it is swooned (*mūrcchita*); and Rudra when it is bound (*baddha*). Other sources (*RRĀ* 1.1.12a–13a, *RM* fol. 1a.8–10; *Rasasindhu*, ASL MSS no. 4267, fol. 1.5) follow this enumeration, adding other hypostases of Śiva (Maheś-

vara, Sadāśiva, Īśāna) to their lists to correspond to further transformations of mercury.

60. *HYP* 2.7–9,35. The final member of the first of the six preliminary practices of yogic purification (the *ṣaṭkarmāṇi*), called *agnisāra* ("the coursing of the inner fire"), involves a similar body of practices which are said to activate the five inner fires (of digestion, etc.). In *agnisāra*, one is to repeatedly fill and empty the abdomen of air, after the fashion of a blacksmith's bellows: Renou and Filliozat, *L'Inde classique*, vol. 2, pp. 52–53.

61. *HYP* 2.69. *HYP* 3.12, calls the outer *nāḍī*s "lifeless"; 3.73 says they are "paralyzed"; and 3.74 calls them "bound," all synonyms for "swooned." See below, n. 89.

62. Brahmānanda's commentary to *HYP* 4.27. *Mūrcchana* has a number of other meanings, including "swelling," "coagulation," "assuming shape," which together lead to an image of a bruise which, taking shape as it swells, becomes deadened to touch: Monier-Williams, *Sanskrit-English Dictionary*, s.v. "murch."

63. *HYP* 3.55–60. *Uḍḍiyāna* is also the name of one of the four original *pīṭha*s of both Buddhist and Hindu tantrism. In the Nāth Siddha system of the nine *cakra*s (which alternates with the 6 + 1 *cakra* system), *uḍḍiyāna* (here called *oḍyāna*) is located at the level of the second cakra, the *svādhiṣṭhāna: SSP* 2.2.

64. *HYP* 3.70–73. *Jālaṃdhara* is also the name of one of the four original *pīṭha*s, located in the Nāth Siddha system of the nine *cakra*s at the level of the *brahmarandhra-nirvāṇa cakra*, the eighth *cakra* identified with the fontanelle: *SSP* 2.8. The Nāth Siddhas locate the two other original *pīṭha*s, *Kāmarūpa* and *Pūrṇagiri*, at the lowest and highest *cakra*s, respectively: *SSP* 2.1, 9. The form of diaphragmatic retention called *mūrccha*, discussed above (n. 60) in fact combines breath retention with the *jālaṃdhara bandha: HYP* 2.69.

65. *HYP* 4.26.

66. On the seven types of alchemical *bandha*s, see *RPS* 2.2, and above, n. 59. The verse concerning the *rākṣasa* named Method is *RA* 12.3, and the commentary is from the glossary to Tripathi's edition, p. 373.

67. See above, chap. 8, n. 220.

68. *Gorakh Bānī* Sabadī 88. Cf. *HYP* 4.91, which calls the *nāda* an elephant goad for stabilizing the wild elephant of the mind. This passage is the first of a series of nine verses (*HYP* 4.91–99) which metaphorically compare the effects of the *nāda* on the mind to all manner of immobilization in nature and culture. In Śaiva ritual, the *aṅkuśā mudrā* (a fist with the index-finger bent in the form of a hook) is employed to generate nectar from within the subtle body: Gonda, *Viṣṇuism*, p. 180.

69. The notion dates back to *Atharva Veda* 11.4.21. On clipping the wings of the cosmic goose, the *haṃsa*, see Carpaṭi jī kī sabadi 47, in Dvivedi, *Nāth Siddhoṃ*, p. 17; and *HYP* 4.92. On the clipping of mercury's wings, see *RHT* 4.5; *BhP* 5.148,

168–69; 6.176; 8.81; 9.81; and *RC* 16.44, 52–55, 75. See also above, chap. 7, n. 166.

70. *RV* 10.113.6, cited in Jean Varenne, *Cosmogonies védiques* (Milan: Archè, 1982), p. 114.

71. The myth of Gorakh's binding of the nine serpent clouds is related in the ca. A.D. 1820 *Śrī Nāth Tīrthāvalī* of Mān Singh, vv. 330–36 and Lévi, *Le Népal*, vol. 1, pp. 351, 372, citing the "lost" Nepali *Buddha Purāṇa*. This binding may be a reference to the nine *cakra*s of a system described in Gorakhnāth's *SSP* (2.1–9). More likely, it refers to a commonplace of Siddha literature, that through a given practice, one becomes more powerful than nine serpents: *KCM* fol. 20a.8; *BhP* (ASL MSS 4401, fol. 3b.49). The *RA* (12.314) raises this figure to ten.

72. *HT*, p. 53, citing *Paramārthasāra* 1.15; and Kaviraj, *Tāntrik Vāṅmay*, p. 58.

73. *Yogabīja* 52: *chedabandhairmukto*. Cf. Abhinavagupta's praise of Matsyendra as one who "tore apart the glowing net," in *TĀ* 1.7. Lee Siegel's delightful *Net of Magic* is a wide-ranging discussion of this entire symbol system.

74. *KJñN* 17.33–37. Cf. Gorakhnāth's statement that "bound in the noose [of Death] one becomes a living creature. Freed from the noose, one becomes Sadāsiva": Sahagal, *Gorakh Darśan*, p. 107 (without citation). The *Paraśurāma Kalpa Sūtra* (1.5) makes a nearly identical statement. Tantrics also have the power to kill. This one of the "six acts" (*ṣaṭkarmāṇi*) of tantric black magic is called *māraṇa: HT*, p. 35.

75. *HYP* 4.17. On the three knots, *HYP* 4.70, 73, 76.

76. *HYP* 4.94.

77. *Yogamārtaṇḍa* 180, in *SSP*, p. 71; *Yogabīja* 52; and *HYP* 3.24. Cf. *HYP* 4.108, which states that the realized yogin is not bound by karma, not eaten by time, and is beholden to no one; and *Gorakh Bānī* Sabadī 85, which makes a similar statement in the context of what it calls the *anāhat bandh*, the "lock of the unstruck [sound]." See also *Akulavīratantra* [B] 30, 49–50, 65, in Bagchi, *KJñN*, pp. 96–99. The *avadhūta* is one who has thrown down (*ava-dhū*) the bonds of existence: *NSC*, p. 126. Cf. *SSP* 6.1.

78. Death (named Yama or Kāla) carries a noose, as does the divine enforcer of order and binding contracts, Varuṇa. The latter, as a first-function god, is a specialist in invisible binding weapons, not unlike the Scandinavian Odin who ensnares enemies on the field of battle with his invisible fetters. The bonds of death are an Indo-European theme, on which see Bruce Lincoln, "Mithra(s) as Sun and Savior," in *Death, War, and Sacrifice: Studies in Ideology and Practice* (Chicago: University of Chicago Press, 1991), especially pp. 78–81. On *kālavañcana*, see *HYP* 3.3; *KJñN* 17.17; *KCM* (ASL MSS no. 3952) fol. 31a.3, 31b.2.

79. *Gopīcandrer Gān*, summarized in Dasgupta, *Obscure*, p. 227. Gorakhnāth does the same: *Gorakṣa Vijaya*, pp. 45–48, cited ibid., p. 222.

80. *Gopīcandrer Pāñcalī*, p. 345, translated in Dasgupta, *Obscure*, p. 226.

81. *Gopīcandrer Sannyās*, p. 418, cited in Dasgupta, *Obscure*, p. 215.

82. Ernest Trump, *The Ādi Granth* (London: 1877), p. xl, cited in Briggs, *Gorakhnāth*, p. 203. Cf. *Padmāvat* 129 [=12.1] for an extended description of a fully equipped Nāth Siddha; and Briggs, *Gorakhnāth*, pp. 6–23 and Dvivedi, *Nāth Sampradāy*, pp. 15–21, for discussion.

83. The wavering mind is itself compared to a gazelle in the *HYP* (4.94, 99), a metaphor dramatized in the legend of Gorakh's disciple Bhartṛhari: Briggs, *Gorakhnāth*, p. 132.

84. *Gorakh Bānī* Sabadī 48a, in which the *kantha* is identified with the five elements. Cf. the Jain legend of Kanthaḍī, a disciple of Gorakh, who transfers the heat of a fever (or his yogic energy) into his *kantha: Prabandha Cintāmaṇi*, pp. 22–23, cited in Dvivedi, *Nāth Sampradāy*, p. 51.

85. On dying to the world and performing one's cremations rites, see Pandurang Vaman Kane, *History of Dharmaśāstra*, 5 vols. 2d ed. (Poona: Bhandarkar Oriental Institute), vol. 2, part 2, pp. 954–55, 985. On the *prāṇāgnihotra*, see *Vaikhānasa Smārta Sūtra* 2.18. This tradition goes back to the *Taittirīya Āraṇyaka:* Madeleine Biardeau and Charles Malamoud, *Le Sacrifice dans l'Inde Ancienne* (Paris: Presses Universitaires de France, 1976), pp. 67–68. A *Prāṇāgnihotra Upaniṣad*, a compilation of earlier Upanisadic descriptions of this practice, is found in Deussen, *Sixty Upanisads*, 2:645–51. Because the renouncer has performed his own cremation rites upon taking up *sannyāsa*, his body is not burned, but rather inhumed or set adrift, upon its apparent "death." On this see *Paiṅgala Upaniṣad* 4.5–8, cited in Kapani, *Notion de saṃskāra*, vol. 1, p. 153.

86. *RA* 1.19. The optimum fixation (*bandha*) of mercury, effected through its "assimilation" in female sulfur and mica, leaves it in an ashen state (*bhasmīkṛta*) in which it has been rendered "lifeless" (*nirjīva:* in opposition to the quite useless *sajīva-bandha*, which leaves mercury subject to evaporation and has little medical use: *RRS* 11.75), i.e., completely immobilized and impervious to heat and thereby most effective against disease: *RRS* 11.76.

87. *Gorakh Bānī* Sabadī 26: marau be jogī marau, maraṇ hai mīṭhā/ tis maranīṃ marau jis maranīṃ goraṣ mari dīṭhā. Cf. *Yogabīja* 57–58a, and Kabir, *Sākhī* 19.13 (= *Doha* 41.8), in Vaudeville, *Kabīr*, p. 260.

88. *Padmāvat* 24.2, in Grierson and Dvivedi, *Padumawāti*, p. 530.

89. *Amaraugha Prabodha* 40b–41, which is nearly identical to *HYP* 3.27b–28. I have translated the problematic *jānīyāt* in this passage as a gerundive. The fourth state of consciousness is called either *mūrcchā* or *turīya* ("trance"). A fifth may be added. This is *maraṇa*, "death": commentary to English translation of *HYP* 4.107, p. 107.

90. *HYP* 3.4. In classical Indian thought as well, one enjoys one's "third" and most glorious birth, this time in heaven, when one's corpse has been incinerated in the cremation fire: *Śatapatha Brāhmaṇa* 11.2.1.1.

91. On *vajrolī*, see above, chap. 7, nn. 90–102. *Sahajolī* and *amarolī* are described in *HYP* 3.92–98. These practices appear to be connected to the broader tantric ritual practice of *amṛtikaraṇa*, which involves the identification of ashes, water, and nectar: on this practice, see Gonda, *Viṣṇuism*, pp. 72, 180.

92. See *RA* 12.79 on the state of the question. It is also called *bhasma-nirmāṇa pārada: MBhT* 5.1. See above, n. 14.

93. *RA* 7.142. Personal communication from Siddhinandan Misra, Benares, March 1985.

94. An early example is *Vājasaneyi Saṁhitā* 40.15: "Now my breath is the immortal wind, my body is *bhasma*," cited in David Knipe, "Night of the Growing Dead: A Cult of Vīrabhadra in Coastal Andhra," in Alf Hiltebeitel, ed. *Criminal Gods and Demon Devotees: Essays on the Guardians of Popular Hinduism* (Albany: SUNY Press, 1989).

95. *Maitrī Upaniṣad* 6.15.

96. Malamoud, "Village et forêt dans l'idéologie de l'Inde brahmanique," in *Cuire le monde*, p. 102; and Kapani, *Notion de saṃskāra*, vol. 1, p. 60 n. 34, citing *Śatapatha Brāhmaṇa* 6.2.2.6; 6.3.1.1.; and 6.5.3.1.

97. Gopīcand's statement (in Temple, *Legends of the Panjāb*, vol. 2, p. 48 [legend no. 18, vv. 499–500) reads *kachā bartan hove jidhar phere phir jāe/ham to jogī hūe gurū ne dīe pakāe*. Cf. *Śvetāśvatara Upaniṣad* (2.12), which states that a body fired by yoga (*yogāgniṃ mayaṃ śarīram*) cannot be reached by either sickness, aging, or death. Whence also the invocation to Agni and the gods, "May we be well cooked!": *RV* 9.83.1. Cf. *Śiva Saṁhitā*, 2.32–34; and *Yogabīja* 34–35, 51, 76, which distinguishes between a body that is "cooked" or "fired" (*pakvā*) by yoga and one that is not (*apakvā*); and evokes a "seven-*dhātu* body fired in the fire of yoga."

98. Here we are paraphrasing the formulation of Benjamin Walker, *Hindu World*, s.v. "ashes."

99. On the Pāśupatas, see Lorenzen, "Śaivism: Pāśupatas," in *Encyclopedia of Religion*, vol. 13, p. 18. On *vibhūti*, Monier-Williams, *Sanskrit-English Dictionary*, s.v. "vibhūti." On the consumption of ashes as a component of *dīkṣā*, see *Manu Smṛti* 6.25, 38.

100. Walker, *Hindu World*, s.v. "ashes." That is, Śiva ejaculated at the sight of Pārvatī, in which case the combination of elements which Śiva smeared over his body evokes those of the *amarolī mudrā*.

101. *Mahābhārata* 3.81.98–118; 9.37.34–50; *Skanda Purāṇa* 5.2.2.2–37; *Padma Purāṇa* 1.27.1–15; 5.18.132; *Vāmana Purāṇa* 17.1–22. A brief *Mahābhārata*

(13.17.92) reference to the same myth has Śiva calling himself *bhasmabhūta,* "made of ashes": O'Flaherty, *Śiva,* p. 245.

102. *Brahmāṇḍa Purāṇa* 1.2.27.106b, 108ab, 109b, 113ab, 121a, 123a, 124b.

103. Kāvya Uśanas's poetic powers are hymned in *RV* 9.87.3; a Brahmanic myth of his rivalry with Indra and the gods is found in *Jaiminīya Brāhmaṇa* 1.125–27. See O'Flaherty, *Tales of Sex and Violence,* pp. 87–90.

104. Georges Dumézil, *Mythe et épopée,* vol. 2, part 2, "Entre les dieux et les démons: un sorcier," pp. 161–66; 197–205, 208. The myth is found in *Mahābhārata* 1.71.2–1.72.25.

105. Dumézil, *Mythe et épopée,* 2:200–4.

106. On the alternation between *kavi* and Kāvya Uśanas's name, see Dumézil, *Mythe et épopée,* vol. 2, part 2, pp. 148–56, 204. On the incantatory element in Vedic healing, see Zysk, *Religious Healing,* pp. 8 and 241, citing Sāyaṇa's commentary to Atharva Veda 4.2.6. It should be recalled here that "magical alchemy" was an affair of Asuras: see above, chap. 3, nn. 35–40. On the alchemical *kavi* and the medical *kavirāj,* see above, chap. 1, nn. 49–50; below, chap. 10, sec. 5.

107. Knipe, "Night," in Hiltebeitel, *Criminal Gods,* pp. 149–50. In the Punjabi Hills cults of the Seven Sisters, the term *piṇḍī* is applied to "a lump of stone, somewhat resembling a Śiva-*liṅga*" that are manifestations of the Goddess herself: Erndl, *Victory to the Mother,* p. 66. An extensive discussion of the term *piṇḍa* is found in Kapani, *Notion de saṃskāra,* vol. 1, pp. 129–37.

108. See above, chap. 7, n. 98 on the *-oli* suffix; and chap. 8, n. 194, on the relationship between the Nāga suborders of the Dasnāmi sects and the Nāth *sampradāya.* On ashen *golās* carried by the former, see Sadananda Giri, *Society and Sannyāsin: A History of the Daśanāmī Sannyāsins* (Benares: n.p., 1976), p. 26.

109. The alchemical texts generally keep the reading *guṭikā;* however, see *RA* 12.330 for *gulikā.* See Monier-Williams, *Sanskrit-English Dictionary,* s.v. "guḍa."

110. Pir Premnath, *Śiva-Gorakṣa,* pp. 29, 61.

111. *Śiva-Gorakṣa,* pp. 29–34, 36, 41–46. Throughout his account, Premnath identifies Vicārnāth with Bhartṛhari. The *Śrī Nāth Tīrthāvalī* of Mān Singh (v. 364) relates that Bhartṛhari revived a dead child (whom this source names Siddha Kāyānāth) in a cave within "Gorakh Ṭilla" which, although it is usually identified with the prestigious Nāth Siddha monastery of of Sialkot (Jhelum dist., Punjab, Pakistan), is located by this author at Pharphing, in the Kathmandu Valley (an A.D. 1393 inscription at this site states that Gorakṣanātha's sandals were established there by Acintanātha; Tibetan traditions identify this figure with Matsyendra: Bagchi, introduction to *Kaulajñānanirṇaya,* p. 23)!

112. Lévi, *Le Népal,* vol. 1, pp. 351, 372 citing the *Buddha Purāṇa;* and Dvivedi, *Nāth Sampradāy,* p. 47, citing the *YSĀ.* This latter account, which includes the

detail concerning milk and menses, is adapted into Hindi in Gautam, *Srī Gorakhnāth Caritra*, p. 6. A Punjabi variant is briefly recounted in Rose, *Glossary*, p. 393. Another version of the same account, from the *Tahqīqāt-i-Ciśtī*, is cited in Briggs, *Gorakhnāth*, pp. 182–83. *NSC* (p. 49) gives a north Indian version of this legend.

113. These specially prepared ashes are in fact twice calcinated, by virtue of which they take on their distinctive snowy-white color. On this process, see Bedi, *Sadhus*, pp. 78–79.

114. Briggs, *Gorakhnāth*, p. 21. The present-day Gorakhnāth temple complex of Gorakhpur houses both an eternal flame (*akhaṇḍ jyoti*) and an eternal *dhūnī* (*akhaṇḍ dhūna*).

115. On Gorakh's initiation, see Dvivedi, *Nāth Sampradāy*, p. 19. On Carpaṭi's conception from Gorakh's *laṅgoti* water and Gūgā's conception from ashes given by Gorakh to his mother, see *NSC*, pp. 193, 256. Gorakh initiates Pūraṇ Bhagat with ashes: Temple, *Legends*, 2:445–46.

116. Temple, *Legends*, 2:436–37; William Crooke, "A Version of the Guga Legend," *Indian Antiquary* 24 (1895), pp. 52–53; Gautam, *Śrī Gorakhnāth Caritra*, p. 106; *NSC*, p. 276.

117. Rose, *Glossary*, vol. 2, pp. 390–2; Srivastav, ed., *"Gorakh" Viśeṣāṅk*, p. 90. On the calcinating breath of the cosmic serpents, see Temple, *Legends*, vol. 1, p. 177 (legend no. 6 ["Guru Gūggā"], v. 641).

118. Above, chap. 8, sec. 4.

119. *HYP* 1.27, 48; 2.66; 3.111, 115; 4.10, 11, 19. Somānanda, in his *Śaktivijñāna*, uses the term *utthāpana* (vv. 12–13) for the act of raising the *kuṇḍalinī*; and *bodhana* (vv. 14–15) for the subsequent act of causing the *kuṇḍalinī* to pierce the *granthi*s of Brahmā, Viṣṇu, Rudra, and enter into Īśvara, who is found between the eyebrows, and finally into Sadāśiva, via the *brahmadvāra*: Silburn, *Kuṇḍalinī*, p. 113.

120. Padoux, *Vāc*, pp. 86–121 (especially p. 87, citing *Śārada Tilaka* 1.7–8) describes this interaction at length. See Gonda, *Medieval*, p. 186 (citing *Mṛgendrāgama*, Kriyāpada 1.2); and Silburn, *Kuṇḍalinī*, p. 3 for alternative terminology.

121. *HT*, pp. 174, 177. On the *Kaulāvalīnirṇaya* of Jñānānandagiri Paramahaṃsa, see *HTSL*, p. 144. For a discussion of the related term *nirodhinī* in the mantric practice of chapter 21 of the pre–10th c. *Netra Tantra*, see Padoux, *Vāc*, pp. 103–4. Suppression (*nirodha*) is used as a synonym for *prāṇāyāma* in *HYP* 2.2 and *Gorakh Bānī* Sabadī 82, 92.

122. Lilian Silburn, "Le vide, le rien, l'abîme," in *Le Vide: Expérience spirituelle* (Paris: Hermes, 1969), pp. 30–33. This technique, also known to Mahāyāna Buddhism, was transmitted via China to the Japanese Zen masters, where it took the form of the *koan*.

123. *RA* 10.11: *jāraṇād bandhanaṃ bhavet.*

124. *RA* 11.50–54.

125. *RA* 11.12: *grāsaṃ gṛhṇa mama prabho.*

126. On the successive absorption by mercury of six times its mass of mica, see *RA* 11.70–73. More recent sources (*Rasacintāmaṇi* 5.73) suggest that sulfur should be used before mica in this process: Misra, *Āyurvedīya*, p. 243. In modern practice, sulfur, rather than mica, is used: Ray, *History*, vol. 2, pp. xliii–xliv; and Dash, *Alchemy*, p. 100. It should be noted here that mercury has six times the atomic weight of sulfur and that synthetic cinnabar is composed of 84% mercury and 16% sulfur: personal communication from Damodar Joshi, Benares, March 1985.

127. *RA* 11.98–106.

128. Personal communication from Damodar Joshi, Benares, August 1984. Cf. Dash, *Alchemy*, p. 100.

129. *Gorakh Bānī* Sabadī 252a. Cf. Sabadī 13b, in which the yogin is enjoined to absorb (*jaranām*) [his mind] in [the words issuing from] his guru's mouth.

130. This practice, dramatized in the legend of Mastnāth (Sankarnath, *Śrī Mastnāth Carit*, pp. 109–10), has for its outward correlate the playing of the *siṅgnād*, the antelope's horn worn by Nāth Siddhas, which is made to emit a (barely audible) sound by blowing: Véronique Bouillier, "La caste sectaire des Kānphaṭā Jogī dans le royaume du Nepal: l'exemple de Gorkhā," in *Bulletin de l'Ecole Française d'Extrême-Orient* 75 (1986), p. 147.

131. Gorakhnāth mentions (*Gorakh Bānī*, Sabadī 85) the *anāhat bandh*, a powerful lock presumably effected at the level of the heart, by which the yogin is rendered invulnerable.

132. *HYP* 4.85–86.

133. *HYP* 4.100.

134. baddhaṃ vimuktacāñcalyaṃ nādagandhakajāraṇāt/ manaḥ pāradam āpnoti nirālambākhyakhe 'ṭanam.

135. *RRS* 11.78.

136. *HYP* 1.17, 27.

137. A *mātra* (4 seconds) is defined as the time it takes for a sleeping man to breathe in and out once: six of these are a *pala* (*Yogacintāmaṇi*, cited by Brahmānanda, in his commentary to *HYP* 2.12). Alternatively, it is the time it takes to circle the knee three times with the palm of the hand, and then snap one's fingers (loc. cit., citing *Yājñavalkya Smṛti*). Geometric progressions of hathayogic *palas* are found in *Amanaska Yoga* 1.50–98; the relation between temporal duration and the successive stages of Pātañjala yoga are also described in Brahmānanda's commentary to *HYP* 2.12. See below, chap. 10, nn. 57–58.

138. *RA* 18.56–60.

139. *Maitrī Upaniṣad* 6.28; *Gorakh Bānī* Sabadī 33, 215.

140. Khakhar, "History," p. 49.

141. Mircea Eliade, *Shamanism, Archaic Techniques of Ecstasy*, tr. Willard R. Trask (Princeton: Princeton University Press, 1972).

142. Although most traditions make Gopīcand a king in Bengal, the oldest recensions of his song cycle appear to be from Nepal: Mukherji, *Gopicandra Nāṭaka*, p. xliv.

143. Legend cycles of Jālandhara (or Hāḍipā) and Gopīcand are found in Bengal (*Govindacandrer Gān*, summarized in Dvivedi, *Nāth Sampradāy*, pp. 184–86), the Punjab (summarized in Rose, *Glossary*, p. 395, and Temple, *Legends*, 2:1–71 [legend 18]); and Rajasthan (Gold, *Carnival*, pp. 159–310). A Marwari recension is the *Gopīcand kā Akhyān*, ed. Sridhara Sivalal (Bombay: Jnan Sagar, 1890). The Bengali Gopīcand cycle intersects that of Gorakh's rescue of Matsyendra from the Plantain Forest, in the trilogy comprising of *Gorakṣa Vijaya*, *Gopīcandrer Gān*, and *Aṇila Purāṇa:* Mukherji, *Gopicandra Nāṭaka*, p. xxxvi. Three *bānīs*, entitled *Gopīcand jī kī Sabadī*, *Rājā Rānī Saṃbād*, and *Rāg Rāmagrī*, offer fragmentary accounts of the Gopīcand legend: Dvivedi, *Nāth Siddhaṃ*, pp. 6–11 (vv. 47–125).

144. Kabīr, in one of his *Sākhīs* (4.8), refers to the Ketakī (vernacular *kevaṛā;* Latin *Pandarnus odoratissimus*), a fragrant shrub whose creamy colored flowers attract bees: Vaudeville, *Kabīr*, p. 179 and n. 7.

145. The motif is an archaic one, going back at least as far as the *Kauṣītaki Brāhmaṇa* (6.1–2, translated in O'Flaherty, *Hindu Myths*, p. 31).

146. Grierson, "The Song of Mánik Candra," *Journal of the Royal Asiatic Society of Bengal* 47 (1878), no. 3, pt. 1, p. 218, stipulates that she survived this ordeal by taking the form of a mustard seed (*siddhārtha*).

147. *Gopīcandrer Pāñcalī*, pp. 366–69; *Govinda-candra-gīta*, pp. 71–73; *Gopīcandrer Gān, Bujhān Khaṇḍa*, pp. 87–130, summarized in Dasgupta, *Obscure*, p. 226.

148. *RA* 18.228.

149. Temple, *Legends*, 2:23, cited in Briggs, *Gorakhnāth*, p. 194. *NSC* (p. 210) maintains that these effigies were made of the seven metals (*sapta-dhātu*); other Bengali accounts say all three are made of gold (Mukherji, *Gopicandra Nāṭaka*, p. xli). The Bengali *Gopīcandrer Gīt* says merely that Kānha-pā made three Gopīcand effigies: Dvivedi, *Nāth Sampradāy*, p. 186.

150. Another version, from the Punjab, states that Gorakh created a man from a blanket, who called himself "Gopīcand" when Jālandharīpā asked him who he was. The angry yogin reduced him to ashes *seven times*, after which the real Gopīcand was brought forward. Jālandharīpā then declared that since he had not been consumed by fire, he should become immortal: Rose, *Glossary*, p. 395. Cf. the

Marwari version, which states that Jālandhara reduced seven Gopīcand effigies to ashes, after which he declared his disciple immortal: Sivalal, *Gopīcand kā Akhyān*, pp. 33–35.

151. *Gorakh Bānī* Pad 34.5, glossed in Srivastav, ed., "*Gorakh Bānī*" *Viśeṣāṅk*, pp. 282–83. Alternatively, he uses magic to restore these limbs, which his stepmother had cut off (see below, for an identical motif, in the legend of Pūraṇ Bhagat): Briggs, *Gorakhnāth*, p. 191. On a parallel, from the Tibetan *Grub thob*, see above, chap. 4, n. 148.

152. *Gorakh Bānī*, Pañc Mātrā 21a, in Srivastav, ed., "*Gorakh Bānī*" *Viśeṣāṅk*, p. 392; and Barthwal, *Gorakh Bānī*, p. 221.

153. Briggs, *Gorakhnāth*, p. 197.

154. Gautam, *Śrī Gorakhnāth Caritra*, pp. 14–16.

155. Ibid., pp. 96–97.

156. Ibid., pp. 59–62.

157. Briggs, *Gorakhnāth*, p. 72.

158. Ibid., p. 187.

159. The principal recensions of the Pūraṇ Bhagat/Cauraṅgīnāth legend are those found in Temple, *Legends*, vol. 2, pp. 375–455 (no. 34); Swynnerton, *Romantic Tales*, pp. 411–41, both of which are Punjabi; and the twenty opening verses of the *Prāṇ Sāṅkalī* of Cauraṅgīnāth (in Dvivedi, *Nāth Siddhoṃ*, pp. 19–20), written in a medieval eastern Rajasthani dialect (ibid., p. 16 of the preface). It is also recounted by Jñāneśvara in his *YSĀ* (p. 372, cited in Dvivedi, *Nāth Sampradāy*, p. 177), and in Gautam, *Srī Gorakhnāth Caritra*, pp. 81–89.

160. *Asian Mythologies*, s.v. "Turkish and Mongolian Shamanism," by Jean-Paul Roux; idem., "Le nom du chaman dans les textes turco-mongols, *Anthropos* 53 (1958), pp. 113–42; Diane M. Coccari, "The Bir Babas of Banaras and the Deified Dead," in Hiltebeitel, ed., *Criminal Gods*, p. 256; and William Crooke, *Religion and Folklore of North India* (London: Oxford University Press, 1926), p. 319. Sialkot, the ancient Śākala, the venue of the Pūraṇ Bhagat legend, was the capital of the central Asian Hūṇas, the Ephthalite Huns, in the latter half of the first millennium: the Punjabi Jāṭs, of which Pūraṇ Bhagat would have been a scion (Briggs, *Gorakhnāth*, p. 239), are descended from this people. On this, see White, *Myths of the Dog-Man*, p. 120. The term *bhagat* is employed for the *rasdhari* actors whose troupe Gorakhnāth joins to release Matsyendra from the clutches of the women of the Plantain Forest: Rose, *Glossary*, p. 394 [n.].

161. *Prāṇ Sāṅkalī*, in Dvivedi, *Nāth Siddhoṃ*, p. 19 [= v. 206]. On the Śaṅkh/Salwān alternation, see Temple, *Legends*, 2:376, 378 [legend 34, vv. 5, 28], who says in a note that Śaṅkh is Salwān's father. Gautam, *Śrī Gorakhnāth Caritra* (p. 82) calls the king Śaśāṅga and maintains that Cauraṅgīnāth was born from Śiva's seed: Śa-

śāṅga was Cauraṅgī's surrogate father. The Punjabi legend recounted in Temple states that Pūraṇ Bhagat was conceived by Acchrān "as soon as the Sun saw her" (v. 93).

162. This he does in spite of Acchrān's warning, which evokes a yogic notion of the body already discussed: "There are nine gates to the city, go not to the tenth, The tenth is the palace of thy stepmother, Nūṇān": Temple, *Legends*, 2:398 (vv. 265–66). See above, chap. 8, sec. 4.

163. Lūṇā, who is said in Temple's Punjabi recension of this legend (*Legends*, 2:392 [v. 187]) to be of the Chamāri (currier) subcaste, is widely known as Loṇā (or Noṇā) Chamāri, the most terrible sorceress of north India. She is said to have gained her powers by eating the corpse of Dhanvantari, the divine founder of Indian medicine, who had died of snakebite at the fangs of the great *nāga* Takṣaka: Crooke, *Religion and Folklore*, p. 437. Veiled references are given in Temple, *Legends*, 2:386 and 413 (vv. 118–19, 441). Curiously, Sālwan is himself said to be the son of another great *nāga*, Vāsuki (Bāsak) in another version of this legend: Briggs, *Gorakhnāth*, p. 184. The Jain *Prabandha Cintāmaṇi* gives Nāgārjuna a similar pedigree: see above, chap. 4, n. 194. Noṇā Chamāri is said to have belonged to an Islamic subdivision of the Nāth *sampradāya*, that of the Ismail Jogis: Rose, *Glossary*, p. 396.

164. Temple, *Legends*, 2:408 (vv. 383–86).

165. Ibid., 2:411 (vv. 418–19).

166. Ibid., pp. 414–15 (vv. 457–468).

167. Ibid., p. 417 (vv. 498–502).

168. Ibid., pp. 419–20 (vv. 517–33). It is Lūṇā's maid, Hīrā ("Diamond"), who tests the blood. It will be recalled that Hīrā was the name of the sorceress who enslaved Gopīcand for twelve years: see above, n. 149.

169. Ibid., p. 422–23 (vv. 555–67). The well is so described in Narharinath, ed., *Śrīnāthkathāsāra*, p. 18.

170. Temple, *Legends*, p. 426 (v. 604). Cf. Kabīr, *Sākhī* 29.2 (in Vaudeville, *Kabīr*, p. 290), quoted above, chap. 8, n. 115.

171. Temple, *Legends*, pp. 428–34 (vv. 630–701).

172. Ibid., pp. 440–46 (vv. 774–846).

173. Ibid., pp. 448–55 (vv. 875–956).

174. See above, chap. 7, nn. 82–83, for alchemical allegory in the *Padmāvat*.

175. Both *śaṅkha* and *[birwā] loṇa* are also herbs used in alchemical operations: *KCM* fol. 12a.9; and *Padmāvat* 310 [= 27.3].

176. On this forest, see above, chap. 8, sec. 2d.

177. This would parallel such Hindi constructions as *dayālū*, from *dayā*, kindness (thus "kind"); or *kṛpālū*, from *kṛpa*, "mercy" (thus "merciful").

178. Sachau, *Alberuni's India*, vol. 1, p. 192. From here, the story takes a turn and becomes an account of the sack of Valabhī, related above: see chap. 4, nn. 200–202.

179. Sachau, *Alberuni's India*, vol. 1, pp. 191–92. Such traditions have remained common in the regions of the Sind and Kacch, on the western fringe of India, down to the 19th c.: Madhihassan, *Indian Alchemy*, pp. 58–59.

180. *Gorakh Bānī*, Pad 6.1–5 in Srivastav, "*Gorakh Bānī*" *Viṣeśāṅk*, pp. 260–61.

181. This is the body that is rejuvenated through its calcination in the fires of yoga: cf. Kabīr, *Doha* 46.64 (in Vaudeville, *Kabir Granthavali*, p. 70). Cf. *Lallā-Vākyāni* 100, cited in Silburn, *Kuṇḍalinī*, p. 45: "Give thou breath to the bellows even as doth the blacksmith. Then will thine iron turn to gold . . ." The Vedic blacksmith's bellows are fanned with birds' wings: Maurice Winternitz, *A History of Indian Literature*, trans. V. Srinivasa Sarma, 5 vols. (Delhi: Motilal Banarsidass, 1981), 1:59.

182. *ra[t]tī kā kām māse kī corī* literally means "the work [or desire, or semen] of one *ratī*'s weight [is] the theft of one *māṣā*'s weight." According to the weights and measures used in precious metalworking, 8 *ratī*s (the seed of *Abrus precatorius*, 2½ grains, 121 milligrams) equal one *māṣā* (lentil; one-twelfth of a *tola*). Below, in verse 5, the unit of one *gadiyānā* is used: one *gadiyānā* equals 6 *māṣā*s and therefore 48 *ratī*s. Kabīr makes poetic use of the terms *ratti* and *tila* (sesame seed, another unit of weight) in *doha* 35.7–8 (in Vaudeville, *Kabir Granthavali*, p. 56).

183. Because I have found it overly "spiritualized" (to the neglect of most of this poem's concrete referents), I have generally avoided the *ṭīkā* provided by Srivastav and the Nāth Siddha editors of the "*Gorakh Bānī*" *Viṣeśāṅk*. Here, however, I find their commentary useful: the grain is the individual soul, into which the universal soul (the lentil's weight) has emanated. Gorakhnāth, who has stolen his way into the universal soul, identifies himself with it and dwells within it, is lost in it. There is, however, another probable reading of this verse: The play of proportions, of a grain acting on a mass eight times its weight, is a common alchemical phenomenon, in which an infinitesimal quantity of perfected mercury can transmute up to a billion times its weight of base metals into gold.

184. Cf. *HYP* 4.56.

185. Here, the triadic void is the *trikuṭi*, the three-crested peak, located in the cranial vault, which is the culminating point of the three channels [*nāḍī*s]. Alternately, it is the downturned triangle from which the nectar of immortality the yogin has generated drips downward, thereby transforming his body. At this point, all of mundane existence, including the pure/impure opposition, has been transcended.

186. *Unmani* or *unmanā* is a transcendent state of consciousness, located at the highest level of the subtle body. It is also a term which connotes equanimity, a pure

level of thought which is sometimes taken to be the homologue of *samarasa*. The gold that comes in (or "permeates"), by its very nature [*sahaja*], refers to the irresistable flow of refined semen realized at the end of one's hathayogic practice and to the effects of the alchemical touchstone, which transmutes all it touches into gold.

Chapter Ten

1. E. M. Forster, *The Hill of Devi* (Harmondsworth: Penguin, 1965), p. 88.

2. In particular, it is the *ojas*, the fluid of life which exists, in extremely limited quantity in the heart, that is to be restored. See above, chap. 2, n. 44; and Anantacharya, *Rasayana*, pp. 20–21.

3. *Gorakh Bānī* Pad 6; 13.1; 50.2; Śiv Gorakṣ Bāvanī 38.

4. *Gorakh Bānī* Sabadī 60, 211; Pad 5.1; 15.1; *BhP* 5.260; 5.297.

5. See above, chap. 5, n. 113.

6. Alchemical and other uses of the root *vedh* likely remount to the metallurgical technique of amalgamation of mercury with gold for the extraction of gold from the ores in which it naturally occurs. The earliest such use of the term (*rasaviddha*) is found in the *Arthaśāstra* of Kauṭilya (2.12.2).

7. On this relationship, see, for example, *Bṛhadāraṇyaka Upaniṣad* 1.4.11; *Mahābhārata* 12.72.9–12 and 13.8.21–22; *Manu Smṛti* 8.37–39. There is a symmetry between the brahman-kṣatriya relationship and that obtaining between the kṣatriyas and the third *varṇa*, the vaiśyas: *Śatapatha Brāhmaṇa* 12.7.3.8.

8. *Śatapatha Brāhmaṇa* 5.4.4.7–19.

9. The myth is related in *Devībhāgavata Purāṇa* 7.17.45–7.18.58 and *Mārkaṇḍeya Purāṇa* 7.1–69; 8.1–270. For a discussion see White, *Myths of the Dog-Man*, pp. 80–86.

10. *The Mārkaṇḍeya Purāṇa* version dates from the 3d–4th c. A.D.

11. *The Caṇḍa-Kauśika*, ed. Sibani Das Gupta (Calcutta: The Asiatic Society, 1962).

12. *Caṇḍakauśika* 4.25ff.

13. *Caṇḍakauśika* 4.30–31. This is a slightly altered version of the old Buddhist set of eight *siddhis*.

14. *Caṇḍakauśika* 4.32, 34.

15. M. A. Stein, *Kalhaṇa's Rājataraṁgiṇī, Chronicle of the Kings of Kashmir*, 2 vols. (London: Constable, 1900; reprint Delhi: Motilal Banarsidass, 1979), 1:102.

16. This is the third and final regnal period of Cakravarman. He had also ruled in A.D. 923–33 and during part of 935: *Rājataraṅginī* 5.288–92, 297–302.

17. Kānha-pā calls himself a Kāpālika who dances with a Ḍombī (before killing

her) in *Caryāpada* 10 (in Kværne, *Anthology*, p. 113). On the Ḍombī as portion of the female sexual organ, see the A.D. 1446 Bengali commentary to the *Laghu Kālacakratantra*, reproduced in Shastri, *Catalogue*, vol 2, p. v.

18. *Ucchiṣṭa Cāṇḍālī* ("Outcaste-Leftover") is a name for the tantric Goddess/consort in a number of traditions: Apfel-Marglin, *Wives of the God-King*, p. 240.

19. Tod, *Annals and Antiquities*, 2:1196. See above, chap. 4, n. 240.

20. Tod, *Annals and Antiquities*, 2:107. This is portrayed graphically in 19th c. miniature paintings, found in miniatures held in the Jodhpur Fort Museum as well as murals on the outer walls of the shrine of the Mahāmandir, of the Marwar king Mān Singh together with his minister "Jālandharanāth." In these miniatures, the king is standing or pictured in a subservient position to his Nāth Siddha, who is seated, in conical cap, under the royal parasol.

21. *Gorakhāvaṃśāvalī*, ed. Yogi Narharinath (Benares: Rashtriya Press, 1964), p. 95 (in Nepali): *duvai hāt thāpnu bhayo ra uhi hātmā dahi chādi lau ṣā bhandā.* Cf. Nayaraj Pant, *Śrī 5 Pṛthivīnārāyaṇ Sahko Upadeś* (Lalitpur: n.p., n.d.), pp. 545, 641–42. This episode is graphically portrayed in a painting on the walls of the Nāth Siddha monastery of Caughera (Srigau district, Dang, Nepal): personal communication from Véronique Bouillier, Paris, January 1993. A Hindi translation of this episode is found in Srivastav, ed., *"Gorakh" Viśeṣāṅk*, p. 338. The crucial phrase, in Hindi, is *gorakhnāthjī ne wahī dahī uskī añjali meṃ mukh se ulaṭ diyā aur kahā ki isko khāo.* In the Hindi, the verb *ulaṭnā* means both "vomit" and "reverse," as in the hathayogic *ulaṭā sādhana.* This latter reading would imply that Gorakhnāth drew the yogurt down to the base of his subtle body before reversing it and bringing it up out of his mouth.

22. For the historical reality and political intrigue behind this legend, see Véronique Bouillier, "The King and His Yogī: Pṛthivinārāyaṇ Śāh, Bhagavantanāth and the Unification of Nepal in the Eighteenth Century," in John P. Neelsen, ed., *Gender, Caste and Power in South Asia: Social Status and Mobility in a Transitional Society* (Delhi: Munshiram Manoharlal, 1991), pp. 1–21.

23. Sachau, *Alberuni's India*, vol 1, p. 180.

24. Stern, "Le temple d'Eklingjī," nn. 8, 19. This detail of Bāppā Rāwal's initiation is not found in the 15th c. *Śrī Ekaliṅga Māhātmya.* It is, however, related in Tod, *Annals and Antiquities*, vol. 1, pp. 264–65. See above, chap. 4, nn. 226–27.

25. Mujtaba and Shah, "Taming of the Serpent," pp. 83–84.

26. Abhinavagupta's discussions of the various *vedha dīkṣā*s are found in *TĀ* 29.236–75. A partial English translation of the description of *vedha-dīkṣā* is found in Silburn, *Kuṇḍalinī*, pp. 91–103; a full Italian translation is in Raineiro Gnoli, *Luce delle sacre scritture* (*Tantrāloka*) (Torino: Unione Tipografico-Editrice Torinese, 1972), pp. 708–12.

27. *Kulārṇava Tantra*, 14.62–68, 78–79.

28. *Śārada Tilaka* 5.128–41. An English translation of this passage is found in *HT*, pp. 86–87.

29. *Gorakṣa Saṁhitā*, vol. 1, ed. Janardana Pandeya. The initiation is called *vedhavatī* in 14.251–52 and loosely described in 14.254–74. This Śākta text also calls itself the *Kādibheda Tantra: HTSL*, p. 55 and n. 92.

30. *TĀ* 29.239–40, citing the *Gahvara Tantra*.

31. *Śārada Tilaka* 5.138b: tam punarguruvaktre tu yojayed. See also above, chap. 7, n. 94; and chap. 8, nn. 213–15.

32. *TĀ* 29.271.

33. *Śārada Tilaka* 5.140.

34. Silburn, *Kuṇḍalinī*, p. 95.

35. Tucci, "Animadversiones Indicae," pp. 138, 154: vaktreṇa vaktraṃ dattvā tadhṛdi dhyānamukhamāpūrya vajrabhṛtā 'ṣṭottaraśatamantritaṃ kṛtvā muhe muhaṃ dei mela [mukhe mukhaṃ dehi, me]. See also Snellgrove, *Indo-Tibetan Buddhism*, vol. 1 pp. 254–62.

36. *Śārada Tilaka* 15.137b. The editor suggests two readings—*vidhuvakkrāntare* and *viṣṇuvakkrāntare*—neither of which makes sense and which I amend to *vidruvaktrāntare*. In the *kaulaketu* rite of the *siddha mārga*, the guru's mouth is said to be "encased" or "interlocked" (*sampuṭa*) in or with that of his disciple: *KM* (London, Wellcome MSS no. g501) fol. 35a.7–8.

37. *Yogakuṇḍalī Upaniṣad* 71–72, in Varenne, *Upanishads du yoga*, p. 132. These verses are borrowed directly from the *KhV*: the *Yogakuṇḍalī Upaniṣad* is composed of the seventy-five verses of chap. 1 of the *KhV*, together with 164 "original" verses: Bouy, *Nāth Yogin*, p. 41 n. 157.

38. Jonathan Parry, "Sacrificial Death and the Necrophagous Ascetic," in Maurice Bloch and Jonathan Parry, eds. *Death and the Regeneration of Life* (Cambridge: Cambridge University Press, 1982, p. 96, citing H. W. Barrow, "On Aghoris and Aghoripanthis," *Journal of the Anthropological Society of Bombay* 3 (1893), p. 241. Cf. the *Hevajra Tantra* (2.12) description of a secret Indo-Tibetan Buddhist initiation ritual, in which the initiate is enjoined to eat the semen that his guru has shed in the pudendum of a "Wisdom Maiden": Snellgrove, *Indo-Tibetan Buddhism*, vol. 1, pp. 258–59.

39. *KJñN* 18.22b–23c (the conclusion of its chapter on initiation): vaktrādvaktraṃ viśeṣeṇa siddhibhāgyaḥ samānyathā/ sāmānye kathitaṃ kumbhe śaṅkhādvaktraṃ viśeṣataḥ.

40. I am grateful to Alexis Sanderson for this reference.

41. rasendreṇa yathā viddhamayaḥ suvarṇatāṃ vrajet/ dīkṣāviddhastathā hyātmā śivatvaṃ labhate priye: *Kulārṇava Tantra* 14.89.

42. *Sādhanamālā* (vol. 1, p. 82 of Bhattacharya's edition); *TĀ* 5.151; *Parāparaprakāśika* 9 and *Bāsava Purāṇa* A.38.87 (both cited in Sadasiv Balwant Kulkarni, ed. and Marathi tr., *Rasaratnasamucchaya*, 2 vols. [Kolhapur: Sivaji University, 1970, 1972], vol. 1 [1970], pp. 23–24); *Amanaska Yoga* 2.48.

43. *RA* 17.164–65. See above, chap. 7, n. 21.

44. *rasaśca pavanaśceti karmayogo dvidhā mataḥ.*

45. The "three fruits" are the fruits of three varieties of myrobalan; the "three hot substances" are dry ginger, long pepper, and black pepper; "rock water" is a naturally occurring mineral acid.

46. *RA* 12.331–37.

47. As a unit of weight, one *pala* equals eight *tola*s (*RA* 10.34b). A *tola* is slightly more than ten grams. Therefore a *pala* is 82.624 grams, or about three ounces. This value of the *pala* is calculated from equivalents given in *RA* 10.32–34. Other alchemical sources yield different equivalents.

48. Other alchemical texts make the same claim. See for example *BhP* 5.255, 7.224.

49. *Amanaska Yoga* 1.50–98, on *tāraka yoga*. Cf. Srivastav, "*Gorakṣa*" *Viśeṣāṅk*, p. 152.

50. As a measure of time, one *pala* equals one sixtieth of a *ghaṭikā* of twenty-four minutes, i.e., twenty-four seconds.

51. This ordering respects the hierarchy of the five elements, with their corresponding senses.

52. The powers acquired between days fourteen and twenty-eight correspond to the eight classical Hindu *siddhi*s.

53. This is Intellect, the second *tattva* or metaphysical category, according to Samkhyan thought. *Puruṣa*, the universal principle alone, is higher than this.

54. I have arrived at this measure of mass by extrapolating data from the *Bhāgavata Purāṇa* (3.11.5–6) and *RA* 10.32–33a. According to the former source, two *paramāṇu*s make one *aṇu*, three *aṇu*s constitute a *trasareṇu* (or *trisareṇu*), and three *trasareṇu*s equal one *truṭi* ("mote"—and one hundred *truṭi*s equal one *vedha*!); according to the latter, six *truṭi*s equal one *likṣa* ("nit"), six *likṣa*s one *yūka* ("louse"), six *yūka*s one *rajas* ("pollen grain"), and six *rajas*es one *sarṣapa* (one mustard grain), which has the mass of approximately 0.004 grams.

55. *Bhāgavata Purāṇa* 3.11.4.

56. Blaise Pascal, *Les Pensées sur la religion et sur quelques autres sujets* (Paris: Éditions du Luxembourg, 1951), pp. 134–39. Douglas Adams, *The Restaurant at the End of the Universe* (New York: Ballantine Books, 1995). A Hindu equivalent of this "restaurant" is the cosmological construct called Lokāloka ("World/non-World"), located at the outermost edge of the disk of the earth, within the cosmic Egg of

Brahmā. On this, see O'Flaherty, *Dreams*, pp. 204–5; and Malamoud, "Cosmologies prescriptives," pp. 307–17.

57. For definitions of this temporal unit, see above, chap. 3, n. 112, and chap. 9, n. 137.

58. *Bhāgavata Purāṇa* 3.11.9–12, 16–22, 32.

59. For the tantric perspective on breath as the basis for all time reckoning, see Abhinavagupta, *Tantrasāra*, chap. 6 (pp. 46–57 of *The Tantrasāra of Abhinavagupta*, ed. with notes by Mukunda Ram Sastri [reprint ed. Delhi: Bani Prakashan, 1982].)

60. For summaries of Gorakhnāth's metaphysics, see Dvivedi, *Nāth Sampradāy*, pp. 114–26; and Aksaya Kumar Banerjea, *Philosophy of Gorakhnāth with Gorakṣa-Vacana-Saṅgraha*, 2d ed. (Delhi: Motilal Banarsidass, 1983).

61. This notion is particularly transparent in *Jñānakārika* (2.2b–4b), a text attributed to Matsyendra (in Bagchi, *KJñN*, p. 116). Cf. Jean-Paul Sartre, *Being and Nothingness*, trans. with an introduction by Hazel E. Barnes (New York: Washington Square Press, 1972), p. 56: "Nothingness lies coiled in the heart of being—like a worm."

62. *Gorakh Bānī* Gyān Tilak 27–28, in Srivastav, *"Gorakh Bānī" Viśeṣāṅk*, p. 362.

63. *Mahāvedha* is treated on p. 47 of this edition, whose versification is totally confused. It quite identical to the description given in the 15th c. *HYP* 3.26–31. For a similar quantification, this time of the progressive *aṅga*s of Pātañjala yoga, see Brahmānanda's commentary to *HYP* 2.12.

64. Cf. Heimann's (*Facets*, pp. 95–100) discussion of the term *śūnya*, which has many of the same valences in the Sanskrit language.

65. See the early *Aitareya Upaniṣad* 1.1–3.12, especially 3.11–12. This notion carries over into the tantric worldview, in which the endpoint of emanated creation is the *adhaḥ-kuṇḍalinī*, who enters the human microcosm through the fontanelle, to slumber at the base of the system of *cakra*s, until she is awakened by yogic practice. On this, see above, chap. 8, sec. 1.

66. Stephen W. Hawking, *A Brief History of Time: From the Big Bang to Black Holes* (New York: Bantam Books, 1988), pp. 81–113, especially p. 89, in which Hawking discusses the improbability of black holes issuing into "wormholes" in another part of space-time.

67. *RA* 18.217–20.

68. On *śabdavedha*, see *RA* 12.70 and *RRS* 8.95. On transmuting with bodily secretions, see *Yogatattva Upaniṣad* 74, and *RA* 18.28.

69. *Gorakh Bāni* Sabadī 171a, 148: nīñjhar jharaṇaiṃ aṃmīṃras pīvaṇāṃ ṣaṭ dal bedhyā jāi / . . . vyand hīṃ jog vyand hīṃ bhog vyand hīṃ harai causaṭhi rog / yā bind ka koī jāṇṇaiṃ bhev / so āpaiṃ karatā āpaiṃ dev.

70. For a discussion of these texts, see above, chap. 5, sec. 2.

71. *Gorakh Upaniṣad,* in Mallik, ed., *SSP,* p. 74, which suggests that the outer piercing of the ears is tantamount to the inner *khecarī mudrā.* Cf. Briggs, *Gorakhnāth* p. 6, citing the testimony of Nāths in Hardwar.

72. See above, chap. 8, nn. 213–15.

73. See above, n. 17.

74. Here, the mythic paradigm for the biological relationship between priestly teacher and disciple may go back to even pre-Vedic times. See above, chap. 9, n. 104.

75. Here I am following the alternative reading suggested in Tripathi's edition of the *RA* (p. 221 n. 1). in place of *hariharamagabhīraḥ,* which makes no sense, the editor suggests the reading *hariharasamavīraḥ.*

76. *Kulārṇava Tantra* 5.93. Cf. *KJñN* 11.21–23.

77. This theme is especially dear to the *KCM,* which devotes over a fourth of its content to techniques for attracting Siddha maidens, nymphs, goddesses, and females of every stripe into one's embrace. Similar themes are the frequent subject of the *BhP:* see above, chap. 5, n. 214.

78. On the Asura *siddhi* of *rasa-rasāyana,* see above, chap. 3, nn. 34–40. On Kāvya Uśanas, see above, chap. 9, nn. 103–6. On the Bengali *kavirāja*s, see Roşu, "Liétard et Cordier," pp. lxxxiv–lxxxv.

79. *KJñN* 7.21a, 14.18a, 26b; *RA* 12.337; *KCM* fol. 24a.8; *Gorakṣa Śataka* 147b; *KhV* (NNA MSS no. 5-6568), fol. 9b, line 3; *Śiva Saṁhitā* 3.73.

80. On the alternation between *kavi* and Kāvya Uśanas's name, see Dumézil, *Mythe et épopée,* vol. 2, part 2, pp. 148–56, 204. On the incantatory element in Vedic healing, see Zysk, *Religious Healing,* pp. 8, 241, citing Sāyaṇa's commentary to *Atharva Veda* 4.2.6. Cf. Padoux, *Vāc,* p. 6.

81. The archaic cults of these beings go back to at least the first centuries of the common era, in Hindu and Buddhist traditions alike. The Siddhas and Vidyādharas are listed as beings "born from divine wombs" in the 6th c. A.D. *Amarakośa* 1.1.11. See also Jean Przyluski, "Les Vidyārāja," *Bulletin de l'Ecole Française d'Extrême Orient* 23 (1923), pp. 301–18; J. A. van Buitenen, "The Indian Hero as Vidyādhara," in Milton Singer, ed., *Traditional India: Structure and Change* (Philadelphia, American Folklore Society, 1959), pp. 99–105; and David Seyfort Ruegg, "Sur les rapports," p. 83. As Przyluski notes (p. 317), these demigods figure in the entourage of Śiva (Gorakh) in Hinduism, and Avalokiteśvara (Matsyendra) in Buddhism.

82. *KJñN* 8.30a. Italics my own. In his *Yogabīja* (63), Gorakhnāth speaks of Siddhas through whose grace (*kṛpa*) one becomes a yogin.

83. *KJñN* 9.1. Yet, one is enjoined to worship the same three figures in 18.4b. The term *yoginī* is employed both for human "witches" or "sorceresses" with whom tantric practitioners had commerce and for the goddesses to whom they offered

their vital fluids, through them. In Matsyendra's *Akulavīra Tantra* (verse 78a of version "A" on p. 91 of Bagchi's edition of the *KJñN*), it is said that "that which is difficult for divine Siddhas is easily accessible for the Yoginīs."

84. *KJñN* 16.47–50; 24.4–12. On the "Nāths of the Four Ages," of which Matsyendra is the fourth in this tradition, see above, chap. 5, n. 93.

85. Matsyendra's recovery of the Kaula teachings is described in chap. 16 of the *KJñN:* see above, chap. 8, sec. 2. Matsyendra appears to identify himself with "Siddhanātha," who revealed the *akulavīra* doctrines to the world: *Akulavīra Tantra* (A), vv. 1–2a; *Akulavīra Tantra* (B), vv. 39b, 142a. Cf. *Jñānakārikā* 2.1 (in Bagchi, *KJñN*, pp. 94, 97, 106, 116). See above, chap. 3, n. 137.

86. *KJñN* 14.40, 55b–56, 63b–65b.

87. *Pāśupata Sūtras* 1.33–38, quoted in Gonda, *Medieval*, p. 218; *Caṇḍakauśika* (ed. Bhattacharya), pp. 109–11. Kṣemīśvara's Kāpālika alchemist is described as possessing eight *siddhi*s that are quite identical to the eight Buddhist "magical powers": see above, chap. 3, n. 14.

88. *Harṣacarita* 3.112–28.

89. *Ocean*, vol. 2, p. 236. Mahāvratin is a generic term for a Śaiva ascetic—a Pāśupata or Kāpālika—referring as it does to the "great vow" (i.e., the slaying of a brahmin followed by twelve years of expiation) undertaken by them in their initiation.

90. *RM* (Paris MSS no. 1222, fol. 28b.8–10; 29a.1; Gondal MSS no. 861, fol. 36b.4–9). This passage is clearly an expansion on *RA* 18.208–28, discussed above, chap. 5, nn. 163–66. This apotheosis corresponds quite closely to the goal of the Pāśupata, as described in the *Pāśupata Sūtras:* "(one) moves unobstructed everywhere; being equipped with these qualities one becomes the great chief of the *gaṇa*s of Bhagavān Mahādeva." See above, chap. 4, n. 85.

91. *RA* 7.58.

92. *MBhT* 7.36.

93. *Śiva Saṁhitā* 4.46; 5.202, 204.

94. For a complete account of this technique, as it is found in the *RRS* and other alchemical sources, see above, chap. 7, n. 109.

95. *ĀK* 1.1.61.

96. *RA* 12.252–58, especially 12.254 and 257.

97. *RA* 11.104b–106. Cf. 12.337.

98. *RA* 18.222b–227. Cf. *Amanaska Yoga* 1.98.

99. *RA* 18.228. See also *RA* 11.107: "There where the gods are absorbed [at the end of a cosmic eon], there too the Siddha is absorbed." In fact, three half-verses follow *RA* 18.228. Cf. *Yogabīja* 65, which states whereas the three great gods pass away with the universal dissolution, the perfected yogin is indestructible.

100. See above, chap. 1, note 13.

101. This is the text of an inscription in the Viśvanāth Temple at Benares Hindu University. Cf. *RM* fol. 8a.8; 26a.2; *BhP* 2.1; and *RA* 15.16: "Eaten, (mercury) effects the destruction of aging and poverty."

102. *Caraka Saṁhitā* 6.1.78, 80.

103. Stein, "Jardins en miniature," pp. 53–55, 58.

104. Ibid., p. 57, citing the *Yun-ki ts'i-tsein* (cited in *P'ei-wen yun-fou*).

105. Ibid., p. 58; and idem, "Architecture et pensée en Extrême-Orient," *Arts Asiatiques* 4:3 (1957), pp. 176, 185.

106. *Bhāgavata Purāṇa* 5.16.7. This passage describes that portion of Meru which rises up from the earth's surface: a mirror image of this mountain extends below the surface of the earth, into the subterranean worlds of the demonic beings who inhabit them. The "lower half" of Meru is of lesser dimensions than the upper half, according to the Puranic texts. On this, see Ali, *Geography*, p. 48.

107. Ibid., p. 49; and I. W. Mabbett, "The Symbolism of Mount Meru," *History of Religions* 23 (1983), pp. 68, 71. The *Bhāgavata Purāṇa* (5.24.4) locates the Siddhas, Vidyādharas, and Cāraṇas at the highest atmospheric (but not heavenly) level, immediately below the spheres of the sun and Rāhu, the "descending node" of the moon. See above, chap. 1, n. 11.

108. Here, I concentrate on *TĀ* 8.119–38 (vol. 4, pp. 1441–51), with the commentary of Jayaratha, who indicates selected passages borrowed from the *Svacchanda Tantra* (10.424–51). On the millennarian importance of this latter text and the cult of Svacchanda Bhairava in Kashmir, see Sanderson, "Śaivism: Śaivism in Kashmir," in *Encyclopedia of Religion*, vol. 13, p. 16.

109. *Vajrāṅka* in *TĀ* 8.128, but *vajrāṅga* ("Lightning-Limbed") in *SvT* 10.446, which adds that the "lowest-level Vidyādharas are travelers on the winds of the mind (*manaḥpavanagaminaḥ*)."

110. *TĀ* 8.133. The names of these Siddhas are *[go]rocanā*, *añjana*, and *bhasma*. *Gorocana* is in fact an organic dye having the same intense yellow color as orpiment (auripigmentum). *Gorocana* is made from the urine of the cow.

111. *SvT* 10.452. "Love's body" is a *siddhi* enjoyed by the consummate alchemist (*RA* 12.366: *madana iva sukāntiḥ*) and yogin (see above, n. 53).

112. See above, chap. 3, n. 137, and chap. 8, n. 68.

113. The thirty-sixth and final chapter of the *Tantrarāja Tantra* (pp. 115–21 of Woodroffe's edition), entitled "The Siddha," seems to second this account of the Siddhas, albeit in a rather tame way (p. 121): "The Siddha has prior (to death) been freed from (attachment to) the body . . . and whenever, wherever, and howsoever he may leave the body, he goes to the Good Path, for he was liberated whilst living (*jīvanmukta*)."

114. The "Raivatācala Māhātmya" constitutes chapters ten through thirteen of the Jain *Śatruñjaya Māhātmya* (translated in James Burgess, *Report on the Antiquities of Kâthiâwâḍ and Kacch, Being the Result of the Second Season's Operations of the Archaeological Survey of Western India, 1874–1875* [London: India Museum, 1876; reprint Delhi: Indological Book House, 1971], p. 157, note). See above, chap. 4, n. 213 for other Jain references to this site.

115. The bulk of the *Matsya Purāṇa* is older than this; the praise of the Narmada River region in which Raivātaka is mentioned is a late addition made by a Śaiva resident of Maharashtra: Surinder Mohan Bharadvaj, *Hindu Places of Pilgrimage in India (A Study in Cultural Geography)* (Berkeley: University of California Press, 1973), pp. 66–67; R. C. Hazra, *Studies in the Purānic Records on Hindu Rites and Customs*, 2d ed. (Delhi: Motilal Banarsidass, 1975), p. 46; S. G. Kantawala, *Cultural History from the Matsya Purāna* (Baroda: M.S. University, 1964), appendix III.

116. *Skanda Purāṇa* 7.2.1–15 (on Girnar). On the dating of this Purāṇa, and of book seven, the Prabhāsa Khaṇḍa in particular, see Hazra, *Purānic Records*, p. 165.

117. Watters, *On Yuan-Chwang's Travels*, vol. 2, pp. 248–49; Beal, *Su-yu-ki*, vol. 2, p. 269. Hsuan-tsang's contemporary, the Indian author Bāṇabhaṭṭa, describing a conclave of such "rishis," names the Pāśupatas: *Harṣacarita* 8.226.

118. On the identification of Raivata and Gomanta, see Vettam Mani, *Purāṇic Encyclopedia* (Delhi: Motilal Banarsidass, 1975), s.v. "Gomanta I." This is the first English edition, a translation of the original 1964 Malayalam edition.

119. *Mahābhārata* 2.13.53 of the Bengali ($B_{1m.2-5}$) and Bombay Government collection (D) manuscripts only. The critical reading is Bhavanta. Another peak mentioned in the *Mahābhārata* has also been identified with Girnar: this is Ujjayanta, which the epic (3.86.18–20) describes as one of the holy places of Saurashtra (i.e., eastern Gujarat). The *Mahābhārata* (2.42.8) names, without describing it, a Raivatāka Hill, which it also locates in Gujarat. The site has also been called Girinagara and Girinārāyaṇa, of which Girnar is a vernacularization.

120. On this king, one of the earliest mythic devotees of Rudra-Śiva, and his use of mountain caves, see Dumézil, *Mythe et épopée*, vol. 2, pp. 96–105.

121. The passage concerning Gomanta is found only in the Bombay and Calcutta recensions of the *Harivaṃśa* (2.40, entitled "The Climbing of Gomanta" or "The Journey to Gomanta"); in the critical edition, it forms a portion of appendix 17 and all of appendix 18, found in vol. 2, pp. 92–98 (lines 380–507). Cf. Mani, *Purāṇic Encyclopedia*, s.v. "Gomanta I."

122. *Harivaṃśa*, appendix 17, lines 381–82, 386. Girnar is a cluster of peaks, of which two twin crags, today identified by Hindus as Gorakh and Dattātreya, are by far the highest. Lines 390–91 state that Kṛṣṇa and Balarāma would later defeat Jarāsandha at that site; the battle is drawn in line 487.

123. *Harivaṃśa,* appendix 18, lines 448–49. See above, n. 106, citing the later (post–6th c. A.D.) *Bhāgavata Purāṇa* (5.24.4), which gives a similar description of Mount Meru.

124. Burgess, *Report,* p. 159.

125. Girnar figures prominently in both the 13th c. *YSĀ* and the early 19th c. *Nātha Caritra* of Mān Singh, which devotes no less than fourteen chapters (1.2; 2.1–13) to the site and in particular to Gopīcand's travels there.

126. Grierson, "The Song of Mánik Candra," p. 209; Temple, *Legends,* vol. 2, p. 375.

127. Dasgupta, *Obscure,* p. 207; and Marie Lecomte-Tilouine, "Des dieux aux sommets (Népal)," in Véronique Bouillier and Gérard Toffin, eds., *Classer les Dieux? Des Panthéons en Asie du Sud* [*Puruṣārtha* 15](Paris: EHESS, 1993), pp. 153–72, esp. pp. 159–62.

128. *Punjab States Gazetteer,* vol. 22A, *Chamba State with Maps, 1904* (Lahore: Civil and Military Gazette Press, 1910), pp. 183–84.

129. See above, chap. 4, n. 156.

130. The Hindu and Jain Vidyādharas had their Buddhist homologues in the Vidyārājas: Reugg, "Sur les rapports," p. 83. In the *Mañjuśrī Mūlakalpa,* the bodhisattva Vajrapāṇi, the foremost of the Vidyārājas, is iconographically placed to the left of Śākyamuni: Snellgrove, *Buddhist Himalaya,* p. 287. I have noted (chap. 3, nn. 75–91) Nāgārjuna's connection with Tārā: as the leader of the Mahāvidyā goddesses, she is called "Vidyārajñī": Bhattacharya, *History,* p. 225.

Epilogue

1. E. M. Forster, *The Hill of Devi* (Harmondsworth: Penguin, 1963), p. 65.

2. See above, chap. 3, n. 143.

3. See above, chap. 4, n. 156.

4. On this process in medieval Europe, see Jacques LeGoff, *Pour un autre Moyen Age, Temps, travail et culture en Occident: 18 essais* (Paris: Gallimard, 1977), p. 231.

5. Personal communication from Siddhinandan Misra, Benares, March 1985.

6. Personal communication from Siddhinandan Misra, Benares, March 1985. A similar experiment, in which the production of gold from mercury was authenticated by a recognized authority, C. P. N. Singh, is documented by S. N. Khandelwal in the 6–12 November 1983 edition of *Saptāhik Hindustān,* pp. 41–44.

7. Sanjukta Gupta, "The *Maṇḍala* as an Image of Man," in Richard Gombrich, ed., *Indian Ritual and Its Exegesis* (Delhi: Oxford University Press, 1988), p. 35.

8. Paramahansa Yogananda, *Autobiography of a Yogi,* 2d Indian ed. (Bombay: Jaico, 1975), p. 70.

9. T. R. Anantharaman, "Transformations—Metallurgical and Mental," Prof. N. P. Gandhi Memorial Lecture, Varanasi, 18 December 1973, pp. 1–25.

10. Personal communication, 3 November 1984, Kathmandu. On this, see also Yogananda, *Autobiography*, p. 163.

11. Personal communications from Surya Kumar Yogi, Bhilbara (Rajasthan), March 1985; and Narharinath Yogi, Kathmandu, Nepal, October 1984. See Kakar (*Shamans*, p. 182) for names and descriptions of a number of similar illustrious figures.

12. Trevor Fishlock, *India File* (London: John Murray, 1983; reprint Calcutta: Rupa and Co., 1984), p. 36, quoting the advertising of a "sex clinic."

13. Tāyumānavar, *Vaṇṇam*, unpublished translation by Swami Sevananda.

14. *MBhT* 2.5–6; *Suśruta Saṁhitā* 1.14.14–15; but see 6.15.32 for a figure of six to seven days.

15. According to both the medical and folk traditions, it takes forty drops of blood to produce one drop of semen: Carstairs, *The Twice-Born*, pp. 83–84. Cf. *SSP* 1.73.

16. Conception joins the four lower *mahābhūtas*, already present in semen, to ether, the empty space of the female womb. Also present are mind and karma, attached to the soul: Dasgupta, *History*, 2:302, 307.

17. *Caraka Saṁhitā* 4.2.11–12; *Śārṅgadhara Saṁhitā* 1.6.12–13; *MBhT* 2.13–14; *SSP* 1.71. When semen is predominant, the fetus is male and spherical; when blood, it is female and elliptical; when equal, is hermaphrodite and hemispherical: Dasgupta, *History*, 2:314. In alchemy, similar genders are assigned to diamonds (*vajras*) of different shapes: *RA* 6.69–71.

18. Gananath Obeyesekere, cited in Kakar, *Shamans*, p. 234. On the myth of King Moon, see above, chap. 2, nn. 38–40.

19. In one of his mystic poems on hathayogic practice, Gorakhnāth identifies the vulva as a vampiress and tigress: *Gorakh Bānī* Pad 48.1–3. An identical sentiment is voiced by Mayanā, mother of the Nāth Siddha Gopīcand, in *Gopicandrer Gān*, cited in Dasgupta, *Obscure*, p. 246 n. 1. The alchemical *RA* (18.103–6) provides a *mantra* by which the practitioner may protect his semen, mercury, blood, flesh, and bones from hordes of goddesses and succubi who would trouble his dreams and suck him dry in the night. This may be a reference to early *kula* tantrism, which imagined the "extraction" of vital fluids from within the body by *yoginīs* and *śākinīs*, who would in turn offer the same to Mahābhairava enthroned in the heart (Sanderson, "Purity," p. 213 n. 89, citing *Netra Tantra* 20.1–40 and other sources). See above, chap. 5, n. 84.

20. Svoboda, *Aghora*, pp. 280–81. On *ojas*, see Dasgupta, *History* vol. 2, p. 343 n. 2, citing Cakrapāṇi's commentary to *Caraka Saṁhitā* 1.30.6.

21. On this and related attitudes as rationales for the practice of widow burning, see the masterful work of Catherine Weinberger-Thomas, *Cendres d'immortalité: la crémation des veuves en Inde* (Paris: Editions du Seuil, 1996; translation forthcoming, University of Chicago Press).

22. This claim was displayed prominently on the billboard over the storefront of a *gupta rog* clinic in the Lanka district of Benares in 1985. Recall here that the eighth and ultimate limb of traditional Āyurveda is *vājīkaraṇa*, sexual therapy: see above, chap. 2, n. 46.

23. Here I am simply summarizing two detailed studies by Véronique Bouillier: "The King and His Yogī," pp. 1–21; and "Growth and Decay of a Kānphaṭā Yogi Monastery in South-west Nepal," *The Indian Economic and Social History Review* 28:2 (1991), pp. 151–70, especially pp. 152–60.

24. This legend forms chapter 20 of the late 19th c. *Śrī Mastnāth Carita* (Acts of the Illustrious Mastnāth) of Śaṅkarnāth Yogī, which places the action in the fortified city of Chittor, in southeastern Rajasthan.

25. Padmaja Sharma, *Maharaja Man Singh of Jodhpur and His Times (1803–1843* A.D.) (Agra: Shiva Lal Agarwala & Company, 1972), pp. 155–56.

26. Tod, *Annals and Antiquities*, vol. 2, pp. 825–27. The most complete and insightful accounts of the relations between Mān Singh and Ayas Dev Nāth and his successors are Sharma, *Maharaja Man Singh*, pp. 153–82; and Daniel Gold, "The Instability of the King: Magical Insanity and the Yogi's Power in the Politics of Jodhpur, 1803–1843," in David N. Lorenzen, ed., *Bhakti Religion in North India: Community Identity and Political Action* (Albany, N.Y.: SUNY Press, 1995), pp. 120–32.

27. Peter van der Veer, *Gods on Earth: The Management of Religious Experience and Identity in a North Indian Pilgrimage Centre*, London School of Economics Monographs on Social Anthropology, 59 (London: Athlone, 1988).

28. The ascetic sects were, by the 1780s, the dominant money-lending and property-owning group in Allahabad, Benares, and Mirzapur: ibid., p. 134, citing C. A. Bayly, *Rulers, Townsmen and Bazaars: North Indian Society in the Age of British Expansion, 1770–1870* (Cambridge: Cambridge University Press, 1983), p. 143.

29. David Lorenzen, "Warrior Ascetics in Indian History," *Journal of the American Oriental Society* 98 (1978), pp. 68–70.

30. Dirk H. A. Kolff, *Naukar, Rajput and Sepoy: The Ethnohistory of the Military Labour Market in Hindustan, 1450-1850* (Cambridge: Cambridge University Press, 1990), pp. 74–85: "The warrior-ascetic in song, ballad, and legend."

31. Ibid., pp. 76, 81.

32. Tod, *Annals and Antiquities*, 1:300; and 2:298 ff., cited in Kolff, p. 82. Italics my own.

33. George A. Grierson, "Some Bihari Folk-Songs," *JRAS* 16 (1884), p. 236, cited in Kolff, p. 77.

34. Van der Veer, *Gods on Earth*, pp. 126–30, 176.

35. Yubaraj Ghimire, "The Rise of the Sādhus," *India Today*, pp. 61–63. A photograph on page 62 shows Avedyanāth seated, sixth from the left, with the other eight members of the VHP brain trust. See also Véronique Bouillier, "La violence des non-violents, ou les ascètes au combat," in Denis Vidal, Gilles Tarabout, and Eric Meyer, eds., *Violences et non-violences en Inde* (Puruṣārtha, vol. 16) (Paris: Editions de l'EHESS, 1994), pp. 213–43 and especially p. 233 for a historical overview of this phenomenon.

36. Cf. Van der Veer, *Gods on Earth*, p. 133: "Ascetics use violence on their own bodies to acquire power over the microcosm of the body and over the connected macrocosm of nature, and they use violence to acquire power in society."

37. See above, chap. 4, n. 204. The dire and irreversible effects of a Yogi's curse are feared throughout India. E. M. Forster takes a different view, as stated in the epigraph to this chapter.

38. See above, chap. 3, n. 6.

39. Oman, *Cults*, "A Group of Yogis, One Man Enjoying His *Churrus* Pipe," facing p. 4; "A Party of Wandering Yogis," facing p. 29. Cf. pp. 7, 29.

40. See above, chap. 4, n. 220.

41. *raṅk se rāv rāv se raṅkā, chinmeṃ karaiṃ nahīṃ kuch śaṅkā:* Śaṅkarnāth, *Śrī Mastnāth Carita*, p. 108.

42. Illustrious Nāth Siddhas are inhumed under burial tumuli called *samādhi*s after death: see above, chap. 4, n. 71; and chap. 9, n. 113.

43. The most common form of greeting between Nāth Siddhas, *ādeś* means "[what is your] command [?]"; a mystic interpretation holds the term means "Ādi [-nāth] is Lord [*īśa*]."

44. On this serpent-keeping and -charming suborder of the Nāth *sampradāya*, see Briggs, *Gorakhnath*, pp. 59–61 (who calls them Sepalas); and Rose, *Glossary*, vol. 2, p. 409.

45. Like many of the itinerant Nāth suborders, the Sampelas generally live by begging (and by snake charming).

46. See above, chap. 9, n. 28, for this Brahmanic identification.

47. See above, chapter 7, part 3.

48. "Om, Victory to the Lord of Animals!" Paśupatināth, located in eastern Kathmandu, is the national shrine of Nepal.

49. See above, chap. 9, n. 173, for this identification.

50. The "wallet" in which Nāth Siddhas carry their numerous paraphernalia. The *jholī* is the Siddha's magical bag of tricks.

51. See above, chap. 8, n. 220.

52. I am grateful to Bob Ladd, of the Department of Materials Sciences at the University of Virginia, for carrying out electromicroscopic spectroscopy on my sample.

SELECTED BIBLIOGRAPHY

Manuscripts

Ānandakanda of Mahābhairava, 907 fols. Jamnagar. GAU MSS no. 830/2. This is a copy of the Tanjore Sarasvati Mahal Sanskrit Library manuscript upon which S. V. Radhakrishna Sastri's 1952 edition is based.

Āścaryayogamālā of Nāgārjuna, 45 fols. Bikaner. ASL MSS no. 3941. A.D. 1674.

Carpaṭ Rasāyan of Carpaṭnāth, 2 fols., incomplete (*pada*s 19–52). Jodhpur. MSL MSS no. 1178/669 (Hindi).

Dattagorakṣasaṃvāda. Jodhpur. MSL MSS no. 1557. This work claims to comprise chapters 27–29 of the *Tantra Mahārṇava.*

Dhātukalpa of the *Rudrayāmala Tantra,* 112 fols. Jamnagar. GAU MSS no. 843/18.

Gandhakakalpa of the *Rudrayāmala Tantra.* Jamnagar. GAU MSS no. 835/7. Itself a work in twenty-three chapters, this work claims, in its colophon, to be a portion of chapter 28 of the Rudrayāmala Tantra.

Ghoḍā Colī. Jaipur. Śrī Rāmacaraṇa Prāya Vidyāpīṭh MSS no. 1.14.ii.19.

Ghoḍācoli-vākya, 1 fol. Jodhpur. MSL MSS nos. 1481, 1482[a], 1483[b].

Gorakṣa Saṁhitā, 34 fols. (incomplete). Jamnagar. GAU MSS no. 841/13. This is a compendium of passages from various tantric works, including the *Kakṣapuṭa.* It bears no resemblance to either the "Śākta" *Gorakṣa Saṁhitā* or the *Bhūtiprakaraṇa.*

Gorakṣa Saṁhitā, Bhūtiprakaraṇa, 174 fols. Jodhpur. MSL MSS no. 1496/1431. 18th c.

———, 59 fols. Jodhpur. MSL MSS no. 1497/1432. 19th c.

Gorakṣa Saṁhitā, Svacchandaśaktyavatāra, Bhūtiprakaraṇa, 119 fol. Jodhpur. MSL MSS no. 1499/1434 (V.S. 1881). See also below, *Svacchandaśaktyavatāra.*

———, *Mahāmanthānabhairava Tantrāntargataḥ.* Jodhpur. MSL MSS no. 1502/1437, 310 fol. This is the manuscript of the "Śākta" *Gorakṣa Saṁhitā* that Pandey edited as *Gorakṣa Saṁhitā,* vol. 1 (1976).

———. Kathmandu. NNA MSS no. 5-3978 (Ayurveda 89). Reel no. A-213/21, 118 fols. This is a copy of the *Bhūtiprakaraṇa.*

Gorakṣa Saṁhitā bhāṣa. Jodhpur. MSL MSS no. 649 (Hindi). This is a Hindi commentary on the "Śākta" *Gorakṣa Saṁhitā*.

Kākacaṇḍeśvarīmata, 32 fols. Kathmandu. NNA MSS no. 5-3969. Reel no. A211/19.

———, 57 fols. Kathmandu. NNA MSS no. 3–118 (Ayurveda 71). Reel no. A-211/8.

———, 37 fols. Kathmandu. Reel no. E-1796-8b.

———. London. Wellcome Institute for the History of Medicine MSS no. g473. This is a copy of NNA MSS no. 3-118.

———, 43 fols. Bikaner. ASL MSS no. 3952.

Kakṣapuṭam of Śrī Nāgārjuna, 140 fols. Jodhpur. MSL MSS no. 2959/1318. 19th c.

——— of Siddha Nāgārjuna, 40 fols. Jodhpur. MSL MSS no. 2960/1319. 18th c.

Kautukacintāmaṇi of Pratāpadeva, 53 fols. Bikaner. ASL MSS no. 3967.

Khecarī Paṭala of Ādinātha, 19 fols. Jodhpur. MSL MSS no. 1469/1375. A.D.1726. This is a manuscript of the *Khecarī Vidyā*.

Khecarī Vidyā of Ādinātha, 16 fols. Jodhpur. MSL MSS no. 1468/1374. 19th c.

———, 23 fols. Jodhpur. MSL MSS no. 1470/1376. 19th c.

———, 15 fols. Jodhpur. MSL MSS no. 1471/1377. A.D. 1683.

———, 9 fols. Jodhpur. MSL MSS no. 1472/1378. 19th c.

———, 15 fols. Kathmandu. NNA MSS no. 6-1636 (Jyautiṣa 7). Reel no. A-999/7. A.D. 1678.

———, 15 fols. Kathmandu. NNA. Reel no. M-23/10.

———, 17 fols. Kathmandu. Kaiser Library MSS no. 316 (Yoga). Reel no. C32/12.

———, 11 fols. Kathmandu. NNA MSS no. 4-1817 (Tantra 347). Reel no. A-1289-9.

Kriyākālaguṇottara Tantra, 14 fols. Kathmandu. NNA MSS no. 3-392 (Śaivatantra 67). Reel no. B25/32. A.D. 1184.

———, 88 fols. Kathmandu. NNA MSS no. 5-4947. Reel no. A149/2.

———, 88 fols. Kathmandu. Kaiser Library MSS no. 297. Reel no. C30/16.

Kubjikāmata. London. Wellcome Institute for the History of Medicine. MSS no. g501. This is a copy of NNA MSS no. 1-285 ka.

Madanavinodanighaṇṭu of Rāmarāja, 71 fols. Kathmandu. NNA MSS no. 4-2224 (Āyurveda no. 199) / reel no. A1289/4

Mahākālatantrarājā. Kathmandu. Reel no. E-1358/7.93 fols. in Newari script. This is the same work as the *Nāthābhyudayatantra*, referred to by Bu-ston in his *History of Buddhism*. See *Chos-hbyung* of Bu-ston.

Mahākālayogaśāstra, 13 fols. NNA MSS no. 5-6568. Reel no. A207/6. This is a manuscript of the *Khecarī Vidyā*.

Matsyendra Saṁhitā, 179 fol. Jodhpur. MSL MSS no. 1604/1782. 19th c.
Nātha Caritra of Mānsiṁha, 85 fol. Jodhpur. MSL MSS no. 1573/1645. 19th c.
Pāradakalpa of the *Rudrayāmala Tantra*, 244 fols. Jamnagar. GAU MSS no. 21/849. Itself a work in twenty-five chapters, this work claims, in its colophon, to be a portion of chapter 28 of the Rudrayāmala Tantra. See also below, *Rudrayāmalatantrapāradakalpa.*
Rasahṛdaya of Śrigovinda-bhagavat-pād. Kathmandu, NNA MSS no. T118/277 (Āyurveda).
Rasakautuka, 5 fols. Bikaner. ASL MSS no. 4203.
Rasaprabodha of Nāgadeva, 13 fols. (incomplete). Bikaner. ASL MSS no. 4216.
Rasarājaśiromaṇi of Paraśurāma. Bikaner. ASL MSS no. 4258.
Rasaratnadīpika of Rāmarāja, 31 fols. Bikaner. ASL MSS no. 4222.
Rasaratnākara of Nityanātha. This work is divided into five sections (*khaṇḍa*s), which appear as separate manuscripts and edited works. They are the (1) Rasa; (2) Rasendra; (3) Vāda; (4) Rasāyana; and (5) Mantra-khaṇḍas. The Rasa, Vāda, and Rasāyana-khaṇḍas have been edited; the Rasendra and Mantra-khaṇḍas only exist in manuscript form.
Rasa Khaṇḍa, 68 fols. Kathmandu. NNA. Reel no. D2/7.
———. *Rasa* and *Rasendra Khaṇḍa*s, 99 fols. Kathmandu. NNA. Reel no. H108/1.
———. *Rasa* and *Rasendra Khaṇḍa*s, 134 fols. Kathmandu. NNA. Reel no. E2086/3.
———. *Siddha [Mantra] Khaṇḍa*, 22 fols. Kathmandu. NNA MSS no. 5-3092 (Āyurveda 266) Reel no. B163/19.
———. *Siddha [Mantra] Khaṇḍa*, 49 fols. Kathmandu. NNA. Reel no. H253/20.
Rasārṇava, 106 fols. Bikaner. ASL MSS no. 4256. A.D. 1675. Erroneously catalogued under the title of *Rasarājaśaṅkara.*
———, 109 fols. Bikaner. ASL MSS no. 4273. A.D. 1627.
———, 100 fols. (incomplete). Bikaner. ASL MSS no. 4274.
Rasasāra of Govindācārya, 81 fols. (incomplete). Bikaner. ASL MSS no. 4260. A.D. 1649.
Rasasindhu of Viṣṇudeva, 129 fols. Bikaner. ASL MSS no. 4267. A.D. 1564.
Rasāvatāra, 10 fols. Bikaner. ASL MSS no. 4269.
Rasendrakalpadruma of Rāmakṛṣṇabhaṭṭa, 51 fols. Bikaner. ASL MSS no. 4280.
Rasendramaṅgala of Nāgārjuna, 45 fol. Bikaner. ASL MSS no. 4281.
———, 39 fols. Paris, Bibliothèque Nationale. Fonds Palmyr Cordier. MSS no. 1222 (Sanscrit). This is a copy of ASL MSS no. 4281.
———, 37 fol. Jamnagar. GAU MSS no. 862/34.
Rudrayāmalatantrapāradakalpa, 144 fols. Bikaner. ASL MSS no. 4290. A.D. 1662. See also *Pāradakalpa* of the *Rudrayāmala Tantra.*

Śivakalpadruma of Śivanātha, 45 fols. Bikaner. ASL MSS no. 4349.
Svacchandaśaktyavatāra of Śrīkaṇṭha, 130 fols. Bikaner. ASL MSS no. 4401. This is the *Bhūtiprakaraṇa*. See also *Gorakṣa Saṁhitā*.
Yogaratnāvali of Śrīkaṇṭha Śiva, 175 fols. Bikaner. ASL MSS no. 4184. A.D. 1640.

Primary Sources:

Advayavajrasaṃgraha. Ed. Haraprasad Shastri. Gaekwad's Oriental Series, no. 40. Baroda: Oriental Institute, 1927.
Aitareya Āraṇyaka. With the commentary of Sāyaṇa. Ed. Rajendralal Misra. Calcutta: Ganesa Press, 1876.
———. Trans. Arthur Berriedale Keith. Oxford: Clarendon Press, 1969.
Aitareya Upaniṣad. Edit. and trans. into French by Lillian Silburn. Paris: Adrien Maisonneuve, 1950.
Amanaskayoga of Gorakṣanātha. Ed. Ramlal Srivastav. Gorakhpur: Gorakhnath Mandir, 1980.
———. Ed. Yognath Swami. Poona: Siddh Sahity Samsodhan Prakasan Mandal, 1967.
Amarakośa. *Śrīmad Amarasiṃhaviracitaṃ nāmaliṅgānuśāsanam Amarakośa*, 2d ed. Ed. with Hindi and Sanskrit commentaries by Brahmananda Tripathi. Chaukhamba Surbharati Granthamala, no. 52. Benares: Chaukhamba Surbharati Prakashan, 1982.
Amaraugha Prabodha of Gorakṣanātha. In *Siddha Siddhānta Paddhati* of Gorakṣanātha.
Amaraughaśāsana of Gorakṣanātha. *Amaraughaśāsanam*. Ed. Mukundaram Shastri. Kashmir Series of Texts and Studies no. 20. Bombay: Nirnay-sagar Press, 1918.
Ānandakanda. Ed. Sri S. V. Radhakrishna Sastri. Tanjore Sarasvati Mahal Series, 15. Tanjore: TMSSM Library, 1952.
Āpastambha Dharma Sūtra. With the commentary of Ujjwala. Ed. A. Chinnaswami Sastri and A. Ramanatha Sastri. Haridasa Sanskrit Granthamala, no. 93. Benares: Chowkhamba Sanskrit Series Office, 1932.
Arthaśāstra of Kauṭilya. *The Kauṭilya Arthaśāstra*, 2 vols. Ed. R. P. Kangle. Bombay: University of Bombay Press, 1960.
Aṣṭāṅga Hṛdaya of Vāgbhaṭṭa. *Aṣṭāṅgahṛdaya* with the commentary of Hemadri. Bombay: Nirnaysagar Press, 1925.
Aṣṭāṅga Saṃgraha. *Śrīmadvāgbhaṭṭaviracita Aṣṭāṅgasaṃgraha*, 2 vols. Ed. with a Hindi translation by Kaviraj Atrideva Gupta. Bombay: Nirnay Sagar Press, n.d.
Atharva Veda. *Atharvaveda Saṁhitā*, 2 vols. Trans. with a critical commentary by William D. Whitney. Revised and edited by Charles R. Lanman. Harvard Oriental Series, vols. 7–8. Cambridge: Harvard University Press, 1905.

bCud len gyi man ngag of Bo dong. In *Encyclopedia Tibetica: The Collected Works of Bo doṅ Pan-chen phyogs-las-rnam-rgyal*, 13 vols. Ed. S. T. Kazi. New Delhi: Tibet House, 1970, vol. 2, pp. 507–601.

Bhāgavata Purāṇa. Śrimadbhāgavata Purāṇa, 2 vols. Ed. and trans. C. L. Goswami and M. A. Sastri. Gorakhpur: Gita Press, 1971.

Bhūtaśuddhi Tantra. In *Tantrasaṃgraha*, vol. 3, pp. 565–625; and vol. 4, pp. 308–16.

Bhūtiprakaraṇa. Gorakṣa Saṁhitā (Part Two). Ed. Janardana Pandeya. Sarasvatibhavana-Granthamala, vol. 111. Benares: Sampurnananda Sanskrit Visvavidyalaya, 1977.

Brahmāṇḍa Purāṇa. Brahmāṇḍa Purāṇa of Sage Kṛṣṇa Dvaipāyana Vyāsa. Ed. J. L. Shastri. Delhi: Motilal Banarsidass, 1973.

Bṛhadāraṇyaka Upaniṣad. Ed. and trans. into French by Emile Sénart. Paris: Les Belles Lettres, 1934.

Bṛhat Saṁhitā of Varāhamihira. *Varāhamihira's Bṛhat Saṁhitā*, 2 vols. Ed. and trans. by M. Ramakrishna Bhat. Delhi: Motilal Banarsidass, 1981, 1982.

Caṇḍakauśika of Kṣemīśvara. *The Caṇḍa-Kauśika*. Ed. Sibani Das Gupta. Calcutta: The Asiatic Society, 1962.

Caraka Saṁhitā, with the commentary of Cakrapāṇidatta. Ed. with Hindi translation by Yadavji Trikamji Acarya, Chaukhamba Ayurvijnan Granthamala, 34. Bombay: 1941; reprint Benares: Chaukhamba Surbharati Prakashan, 1992.

Caraka Saṁhitā. Caraka Saṁhitā: Agniveśa's Treatise Refined and Annotated by Caraka and Redacted by Dṛḍhabala: Text with English Translation. Ed. and trans. Priyavrat Sharma. Jaikrishnadas Ayurveda Series, no. 36. Benares: Chowkhamba Orientalia, 1992.

Caryāgīti. An Anthology of Buddhist Tantric Songs: A Study of the Caryāgīti. Ed. and trans. Per Kværne. Oslo: Universitetsforlaget, 1977; reprint Bangkok: White Orchid, 1986.

Chāndogya Upaniṣad. Ed. and trans. into French by Emile Sénart. Paris: Adrien Maisonneuve, 1930.

Chos-hbyung of Bu-ston. *History of Buddhism (Chos-hbyung) by Bu-ston*, 2 vols. Translated by Ernst Obermiller. Heidelberg: Harrassowitz, 1931–32; reprint Delhi: Sri Satguru Publications, 1986.

Dam-pa'i-chos-rin-po-che-'phags-pa'i-yul-du-ji-ltar-dar-ba'i-tshul-gsal-bar-ston-pa-dgos-'dod-kun-hbyung of Tāranātha. *Taranātha's History of Buddhism in India*. Ed. Debiprasad Chattopadhyaya. Trans. Lama Chimpa Alaka Chattopadhyaya. Simla: Indian Institute of Advanced Study, 1970.

Darśana Upaniṣad. In *Yoga Upaniṣads*.

Dattātreya Tantra. In *Indrajālavidyāsaṃgraha*. Ed. Jivananda Bhattacharya. Calcutta: V. V. Mukherji, 1925, pp. 132–79.

Dhyānabindu Upaniṣad. In *Yoga Upaniṣads.*

Ekaliṅga Māhātmyam. Premlata Sharma, *Ekaliṅgamāhātmyam (Ekliṅg Mandir kā Sthalapurāṇa evaṃ Mewāḍ ke Rāj-Vaṁś kā Itihās.* Delhi: Motilal Banarsidass, 1976.

Gheraṇḍa Saṁhitā. Ed. and trans. Sisa Candra Vasu. Madras: Adyar, 1933.

Gorakṣa Paddhati. Ed. with commentary by Mahidhara Sharma. Bombay: Khemaraja Srikrishnadas, 1983.

Gorakṣa Saṁhitā. Gorakṣa Saṁhitā (Part One). Ed. Janardana Pandeya. Sarasvatibhavana Granthamala, vol. 110. Benares: Sampurnananda Sanskrit Visvavidyalaya, 1976.

Gorakṣa Śataka. Das Gorakṣaśataka. Ed. Karl A. Nowotny. Wetterschlick b. Bonn: Richard Schwarzbold, 1976.

Gorakṣa Siddhānta Saṃgraha. Ed. Gopinath Kaviraj. Benares: Vidya Vilas Press, 1925.

———. Ed. Janardana Pandeya. Sarasvatibhavana Granthamala, no. 110. Benares: Varanaseya Sanskrit Visvavidyalaya Press, 1973.

Gorakṣa Vijay. Gorakha Vijaya of Bhīmasena Rāy. Ed. Pancanand Mandal. Calcutta: Visvabharati Granthalaya, 1949.

Gorakṣa Vijay. Kavikokil Vidyāpati-kṛt Gorakṣavijay. Ed. Harimohan Misra. Patna: Bihar-Rashtrabhasha-Parishad, 1974.

Gorkhavaṃśāvalī. Ed. Yogi Narharinath. Benares: Rashtriya Press, 1964.

Granthāvalī of Kabīr. *Kabīr Granthāvalī.* Ed. Shyam Sundar Das, 5th ed. Benares: Kasi Nagaripracarini Sabha, 1954.

———. *Kabir Granthavali (Doha).* Trans. into French by Charlotte Vaudeville. Publications de l'Institut Français d'Indologie, no. 12. Pondicherry: Institut Français d'Indologie, 1957.

Guhyasamāja Tantra. Ed. Benoytosh Bhattacharyya. Gaekwad's Oriental Series, no. 53. Baroda: Oriental Institute, 1931.

Hārītasaṁhitā. La Hārītasaṁhitā: texte médical sanskrit. Ed. and trans. into French by Alix Raison. Pondicherry: Institut Français d'Indologie, 1974.

Harivaṃśa. The Harivaṃśa Being the Khila or Supplement to the Mahābhārata, 2 vols. Ed. Parasuram Lakshman Vaidya. Poona: Bhandarkar Oriental Research Institute, 1969, 1971.

Harṣacarita of Bāṇabhaṭṭa. *The Harṣacarita of Bāṇabhaṭṭa with Exhaustive Notes [Ucchvāsas I–VIII].* Ed. Pandurang Vamana Kane. Bombay: 1918; reprint New Delhi: Motilal Banarsidass, 1973.

———. *The Harṣacarita,* trans. E. B. Cowell and P. W. Thomas. London: University Press, 1897.

Haṭhayogapradīpikā of Svātmarāman. *Haṭhayogapradīpikā of Svātmarāman.* With the commentary of Brahmānanda. Ed. and trans. Srinivasa Iyengar. Madras: Adyar, 1972.

Himavat Khaṇḍa of the *Skanda Purāṇa. Himavatkhaṇḍaḥ.* Ed. Yogi Narharinath. n.p.: 1957.

Hudūd al-'Alam. Hudūd al-'Alam, "The Regions of the World": A Persian Geography 372 A.H.–982 A.H. Trans. and explained by V. Minorsky. Karachi: Indus Publications, 1980.

Jaiminīya Brāhmaṇa. Jaiminīya Brāhmaṇa of the Sāmaveda. Ed. Raghu Vira and Lokesh Chandra. Sarasvati Vihara Series, vol. 31. Nagpur: Arya Bharati, 1954.

Jaiminīya Upaniṣad Brāhmaṇa. Ed. and trans. Hans Oertel in *Journal of the American Oriental Society* 16:1 (1894), pp. 79–260.

Jñānakārikā of Matsyendranātha. In *Kaulajñānanirṇaya* of Matysyendranātha.

Kādambarī of Bāṇabhaṭṭa. *Bāṇa's Kādambarī (Pūrvabhāga Complete).* Ed. M. R. Kale, 4th revised ed. Delhi: Motilal Banarsidass, 1968.

———. *Kādambarī: A Classical Sanskrit Story of Magical Transformations.* Trans. with an introduction by Gwendolyn Layne. New York: Garland Publishing, 1991.

Kākacaṇḍīśvara Kalpatantra. Ed. Kailashpati Pandey. Kashi Sanskrit Granthamala, no. 73. Benares: Chowkhamba Sanskrit Series Office, 1963.

Kakṣapuṭa of Siddha Nāgārjuna. In *Indrajālavidyāsaṃgrahaḥ.* Ed. Jivananda Bhattacharya. Calcutta: V. V. Mukherji, 1925, pp. 264–390.

———. *Kakṣapuṭa mchan khung gi sbyor ba.* In *Sde-dge mtshal-par bstan 'gyur: A Facsimile Edition of the 18th Century Redaction of Si-tu Chos-kyi-byuṅ-gnas* (Prepared under the Direction of H.H. the 16th rgyal-dbaṅ Karma-pa). Delhi: Karmapae Chodhey Gyalwae Sungrab Partun Khang, 1978. Toh 1609 (P 2480).

Kālikā Purāṇa. Ed. English translation and introduction by B. N. Shastri, 2 vols. Delhi: Chowkhambha Sanskrit Series, 1972. Reprint Delhi: Nag Publishers, 1992.

Kāṭhaka Saṁhitā. 3 vols. Ed. Leopold von Schroeder. Leipzig: F. A. Brockhaus, 1900–12. Reprint. Wiesbaden: Steiner Verlag, 1970–72.

Kathāsaritsāgara of Somadeva. *The Ocean of Story Being C. H. Tawney's translation of Somadeva's Kathā Sarit Sāgara (or Ocean of Streams of Story),* 10 vols. Ed. N. M. Penzer. London: Chas. J. Sawyer, Ltd., 1924–28.

Kaulajñānanirṇaya of Matsyendranātha. *Kaulajñānanirṇaya and Some Minor Texts of the School of Matysyendranātha.* Ed. Prabodh Chandra Bagchi. Calcutta Sanskrit Series, no. 3. Calcutta: Metropolitan, 1934.

Kauṣītaki Upaniṣad. Ed. and trans. into French by Louis Renou. Paris: Adrien Maisonneuve, 1948.

Kṛtyakalpataru of Bhaṭṭa Lakṣmīdhara. Tīrthavivecanakāṇḍa. Ed. K. V. Rangaswamy Aiyangar. Baroda: Oriental Institute, 1942.

Kubjikāmata. Kubjikāmata Tantra, Kulālikāmnāya Version. Ed. Teun Goudriaan and Jan A. Schoterman. Orientalia Rheno-Traiectina, 30. Leiden: Brill, 1988.

Kulānanda Tantra of Matsyendranātha. In *Kaulajñānanirṇaya* of Matysyendranātha.

Kulārṇava Tantra. Ed. Taranatha Vidyaratna with an introduction by Sir John Woodroffe. Madras: Ganesh and Company, 1965; reprint Delhi: Motilal Banarsidass, 1975.

Kulavīra Tantra of Matsyendranātha. In *Kaulajñānanirṇaya* of Matysyendranātha.

Laṅkāvatāra Sūtra. Edited by B. Nanjio. Kyoto: Otani University Press, 1923.

Laṅkāvatāra Sūtra. Trans. Daisetz Teitaro Suzuki. London: Routledge and Kegan Paul, 1932.

Lohasarvasvam of Sureśvara. *The Lohasarvasvam of Śrī Sureśwara.* Ed. Brahmashankar Mishra with Hindi commentary by Pavani Prasad Sharma. Vidyabhavana Ayurveda Granthamala, no. 46. Benares: Chowkhamba Vidyabhavan, 1965.

Mahābhārata, 21 vols. Ed. Visnu S. Sukthankar, et al. Poona: Bhandarkar Oriental Research Institute, 1933–60.

Mahānirvāṇa Tantra. With the commentary of Hariharananda Bharati. Ed. Arthur Avalon [John Woodroffe]. Madras: Ganesh, 1929. Reprint Delhi: Motilal Banarsidass, 1977.

Mahāprajñāparamitāśāstra of Nāgārjuna. *Traité de la grande vertu de sagesse de Nāgārjuna (Mahāprajñāparamitāśāstra),* 4 vols. Ed. and trans. into French by Etienne Lamotte. Louvain: Institut Orientaliste, 1949–1976.

Mahāyāna Saṃgraha. La Somme du Grande Véhicule d'Asaṅga, 2 vols. Ed. and trans. into French by Etienne Lamotte. Bibliothèque du Muséon, nos. 6–7. Louvain: Institut Orientaliste, 1938–39.

Maitrāyaṇi Saṁhitā. Die Saṃhitā der Maitrāyaṇīya-Śākhā. Ed. Leopold von Schroeder. Weisbaden: Franz Steiner Verlag, 1972.

Maitrī Upaniṣad. Ed. and trans. into French by Marie-Louise Esnoul. Paris: Adrien Maisonneuve, 1952.

Mālatī-Mādhava of Bhavabhūti. *Bhavabhūti's Mālati-Mādhava, with the Commentary of Jagaddhara,* 3d ed. Ed. M. R. Kale. Delhi: Motilal Banarsidass, 1967.

Mānasollāsa of Bhūlokamalla Someśvara. *Mānasollāsa of King Bhūlokamalla Someśvara,* 2d ed., 3 vols. Ed. G. K. Srigondekar. Gaekwad's Oriental Series, no. 28. Baroda: Oriental Institute, 1967.

Mañjuśrīmūlakalpa. Ed. T. Ganapati Sastri, 3 vols. Trivandrum Sanskrit Series, nos. 70, 76, 84. Trivandrum: Superintendent, Government Press, 1920–22.

Manu Smṛti. With the commentary of Kullūka Bhaṭṭa. Ed. Gopala Sastri Nene. Kashi Sanskrit Series, no. 114. Benares: Chowkhamba Sanskrit Series Office, 1970.

Mārkaṇḍeya Purāṇa. Śrīvyāsapraṇītaṃ Śrīmārkaṇḍeya Purāṇam, 3 vols. Ed. and trans. into Hindi by Satyavrat Singh and Mahaprabhulal Goswami. Sitapur: Institute for Puranic and Vedic Studies and Research, 1984–1986.

Mātṛkabheda Tantra. Ed. Chintamani Bhattacharya, Calcutta Sanskrit Series, 7. Calcutta: Metropolitan, 1933, 1958.

Mātṛkabheda Tantra. Trans. Michael Magee [Loknath Maharaj]. Delhi: Indological Book House, 1989.

Mṛcchakaṭikā of Śūdraka. *Mṛcchakaṭikā of Śrī Śūdraka.* Ed. Jagdish Chandra Mishra. Benares: Chaukhamba Surbharati, 1985.

Mṛgendrāgama. Mṛgendrāgama, Section des Rites et Section du Comportement avec la Vṛtti de Bhaṭṭanārāyaṇakaṇṭha. Ed. Hélène Brunner-Lachaux. Publications de l'Institut Française d'Indologie, no. 69. Pondicherry: Institut Français d'Indologie, 1962.

Navanāthacaritra of Gauraṇa. Ed. K. Ramakrishnaiah. Madras: Madras University Press, 1970.

Netra Tantra. The Netra Tantram, with the commentary of Kṣemarāja, 2 vols. Ed. Madhusudan Kaul. Srinagar: Research Department, 1926, 1939.

Padmāvat of Muhammad Jāyasī. Lakshmi Dhar. *Padumāvatī: A Linguistic Study of the 16th Century Hindi (Avadhi).* London: Luzac & Co., Ltd., 1949.

———. Rajnath Sharma, *Jayasī Granthāvalī (Padmāvat—Ṭīkā Sahit).* Agra: Vinod Pustak Mandir, 1965.

———. *The Padumawāti of Malik Muhammad Jaisī.* Ed. with a Hindi commentary, translation, and critical notes by George Grierson and Sudhakara Dvivedi. Bibliotheca Indica, n.s. 877. Calcutta: Baptist Mission Press, 1896.

———. A. G. Shirreff, *Padmāvatī of Malik Muhammad Jaisi.* Bibliotheca Indica, 267. Calcutta: Royal Asiatic Society of Bengal, 1944.

Paraśurāmakalpasūtra. With the Sanskrit commentary of Rāmeśvara. Ed. A. M. Sastri and S. Y. Dave. Gaekwad's Oriental Series, no. 22. Baroda: Oriental Institute, 1950.

Parātriṃśikā, with the *Vivaraṇa* commentary of Abhinavagupta. Ed. M. K. Sastri. Kashmir Series of Texts and Studies, vol. 18. Srinagar: Research Department, 1918.

Parātrīśikā Laghuvṛtti of Abhinavagupta. Ed. Jagaddhara Zadoo. Kashmir Series of Texts and Studies, no. 68. Srinagar: Research Department, 1947.

Parātrīśikā Vivaraṇa of Abhinavagupta. *A Trident of Wisdom: Translation of Parātrīśika-vivaraṇa of Abhinavagupta.* Trans. Jaideva Singh, with a foreword by Paul Muller-Ortega. Albany: SUNY Press, 1989.

Pāśupata-Sūtram. With the commentary of Kauṇḍinya. Ed. R. Ananthakrishna Sastri. Trivandrum: Oriental Manuscript Library of the University of Travancore, 1940.

Prabodhacandrodaya of Kṛṣṇamiśra. Ed. and trans. Sita Krsna Nambiar. Delhi: Motilal Banarsidass, 1971.

Prāṇāgnihotra Upaniṣad. In Paul Deussen, *Sixty Upaniṣads* (listed under *Secondary Sources*), vol. 2, pp. 645–51.

Praśna Upaniṣad. Ed. and trans. into French by J. Bousquet. Paris: Adrien Maisonneuve, 1948.

Rāja Mārtaṇḍa of Bhojarāja. *Yoga-sūtras of Patañjali with Bhojavṛtti Called Rājamārtaṇḍa (in English Translation).* Delhi: Parimal Publications, 1990.

Rājataraṃgiṇī of Kalhaṇa. *Kalhaṇa's Rājataraṁginī, Chronicle of the Kings of Kashmir,* 2 vols. Ed. M. A. Stein. London: Constable, 1900. Reprint Delhi: Motilal Banarsidass, 1979.

Rāmāyaṇa of Vālmīki, 7 vols. Ed. G. H. Bhatt et al. Baroda: Oriental Institute, 1960–75.

Rasacintāmaṇi of Anantadeva Sūri. Ed. Jivaram Kalidas. Bombay: Venkatesvara Steam Press, 1967.

Rasahṛdaya Tantra of Govinda. Ed. Yadavji Trikamji Acarya. Lahore: Motilal Banarsidass, 1927.

———. *Śrīmadgovindabhagavatpādaviracita Rashṛdayatantram* with the commentary of Caturbhuja Misra. Trans. into Hindi by Daultarama Rasasastri. Vidyavilas Ayurved Series, 5. Benares: Chaukhamba Orientalia, 1989.

Rasakāmadhenu. Ed. Yadavaji Trikamji Acarya. Bombay, Nirnaysagar Press, 1925. Reprint Benares: Chaukhambha Orientalia, 1988.

Rasakaumudi of Bhiṣagvāra Jñānacandra Śarman. *The Rasakaumudi of Bhiṣagvāra Jñānacandra Śarman.* Ed. Brahmasankar Mishra. Vidyabhavan Ayurveda Granthamala, 47. Benares: Chowkhamba Vidyabhavan, 1966.

Rasamañjari of Śalinātha. *Rasamañjari-vaidyaka.* Ed. Raghunathji Srikrsnalal. Bombay: Venkatesvara Press, 1906.

Rasapaddhati of Bindu. Ed. Yadavji Trikamji. Bombay: Nirnay Sagar Press, 1925.

Rasaprakāśa Sudhākara of Yaśodhara. *Rasaprakaśa.* Edited by Yadavji Trikamji Acharya. Ayurvediya Granthamala, vol. 1. Bombay: Venkatesvara Steam Press, 1910–11.

———. *Rasaprakāśasudhākara by Acarya, Yaśodhara.* With a Hindi translation by Siddhinandan Misra. Jaikrishnadas Ayurveda Series, no. 54. Benares: Chaukhambha Orientalia, 1984.

Rasaratnākara of Nityanātha, *Rasāyanakhaṇḍa. Śrīnityanāthasiddhaviracitaḥ (Rasaratnākarāntargataś caturthaḥ) Rasāyanakhandaḥ,* ed. Yadavji Trikamji Acharya with a Hindi translation by Indradeo Tripathi. Haridas Sansrit Series, no. 95. Benares: Chaukhamba Sanskrit Pustakalaya, 1939, 1982.

Rasaratnākara of Nityanātha, *Ṛddhikhaṇḍa. Śrīparvatīputranityanāthasiddhaviracitaḥ*

Rasaratnākarāntargataś caturtho [*sic*] *Ṛddhikhaṇḍaḥ-Vādikhaṇḍaḥ*, ed. Jivaram Kalidas Shastri. Rasashala Granthamala, no. 9. Gondal: Rasashala Aushadhashram, 1940.

Rasaratnasamuccaya of Māṇikyadeva Sūri. *The Rasa-ratna-samuccaya of Māṇikyadeva Sūri*. Ed. and trans. J. C. Sikdar. Jaipur: Prakrta Bharati Academy, 1986.

Rasaratnasamucchaya of Vāgbhaṭṭa. *Rasaratnasamucchaya*, 2 vols. Ed. with Marathi translation by Sadasiv Balwant Kulkarni. Kolhapur: Sivaji University, 1970, 1972.

———. *Śrīvāgbhaṭācāryaviracitaḥ Rasaratnasamucchaya*. Ed. with a Hindi commentary by Dharmananda Sharma. Benares: Motilal Banarsidass, 1962.

Rasārṇava. *Rasārṇava*. Ed. P. C. Ray and Hariscandra Kaviratna. Bibliotheca Indica, 174. Calcutta: Baptist Mission Press, 1910.

———. *Rasārṇavam nama Rasatantram*. Ed. with Hindi translation by Indradeo Tripathi and notes by Taradatta Panta. Haridas Sanskrit Series, 88. Banares: Chowkhamba, Sanskrit Series Office, 1978.

Rasārṇavakalpa. *Rasārṇavakalpa (Manifold Powers of the Ocean of Rasa)*. Ed. Mira Roy and B. V. Subbarayappa. New Delhi: Indian National Science Academy, 1976.

Rasasaṅketakālikā of Camuṇḍakāyastha. Ed. with notes by Yadavji Trikamji Acarya and Hindi commentary by Indradeo Tripathi. Chaukhamba Ayurveda Granthamala, 10. Benares: Chaukhamba Amarabharati Prakashan, 1984.

Rasendra Bhāskara of Lakṣminārāyaṇa. Jaipur: n.p., 1896.

Rasendracintāmaṇi of Ḍhuṇḍhukanātha. Ed. Manirama Sastri. Bikaner: Maniramasarma, 1934.

Rasendracūḍāmaṇi of Somadeva. *Rasendracūḍāmaṇi*. Ed. Yadava Sharman. Lahore: Motilal Banarsidass, 1932.

———. *Rasendracūḍāmaṇi by Ācārya Somdeva*. Ed. Siddhinandan Misra. Varanasi: Chowkhambha Orientalia, 1984.

Rasopaniṣat. Ed. Sambhasiva Sastri. Trivandrum: Superintendent, Government Press, 1928.

———. *Rasopaniṣat*, 2 vols. Ed. with a Hindi translation and commentary by Badrinarayan Sarma. Ajmer: Krsna Gopal Ayurved Bhavan, 1959.

Ṛg Veda. *Ṛg Veda Saṁhitā, Together with the Commentary of Sāyaṇāchārya*, 4 vols. Ed. F. Max Müller. 2d ed. London: Henry Frowde, 1890–92; first Indian ed. Chowkhamba Sanskrit Series no. 99. Varanasi: Chowkhamba Sanskrit Series Office, 1966.

Rudrayāmala Tantra. *Rudrayāmalam*. Ed. the Yogatantra Department. Yogatantra Granthamala, no. 7. Benares: Sampurnanand Sanskrit Vishvavidyalaya Press, 1980.

Sādhanamālā. *Sādhanamālā*, 2 vols. Ed. Benoytosh Bhattacharya. Gaekwad's Oriental Series nos. 26, 41. Baroda: Oriental Institute, 1925, 1928.

Sākhī of Kabīr. *Kabīr*, vol. 1. Trans. Charlotte Vaudeville. Oxford: Clarendon Press, 1974.

Śaṅkaradigvijaya of Vidyāraṇya. *Śrīmacchaṅkaradigvijaya*. Ed. K. S. Venkata Ramashastri. Srirangam: Srivanivilasamudralaya, 1972.

Śaṅkaravijaya of Ānandagiri. *Śrīśaṅkaravijaya of Anantānandagiri*. Ed. N. Veezhinathan, with an introduction by T. M. P. Mahadevan. Madras: University of Madras, 1971.

Śārada Tilaka of Lakṣmaṇadeśikendra. *The Śārdatilakam of Lakṣmaṇadeśikendra with the Padārthadarśa Commentary by Rāghavabhaṭṭa*, 3d ed. Ed. Mukunda Jha Bakshi, Kashi Sanskrit Granthamala, 107. Varanasi: Chowkhamba Sanskrit Series Office, 1986.

Śārṅgadhara Paddhati. *The Paddhati of Śarṅgadhara: A Sanskrit Anthology*. Ed. Peter Peterson. Bombay Sanskrit Series, no. 37. Bombay: Government Book Depot, 1888.

Śārṅgadhara Saṁhitā. Ed. and trans. K. R. Srikanta Murthy. Benares: Chaukhamba, 1984.

Sarvadarśanasaṃgraha of Mādhava. *Sarvadarśana-saṃgraha of Sāyaṇa-Mādhava*. Ed. with Commentary by Vasudev Shastri Abhyankar. Government Oriental Series, Class A, no. 1. Poona: Bhandarkar Oriental Research Institute, 1924. Reprint Poona: Bhandarkar Oriental Research Institute, 1978.

———. *The Sarva-darśana-saṃgraha or Review of the Different Systems of Hindu Philosophy by Madhava Āchārya*, trans. E. B. Cowell and A. E. Gough. London: Kegan Paul, Trench & Trubner, 1882. 7th reprint ed. Benares: Chaukhamba Amarbharati, 1978.

Śatapatha Brāhmaṇa. *The Śatapatha Brāhmaṇa in the Mādhyandina-Śākhā, with Extracts from the Commentaries of Sāyaṇa, Harisvāmin, and Dvivedagaṅgā*. Ed. Albrecht Weber. London-Berlin, 1855. Reprint ed. Chowkhamba Sanskrit Series, no. 96. Benares: Chowkhamba Sanskrit Series Office, 1964.

———. *The Śatapatha Brāhmaṇa According to the Mādhyandina School*. Trans. Julius Eggeling. Sacred Books of the East, vols. 12, 26, 41, 43, 44. Oxford: Clarendon Press, 1882–1900; reprint Delhi: Motilal Banarsidass, 1968.

Ṣaṭsāhasra Saṁhitā. *The Ṣaṭsāhasrasaṁhitā, Chapters 1–5*. Trans. J. A. Schoterman. Leiden: Brill, 1982.

Siddha Siddhānta Paddhati of Gorakṣanātha. Edited with an introduction by Kalyani Mallik in *Siddha Siddhānta Paddhati and Other Works of the Nātha Yogīs*. Poona: Oriental Book House, 1954.

Siṁhāsanadvatriṃśika. *Vikrama's Adventures or the Thirty-two Tales of the Throne*, 2 vols. Trans. Franklin Edgerton. Harvard Oriental Series, 26. Cambridge: Harvard University Press, 1926.

Śiva Saṁhitā. Ed. and trans. Sisa Chandra Vasu, 2d ed. Allahabad: Panini Office, 1914; reprint New Delhi: Munshiram Manoharlal, 1975.

Skanda Purāṇa. Ed. Nag Sharan Singh, 3 vols. Delhi: Nag Publishers, 1984.

Smṛticandrikā of Devaṇṇabhaṭṭa. *Smṛticandrikā of Devaṇṇabhaṭṭa*, Āhnika Kāṇḍa. Trans. with notes by J. R. Gharpure. Bombay: V. J. Gharpure, 1946.

Solah Somvār tathā Somvār aur Saumya Pradoṣ Vrat Kathā. Hardwar: Ranadhir Book-sales, n.d.

Śrī Mastnāth Carit (Śrī Mastnāth adbhut līlā prakāś) of Śrī Śaṅkarnāth Yogiśvar. Ed. Sankarnath Yogisvar. Delhi: Dehati Pustak Bhandar, 1969.

Śrīnāthakathāsāra of Dwarkanāth. *Śrīnāthakathāsāra*. Ed. Narharinath Yogi. Benares: n.p., 1951.

Śrīnāth Tīrthāvalī of Rājā Mān Singh. Churu, Rajasthan: n.p., 1951.

Śūnyasampādane of Śrī Gūḷūra Siddhavīraṇāryaru, 5 vols. Ed. and trans. S. C. Nandimath, L. M. A. Menezes, R. C. Hiremath et al. Dharwar: Karnataka University Press, 1965–72.

Suśruta Saṁhitā with the commentary of Atrideva. Ed. Bhaskara Govinda Ghanekar. 5th ed. Delhi: Motilal Banarsidass, 1980.

Su yu ki of Hsuan-tsang. *Buddhist Records of the Western World, Translated from the Chinese of Hiuen Tsiang (A.D. 629)* by Samuel Beal, 2 vols. London: Trubner & Co., 1884; reprint Delhi: Munshiram Manoharlal, 1969.

Svacchanda Tantra. *Svacchandatantram*, with the commentary of Kṣemarājā, 2 vols. Ed. Vrajavallabha Dvivedi. Delhi: Parimal Publications, 1985.

Śvetāśvatara Upaniṣad. Ed. and trans. into French by Aliette Silburn. Paris: Adrien Maisonneuve, 1948.

Taittirīya Saṁhitā. With the commentary of Mādhava. Ed. Rajendralal Misra. Calcutta: Bibliotheca Indica, 1860.

Taittirīya Upaniṣad. Ed. and trans. into French by Emile Lesimple. Paris: Adrien Maisonneuve, 1948.

Tanjur. sde-dge mtshal-par bstan 'gyur: A Facsimile Edition of the 18th Century Redaction of Si-tu Chos-kyi-byuṅ-gnas (Prepared under the Direction of H.H. the 16th rgyal-dbaṅ Karma-pa). Delhi: Delhi Karmapae Chodhey Gyalwae Sungrab Partun Khang, 1978.

Tantrāloka of Abhinavagupta. *The Tantrāloka of Abhinavagupta with Commentary by Rājānaka Jayaratha*, ed. with notes by Mukund Ram Shastri, 12 vols. Allahabad: Indian Press, 1918–38. Reprinted with introduction and notes by R. C. Dwivedi and Navjivan Rastogi, 8 vols. Delhi: Motilal Banarsidass, 1987.

———. *Luce delle sacre scritture (Tantrāloka)*. Trans. Raniero Gnoli. Torino: Unione Tipografico-Editrice Torinese, 1972.

Tantrasaṃgraha, 4 vols. Ed. Gopinath Kaviraj (vols. 1–3) and Ramaprasada Tripathi (vol. 4). Benares: Sampurnanand Sanskrit Visvavidyalaya, 1973–81.

Tantrasāra of Abhinavagupta. *The Tantrasāra of Abhinavagupta.* Ed. with notes by Mukunda Ram Sastri. Bombay: Nirnaya Sagar, 1918; reprint Delhi: Bani Prakashan, 1982.

Tantratattva. Principles of Tantra: The Tantratattva of Śrīyukta Śiva Candra Vidyārṇava Bhaṭṭācārya, 2 vols. Ed. John Woodroffe. Madras: Ganesh, 1970.

Tārā Tantra. Tārā-Tantram, ed. Girish Chandra Vedantatirtha. With an introduction by A. K. Maitra. Rajshahi: Varendra Research Society, 1914; reprint Delhi: Bani Prakashan, 1983.

Toḍala Tantra. Toḍala Tantram. Ed. Bhadrashil Sharma. Allahabad: Kalyan Mandir, 1961.

Vaikhānasa Smārta Sūtra. Ed. Wilhelm Caland. Calcutta: Baptist Mission Press, 1927.

Vājasaneyi Saṁhitā. Vājasaneyi Saṁhitā, 2d ed. With the commentaries of Uvaṭa and Mahīdhara. Ed. Vasudeva Laksman Sastri Pansikar. Bombay: Pandurang Jawaji, 1929.

Varṇaratnākara of Kaviśekharācārya Jyotīśvara. Ed. S. K. Chatterji and Babua Misra, Bibliotheca Indica, no. 262. Calcutta: Bibliotheca Indica, 1940.

Vāsavadattā of Subandhu. *The Vāsavadattā* of Subandhu. Ed. Fitz-Edward Hall. Calcutta: Asiatic Society of Bengal, 1859.

Vāyutattvaṃ-bhāvanopadeśa of Ghorakṣa. *Esoteric Instruction on the Cultivation of the Wind Principle (vāyutattvaṃ-bhāvanopadeśa; rlung gi de nyid bsgom pa'i man ngag)* in *sde-dge mtshal-par bstan 'gyur: A Facsimile Edition of the 18th Century Redaction of Si-tu Chos-kyi-byuṅ-gnas* (Prepared under the Direction of H.H. the 16th rgyal-dbaṅ Karma-pa). Delhi: Delhi Karmapae Chodhey Gyalwae Sungrab Partun Khang, 1978. Toh. 2377; P 3219.

Vimalaprabhā. Portions trans. in Fenner, Edward Todd, *Rasāyan Siddhi* (listed under *Secondary Sources*).

Vināśikhatantra. Ed. with an introduction and a translation by Teun Goudriaan. Benares: Motilal Banarsidass, 1985.

Viṣṇudharmottara Purāṇa. Bombay: Venkatesvara Press, 1912.

Yājñavalkya Smṛti, 2d ed. Ed. T. Ganapati Sastri. New Delhi: Munshiram Manoharlal, 1982.

Yogabīja of Gorakṣanātha. Ed. Ramlal Srivastav. Gorakhpur: Gorakhnath Mandir, 1982.

Yogadarśana Upaniṣad. In *Yoga Upaniṣads.*

Yogakuṇḍalī Upaniṣad. In *Yoga Upaniṣads.*

Yogamārtaṇḍa of Gorakṣanātha. In *Siddha Siddhānta Paddhati of Gorakṣanātha.*

Yogaratnamālā of Nāgārjuna. *Nāgārjuna's Yogaratnamālā with the Commentary of Śvetāmbara Bhikṣu Guṇākara.* Ed. Priyavrat Sharma. Benares: Chaukhambha Orientalia, 1977.

Yoga Śāstra of Dattātreya. Ed. and trans. Amita Sharma. Delhi: Swami Keshawananda Yoga Institute, 1985.

Yogaśataka of Nāgārjuna. *Yogaśataka: texte médicale attribué à Nāgārjuna.* Ed. and French trans. by Jean Filliozat. Pondicherry: Institut Français d'Indologie, 1979.

Yoga Sūtras of Patañjali. *Sāmkhya Yogadarśana or Yogadarśana of Patañjali.* Ed. Goswami Damodara Sastri et al. Benares: Chaukhambha Sanskrit Sansthan, 1990.

———. *Yoga Philosophy of Patañjali* with the commentary of Vyāsa. Ed. and trans. Swami Hariharananda Aranya. Calcutta: University of Calcutta, 1981.

Yoga Upaniṣads. The Yoga Upaniṣads with the Commentary of Śrī Upaniṣad-Brahmayogin. Ed. A. Mahadeva Sastri. Adyar Library Series, vol. 6. Madras: Adyar Library and Research Center, 1968. English translation by Srinivasa Iyengar. Madras: Adyar, 1952. French translation by Jean Varenne. *Upanishads du Yoga.* Paris: Gallimard, 1971.

Yogatattva Upaniṣad. In *Yoga Upaniṣads.*

Yogaviṣaya of Matsyendranātha. In *Siddha Siddhānta Paddhati of Gorakṣanātha.*

Yogimuni 1000 of Yogimuni. Ed. and trans. S. Raghunathan. Madurai: Madurai University, 1982.

Yogisampradāyāviṣkṛti of Jñāneśvara. Trans. into Hindi by Candranāth Yogī. Ahmedabad: Sivanath Yogi, 1924.

Yoni Tantra. Yonitantra. Ed. with an introduction by J. A. Schoterman. Delhi: Manohar, 1980.

Secondary Sources

Aiyar, C. S. Narayanaswami. "Ancient Indian Chemistry and Alchemy of the Chemico-Philosophical Siddhānta System of the Indian Mystics." In *Proceedings and Transactions of the Third All-India Oriental Conference*, Madras, 22–24 December 1924. Madras: Law Printing House, 1925.

Alexander, Ernst Bruce. *Statistical Description and Historical Account of the Northwestern Provinces of India.* Gazetteer, Northwest Provinces, vol. 6. Allahabad: Northwest Provinces and Oudh Government Press, 1881.

Ali, S. M. *The Geography of the Purāṇas*, 2d ed. New Delhi: People's Publishing House, 1973.

Alper, Harvey, ed. *Mantra.* Albany: SUNY Press, 1989.

Anantacharya, E. *Rasayana and Ayurveda.* Vishakapatnam: World Teacher Publications, 1935, 1982.

Anantharaman, T. R. "Transformations—Metallurgical and Mental," Prof. N. P. Gandhi Memorial Lecture, Varanasi, 18 December 1973.

Apfel-Marglin, Fréderique. *Wives of the God-King.* New York: Oxford University Press, 1985.

Aung, Maung Htin. *Folk Elements in Burmese Buddhism.* London: Oxford University Press. 1962. Reprint Westport, Conn.: Greenwood Press, 1978.

Babb, Lawrence. *The Divine Hierarchy: Popular Hinduism in Central India.* New York: Columbia University Press, 1975.

Bachelard, Gaston. *La poétique de l'espace.* Paris: Presses Universitaires de France, 1974.

Bagchi, Prabodh Chandra. "Compte-rendu de Benoytosh Bhattacharya, édition de la *Sādhanamālā.*" *Indian Historical Quarterly* 6 (1930): 574–87.

———. "The Cult of the Buddhist Siddhācāryas." In *Cultural Heritage of India,* ed. Haridas Bhattacharyya, vol. 4, pp. 273–79.

———. *Studies in the Tantras.* Calcutta: University of Calcutta, 1939, 1975.

Bali, Krsna Kumar. *Ṭillā Gorakṣanāth.* Haridwar: Pir Kala Nath Trust, 1983.

Bandyopadhyay, Pradip Kumar. *Nātha Cult and Mahānād.* Delhi: B. R. Publishing Company, 1992.

Banerjea, Aksaya Kumar. *Philosophy of Gorakhnāth with Gorakṣa-Vacana-Saṅgraha.* 2d ed. Delhi: Motilal Banarsidass, 1983.

Banerji, R. D. *The Haihayas of Tripuri and Their Monuments.* Memoirs of the Archaeological Survey of India, no. 23. Calcutta: Government of India Central Publication Branch, 1931.

Barrow, H. W. "On Aghoris and Aghorapanthis." *Anthropological Society of Bombay* 3:4 (1893): 197–251.

Barthwal, Pitambaradatta. *Gorakh Bāṇī.* Allahabad: Hindi Sahitya Sammelan, 1955 (1st ed. 1942).

———. *Yog Pravāh.* Benares: Kashi Viyapith, 1946.

Bayly, C. A. *Rulers, Townsmen and Bazaars: North Indian Society in the Age of British Expansion, 1770–1870.* Cambridge: Cambridge University Press, 1983.

Bedi, Rajesh and Ramesh. *Sadhus: The Holy Men of India.* New Delhi: Brijbasi Printers Private Ltd., 1991.

Bernier, François. *Voyage dans les Etats du Grand Mogol.* Ed. with an introduction by France Bhattacharya. Paris: Fayard, 1981.

Beyer, Stephan. *The Cult of Tārā.* Berkeley: University of California Press, 1973.

Bharati, Aghehananda. *The Tantric Tradition.* London: Rider and Co., 1965; New York: Grove Press, 1975.

Bharati, Dharmavir. *Siddh Sāhity.* 2d ed. Allahabad: Kitab Mahal, 1955, 1968.

Bhardwaj, Surinder Mohan. *Hindu Places of Pilgrimage in India.* Berkeley: University of California Press, 1973.

Bhattacarya, Jivananda, ed. *Indrajālavidyāsaṃgraha.* Calcutta: V. V. Mukherji, 1925.

Bhattacharya, Benoytosh. *An Introduction to Buddhist Esoterism.* Oxford: Oxford University Press, 1932.

Bhattacharyya, Haridas, ed. *Cultural Heritage of India.* 5 vols. Calcutta: Ramakrishna Mission, 1956.

Bhattacharyya, Nagendranath. *History of the Tantric Religion (A Historical, Ritualistic and Philosophical Study).* Delhi: Munshiram Manoharlal, 1982.

Biardeau, Madeleine. *L'Hindouïsme: Anthropologie d'une civilisation.* Paris: Flammarion, 1981.

———. *Histoires de poteaux: Variations autour de la Déesse hindoue.* Publications de l'Ecole Française d'Extrême Orient, 154. Paris: Ecole Française d'Extrême Orient, 1989.

———. "Puranic Cosmogony." In *Asian Mythologies,* compiled by Yves Bonnefoy and translated under the direction of Wendy Doniger. Chicago: University of Chicago Press, 1989, pp. 43–50.

Biardeau, Madeleine, and Charles Malamoud, *Le Sacrifice dans l'Inde Ancienne.* Paris: Presses Universitaires de France, 1976.

Blackburn, Stuart H., Peter J. Claus, Joyce B. Fluekiger, and Susan Wadley, eds. *Oral Epics in India.* Berkeley: University of California Press, 1989.

Bose, D. M., ed. *A Concise History of Science in India.* New Delhi: Indian National Science Academy, 1971.

Bouillier, Véronique. "La caste sectaire des Kānphaṭā Jogī dans le royaume du Nepal: l'exemple de Gorkhā." *Bulletin de l'Ecole Française d'Extrême-Orient* 75 (1986): 125–67.

———. "Growth and Decay of a Kānphaṭā Yogi Monastery in South-west Nepal." *The Indian Economic and Social History Review* 28:2 (1991): 151–70.

———. "The King and His Yogī: Pṛthivinārāyaṇ Śāh, Bhagavantanāth and the Unification of Nepal in the Eighteenth Century." In John P. Neelsen, ed., *Gender, Caste and Power in South Asia: Social Status and Mobility in a Transitional Society,* pp. 1–21.

———. "La violence des non-violents, ou les ascètes au combat." In Denis Vidal, Gilles Tarabout and Eric Meyer, eds., *Violences et Non-Violences en Inde,* pp. 213–43.

Boulnois, Lucette. *Poudre d'or et monnaies d'argent au Tibet.* Paris: Editions du C.N.R.S., 1983.

Briggs, George Weston. *Gorakhnāth and the Kānphaṭa Yogis.* Calcutta: Y.M.C.A. Press, 1938; New Delhi: Motilal Banarsidass, 1982.

Brooks, Douglas Renfrew. *The Secret of the Three Cities: An Introduction to Hindu Śākta Tantrism.* Chicago: University of Chicago Press, 1990.

Buoy, Christian. *Les Nātha-yogin et les Upaniṣads.* Publications de l'Institut de Civilisation Indienne, no. 62. Paris: De Boccard, 1994.

Burgess, James. *Report on the Antiquities of Kâthiâwâḍ and Kacch, Being the Result of the Second Season's Operations of the Archaeological Society of Western India, 1874–1875.* London: India Museum, 1876; reprint Delhi: Indological Book House, 1971.

Carstairs, G. Morris. *The Twice Born.* London: Hogarth Press, 1958.

Chambard, Jean-Luc. "Les trois grands dieux aux enfers: Tradition orale et cycle des fêtes hindoues dans un village de l'Inde centrale (M.P.). In Catherine Champion, ed. *Littérature Populaire et Tradition Orale en Inde (Puruṣārtha 17).* Paris: Éditions de l'E.H.E.S.S., 1994.

Chénu, Marie-Dominique. *Nature, Man and Society in the Twelfth Century.* Ed. and trans. Jerome Taylor and Lester K. Little. Chicago: University of Chicago Press, 1969; reprint Chicago: Midway Books, 1979.

Cordier, Palmyr. *Catalogue du fonds tibétain de la Bibliothèque nationale,* vol. 3. Index du Bstan-hgyur (Tibétain 180–332). Paris: Bibliothèque Nationale, 1915.

———. "Histoire de la médecine indienne: La phtisie pulmonaire." *Annales d'hygiène et de médecine coloniales* 15 (1912) 255–66, 535–48.

———. *Nāgārjuna et l'Uttaratantra de la Suçrutasamhitā.* Antananarivo: n.p., 1896.

———. "Récentes découvertes de mss. médicaux sanscrits dans l'Inde (1898–1902)." *Le Muséon,* n.s. 4 (1903): 321–52.

———. *Vāgbhaṭa et l'Aṣṭāṅgahṛdayasaṁhitā.* Besançon: n.p., 1896.

Cort, John. "Twelve Chapters from *The Guidebook to Various Pilgrimage Places,* the *Vividhatīrthakalpa* of Jīnaprabhāsūri," in Phyllis Granoff, ed., *The Clever Adulteress and the Hungry Monk.*

Crooke, William. "Hiṅglāj." In *Encyclopedia of Religion and Ethics,* vol. 6, pp. 715–16. New York: Scribner's, 1914.

———. *Religion and Folklore of Northern India.* London: Oxford University Press, 1926; reprint Delhi: Munshiram Manoharlal, 1968.

———. "A Version of the Guga Legend," *Indian Antiquary* 24 (1895): 49–56.

Ctesias. *Indika.* In Photios, *Bibliotheca,* 6 vols. Ed. and trans. into French by René Henry. Paris: Les Belles Lettres, 1959.

Baba Cunninathji. *Tan-Prakāś.* Gorakhpur: Eureka Press, 1981.

Cunningham, Alexander. *Archaeological Survey of India, Four Reports Made during the Years 1862–63–64–65.* Simla: Government Central Press, 1871.

———. *A Report of a Tour in the Central Provinces in 1873–74 and 1874–75.* Archaeological Survey of India, vol. 9. Calcutta: Archaeological Society, 1879; reprint Benares: Indological Book House, 1966.

Dasgupta, Shashibhushan. *An Introduction to Tantric Buddhism.* 2d ed. Calcutta: University of Calcutta Press, 1958.

———. *Obscure Religious Cults.* 3d ed. Calcutta: Firma KLM Limited, 1976.

Dasgupta, Surendranath. *A History of Indian Philosophy*, 5 vols. Cambridge: Cambridge University Press, 1922; reprint Delhi: Motilal Banarsidass, 1951–55.

Dash, Bhagwan. *Alchemy and Metallic Medicines in Āyurveda.* New Delhi: Concept Publishing, 1986.

———. *Fundamentals of Ayurvedic Medicine.* Delhi: Bansal & Co., 1978.

Davis, Richard H. *Ritual in an Oscillating Universe: Worshipping Śiva in Medieval India.* Princeton: Princeton University Press, 1991.

Detienne, Marcel. *L'invention de la mythologie.* Paris: Gallimard, 1981.

Deussen, Paul. *Sixty Upanisads.* Trans. V. M. Bedekar and G. B. Palsule. Delhi: Motilal Banarsidass, 1980.

Devi, Konduri Sarojini. *Religion in the Vijayanagara Empire.* New Delhi: Sterling, 1990.

Dhoundiyal, B. N. *Rajasthan District Gazateers: Sirohi.* Jaipur: Government Central Press, 1967.

Digby, Simon. "Encounters with Jogīs in Indian Sūfī Hagiography." Typescript of paper read at the School of Oriental and African Studies, London, 27 January 1970.

———. "To Ride a Tiger or a Wall? Strategies of Prestige in Indian Sufi Legend." In *According to Tradition: Hagiographical Writing in India.* Ed. Winand Callewaert and Rupert Snell. Wiesbaden: Harrassowitz, 1994, pp. 99–129.

Dikshit, Rajesh. *Śrī Navanāth Caritr Sāgar.* Delhi: Dehati Pustak Bhandar, 1969.

Dimmitt, Cornelia, and J. A. Van Buitenen. *Classical Hindu Mythology.* Philadelphia: Temple University Press, 1978.

Dimock, Edward C., Jr. *The Place of the Hidden Moon: Erotic Mysticism in the Vaiṣṇava-sahajiyā Cult of Bengal.* With a new Foreword by Wendy Doniger. Chicago: University of Chicago Press, 1966; reprint Delhi: Motilal Banarsidass, 1991.

Dobbs, Betty Jo Teeter. *The Foundations of Newton's Alchemy or "The Hunting of the Greene Lyon."* London: Cambridge University Press, 1975.

Dowman, Keith. *Masters of Mahāmudrā: Songs and Histories of the Eighty-Four Buddhist Siddhas.* Albany: SUNY Press, 1985.

Dumézil, Georges. *Mythe et épopée*, 3 vols: Vol. 1. *L'idéologie des trois fonctions dans les épopées des peuples indo-européens*, 5th ed. Paris: Gallimard, 1986. Vol. 2. *Types épiques indo-européens: un héros, un sorcier, un roi*, 4th ed. Paris: Gallimard, 1986. Vol. 3. *Histoires romaines*, 3d ed. Paris: Gallimard, 1981.

Dumont, Louis. *Homo hierarchicus: Le système des castes et ses implications.* Paris: Gallimard, 1978.

Dutt, N. "Notes on the Nāgārjunikoṇḍa Inscriptions." *Indian Historical Quarterly* 7:3 (September 1931): 633–53.

Dvivedi, Hazariprasad. *Nāth Sampradāy.* 3d ed. Allahabad: Lokabharati Prakasan, 1981.

———, ed. *Nāth Siddhoṃ kī Bāniyāṃ.* 2d ed. Benares: Kasi Nagaripracarini Sabha, 1980 (first ed. 1957).

Dwarkanath, C. *Introduction to Kāyacikitsā.* Bombay: Popular Book Depot, 1959.

Dyczkowski, Mark S. G. *The Canon of the Śaivāgama and the Kubjikā Tantras of the Western Kaula Tradition.* Albany: SUNY Press, 1988.

———. "Kuṇḍalinī the Erotic Goddess: Sexual Potency, Transformation and Reversal in the Heterodox Theophanies of the Kubjikā Tantras." Typescript of paper read at American Academy of Religion Annual Meeting, San Francisco, 23 November 1992.

Eck, Diana. *Banaras: City of Light.* Princeton: Princeton University Press, 1983.

Eliade, Mircea. *Forgerons et alchimistes.* 2d rev. ed. Paris: Flammarion, 1977.

———. *The Sacred and the Profane: The Nature of Religion.* Trans. Willard R. Trask. New York: Harcourt Brace Jovanovich, 1959.

———. *Shamanism, Archaic Techniques of Ecstasy.* Trans. Willard R. Trask. Princeton: Princeton University Press, 1972.

———. *Yoga: Immortality and Freedom.* 2d ed. Trans. Willard R. Trask. Princeton, N.J.: Bollingen, 1973.

Encyclopedia of Religion and Ethics. 12 vols. Ed. James Hastings. New York: Scribner's, 1908–26.

Encyclopedia of Religions. Ed. Mircea Eliade. Chicago: University of Chicago Press, 1986.

Enthoven, R. E. *The Tribes and Castes of Bombay.* 3 vols. Bombay: Government Central Press, 1923.

Erndl, Kathleen M. *Victory to the Mother: The Hindu Goddess of Northwest India in Myth, Ritual, and Symbol.* New York: Oxford University Press, 1993.

Ernst, Carl. "The Arabic Version of "The Pool of the Water of Life (Amṛtakuṇḍa)." Typescript of paper read at American Academy of Religion, Annual Meeting, Washington, D.C., 20 November 1993.

Fenner, Edward Todd. *Rasāyan Siddhi: Medicine and Alchemy in the Buddhist Tantras.* Ph.D. dissertation, University of Wisconsin, 1979.

Filliozat, Jean. "Al-Biruni and Indian Alchemy." In *Studies in the History of Science in India.* 2 vols. Ed. Debiprasad Chattopadhyaya. New Delhi: Educational Enterprises, 1982, vol. 1, pp. 338–43.

———. "La discipline psychosomatique du yoga et ses fondament théoriques." *Annuaire du Collège de France* (1965–66): 383–87.

———. *La doctrine classique de la médecine indienne: Ses origines et ses parallèles grecs.* 2d ed. Paris: Ecole Française d'Extrême Orient, 1949, 1975.

———. *Etude de démonologie indienne: Le Kumāratantra de Rāvaṇa et les textes parallèles indiens, tibétains, chinois, cambodgien et arabe.* Cahiers de la Société Asiatique, 1è série, vol. 4. Paris: Imprimerie Nationale, 1937.

———. "Liste des manuscrits de la Collection Palmyr Cordier conservés à la Bibliothèque Nationale." *Journal Asiatique* 224 (1934): 155–73.

———. "Le Kumāratantra de Rāvaṇa." *Journal Asiatique* 226 (1935):1–66.

———. "Les mechanismes psychiques d'après les textes de yoga." *Annuaire du Collège de France* (Paris: 1970–71): 415–16; (Paris: 1971–72): 397–99.

———. "Taoïsme et yoga." *Journal Asiatique* 257 (1969): 41–87.

Filliozat, Jean, and Louis Renou. *L'Inde classique: Manuel des études indiennes.* 3 vols. Paris: Imprimerie Nationale, 1947–53.

Fishlock, Trevor. *India File.* London: John Murray, 1983; reprint Calcutta: Rupa and Co., 1984.

Forbes, Alexander Kinloch. *Rās-mālā: Hindu Annals of Western India, with particular Reference to Gujarat.* London: Richardson, 1878; reprint New Delhi: Heritage Publishers, 1973.

Forster, E. M. *The Hill of Devi.* Harmondsworth: Penguin, 1963.

Gairola, C. Krishna. "Les conditions sociales et religieuses à l'époque de Śātavāhana dans l'Inde (Ie siècle av. J.-C.–IIe siècle ap. J.-C)." *Journal Asiatique* 243 (1955): 281–95.

Gaston, Anne-Marie. *Śiva in Dance, Myth and Iconography.* Delhi: Oxford University Press, 1982.

Gautam, Camanlal. *Śrī Gorakhnāth Caritr.* Bareilly: Samskrti Samsthan, 1981.

Gellner, David N. *Monk, Householder, and Tantric Priest: Newar Buddhism and Its Hierarchy of Ritual.* New Delhi: Cambridge University Press, 1992.

Gharote, M. L., and V. A. Bedekar, eds. *Descriptive Catalogue of Yoga Manuscripts.* Lonavla: Kaivalyadhama S.M.Y.M. Samiti, 1989.

Ghimire, Yubaraj. "The Rise of the Sādhus." *India Today* (31 January 1993): 61–63.

Giri, Sadananda. *Society and Sannyāsin: A History of the Daśanāmī Sannyāsins.* Benares: n.p., 1976.

Gold, Ann Grodzins. *A Carnival of Parting: The Tales of King Bharthari and King Gopi Chand as Sung and Told by Madhu Natisar Nath of Ghatiyali, Rajasthan.* Berkeley: University of California Press, 1992.

———. "Gender and Illusion in a Rajasthani Yogic Tradition." In *Tale, Text and Time: Interpreting South Asian Expressive Traditions.* Ed. Frank Korom, Arjun Appadurai, and Margaret Mills. Philadelphia: University of Pennsylvania Press, 1990, pp. 102–35.

Gold, Daniel. "The Instability of the King: Magical Insanity and the Yogi's Power in the Politics of Jodhpur, 1803–1843." In David N. Lorenzen, ed., *Bhakti Religion in North India: Community Identity and Political Action.* Albany: SUNY Press, 1995, pp. 120–32.

Gonda, Jan. *Change and Continuity in Indian Tradition.* The Hague: Mouton, 1965.

———. *Medieval Religious Literature in Sanskrit.* History of Indian Literature, II, 1. Wiesbaden: Harassowitz, 1977.

———. *Triads in the Veda.* Amsterdam: North-Holland, 1976.

———. *Viṣṇuism and Śivaism, A Comparison.* London: Athlone, 1970.

Goswamy, B. N., and J. S. Grewal. *The Mughals and the Jogis of Jakhbar: Some Madad-i-Ma'ash and Other Documents.* Simla: Indian Institute of Advanced Study, 1967.

Goudriaan, Teun, ed. *The Sanskrit Tradition and Tantrism.* Panels of the VIIth World Sanskrit Conference, Kern Institute, Leiden, 3–29 August 1987. Leiden: Brill, 1990.

Goudriaan, Teun, and Sanjukta Gupta. *Hindu Tantric and Śākta Literature.* History of Indian Literature, II, 2. Wiesbaden: Harrassowitz, 1981.

Granoff, Phyllis, ed. *The Clever Adulteress and the Hungry Monk: A Treasury of Jain Literature.* New York, Mosaic Press, 1990.

Granoff, Phyllis, and Koichi Shinohara, eds. *Monks and Magicians: Religious Biographies in Asia.* Oakville, Ontario: Mosaic Press, 1988; reprint Delhi: Motilal Banarsidass, 1994.

———. "The Song of Mánik Candra." *Journal of the Royal Asiatic Society of Bengal* 47:3, pt. 1 (1878): 135–238.

———. "Two Versions of the Song of Gopīcand." *Journal of the Royal Asiatic Society of Bengal* 55 (1885): 35–55.

Gupta, Mataprasad. *Prācīn Bhāṣā Nāṭak Saṅgrah.* Agra: Agra University Press, 1970.

Gupta, Sanjukta. "The *Maṇḍala* as an Image of Man." In Richard Gombrich, ed., *Indian Ritual and Its Exegesis.* Delhi: Oxford University Press, 1988, pp. 32–41.

Gupta, Sanjukta, Dirk Jan Hoens, and Teun Goudriaan. *Hindu Tantrism.* Handbuch der Orientalistik, 2.4.2. Leiden: Brill, 1979.

Harzer, Edeltraud. "Sāmkhya," In *Encyclopedia of Religion,* vol. 13, pp. 47–51.

Hawking, Stephen W. *A Brief History of Time: From the Big Bang to Black Holes.* New York: Bantam Books, 1988.

Hazra, R. C. *Studies in the Purāṇic Records on Hindu Rites and Customs.* 2d ed. Delhi: Motilal Banarsidass, 1975.

Heesterman, Jan. *The Broken World of Sacrifice.* Chicago: University of Chicago Press, 1993.

———. *The Inner Conflict of Tradition.* Chicago: University of Chicago Press, 1985.

Heimann, Betty. *Facets of Indian Thought.* London: Allen and Unwin, 1964.

Helffer, Mireille and Gaborieau, Marc. "A propos d'un tambour du Kumaon et de l'ouest du Népal: Remarques sur l'utilisation des tambours-sabliers dans le monde indien, le Népal et le Tibet." In *Studia instrumentorum musicae populares,* Festschrift to E. Emsheimer on the occasion of his 70th birthday. Stockholm: Musikhistorika Museet, 1974.

Hiltebeitel, Alf, ed. *Criminal Gods and Demon Devotees: Essays on the Guardians of Popular Hinduism.* Albany: SUNY Press, 1989.

Hou, Ching-lang. *Monnaies d'offrande et la notion de Trésorerie dans la religion chinoise.* Paris: Mémoires de l'Institut des Hautes Etudes Chinoises, 1975.

Hulin, Michel. *La face cachée du temps: L'imaginaire de l'au-delà.* Paris: Fayard, 1985.

I-Ching. *A Record of the Buddhist Religion as Practiced in India and the Malay Arhcipelago (AD 671–695).* Trans. J. Takakusu. London: Clarendon Press, 1896; reprint Delhi: Munshiram Manoharlal, 1966.

Jacobi, H. "Abode of the Blest (Hindu)." In *Encyclopedia of Religion and Ethics,* vol. 1, pp. 698–700.

Jaggi, O. P. *Yogic and Tantric Medicine.* History of Science and Technology in India, vol. 5. Delhi: Atma Ram and Sons, 1973.

Jamison, Stephanie W. *The Ravenous Hyenas and the Wounded Sun: Myth and Ritual in Ancient India.* Ithaca, N.Y.: Cornell University Press, 1991.

Joshi, Damodar. "Mercury in Indian Medicine." *Studies in History of Medicine* 3 (1979):234–97.

Joshi, Rasik Vihari. "Notes on Guru, Dīkṣā and Mantra." *Ethnos* 37 (1972): 103–12.

Kaelber, Walter O. *Tapta-Mārga: Asceticism and Initiation in Vedic India.* Albany: SUNY Press, 1989.

Kakar, Sudhir. *The Inner World: A Psychoanalytic Study of Childhood and Society in India.* New York: Oxford University Press, 1978.

———. *Shamans, Mystics and Doctors: A Psychological Inquiry into India and Its Healing Traditions.* New York: Alfred A. Knopf, 1982; New Delhi: Oxford India Paperbacks, 1990.

Kalyāṇ Śakti Aṅk. Gorakhpur: Gita Press, 1934.

Kamat, Ashok Prabhakar. *Mahārāṣṭr ke Nāthpanthīy Kaviyoṃ kā Hindi Kāvy.* Mathura: Jawahar Pustakalaya, 1976.

Kane, Pandurang Vaman. *History of Dharmaśāstra.* 5 vols. 2d ed. Poona: Bhandarkar Oriental Research Institute, 1968–75.

Kantawala, S. G. *Cultural History from the Matsya Purāṇa.* Baroda: M. S. University, 1964.

Kapani, Lakshmi. *La notion de saṃskāra.* 2 vols. Publications de l'Institut de Civilisation Indienne, no. 59. Paris: De Boccard, 1991, 1993.

Karambelkar, V. W. "Matsyendranāth and His Yoginī Cult." *Indian Historical Quarterly* 31 (1955):362–74.

Kardaswamy, Thiru N. *History of Siddha Medicine.* Madras: n.p., 1979.

Kaul, Jayalal. *Lal Ded.* New Delhi: Sahitya Akademi, 1973.

Kaviraj, Gopinath. *Aspects of Indian Thought.* Calcutta: University of Burdwan, 1966.

———. *Bhāratīy Saṃskṛti aur sādhanā.* 2 vols. Patna: Bihar Rashtrabhasha Parishad, 1962–64.

———. *Tāntrik Sādhanā aur Saṃskṛti.* Patna: Bihar Rashtrabhasha Parishad, 1979.

———. *Tāntrik Vāṅmay meṃ Śākta Dṛṣṭi.* Patna: Bihar Rashtrabhasha Parishad, 1963.

Khakhar, Dalpatram Pranjivan. "History of the Kānphaṭas of Kacch." *Indian Antiquary* 7 (February 1878):47–53.

Khan, Dominique-Sila. "L'Origine ismaélienne du culte hindou de Rāmdeo Pīr." *Revue de l'Histoire des Religions* 210 (1993):27–47.

———. "Rāmdeo Pīr and the Kāmaḍiyā Panth." In N. K. Singhi and Rajendra Joshi, eds. *Folk, Faith, and Feudalism.* Jaipur: Rawat Publications, 1995, pp. 295–327.

Knipe, David M. "The Heroic Theft: Myths from Ṛgveda IV and the Ancient Near East." *History of Religions* 6 (1967):328–60.

———. "Night of the Growing Dead: A Cult of Vīrabhadra in Coastal Andhra." In Alf Hiltebeitel, ed. *Criminal Gods and Demon Devotees: Essays on the Guardians of Popular Hinduism.*

———. "One Fire, Three Fires, Five Fires: Vedic Symbols in Transformation," *History of Religions* 12 (1972):28–41.

Kolff, Dirk H. A. *Naukar, Rajput and Sepoy: The Ethnohistory of the Military Labour Market in Hindustan, 1450–1850.* Cambridge: Cambridge University Press, 1990.

Kramrisch, Stella. *The Hindu Temple.* 2 vols. Calcutta: University of Calcutta, 1946; reprint Benares: Motilal Banarsidass, 1976.

———. *The Presence of Śiva.* Princeton: Princeton University Press, 1981.

Kraus, Paul. *Jabir ibn Hayyan: Contribution à l'étude des idées scientifiques dans l'Islam: Jabir et la science grecque.* Paris: Les Belles Lettres, 1986.

Lamb, Alastair. *British India and Tibet, 1766–1910.* 2d ed. London: Routledge and Kegan Paul, 1986.

Lamotte, Etienne. *Histoire du Bouddhisme indien, des origines à l'ère Śaka.* Bibliothèque du Muséon, vol. 43. Louvain: Université de Louvain, 1958.

Lapoint, E. C. "The Epic of Gūgā: A North Indian Oral Tradition." In S. Vatuk, ed., *American Studies in the Anthropology of India.* New Delhi: Manohar, 1978.

Larson, Gerald James. *Classical Sāṃkhya: An Interpretation of its History and Meaning.* 2d ed. Delhi: Motilal Banarsidass, 1979.

Lecomte-Tilouine, Marie. "Des dieux aux sommets (Népal)." In Véronique Bouillier and Gérard Toffin, eds. *Classer les Dieux? Des Panthéons en Asie du Sud* [*Puruṣārtha* 15]. Paris: EHESS, 1993, pp. 153–72.

Lester, Robert C. *Theravada Buddhism in Southeast Asia.* Ann Arbor: University of Michigan Press, 1973.

Lévi, Sylvain. "Kaniṣka et Śatavahana: deux figures symboliques de l'Inde au premier siècle." *Journal Asiatique* 228 (1936):61–121.

———. "Maṇimekhalā, divinité de la mer." In *Mémorial Sylvain Lévi.* Paris: P. Hartmann, 1937, pp. 371–83.

———. *Le Népal.* 3 vols. Paris: Ernest Leroux, 1905; reprint Paris: Toit du Monde & Errance, 1985.

Lincoln, Bruce. *Death, War, and Sacrifice: Studies in Ideology and Practice.* Chicago: University of Chicago Press, 1991.

Locke, John K. *Karunamaya: The Cult of Avalokitesvara-Matsyendranath in the Valley of Nepal.* Kathmandu: Sahayogi Press, 1980.

Lorenzen, David. *The Kāpālikas and Kālamukhas: Two Lost Śaivite Sects.* New Delhi: Thomson Press, 1972.

———. "Śaivism: Pāśupatas." In *Encyclopedia of Religion,* vol. 13, pp. 18–19.

———. "Warrior Ascetics in Indian History." *Journal of the American Oriental Society* 98 (1978):61–75.

Mabbett, I. W. "The Symbolism of Mount Meru." *History of Religions* 23 (1983):64–83.

MacDonald, Ariane. *Le maṇḍala du Mañjuśrīmūlakalpa.* Paris: Adrien Maisonneuve, 1962.

Madhavan, V. R. *Siddha Medical Manuscripts in Tamil.* Madras: International Institute of Tamil Studies, 1984.

Madhihassan, S. *Indian Alchemy or Rasāyana.* New Delhi: Vikas, 1979.

Mahapatra, Piyush K. "The Nath Cult of Bengal." *Folklore* (Calcutta) 12:10 (October 1971): 376–96.

Majumdar, M. R. et al. *Historical and Cultural Chronology of Gujarat.* 2 vols. Baroda: University of Baroda, 1960.

Malamoud, Charles. "Cosmologie prescriptive: Observations sur le monde et le non-monde dans l'Inde ancienne." *Le temps de la réflexion* 10 (1989):303– 25.

———. *Cuire le monde: Mythe et pensée dans l'Inde ancienne.* Paris: Editions de la Découverte, 1989.

Mallmann, Marie-Therèse de. "Divinités hindoues dans le tantrisme bouddhique." *Arts Asiatiques* 10 (1964):67–86.

Mariadassou, Paramananda. *Médecine traditionelle de l'inde.* 4 vols. Pondicherry: Sainte Anne, 1934–36.

Maspero, Henri. *Le Taoïsme et les religions chinoises.* With a preface by Maxime Kaltenmark. Paris: Gallimard, 1971.

McDaniel, June. *The Madness of the Saints: Ecstatic Religion in Bengal.* Chicago: University of Chicago Press, 1989.

McGregor, Ronald Stuart. *Hindi Literature from Its Beginnings to the Nineteenth Century.* Wiesbaden: Harrassowitz, 1984.

Meister, Michael, ed. *Discourses on Śiva: Proceedings of a Symposium on the Nature of Religious Imagery.* Philadelphia: University of Pennsylvania Press, 1984.

Mely, M. F. de. "L'alchimie chez les chinois et l'alchimie grecque." *Journal Asiatique,* 9è série, vol. 6 (September–October 1895): 314–40.

Meulenbeld, Jan G. *History of Indian Medical Literature.* Leiden: Brill, 1996.

Michaels, Axel. "On 12th–13th Century Relations between Nepal and South India." *Journal of the Nepal Research Center* 7 (1985):69–72.

Misra, Sarat Chandra. "On the Cult of Gorakṣanāth in Eastern Bengal." *Journal of the Department of Letters* (University of Calcutta) 14 (1927):1–41.

Misra, Shiva Sheikhar. *Fine Arts and Technical Sciences in Ancient India with Special Reference to Someśvara's Mānasollāsa.* Benares: Krishnadas Academy, 1982.

Misra, Siddhinandan. *Āyurvedīya Rasaśāstra.* Jaikrishnadas Ayurveda Series, 35. Benares: Chowkhamba Orientalia, 1981.

Mitra, Debala. *Buddhist Monuments.* Calcutta: Sahitya Samsad, 1971.

Monier-Williams, Monier. *A Sanskrit-English Dictionary.* London: Oxford University Press, 1899; reprint Delhi: Motilal Banarsidass, 1984.

Mookerji, Bhudeb. *Rasa-jala-nidhi or Ocean of Indian Chemistry and Alchemy.* 5 vols. Calcutta: K. C. Neogi, 1926–38.

Mukherji, Tarapada. *Gopicandra Nāṭaka.* Calcutta: University of Calcutta Press, 1970.

Muller-Ortega, Paul Eduardo. *The Triadic Heart of Śiva: Kaula Tantricism of Abhinavagupta in the Non-dual Shaivism of Kashmir.* Albany: SUNY Press, 1989.

Murty, K. Satchidananda. *Nāgārjuna.* New Delhi: National Book Trust, 1971.

Mus, Paul. *Barabudur.* Hanoi: Imprimerie d'Extrême Orient, 1935.

———. "La notion de temps réversible dans la mythologie bouddhique." *Ecole Pratique des Hautes Etudes. Annuaire 1938–1939.* Melun: Imprimerie Administrative, 1938.

Yogi Narharināth. *Nav Nāth Caurāsī Siddh.* Benares: Rashtriya Press, 1968.

Needham, Joseph, et al. *Science and Civilisation in Ancient China.* 6 vols. in 17 tomes. Cambridge: Cambridge University Press, 1954–88.

Neelsen, John P., ed. *Gender, Caste and Power in South Asia: Social Status and Mobility in a Transitional Society.* Delhi: Munshiram Manoharlal, 1991.

Newman, John. "A Brief History of the Kālacakra." In *The Wheel of Time: The Kālacakra in Context.* Madison, Wis.: Deer Park Books, 1985.

Obermiller, Ernst. *History of Buddhism (Chos-hbyung) by Bu-ston.* 2 vols. Heidelberg: Harrassowitz, 1931–32; reprint New Delhi, Sri Satguru Publications, 1986.

O'Flaherty, Wendy Doniger. *Dreams, Illusion and Other Realities.* Chicago: University of Chicago Press, 1984.

———. *The Rig Veda.* Harmondsworth: Penguin, 1981.

———. *Śiva: The Erotic Ascetic.* New York: Oxford University Press, 1981.

———. *Tales of Sex and Violence: Folklore, Sacrifice, and Danger in the Jaiminīya Brāhmaṇa.* Chicago: University of Chicago Press, 1985.

———. *Women, Androgynes and Other Mythical Beasts.* Chicago: University of Chicago Press, 1980.

Oguibenine, Boris. "Sur le terme *yoga*, le verbe *yuj-* et quelques-uns de leurs dérivés dans les hymnes védiques." *Indo-Iranian Journal* 27 (1984):85–101.

Ojha, Gaurishankar H. "A Gold Coin of Bāppā Rāwal." *Journal of the Asiatic Society of Bengal,* new series, 23:6, numismatic supplement no. 40 (1926–27):14–18.

Oman, John Campbell. *Cults, Customs, and Superstitions of India.* London: T. Fisher Unwin, 1908.

———. *The Mystics, Ascetics and Saints of India.* London: 1903; reprint Delhi: Oriental Publishers, 1973.

Oosten, Jarich G. *The War of the Gods: The Social Code in Indo-European Mythology.* London: Routledge & Kegan Paul, 1985.

Padoux, André, ed. *L'Image divine: Culte et méditation dans l'hindouisme.* Paris: Editions du CNRS, 1990.

———, ed. *Mantras et diagrammes rituels dans l'hindouisme.* Table Ronde, Paris, 21–22 June 1984. Paris: Editions du CNRS, 1986.

———. "The Body in Tantric Ritual: The Case of the Mudrās." In Teun Goudriaan, ed., *The Sanskrit Tradition and Tantrism,* pp. 65–77.

———. *Vāc: The Concept of the Word in Selected Hindu Tantras.* Albany: SUNY Press, 1989.

Pal, Pratapaditya. *Hindu Religion and Iconology According to the Tantrasāra.* Los Angeles: Vichitra Press, 1981.

Pandey, Divakar. *Gorakhnāth evam unkī Paramparā kā Sāhity.* Gorakhpur: Gorakhpur University, 1980.

Pandey, Raj Bali. *Hindu Saṃskāras (Socio-Religious Study of the Hindu Sacraments).* 2d ed. Delhi: Motilal Banarsidass, 1969.

Parry, Jonathan. "Sacrificial Death and the Necrophagous Ascetic." In Maurice Bloch and Jonathan Parry, eds. *Death and the Regeneration of Life.* Cambridge: Cambridge University Press, 1982.

Philostratus. *Life of Apollonius.* Trans. C. P. Jones and edited, abridged, and introduced by G. W. Bowersock. Harmondsworth: Penguin, 1970.

Prakash, Satya. *Prācīn Bhārat meṃ Rasāyan kā Vikās.* Allahabad: Prayag Visvavidyalaya, 1960.

Pranke, Patrick. "On Becoming a Buddhist Wizard." In Don Lopez, ed., *Buddhism in Practice.* Princeton: Princeton University Press, 1995, pp. 343–58.

Pir Premnath, *Śiva-Gorakṣa.* New Delhi: Vijnana Prakashan, 1982.

Przyluski, Jean. "Les Vidyārāja," *Bulletin de l'Ecole Française d'Extrême Orient* 23 (1923): 301–18.

Puhvel, Jaan. *Comparative Mythology.* Baltimore: Johns Hopkins University Press, 1986.

Punjab States Gazetteer, vol 22A. *Chamba State with Maps, 1904.* Lahore: Civil and Military Gazette Press, 1910.

Rama Rao, B. and Reddy, M. V. "A Note on Gorakṣanātha and His Work *Yogadīpikā.*" *Bulletin of the Indian Institute of the History of Medicine* (Hyderabad) 12 (1982):34–38.

Ramachandra Rao, S. K. *Śrī-Cakra.* Delhi: Sri Satguru Publications, 1989.

Raman Shastri, V. V. "The Doctrinal Culture and Tradition of the Siddhas." In *Cultural Heritage of India*, ed. Haridas Bhattacharyya, vol. 4, pp. 300–8.

Ramanujan, A. K. *The Inner Landscape: Love Poems from a Classical Tamil Anthology.* Bloomington: Indiana University Press, 1975.

———. "The Myths of Bhakti: Images of Śiva in Śaiva Poetry. In Michael Meister, ed., *Discourses on Śiva: Proceedings of a Symposium on the Nature of Religious Imagery.*

———. *Speaking of Śiva.* Harmondsworth: Penguin, 1979.

Rao, T. A. Gopinath. *Elements of Hindu Iconography.* 2 vols. Madras: Law Road Printing House, 1914–16.

Rastogi, Navjivan. *Introduction to the Tantrāloka: A Study in Structure.* Albany: SUNY Press, 1987.

———. *The Krama Tantrism of Kashmir.* Vol. 1. Delhi: Motilal Banarsidass, 1979.

Ray, Prafulla Chandra. *A History of Hindu Chemistry from the Earliest Times to the Middle of the 16th Century* A.D. 2 vols. Calcutta: Prithwis Chandra Ray, 1902, 1909.

Ray, Priyanaranjan. *History of Chemistry in Ancient and Medieval India Incorporating the History of Hindu Chemistry by Acharya Prafulla Chandra Ray.* Calcutta: Indian Chemical Society, 1956.

Renou, Louis. "Études védiques," *Journal Asiatique* 243 (1955):405–38.

Rhys-Davids, Caroline A. F. "Original Buddhism and Amṛta." *Mélanges chinois et bouddhiques* [Brussels], vol. 6 (1938–39), pp. 371–82.

Robinson, James B. *Buddha's Lions: The Lives of the Eighty-four Siddhas.* Berkeley: Dharma Publishing, 1979.

Rose, H. A. *A Glossary of the Tribes and Castes of the Punjab and Northwest Frontier Province*, 3 vols. Lahore: Superintendent, Government Printing, Punjab, 1911–19; reprint Delhi: Asian Educational Services, 1990.

Roşu, Arion. "A la recherche d'un *tīrtha* énigmatique du Deccan médiéval." *Bulletin de l'Ecole Française d'Extrême Orient* 60 (1969):23–57.

———. "Alchemy and Sacred Geography in the Medieval Deccan." *Journal of the European Ayurvedic Society* 2 (1992):151–56.

———. "Considerations sur une technique du *Rasāyana* Āyurvédique." *Indo-Iranian Journal* 17 (1975):1–29.

———. *Gustave Lietard et Palmyr Cordier: Travaux sur l'Histoire de la médecine indienne.* Publications de l'Institut de Civilisation Indienne, no. 56. Paris: De Boccard, 1989.

———. "*Mantra* et *Yantra* dans la médecine et l'alchimie indiennes." *Journal Asiatique* 274:3–4 (1986):205–68.

———. "Le renouveau contemporain de l'Āyurveda." *Wiener Zeitschrift für die Kunde Südasiens* 26 (1982):59–82.

———. "Yoga et alchimie." *Zeitschrift der Deutschen Morgenländischen Gesellschaft* 132 (1982):363–79.

Roux, Jean-Paul. "Turkish and Mongolian Shamanism." In *Asian Mythologies*, compiled by Yves Bonnefoy and trans. under the direction of Wendy Doniger. Chicago: University of Chicago Press, 1989, pp. 329–30.

Ruben, Walter. *Eisenschmiede und Dämonen in Indien.* Internationales Archiv Für Ethnographie, 37, suppl. Leiden: Brill, 1939.

Ruegg, David Seyfort. "Sur les rapports entre le Bouddhisme et le 'substrat religieux' indien et tibétain." *Journal Asiatique* 252 (1964):77–95.

Sachau, Edward, ed. *Alberuni's India.* 2 vols. London: Kegan Paul, Trench, and Trubner, Inc., 1910; reprint Delhi: Munshiram Manoharlal, 1983.

Sahagal, Sarasvati. *Gorakh Darśan.* Hyderabad: Madhu Printers, 1979.

Saletore, Bhasker Anand. *Ancient Karnataka.* 2 vols. Poona: Oriental Books Agency, 1936.

———. "The Kānaphāṭa Jogis in Southern History." *Poona Orientalist* 1 (January 1937):16–22.

———. *Social and Political Life in the Vijayanagara Empire* (A.D. *1346*–A.D. *1646*). 2 vols. Madras: B. G. Paul & Co., 1934.

Saṃkṣipt Hindi Śabd Sāgar. Edited by Ramcandra Varma. Benares: Nagaripracarini Sabha, 1981.

Sanderson, Alexis. "Maṇḍala and Āgamic Identity in the Trika of Kashmir." In André Padoux, ed., *Mantras et diagrammes rituels dans l'hindouisme*, pp. 169–207.

———. "Meaning in Tantric Ritual." In Ann-Marie Blondeau, ed., *Le Rituel.* vol. 3. Paris: Ecole Pratique des Hautes Etudes, 5è section, 1996, pp. 15–95.

———. "Purity and power among the Brahmins of Kashmir." In *The category of the Person: Anthropology, Philosophy, History.* Ed. Michael Carrithers, Steven Collins, and Steven Lukes. Cambridge: Cambridge University Press, 1985, pp. 191–216.

———. "Śaivism and the Tantric Tradition." In *The World's Religions.* Ed. S. Sutherland et al. London: Routledge and Kegan Paul, 1988, pp. 660–704.

———. "Śaivism: Krama Śaivism"; "Śaivism: Śaivism in Kashmir"; "Śaivism: Trika Śaivism." In *Encyclopedia of Religion*, vol. 13, pp. 14–17.

———. "The Visualization of the Deities of the Trika." In André Padoux, ed., *L'image divine: Culte et méditation dans l'hindouisme.* Paris: CNRS, 1990.

Sankrtyayana, Rahula. "(Recherches Bouddhiques II) L'Origine du Vajrayāna et les quatre-vingt siddhas." *Journal Asiatique* 225:2 (October–December 1934): 209–30.

Sastri, Devadatt. *Āgneya tīrth Hiṅglāj.* Bombay: Lokaloka Prakashan, 1978.

Schmidt, Toni. "Fünfundachtzig Mahāsiddhas." *Ethnos* 2–3 (1955):103–21.

Schwartzberg, Joseph E., ed. *A Historical Atlas of South Asia.* Chicago: University of Chicago Press, 1978; second impression, with additional material, New York: Oxford University Press, 1992.

Sen, Gananath. *Āyurved Paricay.* Shantiniketan: Visva Vidya Samgraha, 1943.

Sen, Sukumar. *History of Bengali Literature.* New Delhi: Sahitya Academy, 1960.

Sethi, V. K., ed. *Kabir: The Weaver of God's Name.* Beas, Punjab: Radha Soami Satsang Press, 1984.

Sethu Raghunathan, N. "Contribution of Yoogi Munivar for Siddha System of Medicine." In *Heritage of the Tamils: Siddha Medicine.* Ed. S. V. Subrahmanian and V. R. Madhavan.

Shanmuga Velan, A. *Siddhar's Science of Longevity and Kalpa Medicine of India.* Madras: Sakthi Nilayam, 1963.

Shah, Shersingh. *Śrī Kedārnāth Māhātmya (Yātrā Gāīḍ).* Kedarnath: Shersingh Shah, n.d.

Sharma, Brijendra Nath. *Iconography of Sadāśiva.* New Delhi: Abhinava Publications, 1976.

Sharma, Padmaja. *Maharaja Man Singh of Jodhpur and His Times (1803–1843 A.D.).* Agra: Shiva Lal Agarwala & Company, 1972.

Sharma, Priyavrat. *Āyurved ka Vaijñānik Itihās.* Jaikrishnadas Ayurveda Series, no. 1, 2d ed. Benares: Chowkhamba Orientalia, 1982.
———. *Indian Medicine in the Classical Age.* Chowkhamba Sanskrit Series, 85. Benares: Chowhkamba Sanskrit Series Office, 1972.
Sharpe, Elizabeth. *An Eight-Hundred Year Old Book of Indian Medicine and Formulas, Translated from the Original Very Old Hindi into Gujarati Character and Thence into English.* London: Luzac & Co, 1937; reprint New Delhi: Asian Educational Services, 1979.
Shastri, Haraprasad. *A Catalogue of Palm-Leaf and Selected Paper Manuscripts Belonging to the Durbar Library, Nepal.* 2 vols. Calcutta: n.p., 1905, 1915.
Shorter Oxford Economic Atlas of the World. 2d ed. Prepared by the Economist Intelligence Unit. London: Oxford University Press, 1959.
Siegel, Lee. *Net of Magic: Wonders and Deceptions in India.* Chicago: University of Chicago Press, 1991.
Silburn, Lilian. *Kuṇḍalinī: Energy of the Depths.* Trans. Jacques Gontier. Albany: SUNY Press, 1988.
———. "Le vide, le rien, l'abîme." In *Le Vide: Expérience spirituelle.* Paris: Hermes, 1969.
Singh, Moti. *Nirguṇ Sāhity: Sāṁskṛtik Pṛṣṭhabhūmi.* Benares: Nagaripracarini Sabha, 1963.
Singh, Raya Bahadur Munshi Haradayal. *Ripoṛt Mardumaśumārī Rāja Mārvāḍ Bābat san[vat] 1891 Īsvī, Tīsarābhissā.* 2 vols. Jodhpur: Vidyasal, 1895.
Sinha, S., and B. Saraswati. *Ascetics of Kashi: An Anthropological Exploration.* Varanasi: N. K. Bose Memorial Foundation, 1978.
Sircar, D. C. *Cosmography and Geography in Early Indian Literature.* Calcutta: Indian Studies: Past and Present, 1967.
———. *The Guhilas of Kiṣkindhā.* Calcutta: Sanskrit College, 1965.
———. *The Śākta Pīṭhas.* 2d rev. ed. Delhi: Motilal Banarsidass, 1973.
———. *Studies in the Geography of Ancient and Medieval India.* 2d rev. ed. Delhi: Motilal Banarsidass, 1977, 1990.
Sivalal, Sridhar, ed. *Gopīcand kā Ākhyān.* Bombay: Jnan Sagar, 1890.
Smith, Brian K. *Reflections on Resemblance, Ritual, and Religion.* New York: Oxford University Press, 1989.
Snellgrove, David. *Buddhist Himalaya: Travels and Studies in Quest of the Origins and Nature of Tibetan Religion.* Oxford: Cassirer, 1957.
———. *Indo-Tibetan Buddhism: Indian Buddhists and Their Tibetan Successors.* 2 vols. Boston: Shambhala, 1987.
Spiro, Melford. *Buddhism and Society: A Great Tradition and Its Burmese Vicissitudes.* New York: Harper & Row, 1970.

Srivastav, Ramlal, ed. *"Gorakh" Viśeṣāṅk* [*Yog Vāṇī* special issue no. 1 for 1977]. Gorakhpur: Gorakhnath Mandir, 1977.

———, ed. *"Gorakh Bānī" Viśeṣāṅk* [*Yog Vāṇī*, special issue no. 1 for 1979]. Gorakhpur: Gorakhnāth Mandir, 1979.

———, ed. *"Nāth Siddh Carit" Viśeṣāṅk* [*Yog Vāṇī*, special issue no. 1 for 1984]. Gorakhpur: Gorakhnath Mandir, 1984.

Stein, R. A. *Grottes-Matrices et Lieux Saints de la déesse en Asie orientale.* Paris: Ecole Française d'Extrême Orient, 1988.

Stein, Rolf. "Architecture et pensée en Extrême-Orient." *Arts Asiatiques* 4:3 (1957): 163–86.

———. "Jardins en miniature d'Extrême Orient." *Bulletin de l'Ecole Française d'Extrême Orient* 52 (1942):1–104.

Stern, Henri. "Le temple d'Ekliṅgjī et le royaume de Mewar (Rajasthan) (rapport au divin, royauté et territoire: sources d'une maîtrise)." In Jean-Claude Galey, ed., *L'Espace du Temple (Puruṣārtha 10)* (1986), pp. 15–30.

Subrahmanian, S. V., and V. R. Madhavan, eds. *Heritage of the Tamils: Siddha Medicine.* Madras: International Institute of Tamil Studies, 1983.

Sukul, Kubernath. *Varanasi Down the Ages.* Benares: Bhargava Bhushan Press, 1974.

Sutherland, Gail Hinich. "*Bīja* (Seed) and *Kṣetra* (Field): Male Surrogacy or *Niyoga* in the Mahābhārata." *Contributions to Indian Sociology*, n.s. 24 (1990): 77–103.

Svoboda, Robert. *Aghora: At the Left Hand of God.* Albuquerque: Brotherhood of Life, Inc., 1986.

Swynnerton, Charles. *Romantic Tales from the Panjāb.* Westminster: Archibald Constable & Co., 1903.

Temple, Richard Carnac. *The Legends of the Panjāb.* 3 vols. London: Turner and Company, 1884–86; reprint Patiala: Department of Languages, Punjab, 1963.

Thapar, Romila. "The Image of the Barbarian in Early India." *Comparative Studies in Society and History* 13:3 (July 1971):408–36.

Tod, James. *Annals and Antiquities of Rajasthan.* Ed. with an introduction by William Crooke. 3 vols. London: H. Milford, 1920; reprint Delhi: Low Price Publications, 1990.

Treloar, Francis E. "The Use of Mercury in Metal Ritual Objects as a Symbol of Śiva." *Artibus Asiae* 34 (1972):232–40.

Tucci, Giuseppe. "Animadversiones Indicae." *Journal of the Royal Asiatic Society of Bengal* n.s. 26 (1930):125–60.

———. *Tibetan Painted Scrolls.* 3 vols. Rome: Libreria dello Stato, 1949.

Tulpole, Shankar Gopal. *Mysticism in Medieval India.* Wiesbaden: Harrassowitz, 1984.

Upadhyaya, A. N. "On Some Undercurrents of the Nātha-sampradāya or the *Carpaṭa-śataka*." *Journal of the Oriental Institute* (Baroda) 48:3 (1968–69):198–206.

Vaidyaraj, Vansidhar Sukul. *Vāmamārg*. Allahabad: Kalyan Mandir, 1951.

Vaidyaraja, Yogiraja. "Yoga Research on Mercury and the Dhātus." *Cakra: A Journal of Tantra and Yoga* [New Delhi] 4 (March 1972):186.

Vaisya, Syamasundaracarya. *Rasāyan Sār.* 2 vols. 5th ed. Benares: Syamasundar Rasayansala, 1971.

Vallée Poussin, Louis de la. "Le Bouddhisme et le Yoga de Patañjali." *Mélanges chinois et bouddhiques* [Brussels] 5 (1936–37): 223–42.

Van Buitenen, J. A. "The Indian Hero as Vidyādhara." In *Traditional India: Structure and Change.* Ed. Milton Singer. Philadelphia, American Folklore Society, 1959, pp. 99–105.

Van der Veer, Peter. *Gods on Earth: The Management of Religious Experience and Identity in a North Indian Pilgrimage Centre*, London School of Economics Monographs on Social Anthropology, 59. London: Athlone Press, 1988.

Van Kooij, Karel R. *Worship of the Goddess According to the Kālikā Purāṇa*, part 1: A Translation with an Introduction and Notes of Chapters 54–69. Leiden: Brill, 1972.

Varenne, Jean. *Cosmogonies védiques.* Milan: Archè, 1982.

———. *Upanishads du yoga.* Paris: Gallimard, 1971.

Vaudeville, Charlotte. *Kabīr*, vol. 1. Oxford: Clarendon Press, 1974.

Venkata Ramanan, K. *Nāgārjuna's Philosophy: As Presented in the Mahā-Prajñāpāramitā-Śāstra.* Delhi: Motilal Banarsidass, 1975.

Vidal, Denis, Gilles Tarabout, and Eric Meyer, eds. *Violences et non-violences en Inde (Puruṣārtha 16).* Paris: Editions de l'EHESS, 1994.

Vostrikov, A. I. *Tibetan Historical Literature.* Trans. Harish Chandra Gupta. Calcutta: R. D. Press, 1970.

Waley, Arthur. "Notes on Chinese Alchemy," *Bulletin of the School of Oriental Studies* (1930–32):22–24.

Walker, Benjamin. *Hindu World: An Encyclopedic Survey of Hinduism*, 2 vols. New York: Praeger Books, 1968.

Walleser, Max. "The Life of Nāgārjuna from Tibetan and Chinese Sources." In Bruno Schindler, ed., *Asia Major: Hirth Anniversary Volume.* London: 1923.

Walter, Michael Lee. "Preliminary Results from a Study of Two Rasāyana Systems in Indo-Tibetan Esoterism." In *Tibetan Studies in Honor of Hugh Richardson*, ed. Michael Aris and Aung San Sun Kyi. Warminster, Eng.: Aris and Phillips, 1979.

———. *The Role of Alchemy and Medicine in Indo-Tibetan Tantrism:* Ph.D. dissertation, Indiana University, 1980.

Watt, George. *Dictionary of the Economic Products of India.* 9 vols. Calcutta: Superintendent of Government Printing, 1889–96. Second reprint in 10 vols. Delhi: Periodical Exports, 1972.

Watters, Thomas. *On Yuan-Chwang's Travels in India, 629–645 A.D.* 2 vols. London: Royal Asiatic Society, 1904–05.

Wayman, Alex. *The Buddhist Tantras: Light on Indo-Tibetan Esotericism.* Delhi: Motilal Banarsidass, 1973.

———. *Yoga of the Guhyasamājatantra: The Arcane Lore of Forty Verses.* New York: Samuel Weiser, 1977.

Weinberger-Thomas, Catherine. *Cendres d'immortalité, la crémation des veuves en Inde.* Paris: Editions du Seuil, 1996.

White, David Gordon. "*Dakkhina* and *Agnicayana:* An Extended Application of Paul Mus's Typology." *History of Religions* 26:2 (November 1986): 188–213.

———. *Myths of the Dog-Man.* Chicago: University of Chicago Press, 1991.

———. "Why Gurus Are Heavy." *Numen* 33 (1984), pp. 40–73.

Wink, André. *Al-Hind: The Making of the Indo-Islamic World.* Vol. 1: Early Medieval India and the Expansion of Islam, Seventh to Eleventh Centuries. Delhi: Oxford University Press, 1990.

Woodroffe, John. *The Serpent Power.* 9th ed. Madras: Ganesh, 1973.

———. *Tantrarāja Tantra: A Short Analysis.* 3d ed. Madras: Ganesh, 1971.

———. *Tantra of the Great Liberation.* London: Luzac & Co., 1913; reprint New York: Dover Publications, 1972.

Wujastyk, Dominik. "An Alchemical Ghost: The Rasaratnākara by Nāgārjuna." *Ambix* 31:2 (July 1984):70–83.

———. "Ravigupta and Vāgbhaṭa." *Bulletin of the School of Oriental and African Studies* 48:1 (1985):74–78.

Yazdani, G., ed. *The Early History of the Deccan.* 2 vols. London: Oxford University Press, 1960–61.

Zbavitel, Dušan. *Bengali Literature.* History of Indian Literature, vol. 9, fasc. 3. Leiden: Brill, 1976.

Zimmerman, Francis. *Le discours des remèdes au pays des épices: Enquête sur la médecine hindoue.* Paris: Payot, 1989.

———. "Ṛtu-Sātmya: Le cycle des saisons et le principe d'appropriation." *Puruṣārtha* 2 (1975):87–105. (English translation: "Rtu-Satmya: The Seasonal Cycle and the Principle of Appropriateness." In *Social Science and Medicine* 14B [1980]:94–106.)

Zvelebil, Kamil V. *The Poets of the Powers.* London: Rider and Company, 1973.

Zysk, Kenneth. *Religious Healing in the Veda.* Transactions of the American Philosophical Society, vol. 75, part 7. Philadelphia: The Society, 1985.

INDEX

Carpaṭi, 2, 71, 91, 98, 106, 109, 121, 125, 143, 369; "fathered" by Gorakh, 289, 296, 501; in Siddha lists, 81–84, 86, 92–93; works attributed to, 126, 132, 160, 415, 417, 434
Caryāpadas, 81, 89, 107, 117, 224, 252, 394, 404, 422, 507
Caturaśītisiddha Pravṛtti of Abhayadatta. See *Grub thob*
Caturbhujamiśra, 83
Catuṣpīṭhatantra, 470
Cauraṅgi[nāth], 94, 106–7, 109, 132–33, 239, 294, 296, 297, 298, 351, 391, 403, 404, 413, 460, 503–4; in Siddha lists, 80–81, 84, 86, 91–93. *See also* "Prāṇ Saṅkalī"; Pūraṇ Bhagat
caves, 115, 195, 196, 240, 294, 310, 333, 397, 412, 451, 480, 500, 515; Aṭaka, 246–47; Ca-ri, 216, 247, 452
Central Asia, exchanges with India, 2, 62, 66, 251, 298, 377–80, 385, 471
Chambard, Jean-Luc, 362
charismatic impersonation, 387
China, exchanges with India, 2, 53–55, 60–65, 68, 71, 194, 203–4, 250, 376–79, 381–82, 385, 409, 482, 501. *See also* Hsuan-tsang
Chinese alchemy, 53–54, 56, 63–64, 72, 189, 194, 244, 250, 327, 328, 333, 363, 372, 376, 378, 384, 455, 470, 476, 479, 482. *See also* Immortals (China); Ko Hung
Chinese literature, 68–69
Chos hbyung of Bu-ston, 70, 231, 381, 383, 471
Chou I Tshan Thung Chhi of Wei Po-Yang, 372
Cikitsāsaṃgraha of Cakrapāṇidatta, 76, 388
Cikitsāsārasaṃgraha of Vaṅgasena, 388
ciñcinī (tamarind): name of Kubjikā, 88, 194, 450; *Ciñcinimatasārasaumucchaya*, 88, 231, 356, 386, 388; Ciñcinīśvara, 86–88
cinnabar, 62, 64–66, 117, 192, 193, 195–96, 198, 206, 247–48, 377, 380, 387, 446, 449, 450, 480, 501; in Chinese alchemy, 194, 250, 482. See also *darada*
clan nectar, 79, 101, 137–38, 172, 195, 199, 200, 435, 473. See also *yonitattva*
clans, Siddha and tantric, 78, 88. See also *kula*
Clémentin-Ojha, Catherine, 450
code language, 173
Congress Party, 348
cooking, 20, 186, 207, 221, 232, 283, 339, 446, 499
Cordier, Palmyr, 363, 380, 387, 401
Corpus Hermeticum, 447
corresponding hierarchies, 139, 184–217 passim, 240
Cort, John, 479
cosmic egg, 189, 190, 215, 216, 218, 295, 326, 450, 463, 510. *See also* Lokāloka; Meru
cranial vault, 28, 39, 41, 45, 150, 170, 201, 202, 211, 216, 218, 230, 231, 233, 240–43, 245–49, 252–55, 277, 293, 301, 308, 312, 319, 320, 333, 341, 367, 469, 471, 477, 481, 506. See also *ājñā*; *brahmarandhra*;

Jwālamukhī, 234, 414; *jvālamukhī-bīḍa*, 449; *jvālamukhī-rasa*, 436
jyotirliṅgas. See *liṅga*

Kabīr, 85, 233, 238, 242, 243, 404, 456, 503
Kacch. *See* Gujarat
Kadalī (Plantain): City, 113; Forest, 113, 162, 223, 234, 238–39, 240, 261, 466, 474, 489, 502, 504 (see also *kajjalī*); Kingdom, 236–37, 296, 475. *See also* Kingdom of Women.
Kadalīmañjunātha Māhātmya, 113
Kādambarī of Bāṇabhaṭṭa, 53, 62
Kadri, 86, 94–97, 109–10, 396, 404, 406, 474
Kailash, Mount, 152, 225, 260, 284, 298, 475, 488
Kaivartta, subcaste of fishermen, 467, 475
kajjalī (black mercuric sulphide) 267, 300, 388, 420, 449; Forest of, 238–39, 299–300, 476, 505
Kākacaṇḍeśvarī, 127, 152, 163, 416; in Siddha lists, 86
Kākacaṇḍeśvarīmata, 127, 130–31, 145, 152–55, 159, 160, 163, 164, 166, 167, 176, 209, 324, 371, 416, 420, 428, 430, 431, 453, 481, 512
Kākacaṇḍīśvara, 83, 127
Kākacaṇḍīśvara Kalpa Tantra, 152, 416, 428, 430
Kakṣapuṭa Tantra of Siddha Nāgārjuna, 76, 104, 112, 114, 116, 155, 419, 435; adapted from Siddha Khaṇḍa of the *Rasaratnākara*, 129, 131, 161, 164; name of a work in the *Tanjur*, 383
Kāla, God of Death. *See* Yama
Kālacakra Tantra, 71, 105, 148, 380, 384, 402, 438, 454, 488, 508
Kalacuris of Tripura, 147–48, 428. *See also* Madana
kālāgni. *See* fire
Kālāgnirudra, 40, 215, 220, 232–33, 240, 367, 472; Śiva Kālaghna, 440
Kālamukhas, 97–98, 102, 110; -rāśi name endings of, 413 (*see also* Pāśupatas)
kalās (lunar digits), 18, 25, 36–43, 170, 367–68, 475, 477; *amṛta kalā*, 37–38; *nivṛtti kalā*, 39
kāla-vañcana (skewing Time), 42, 145, 154, 167, 222, 255, 280, 475, 497
Kālī, 79, 89, 152, 286, 357, 416, 438, 444; circle of Kālīs, 291; Guhyakālī, 152; *Kālī Tantra*, 163; *mantra* (see *mantras*)
kalpa, 3, 17, 42, 46–47, 215–16, 251, 318, 326 (*see also* cycles, temporal); *kalpa sādhana* (*see* reversal, yogic).
Kāma, 232, 284, 289, 463
Kāmākhyā/Kāmākṣī. *See* Kāmarūpa
Kamalā, Queen of the Plantain Forest, 236–37, 297, 474
Kāmarūpa (Assam), 62, 73, 89, 108, 115, 134, 195–96, 223, 224, 234–36, 240, 244–45, 260, 386, 435, 451, 460, 466, 467, 473, 475, 479, 480, 482, 488, 495; location in subtle body, 112, 163, 239, 389, 467; name of a *siddhi*, 317, 330, 514
Kambali, name of a Siddha, 82, 87, 124, 390

khānepāne (vernacular term for *siddhi*), 158, 433
khecara, 253; Khecarī (name of a Dūtī in alchemical *maṇḍalas*), 441; *khecari cakra*, 198, 253, 484; *khecarī gutikā*, 153, 316, 427, 430, 487, 496; *khecari jāraṇa*, 292, 326; *khecari kula*, 443, 461; *khecari mantra*, 170, 253; *khecarī mudrā*, 135, 146, 150, 158–59, 170, 173, 230, 252, 254, 257, 258, 276, 481, 483, 487, 512; *khecarī śakti*, 487; *khecari siddhi* (*see* flight, power of)
Khecarī Vidyā, 146, 169–70, 253, 324, 370, 484, 509
Kingdom of Women, 119, 139, 219, 223, 236, 251, 466, 489. *See also* Kadalī
Kiraṇāgama, 213, 397
Kirātas, 147–48
Ko Hung, Chinese alchemist, 64
koans, 501
Kolff, Dirk, 345
Koṅganar, name of a Siddha, 61, 87, 111; works attributed to, 202
Koṅkaṇā, consort of Macchanda in Siddha Cakra, 89, 135
Koṅkaṇa, west coast of India, 73, 88, 91, 94, 230, 393
Koṅkaṇeśvara, name of a Siddha, 86–89, 168
Korakkar. *See* Gorakh, south Indian traditions of
Kosinski, Jerzy, 455
Krama, 79, 181, 291, 416
krāmaṇa (progression of mercury), 149, 268, 492
Kraus, Paul, 457
Kriyā Tantras, 129, 131, 146, 152–54, 160, 162, 165, 308, 397, 409, 418–20, 428, 431, 432, 442, 496. See also *Kautukacintāmaṇi* of Pratāpadeva; *Kriyākālaguṇottara*
Kriyākālaguṇottara, 129, 131, 151
Kriyātantrasamucchayī, in Rasa Siddhạ lists, 83, 129
Kṛṣṇa, 410, 515
Kṣāntaśīla, name of a tāntrika in the *Vetālapañcaviṃśati*, 306, 307
Kṣemarāja, disciple of Abhinavagupta, 136, 138, 142, 178, 418, 465
kṣetrīkaraṇa (preparation of the body in alchemy and fiyurveda), 266, 270–71
Kubera, 58, 259, 415
Kubjikā, goddess of Western Transmission, 2, 79, 88–89, 91, 134–35, 151, 168, 180, 194, 255, 390, 443, 481; *kubjikā mudrā*, 429; Kubjika the name of Buddhist Mahāsiddha, 74, 387. See also *mantras*; Western Transmission
Kubjikāmata, 88, 90, 105, 134–35, 145, 180, 230, 233, 260, 386, 392, 422, 423, 471
Kubjikānityāhnikatilaka, 73, 88, 91, 181, 230, 330, 386, 392, 422
Kubjikāpūjāpaddhati, 421
kula, 200; as tantric clan or lineage, 35, 137–38, 172, 210, 330, 357, 443, 460, 461 (see also *khecari kula*); *kula-parvata*, 112; *kula-siddhas*, 324, 444; *kulayāga*, 255; Kuleśvara and Kuleśvarī, 135; term for early tantrism of the Vidyā Pīṭha, 73, 88, 90, 101, 136, 224, 230, 438, 517
kuladravya. *See* clan nectar

367, 393. *See also* Candradvīpa; Candragiri; Candrapuri; cranial vault; *kalās*; month, lunar; sun
mother goddesses, 43, 135, 157, 176, 324, 361, 424, 457; Seven Sisters, 29, 499
Motināth, 350
mountains, sacred, 114–19, 327–34. *See also* Abu (Mount); Girnar; Himalayas; Kedārnāth; Meru (Mount); Srisailam
mouth, 193, 200, 212, 252–58, 471, 482, 487; mercury becomes possessed of, 6, 256, 267 (see also *grāsa*); passage of sublimated sexual fluids from mouth to mouth, 137, 200, 255, 312, 313, 321, 322, 439; sealing of (see *samputa*); Yoginī's upper and lower, 234–35, 240, 254, 256, 454, 464, 467, 476, 482, 485, 486 (see also *kuṇḍalinī*; *śaṅkinī*; Yoginī; *yoni*)
Mṛcchakaṭikā of Śūdraka, 60, 422
Mṛgendrāgama, 134, 491, 501
mudrās: alchemical seals, 256; *aṅkuśā mudrā*, 432, 496; earrings worn by Nāth Siddhas, 281, 299, 310, 321 (see also *kuṇḍalas*); one of the *pañcamakāra*, 234; *śāmbhavī*, 248, 481; yogic seals, 220, 265, 274, 276 (see also *khecarī*; *kubjikā*; *vajrolī*)
muktivāda. See *mokṣa*
mūla bandha. See *bandhana* and *bandhas*
mūlādhāra (the root *cakra*), 40, 163, 208, 234, 241, 243, 256, 293, 301, 319, 469, 482, 490
Mūlanātha, 85, 87–88, 168, 392
Muller-Ortega, Paul, 468
mūrcchana (swooning), of mercury, 266, 273–75, 290, 492, 495; yogic, 228, 257, 274–75, 495, 498. *See also* swooned, killed, and bound mercury
Murthy, K. R. Srikanta, 420, 437
Murugan. *See* Skanda
Mus, Paul, 360
Muslim conquest of India, 49, 70–71, 103–7, 116, 305, 345, 394, 402, 476
Muslims and Hindus. *See* syncretism, Hindu-Muslim

nāda (resonance), 43, 202, 211, 236, 251, 274, 280, 291, 301, 444, 456, 484, 496, 501; location within subtle body, 178, 368; reversing the, 293. See also *anāhata*; phonemes
nāḍīs (breath and energy channels), 111, 170, 226–28, 232, 247, 251–54, 257, 260, 273, 276, 277, 282, 301, 319, 321, 464, 469, 480, 495, 506; three portrayed as primal Siddhas Sun, Moon, and Fire (*see* Siddhas, three primal). See also *baṅka nāla*; medial channel; *śaṅkhinī*
Nāgabodhi, 69, 81–82, 104, 124–25, 390. *See also* Nāgārjuna
Nāgārjuna, 60, 62, 64–70, 73, 75–76, 103, 106, 110–11, 113–14, 117, 121, 125–26, 131, 133, 143, 150–51, 158, 160, 165, 215, 218, 312, 327, 333, 339, 378, 380–82, 387, 410, 411, 414, 415, 422, 430, 464, 516; as Ayurvedic author, 370, 372, 381, 388, 431 (see also *Rasavaiśeṣika Sūtra*); as honorific title,

nectar, 5, 76, 173, 184, 190, 192, 199, 207, 212, 285, 299, 300, 309, 313, 320, 328, 349, 355, 437, 455, 462, 481–84, 496, 498, 506; in the Vedas, 10–11, 358; "red-white," 202; three types, 327; yogic generation of, in cranial vault, 28, 38–39, 41, 218, 221–22, 242–43, 247–50, 252–54, 257, 258, 272, 277, 282. *See also* waters, magical; extraction; clan nectar; *soma*
Needham, Joseph, 63, 204
Nemināth/Nimnāth, 93, 119, 298, 331–32, 399, 475
Neoplatonism, 189, 490
Nepal, 2, 65, 89, 98, 105, 109, 119, 134, 152, 224, 251, 278, 288, 310–12, 321, 333, 349–51, 380, 389, 391, 393, 431, 435, 465, 467, 473, 502, 508; Gurkhas in, 310–11, 335, 343–44, 357 (*see also* Pṛthivinārāyaṇ Śāh); National Archives, 418, 421, 423, 426, 431, 434, 472. *See also* Kathmandu [Valley]
Nepali literature, 108, 465, 474
Netra Tantra, 178, 418, 419, 442, 501
Newman, John, 384
Nicholas, Ralph, 475
Nīlakaṇṭha, 97, 126, 142, 221, 447
nine doors, 163, 254, 489, 504. *See also* tenth door
Nine Nāths, 85–88, 90–100, 109, 112, 123, 135, 169, 181, 260, 330, 332, 339, 356, 391, 394, 395, 396, 408, 484, 488; identified with Nine Nārāyaṇas in Marathi traditions, 395, 411. *See also* Nāth Siddhas, lists of
nirvāṇa, 33, 35, 201, 375, 482
Nityānanda Siddha, 390, 418
Nityanātha Siddha, 83, 129, 160, 407, 408, 417; "son of Pārvatī," 129–30, 160, 418, 435. See also *Rasaratnākara*; *Śabaracintāmaṇi*
Nityaṣoḍaśika Tantra, 163, 394
nivṛtti. See withdrawal and return, yogic
Nivṛttināth, 113, 396
niyamana (regulation, restraint of mercury), 267, 290, 461
numbers and number symbolism, 15–47 passim. *See also* five; geometric progressions; six; sixteen; three; twelve
nummelite, 196.
nyāsa. *See* worship, tantric
Nyingma. *See* Vajrayāna Buddhism

Obermiller, Ernst, 471
Obeyesekere, Gananath, 341, 517
Ocean of Milk, 190, 192, 221, 234, 289, 447, 466, 475
oghas ("streams" of Siddhas), 3, 92, 135, 327, 332, 356, 386, 394, 415
ojas (the "eighth *dhātu*"), 184, 341, 363, 477, 506, 517
Old Bengali language, 81, 107, 236, 390. See also *Caryāpadas*
Old Kannada language, 140, 407. See also *Yogadīpikā*
Old Punjabi language, 96, 132
Old Rajasthani language, 96, 132
Oṃ. See *mantras*, *praṇava*
Oman, John Campbell, 51–52, 349, 370
opium, 159, 167, 434
oral transmission, 2, 145, 161. *See also* written transmission

Peshawar. *See* Pakistan
phonemes, 43, 179–80, 274, 367, 368, 452, 471, 486; identified with *mātṛka*s, 291. See also *bindu*; *nāda*
piercing, 289, 303, 313, 320, 463; of *cakra*s, 40, 135, 293, 314–18, 319, 489, 511. *See also* ear-boring; *vedha*
Pietro della Valle, 94–95
Pigalle, Paris red-light district, 341
*piṇḍa*s, 287, 500
piṅgalā. See *nāḍī*s
*pīṭha*s: Buddhist, 72, 260, 385, 389, 482 (*see also* Jālandhara; Kāmarūpa; Uḍḍiyāna); chasing in which a Śiva *liṅga* housed, 258; *śākta pīṭha*s, sacred sites of the Goddess, 91, 112, 195, 210, 260, 245, 246, 467, 488 (*see also* worship, tantric); tantric literary classification system, 79–80, 181, 389, 424 (*see also* Mantra Pīṭha; Vidyā Pīṭha)
pitṛyāna. *See* year, solar
Plantain Forest. *See* Kadalī
poison; 164–65, 190, 209, 221, 222, 239, 289, 329, 338, 376, 447, 465, 476; Tantras, 131, 419, 465 (*see also* Garuḍa Tantras; *Yogaratnāvali*)
power substances, 4, 135, 137, 153, 158, 163, 167, 173, 183, 198–200, 323, 430, 433, 454. *See also* clan nectar; *yonitattva*
Prabandhacintāmaṇi of Merutuṅga, 114, 409, 504
Prabandhakośa, 114, 119
Prabhudeva. *See* Allama Prabhu
Prabhuliṅgalīlā of Piḍapatti Somanātha Kavi, 111
Prajāpati, 12–13, 17, 23, 32–33, 189, 271, 272, 283, 286, 351, 365, 492
Prajñā[-paramitā], 67, 72, 104, 152, 164, 378, 382; and Upaya, 247, 251
prakāśa. *See* light
Prakṛti (Nature, feminine principle of materiality), 20–21, 33–34, 36, 195, 210, 215, 218, 473, 492
pralaya (cosmic dissolution), 3, 232–33, 289, 296, 297, 317, 326, 463, 513; as withdrawal of cosmic yogin, 33, 41, 46–47, 221, 251, 263, 294, 463 (*see also* Viṣṇu Nārāyaṇa); provoked by dance of Śiva and Kālī, 286; within subtle body, 40. Seẹ also *saṁhāra*; *sṛṣṭi*
"Prāṇ Sāṅkalī" of Cauraṅgi[nāth], 133, 260, 404, 416, 504
prāṇa, 22, 39, 184, 185, 200, 211, 226, 316, 359, 445, 454. *See also* breath
prāṇāyāma. *See* breath, control
prasāda (gift of grace from god or Siddha), 174, 288, 311, 512
pravṛtti. *See* withdrawal and return, yogic
Pṛthivīnārāyaṇ Śāh, Gurkha king of Nepal, 310, 311, 313, 321, 335, 343–44, 348
Pseudo-Zosimus, 203–5, 447
Ptolemy, 205
Punjab, Indian state of, 1, 98, 398; Pakistani state of 62, 239, 298–99, 333, 404, 479, 500 (*see also* Jhelum)
Punjabi literature, 92–93, 239, 244, 298, 333, 476, 500, 502, 503
Pūraṇ Bhagat, 92, 239, 244, 261, 289, 298–301, 333, 403, 476, 484, 489, 500, 503, 504. *See also* Carangi[-nāth]; wells

(*see also* Ardhanarīśvara); relationship to the moon (*see* moon); revealer of Tantras, 54, 127, 142, 145, 161, 172, 223, 225, 229, 236, 447, 468; Siddhas in retinue of, 331, 512; Siddheśvara (temples of), 60, 95–96, 103, 110, 367, 375, 398; Tripurāntaka, 438. *See also* Bhairava; Kālāgnirudra; *liṅga*; *and names of deities identified with Śiva*
Śiva Saṁhitā, 324, 325
Śivahood, 4, 6, 42, 52–53, 143, 157, 163, 166, 173, 181, 188, 220, 228; 234, 240, 312–25 passim, 331, 322, 432, 439, 465
Śivakalpadruma of Śivanātha, 130, 448
six: metals, 189, 190; months, 170, 294; *rasa*s, 185; schools of Indian philosophy, 174
sixteen, 17, 36–44, 365, 368, 392; *ādhāra*s, 366; expansion to eighteen, 43–44, 265, 491; Mondays vow, 37, 366; number of women in Plantain Kingdom, 475; *saṃskāra*s, 43–44, 265–69; Siddhas, 85, 91, 169
Skanda, 131, 159, 189–91, 224, 329, 359, 376, 440, 441, 447, 448, 472
snake charming, 99, 222, 350, 399, 519
Soḍhala, 106, 114. See also *Gadanigraha*
śodhana. *See* purification
soma: as herbal medicine, 365, 366; as moon god, 11, 16, 184, 359 (*see also* moon); as sacrificial oblation, 24, 36, 365, 455, 478; as Vedic draft of immortality, 10–11, 25, 28, 189, 232, 242, 243, 259, 285; theft of, 190, 462.
Somnath. *See* Gujarat
sorcery, tantric. *See* Kriyā Tantras
soteriology, 72, 385
soul, individual. See *ātman*
soul, universal. See *bráhman*
sound, body of, 72; substrate of, 291, 293, 477
south India, 49, 53, 55, 61, 67–68, 77, 80, 105–6, 110–11, 124, 126, 131, 168, 169, 307, 372, 376, 379, 382, 393, 431. *See also* Andhra Pradesh; Kadri; Karnataka; Kerala; Konkaṇa; Malabar coast; Sittars; Srisailam; Tamil Nadu
Southeast Asia, exchanges with India, 48, 55, 61, 64, 103, 369, 384, 389, 401, 457, 487
Southern Transmission. *See* Śrīvidyā
Spanda Kārika of Vasugupta, 222
sparśamaṇi. *See* transmutation
spitting. *See* initiation
Śrī Cakra or Śrī Yantra. See *maṇḍala*s
Sri Lanka, 55, 60–61, 119, 126, 236, 260, 262, 299, 415, 489
Śrī Nāth Tīrthāvalī of Mān Singh, 496, 500
Śrīkaṇṭha, 73, 97–98, 126, 128–29, 131, 133, 158, 230, 250, 416, 418, 442, 465; revealer of *Bhūtiprakaraṇa*, 140, 142, 156, 157, 158
Śrīmatottara Tantra, 156, 157, 386, 425, 433
Śrīnātha, 73–74, 91, 129, 135, 230, 255, 330, 418
Śrīparvata. *See* Srisailam
Srisailam, 49, 53, 60, 68–69, 76–77, 92, 103–4, 110–12, 136, 152, 161–62, 164–65, 168, 196, 238, 245, 260, 331, 375, 398, 405, 408, 409,

Swami Sevananda, 517
swooned, killed, and bound mercury, 6, 144, 146, 149, 158, 159, 162, 274, 384. See also *bandhana*; *māraṇa*; mercury; *mūrcchana*
syncretism, Hindu-Buddhist, 53, 55, 57–59, 61, 66, 70–71, 74, 78, 94, 104–11, 118, 136, 148, 152, 187, 196, 206, 361, 373, 375, 383, 390, 513 (*see also* Buddhist alchemy; Vajrayāna Buddhism; Highest Yoga Tantra); Hindu-Jain, 57, 80, 93, 99, 114–19, 331–34, 399, 410, 475, 479, 498, 515 (*see also* Jainism, Siddha and tantric traditions of; Nemināth/Nimnāth; Pārasnāth/Parśvanāth); Hindu-Muslim, 80, 99, 106, 121, 171, 205, 228, 238, 311, 399, 403–5 (*see also* Bāuls; Jogis, Muslim; Rāwals); Hindu-Sikh, 126; Hindu-Taoist, 62, 71, 196

Tahqīqāt-i-Ciśtī, 395, 501
Taishang suling dayou miaojing, 250
Taittirīya Saṁhitā, 24, 359
Tamil Nadu, 2, 60–61, 63–64, 77, 87, 97, 106, 124, 178, 340, 357, 376, 378, 392, 398, 407, 415, 447, 450, 504
Tanjur, 70–71, 81, 105, 108, 125, 224, 380, 383, 386, 387, 390, 403, 416, 425
Tanti-pā, in Siddha lists, 81, 83–84, 86, 91–92
tantra, etymology of, 1–2
Tantra Mahārṇava, 91, 113, 394, 408, 425
Tantrāloka, 73, 88, 137, 225, 312–14, 329, 331, 395, 424. *See also* Abhinavagupta
Tantrarāja Tantra, 91, 394, 514
tantric alchemy, 51–55, 72, 78, 104, 109–22 passim, 145, 171–83 passim, 187, 372; "tantric element" in, 139, 141–44
Tao te ching, 62, 377
Taoism and Hinduism. *See* syncretism, Hindu-Taoist
Taoist alchemy. *See* Chinese alchemy
tapas (ascetic ardor), 18, 27, 39, 184, 243, 270, 281, 284, 295. *See also* thermal energy
Tārā, 64–65, 69–70, 110, 378, 380, 387, 465, 516; *Tārā Tantra*, 394, 412
Tāranātha, 70, 107–8, 383, 403
tattvas, 33–36, 43, 210, 214, 317, 365, 477, 510. *See also* five, elements; Prakṛti; Puruṣa
Tāyumānavar, 340
Telugu literature, 92–93, 111–12, 369, 429. See also *Navanātha Caritra* of Gauraṇa; *Śūnyasampādane*
tenth door, 252, 254, 256, 260, 261, 483–85, 489, 504. *See also* nine doors
thermal energy, 13, 39, 284. *See also* geothermal phenomena; *tapas*
Tibet, exchanges with India, 2, 55, 64–66, 69, 80, 105, 196, 247, 251, 379, 380, 384
Tibetan literature, 64, 67–71, 80, 218, 447. See also *bCud len gyi man ngag bshad pa* of Bo dong; *Chos hbyung* of Bu-ston; *Dragpa jets'en*; *Grub thob*; *Kanjur*; *Tanjur*; Tāranātha

Weber, Max, 385, 387
weights and measures, 510. See also *pala*
Weikzas. *See* Zawgyis and Weikzas
Weinberger, Steven, 404
Weinberger-Thomas, Catherine, 517
Wellcome Institute for the History of Medicine, 435
wells, 237, 239, 240–53 passim, 280, 288, 289, 294, 297, 344, 449, 478–79, 505; dedicated to Goddess, 245; inverted, 242–44; *jīrṇāndhakūpa*, 244; of mercury, 115, 117, 159, 162, 168, 191, 202, 205, 208, 212; Pūraṇ's Well, 245, 299–300, 478; *romakūpa* (pores), 273, 495; water pots represented as, 242–43, 478; Well of Truth, 457
West, Indian exchanges with, 2, 87, 203–6, 376, 456
western India, 110–22, 422, 476
Western Transmission, 2, 4–5, 73, 79, 87–90, 94, 112–13, 126, 129, 133–35, 139–40, 143, 151, 180–81, 228, 230, 255, 389, 423, 481. See also *Gorakṣa Saṁhitā*; Kubjikā; *Kubjikāmata*; *Manthānabhairava Tantra*; *Ṣaṭsāhasra Saṁhitā*
Wilkinson, Chris, 386
wine, ritual use of, 137, 220, 231, 234, 252, 455. See also *pañcamakāra*
Wink, André, 412
withdrawal and return, yogic, 33, 38–39, 42, 46–47, 185, 221, 251, 263, 290, 293, 318, 463
Work in Two Parts, 14, 57, 173, 263–65, 266, 274, 275, 277, 281, 294, 315, 372
worship, of chemicals. See *rasacikitsā*
worship, tantric, 4, 54, 79, 89, 131, 135–40, 143–45, 150, 152, 157, 163, 167, 168, 169, 172, 173, 176, 179–81, 241, 258, 284, 306, 324, 355, 391, 424, 430, 440, 441, 442, 443, 450, 454, 473, 488. *See also* erotico-mystical practice; *pañcamakāra*; *yoni-pūjā*
written transmission, xii, 145, 161. *See also* oral transmission
Wujastyk, Dominik, xiii, 104, 115, 410, 435

Yādavas of Devagiri, 94, 104–6, 112–14, 127, 147, 167, 393, 408–9. *See also* Devagiri; Siṅghaṇa
Yadavji Trikamji Acarya, 117
Yājñavalkya Smṛti, 37, 494
Yajur Veda, 189, 499
Yakṣas (Dryads), 58–59; Yakṣiṇīs, 104, 153, 475
Yama, 11, 23, 46, 171, 259, 280, 295, 340, 409, 429, 475, 497; iron arises from seed of, 190
Yamāntaka, 220–21. *See also* Bhairava
Yamunā River, 225–26, 277, 480
*yantra*s (alchemical apparatus), 78, 145, 160, 169, 181, 183, 241, 248, 250–51, 257–58, 327, 333, 426, 480; bicameral configuration, 247–52, 256, 328, 479. See also *ḍamaru*; *pātana*; Vidyādharas
Yaśodhara [Bhaṭṭa], 82, 159. See also *Rasaprakāśa Sudhākara*
year: solar, 23–25, 28, 362, 469; semesters of, 22–26, 30, 41, 46, 318, 363; seasons of, 23–24, 29, 362